POLITICAL AND SOCIAL GROWTH
OF THE UNITED STATES

1852–1933

POLITICAL AND SOCIAL GROWTH OF THE UNITED STATES

VOLUME I (1492–1852)

BY HOMER C. HOCKETT

PROFESSOR OF HISTORY
OHIO STATE UNIVERSITY

VOLUME II (1852–1933)

BY ARTHUR MEIER SCHLESINGER

PROFESSOR OF HISTORY
HARVARD UNIVERSITY

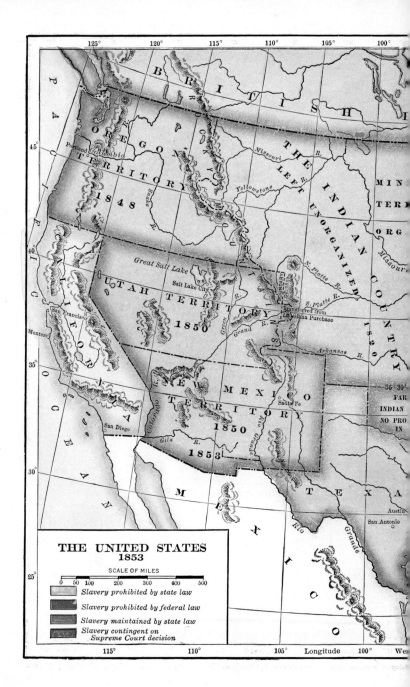

THE UNITED STATES
1853

SCALE OF MILES

0 50 100   200   300   400   500

Slavery prohibited by state law
Slavery prohibited by federal law
Slavery maintained by state law
Slavery contingent on
  Supreme Court decision

Adapted from *American Nation*, Volume 18, "Parties and Slavery," by T. C. Smith, Harper & Brothers, publishers

POLITICAL AND SOCIAL GROWTH OF THE UNITED STATES · 1852-1933

BY ARTHUR MEIER SCHLESINGER

PROFESSOR OF HISTORY AT HARVARD UNIVERSITY

REVISED EDITION

1933

THE MACMILLAN COMPANY · NEW YORK

PREFACE

THAT five "real daughters" of the American Revolution still live suggests the brief moment in the world's history occupied by the whole course of American development since independence. The present volume deals with a still shorter time, that since 1852, a period of whose events the "real daughters" doubtless have a lively recollection. Few as these years are, however, they were so crammed with adventure, aspiration and national achievement as to give them the character of an epoch. The United States was transformed from a rural and agricultural society to an urban and industrial one, from a loose federation of states to a consolidated republic, from a continent-wide country to one with far-flung insular possessions, from a people deriving their cultural life largely from Europe to one who have contributed their full share to world civilization, from the principal nation in the Western Hemisphere to one of the Great Powers of the globe. The United States has never been so greatly isolated from the international flow of ideas and practices as statesmen have usually asserted. During these years the fine line between what is strictly American history and what is world history has grown so thin that in our own day it is scarcely perceptible.

It may well be beyond the power of the human mind to comprehend the intricate drama played on so vast and ever shifting a stage. Yet we should be like the ants, who also live in a complex social order they do not understand, did we not continually make the effort to arrive at some sort of a picture portraying as a whole the events and conditions out of which has emerged our own cross section of life. "History," says Santayana, "is merely memory aided and directed." If political developments usually occupy the foreground of the present narrative, it is not for their own sake but as a means of revealing and illustrating deeper social forces at work. As in the volume out of which this one has grown, the major emphasis is put on the evolution of nationality, the influence of industrial growth and technological change, the trend toward imperialism and larger participation in world affairs, the struggle for broader democracy, and the unceasing quest for social amelioration and humanitarian reform. These themes are considered not merely as they affected governmental decisions but also as they touched the material and intellectual life of the people. Kindred interests, of course, formed the central concerns of

v

European history during the same period. So far as space has permitted, an effort has been made to show the essentially international character of these movements.

The lapse of eight years since the original edition of this work has afforded an opportunity to introduce much new material, reorganize the presentation and revise certain judgments in the light of later evidence. Because of space limitations the "Select Bibliography" at the end of each chapter is confined to historical accounts of book length. A full list of the authors and books cited appears at the close of the volume. Among the persons who have made suggestions that have been incorporated in the book I wish particularly to mention my colleague Dr. Paul H. Buck, Professor F. A. Shannon of the Kansas State College of Agriculture and Applied Science, and Professor H. C. Hockett and Dr. E. H. Roseboom of the Ohio State University. I am under a special debt to Miss Elizabeth F. Hoxie of Belmont and Mr. Donald Born of the Harvard Graduate School of Arts and Sciences for seeing the manuscript through the press. At all stages I have had the counsel and coöperation of my wife Elizabeth Bancroft.

A. M. S.

CAMBRIDGE, MASS.
September, 1933.

CONTENTS

PART ONE. THE ORDEAL OF NATIONALITY

MAPS AND TABLES

PART ONE
THE ORDEAL OF NATIONALITY

CHAPTER I

THE UNDOING OF THE SECTIONAL TRUCE
OF 1850

MID-CENTURY AMERICA

THE Compromise of 1850 was consummated amidst piping times of peace and plenty. The generation which had been vexed with endless strife over gag resolutions, the return of fugitive slaves, Texas annexation and the disruption of Mexico had witnessed at the same time what President Pierce in his inaugural address called an "unparalleled progression" in population and national wealth. Thanks to Polk's masterful handling of foreign affairs, the national territory now stretched continent-wide over forest, plain and mountain, while within these far-flung limits dwelt a hardy, industrious people, numbering in 1850 twenty-three million. The Union comprised thirty-one states, including the newly admitted California. Save for some three million Negroes held in bondage and a hundred thousand or so Indians in the trans-Mississippi borderlands, the land of promise had never before seemed so demonstrably the land of performance. In the East every branch of industry boomed, in the Midwest and the South agriculture returned unusual profits, while the railways knitted the settled parts of the country in ever tighter bonds and the mines of California poured a golden stream into all the channels of trade. Prosperity acted like an opiate upon the people. Without its soothing effects the politicians would have found the public less ready to accept the Compromise measures. Its continuance seemed to offer the best assurance that this new era of good feelings would last.

Yet the material development itself held latent dangers for the maintenance of sectional harmony, for in its nature and variety it served to sharpen the differences that underlay the economic systems of North and South. New England and the Middle Atlantic states were the principal centers of manufacturing, commerce and finance. Compared with later times the

3

output of mill and mine is not impressive, but to the compilers of the census of 1860 the advance during the decade was one of "startling magnitude." The amount of capital invested in manufacturing (including fisheries and mines) doubled, totaling more than a billion dollars on the eve of the Civil War. First in order of importance was the making of flour and meal, then boots and shoes, cotton textiles, and lumber products, with clothing, machinery, leather and woolen goods forging rapidly to the fore. In 1849, for the first time, the patents granted for new inventions passed the thousand mark, to reach nearly six times that number in 1860.

Of the new mechanisms employed in industry the census officials in 1860 characterized the sewing machine as "altogether a revolutionary instrument." Elias Howe of Massachusetts, after ceaseless tinkering, had invented it in 1846, and in the next decade A. B. Wilson, Isaac M. Singer and other ingenious persons made improvements which greatly widened its usefulness. Not only did the contrivance simplify one of the age-old tasks of the housewife, but, as it was introduced into the factory and harnessed to steam or water power, it also helped usher in the era of cheap ready-made clothing for general sale. Men's shirts, which had taken fourteen hours and twenty minutes to make by hand, could now be finished in an hour and sixteen minutes at greatly reduced cost. Between 1850 and 1860 the annual output of clothing factories rose from $48,000,000 to $80,000,000.

At the same time shipping reached the high noon of its prosperity. Vessels flying the American flag plied the seven seas, distributing the wares of all nations and excelling the British at their own game. Again American inventive genius was a factor, for the *Rainbow*, a clipper ship designed in 1845 by John W. Griffiths of New York, had pointed the way to a superior kind of craft, long of beam with slender concave bows and a great cloud of sail, and characterized by grace, beauty and speed. Soon the shipyards at Boston, New York and other Northern ports were busily constructing the new type of sailing vessel, and the clippers found a rush of employment in the continued migration to California, the British East India commerce, thrown open to the world in 1849, and the China trade. Meanwhile, beginning in 1845, Congress sought to promote ocean steam navigation by liberal subsidies. New steamship lines were established, including one connecting the Atlantic ports with the Isthmus of Panama and another joining the isthmus with California and Oregon.[1] For a time the American Collins line vigorously competed with the British Cunard line in the transatlantic trade. But a series of disasters culminating in the Panic of 1857 forced Collins into bankruptcy.

The triumphs of the merchant marine had reverberations in diplomatic relations. In 1844 the United States had concluded its first treaty with China, opening certain Chinese ports to trade and obtaining for American merchants extraterritorial privileges, that is, the right of accused persons to be tried by American tribunals according to American law. The motives guiding later phases of American policy are suggested in the instructions borne by Commodore M. C. Perry on his historic mission to Japan: "Recent events — the navigation of the ocean by steam, the acquisition and rapid settlement by this country of a vast territory on the Pacific, the discovery of gold in that region, the rapid communication established across the isthmus which separates the two oceans — have practically brought the countries of the East in closer proximity to our own."

In 1850 the United States made the Clayton-Bulwer treaty with Great Britain, designed to secure international control of any future interoceanic canal in Central America and at the same time to check the encroachments of the British authorities on near-by territory from their base at Belize (British Honduras). The next year the United States, suspicious of French intentions, affirmed its opposition to the seizure of Hawaii by any European power. So vital did the Hawaiian group seem to the growth of American commerce in the Pacific that a few years later the government proposed to annex the islands, a plan wrecked, however, in 1854 by the death of the well-disposed insular monarch. The same year Commodore Perry, with a show of force, coerced Japan into departing from its ancient seclusion by opening two ports to American trade — an event which rang the knell of feudalism and marked the beginning of modern times for the

---

[1] Besides, a railway for transporting passengers and goods across the isthmus, undertaken with American capital, was completed in 1855.

island kingdom. "Manifest Destiny" was not merely a doctrine of New World territorial expansion. Regardless of party, "Young America" also visioned possibilities of trade and even territorial advantage in the great ocean stretching toward Asia. But for the renewal of the slavery controversy and the exhausting war that followed, the United States might have embarked upon a career of colonial empire a half-century before it did.

While manufacturing and shipping flourished in the East, prosperity smiled with equal favor upon the South. There, despite the attention given rice culture along the coast, sugar growing in Louisiana and tobacco raising in the border states, not to mention scattered local manufacturing, the chief fount of wealth was the cotton crop. With the fuller development of the rich black lands of the Gulf shore production doubled during the decade, but the world's demand for cotton remained unappeased and the market price soared to new levels. From all parts of Dixie wagon, steamer and railroad brought the bulky bales to the points whence they were dispatched to more remote markets. Cotton furnished directly more than half the nation's foreign exports, most of it going to England. At the same time it shed benefits upon Northern mill owners, merchants and bankers and, by centering Southern energies upon its cultivation, created a demand for the farm produce of the Midwest. In the South itself the wealth invested in cotton culture and its peculiar labor system represented a power which ramified into all phases of political, economic and social life. Little wonder that the people south of Mason and Dixon's line attached an almost fantastic importance to their great staple. "What would happen if no cotton was planted for three years?" asked Senator J. H. Hammond of South Carolina in a speech in 1858. "I will not stop to depict what every one can imagine, but this is certain, England would topple headlong, and carry the whole civilized world with her save the South. No, you dare not make war on cotton. No power on the earth dares to make war on it. Cotton is King."

The Midwest with its boundless prairies and swiftly growing population shared fully in the good times. Thanks to the Irish famine and a little later the Crimean War, England as well as the older settled parts of America demanded its wheat and other cereals, while the rapid introduction of labor-saving implements made possible an unexampled increase of production.[1] Of the new devices the most important was the McCormick reaper. Patented originally in 1834 by Cyrus H. McCormick, a Virginia blacksmith, the first model had been continually improved until it became possible for one person with a team of horses to cut as much grain as seven men swinging cradles in the immemorial fashion. When McCormick in 1847 moved his factory to Chicago, a town of hardly seventeen thousand but near the center of the prairie grain belt, a new era opened in the mechanization of agriculture. He manufactured 500 machines for the harvest of 1848, 1600 in 1850 and 4000 in 1856. Over 100,000 machines of his and other makes were in use before the end of the decade. Meantime the grain crops of the land swelled from 100,000,000 bushels in 1850 to 171,000,000 in 1860, more than half being grown in the Midwest. With profits attractive and the demand for grain apparently unlimited, it is not surprising that the farmers of the upper Mississippi Valley eagerly welcomed any move which might open to them on favorable terms the fertile country west of Iowa and Missouri.

An important stimulus to Western prosperity was the great improvement in transportation facilities with the East. Until mid-century, except for the turnpikes over the mountains, the only routes for hauling goods were by way of the Great Lakes and the Erie Canal or down the Mississippi and around through the Gulf. The economic attachment of the Midwest had been southward rather than eastward. But from 1850 to 1857 the Appalachian barrier was pierced by five railway trunk lines and these, by their connections in the interior, reached the Ohio River at eight points and the Mississippi at ten. Railroad building became a mania, cities and counties vying with one another in subsidizing new routes and the national government assisting by land grants to states for transfer to projected lines. In 1850 Stephen A. Douglas helped secure a princely grant for the Illinois Central Railroad with which eventually to link Chicago, by way of Cairo at the southern tip of the state, with Mobile

---

[1] The act of Parliament repealing the "corn" laws in 1846 had thrown open the door to foreign cereals, but its full effect on the normal grain trade with America was not felt until the sixties.

on the Gulf. Soon he was visioning the advantages to his home city of like communications across the plains with California. By 1860 Illinois had more track completed than any other state in the Union. The iron bonds uniting East and West not only gave rise to mutually profitable trade but, by emphasizing the economic interdependence of the two regions, tended to create a harmony of political outlook as well. This fact, far more than abolitionist agitation, was to account for Northern unity when Southern guns boomed out against Fort Sumter in 1861.

In the expansion of the railway net the South, hampered by the absorption of capital in land and slaves, had much less part. Despite their strict-construction objections to internal improvements at national cost, a number of Southern states secured federal land grants to aid railroad construction. But not until late in the decade did a continuous line through the mountains, running from Memphis to Norfolk, connect the lower Mississippi with the Southern Seaboard, and this was the only one to do so. A series of commercial conventions met in the fifties to whip up enthusiasm for railway building, particularly for a road linking the South with California. The speakers also urged the promotion of manufactures and the establishment of direct steamship lines to Europe. But such efforts to keep pace with the North and free the South from "vassalage" to that section met with little success.

As each year passed, the antagonism of interest between the two economic systems became increasingly manifest. Southerners resented the large profits amassed by Northern business men and capitalists from marketing the cotton crop as well as from conducting the foreign and much of the domestic trade of their section. Nor was this all. "In one way or another," protested a Southern writer in 1857, "we are more or less subservient to the North every day of our lives. In infancy we are swaddled in Northern muslin; in childhood we are humored with Northern gewgaws; in youth we are instructed out of Northern books; at the age of maturity we sow our 'wild oats' on Northern soil; . . . in the decline of life we remedy our eye-sight with Northern spectacles . . .; in old age we are drugged with Northern physic; and, finally, when we die, our inanimate bodies, shrouded in Northern cambric, are stretched upon the bier, borne to the grave in a Northern carriage, entombed with a Northern spade, and memorized with a Northern slab!"

To be sure, the protective tariff no longer formed a political issue between the sections, and in 1857 Congress scaled down the already low duties of 1846 by about five per cent, at the same time enlarging the free list. Yet the South, not content, forced through a law in 1858 withdrawing the subsidies for steamship lines. On the other hand, the rising price of slaves caused agitation among the planting interests toward the close of the decade for reopening the African slave trade. The growing sense of economic inferiority on the part of the South might eventually have unsettled the sectional peace of 1850, but other forces were at work to disrupt it in a more dramatic way.

FOREIGN INFLUENCES

From a world point of view the middle of the nineteenth century was a time of reform aspiration and domestic strife rather than of compromise and peaceable accommodation. A popular upheaval in France in 1848 acted as a spark to a powder train that reached from the English Channel to the Russian border and from the Mediterranean to the Baltic. The system of reaction and repression which had succeeded the uprisings of 1830 crashed in sudden confusion before the revivified forces of democracy and nationality. Within a few months half the monarchs of Europe had been deposed or forced to concede constitutions. In France the people set up the Second Republic on a basis of manhood suffrage, a victory followed four years later, however, by a return to monarchy under Louis Napoleon. The Hapsburg ruler in great fright granted a short-lived constitution to Austria, while the oppressed nationalities of his conglomerate empire — Hungarians, Italians, Poles, Bohemians — strove desperately, if vainly, to cast off the Austrian yoke. Equally unavailing was the movement to forge the loosely attached German States into a strongly united Fatherland under a representative parliament. On the other hand, the kings of Prussia, Holland, Denmark and Sardinia made important concessions to popular demands, and the various Swiss communities after much bickering established an effective federal government modeled on that of the United States. Even Great Britain was shaken by democratic unrest.

The "Chartists," championing the rights of the lower classes
ignored by the reform act of 1832, demanded a government
based upon universal manhood suffrage. The desired step, however, had to await a later time. If the "Year of Revolutions"
was disappointing in some of its immediate fruits, yet the foundations of the Old Order were irretrievably shaken. The remnants
of feudal privilege were swept away in many lands, and the next
two decades— so momentous for similar reasons in the history
of the American republic—were to witness the triumph of nationality and substantial gains for democracy in nearly every
great European state.

The people of the United States watched with approval
these restless stirrings across the Atlantic. In many of the
larger cities public meetings and parades celebrated the glad
tidings. The national Democratic convention of 1848 sent
"fraternal congratulations" to the new French republic, and rejoiced that the spirit of popular rule was "prostrating thrones
and erecting republics on the ruins of despotism in the Old
World." Even the gentle Longfellow said, "So long as a king is
left upon his throne there will be no justice in the earth."
Two years later Daniel Webster as Secretary of State sent a note
to Austria, justifying the right of the American people "to cherish
always a lively interest in the fortunes of nations struggling for
institutions like their own," and declaring grandiloquently that,
compared with free America, "the possessions of the House of
Hapsburg are but as a patch on the earth's surface." Privately
Webster defended the boastful tone of this letter on the score
of his desire to "touch the national pride" and shame Americans "who should speak of disunion."

As military reverses or loss of popular support cheated the
hopes of the revolutionists, many of their leaders sought temporary refuge in the New World. New York City in 1850 presented
a strange sight. Ledru-Rollin was a shore porter there, Louis
Blanc a dancing master, Felix Pyat a scene shifter, Lamartine a
mendicant. Besides these French radical leaders, a member of
the late German parliament worked as a barber and the Italian
revolutionist Garibaldi made tallow candles in a back street on
Staten Island. The next year President Fillmore, at the behest
of Congress, sent a warship to Turkey to convey the exiled Hun-

garian patriot, Louis Kossuth, to the United States. Arriving
in December, 1851, he received great ovations in the Eastern
cities, was dined by the President in Washington and formally
greeted by each House of Congress. Yet, despite his vociferous
reception, the American people still considered the Atlantic a
bar to armed intervention in European affairs. Kossuth had to
content himself with what benefit his cause might derive from
their moral support and financial contributions.

As in 1830, the new series of revolutionary outbreaks sent
thousands of refugees flying to the United States for a permanent
abode. The greatly increased immigration at mid-century was
due mainly, however, to bad economic conditions abroad.
"America letters," written by successful migrants to their
countrymen at home, extolled the advantages and rewards of
life in the New World, while steamship and railway representatives and the immigration agents of Western states added their
efforts to swell the flow of settlement. From 23,000 in 1830 the
number of annual arrivals rose to 84,000 in 1840 and to 297,000
in 1849, reaching high tide five years later with 428,000. Approximately three million came in the decade from 1845 to 1855 —
three times as many as in the whole earlier period of national
independence. "From every degree of latitude and longitude,
and from every isle and continent under the whole heaven, the
flood of emigration has poured in upon the United States,"
wrote a sympathetic observer in the *Democratic Review* in 1850.
"There has been nothing like it in appearance since the encamp-
ment of the Roman empire, or the tents of the Crusaders."
Many of the newcomers were desperately poor, and the hardships and sufferings of the voyage across the Atlantic severely
tested their mettle. Though small numbers of Scandinavians
and certain other peoples formed a part of the influx, the great
bulk consisted, on the one hand, of peasant farmers from south-
western Germany, discouraged by crop failures and oppressive
agrarian laws, and, on the other, of peasants from central and
southern Ireland, forced to flee because of the potato famine in
1845–1846 and later years.

In the decade after the German revolution nearly a million
Teutons arrived in the United States, including such prominent
"Forty-eighters" as Carl Schurz, Franz Sigel and other leaders

of education and talent. Most of them settled in the newer parts of the country north of the Ohio or beyond the Mississippi. St. Louis, Milwaukee, Chicago, Cincinnati and Cleveland attracted strong colonies. In about half the cities of Ohio the Germans and "Pennsylvania Dutch" (descendants of German immigrants of colonial days) held nearly or quite the balance of political power. But the great majority sought the soil, usually in company with their kind, and proved to be thrifty and successful farmers. Wherever they went they carried with them their zeal for schools and education, their love of music and the liberal social customs of the Fatherland. In large degree, they planted the first seeds of æsthetic appreciation in the raw West. Staunch believers in free-homestead legislation, they were ever ready to do what they could to support that cause. The Irish, on the other hand, hived in the crowded cities of the East, or became workers on turnpikes, canals and railroads. Indeed, the hard manual labor upon the great public improvements of the time was performed mainly by their brawn and energy. They lived, for the most part, in wretched poverty in the city tenements; and everywhere they settled they added to the traditional anti-British feeling of Americans their own bitter hatred of that country — a fact quickly observed and capitalized by vote-seeking politicians.

This sudden growth of immigration inevitably begot a strong nativist, or antiforeign, sentiment on the part of Americans of older stock. In the seaboard industrial districts the working-men were dismayed by the increase of cheap Irish laborers with their lower standard of living. Moreover, most of the Irish were Catholics, and the spread of Catholic churches, convents and parochial schools alarmed the deep-seated Protestant sentiment in New England and the Middle Atlantic states. The ease with which unscrupulous native politicians managed to corrupt newly naturalized voters gave further cause for fear, seeming to threaten the integrity of American republican institutions. In the West, the chief source of friction grew out of the unfamiliar social customs of the Germans, especially in regard to beer drinking and their lax observance of the Sabbath — practices which offended the inherited Puritan austerity of the older inhabitants. Though the presence of slave labor turned most immigrants away from the South, there, too, nativist feeling flourished. The planters ascribed the alarming growth of Northern population and political power to the large foreign infusions, and viewed immigration as an inexhaustible stream which would flood the federal territories with the foes of slavery.

As early as the thirties the hostility to the Irish had broken out in the form of mob violence. In 1834 a convent in Charlestown, Massachusetts, was burned. A few years later the Irish quarter of Boston was sacked, similar outrages occurring in other cities. The movement entered local politics, and on one or two occasions Native American parties in New York and Philadelphia undertook to prevent the election of naturalized citizens to municipal office. In 1845 a national organization of Native Americans was effected with a membership, it was claimed, of more than a hundred thousand. In 1850 the movement assumed the form of a secret society under the name (known only to its members) of the Supreme Order of the Star-Spangled Banner. For a few years the society showed little sign of thriving, although presently, under unexpected circumstances, it was to form the backbone of the spectacular Know Nothing movement.

The deeper significance of this peaceful alien invasion appears less in the short-lived manifestations of nativist feeling than in the influence the immigrant elements exerted upon the growing sectional controversy. Between 1850 and 1860 the total number of foreign-born leaped eighty-four per cent, a rate of increase far surpassing that of the native stock. A contemporary observer testified that "over this confused diversity there broods, after all, a higher unity, . . . in this chaos of peoples the traces of a specifically American national character may be discerned." Yet, almost inevitably, the newcomers' conception of American nationality became patterned upon that of the North rather than that of the South since nine tenths of them dwelt in the free states and territories. The Irish excepted, they naturally gravitated to the party that opposed slavery, favored free farms and espoused an indivisible Union, for slavery was unknown in Western Europe, most of them were farmers and many had fought in wars for national unification. Temporarily some of them joined the Democratic ranks because of the appeal of the party name; but as the issue between the sections sharpened, the Germans in particular, and also the Scandinavians and the Hollanders, flocked into the antislavery party. The Irish, for the most part, remained incurably Democratic.

THE RISE OF A NEW GENERATION

A greater immediate danger to the maintenance of sectional harmony was the advent of a new generation to the control of public affairs. By the close of 1852 the master figures of the older generation had passed from the scene. Calhoun died in the Compromise year; Clay and Webster followed before Pierce's election. Van Buren definitely dropped out of politics after his unsuccessful run as Free Soil candidate in 1848, and Benton was retired by Missouri from the Senate in 1851 after thirty years' service. Calhoun perhaps excepted, the distinguishing trait of these men had been their single-minded devotion to the Union, for their public life had been shaped by the great surge of nationalism which followed the second war with Great Britain. The new leaders, on the contrary, had been reared in an era of sectional controversy. Younger in years and experience, they lacked the poise and caution of the seasoned statesmen. They faced the problems of the age with all the jaunty assurance which fresh generations are apt to bring to a consideration of grave public issues. On the central question of the time they held intense convictions, and felt lightly the obligation of maintaining a patchwork peace that had been dictated by leaders of a departed era.

The new generation, moreover, represented two radically different points of view. From the free states came William H. Seward of New York, Salmon P. Chase of Ohio, Charles Sumner of Massachusetts and Thaddeus Stevens of Pennsylvania, all of whom entered Congress in the years 1849–1851 as uncompromising foes of slavery extension and of the "Slave Power." While ever professing to cherish the Union, they were ready to risk harmony and peace within the Union for the sake of advancing the cause to which they were committed. Southern interests were no less stoutly championed by Jefferson Davis of Mississippi, on whom fell the mantle of Calhoun, and by W. L. Yancey of Alabama, and Alexander H. Stephens, Robert Toombs and Howell Cobb of Georgia. These men frankly calculated the value of the Union in terms of sectional advantage, proclaiming on every occasion the right of secession as a means of Southern redress. The Compromise ideals of the preceding era found spokesmen in John J. Crittenden of Kentucky, Clay's successor in the Senate, and in Senator John Bell of Tennessee, men of lesser stature, however, than the sectional chieftains.

Stephen A. Douglas, the Illinois Senator, is harder to classify, but he was one of the dominant political figures of the decade. Short in stature but with powerful shoulders, idolized by his Western followers as the "Little Giant," he embodied the two ideals dear to the frontier: ardent attachment to nationality and an unfaltering faith in local self-rule as a solvent of human ills. He was also interested in the rapid economic development of the West and particularly in the growth of Chicago where he had heavy real-estate investments. As the foremost Democrat in the free states, his position gave him an unusual opportunity to act as conciliator and arbiter between Northern radicals and Southern "fire-eaters." The fifties, however, were not a time when one who sought a middle ground between extremes could attain success — certainly not a man who, like Douglas, failed utterly to comprehend the intensity of the moral opposition to slavery. His solution for the slavery question in the territories, that of "popular sovereignty," deserved a better reception than it received, but at the same time it revealed that in his political thinking he still adhered blindly to the democratic philosophy of Jackson's day. A believer in the destiny of Middle America and an exemplar of its aspirations, he retained his hold on his section unshaken until Abraham Lincoln emerged from private life in 1858.

Despite twenty years of abolitionist activity and propaganda in the North, the new antislavery leaders had much popular inertia and indifference to overcome if their cause was to be successful. In accomplishing this object, certain literary forces proved of incalculable value. The first was the advent of a new type of journalism. By 1852 the official party organs, located at Washington and subsidized by government printing, were rapidly on the decline, to disappear entirely by the close of the decade. Such journals made dull reading for any but bigoted partisans, and their high subscription price further narrowed the circle of their influence. The gradual assumption by the government itself, after 1846, of the task of executing the public printing foreshadowed the end. But the end was inevitable in any case, for the masses educated in the free public schools demanded a different type of newspaper, and New York City, thanks to the improved news facilities afforded by the telegraph and the railroad, was fast replacing Washington as the principal news center of the nation.

The new journalism flowered most luxuriantly in New York and the East. Selling at a price within the reach of all, the papers sought to make a broad popular appeal with headlines, sprightly news "stories" and trenchant editorials.[1] The period produced the greatest editorial writers in our history. Unlike those today they usually owned the journals they directed — men such as Horace Greeley of the *New York Tribune*, Henry J. Raymond of the *New York Times*, James Gordon Bennett of the *New York Herald*, Samuel Bowles of the *Springfield* (Massachusetts) *Republican* and Joseph Medill of the *Chicago Tribune*. William Cullen Bryant, who at the helm of the *New York Evening Post* had steered a course of vigorous independent journalism since 1826, continued to make a special appeal to the educated classes in the East. In national circulation and influence no other newspaper equaled the *Tribune*, edited by the brilliant but eccentric Greeley. He was by temperament a reformer, and none of the agitations of the time, from spiritualism to scientific farming and Irish freedom, failed to challenge his interest. But his soul-consuming passion was hatred of slavery, and to this cause he gave increasing devotion during the fifties. The *Tribune's* circulation grew fivefold from 1850 to 1860; but its sectional character is evidenced by the fact that virtually all its subscribers lived in the free states. The weekly edition was preëminently the journal of the rural districts which regarded it as a sort of political Bible. The antislavery forces could hardly have found a more potent vehicle of agitation and education.

No less effective in molding Northern opinion, though in a

---

[1] The change had begun as early as 1833 when the *New York Sun* was founded as a "penny paper" catering particularly to working-class readers. Of the newspapers here named, the *Times* (1851) was the only one established after 1850. Medill formed his connection with the *Chicago Tribune* in 1855.

/ 7 6 4
C 2

different way, was the appearance of that great propagandist
novel, *Uncle Tom's Cabin*, written by Harriet Beecher Stowe of
Cincinnati. Others had long inveighed against slavery in the
abstract, but Mrs. Stowe portrayed concretely and with moral
intensity the cruelty and injustice that the system could inflict
even upon a faithful liegeman like the lovable Uncle Tom. She
depicted not the average condition of slaves but, rather, the
melodramatic contrast between the best and worst possibilities
of their existence. Appearing originally as a serial in an antislavery newspaper at the capital, the story was published in
book form in March, 1852. At once it began its record-breaking
career with a sale of three hundred thousand copies in the first
year. The stage possibilities of the story appealed first to theatrical managers, then to political managers. Presently thousands
of men and boys who would not have read the book were thrilled
and swayed by the dramatized version. Mrs. Stowe's interpretation of slavery deeply influenced the thinking of Northern
youths who came of voting age in the years from 1852 to 1860.
In the South it was anathema.

THE REVIVAL OF SECTIONAL DISCORD

The first actual steps toward a disturbance of the sectional
accord were taken by moral enthusiasts of the North in defiance
of the new fugitive-slave act. Because the Supreme Court had
decided in Prigg *v.* Pennsylvania (1842) that state authorities
need not assist in recovering runaways, the law of 1850 had
clothed the federal government with far-reaching powers for
the purpose, even to the extent of denying trial by jury and other
customary legal safeguards to the Negro whose freedom was
at stake. The provisions were energetically put into operation
by the slave owners. In some instances, fugitives who had been
living on free soil for many years and had married there were
seized and carried off into bondage again. Northern communities, which thus saw some of the harshest features of the slavery
system enacted before their very eyes, were easily incited to
riotous opposition. One case that attracted nation-wide attention occurred in Boston in February, 1851, when a runaway
named Shadrach was forcibly taken from the United States
marshal and spirited away into Canada. Some months later, in

October, the seizure of Jerry McHenry, for several years a resident of Syracuse, New York, led to another lawless rescue, under Gerrit Smith's leadership, followed by the Negro's flight across the border.

Nor did the course pursued by the new administration at Washington augur well for the finality of the Compromise. Franklin Pierce, a small-town New Hampshire lawyer chosen to head his party because none of the real leaders could be nominated, lacked both the experience and ability to cope with the complex forces that portended a renewal of sectional strife. When taking the oath of office on March 3, 1853, he expressed the fervent hope that "no sectional or ambitious or fanatical excitement may again threaten the durability of our institutions or obscure the light of our prosperity." Yet a definite proslavery influence was reflected in his choice of a cabinet. Under Southern pressure he withdrew his offer of the post of Secretary of State, first made to a New Yorker with antislavery leanings, and appointed instead another New Yorker, William L. Marcy, who more nearly met the Southern requirements. Jefferson Davis, noted as an implacable opponent of the Compromise, received the important office of Secretary of War.[1]

Moreover, in his inaugural address Pierce, while expressing interest in developing "new channels of trade," placed chief emphasis on his intention of not having his course as President deterred "by any timid forebodings of evil" from territorial expansion. The reference, as everyone knew, was to the scheme of annexing Cuba, which Polk and his Secretary of State, James Buchanan, had fostered but which their Whig successors had failed to press. This proposal to enlarge the slave area of the United States greatly pleased Southern extremists who during the Whig lease of power had helped fit out filibustering expeditions in a fruitless endeavor to free the island from Spain. With Marcy's assistance Pierce prepared to translate his words into action. In August, 1854, Buchanan, Pierre Soulé and John Y. Mason, the American Ministers to Great Britain, Spain

[1] The other members of the cabinet were James Guthrie of Kentucky, Secretary of the Treasury; James C. Dobbin of North Carolina, Secretary of the Navy; Robert McClelland of Michigan, Secretary of the Interior; James Campbell of Pennsylvania, Postmaster-General; Caleb Cushing of Massachusetts, Attorney-General.

and France, were instructed to confer as to the best means of acquiring Cuba. In Belgium in October, they drew up a remarkable document, known in history as the Ostend Manifesto. Their recommendation, in brief, was that, if Spain refused to sell the island and should our national interests require, we would be justified "by every law, human and divine," in wresting it from her by force. The President, however, was not prepared to go to such lengths. The recommendation was coldly pigeonholed, but it produced wild excitement in the free states when its contents leaked out.

The administration also coveted territory across the Mexican border, including Lower California. Pierce's diplomatic approaches, however, fruited in an acquisition of unimpressive extent. In 1853 James Gadsden, acting for the United States, negotiated the purchase of an irregular tract south of the Gila River for $10,000,000. By this act a boundary difficulty was settled with Mexico and, at the same time, land acquired which Secretary of War Davis deemed desirable for a Southern railway route to the Pacific. The Gadsden Purchase was the sole consequence of the administration's efforts at expansion southward.

Meantime other events were rendering unavoidable that revival of sectionalism which Pierce's imperialistic program prefigured. A chance combination of circumstances afforded an unexpected opportunity for extending the slave area within American borders. The region between the Rockies and the western boundary of Missouri, Iowa and Minnesota had never been given territorial organization, remaining, for the most part, a vast reserve for wild Indians and roving buffaloes. Located north of the parallel 36° 30′, the entire domain was destined to be free soil by the Missouri Compromise of 1820. The need for opening the country to settlers was fast becoming urgent. As population thickened in the upper Mississippi Valley, more and more people hankered for the virgin lands to the west. Furthermore, national security made desirable a continuous zone of settlement from the heart of the continent to the distant communities on the Pacific Coast. Still others desired to have the region inhabited and the Indian title extinguished in order to facilitate their plans of obtaining governmental support for a transcontinental railway.

On January 4, 1854, Douglas as chairman of the Senate committee on territories offered a bill for organizing the whole domain as the "Territory of Nebraska." His accompanying report
explained that the status of slavery in the proposed territory
should be determined in conformance with the principles underlying the Compromise of 1850. These were said to be the right
of the territorial legislature to admit or exclude slavery (popular

KANSAS AND NEBRASKA, 1854

sovereignty), and the final determination of all questions involving legality of slave ownership by the Supreme Court. Greeted
by a storm of criticism and protest, Douglas was obliged to change
the bill in certain particulars. In its final form it provided not
for one territory but for two, Kansas and Nebraska, with the
fortieth parallel dividing them. The Missouri Compromise was
explicitly repealed, and the people of the territories were authorized to regulate their domestic institutions as they chose, "subject only to the Constitution of the United States." All questions involving title to slaves might be appealed to the Supreme
Court.

From the standpoint of practical politics Douglas undoubtedly won favor for his cause by claiming that the regulations in the Compromise of 1850 as to slavery in New Mexico and Utah had been intended as a rule of universal application; but historians find no warrant for this assumption. He was on equally unsafe ground in alleging that these regulations embodied the principle of popular sovereignty.[1] Indeed, not all who supported the Kansas-Nebraska act believed popular sovereignty to be the import even of that measure. Senator A. G. Brown of Mississippi went so far as to say, "If I thought that in voting for the bill as it now stands I was conceding the right of the people in a territory to exclude slavery, I would withhold my vote. . . . It leaves the question where I am willing it should be left — to the ultimate decision of the courts."[2] The provision for two territories instead of one aided passage, for it was believed that Kansas, lying next to Missouri, would become slave soil while Nebraska would fall to the antislavery Northerners.

The passage of the bill through Congress precipitated a desperate struggle. The Missouri Compromise was consecrated in the hearts of the people as if a part of the Constitution itself. Though Congress possessed the legal power to undo what it had once done, the proposal for repeal deeply outraged the moral sense of the North. The opposition in the Senate was directed by Chase and Sumner, but the Little Giant, ceaselessly active, proved more than their match. In the House the shrewd assaults of ex-Senator Benton were counteracted by the parliamentary adroitness of the proslavery Whig, Alexander H. Stephens. President Pierce, abetted by Jefferson Davis, threw all his prestige and power of patronage in favor of the bill. Its success was assured by the support of an almost solid South, seconded by Democrats from the Midwest. The bill, signed by the President on May 30, 1854, was avowedly a Democratic measure, but

[1] See H. C. Hockett, *Political and Social Growth of the United States, 1492-1852*, 602–603.

[2] Douglas himself later said of the Kansas-Nebraska act: "We did not pretend to decide the question whether the Territorial Legislature had the power or not to prohibit slavery, but we did agree to give them all the power we had; and, if they exercised it in such manner as to violate the constitutional rights of any portion of the people, their remedy is to be found in an appeal to the Supreme Court, and not to Congress."

throughout the stormy contest sectional rather than party advantage had been the prime consideration.

So far-reaching were the effects of the Kansas-Nebraska act that the motives which led to its introduction are a matter of continuing interest. At the time, Douglas was accused by his antislavery foes of making a conscienceless bid for Southern support for the presidency, but it is hardly probable that a man of his political acumen would have risked Northern defections to gain additional favor in the South. Douglas himself found ample justification for his course in the democratic character of his plan and in the belief that popular sovereignty would permanently "withdraw the question of slavery from the halls of Congress and the political arena." In any case, as he pointed out, climate would make impossible the deep rooting of slavery in the new territories. It is only fair to say that nothing in his career, either before or after 1854, warrants us in doubting his unselfish devotion to the principle of local self-determination.

Other factors, however, were involved in the situation. The agitation for a transcontinental railroad had created rivalry between the Northwest and the Southwest, each seeking new means of nourishing its own sectional prosperity. Though an engineering survey of the War Department reported the superior feasibility of a Southern route, enterprising men in the Northwest were not willing to yield the point, and they believed that rapid settlement of the Nebraska country would be a potent argument for a centrally located line. Douglas, eager for the commercial preëminence of Chicago, was a natural leader in any such movement. Thus the economic interest of the Northwest, as well as its democratic idealism, favored the bill. The South was willing temporarily to weaken its chances because of the opportunity for slavery extension afforded by popular sovereignty.[1] As a matter of fact, sectional rivalry was to prevent

[1] Additional support for the bill resulted from a factional fight in Missouri within Democratic ranks. Senator D. R. Atchison, seeking reëlection and finding a bold course necessary to rally his slaveholding constituents, publicly promised that when he returned to Congress in December, 1853, he would work to have the rich prairie lands west of the state opened to settlers without the Missouri Compromise restriction. Besides, like the Illinois Senator, he desired to connect his state with California by rail. Had not Douglas fathered the Kansas-Nebraska bill, it seems certain that Atchison would have.

federal aid to any transcontinental project until after secession caused the withdrawal of Southern representatives from Congress and left the North in control.

SELECT BIBLIOGRAPHY

The Ordeal of Nationality. The years from 1853 to 1865 are treated, with a wealth of detail and from differing points of view, in the standard comprehensive histories, notably Channing, *A History of the United States*, embracing the period 1000–1865; Von Holst, *The Constitutional and Political History of the United States*, covering the period 1750–1861; McMaster, *A History of the People of the United States*, dealing with the period 1784–1865; Rhodes, *History of the United States from the Compromise of 1850 to the Final Restoration of Home Rule at the South in 1877;* and Schouler, *History of the United States*, covering the years from 1783 to 1877. In a class with these large-scale treatments by a single hand are the major coöperative works, dealing with American history from the beginning: Hart, ed., *The American Nation: A History;* Johnson, ed., *The Chronicles of America Series;* and Schlesinger and Fox, eds., *A History of American Life*, the last a social and intellectual history. Individual volumes of these series are cited later in appropriate connections. Various aspects of American development are treated pictorially in Gabriel, ed., *The Pageant of America*. Among the standard biographical series are Morse, ed., *American Statesmen;* Oberholtzer, ed., *American Crisis Biographies;* Howe, ed., *The Beacon Biographies;* and Nevins, ed., *American Political Leaders*. For briefer reference, the *Dictionary of American Biography*, edited by Allen Johnson and Dumas Malone, is indispensable. The most useful historical atlas is Paullin, *Atlas of the Historical Geography of the United States*.

Special phases of American history have received separate attention. Stanwood, *A History of the Presidency*, is concerned with presidential elections. General sketches of economic development include Bogart, *An Economic History of the United States;* Faulkner, *American Economic History;* and Kirkland, *A History of American Economic Life*. More particularized are Clark, *History of Manufactures in the United States;* Dewey, *Financial History of the United States;* Taussig, *Tariff History of the United States;* Commons and others, *History of Labour in the United States;* Schmidt and Ross, eds., *Readings in the Economic History of American Agriculture;* and Frederick, *The Development of American Commerce*. Textbooks on diplomatic relations include Fish, *American Diplomacy*, and Latané, *History of American Foreign Policy*. Bemis, ed., *The American Secretaries of State and Their Diplomacy*, provides a biographical approach to the subject.

Mid-century America. Cole, *The Irrepressible Conflict*, treats the subject as a whole. Industrial and technological changes may be followed in Clark, *History of Manufactures in the United States*, and Byrn, *The Progress of Invention in the Nineteenth Century*. Johnson and others, *History of the Domestic and Foreign Commerce of the United States*, the most extensive general account, should be supplemented by Spears, *The Story of the American*

Merchant Marine; Clark, *The Clipper Ship Era, 1843–1869;* and Morison, *The Maritime History of Massachusetts, 1783–1860,* which joins scholarship with unusual literary charm. On railway development the standard works are Sanborn, *Congressional Grants of Land in Aid of Railways;* Haney, *A Congressional History of Railways in the United States, 1850–1887;* MacGill and others, *History of Transportation in the United States before 1860;* and Riegel, *The Story of the Western Railroads.* Bidwell and Falconer, *History of Agriculture in the Northern United States, 1620–1860,* and Gray, *History of Agriculture in the Southern United States to 1860,* contain much information in regard to the fifties. Hutchinson, *Cyrus Hall McCormick, Seed-Time, 1809–1856,* describes the rôle played by the chief inventor and maker of farm implements. Phillips, *Life and Labor in the Old South,* includes material on economic and social conditions in the fifties, while Ingle, *Southern Sidelights,* supplements Phillips at various points. Bancroft, *Slave-Trading in the Old South,* is the best treatment of its subject. Russel, *Economic Aspects of Southern Sectionalism, 1840–1861,* and Wendell, *Southern Commercial Conventions,* show, with full documentation, the importance of economic inferiority as a factor in the movement for Southern independence. Diplomatic phases of the era are treated in Dennett, *Americans in Eastern Asia;* Treat, *Diplomatic Relations between the United States and Japan, 1853–1865;* and Williams, *Anglo-American Isthmian Diplomacy, 1815–1915.*

Foreign Influences. The interest of the American people in the mid-century European revolutions appears in Curtis, *The French Assembly of 1848 and American Constitutional Doctrines;* Gazley, *American Opinion of German Unification;* and Marraro, *American Opinion on the Unification of Italy, 1846–1861.*   General accounts of immigration include Fairchild, *Immigration;* Garis, *Immigration Restriction;* and Stephenson, *A History of American Immigration.* For particular racial elements Adams, *Ireland and Irish Emigration to the New World,* Faust, *The German Element in the United States,* and Blegen, *Norwegian Migration to America, 1825–1860,* should be consulted.

The Rise of a New Generation. For biographies of Northern leaders, see Bancroft, *The Life of William H. Seward;* Hart, *Salmon Portland Chase;* Haynes, *Charles Sumner;* Woodburn, *The Life of Thaddeus Stevens;* Johnson, *Stephen A. Douglas;* and Linn, *Horace Greeley.* Lives of outstanding Southern figures include Dodd, *Jefferson Davis;* Pendleton, *Alexander H. Stephens;* Phillips, *The Life of Robert Toombs;* Craven, *Edmund Ruffin, Southerner;* White, *Robert Barnwell Rhett;* Merritt, *James Henry Hammond;* and Flippin, *Herschel V. Johnson of Georgia.* Bleyer, *Main Currents in the History of American Journalism,* portrays the new era in the newspaper world.

The Revival of Sectional Discord. Political development and party conflict during the decade are traced in Smith, *Parties and Slavery;* Cole, *The Irrepressible Conflict,* deals with the divisive economic and social forces. Nichols, *Franklin Pierce,* appraises Pierce's presidency with relentless honesty. Two phases of foreign policy are treated in Garber, *The Gadsden Treaty,* and Ettinger, *The Mission to Spain of Pierre Soulé, 1853–1855.* Difficulties of enforcing the fugitive-slave act may be followed in Siebert,

The Underground Railroad from Slavery to Freedom. The question of the motives behind the Kansas-Nebraska act has provoked considerable discussion among historians. Rhodes lays it all to Douglas's personal ambition for the presidency. According to Ray, *The Repeal of the Missouri Compromise,* the act should be understood as the execution of a campaign pledge made by Senator Atchison of Missouri in his contest for reëlection. Hodder in his "Genesis of the Kansas-Nebraska Act," Wisconsin Historical Society, *Proceedings for 1912,* 69–86, and elsewhere, represents the act as one phase of the rivalry between Northern and Southern commercial interests to secure the terminus of the proposed Pacific railway.

CHAPTER II

THE DRIFT TOWARD DISUNION, 1854–1860

THE PARTY REVOLUTION

NO law ever passed by Congress produced such momentous consequences as the Kansas-Nebraska act. While the bill was yet before Congress, Chase predicted, "It will light up a fire in the country which may, perhaps, consume those who kindle it." The reasons are not far to seek. The measure not only revived all the old rancors over slavery extension, which Pierce had promised were at an end, but did so at the cost of annulling a long-standing sectional pact which, in the North at least, had assumed an almost sacred character. Hardly less important was the fact that the self-interest of the Northern farmers, both native and foreign-born, was directly threatened by the law. Accustomed to think of the new territories as a Promised Land to which they would eventually fall heir, they now faced possible competition with slave labor there. Nor were they made less apprehensive by the fact that, while the Kansas-Nebraska measure was under consideration, a bill which would have encouraged Northern settlement through free homesteads had been blocked by the proslavery Senate after passing the House. Greeley declared that Douglas and Pierce had made more abolitionists in three months than William Lloyd Garrison and Wendell Phillips could in half a century.

To the Whig party the act dealt a death blow. Already weakened by sectional differences, the two factions of the party now found themselves occupying opposing camps. Most of the Southern members in Congress had voted for the measure while every Northern one had opposed it. The next few years witnessed the dispersion of the Whigs into the ranks of other parties. The Democrats also suffered, though in less degree. If their numbers were diminished in the North by the desertion of "Anti-Nebraska" Democrats, the loss was in considerable degree offset by accessions from the Southern Whigs. A. H. Stephens and Robert Toombs who now turned Democrat were hosts in themselves. Under the circumstances the party became more firmly allied than ever with the interests of cotton capitalism.

The most significant outcome of the Kansas-Nebraska contest, however, was the rise of two new organizations. One was the Republican party. While the act was yet pending in Congress, antislavery leaders there had issued an appeal to the people, branding it as "a gross violation of a sacred pledge" and "an atrocious plot to exclude from a vast unoccupied region immigrants from the Old World and free laborers from our own States." Three political factions were ripe for union on a program opposed to slavery extension: most of the Northern Whigs, the old Free Soilers (who had called themselves Free Democrats in the campaign of 1852) and the Anti-Nebraska Democrats. Another source of strength lay in the immigrant farmers of the Midwest, whose probable political course was charted by the anti-Nebraska editorials in eighty out of eighty-eight German newspapers. Horace Greeley took a leading part in urging independent political action, but the party actually sprang into being from a spontaneous uprising of the people in the Midwest. On February 28, 1854, a local gathering at Ripon, Wisconsin, heralded the new party; other localities fell into line; and on July 6 a giant mass meeting in an oak grove near Jackson, Michigan, organized the party on a state-wide basis. By the fall of 1854 the new organization was active in all the Western states and in some Eastern ones, though the name Republican was not yet everywhere employed.

In the East progress was slower because of the powerful competition offered by the newly formed American party. This party was an outgrowth of the strong nativist prejudice against immigrants and especially Catholics. Having as its nucleus the Supreme Order of the Star-Spangled Banner, it was organized as a secret society with grips, passwords and ritualistic ceremonies. Since members declined to satisfy outside curiosity in regard to the organization, they were popularly called "Know Nothings." As a matter of fact, each member swore a solemn oath to oppose any but American-born Protestants for office. The secrecy and charm of novelty won many persons to the party, especially in the East where aliens were least welcome and most in evidence. At the same time, important accessions came from people all over the North, who hoped by magnifying the new issue to drive the slavery question out of politics. Many Southern Whigs joined because loath to make common cause with their traditional enemies, the Democrats; indeed, to oppose immigration seemed a means of curbing the growth of anti-slavery power.

The fall elections of 1854 revealed the remarkable advance of the two new parties. With no public campaign the Know Nothings cast over a fourth of the total vote in New York and more than two fifths in Pennsylvania. In Massachusetts they elected every state officer and nearly the entire legislature, while lesser successes greeted them elsewhere. The Republicans swept Maine, Vermont and all the Midwestern states but Illinois. The Democrats lost control not only of the House of Representatives but of nine states besides. Nearly everywhere the Whigs revealed great weakness, their success in New York being due to Seward's reluctance to leave the party until after his reëlection as Senator. Vastly elated, the Know Nothings laid plans to capture the presidency two years later. In order to consolidate the support which had come from voters averse to sectional strife, they now added to their ritual a "Union oath," pledging all members to resist the election to office of disunionists as well as immigrants. But with the political waters in turmoil it was impossible for any party to steer a middle course. The Northern and Southern sections inevitably fell into contentions over slavery, and by 1856 the Know Nothings found themselves officially committed to popular sovereignty. Since this doctrine was, in a political sense, copyrighted by the Democrats, the fate of the party was sealed. Its activities in local politics, however, were not without effect, for Know Nothing influence was responsible for the enactment of literacy tests for voting in Connecticut in 1855 and in Massachusetts two years later — the first laws of the kind in our history.[1] The object was to reduce the number of naturalized voters.

Meantime the Republican-controlled states proceeded to take whatever legal steps they could to impede or defeat the operation

---

[1] These states stood alone until 1889 when Wyoming and presently certain other commonwealths imposed literacy requirements.

of the fugitive-slave act. Such statutes usually prohibited the use of local jails to confine fugitives and punished severely the seizure of a free Negro with intent to enslave him. The personal-liberty laws, as they were called, were hailed by the South as proof positive of the aggressive and lawless character of the party. In the free states, however, the Republicans steadily gained in popular favor. Seward, a giant of strength, took over the reins of leadership in the East in 1855; the fiery partisan discussions in Congress helped educate the Northern masses; and in May, 1856, occurred a brutal assault on Senator Sumner which, in a different way, aided the Republican cause. A few days after Sumner had made a violent speech against Southern machinations in Kansas, he was attacked and caned into insensibility by Preston Brooks, a member of the House and nephew of a Southern Senator whom Sumner had assailed with particular venom. The deed enraged the North which saw in it additional evidence of the ruthlessness of the "Slave Power." An attempt to expel Brooks from his seat failed, every Southern member but one voting to sustain him.

The Republicans faced the campaign of 1856 in a resolute mood, meeting at Philadelphia on June 17, the anniversary of Bunker Hill. The presidential nomination went to John C. Frémont of California, a popular figure by reason of his explorations in the Far West and at the same time a man unhampered by past political antipathies such as embarrassed Seward and Chase. For second place W. L. Dayton of New Jersey was chosen over Abraham Lincoln, the Midwestern candidate. The platform called for the exclusion of slavery from all territories as a requirement of the Constitution, flayed the Pierce administration for the efforts it was making to impose slavery on Kansas, and stigmatized the Ostend Manifesto as "the highwayman's plea that 'might makes right.'" The convention of the Know Nothings was marked by angry debates, ending in the withdrawal of most of the antislavery delegates. In their platform the Know Nothings denounced the election of immigrants and Catholics to office, demanded twenty-one years' residence for naturalization, and advocated an indestructible Union with popular sovereignty in the territories. Millard Fillmore, whose signature had given legal effect to the Compromise of 1850, was nominated for President with A. J. Donelson of Tennessee as his running mate. Later in the year these nominations were indorsed by a national convention composed of remnants of the old Whig party.

The Democrats, fearing to nominate either Pierce or Douglas as too deeply tainted by their sponsorship of the Kansas-Nebraska bill, chose instead James Buchanan of Pennsylvania, who had been Minister to Great Britain during most of the controversy. With him was associated John C. Breckinridge of Kentucky. The platform vindicated popular sovereignty and the Kansas-Nebraska act as consistent with the Compromise of 1850, while condemning the "political crusade" of the Know Nothings as contrary to the American "spirit of toleration and enlightened freedom." The campaign that followed was a thrilling one. In the North the Republicans conducted a canvass rivaling that of 1840 in enthusiasm and having behind it what the earlier campaign lacked — a dynamic moral drive. With the slogan of "Bleeding Kansas" they sought to arouse the latent fear of every Northerner against the proslavery "Buchaneers." They made an especial appeal to the wage-earners, circulating campaign material which represented slaveholders as declaring, for example, that "Slavery is the natural and normal condition of the *laboring man*, whether WHITE or *black*." Alarmed by the success of such tactics, the conservative elements of the country assailed the Republicans as a radical sectional party. Both Buchanan and Fillmore maintained that Frémont's election would cause a break-up of the Union. It was repeatedly declared in Philadelphia that, if Buchanan should be defeated, the South would decline to pay the $60,000,000 which it owed the merchants and manufacturers of that city. Southern pamphleteers recklessly charged that the antislavery men were "committed to Socialism and Communism — to no private property, no church, no laws, no government — to free love, free lands, free women and free churches." Conservatism triumphed. Buchanan polled 174 electoral votes, including every slave state except Maryland whose eight votes alone Fillmore succeeded in winning. Frémont received 114 votes from eleven Northern states. Though the Democratic party was returned to office, the surprising vote polled by the Republicans marked them as a political force to be reckoned with.

THE DRIVE FOR SLAVERY EXTENSION

Buchanan, the new President, had behind him a record of holding public offices of one sort or another for forty years without having attained real distinction in any of them. A Northerner by birth and upbringing, he had always been favorable to the political objects of cotton capitalism. Reaching the goal of his ambitions at the age of sixty-six, he surrounded himself with advisers who shared the same point of view. Lewis Cass of Michigan, head of the cabinet and a man older than his chief, was widely known because of his Southern sympathies as the "archdoughface." Four other members were from slave states and two from free states.[1] To the new administration fell the difficult and delicate task of healing the wounds inflicted by the revival of sectionalism. But this was a course for which Buchanan was ill fitted since one of his dominant purposes was to find new territory for Southern expansion. The admission of California as a part of the Compromise of 1850 had destroyed the "sacred balance" of free and slave states in the Senate, and the rapid increase of Northern population produced two more free-soil states during Buchanan's term — Minnesota in 1858 and Oregon in 1859. In the President's mind the permanence of the Union depended upon a restoration of the old equality. From this point of view he approached all the great problems of the time.

Like his two Democratic predecessors, he espoused a policy of tropical annexation. Since westward expansion had built up the power of the free states, why should not Manifest Destiny now direct the course of empire southward? In three annual messages he urged upon Congress the acquisition of Cuba "by fair purchase." Central America, he predicted in his message of 1858, would fall to the United States "at no distant day" by the natural course of events. Upon the same occasion he proposed a protectorate over northern Mexico. Repeating his recommendation the next year, he asked authority to invade Mexico to restore order. But his efforts were ill timed. With the coun-

---

[1] Howell Cobb of Georgia, Secretary of the Treasury; J. B. Floyd of Virginia, Secretary of War; Isaac Toucey of Connecticut, Secretary of the Navy; Jacob Thompson of Mississippi, Secretary of the Interior; A. V. Brown of Tennessee, Postmaster-General; Jeremiah S. Black of Pennsylvania, Attorney-General.

try embroiled over the question of extending slavery within boundaries already possessed, Congress declined to heed the President's call to foreign adventure.

The attempt to apply popular sovereignty had reached a critical stage when Buchanan entered office. The Republican campaign slogan of "Bleeding Kansas" hardly exaggerated conditions. If the new territory had contained a settled population when Pierce signed the law, the slavery question might perhaps have been peaceably decided. Since the region was virtually unoccupied, however, the Kansas-Nebraska act precipitated a mad scramble on the part of each section for political control. Many organizations were formed in the North, among which the New England Emigrant Aid Company was outstanding, to urge colonization and assist settlers with reduced transportation fares and necessary equipment. While the Southern planters, hampered by smaller numbers and an undersupply of slaves, could not meet this competition in kind, secret lodges along the Missouri border held themselves ready to cross into Kansas and stuff the ballot boxes in behalf of Southern interests. The intense rivalry resulted in the establishment of two groups of settlements. The Northerners flocked into the Kansas River Valley, naming their principal town Lawrence in honor of the chief patron of the New England Emigrant Aid Company. The proslavery strongholds, on the other hand, were Atchison and Leavenworth on the Missouri River and Lecompton on the Kansas.

The free-soil settlers already outnumbered their antagonists when the first territorial legislature was chosen on March 30, 1855, but the pro-Southern forces carried the day with the illegal help of the "Border Ruffians." While the legislature thus elected proceeded to adopt laws establishing slavery, the free settlers in protest set up a *de facto* government of their own and, in October, held a constitutional convention at Topeka which proposed to Congress a state constitution banning slavery.[1] President Pierce, had he been so disposed, might at this juncture have solved the difficulties by declaring both governments irregular and holding a fresh election under the protection of

[1] A bill to admit Kansas under the Topeka constitution passed the House of Representatives on July 3, 1856, but received scant consideration in the Senate.

federal bayonets. Instead, he adopted a narrowly legal view, siding with the proslavery legislature and pledging the full power of his office "to support public order." Emboldened by such high sanction, the pro-Southern leaders took vigorous steps to crush the Topeka government. The free-soil "governor" and his chief associates were indicted for treason and on May 21, 1856, a proslavery force, acting as a posse, invaded Lawrence and sacked it.

A few days passed and then the country, for the first time, heard the name of John Brown. Born in Connecticut, he had grown to manhood amidst frontier conditions in northern Ohio. Both his mother and grandmother had died insane and a sister and five cousins suffered from the same affliction. Imbibing an intense hatred of slavery in childhood, he became convinced that he was, in some way, divinely appointed to accomplish its doom. In August, 1855, he set out for Osawatomie, Kansas, where his five sons had preceded him, traveling in a one-horse wagon filled with guns and ammunition. Incensed by the attack on Lawrence, he resolved, in the spirit of Old Testament justice, to slay five pro-Southerners to atone for an equal number of deaths of free-soilers. On the night of May 24 he and his band fell upon a settlement on Pottawatomie Creek and ruthlessly executed his purpose. The massacre served as fuel to the spreading flames. For several months parties of men from each side roamed the country, plundering and killing. In all, two hundred lives were lost and two million dollars' worth of property destroyed. Only a vigorous employment of United States troops finally brought the guerrilla warfare to an end in November, 1856.

Though the proslavery party occupied the seats of power in the territory, it was certain that the next election would go against them. In anticipation of the event they summoned a constitutional convention which, meeting at Lecompton in September, 1857, drew up a proslavery constitution. To make assurance doubly sure, the convention refused to give the people a clear choice between accepting or rejecting the instrument. The voters were, in effect, permitted merely to affirm whether they favored the Lecompton constitution with or without the further introduction of slaves. Outraged by this fresh perversion of popular sovereignty, the free-soil partisans, who had already declined to participate in the election of delegates, once more stayed away from the polls. The constitution was ratified with the extreme slavery clause by a vote of 6226 to 569. When the free-soilers captured the new legislature in October, they resubmitted the constitution to the people on the express issue of acceptance or rejection. It was defeated by 10,226 to 162, the pro-Southerners this time refusing to vote.

However irregular these proceedings, it was clear that a large majority opposed the proslavery constitution. Yet President Buchanan, as narrowly legalistic as his predecessor and laboring under a similar influence, urged Congress to grant statehood to Kansas under the Lecompton instrument. One Democratic chieftain, however, none other than the great proponent of popular sovereignty himself, held differently. Douglas warned Congress that he would not have the doctrine used as "trickery and jugglery to defeat the fair expression of the will of the people." In bold defiance of the administration he set about to prevent favorable action. Feeling ran high in Congress, Buchanan personally threatened the Little Giant with political oblivion, and the administration press charged him with having turned "Black Republican." Though Douglas's efforts proved unsuccessful in the Senate, the House on April 1, 1858, defeated the President's proposal.

For a month the Kansas matter stood at a halt; then the deadlock was broken by a compromise measure, the so-called English bill. This act authorized a third submission of the Lecompton constitution to popular vote, with the provision, however, that, in case of acceptance, Kansas should receive a specified grant of government lands within the state and, in case of rejection, statehood should wait until the population reached the number (93,560) necessary for a Representative in Congress. Though the bill was manifestly unfair and Douglas voted against it, it at least gave the people a chance to reject the instrument entire. This the voters proceeded to do in August, 1858, by a majority of 11,300 to 1788. The protracted conflict over Kansas added immeasurably to sectional ill will, for the nation was deeply stirred by the dramatic and ruthless struggle. Though the contest was conducted by fanatics on the two sides, the law-abiding citizens of each section came to regard the extremists of the other as representing the general state of mind. Meantime Kansas remained a territory until January, 1861, when the withdrawal of Southern Congressmen made possible its admission as a free state.

THE SUPREME COURT AND SLAVERY EXTENSION

In his inaugural address Buchanan had voiced the hope that all contention over the status of slavery in the territories would soon be stilled by a forthcoming judgment of the Supreme Court. Two days later, on March 6, 1857, the famous decision of Dred Scott v. Sandford was announced. Dred Scott was a Missouri slave who some twenty years before had been taken by his then master, an army surgeon, to reside at various posts in the free state of Illinois and, later, to a fort in the northern part of the Louisiana Purchase where slavery was forbidden by the Missouri Compromise. Returning to Missouri and becoming discontented with his lot, Dred was prompted by some antislavery lawyers to begin suit for liberation on the score of his residence on free soil.[1] Meantime he was sold to an absentee master residing in another state. After a long period of litigation the case finally reached the federal Supreme Court. The Negro's right to sue there rested upon the constitutional provision granting the federal judiciary jurisdiction in cases arising between citizens of different states. The Supreme Court, therefore, had to decide the preliminary question, was Dred really a citizen? before it could consider the question, was he a freeman? If it decided against his citizenship, the customary practice of the court dictated that it would not then pass upon the more important question of his freedom.

The majority of the court held that he was not a citizen, asserting that Negroes had not been citizens of any state at the time of the formation of the Constitution, and that the Constitution, in their judgment, was intended to apply only to the white race. Here, according to precedent, the case should have ended, but Chief Justice Roger B. Taney and his associates felt that an opinion on the merits of the case from the preëminent judicial

[1] The fact that the Missouri Compromise was repealed in 1854 had, of course, no bearing upon Dred Scott's rights under that law while it was still in force.

tribunal would remove a dangerous question from the political arena. The court, therefore, went on to declare that the Missouri Compromise had all along been void, for Congress lacked the constitutional right to enact a law which arbitrarily deprived persons of their property, slave or otherwise, in the territories of the United States.[1] Accordingly, Dred Scott was not entitled to freedom and, by the same token, masters had a constitutional right to hold slaves anywhere in the federal domain. The court attached no importance to Dred Scott's sojourn in Illinois, arguing that, since his residence was only temporary, his status as slave or freeman depended upon the laws of Missouri, not Illinois.

The decision created fierce excitement throughout the North, increased by the fact that the court itself had not been in agreement, two members from the free states dissenting. Mr. Justice B. R. Curtis, challenging the assumption that Negroes had never been citizens in any of the states, insisted that Dred Scott was a citizen within the meaning of the Constitution. He justified the Missouri Compromise by the constitutional power of Congress to "make all needful rules and regulations" for the federal territories, rejecting Taney's view that this grant of authority was limited to the original area of the United States. He further contended that the judgment of the court in regard to the Missouri Compromise was an *obiter dictum*, that is, a pronouncement on matters not properly before the judges. As such, it had no legal binding effect.

Republican indignation was unrestrained. Not even in Jefferson's time had the judiciary come in for such bitter condemnation. Republican spokesmen made the most of the fact that seven of the nine judges were Democrats, five of them from slave states. Greeley declared in the *Tribune* that Taney's decision was "entitled to just so much moral weight as would be the judgment of a majority of those congregated in any Washington bar-room." Thousands of copies of the dissenting opinions were printed and circulated as campaign documents. In reality, the party was in a bad predicament, for, if the Dred Scott decision were binding, then the Republican platform was unconstitutional

---

[1] "Nor shall any person . . . be deprived of life, liberty, or property, without due process of law." Constitution, Amendment V.

and the party must disband. For the Southern Democrats the decision was a great victory, since it gave judicial sanction to the extreme theory of slavery in the territories. Northern Democrats, on the other hand, accepted it with mental reservations. Douglas and his followers did not fail to see that the doctrine of the Dred Scott case ran counter to, if it did not outlaw, the theory of popular sovereignty.

THE WIDENING OF THE SECTIONAL BREACH

The Republicans, conscious of the growing appeal of their party in the North, looked eagerly to a new trial of strength in the fall elections of 1858. To Northern wrath over "Bleeding Kansas" was now added resentment over the Dred Scott decision; and both meant converts to the cause. In 1857 occurred another event which, in the minds of the unthinking, further discredited the party in power: a financial storm burst upon the country that did not entirely clear away during Buchanan's term of office. The Panic of 1857 was the price exacted for the excessive commercial and industrial development which had marked the years that went before. Flush times had produced the usual orgy of speculation and imprudent investment. In anticipation of the future growth of the country, railroads, manufacturers and promoters of all kinds had burdened themselves with indebtedness beyond their existing power to repay. The crash came in the summer and autumn. Fourteen railway corporations failed; banks and insurance companies suspended; factories closed their doors. As untold numbers of wage-earners faced the winter of 1857–1858 without work, "hunger meetings," often tinged with revolutionary bitterness, took place in Eastern centers. The Western farmers, too, were involved in the disaster. Crops were scarcely moved in some localities and grain exports diminished by half. Even the South, despite the relative absence of speculation there, did not wholly escape. According to Senator Hammond of South Carolina, the Northern failure to advance money as usual to market its crops inflicted a loss of $35,000,000. Many Southerners discovered in this default a fresh reason why their section should live its economic life apart from the North.

As the country recovered from the shock of the panic, the autumn elections were at hand. Throughout the North the

Republicans waged active campaigns and in every state but Illinois and Indiana their opponents lost ground. Even the President's own state of Pennsylvania turned from him because of umbrage at the tariff of 1857 (see page 9) and the inroads of the panic on the iron industry. The senatorial contest in Illinois possessed unusual features of interest. The Republicans there had nominated Abraham Lincoln, a lawyer of local repute with some slight experience in the state legislature and Congress. Opposed to him was the veteran Douglas whose recent break with Buchanan over the Lecompton constitution had earlier prompted Greeley and other Easterners to advise their Illinois brethren not to put up a candidate against him. They saw in the Little Giant a possible accession of strength to their own party.

As the new Senator was to be chosen by a legislature not yet elected, the rival candidates went before the voters of Illinois in a series of seven joint debates to acquaint them with the issues. Upon the lean and ungainly Lincoln rested the burden of the attack. Not only was he challenging Douglas's right to continue in the Senate, but he was also spokesman for a new party. Striking the first blow in his speech accepting the nomination, he undertook to convince the people of the aggressive proslavery purposes of the Democrats. Before it was too late, he asserted, the free-soil North must take a bold stand against the "Slave Power," for the Dred Scott decision was merely an entering wedge for a later pronouncement that would legalize slavery throughout the land. "'A house divided against itself cannot stand.' I believe this government cannot endure permanently half slave and half free. . . . It will become all one thing or all the other." Lincoln, of course, was expressing not a purpose but the perception of a great truth; but Douglas, seizing the opportunity, made an adroit countercharge that the Republicans were plotting to destroy slavery within the Southern states.

Lincoln next undertook to show that Douglas, despite his stand against the Lecompton constitution, was unworthy of Republican support. Douglas's opposition, he pointed out, had been actuated not by antislavery motives but by his attachment to popular sovereignty. With fine rhetorical effect he quoted Douglas's own words in Congress: "If Kansas wants a slave-state Constitution, she has a right to it; if she wants a free-state Constitution, she has a right to it. . . . I care not whether it [slavery] is voted down or voted up." Finally, Lincoln took occasion to bring to sharp public notice the contradiction between the Dred Scott pronouncement, which legalized slavery in all federal territories, and Douglas's doctrine of 1854, which left the matter to the territorial legislature. By asking Douglas to reconcile the two positions Lincoln placed him in a dilemma.[1] If he reaffirmed the right of popular sovereignty, he would retain the loyalty of the Illinois farmers, imbued with frontier ideals of democracy, but such a declaration would deprive the Dred Scott decision of its force and alienate Southern backing for the presidency in 1860. On the other hand, a confession that popular sovereignty had been outlawed by the action of the Supreme Court would insure his defeat in the election at hand.

Douglas's reply is known as the Freeport Doctrine or, as the Southern Democrats called it, the Freeport Heresy. He drew a distinction between theory and practice in the application of the Dred Scott decision. In theory, slavery might exist throughout the federal domain; in practice, no master would go where his right of slaveholding was not fully protected by territorial law. Therefore, he concluded, the failure of a legislature to enact such a body of law, or "slave code," would have the practical effect of excluding slavery.[2] Whatever other motives may have influenced him, Douglas's stand at Freeport revealed his fidelity to cherished convictions long held. Taking the side of his neighbors and friends, he won reëlection to the Senate, but his utterance cast dismay into the ranks of the Southern members of his party.

The year 1859 found sectional strife once more assuming the ominous form of anarchy and bloodshed. Since his gory exploit three years before in Kansas, John Brown's ill-balanced mind had continued to brood over the evils of slavery. Now, aided

---

[1] Lincoln's question was: "Can the people of a United States territory, in any lawful way, against the wish of any citizen of the United States, exclude slavery from its limits prior to the formation of a state constitution?"

[2] This was his soundest contention, but, as a matter of fact, he also claimed that, since the Dred Scott decision merely forbade *Congress* to exclude slavery from the territories, the *territorial legislature* still retained that power, at least until the Supreme Court should declare to the contrary. In other words, a free-soil legislature might prevent the existence of slavery by "unfriendly legislation."

and abetted by a few antislavery extremists in New England, he planned a more desperate stroke against it. Gathering a band of twenty-one followers, five of them Negroes, he seized the federal arsenal at Harper's Ferry, Virginia, on Sunday night, October 16. His scheme was to summon the slaves of the South to his standard and, from the mountain fastnesses near by, dictate the terms of their liberation. When dawn came, men armed with a medley of weapons poured into the village and, with the help of some militia companies, began a counterattack. That night Colonel Robert E. Lee arrived with a company of United States marines, and early the next morning Brown and his surviving men were overpowered and made prisoners.

A thrill of horror ran through the nation. For many Southerners Brown's fanatical attempt confirmed their worst fears as to the hidden purposes of the "Black Republicans." In retaliation, governors of several states recommended opening Southern ports to foreign trade and levying high excise taxes on Northern-made goods. Antislavery zealots, on the other hand, hailed Brown as a noble martyr to a great cause. Most Northerners, however, repudiated the exploit, for they rightly saw in it an assault not against the South but upon all organized society and democratic methods of securing progress. Brown was promptly tried for conspiracy, treason and murder. Seventeen affidavits by neighbors and friends attesting their belief that he was insane were not considered, and on December 2, 1859, he was publicly hanged. The nobility of his bearing in these last weeks impressed all who saw him. To the end he believed he was an instrument in the hands of God.

THE CRUCIAL ELECTION OF 1860

In the new Congress which met a few days after John Brown's execution, the Northern and Southern members faced each other like enemies belonging to hostile nations rather than like brethren of a common country. Charges and countercharges punctuated the discussions. Threats of secession were made with increasing vehemence by Southern "fire-eaters," and Senator Seward was openly accused of having instigated Brown's criminal adventure. "The members on both sides are mostly armed with deadly weapons," Senator J. W. Grimes of Iowa wrote to his wife, "and it is said that the friends of each are armed in the galleries." On several occasions violent clashes between members were only narrowly averted. While the administration party still controlled the Senate, in the House a Democratic majority of twenty-five had changed to a Republican plurality of twenty-one. The Republicans lacked an absolute majority, however, and it required nearly two months before they could elect one of their number Speaker.

The bitterness of the struggle over the speakership was sharpened by angry allusions of Southern members to an abolitionist tract, Hinton R. Helper's *The Impending Crisis of the South*, which sixty-four Republican Congressmen had formally indorsed in print. The animus of this latest assault on slavery was different from that of *Uncle Tom's Cabin*. The author, himself a nonslaveholding North Carolinian, asked the pregnant question: for whose good was slavery? Fortified by a mass of facts gleaned from the census reports, he answered that its direct benefits accrued to but a fraction of the white population, the "lords of the lash." This minority alone possessed the wealth, luxury and culture of which the Southland boasted, leaving the bulk of the people in "galling poverty and ignorance," deprived of equal economic, social and political opportunities. The slavery system had cursed Dixie with "comparative imbecility and obscurity," while the North without this incumbrance had attained "almost unexampled power and eminence." Helper's book was a forthright and convincing argument on behalf of the Southern white proletariat against cotton capitalism and all its works. Though virtually without circulation in the slave states, the Republicans printed a hundred thousand copies for Northern reading in the approaching presidential campaign, winning many converts to their cause among voters who had been left untouched by the real or fancied wrongs of the Negro.

The basic antagonism between the slavery and free-labor systems was further impressed upon the Northern farming and wage-earning classes by Buchanan's veto of a homestead bill in June, 1860. For more than a decade efforts had been made to secure a law giving actual settlers free farms of 160 acres from the public domain. In the House Andrew Johnson, a "poor-white" member from Tennessee, had pressed the matter, workingmen's associations in the North had championed it, and it will be recalled that in 1854 a bill for the purpose had passed the lower branch, only to suffer defeat in the upper. Again in February, 1859, a similar proposal, adopted by the House, failed in the proslavery Senate. The Southern members, viewing the measure through the distorting lenses of sectional hostility, saw truly that such a law, if enacted, would quickly fill the federal territories with antislavery Northerners who would lightly brush aside court decisions opposed to their interests or convictions.

When the matter came before Congress once more, in the spring of 1860, the Democrats had to tread warily for fear of offending possible Northern support in the coming national election. The demand for free land was particularly popular in the Midwest, and everywhere it enlisted the enthusiasm of the Germans and other recent citizens. The Senate, however, could not quite bring itself to accept a new House bill for free homesteads. Instead, it finally compromised upon a measure authorizing the sale of tracts of 160 acres at the low price of twenty-five cents an acre, one fifth the existing rate. But Buchanan, bolder than his party associates in Congress, vetoed the bill, alleging it would tend to depopulate the older states, sap the frontiersmen's "noble spirit of independence," and even propagate "pernicious social theories which have proved so disastrous in other countries."

Meantime, while fighting the common enemy, the members of the President's party had sought vainly to patch up their internal differences. Douglas's independent course, begun at the time of the Lecompton fight and continued in the Freeport Heresy, had made him a frail reed for the planting interests to lean on. Without delay the proslavery leaders notified him of the price he must pay for their backing in the impending Democratic convention: he must agree to support the passage of a congressional slave code applicable to the entire federal domain. This was their reply to his assertion at Freeport that slavery could be barred from a territory by the failure of the local legislature to enact protective laws. Resolutions framed by Jefferson Davis and declaring the obligation of Congress to provide a territorial slave code were presented in the Senate in February, 1860, and eventually adopted by the Democratic majority. But Douglas disregarded the ultimatum.

When the party convention met on April 23 at Charleston, South Carolina, the matter was pressed to a decision. Two platforms were submitted to the delegates, one embodying in substance Davis's demand and the other phrased in the spirit of Douglas's Freeport utterance. The Northern faction carried the day, though at the cost of the withdrawal of eight Southern delegations from the hall. In the voting for the presidential nomination Douglas led on all fifty-seven ballots, but could not command the necessary two thirds of the convention's original membership. His nomination, however, was accomplished several weeks later at an adjourned session in Baltimore under a rule requiring a two-thirds majority of only those present. As a sop to the South, Herschel V. Johnson of Georgia was associated with him as running mate. Meantime, the Southern Democrats, deciding to place their own ticket in the field, held a convention at which they unanimously adopted the proslavery platform rejected at Charleston and chose as their candidates John C. Breckinridge of Kentucky and Joseph Lane of Oregon. Apart from the central question, the rival platforms agreed in demanding the acquisition of Cuba on "honorable" terms and the building of a Pacific railway.

While the Democrats were quarreling among themselves the Republicans proceeded exultantly to their own nominations. The chief aspirants for head of the ticket were Seward and Lincoln. The former, an Easterner long prominent in national affairs, seemed to have a prior claim to the honor. Though generally moderate in his views, he had recently won Northern applause by his resounding declaration that the issue between North and South was "an irrepressible conflict between opposing and enduring forces." Lincoln's greatest asset, on the other hand, was his relative obscurity. Unlike the New Yorker, he bore no obvious handicap of old political enmities, no burden of past antagonisms likely to prove harmful in doubtful states. Besides, as a son of "poor-white" parents and a self-made man, "Honest Abe, the Rail-Splitter," would appeal strongly to the plain people of the North.

When the convention assembled in Chicago on May 16, his

friends left nothing undone to bring success. The Indiana and Pennsylvania delegations were won over by promises of cabinet positions, agreements to which Lincoln himself was not a party though he later carried them out. Seward's supporters were no less active, but on the third ballot the Westerner captured the prize. The second place went to Hannibal Hamlin of Maine. The platform was marked by moderation, being framed especially to attract Northern voters who had not yet identified themselves with the party. Reaffirming opposition to slavery in the federal domain, it demanded statehood for Kansas and denounced "the new dogma that the Constitution, of its own force, carries slavery into any or all the territories." With an eye to the Midwest the party promised free homesteads and, with a squint at the Pennsylvania iron districts, advocated a tariff to encourage "the industrial interests." No mention was made of the fugitive-slave law, and John Brown's raid was branded as "among the gravest of crimes." Like their opponents, the Republicans indorsed a transcontinental railway. As for threats of disunion, they declared that "the union of the States must and shall be preserved."

Still another convention was held on May 9, composed mostly of old men who were one in spirit with the venerable statesmen who had saved the nation in 1850. Adopting the name of the Constitutional Union party, they drew up a brief platform recognizing "no political principle other than the Constitution of the country, the union of the States, and the enforcement of the laws." They hoped to settle the sectional question by ignoring it. As candidates they named John Bell of Tennessee and Edward Everett of Massachusetts. Though the ensuing campaign was less exciting than that of 1856, James Russell Lowell in the newly established *Atlantic Monthly* rightly called it "a turning-point in our history." The shrewdness of the Republican tactics became quickly evident. Everywhere profiting from Northern resentment against the "Slave Power," the party found the tariff a particularly potent issue in Pennsylvania and New Jersey, while the slogan, "Free Homes for the Homeless," proved equally effective among the Western farmers. Special efforts were made, with the help of Carl Schurz and other immigrant leaders, to mobilize the German and Scandinavian vote.

Seward, campaigning vigorously for his erstwhile rival, took occasion in St. Louis and other appropriate places to praise the "onward striving, freedom-loving German inhabitants." [1]

The large moneyed interests of the East, on the other hand, feared lest Republican victory bring secession and a general derangement of business. William B. Astor and other financial magnates are said to have raised two million dollars to defeat the ticket in New York state. In most of the South the Republi-

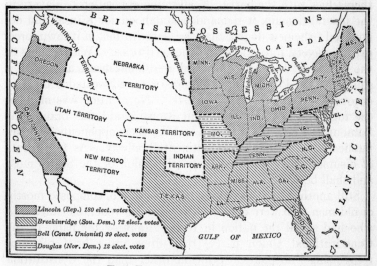

THE ELECTORAL VOTE IN 1860

cans made no efforts, for their platform "could not cross the Ohio River." Indeed, many voters in Dixie supposed that Lincoln's running mate was a mulatto. As election time drew near, Douglas, alarmed by the increasing violence of Southern threats of secession in the event of a Republican triumph, made a speaking tour through five slave states. Everywhere he pledged his support to an undivided country. At Norfolk, Virginia, he declared flatly that the next President, "whoever he may be, should

[1] It is noteworthy that shortly before the Republican convention a group of representative Germans, meeting in Chicago, had called upon the party to favor a homestead law, oppose the extension of slavery and resist measures unfriendly to naturalized citizens. Lincoln himself, while angling for the nomination, had found it expedient to become owner of a German paper in Springfield for a period lasting until after his election as President.

treat all attempts to break up the Union by resistance to its laws, as Old Hickory treated the nullifiers of 1832." In the electoral count Lincoln received 180 votes, all from free states, Breckinridge 72, all from slave states, while Bell and Douglas divided the border states between them, receiving 39 and 12 votes respectively. These figures, however, do not correctly reflect the relative popular following of each candidate, for Lincoln polled about forty per cent of the popular ballots, Douglas more than twenty-nine, Breckinridge eighteen and Bell nearly thirteen. Lincoln's three opponents commanded a total vote of almost a million more than he. Yet if all the ballots cast for them had been given to any one of the three, the Republican candidate would still have won a majority in the electoral college. The party, however, failed to carry either branch of Congress.

SELECT BIBLIOGRAPHY

The Party Revolution. The disintegration of the old Whig organization is treated in Cole, *The Whig Party in the South*, and Mueller, *The Whig Party in Pennsylvania*. Scisco, *Political Nativism in New York State*, is the best of the state studies of the Know Nothing movement. The other new party is the special theme of Crandall, *The Early History of the Republican Party, 1854–1856*, while further light is thrown on it by Nevins, *Frémont*, and Bartlett, *John C. Frémont and the Republican Party*.

The Drive for Slavery Extension. Curtis, *Life of James Buchanan*, is useful for this period. Efforts to secure Cuba receive detailed discussion in Callahan, *Cuba and International Relations*. Of the many accounts of the Kansas struggle perhaps the most objective is Spring, *Kansas; the Prelude to the War for the Union*.

The Supreme Court and Slavery Extension. Two excellent discussions of the Dred Scott decision may be found in Warren, *The Supreme Court in United States History*, and Beveridge, *Abraham Lincoln*, the latter a detailed biography carrying its subject through the year 1858.

The Widening of the Sectional Breach. The Panic of 1857 is given special study in Dunbar, *Economic Essays*. The Lincoln-Douglas debates are fully treated in Beveridge's *Lincoln*, II. Of the numerous lives of Brown, Villard, *John Brown, 1800–1859*, is the best balanced.

The Crucial Election of 1860. The efforts for a homestead law are painstakingly traced in Stephenson, *The Political History of the Public Lands from 1840 to 1862*. The major aspects of the presidential contest of 1860 can be followed in Fite, *The Presidential Campaign of 1860*, which has an anti-Douglas bias, and the early chapters of Dumond, *The Secession Movement, 1860–1861*.

CHAPTER III

THE GREAT DECISION, 1860-1861

THE MOVEMENT FOR SOUTHERN INDEPENDENCE

THE election of Lincoln roused a storm of emotions in the breasts of Southern leaders. Did Republican success justify execution of the oft-threatened withdrawal from the Union? Notwithstanding the fulminations of the "fire-eaters," the tide of American nationality ran strong in Dixie, and a decision involving dismemberment of a nation which Southern statesmen had done so much to build was not lightly to be made. The right of separation was generally admitted, but did the existing circumstances justify the exercise of the right? In an address before the Georgia legislature on November 14 Alexander H. Stephens declared emphatically in the negative. He pointed out that the President could "do nothing unless backed by power in Congress," and in that body the Republicans lacked a majority. If the new chief executive should violate the Constitution, then would come the time for action. Certain other leaders also counseled delay, but for the purpose of insuring that the several slave states should act as a unit in the crisis. Still others favored secession, not as an irrevocable step, but as a temporary expedient, believing with the Georgian, T. R. R. Cobb, that "We can make better terms out of the Union than in it."

The psychology of the situation, however, played inevitably into the hands of the extremists. Twenty-five years of sectional bickering had tended to make Southerners and Northerners forget they were two branches of the same people. All the influential agencies for the dissemination of propaganda — the printing press, the church, the school — had fed the flames of mutual distrust, hatred and fear. As Dr. Francis Lieber, a political economist who had lived in both sections, wrote in 1860, "What Thucydides said of the Greeks at the time of the Peloponnesian War applies to us at the present. 'The Greeks,' he said, 'did not understand each other any longer, though they spoke the same language; words received a different meaning in different parts.'" Exaggerated fears of what *might* happen under a "Black Republican" administration became transformed into a conviction of assured calamities. Moreover, Lincoln's kindly and essentially conservative nature was unknown to most Southerners, who, however, were well apprised of his threatening sentiment that the Union must become all slave or all free. Was it not better to secede, they argued, before the abolition party completely dominated the federal government?

The extreme secessionists were strongest in the seaboard and Gulf states from South Carolina to Texas. Here, amidst a dense slave population, where King Cotton reigned supreme, sensitiveness to antislavery criticism was keenest. Under the urging of such men as Toombs in Georgia, Yancey in Alabama and Hammond and R. B. Rhett in South Carolina, the movement for disunion plunged on. Jefferson Davis, though at first advising delay and cautious action, soon joined the others. While most Southerners held that, in any case, the inalienable right of revolution justified their course, the seceding states nevertheless took care to observe legal forms in severing the bonds of union. In conformity with the teachings of Calhoun, special state conventions were summoned to adopt ordinances of secession, thus reversing the process by which the Constitution had originally been accepted. Appropriately enough, South Carolina took the lead. Upon receiving word of Lincoln's election, the legislature, having remained in session for the express purpose, issued a call for a state convention. On December 20, 1860, amid intense excitement, that body formally repealed the act of 1788 ratifying the Constitution, and "dissolved" the "union now subsisting between South Carolina and other States, under the name of the 'United States of America.'" By February 1, 1861, similar action had been taken successively by Mississippi, Florida, Alabama, Georgia, Louisiana and Texas.

The ordinances of secession were usually accompanied by a formal statement of the justifying causes. In general, four reasons were assigned. The growing preponderance of the North in Congress was pointed to as the prolific source of policies and legislation designed to promote Northern economic welfare at the cost of the South. Much was made, also, of the waxing strength and increasing aggression of the antislavery forces, as exemplified by the personal-liberty laws, defiance of the Supreme Court and John Brown's raid. Such acts were held to violate the "constitutional compact" and thereby to release the Southern states from their obligations. Next, slavery was justified as a positive good. In the words of the Mississippi convention, slave labor "supplies the product which constitutes by far the largest and most important portions of the commerce of the earth . . . and by an imperious law of nature none but the black race can bear exposure to the tropical sun. These products have become necessities of the world, and a blow at slavery is a blow at commerce and civilization." But the most fundamental justification of all, in the minds of Southerners, may be summed up in the modern expression: the right of self-determination. The South demanded the right to live its own life in its own way under such social institutions as it found satisfactory. In this sense, the official statements of causes may be regarded as declarations of independence. As Mississippi said, "We must either submit to degradation and to loss of property worth four billions of money or we must secede from the Union framed by our fathers, to secure this as well as every other species of property. For far less cause than this our fathers separated from the Crown of England."

That the seceding states, in following their separate courses, acted in response to an underlying sense of Southern nationality became quickly apparent. Delegates from the several states, meeting at Montgomery, Alabama, on February 4, 1861, organized a new federal government under the name of the Confederate States of America. Davis was chosen President, though much against his wishes, for he aspired to command one of the armies of the new nation. As a concession to the moderates, the vice-presidency was bestowed upon Stephens, who had done more than any other Southerner to postpone and defeat secession. The Confederate Constitution was closely modeled upon that of the United States, but there were certain significant differences. One body of provisions aimed to establish beyond question the Southern position on the various sectional questions that had arisen in the past. Congress was forbidden to subsidize internal improvements (except as an aid to navigation), or to lay protective tariffs, or to grant bounties. Negro bondage was to be safe-guarded in all territories, and property in slaves should never be impaired. Nothing specific, however, was said about the right of secession, though three distinct proposals to affirm the right had been presented in the convention. A second group of clauses provided for certain reforms in governmental procedure, suggested by experience under the old Constitution. For ex-ample, the President was limited to a single six-year term, he could veto individual items in appropriation bills, and an executive budget system was provided for.

Only seven states were represented at Montgomery, but the architects of the new republic expected the early adhesion of the eight slave states which, as yet, continued loyal to the old Union. Indeed, in their high enthusiasm, they anticipated an extension beyond these natural limits. Stephens, now an ardent supporter of the Confederacy, predicted in a notable speech at Savannah, "Looking to the distant future, and perhaps not very far distant either, it is not beyond the range of possibility, and even prob-ability, that all the great states of the north-west will gravitate this way." The sequel was to show that the Confederate leaders were too optimistic, even in regard to all those states which had domestic institutions like those of the Lower South.

THE NORTH AND SECESSION

The Northern people watched these developments in the Lower South with bewilderment and indecision. Few had antic-ipated such an eventuality, for Southern threats of secession had been looked upon as mere bombast and brag. Nor was the North a unit on the slavery question — a fact amply evident from Douglas's success in polling well over a million votes in the free states. In any contingency, many people preferred a perma-nent disruption of the Union to the terrible alternative of a fratricidal war. Antislavery radicals, for their part, declared publicly that the departure of the slave states was good riddance. "If the cotton States shall decide that they can do better out of the Union than in it," asserted the *New York Tribune*, "we insist on letting them go in peace." A national convention of working-men at Philadelphia in February, 1861, agreed that "our Gov-ernment never can be sustained by bloodshed but must live in the affections of the people; we are, therefore, utterly opposed to any measures that will evoke civil war." On the other hand, there were those who could declare, like Senator E. D. Baker of Oregon, "We of the North are a majority of the Union, and we will govern our Union in our own way."

The responsibility for formulating a policy to cope with the crisis devolved upon the outgoing President and his Congress, but their course was inevitably influenced by the uncertain state of public opinion. Buchanan was at this time nearly seventy years of age, by nature timid, and a strict constitutionalist accustomed to view public questions through Southern spectacles. Flinching from any action likely to precipitate civil conflict, he felt also an obligation to maintain the *status quo* until the new administration took hold. In his message of December 4, 1860, he outlined his policy. He denied absolutely the constitutionality of secession, but at the same time declared the Constitution nowhere gave the federal government authority to compel a state to remain in the Union by force.[1] Placing the chief blame for the difficulties upon the North, he proposed an amendment to the Constitution, which would concede the extreme Southern contentions in regard to the Dred Scott decision, the fugitive-slave act, and the unconstitutionality of the personal-liberty laws.

Unfortunately for the President's peace of mind the situation called for more than well-intentioned words. What should be done about the seacoast forts and other federal property within the borders of the Confederacy? Buchanan was torn alternately between the advice of proslavery disunionists and Northern nationalists. The most critical situation existed at Charleston, South Carolina, where Major Robert Anderson and a small body of men occupied Fort Sumter on an island in the harbor. Old General Winfield Scott urged swift and decisive action, seeking to stiffen the President's resolution by recounting the military measures he had taken years before at Jackson's behest to meet

---

[1] In one portion of his message, he made allusion to the obligation of the President to enforce the laws throughout the land, but, unlike either Jackson in 1832 or Lincoln when he entered office, he failed to find therein ample power for the suppression of an unlawful movement against federal authority. Yet, if Buchanan had begun a second term in March, 1861, it is not impossible that his course might have been much like Lincoln's.

the nullification crisis in South Carolina. Buchanan's indecision caused Cass's resignation as Secretary of State in December. Finally, in January, 1861, Buchanan dispatched an armed steamer, the *Star of the West*, to Fort Sumter with military supplies and reënforcements of two hundred men. Upon her arrival at daybreak on January 9, the Confederate batteries on the shore opened fire. Since Major Anderson, ignorant of the government's plans, was unprepared to lend prompt support, she hurried back to New York. The firing upon the *Star of the West* was really an act of war, but Buchanan did not make an issue of it. Meantime, the secessionists took peaceable possession of two unoccupied forts in Charleston Harbor and of the customhouse and arsenal. Elsewhere in the Confederacy the federal forts and arsenals, left unprotected, were also quietly taken over, save only Fort Pickens at Pensacola, which remained in Union hands throughout the war.

Buchanan's inaction may, in part, be accounted for by the belief of statesmen in both sections that civil war might yet be averted, as in 1850, through compromise measures. The most conspicuous champion of this solution, Crittenden of Kentucky, Clay's successor in the Senate, proposed a constitutional amendment reëstablishing the Missouri Compromise line in the territories, with the protection of slavery south of the line. But the Republican Congressmen would have none of it, believing with their President-elect that such an arrangement would merely redouble proslavery exertions for territorial expansion southward. "The tug has to come, and better now than later," advised Lincoln. While countless other proposals were aired in Congress, the only measure actually adopted fell pathetically short of the needs of the occasion — the submission to the states on March 2, 1861, of an amendment pledging Congress never to interfere with slavery within a state. Meanwhile, efforts for conciliation had been undertaken outside of Congress. In December, 1860, seven Republican governors, meeting in New York, agreed to recommend to their legislatures the repeal of the personal-liberty laws. Such a step was taken by Rhode Island in January, Massachusetts and Vermont soon following with drastic changes in their statutes. Had any real hope inhered in this plan, other Northern states would probably have done likewise. A final attempt at adjustment was made at a "Peace Convention," presided over by ex-President John Tyler of Virginia and attended by delegates from twenty-one states. Assembling in Washington on February 4, 1861, at the call of Virginia, the gathering drafted a series of proposed amendments. The principal one provided that no new territory should be acquired without the consent of a majority of the Senators from the free and from the slave states. Apart from Crittenden and Douglas, however, the proposals found little favor when they were offered in the Senate.

As James Russell Lowell wrote in the *Atlantic Monthly*, the "panacea of palaver" had failed. Nevertheless, the months of discussion served the purpose of convincing the Northern people that, peaceable means of settlement having come to naught, no alternative remained but war. Responsibility for the next move fell upon the man whose election had precipitated the crisis. It was the act of an inscrutable providence that Abraham Lincoln should have been called to the helm of state to undertake a task which, as he told his neighbors in Springfield upon departing for the capital, was "greater than that which rested upon Washington." Born in 1809 in the border state of Kentucky, there coursed through his veins the blood of a vigorous stock inherited on the one side from New England and on the other from Virginia. Migrating with his parents to Indiana and then to Illinois, he imbibed from his youthful pioneer surroundings a passionate belief in American nationality and an ardent faith in the common man. His broad humanity arrayed him instinctively on the anti-slavery side. Yet he had little patience with the precipitate methods of the abolitionists, who, he believed, hurt rather than helped their cause, and even less with those zealots who valued the freedom of the Negro above national preservation.

To the great majority of his countrymen he was but an uncouth backwoodsman when he entered the presidency. Indeed, his true greatness did not dawn on most men until after his death. Of the common clay himself, his mind was attuned to the unspoken hopes of the masses. "The Lord must love the plain people," he once said in his whimsical way, "that's why he made so many of them." But unlike the first great American commoner, Jackson, he regarded himself as an instrument, rather than the dictator, of events. Conscious of his political inexperience, he counseled with all sorts and conditions of men. Yet, once having formed his political principles, he never yielded them. He displayed endless tact and patience in the management of his cabinet with its contentious personalities, and submitted to discourteous treatment from overbearing men like E. M. Stanton and G. B. McClellan for the good of the cause. He had a deep understanding even of those who were seeking to destroy his beloved Union, adjudging them misguided rather than depraved. "Destruction for the idea, infinite clemency for the person — such was his attitude." Lincoln would have been the first to protest against the attempts of posterity to idealize him. Human in every pore, homely to the verge of ugliness, awkward in manner, he sometimes shocked dignified statesmen by receiving them in slippered feet. Nor were his humorous stories always in the best taste, thereby winning him a reputation for flippancy on grave occasions. His greatest mistakes were made as an administrator, for he was often unfortunate in his judgment of men. But these qualities made him resemble the average man and endeared him to the plain people.

Lincoln arrived in Washington ten days before the close of Buchanan's term, escaping a plot to assassinate him as he passed through Baltimore. The day of the inauguration dawned, disagreeable and stormy. Most of the participants were agitated and apprehensive. General Scott kept an anxious eye upon the crowd, which was commanded by cannon. Chief Justice Taney, author of the Dred Scott decision, administered the oath of office in words scarcely intelligible from emotion. Then came Lincoln's inaugural address, delivered with deep feeling and a trace of nervousness, and containing his long-awaited announcement of policy. Dwelling first upon the nature of the Union, he affirmed that it was "older than the Constitution," for it grew out of the fundamental sense of nationality which had animated the colonies in their struggle against Britain. The so-called ordinances of secession were "legally void," from which it followed that violent efforts to uphold them were "insurrectionary or revolutionary." As for his own duty in the crisis, the Constitution expressly enjoined the President to execute the federal laws in all the states. "The power confided to me will be used to hold, occupy, and possess the property and places belonging to the Government and to collect the duties and imposts." He closed with an eloquent and touching plea for a restoration of the ancient bonds of affection.

The address was phrased cautiously, with the object of preventing the secession movement from spreading to the eight slave states still loyal. Yet Lincoln announced the principle upon which the federal government was later to wage war against the South. Ignoring Buchanan's assertion that the federal government could not legally coerce a state, he dwelt on his constitutional duty to execute the laws in all parts of an indivisible country. In his mind, the whole situation reduced itself to a transaction between the national authority, on the one hand, and lawless persons or groups, on the other. This view, he held, was in accord with the central principle of the Constitution that the federal government operates directly upon individuals, not upon states.

Lincoln chose a cabinet that at once commanded Northern confidence. All elements which had contributed to Republican success were represented, including his chief rivals for the nomination. Seward was appointed to the State Department, Chase, head of the Treasury, Simon Cameron of Pennsylvania, Secretary of War, and Gideon Welles of Connecticut, Secretary of the Navy. Two border slave states were recognized by the choice of the Missourian, Edward Bates, as Attorney-General and of Montgomery Blair of Maryland as Postmaster-General.[1] Almost at once events forced the President to put into effect the course he had forecast in his inaugural address. Word came from Major Anderson that he would have to surrender Fort Sumter unless he were reënforced and provisions sent. All the members of the cabinet, except Chase and Blair, advised evacuation, while General Scott gave his weighty opinion that, to relieve the fort now, would require a force of twenty thousand — which did not exist.

Lincoln, almost without support, pitted his judgment against that of his more experienced counselors. It seemed to him that

[1] Caleb B. Smith of Indiana was appointed Secretary of the Interior. Cameron was succeeded by Edwin M. Stanton of Pennsylvania as Secretary of War in January, 1862. There were also other changes.

the abandonment of Sumter without resistance would not only impair Northern morale, but would, in a sense, constitute a recognition of the Confederacy. In accordance with a prior agreement, he therefore served formal notice on the government of South Carolina of his intention to reprovision the fort and, on April 6, ordered the dispatching of a relief expedition. The Confederates summoned Anderson to surrender and, when he refused, their batteries opened fire. By the next day, the thirteenth, his position had become untenable, and just as the relief ships — which could in no case have really helped him — appeared in the offing, he surrendered with the honors of war. The period of irresolution was ended. The nation — "a house divided" — faced the terrible certainty of a brothers' war.

THE APPEAL TO ARMS

The bombardment of Fort Sumter had a galvanic effect upon the men of both sections. All hesitation was now swept from the minds of the Northern people. On April 15, 1861, President Lincoln issued a call for 75,000 volunteers for three months, followed early in May by a request for 42,000 more for a term of three years. Other proclamations added about 23,000 men to the regular army and 18,000 to the navy, and declared the coast of the Confederacy under blockade. The drums beat in every town and village, and the rush to arms of the young men was universal. Although the Northern people were of many minds concerning the Negro question, patriotism clearly demanded of them the maintenance of an undivided nation. Greeley and other editors, casting aside their earlier timidity, rallied strongly to the cause. Douglas, having but a few more months to live, declared in a great speech in Chicago, "There can be no neutrals in this war; only patriots — or traitors." "For my own part," wrote Lincoln, "I consider the central idea pervading this struggle is the necessity of proving that popular government is not an absurdity. We must settle this question now, whether, in a free government, the minority have the right to break up the government whenever they choose." Meanwhile, with equal fervor, the people of the seven seceded states responded to President Davis's appeal for 100,000 men. Regiments sallied gayly forth from the Southern towns and hamlets, as if on holiday parade, little dreaming how awful a struggle was about to begin.

Even the religious world felt the shattering blow. The Methodists and Baptists had split along geographic lines nearly twenty years before. As the fifties advanced, six Southern synods comprising 15,000 communicants withdrew (1857) from the New School Presbyterian Church; and sectional antagonisms plagued other sects as well. A contributor to the *Southern Presbyterian*, writing shortly after the fall of Sumter, believed, "This revolution has been accomplished mainly by the churches." While B. M. Palmer, the Southern Presbyterian divine, proclaimed that "In this great struggle, we defend the cause of God and religion," the Philadelphia synod of the same denomination prayed for the suppression of "the most groundless, cruel, and wicked rebellion in the history of any people." The outbreak of war precipitated the division of the Old School Presbyterians and the Protestant Episcopalians into sectional bodies. Of the principal nation-wide religious groups, only the Roman Catholics, held together by a central authority outside the national borders, escaped organic rupture.

Both sections anxiously awaited the action of the eight slave states which had thus far continued loyal. Bordering the Confederacy on the north were Arkansas, Tennessee, North Carolina and Virginia. These states were less identified with cotton production than the Lower South, having fewer slaves as well as a larger proportion of slaveless whites. The majority of the inhabitants believed in the right of secession, yet until now had denied that sufficient provocation existed. But their doubts were dispelled by the attempt to relieve Sumter, followed by Lincoln's call for troops. Virginia took the fateful step on April 17, Arkansas on May 6, North Carolina two weeks later and Tennessee on June 24. No state left the Union with greater reluctance than the Old Dominion. Her statesmen had not only been indispensable to the winning of independence and the framing of the Constitution, but she had also furnished five Presidents. On April 5 her state convention had rejected secession, only to be overwhelmed by the whirlwind of disunionism raised by Lincoln's warlike proclamations. With Virginia went Colonel Robert E. Lee, a man of noble character and superb military ability, who declined the command of the Union army out of loyalty to his state. The importance of Virginia's action to the South is indicated by the prompt removal of the Confederate capital from Montgomery to Richmond.

The mountaineers of northwestern Virginia, however, refused to abide by the decision of the state. These folk, prevailingly Scotch Irish and Pennsylvania German in stock, owned few slaves, and had long been pitted against their tidewater brethren

THE PROGRESS OF SECESSION

in state politics. Shielded from Southern interference by federal troops, they determined to erect a state of their own. As a preliminary move, a convention at Wheeling in June, 1861, set up a loyal government of Virginia, composed chiefly of men from the upland counties and those districts under federal military control adjoining Washington. A later convention representing only the people of forty-six northwestern counties was held in November and, with the consent of the rump "state government," made application for admission into the Union as the state of West Virginia. Congress acted tardily, statehood being finally granted in June, 1863, with a constitution providing for gradual emancipation. Since West Virginia runs up like a wedge between Ohio and Pennsylvania, the disaffection of the inhabitants had the important military result of securing to the federal authorities the command of essential rail and telegraph facilities between the East and the Ohio Valley.

Between the enlarged Confederacy and the free-soil North lay the four remaining slave commonwealths — the border states of Maryland, Delaware, Kentucky and Missouri. Cotton capitalism was negligible in these states, and slaves, being relatively scarce, were regarded as only one among many forms of property. Torn in their affections between South and North, and bound by substantial economic ties with both, these states knew not which way to turn. Vigorous action by the federal authorities saved Maryland to the Union. Hemming in the District of Columbia on three sides, it would have been a fatal military blunder to permit the state to pass under enemy control. When Maryland disunionists severed telegraphic communications between Washington and the North and sought to prevent the passage of Union troops, Lincoln suspended the writ of *habeas corpus*, ordered the arrest of suspects, and stationed troops at strategic points throughout the state. By the middle of May, 1861, all danger of secession had vanished. With Maryland went Delaware, as a matter of course; in any case, slaves formed an insignificant fraction of the latter's population.

Farther to the west, Lincoln's native state of Kentucky, lying athwart the military highway between North and South and rent by internal dissension, found a temporary solution for her problem in May, 1861, in a declaration of neutrality. Lincoln's policy here was in marked contrast with his treatment of Maryland. Feeling confident of Kentucky's eventual decision, he respected her negative attitude, while quietly laboring to promote the spread of nationalist sentiment. When Confederate troops violated her neutrality in September by occupying Columbus, the newly chosen legislature declared for the Union. In Missouri, on the other hand, the state government was openly disunionist. But the special convention, called to consider secession, proved unexpectedly nationalist in sentiment. Each body claimed to voice the true will of the people, and each summoned military force to its support. Led by Francis P. Blair, Jr., and Captain

Nathaniel Lyon, and supported by militia companies of St. Louis Germans, the forces of nationalism triumphed. The state convention in July, 1861, deposed the pro-Southern governor and established a loyal government. While conflict between the antagonistic elements continued sporadically throughout the war, the crisis was safely passed. In all the border states save Delaware, thousands of citizens, unwilling to accept the decision of the majority, flocked into the Confederate armies.

THE EMBATTLED HOSTS

The people of each section entered the war with high hopes for an early victory. In material resources, however, the North enjoyed a decided advantage. Twenty-three states with a population of twenty-two million, including about half a million slaves, were arrayed against eleven states containing nine million people, of whom three and a half million were slaves. Though the Southern white population was more homogeneous, the diversified make-up of the Northern people proved a source of strength rather than weakness, for, in proportion to their numbers, more English, German and Irish immigrants served in the Union armies than native-born Northerners.[1] The industrial superiority of the North even exceeded its preponderance in man power. Unlike the rural South, the free states had abundant facilities for the manufacture of arms and ammunition, clothing and other supplies. Their investment in manufacturing was nearly ten times as great.

Indeed, three of the most powerful allies of the North in the war were mechanical agencies that had been developed to high efficiency in the decade or so preceding. One of these, the McCormick reaper with its various competitors, caused the Secretary of War to declare in 1861: "The reaper is to the North what slavery is to the South. By taking the places of regiments of young men in the Western harvest fields, it releases them to do battle for the Union at the front, and at the same time keeps up the supply of bread for the nation and the nation's

[1] Franz Sigel, Carl Schurz and other Germans prominent in the Revolution of 1848 gave the benefit of their military experience to the untrained federal armies, rising high in the service. Count Zeppelin, who later perfected the dirigible airship in Germany, served as a cavalry officer and engineer from 1863, making his first ascent in a military balloon in this country.

armies." Hardly less important was the sewing machine. Besides providing factory-made garments in unlimited quantities, the introduction of the McKay sewing machine in 1861 made possible the large-scale production of well-made, low-priced shoes. In the first year 1,500,000 pairs were manufactured, twice as many as in any previous year. Though factory workers joined the army in large numbers, the output of clothing, undergarments and shoes, so necessary for the comfort of both soldiers and civilians, actually increased during the war.

The rapid spread of rail mileage in the North after 1850 had an even more direct relationship to federal military success. Assisted by the telegraph, the railroad helped promote the rapid movement of troops and supplies. Among the early war-time laws was one of January, 1862, giving the President authority to commandeer the rail and telegraph lines, if necessary for military purposes. A director of railroads was appointed, charged with responsibility for more than two thousand miles of track, chiefly in the border states, which were taken over and operated by the government during the conflict.[1]

The principal advantage of the South in the struggle consisted in its geographic position, added to the fact that the people were fighting on their own soil. Though adequate railway facilities were lacking, the Confederacy, with a compact, well-watered territory, could protect its military front with a minimum of exertion and upon a smaller war budget than the North. The Union forces, on the other hand, operating on unfamiliar ground, were constantly drawing farther away from their base of supplies. Besides, the aristocratic social system of the South was conducive to the development of natural leaders and the cultivation of the martial spirit. Many of the Confederate generals had fought in the Mexican War and, when secession occurred, an undue proportion of able officers resigned their federal commissions to join the

[1] Curiously enough, another invention was neglected, which would have greatly increased the destructive power of the army adopting it. This was the breech-loading rifle. In 1857 a board appointed by the Secretary of War had reported unanimously in favor of a single-shot breechloader. Since the old muzzle-loader required sixty seconds to load and fire as against four seconds for the new gun, the superiority of the latter would seem obvious. After the battle of Gettysburg 18,000 muzzle-loaders were picked up with two or more unexploded charges in them. Yet the purchase of the newer type did not become a regular policy until 1864. Perhaps 100,000 breechloaders were in use when the war closed.

South. It was a common boast in Dixie that any Confederate could lick three Yankees, which provoked President Davis's sober retort, "Only fools doubt the courage of the Yankees or their willingness to fight when they see fit."

The chief hope of the Confederacy lay in a speedy victory, or else in foreign intervention. For the latter, they relied upon their virtual monopoly of the world's cotton supply, a product so necessary for the operation of British textile mills. Time fought on the side of the North, for, given sufficient time, raw armies might be whipped into shape, material resources utilized and effective military leadership developed. In reality, from a military point of view, neither section was prepared for a great war. Few officers on either side had ever commanded so much as a regiment, and as for commanding armies there was no experience. Many of the opposing generals were West Point men, oftentimes classmates; but the regimental and company officers in the volunteer armies were commissioned by the governors. Though this system was quickly altered in the South, politicians continued to secure high military posts in the North, where 2537 generals of all grades made their appearance during the war. Moreover, the insistent clamor and officious meddling of Greeley and of busybodies in Congress embarrassed the success of Northern military plans, sometimes even serving as a source of information to the enemy. In the Confederacy, too, there was lacking that unity of support so necessary for an infant nation struggling for existence. The old conception of state rights constantly battled with the new ideal of Southern nationalism.

Both sides faced the task of creating efficient fighting units out of the ranks of a people who, however warlike, were essentially unmilitary in their habits. In the first flush of war enthusiasm the call for troops was met in both sections by an excess of volunteers. Training camps were established, where the raw recruits, many of them mere youths, hastily learned the manual of arms and were then rushed to the front. Enthusiasm began to wane, however, as the war showed signs of lasting much longer than at first expected, and as individuals saw a chance to reap unusual profits in civilian jobs. The private's pay of $13 a month (later raised to $16) was hardly sufficient to counteract such influences. Under the circumstances, both governments supplemented the system of voluntary enlistments with the inducement of bounties and, when that failed to raise sufficient troops, with compulsory recruiting.

The bounty system was first employed in July, 1861, when the federal government offered a bonus of $100 to each volunteer, a sum increased during 1863 to $302 for raw recruits and $402 for veterans. States, counties and cities granted additional amounts. In 1864 a volunteer in New York county could obtain $300 from the county and $75 from the state, besides the still larger federal bounty. At the same time an Illinois district paid an average bounty of $1056. The system was bad, for it led to the crime of "bounty-jumping." Unprincipled men would enlist, claim the bounty, desert and reënlist elsewhere under a different name, repeating the process indefinitely. In all, the federal government paid out $300,000,000 in bounties, while the state and local governments expended an additional $286,000,000.

Conscription was first resorted to on August 4, 1862, when President Lincoln ordered a draft of 300,000 militia through the medium of the states. The results were unsatisfactory, and on March 3, 1863, Congress enacted the statute upon which all later drafts were based. This law operated directly upon the people of the nation. It applied only to those districts which failed to furnish their quota of volunteers—a fact which helps to explain the generous bounties offered by local authorities. All unmarried men between the ages of twenty and forty-five and all married men between twenty and thirty-five were made subject to compulsory enlistment at the President's call, the names in each draft to be selected by lot. Certain classes were exempt: high public officials, men who were the sole support of dependent families, the physically unfit and criminals. A drafted man might avoid service by providing a substitute or by paying $300.

The conscription act provoked much discontent in the North, for it ran counter to the traditional military policy of the nation. Moreover, the laboring classes and poor people generally objected to the provision which made it easy for the well-to-do to purchase exemption. When the first draft under the new law was undertaken, the provost marshal general admitted that "Every imaginable artifice was adopted to deceive and defeat the enrolling officers. Open violence was sometimes met with. . . . In certain mining regions organized bodies of men openly opposed the enrollment, rendering it necessary that the U. S. authorities should send troops to overcome their opposition." The most notorious resistance took place in New York in July, 1863. When it appeared that most of those drafted in that city were working-men, rioting ensued. For four days the citizens were at the mercy of a mob which pillaged, burned and, in particular, vented their hatred against Negroes, who were blamed as the cause of the war and the draft. No less than a thousand persons were killed or wounded. In most parts of the North, however, the draft went quietly into effect. While it did not directly furnish many new soldiers, it did serve to speed up volunteering.

In the South, also, bounties were offered to accelerate enlistments. Conscription was resorted to earlier than in the North. By acts of April and September, 1862, President Davis was empowered to impress into service all able-bodied male whites between the ages of eighteen and forty-five. The exempted classes included state and Confederate officials, preachers and teachers, persons employed in rail transportation and important war industries, newspaper proprietors and overseers on the larger plantations. Toward the end of the war an act of March, 1865, even provided for the enforced service of Negro slaves. The exercise of conscription by the Confederate government violated the strong state-rights tradition, and produced spirited opposition on the part of Rhett and Stephens as well as by some of the states. Governor J. E. Brown of Georgia, pronouncing the law unconstitutional, refused to permit its enforcement within his jurisdiction, though he was zealous enough in raising troops by state action. The North Carolina legislature, after formally protesting against conscription, passed an act, in direct contravention of the Confederate law, exempting additional classes from military service.

Faulty statistics make it impossible to know just how many men actually served under the opposing flags. Yet it is probably within the range of truth to assume that approximately 800,000 individuals fought on the Southern side, and from two to three times as many on the Northern. Of the latter number, it should not be overlooked that over 50,000 whites and more than 100,-000 Negroes were recruited from within the seceded states.

SELECT BIBLIOGRAPHY

The Movement for Southern Independence. Stephenson, *The Day of the Confederacy*, gives a good general account. Carpenter, *The South as a Conscious Minority, 1789–1861*, traces the evolution of Southern political thought to the goal of secession. Dumond, *The Secession Movement, 1860–1861*, is a detailed, analytical study. Biographies of Southern leaders are listed at the end of Chapter I.

The North and Secession. A special study is Scrugham, *The Peaceable Americans, 1860–1861*. In *James Buchanan and His Cabinet on the Eve of Secession* Auchampaugh offers an antidote to the received opinion of Buchanan as timorous and time-serving. Among the best of the many biographies of the war President are Charnwood, *Abraham Lincoln;* Stephenson, *Lincoln;* and Barton, *The Life of Abraham Lincoln.*

The Appeal to Arms. Smith, *The Borderland in the Civil War*, is a special study of the rôle of Kentucky, Missouri, northwestern Virginia and the southern halves of Ohio, Indiana and Illinois in the secession movement and the war. Further consideration is given certain of these states in McGregor, *The Disruption of Virginia;* Coulter, *The Civil War and Readjustment in Kentucky;* and McElroy, *The Struggle for Missouri.* The impact of the secession movement on organized Christianity is discussed in Vander Velde, *The Presbyterian Churches and the Federal Union, 1861–1869;* Heathcote, *The Lutheran Church and the Civil War;* and Sweet, *The Methodist Episcopal Church and the Civil War.*

The Embattled Hosts. In *The Organization and Administration of the Union Army* Shannon deals authoritatively with the problems of raising, equipping and maintaining the armed forces, with particular reference to the common soldier. Lonn, *Desertion during the Civil War*, is the standard treatment of that embarrassing subject. Northern military legislation is summarized in Huidekoper, *The Military Unpreparedness of the United States.* The military problems of the Confederacy behind the lines are dealt with in Moore, *Conscription and Conflict in the Confederacy;* economic problems in Schwab, *The Confederate States of America;* and political problems in Owsley, *State Rights in the Confederacy.*

CHAPTER IV

THE WAR OF AMERICAN NATIONALITY

NAVAL OPERATIONS OF THE CIVIL WAR

THE Confederate armies, for the most part, fought on the defensive in the Civil War. To the North fell the task of invading and conquering a country three times the size of France. For success in this effort two objects must be secured: the sealing of Southern ports against munitions and supplies from abroad, and a clear military preponderance in the field of fight. Had the first purpose failed of accomplishment, it may be doubted whether the second could have been attained. Yet, when Lincoln inaugurated the blockade in April, 1861, the federal navy consisted of but ninety-odd vessels, most of them small and antiquated and some of them absent on distant cruises; and the seacoast to be guarded was 3500 miles in length. Nevertheless, by pressing all sorts of vessels into service, the blockade was already reasonably effective by summer. Federal naval operations were, in general, lacking in spectacular exploits, though constant watchfulness was required to thwart the efforts of blockade runners. Evasion of the blockade was not only an adventurous but also a lucrative business; occasional vessels, like the steamer *Kate* which made forty-four successful trips, disclosed the possibilities of the traffic. Charleston and Wilmington were the principal ports for this irregular trade, but it never assumed formidable proportions. As prewar supplies became depleted, the Southern people began to suffer acute discomfort. Coffee, tea, soap, paper, clothing and matches were extremely hard to get at any price. Even more serious was the scarcity of common medicines, like quinine and morphia, indispensable for the treatment of sick and wounded soldiers. Lack of salt also created difficulties, for salt meat formed a large part of the army ration.

The Confederates made one ingenious but unsuccessful effort to relieve the situation. On March 8, 1862, there suddenly appeared off Hampton Roads, Virginia, a Confederate vessel, the *Virginia*, made over from the former United States frigate *Merrimac* and plated with iron. The wooden ships of the block-ading fleet were helpless before the iron monster, two being sunk and another driven aground. But the federal authorities had also been experimenting with the new type of vessel and, thanks to the ingenuity of John Ericsson, a Swedish immigrant, had contrived an armored craft of a different model. On the next day the *Monitor*, a low-decked ironclad vessel with a revolving turret carrying heavy guns, took up the gage of battle. While neither won a decisive victory, the *Virginia* was prevented from doing further mischief. This marine duel was epoch-making in the history of nautical architecture, for it proved conclusively what the naval constructors of leading maritime powers abroad already knew — that the day of the wooden warship was past. A fleet of "monitors" was presently built by the United States, and performed valuable service during the remainder of the war.

The work of the navy was not confined to maintaining the blockade, for vessels of war coöperated with the land forces in opening up the Mississippi and other rivers. In Lincoln's ex-pressive language, "Uncle Sam's web-feet" were present not only on "the broad bay, and the rapid river, but also up the narrow, muddy bayou, and wherever the ground was a little damp." The navy was also responsible for the eventual destruc-tion of the Confederate raiders engaged in harassing Northern commerce on the high seas.

MILITARY ACTIVITIES IN THE WEST

The federal operations on land were determined in part by the objectives of the fighting and in part by the physical con-tour of the country. From the early days of the war, one of the major purposes was the capture of the Confederate capital. Other important objectives were the military control of moun-tain passes and navigable streams and the seizure of railway junctions — means whereby the economic life of Dixie and the transportation of troops and munitions might be paralyzed. The Appalachian system, one hundred and fifty miles wide, divides the South into two unequal parts: each area became promptly a theater of war. During the first three years and more,

MAJOR OPERATIONS OF THE CIVIL WAR ON ALL FRONTS

In the West	In the East
	April 12–14 Attack on Fort Sumter.
	June 3 Engagement at Philippi, W. Va.
	June 10 Engagement at Big Bethel, W. Va.
July 5 Engagement at Carthage, Mo.	
	July 8 Engagement at Laurel Hill, W. Va.
	July 21 First battle of Bull Run, Va.
Aug. 10 Engagement at Wilson's Creek, Mo.	
	Aug. 28–29 Capture of Fort Hatteras, N. C.
Sept. 2 Capture of Fort Scott, Mo.	
	Sept. 12–15 Fighting at Cheat Mt., W. Va.
	Oct. 21 Engagement at Ball's Bluff, Va.
Nov. 7 Battle of Belmont, Mo.	Nov. 7 Capture of Port Royal, S. C.
Jan. 19–20 Battle of Mill Springs, Mo.	
Feb. 6 Capture of Fort Henry, Tenn.	
Feb. 16 Capture of Fort Donelson, Tenn.	
Mch. 5–8 Battle of Pea Ridge, Ark.	
April 6–7 Battle of Shiloh, Tenn.	
April 7 Capture of Island No. 10.	
April 28 Capture of New Orleans, La.	
	May 4 Capture of Yorktown, Va.
	May 5 Battle of Williamsburg, Va.
	May 25 Battle of Winchester, Va.
May 30 Capture of Corinth, Miss.	May 31–June 1 Battle of Seven Pines, Va.
June 5 Capture of Fort Pillow, Tenn.	
June 6 Occupation of Memphis, Tenn.	
	June 25–July 1 Seven Days' Battles, Va.
	Aug. 9 Battle of Cedar Mt., Va.
	Aug. 30 Second battle of Bull Run, Va.
Sept. 14–16 Battle of Munfordsville, Ky.	Sept. 14 Battle of South Mt., Md.
	Sept. 17 Battle of Antietam, Md.
Sept. 19 Battle of Iuka, Miss.	
Oct. 3–4 Battle of Corinth, Miss.	
Oct. 8 Battle of Perryville, Ky.	
	Dec. 13 Battle of Fredericksburg, Va.
Dec. 29 Sherman's repulse at Vicksburg, Miss.	

(Left margin: 1861, 1862. Right margin: 1861, 1862.)

simultaneous campaigns were waged on opposite sides of the mountain barrier, usually with little or no relation to each other. West of the Mississippi River lay a third area of conflict, involving military movements of distinctly minor consequence.

To take a look ahead, the subjugation of the South proved a slow, difficult and much interrupted process. Having been blockaded by sea, the Confederacy was gradually cut off from its western territory and deprived of its main internal lines of communication. The Southern capital, against which the North began to move within the first three months of the war, did not fall until nearly four years later, after the victorious Union army in the West, sweeping all before it, had rounded the southern end of the mountains and advanced northward along the coast, prepared to join forces with the troops assailing Richmond.

MAJOR OPERATIONS OF THE CIVIL WAR ON ALL FRONTS

	In the West	In the East	
1863	Dec. 31–Jan. 2 Battle of Murfreesboro, Tenn. May 16 Fighting at Champion Hill, Miss. July 4 Capture of Vicksburg, Miss. July 9 Capture of Port Hudson, La. Sept. 9 Occupation of Chattanooga, Tenn. Sept. 19–20 Battle of Chickamauga, Ga. Nov. 23–25 Battle of Chattanooga, Tenn. Dec. 6 Occupation of Knoxville, Tenn.	May 2–5 Battle of Chancellorsville, Va. June 13–15 Fighting at Winchester, Va. July 1–3 Battle of Gettysburg, Pa. Sept. 7 Capture of Fort Wagner, S. C.	1863
1864	Feb. 14 Occupation of Meridian, Miss. April 8 Battle of Sabine Cross Roads, La. May 13–16 Fighting at Resaca, Ga. May 18 Fighting at Rome, Ga. June 27 Battle of Kenesaw Mt., Ga. July 22 First battle before Atlanta, Ga. Aug. 5 Capture of Mobile Bay, Ala. Sept. 2 Capture of Atlanta, Ga. Sept. 26–27 Fighting at Ironton, Mo. Nov. 30 Battle of Franklin, Tenn. Dec. 15–16 Battle of Nashville, Tenn. Dec. 20 Capture of Savannah, Ga.	May 5–6 First battle in Wilderness, Va. May 8–12 Battle of Spottsylvania C. H., Va. June 1–3 Battle of Cold Harbor, Va. June 19 Siege of Petersburg, Va., begins. Sept. 19 Battle of Opequon, Va. Sept. 21 Battle of Fisher's Hill, Va. Oct. 19 Battle of Cedar Creek, Va.	1864
1865	May 26 Kirby Smith's surrender at Baton Rouge, La.	Jan. 15 Capture of Fort Fisher, N. C. Feb. 17 Capture of Columbia, S. C. Feb. 18 Capture of Charleston, S. C. Feb. 22 Capture of Wilmington, N. C. Mch. 19 Fighting at Goldsboro, N. C. April 1 Battle of Five Forks, Va. April 2 Occupation of Petersburg, Va. April 3 Occupation of Richmond, Va. April 9 Lee's surrender at Appomattox, Va. April 26 Johnston's surrender at Hillsboro, N. C.	1865

The North enjoyed an initial advantage in the West, for the decision of Missouri, Kentucky and West Virginia to remain with the Union placed the original battle front on a line somewhat north of the center of those states. The Confederates were thus deprived of the Ohio River, which would have formed a splendid boundary for defense and offense. When the campaign of 1862 began, the federal forces set about to open up the Mississippi, and thereby accomplish the double purpose of isolating the Confederate states west of the river and of providing the upper Mississippi Valley with its accustomed channel of commerce. The key to the situation was the control of the Tennessee and Cumberland rivers, two tributaries of the Ohio, which penetrated southward toward the heart of the enemy country. The first major movement, therefore, was an expedition up these streams by a combined gunboat fleet and army under command of General U. S. Grant. In the early weeks of February, 1862, Forts Henry and Donelson, situated on these rivers near the Kentucky-Tennessee border, surrendered with more than 14,000 prisoners. The expedition pushed on, capturing Nashville, the Tennessee capital, on the Cumberland, while continuing the southward advance along the Tennessee. Grant's objective now was the village of Corinth in northern Mississippi, one of the principal railway centers of the South, lying at the junction of lines from Memphis, Vicksburg, Mobile and Chattanooga. After desperate fighting on April 6–7 at Pittsburg Landing and at Shiloh, where the federals departed from the river, the advance was resumed under General H. W. Halleck. On May 30 Corinth was occupied.

Meantime, corresponding progress had been made elsewhere in relaxing the Confederate hold on the Mississippi. Union forces operating from the north under General John Pope captured Island No. 10 (April 7), an important river fort near the Kentucky-Tennessee border, while the occupation of Corinth obliged the Confederates to abandon Fort Pillow and Memphis. A northward thrust from the Gulf by a naval force under D. G. Farragut secured also the fall of New Orleans on April 28 after ten days' fighting. In September and October the Confederates made a bold attempt to compel the withdrawal of the Union forces by a raid into the North. Braxton Bragg and Kirby Smith, moving rapidly into Kentucky, actually approached within a few miles of Cincinnati. But the Kentuckians failed to rally to the Confederate cause; and, fearing disaster, the invaders retreated, fighting notable battles at Perryville, Kentucky, and at Murfreesboro in Tennessee. The year 1862 closed with the North in possession of the western half of Tennessee, and in control of the Mississippi River save for a two-hundred-mile stretch guarded at either end by the Confederate strongholds of Vicksburg and Port Hudson.

The first business of the campaign of 1863, on the part of the North, was to complete the task begun in the preceding year —

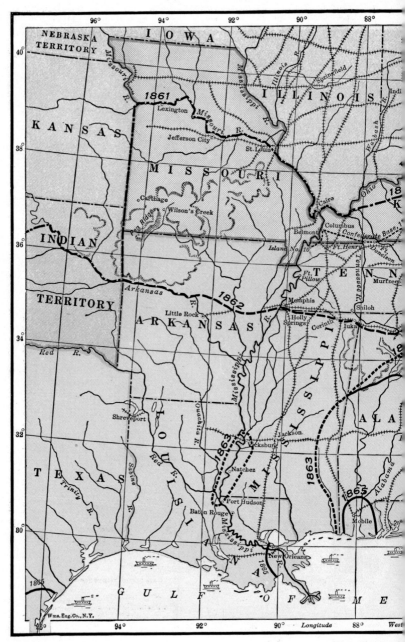

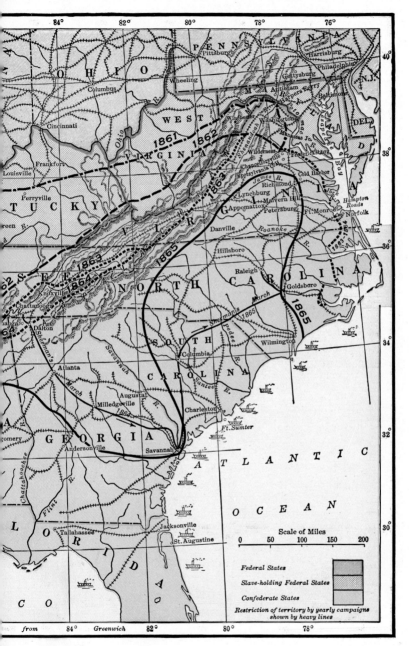

that of freeing Mississippi navigation. This involved one of the most difficult operations of the war, for Vicksburg was a natural fortress, perched on a high bluff commanding the Mississippi, and almost unapproachable from the north or northeast because of swamps. In April Grant began his active movement against Vicksburg, assisted by a gunboat flotilla. Many weeks passed with nothing to show but blocked attacks, heavy losses in battle and deaths from malaria and smallpox. Finally, on July 4, the Confederates, themselves stricken with disease and on the verge of starvation, gave up the fight. Thirty thousand men surrendered. Five days later, when Port Hudson was taken, the "Father of Waters," in Lincoln's phrase, again flowed "unvexed to the sea." The Union forces in Tennessee were now ready to press forward the conquest of the remainder of that state, their special objective being Chattanooga in the extreme southeastern portion, which commanded the shortest rail route between Richmond and Atlanta. A skillful campaign, conducted by General W. S. Rosecrans, brought the desired culmination on September 9; but General Bragg's army, strengthened by reenforcements from Lee, turned on the federals at Chickamauga Creek on September 19–20, driving them back into Chattanooga, to which it laid siege. Grant, now taking command in person, waged a hot battle from November 23 to 25, dislodging the Confederates and forcing their retreat into Georgia.

The campaign of 1863 marked a turning point in the war. Not only did it complete the conquest of Tennessee, but it rent the enemy country in twain, crippled the Southern transportation system, and placed the Union army in a strategic position to rive the Confederacy in a new direction. Hardly less significant was the fact that it brought to the fore the greatest military genius on the Northern side, thereby causing Lincoln to appoint Grant to the supreme command of the nation's armies. With Grant's removal to the Eastern theater of war, W. T. Sherman, who had proved one of his ablest generals, took charge at Chattanooga as the campaign of 1864 got under way. To him fell the task of breaking through the mountains of northwestern Georgia and capturing Atlanta, the principal railroad center left to the Confederacy and its chief manufacturing city. His army outnumbered the foe almost two to one, but it took him from May to

July to arrive before Atlanta, where after weeks of hard fighting he took possession on September 2. The Confederate general, J. B. Hood, who had saved his army only by evacuating the city, set about to imperil Sherman's line of communications and base of supplies at Nashville, and thus compel his withdrawal. But Hood suffered irreparable defeat at the battle of Nashville on December 15–16 at the hands of General G. H. Thomas.

Meantime Sherman, undeterred by Hood's operations in his rear, resolved upon a southeasterly march across Georgia to the ocean. This would enable him to establish a safe base which could be supplied by sea from the North and, at the same time, to strike a disastrous blow at the granary which fed Lee's army. He believed that if the war in all its frightfulness and ruin were brought home to the people of the Lower South their morale would break and the Confederate armies melt away. Beginning the advance on November 12, 1864, his army of sixty thousand, marching in four columns and foraging off the country, destroyed 265 miles of railway, and left in its wake a belt sixty miles wide in which nothing of military value remained. According to Sherman's own estimate, the damage amounted to a hundred million dollars, four fifths of it "simple waste and destruction." He met with no opposition worthy of the name and, on December 20, took possession of Savannah. Thus the campaign of 1864 ended with the Confederacy cut into three parts, and Sherman in a position to sweep northward along the coast toward the Union forces massed in Virginia.

The fighting west of the Mississippi River had little effect upon the campaigns farther east, most of it being desultory and guerrilla in character. It was not until the spring of 1862 that the Confederates gave up hope of imposing their will upon Missouri. They had succeeded in regaining a good part of the state by September, 1861, but the issue was definitely settled against them at the bloody battle of Pea Ridge, in northwestern Arkansas, on March 5–8 of the next year. General S. R. Curtis, the victor in this fight, rapidly enlarged his area of authority until at the close of 1862 the northern half of Arkansas was in Union hands. The center of Confederate power was at Shreveport in the Red River Valley in northwestern Louisiana. Various unsuccessful attempts were made by the Union forces to dislodge

the foe from this region in 1863 and 1864, but General Kirby
Smith retained possession until the end of the war.

THE CAMPAIGNS IN THE EAST

Meanwhile the Eastern theater of war presented a different
story. From the very first both sides had realized the importance
of decisive action in Virginia. The rival capitals stood only a
hundred miles apart, one on the Potomac, the other on the
James — rivers running approximately parallel to each other.
The intervening country, rough and wooded, was traversed by
numerous streams which lay athwart an invader's path, while
furnishing the Confederates natural moats of defense. Still
another feature of Virginia topography gave the South a military
advantage. Along the northwestern border of Virginia lie two
mountain ranges, cradling the Shenandoah, a river flowing
northerly into the Potomac at Harper's Ferry, above the federal
capital. This valley formed a natural passageway into the North
and, under the protective screen of the mountains, Confederate
commanders were constantly able to threaten Washington or
harry the rear of federal armies.

Lincoln's enterprise in preventing the secession of Maryland
in the spring of 1861 had the strategic value of saving to the
United States the control of the Potomac River. Spurred by the
popular cry of "On to Richmond," General Irvin McDowell
attacked the enemy at Manassas Junction on the little stream
of Bull Run, twenty-five miles west of Washington, on July 21,
1861. Both armies were raw and undisciplined, but the superior
leadership of the Confederate general, Joseph E. Johnston, threw
the Union forces into confusion, causing a disgraceful rout.
Lincoln now placed General George B. McClellan in command.
Though he showed marvelous energy and success in whipping his
armed mob into an efficient fighting unit, the remainder of the
year passed without offensive operations.

The campaign of 1862 opened with McClellan's decision to
launch a drive against Richmond from an unexpected quarter —
the shore of Chesapeake Bay — thereby avoiding the difficult
overland march. His plan was to ship his army to Fortress Monroe, then advance up the peninsula between the York and James
rivers and capture Richmond. The Peninsular campaign was

marked by McClellan's characteristic timidity and overcaution. It required a month for him to take Yorktown, his first objective. Proceeding slowly in the teeth of stubborn resistance, he battled his way across the Chickahominy and, by early June, came within sight of Richmond. Though his force outnumbered Lee's army of defense by thirty thousand, he allowed the latter to assume the offensive. In the Seven Days' Battles (June 25–July 1), the Union troops were driven steadily backward, both sides suffering terrible losses.

Realizing the moment for victory had passed, Lincoln recalled the army, replacing McClellan with Pope who was enjoying temporary fame for his capture of Island No. 10 on the Mississippi. Boastful and overconfident, Pope began the overland march against Richmond, only to meet needless disaster at the second battle of Bull Run on August 30, 1862. Lee, seizing the opportunity, undertook a counterinvasion of the free states, crossing into Maryland by way of the Shenandoah Valley. With such a bold stroke he might hope to incite a pro-Southern uprising in Maryland, capture the federal capital, and force the war to an abrupt close. But as Lee advanced northward, McClellan, again in command, paralleled his movements with a force vastly superior in numbers. On September 17 the two armies met at Antietam Creek, near Sharpsburg, Maryland. Desperate fighting ensued with heavy casualties. Lee was forced to give way, but, thanks to McClellan's inactivity, he effected an orderly retreat into Virginia. Late in October, when the federals once more undertook the overland march on Richmond, McClellan was presently replaced by General A. E. Burnside. Oddly enough, the latter had protested against his own appointment on the plea of incapacity, and the sequel justified his candor, for he was defeated with heavy slaughter at the battle of Fredericksburg on December 13. The Eastern campaign of 1862 thus ended in a draw, though with the advantage distinctly on the side of the South.

The next year's campaign began badly for the North. Under "Fighting Joe" Hooker, the Union forces once more attempted the overland advance on Richmond. At Chancellorsville a bloody battle from May 2 to 5, 1863, resulted in a severe repulse for the federals. The Confederate victory was gained at a

high price, for it cost the life of General T. J. ("Stonewall")
Jackson, who, next to Lee, was the ablest Southern commander.
Lee, seeing the way open for a new invasion of the North, and
again using the Shenandoah Valley for the purpose, crossed the
Potomac late in June. Meantime the Union army, with General
G. G. Meade in command, occupied the heights at Gettysburg,
which commanded several important highways, and awaited
attack. Here, in southern Pennsylvania, occurred three days of
terrific fighting on July 1–3, involving casualties of nearly forty
thousand men, shared almost equally by the two sides. In the
end Meade won the advantage, for Lee's invasion was checked.
Yet Lee retired southward in such good order that the Union
general dared not risk another battle. The remaining months
passed with small skirmishes but no general engagement. Accordingly, the close of the year 1863 saw the Northern army as
far away from Richmond as when the war began.

The federals had all along possessed an advantage over the
enemy in man power and equipment, but had suffered from inferior leadership. With unexampled patience Lincoln had tried
a succession of generals, but without satisfactory result. The
campaign of 1864 opened with the choice of yet another commander, Ulysses S. Grant. A former West Pointer, he had entered the war in 1861 as a colonel of Illinois volunteers and,
through his military successes in the West, had won rapid promotion. On March 9, 1864, he was appointed to the newly revived
position of lieutenant general with supreme command, under the
President, of all the Union armies. Grant differed from his
predecessors mainly in his pertinacity and in his resolution to
crush the South by his superiority in men and resources. Furthermore, his plans embraced concerted movements by the armies
East and West. For himself he reserved the Eastern command.

On the night of May 3, 1864, Grant began the oft-attempted
march on the Confederate capital by crossing the Rapidan, en-
camping the next day in the Wilderness, a densely wooded,
marshy tract ten miles across. Here Lee measured his strength
with his new opponent in an inconclusive two days' battle
(May 5–6). Grant now moved southeastward toward Spottsylvania Court House and, for the next month, was almost constantly engaged in desperate combat while battering his way

stubbornly toward Richmond. Lee was the abler strategist, and Grant's men were constantly being hurled against well-chosen intrenched positions, protected by the new device of wire entanglements. Two costly engagements — at Spottsylvania on May 8–12, and at Cold Harbor on June 1–3, the latter near the scene of McClellan's misadventure — caused Grant to shift his base to the James River, south of Richmond. By this time he had lost 55,000 men, or about half his original force, but fresh troops kept his ranks full. Still, repeated attacks failed to pierce the Confederate defense. Grant laid siege to Petersburg, an important railroad junction connecting Richmond with the South. When Lee sought to draw him off in July by sending General J. A. Early down the Shenandoah Valley in a raid against Washington, Grant retaliated by dispatching General P. H. Sheridan with a force which defeated Early by weight of numbers at Opequon Creek and elsewhere. Sheridan ravaged the valley so thoroughly that it could never be used again for a Confederate invasion. The year closed with Grant still before Petersburg, twenty-two miles from Richmond.

Grant's inexorable advance in 1864 foreshadowed the end. From all sides Yankee troops were closing in on Richmond. On February 1, 1865, Sherman began his march northward from Georgia. The lay of the land made it necessary for his men to cross innumerable streams swollen by spring freshets. Everywhere a desperate enemy obstructed their progress. The Union soldiers, living off the country, systematically destroyed railways and machinery. The march through South Carolina was marked by pillaging and general lawlessness. On February 17, the Confederates abandoned Columbia, the South Carolina capital, and in the confusion of federal occupation it was partly destroyed by fire. Charleston fell into the hands of the federal fleet without a battle when her railroad connections with the interior were cut. On March 19 Sherman's advance ran into the Confederate forces under General J. E. Johnston at Goldsboro in central North Carolina, and was temporarily checked.

Meantime, the Confederate positions in Petersburg and Richmond had proved no longer tenable, and on April 2 Lee abandoned them, intending to effect a junction with Johnston or, if that failed, to secure himself in the mountain fastnesses. But

Northern cavalry got ahead of him, tearing up railways he had hoped to use, and blocking possible mountain passes. On April 9 Lee found himself at Appomattox Court House, some seventy miles west of Petersburg, hemmed in by the enemy and with no alternative but surrender. A conference ensued between the two generals — Lee, erect in a new full-dress uniform of Confederate gray with a jeweled sword; Grant in the shabby blue of a private, wearing the straps of lieutenant general but no sword. The terms of surrender were magnanimous. The officers were permitted to retain their sidearms, and both officers and men rode off on their own horses. On his return from the conference, Grant quieted the noisy demonstrations of his soldiers by reminding them, "The rebels are our countrymen again." When the news reached Johnston, he asked Sherman for terms. The two men met at Hillsboro, and on April 26 Johnston yielded on the same conditions as Lee. The two events occurred within ninety miles of each other. A month later Kirby Smith at Baton Rouge surrendered his force of 18,000 men. The war for Southern independence had become the "Lost Cause."

FILLING THE WAR PURSE

The financing of the war placed an enormous burden upon a people unused to heavy taxation. In the four years the governmental expenditures overtopped those of the whole previous period of national independence. Yet, when Lincoln entered office, custom receipts were almost at a standstill, the treasury was nearly empty and public credit on the ebb. In December, 1861, the banks of the North suspended specie payments, an action soon followed by the government. People promptly began to hoard gold and silver coins, and the country went on a paper-money basis. In a frantic effort to meet the mounting war costs and restore confidence, Secretary of the Treasury Chase and Congress resorted to every known device for obtaining revenue. There were three principal sources to draw upon: taxation, legal-tender issues and loans. In all these respects the crying need for funds caused the government to depart widely from time-honored policies.

Hardly a session of Congress passed without some increase in the tariff until the act of 1864 advanced the average rate to forty-seven per cent, an unprecedented figure at that time, though not excessive according to later standards. The chief purpose of such legislation was to protect Northern industrialists from foreign competition, in order to enable them to pay high domestic taxes. A total of $305,360,000 was raised from tariff duties during the war. In imposing internal taxes Congress broke even more sharply with the past. Such levies had been unknown for more than a generation, while an income tax had never been tried. The first comprehensive law, that of July, 1862, left hardly anything untaxed — from tobacco, liquors and billiard tables to advertisements, occupations, manufactures, railroads and inheritances. Two years later these rates were increased. The first tax on incomes, in 1861, levied three per cent on incomes above $800, but by 1865 the rates had risen to five per cent on those between $600 and $5000 and to ten per cent on larger ones. The total yield from internal taxes of all kinds during the war was $356,846,000.

A second financial expedient — one whose effects were to plague the country for years to come — was the issue of legal-tender notes or "greenbacks." By the simple process of working the printing press, the United States acquired abundant funds to expend for soldiers' wages and war supplies. This paper money was not unlike the Continental currency of Revolutionary days, being fiat money, unsupported by a gold reserve. Creditors were required to take the greenbacks at face value, and their ultimate redemption in gold depended on the good faith and future financial ability of the nation. In February, 1862, Congress authorized $150,000,000 worth of these notes, to be receivable for all debts due to or from the federal government, except import duties and interest on bonds. Further inflation was provided for in 1862 and 1863 until, at the close of the war, greenbacks to the amount of $431,000,000 were in circulation. In addition, the government issued $50,000,000 in fractional currency in denominations as low as three cents. These shinplasters, as they were called, were needed to replace the smaller metal coins that, as the war went on, disappeared from use. From a fiscal point of view, all such issues amounted to a forced loan from the people, for the notes quickly declined in value, both because of their superabundance and because of the people's wavering faith in the government in times of military misfortune. As is always the case, there resulted a rapid rise in the cost of living. In July, 1864, a hundred greenback dollars were worth thirty-nine dollars in gold; in April, 1865, with victory assured, but sixty-seven dollars.

The government's main reliance, however, was on borrowing money through the sale of bonds and treasury notes. In order to compete with commercial investments, high rates of interest had to be offered. The two issues of "five-twenties" (bonds redeemable at the government's option from five to twenty years after date), authorized in 1862 and 1864, bore interest at six per cent; the "ten-forties," issued in 1864, paid five per cent. Short-term loans were effected through treasury notes, offered in smaller denominations, and sometimes carrying interest as high as 7.3 per cent (the "seven-thirties"). In all, the government obtained a revenue of $2,621,917,000 by such means — more than three times as much as from all other sources combined.

The need for speeding up the sale of bonds hastened the adoption of the national banking act. Other causes, however, were more fundamental. On January 1, 1862, there were fifteen hundred banks that issued notes. Chartered by the several states, they possessed different privileges and operated under different restrictions, their bank notes being based on a wide variety of securities, unlike in quality or amount. In some states, boards of bank commissioners made frequent and thorough examinations, while elsewhere no such boards existed or existed in name only. All told, about seven thousand different kinds of notes were in circulation apart from successful counterfeits. The situation was improved over that of Jackson's day, but depositors in many states were still uncertain as to the security of their funds, and bank notes in constant use might, or might not, be worth their face value. Some system of federal regulation and control was clearly called for. The national banking act of 1863 (amended in 1864) did away with these irregularities, supplied a safe and uniform bank currency and, at the same time, provided a new market for government bonds. Incidentally, it enlisted a strong and active financial interest for the preservation of the Union. Banks chartered under the system were required to buy federal bonds to the extent of a third of their capital stock, and to deposit them with the Secretary of the Treasury. On the basis of this security they might issue bank notes up to ninety per cent of the market value of the bonds they owned. They must also keep on hand a cash fund for the current redemption of notes and as a safeguard for their depositors. Depositors were further protected by the provision for periodical examination by federal inspectors. Though a large number of state banks, because of the many restrictions, at first held aloof from the national system, Congress brought most of them into line by providing in March, 1865, for a ten-per-cent tax on their bank notes, thus reserving the note-issuing function for national banks alone. The legislation of 1863–1865 remains the foundation of our national banking system to this day.[1]

Federal expenditures for the army and navy from 1861 to 1865 amounted to more than three billion dollars. This figure, however, does not include the interest charges on the war debt. Furthermore, several years elapsed after the peace before the appropriations for military and naval purposes returned to a normal basis, and already in the last year of the conflict pensions began to swell the government's outlay. In 1879 an estimate was made of the expenditures growing out of the war down to that date, showing a total of $6,190,000,000. But even this amount does not take into account the extraordinary expenses for war purposes borne by the state and local governments.

The financial difficulties of the Confederacy were incomparably greater. While the North had the revenue machinery of the United States government to work through, the South had to build from the ground up. At the outset, however, the Confederacy had over a million dollars in its treasury, nearly all of it confiscated from federal mints and customhouses within its borders. Like the United States, the Richmond government expected to obtain a substantial revenue from custom duties. The blockade, however, quickly put an end to this expectation.

[1] The system was changed in detail by subsequent acts, notably the one of 1908, which permitted a national bank to deposit certain other securities besides United States bonds as a basis for its note circulation. It was also affected, in certain respects, by the establishment of the federal reserve system in 1913 (see pages 345–346).

The Confederate Congress then asked each state to levy a property tax for the general treasury — the old requisition system of the Articles of Confederation — but the results proved disappointing. Finally, in April, 1863, the Congress adopted an internal-revenue measure, comparable to the federal act of 1862, and including even a ten-per-cent tax on farm produce, payable in kind. The levy on farm products caused bitter resentment among the agricultural classes, particularly in North Carolina.

Borrowing was also resorted to, through long-term bonds and short-term treasury notes, but this method proved less successful than in the North where money for investment was plentiful. Since the first bond issue, in 1861, absorbed most of the available specie, the issue of 1862 was made payable in produce. As a result, the government came into possession of vast stores of cotton, tobacco and other commodities that had no sale. In 1863, however, some success was met in selling a bond issue of $15,000,000 abroad. As in the North, the tempting expedient of irredeemable paper money was also adopted. In its extremity, the Confederacy printed nearly a billion dollars of this currency, with the inevitable sequel of rapid depreciation and inflated prices. The total volume of such money was swollen by unrecorded issues of state governments, banks and private business firms. Of course, the enormous war debt of the South was outlawed by the failure of the rebellion, and the Fourteenth Amendment of the federal Constitution, adopted in 1868, forbade either the United States or any state to pay any part of it.

SELECT BIBLIOGRAPHY

Naval and Military Operations. Well-balanced, brief accounts may be found in Rhodes, *History of the Civil War* (condensed and revised from his more elaborate work); Hosmer, *The Appeal to Arms*, and his *Outcome of the Civil War;* Wood, *Captains of the Civil War;* Paxson, *The Civil War;* Eggleston, *The History of the Confederate War;* Dodge, *A Bird's Eye View of Our Civil War;* and Wood and Edmonds, *A History of the Civil War in the United States.* Among the best war biographies are Henderson, *Stonewall Jackson and the American Civil War;* Maurice, *Robert E. Lee, the Soldier;* and Coolidge, *Ulysses S. Grant.* Meneely, *The War Department: 1861,* is a special study. The war on the water in its various aspects is the concern of Baxter, *The Introduction of the Ironclad Warship;* Mahan, *Admiral Farragut;* Porter, *The Naval History of the Civil War;* and Scharf, *History of the Confederate States Navy.* Bradlee, *Blockade Running during the Civil War and the Effect* *of Land and Water Transportation on the Confederacy,* is the best treatment of its subject. In *The Irrepressible Conflict* Cole gives an intimate picture of the conditions of fighting.

Filling the War Purse. A concise analysis of federal finances and the new national banking system appears in Dewey, *Financial History of the United States.* A biographical approach is afforded by Hart, *Salmon Portland Chase;* Oberholtzer, *Jay Cooke, Financier of the Civil War;* and Burton, *John Sherman.* For Southern finances, Schwab, *The Confederate States of America,* is important.

CHAPTER V

SOCIAL AND POLITICAL CONDITIONS IN WAR TIME

LIFE BEHIND THE LINES

SOUTHERN secession came as a severe blow to Northern industry. As the banks suspended specie payments, mercantile failures multiplied until over 12,000 firms were driven to the wall. Not only was business subjected to the usual shocks incident to the outbreak of a great war, but merchants and bankers were confronted with the loss of $300,000,000 owing them from the South — private debts which the Confederate and state authorities promptly outlawed. After 1861, however, a boom set in, which lasted through the remainder of the conflict. The enormous purchases and high prices paid by the government for uniforms, munitions and other supplies kept factory after factory running month after month; and the closing of the Mississippi greatly augmented the freight traffic of the railroads. At the same time, currency inflation and the steadily ascending protective tariff acted as a powerful stimulant to industry.

As the cost of living shot upward, the wage-earner's pay lagged far behind, causing a widespread revival of trade unions and an increasing resort to strikes, until by 1864 labor had regained much of the ground it had lost. Meanwhile, the farmer made rich profits, thanks to the army demand for food and to bad crops abroad. Wheat production had never been so great as during the war. The general well-being was mirrored in the growth of savings-bank deposits in the five-year period from $149,278,000 to $242,619,000, and of the number of depositors from 694,000 to 981,000. In only one respect did Northern enterprise suffer a serious setback. The increased hazards to shipping from the depredations of the *Alabama* and other Confederate raiders enabled the British to take over much of the trade hitherto carried in American vessels. All together, there was a loss of a million tons during the conflict. An injury was inflicted upon the merchant marine from which it never recovered, for, when peace returned, capitalists preferred the certain profits to be gained from factories and railways to the doubtful venture of restoring American shipping.

In the train of war-time prosperity came the usual brood of war-time evils: corruption, profiteering and fast living. The government was cheated without conscience in its purchases of military supplies. A committee of the War Department in 1862 exposed frauds of $17,000,000 in contracts amounting to $50,000,-000. The Michigan legislature formally charged that "traitors in the disguise of patriots have plundered our treasury," and James Russell Lowell, agreeing, asserted, "Men have striven to make the blood of our martyrs the seed of wealth." The term, "shoddy aristocracy," came to stigmatize those who reaped fortunes out of government contracts, particularly from supplying the soldiers with inferior clothing. In the mad strife for gain Northerners even engaged in illicit traffic in cotton with the enemy, often with the corrupt connivance of army officers in the field. Not only food and money but also powder and bullets reached the Confederates by this means. Before the trade was effectively regulated in 1864, the South had sold more cotton to the North than it managed to send through the blockade to England. As profiteers multiplied and wealth piled up, luxury flaunted itself in American cities as never before. "The indulgence in every variety of pleasure, luxury, and extravagance is simply shocking," reported the correspondent of the *London Times* in 1863. "Washington is mad with gayety, reeling in the whirl of dissipation," declared the *Springfield Republican* a year later.

Against this unedifying picture, however, must be set another and more inspiring one. No previous war in history had called forth such heroism and self-sacrifice on the part of noncombatants associated with the troops or from the bulk of civilians behind the lines. The army casualties mounted so rapidly that the medical department was obliged to make use of volunteer nurses. Clara Barton, future founder of the American Red Cross, who resigned a government clerkship to take up nursing and the work of organizing hospital supplies, was merely more famous than the countless others whose labors were no less devoted. To the service of medical treatment came an epochal discovery, for which chief credit belongs to Americans in the years before the war. In 1844 Horace Wells, a dentist in Hartford, Connecticut, demonstrated that nitrous oxide gas might be used to deaden the pain of operations. Two years later a Boston dentist, W. T. Morton, acting upon the advice of C. T. Jackson, a chemist, first employed ether as an anæsthetic.[1] Before these discoveries, a patient in a severe surgical operation had to be restrained by force, or even bound by straps to the table. Since a patient's movement might fatally deflect the surgeon's knife, anæsthesia — so named by Dr. Oliver Wendell Holmes from the Greek word meaning "without pain" — added greatly to the number of recoveries as well as to the relief of suffering. Chloroform was most widely used for this purpose during the Civil War. Unfortunately, the era of antiseptic surgery had not yet arrived and, in order to prevent wound infections, surgeons resorted freely to amputations. Of the thirty thousand that were performed in the Union army, the great majority were successful. For many years following the war, armless and legless veterans were a pathetic reminder of the great conflict. Sanitary science also lingered in the dark ages, with the result that, despite the heavy losses incurred in fighting, deaths from dysentery, camp fevers, pneumonia and other diseases proved almost twice as great.

In no armed conflict in history before the World War was civilian relief work organized on so vast a scale. Every local community in the North had its Ladies' Aid Society for making bandages, shirts and other necessaries and comforts; and these groups coöperated with a national body, the United States Sanitary Commission, which the government created in June, 1861, to help in looking after disabled soldiers and their dependent families. The Sanitary Commission developed an elaborate organization, employing at times five hundred agents. Storehouses were maintained in Boston, New York, Cincinnati, Chicago and other centers, to which local branches sent their supplies with the assistance of free transportation by the railroads

---

[1] A Georgia physician, C. W. Long, had made the same discovery in 1842, but failed to publish his results. The third common anæsthetic, chloroform, was first used for this purpose in 1847 by Sir James Y. Simpson of Edinburgh.

and express companies. Through its labors, conditions of camp life were greatly improved, and assistance was given in caring for the wounded on the field of battle and in hospitals. In the few days following Gettysburg, clothing and food valued at $75,000 were distributed among the men, including such delicacies as poultry, butter, eggs, milk and ice. To provide funds for the Commission's activities, "sanitary fairs" were held in all the leading cities, a total of $7,000,000 being raised in this and other ways. The services rendered by the countless women connected with the work inspired Lincoln's oft-quoted eulogy: "If all that has been said by orators and poets since the creation of the world in praise of women were applied to the women of America, it would not do them justice for their conduct during this war." Nor were the soldiers' spiritual needs neglected. For this purpose the United States Christian Commission was formed in November, 1861, upon the initiative of the Young Men's Christian Association. Besides providing the camps with free reading rooms, where magazines, newspapers and religious literature might be perused, it set up a system of diet kitchens for injured soldiers extending to every corps of the army.

In the South the burdens borne by the noncombatant population were even heavier than in the free states, for a larger proportion of the white men were at the front. Relief work was not organized; but the proud Southern women brought into use old spinning wheels and looms in order to make clothing for the soldiers, they denied themselves meat and drink that it might be sent to the army, and, like their Northern sisters, they nursed the wounded and worked in munition plants. Living in an invaded country, they experienced the horrors of war all about them — homes destroyed, fields ravaged, hostile soldiers at every hand. Nothing was more remarkable perhaps than the peaceable labor of the several million slaves, whose presence in the South had caused the "irrepressible conflict" and whose freedom became a major purpose of the invading hosts.

THE RESTRAINT OF CIVIL LIBERTY

Among the most perplexing problems that confronted the nation was the question of the limits to which criticism of the government might be allowed to go. The democratic system is better adapted to peace than to war, for the efficient conduct of war requires the assumption of extraordinary powers by the government, with a consequent tendency to override the lawful rights of individuals and minorities. During the Civil War President Lincoln performed acts that in peace time would have been unconstitutional, and which could be justified only by his authority as commander-in-chief of the army and navy. Not only was the administration determined to permit nothing to cripple its efforts to maintain public safety, but, under guise of his war powers, Lincoln even accomplished the great humanitarian feat of freeing the slaves. If President Davis was more cautious in the lengths to which he went, minority groups in both sections denounced the course of government as intolerable and despotic.

Lincoln's suspension of the writ of *habeas corpus* called forth particular condemnation. Early decisions of the Supreme Court had implied that this cherished safeguard of the individual could be set aside only by Congress. But without consulting that body Lincoln temporarily suspended the writ in Maryland in 1861 at a time when the arbitrary arrest of suspects seemed necessary to nip the developing secession movement in the bud. In a proclamation of September 24, 1862, he went even further, denying the privilege of *habeas corpus* in the case of all persons, wherever found, who sought to discourage enlistments or were guilty of any other "disloyal practice." Thousands of men in all parts of the North were promptly arrested upon suspicion and imprisoned without hearing or trial, or else sentenced by military tribunals without jury. To still criticism, Congress passed a law on March 3, 1863, providing that suspects should not be detained longer than twenty days without indictment by a grand jury. The President, however, ignored this statute, and arrests continued to be made by executive or military order. On the other hand, Lincoln sought to mitigate the rigors of this policy by paroling many political prisoners. That the government acted with excess zeal, and often unlawfully, was made clear by the Supreme Court in the case of *Ex parte* Milligan. This decision, however, rendered in 1866, came too late to be of service. Milligan, an Indiana Democrat, had been sentenced to death for conspiracy by a military tribunal in 1864. The Supreme

Court reversed the judgment, holding that the constitutional rights of an individual under criminal prosecution could not be denied in places where the regular civil courts were "in the proper and unobstructed exercise of their jurisdiction."

Meanwhile, in the South, President Davis had in February, 1862, declared martial law and suspended the writ of *habeas corpus* in disaffected districts and at important military points. Though, unlike Lincoln, he acted with express sanction of his Congress, strong opposition developed against this interference in the accustomed sphere of state action. The North Carolina courts contested its legality, freely issuing the writ to persons imprisoned by Confederate authority. A Georgia statute in 1864 declared that refusal to grant *habeas corpus* would subject the judge to a penalty of $2500. In this campaign of protest Vice-President Stephens took an active part; and "military despotism" was roundly denounced in resolutions of public meetings and legislative memorials. The Confederate Congress gradually restricted the President's authority in this respect, finally withdrawing it entirely on August 1, 1864.

THE ABOLITION OF SLAVERY

The freeing of the Negro was by no means a necessary consequence of the collision of arms. The avowed object of the victorious party in the election of 1860 was only to confine slavery to the states where it already existed. Even after the war began, Congress announced in July, 1861, that the government was actuated by no "purpose of overthrowing or interfering with the rights or established institutions" of the South, but sought merely "to preserve the Union with all the dignity, equality, and rights of the several States unimpaired; and that as soon as these objects are accomplished the war ought to cease." In the same session, acts were passed to organize the territories of Colorado, Dakota and Nevada with no restriction against slavery. When the popular outcry for emancipation rose high in 1862, Lincoln took further occasion to define his position in a letter of August 22, elicited by a sharply critical editorial in Greeley's *Tribune*. "My paramount object in this struggle," he declared, "is to save the Union, and is not either to save or destroy slavery. If I could save the Union without freeing any slave, I would do it; and if I could save it by freeing all the slaves, I would do it; and if I could save it by freeing some and leaving others alone, I would also do that."

Lincoln's personal convictions as to the evil of human bondage had not altered since his debate with Douglas in 1858; but as President of the whole American nation, he shrank from righting one wrong at the cost of another, and no principle of the federal system went deeper than the right of each state to control its own domestic institutions. Furthermore, he realized the folly of committing the Northern people to a policy which many of them were not yet prepared to accept. Not only had he divided the vote of the North with Douglas, but those who supported him had voted against the extension, not the existence, of slavery. Many who sprang to the defense of the Union would have refrained had they believed they were fighting a "nigger war." Nor did he ever lose sight of the fact that the four border slave states had sided with the North. Abolition would not only be an act of injustice to the loyal whites in those states, but might drive them into the arms of the enemy. Had Lincoln been permitted, undisturbed by men or events, to work out his own solution, he would have instituted everywhere a program of gradual emancipation, with compensation to the masters and removal of the freedmen to Liberia or Latin America.

Under the prod of circumstances, however, steps were taken, almost from the beginning of the war, looking to the further restriction or eventual doom of slavery. On April 16, 1862, Congress provided for the compensated liberation of the three thousand slaves in the District of Columbia. Two months later (June 19) the Republicans enacted into law the principle which had brought their party into being eight years before — the exclusion of slavery from the federal territories. Lincoln desired, further, to bring about emancipation in the border states, for he realized that their permanent loyalty could not otherwise be assured. At his suggestion, Congress in April, 1862, offered to aid these states financially in a program of gradual abolition, and Lincoln held earnest conferences with the border-state Congressmen to the same end. The latter, however, remained unmoved, asserting their constitutional right to hold slaves, and declaring that any scheme of compensation, even with federal help, would inflict ruinous taxation on their people.

The problem of dealing with the question in the seceded states proved far more difficult. To antislavery extremists the war presented a providential opportunity to deal a deathblow to slavery in the South, for, in their minds, the disloyal conduct of the planting class absolved the government from all obligations to respect Southern property rights. They entirely misunderstood Lincoln's legal scruples and political caution, fiercely assailing him as a traitor to the holy cause of freedom. Such Republicans called themselves Radicals, and their quarrel with the President over emancipation led them to criticize him on other scores as well. In the cabinet they had an outspoken champion in Chase; in the House, in Thaddeus Stevens. Outside of Washington their great spokesmen were Greeley of the *Tribune* and John C. Frémont, the latter an ambitious politician as well as a mediocre soldier.

The matter was not merely one for abstract disputation. The invasion of the South brought the troops into direct contact with the slaves, raising questions which called for immediate decision. In the early weeks of the war an overwhelming number of Negroes flocked into the camp of General B. F. Butler in Virginia. Should these be returned to their masters under the fugitive-slave act? Butler propounded the ingenious doctrine that the fugitives were contraband of war, being a form of property used by the foe in hostile war service, and hence subject to confiscation. His position was promptly approved by the War Department, and, when Congress passed a confiscation act on August 6, 1861, it provided for the seizure of slaves as well as other property when used for insurrectionary purposes.

No sooner was this question decided than General Frémont, then in command in Missouri, raised the issue in a different form. By a proclamation of August 30, 1861, he decreed the forfeiture of all property, including slaves, belonging to disloyal citizens there. This overstepped the provisions of the confiscation act, for the cause he assigned for liberation was the hostile service of the master, not of the slave. Lincoln, believing the action premature, overruled it. When General David Hunter, commanding the recovered territory around Beaufort, imitated Frémont's example in May, 1862, by declaring free the slaves of South Carolina, Georgia and Florida, Lincoln again intervened and revoked the order. On July 17, however, Congress passed a second confiscation act, which applied, in modified form, the principle for which Frémont and Hunter had stood. After inflicting drastic penalties on all persons convicted of treason, the law declared that, when the slaves of rebel masters fell into federal hands, they should "be forever free of their servitude." Two months later Lincoln said, "I cannot learn that that law has caused a single slave to come over to us."

In revoking General Hunter's order, Lincoln had declared, "Whether it be competent for me, as Commander-in-Chief of the Army and Navy, to declare the slaves of any State or States, free, and whether at any time, or in any case, it shall have become a necessity indispensable to the maintenance of the Government . . ., are questions which, under my responsibility, I reserve to myself." This pivotal question was never absent from his mind. He was constantly weighing the political considerations involved, at home and abroad, and particularly whether an act of liberation would prove effective in weakening the enemy. At a cabinet meeting on July 22, 1862, he at last announced his readiness to take the fateful step. But Seward counseled further delay, for, in view of recent military reverses, a proclamation of emancipation might be regarded as a "last shriek on the retreat." The wisdom of this advice was at once recognized. Ignorant of what was in store, the Radicals redoubled their clamor. The Confederate repulse at Antietam provided a fit occasion, and on September 22 the President issued the preliminary proclamation. Justifying his action as a "necessary war measure," he declared all slaves free in those parts of the Confederacy that should continue in rebellion on January 1, 1863.

When New Year's Day came, he issued the final proclamation, designating the states and districts affected, and inviting exslaves to join the armed forces of the nation. The proclamation, of course, did not apply to the four border states, nor did it involve the status of slavery in Tennessee or those parts of Virginia and Louisiana already occupied. Elsewhere Negroes became legally free by the executive edict, though actual liberation had to await the victorious advance of the Union forces.

The propriety of emancipation as an exercise of war powers can be gauged only by the results which flowed from it. While it is doubtful whether more slaves than before sought refuge within federal lines, over 100,000 Southern Negroes enlisted as soldiers, performing services as fighters and in guarding and repairing railways, which, in Lincoln's judgment, hastened the final victory. Of even greater import was the effect of the proclamation on public opinion abroad, for, as we shall see, it precluded further danger of foreign intervention.

THE PROGRESS OF EMANCIPATION, 1863–1865

Lincoln's action led by swift stages to the eradication of slavery everywhere. Several of the states unaffected by the proclamation fell into line. The Missouri convention, after providing in June, 1863, for a gradual process, changed its plan to immediate freedom in January, 1865. During 1864 abolition was decreed by Maryland and by conventions of unionists in Virginia, Arkansas and Louisiana, with Tennessee following shortly after. Meanwhile, a strong sentiment had been developing to make abolition both universal and irrevocable by a provision in the federal Constitution. In April, 1864, the Senate approved the Thirteenth Amendment, forbidding slavery or involuntary servitude save as a punishment for crime. Though the House was unable at first to marshal the necessary two-thirds majority for its passage, the nation spoke unmistakably in the presidential election of 1864, causing the House in January, 1865, to reverse its earlier vote. (The amendment became a part of the organic law on December 18, 1865.) Its direct practical effect was to free the slaves in Kentucky and Delaware, and to substitute immediate for gradual emancipation in West Virginia.

POLITICAL DIVISIONS IN THE NORTH

Largely because of strife over the emancipation question, the Republican party throughout the war was plagued by internal dissension. The Radical wing also criticized Lincoln's management of the war, while the Conservatives stoutly defended the President and agreed with him in placing national preservation before Negro freedom. In elections the two factions maintained a united front and, since the Republicans early in the war adopted the practice of nominating candidates under the name of the Union party, they also succeeded in commanding the support of one section of the Democrats. These War Democrats, as they were called, retained their belief in the historic economic doctrines of their party, but believed that, in the existing crisis, the question of the Union overshadowed all other issues.

Most Democrats, however, continued in the regular party organization, doggedly contesting with the administration forces for political control. The great majority of them supported the war, but charged Lincoln with incompetence and condemned his assumption of autocratic power. Their slogan became, "The Constitution as it is and the Union as it was," and in Horatio Seymour of New York they possessed their ablest leader. But a militant minority, headed by C. L. Vallandigham, an Ohio Congressman, opposed the war and demanded immediate peace without terms. The stronghold of the Peace Democrats was the old Northwest, particularly those parts whose inhabitants, like Vallandigham himself, were descended from settlers of Southern origin. In order to carry on their propaganda more effectively, many of their number joined a secret, oath-bound order variously known as the Knights of the Golden Circle, the American Knights and the Sons of Liberty. Execrated by the public at large, this pacifist element quickly won the name of Copperheads, an epithet soon applied indiscriminately to all Democrats.

The first test of strength between the contending forces came in the fall elections of 1862. The voters, suffering a reaction from the buoyant patriotism of 1861, were dismayed by the almost unbroken succession of military defeats as well as by the disclosures of graft in government contracts. The increasing number of arbitrary arrests gave additional cause for dissatisfaction, while many were disconcerted by Democratic jibes that the Emancipation Proclamation had changed the struggle to an "abolition war." [1] As a result, the Union party lost ground in many parts of the country. Besides electing Seymour governor of New York, the Democrats carried New Jersey, Pennsylvania and the states from Ohio to Wisconsin. The administration, however, managed to save its majority in Congress.

The next year proved an even more critical one. In Indiana the Peace Democrats in the legislature blocked every measure for the support of the war, and the lower house of the Illinois legislature declared for an immediate armistice and a peace convention. The President told Sumner he feared "the fire in the rear" more than he did the enemy's military prowess. In the fall of 1863 the efforts of the defeatists reached a dramatic climax. The Democrats in Ohio chose as their candidate for governor Vallandigham, who at the time was under sentence of exile because of his denunciations of "King Lincoln." Conducting his campaign from a safe refuge in Canada, it seemed for a while that he might be successful. [2] Though he received 187,000 votes, he lost the election by a majority of 101,000. The federal victories at Vicksburg and Gettysburg proved a decisive argument against him.

Vallandigham's defeat marked the turning of the tide, though Lincoln still had much opposition to encounter both within and without his party. A mass convention of Radical Republicans

---

[1] A favorite bit of Democratic verse ran as follows:

> Honest old Abe, when the war first began,
> Denied abolition was part of his plan;
> Honest old Abe has since made a decree,
> The war must go on till the slaves are all free.
> As both can't be honest, will some one tell how,
> If honest Abe then, he is honest Abe now?

[2] Edward Everett Hale's famous story, "The Man without a Country," was written for the purpose of affecting public sentiment at the time of this campaign.

at Cleveland on May 31, 1864, even tried to prevent his renomination by putting forward Frémont as their candidate on a platform demanding sterner prosecution of the war and a constitutional amendment against slavery. But the maneuver failed. When the Union party convened a week later at Baltimore, they named the President on the first ballot, thus deciding, in Lincoln's homely phrase, that it was "best not to swap horses while crossing the river." With him was associated Andrew Johnson, then military governor of Tennessee and a War Democrat. The platform praised Lincoln's conduct of the war and promised universal freedom by constitutional amendment. The ticket, however, evoked little popular enthusiasm. The prospects for success, especially during the military misfortunes of July and August, were decidedly gloomy. Advised by Greeley and others of his almost certain defeat, Lincoln recorded his own impressions on August 23. "This morning as for some days past," he wrote in a private memorandum, "it seems exceedingly probable that this Administration will not be reëlected."

The party's chances, however, were somewhat improved by the action of the Democrats at Chicago on August 29. After declaring the war a failure, their platform, written under Vallandigham's influence, called for an immediate armistice with a peace convention to restore the federal Union. But General McClellan, the victor of Antietam, chosen as the Democratic candidate, virtually repudiated this pronouncement in his letter of acceptance. The effect of such divided counsels upon the country was indicated by the *New York Tribune's* version of the platform: "Resolved that the war is a very good war, and most unrighteous war, and while it should be stopped at once, it must be carried on with vigor." Yet success for the Union ticket was far from assured. In order to rally the support of the wage-earners, a campaign circular appealed, "Workingmen, stand by your order. Lincoln and Johnson were poor men and worked for their living." A few months earlier Lincoln had taken occasion to declare, "Labor is the superior of capital and deserves much the higher consideration," while pointing out that the war, in fact, was a "war upon the rights of all working people." In September, Sherman, Sheridan and Farragut won their great victories and, as Seward said, this news "knocked the bottom out of the

Chicago nominations." Frémont now withdrew from the contest, and Lincoln was chosen by an electoral majority of 212 to 21. But he secured only fifty-five per cent of the popular vote.

EUROPE AND THE AMERICAN WAR

With a single exception the Great Powers of Europe sympathized with the South in the struggle. It was the purpose of the Confederacy to convert this sympathy into a recognition of independence, coupled, if possible, with armed intervention. The government at Washington, on the other hand, strove to defeat this expectation and, at the same time, to keep the South from procuring war vessels abroad. The efforts of both sides centered upon Great Britain since it was known that Napoleon III of France would not act alone. British opinion on the American conflict was far from unanimous. The ruling class was friendly to the Confederacy, for the nobility and landed gentry looked upon the Southern planters as fellow aristocrats, and rejoiced that the great American experiment in popular government seemed on the verge of collapse. Citing Congress's own declaration at the opening of the war, they denied the North was fighting to abolish slavery, and held with the *London Times* that "The contest is really for empire on the side of the North and for independence on that of the South." On the other hand, the manufacturing and commercial classes were divided. They heartily disliked the Northern protective-tariff system and greatly feared a cotton famine, but a prewar surplus of cotton tided them over for more than a year, and the shipping interests reaped golden profits from their inroads on the Northern merchant marine.

From the outset the United States had influential friends in Parliament, who, though in the minority, were strong enough to prevent the government from taking extreme measures. Reform leaders like John Bright, Richard Cobden and William E. Forster identified the contest with their own struggle for greater democracy, and declared insistently that the cause of the South was the cause of slavery and the "Slave Power." In this position they were joined by the wage-earners despite the fact that the latter became the chief sufferers from the cotton stringency. It is possible, too, that pro-Northern sentiment was strengthened by English crop failures in 1860–1862, which caused Northern grain

for a time to be in greater demand than Southern cotton.[1]
Tennyson and Darwin were warm supporters of the Union,
offsetting Dickens and Carlyle, who sided with the Confederacy.

Relations between the two countries were sorely strained in
the early years of the war. On May 13, 1861, the British government issued a proclamation of neutrality, an action quickly
followed by other countries. Such a proclamation did not
amount to recognition of Southern independence, but it granted
Confederate ships of war and commerce the same privileges in
British ports all over the world as those accorded Northern
vessels. The act also contravened Lincoln's contention that a
rebellion, and not an international war, was in progress — a
position from which Lincoln himself had unwittingly departed
when he established the blockade. However justified the proclamation may have been, it bore the appearance of action taken
precipitately since it was issued on the very day the American
Minister, Charles Francis Adams, arrived in England.

Six months later occurred the *Trent* affair, which brought the
two nations dangerously near war. Captain Charles Wilkes
commanding an American warship stopped the British steamer
Trent on the high seas on November 8, forcibly removing the
Confederate commissioners, J. M. Mason and John Slidell and
their secretaries, who had taken passage from Havana for South-
ampton, both neutral ports. The news, greeted with extravagant
joy in the North, caused England to blaze with resentment.
Peremptorily demanding liberation of the prisoners, the British
government hurried eight thousand troops to Canada and engaged in naval preparations. Since the seizure had been un-
authorized and, indeed, ran counter to all previous American
policy as to freedom of the seas, Lincoln allowed sufficient time
to pass for public sentiment to cool and then, on December 26,
ordered the men surrendered with a suitable explanation.

No sooner was this incident closed than a new difficulty arose
from Great Britain's lax interpretation of her neutral duties
toward the clandestine construction of Confederate cruisers.
In March, 1862, the authorities allowed the newly built *Florida*

---

[1] Thus, Forster in a speech in Parliament in 1863 declared that, if Britain had
an economic motive for intervention because of the cotton shortage, "it was al-
lowable to ask, 'What would be the cost of the war in corn [wheat]?'"

to slip out of Liverpool, and in July the *Alabama* departed in a similar manner. In both instances Adams protested vigorously, presenting evidence in advance to prove Confederate ownership of the raiders. That the officials were swayed by friendship for the South cannot be gainsaid. Indeed, in September, Lord Palmerston, the Prime Minister, deciding the time had arrived to recognize Confederate independence, arranged for a cabinet meeting with a view to proposing to France and other powers joint action in the matter. But before the meeting was held, the situation changed. For one thing, Adams let it be known that the United States would sever diplomatic relations. A more important influence was the Union victory at Antietam on September 17, followed by the Emancipation Proclamation. With her own strong antislavery traditions, Great Britain could not adopt a policy which would serve to perpetuate human bondage in America. From this time to the close of the war, the government stringently enforced its neutrality obligations. In 1863 the authorities seized three vessels destined for the Confederacy, two of them ironclad rams of great destructive power. Meantime, the *Florida* and the *Alabama*, engaged in their mission of harassing Northern commerce, wrought damage to the extent of more than fifteen million dollars before their capture.

Napoleon III was even more friendly to the South than the British leaders. He encouraged Confederate emissaries to build commerce destroyers in French shipyards, though only one, the *Stonewall*, was actually completed and delivered. Though the cotton shortage caused unemployment in certain sections of his country, Napoleon's chief motive was to cripple the military strength of the United States, so as to create conditions favorable for the realization of the long-cherished dream of reëstablishing a French empire in the New World. About six months after the war began, he induced Great Britain and Spain to join him in an armed expedition against Mexico to collect the unpaid claims of their subjects. In April, 1862, after the allied forces occupied a number of customhouses, Great Britain and Spain came to terms with Mexico and withdrew. The French, left to their own devices, proceeded to overthrow the existing Mexican government and place Maximilian, an Austrian archduke, on a throne supported by French bayonets. All this, of course, was in direct violation of the Monroe Doctrine, but America, being engaged in a struggle for national existence, could do nothing but protest and bide her time. With the return of peace she became mistress of the situation. Napoleon was warned once more, and the French troops finally withdrew in the spring of 1867. Without foreign support Maximilian's bubble monarchy collapsed.

Like France, Spain sought to profit by America's preoccupation with internal embroilments. In 1861 she annexed the Dominican Republic, a part of the island of Santo Domingo. Three years later, having declared war on Peru, she seized the Chincha Islands, valuable for guano. The United States protested sharply, announcing again the principles of the Monroe Doctrine. Early in 1865 Spain quietly relinquished both claims. On the other hand, Russia, Prussia and the Scandinavian countries were favorable to the North, Russia conspicuously so. Czar Alexander II, who had emancipated the serfs in 1861, was strongly influenced by antislavery sympathies, and even more so by the fact that the European powers friendly to the South were unfriendly to his own country. At a critical time in the war (September, 1863), one Russian fleet visited New York and another San Francisco, where their presence gave much moral support to the cause of the Union both at home and abroad.

Though Russia had acted from motives connected with her own national interests, the Northern people felt a deep debt of gratitude. Consequently, shortly after the peace, when she offered to sell Russian America (Alaska) to the United States, the government was agreeably disposed, though "Walrussia," as some wag proposed calling it, was looked upon as a frozen expanse with no possibilities of development. The purchase price being fixed at $7,200,000, the Senate ratified the treaty on April 9, 1867, with but two dissenting votes. As the future was to disclose, the United States had unwittingly made a noble purchase. Thereby, too, another European monarchy was eliminated from the Western Hemisphere.

THE SIGNIFICANCE OF THE CIVIL WAR

The decision that the United States should be one, not two nations, marks an epoch in the history of the American people. The great constitutional issue upon which the war was avowedly fought was resolved, once for all, in favor of the supremacy of the Union. Though this conclusion was reached under purely American conditions, it coincided with a world-wide movement for the consolidation of nationality. The Austrians having been driven out, the several Italian states in 1861 united under a king of their own choosing. In 1867 the dual monarchy of Austria-Hungary was founded with rights of self-government for both peoples. Three years later the third French Republic came into being, and the next year brought the final achievement of German unification. America was the first to recognize the new French government; and President Grant told Congress he saw in the united German Empire "an attempt to reproduce some of the best features of our own Constitution." Meanwhile, to the north of the United States, the provinces from Ontario east (Newfoundland excepted) combined in 1867 to form the Dominion of Canada, with full powers of local autonomy and provision for enlarging the dominion by the admission of the western territories. Northern triumph in the Civil War accorded with a deep-flowing historical trend.

The war also resulted in the destruction of slavery and of the power of the cotton capitalists — the real, though unconfessed, cause of the struggle. The United States was the last of the great Western nations to do away with human bondage, Russia having preceded her by a few years. Yet the abolition of slavery solved one problem only to create another, the Negro problem, which would vex the nation for many years to come. The undoing of the "Slave Power" removed from the political scene an aggressive force seeking objects peculiar to a section, but its going merely hastened the emergence of a new and more powerful economic class, domiciled in the North and intent on molding the entire nation to its will. The collapse of plantation capitalism signalized the rise of industrial capitalism.

Posterity may properly ask whether the gains of the Civil War repaid for the terrific expenditure of blood and treasure. Slavery could hardly have lasted very much longer in any case: it was not only a costly system for the master, but it flew in the face of the conscience of the nineteenth century. If a divided country was not easy for a Northern patriot to contemplate, it may well be questioned whether the Southern Confederacy could long have maintained its life apart. The return of peace, moreover, thrust upon the nation problems such as it had never before been called to face. The seceded states must be accorded their proper legal relations with the triumphant North and, what was equally important, the love of a common nationality must somehow be restored. An unprecedented war debt awaited payment, and some means had to be found to cure the ills arising from greenback inflation. Finally, the presence of several million ex-soldiers among the voters portended a political influence that would not only help keep alive war-time bitterness, but would burden the country for more than a generation with a staggering debt for pensions.

Yet no such thoughts ruffled people's minds when the war ended at Appomattox. All was rejoicing in the North. Even in Dixie the sense of disappointment and blighted hopes was mingled with a feeling of relief. The disbanding of the troops and their dispersion into peace-time employments occurred without shock or incident. Nearly a million Northern soldiers were mustered out in 1865. Most of them took their final payment with them as a "nest egg" and, with free farms awaiting in the West and abundant jobs in the new manufacturing industries, they were quietly absorbed into the ranks of civil life. The Confederates wandered home, on foot and horseback, penniless. Bereft of their slaves, their plantations laid waste or unworked, peace meant to them the building of a new South.

SELECT BIBLIOGRAPHY

Life behind the Lines. Fite, *Social and Industrial Conditions during the Civil War*, is the best guide for the free states; Wesley, *The Collapse of the Confederacy*, for the South. Stephenson, *The Day of the Confederacy*, also gives a good picture of Southern life and politics. A detailed discussion of the discovery of anæsthetics is appended to Packard, *The History of Medicine in the United States . . . to the Year 1800*. The most complete account of the principal relief organization is Stillé, *History of the United States Sanitary Commission;* and the services of women are more particularly treated in Brockett and Vaughan, *Woman's Work in the Civil War*, and Underwood, *The Women of the Confederacy*.

The Restraint of Civil Liberty. Randall, *Constitutional Problems under Lincoln*, supersedes all earlier treatments of the subject.

Political Divisions during the War. The Peace Democrats receive careful study in Benton, *The Movement for Peace without Victory during the Civil*

War, which should be supplemented by Kirkland, *The Peacemakers of 1864.* Other aspects of the political scene are treated at length in the standard histories by Channing, McMaster, Rhodes and Schouler.

Europe and the Civil War. The most useful accounts are Adams, *Great Britain and the American Civil War;* Jordan and Pratt, *Europe and the American Civil War;* West, *Contemporary French Opinion on the American Civil War;* and Thomas, *Russo-American Relations, 1815–1867.* Additional material may be gleaned from Perkins, *The Monroe Doctrine, 1826–1867;* Bancroft, *W. H. Seward;* Adams, *Charles Francis Adams;* and Harris, *The Trent Affair.* For the Confederate side, consult Owsley, *King Cotton Diplomacy;* Callahan, *The Diplomatic History of the Southern Confederacy;* and Bonham, *The British Consuls in the Confederacy.* Martin, *Maximilian in Mexico*, is the standard treatment of that subject.

CHAPTER VI

THE POSTWAR SOUTH

DIRECTION of the process of Southern reconstruction belonged, as a matter of course, to the government at Washington. Since a rebellion does not end in a treaty of peace, the conditions imposed by the President and Congress in the form of executive and legislative enactments and constitutional amendments were, in effect, the terms of Southern defeat. The problem was really a threefold one: humanitarian in so far as it involved helping the ex-slave learn the difficult ways of freedom; political in so far as it involved reëstablishing the state governments and according them their former place in the federal system; and economic in so far as it affected reviving the war-deranged economic life on a free-labor basis. Unhappily, the solution of these questions could not wait until war passions had cooled; action must be taken as need arose. Partisan prejudice, sectional bitterness and motives of revenge colored the purposes of both victor and vanquished, and even embroiled the government itself. Negro welfare, at first envisaged simply as a philanthropic undertaking, assumed a different guise when the politicians made it a party issue. The President and Congress soon found themselves at loggerheads over fundamental policies, and the South grudgingly made such concessions as it must. Only in the matter of economic readjustment were the defeated people allowed to work out their salvation unhindered and unhelped.

From the early days of the war when fugitive slaves began pouring into Union camps, relief work was carried on among them by the American Missionary Association and other Northern bodies. Presently more than three thousand men and women were active in this service, including agents of the Sanitary Commission and of British benevolent societies. Not only physical aid but educational and religious instruction was given.

Nevertheless, as the federal troops occupied additional territory, the scope of the work became too vast for private agencies to handle efficiently, and the chief responsibility inevitably fell upon the government itself.   After some delay, Congress in March, 1865, established the so-called freedmen's bureau, charged for the period of the war and a year thereafter with the duty of relieving distress among refugees and freedmen, and of allotting them land from abandoned estates (not to exceed forty acres) at a low rental, with the privilege of eventual purchase. Placed at the head of the work, Major General O. O. Howard performed competent service in a difficult situation.   Besides coördinating the activities of the private societies, the bureau organized local branches and assumed a general guardianship over the emancipated people.   At a time when they were dazed and distracted by their new-found liberty, unprepared for its responsibilities, the bureau strove to impress them with the idea that freedom did not mean idleness, and to assist them in their dealings with the former master class.   In its eventual four and a half years of existence, it issued 15,500,000 rations to freedmen, gave medical care to a million and expended more than $5,000,000 on colored schools.   That it speeded the process of social re-organization cannot be doubted, though the subordinate officers often proved trouble makers, doing much to antagonize white sentiment as well as to raise rainbow hopes in the breasts of the untutored blacks.

Meanwhile, the question arose of how a "seceded" state might regain its former place in the Union.   In the absence of any specific provision in the Constitution, both the executive and Congress claimed prior authority in the matter. The President held that, since he as head of the army and navy had imposed military law on the South, he alone might declare the conditions of its withdrawal.   The lawmaking branch, on the other hand, asserted its priority because of the constitutional guarantee of a republican form of government for every state and Congress's right to judge of the admission of its own members.   Back of this abstract question, however, lay a more practical one, the fact that Lincoln favored a policy of generosity and speedy reconciliation as contrasted with Congress's insistence upon a more drastic course.   In his eyes the war had been fought to prove that the

Union could not be broken and he planned to welcome the states back with as little offense to their pride as possible.

From the early days of the war Lincoln had recognized as legal the makeshift government of Virginia which had been set up to sanction the separation of West Virginia (see page 58), for he believed that, once the Confederate power was crushed, the loyal legislature would quietly extend its authority over the entire state. When Tennessee, Louisiana and Arkansas came under federal control in 1862 and 1863, he appointed military governors to take charge until acceptable civil governments could be organized. Then, on December 8 of the latter year, he issued a proclamation of amnesty, which indicated a general procedure for guidance of the Southern people. All who took a prescribed oath of loyalty might again become voters, certain classes being excepted, such as prominent Confederate officials and persons who had joined the rebellion after resigning high federal posts. Whenever as many as a tenth of the electorate in 1860 should thus qualify in any state, they might establish a state government which he would recognize as the true government. Congress, he pointed out, must decide for itself whether members from the state should be admitted to seats. From other sources we know Lincoln did not favor the granting of Negro suffrage, except possibly to educated men and ex-soldiers. Under this "ten-per-cent plan" constitutional conventions were held and state governments organized during 1864 in Tennessee, Louisiana and Arkansas. Though these governments were but "as the egg is to the fowl," Lincoln believed "we shall sooner have the fowl by hatching the egg than by smashing it."

Congress viewed this progress with growing concern. Members chosen from the ten-per-cent states were refused admission; and in July, 1864, the body set forth its own terms in a proposed law known, from its chief authors, as the Wade-Davis bill. This measure not only made Congress, instead of the executive, the ultimate authority on reconstruction, but it also imposed more stringent conditions, notably the requirement that a majority of the white men must take an oath of allegiance. To this bill Lincoln applied a pocket veto, though by proclamation he offered it as a possible alternative to his own plan. He was disinclined to quibble over details if the end he was seeking could be as well attained otherwise. His attitude toward the Wade-Davis bill is an augury of how he might have dealt with Congress when the return of peace made reconstruction the paramount public issue. But hardly had Lee and Johnston surrendered before he fell victim to an assassin's bullet. In consequence, his place was taken on April 15, 1865, by a man ill fitted by temperament and training to assume the reins of government at so critical a juncture.

JOHNSON, CONGRESS AND THE SOUTHERN PROBLEM

The rise of Andrew Johnson from humble origins was even more remarkable than that of Lincoln himself. Starting in poverty and ignorance as a tailor's apprentice, unable to write until taught by his wife, he had fought his way upward by sheer pluck and native ability against tremendous odds and the scorn of the planting aristocracy. When scarcely of age, he was chosen mayor of his little mountain village in eastern Tennessee, an event which proved the first step in a political ascent that took him to the state legislature, the national House of Representatives, the governor's chair and, in 1857, to the United States Senate. Thick-set, swarthy, somber of countenance, he had many of Jackson's mental traits, being pugnacious, self-assertive, immovable in his loyalty to duty as he saw it. He stoutly opposed the secession of Tennessee, and his selection as Lincoln's running mate was a sop to the War Democrats in the Union party. Long experience in public life wore off some of his rough edges, revealing his sterling qualities of intellectual courage and inflexible purpose. Unfortunately, the situation before him called also for tact and patience, and these qualities were utterly foreign to his make-up.

Lincoln's death at the hands of a drink-crazed Southern zealot put the North in an ugly humor. While the excitement was at fever heat, Johnson offered rewards for the arrest of Jefferson Davis and other leaders as accomplices in the terrible deed. Misled by this rash action, Radical chieftains hailed the removal of the gentle Lincoln as a "godsend to the country," and awaited his successor's announcement of a vengeful policy toward the South. On cooler thought, however, Johnson declared his acceptance of the governments in Virginia, Tennessee, Louisiana and Arkansas, retained his predecessor's cabinet intact, and on May 29, 1865, issued a proclamation with reference to the remaining states, which revealed his essential agreement with Lincoln's course. While excluding certain additional classes from amnesty, he directed that constitutional conventions be held as speedily as practicable on the basis of a loyal white suffrage. When these conventions met, he further made known his expectation that they should declare invalid the ordinances of secession and repudiate their war debts, and that their first legislatures should ratify the pending Thirteenth Amendment. The reorganization of the remaining seven states proceeded along these lines, and by December 4, 1865, when Congress assembled for the first time under the new President, all the states save one had substantially complied with his terms, Texas completing her handiwork the following April.

Congress, faced with the question of admitting members from the ex-Confederate states, decided in the negative. The President's lenient policy affronted both Congress's sense of its own proper rôle in reconstruction and its desire to impose conditions to insure the South's future good behavior. Idealists like Charles Sumner, driven by conscience, maintained, further, the Negro's right to the ballot as an inherent human right; while other Radicals like Thaddeus Stevens, driven by ambition and party loyalty, favored the same measure as a means of building up Republican strength in Dixie. Thanks to abolition, the white South, unless checkmated by the black South, would actually secure additional members in the House and the electoral college, since the constitutional provision for counting three fifths of the slaves in apportioning representation no longer held. Nor did the conduct of the newly organized state governments excite confidence in the President's course or in the defeated people's penitence. Prominent ex-Confederates, such as Alexander H. Stephens who had just been chosen Senator from Georgia, were again entering politics, while the so-called loyal legislatures were adopting "black codes" that, in Northern eyes, seemed singularly like the old "slave codes." This legislation aimed chiefly to impose restraints which might discourage idleness, vagrancy and race friction. Thus, while according freedmen ordinary civil rights like making contracts and owning property, it affixed in some states special penalties for breaking labor contracts, excluded their testimony in cases involving whites, and forbade them to bear arms without a license. A few legislatures even provided that idle Negroes should be subjected to a fine which, if unable to pay, they must work out in the service of an employer. However justifiable from the standpoint of the former master class, such laws seemed to the Radicals a deliberate effort to nullify the result of the war.

The Congress which passed these matters under review contained conservative, moderate and radical Republicans. If Johnson had been prudent enough to conciliate the moderates, he might, with the help of his conservative supporters and the Democrats, have commanded a majority for a slight modification of his own plan. On the contrary, his dogmatism and violence soon drove many of his natural allies into league with the Radical leaders, Stevens and Sumner, iron-willed, imperious men who for two years were virtual dictators of the political scene. After the two Houses set up a joint committee on reconstruction to consider conditions of admitting the Southern members, they proceeded to take action to safeguard the former slaves against the black codes. The first effort in this direction, the freedmen's-bureau bill of February 6, 1866, besides extending indefinitely the bureau's life, enlarged its powers and authorized it to seek military aid when the Negro's civil rights were denied. The bill, promptly negatived by the President as inexpedient and unconstitutional, caused him in an intemperate speech to class Sumner and Stevens with Jefferson Davis as traitors to the American system of government. Never again, however, was Johnson able to thwart the will of the lawmaking branch. In April Congress adopted over his veto the civil-rights act, which accomplished the purpose of the earlier bill but in a more thorough way. All persons born in the United States (excluding untaxed Indians) were declared to be citizens of the United States and, as such, entitled to equality of treatment before the law, any "statute . . . to the contrary notwithstanding." Not only were heavy penalties inflicted for violations, but the military power might, if necessary, be employed to secure enforcement. A little later Congress assured the continuance of the freedmen's bureau.

After months of taking evidence as to Southern conditions, the joint committee on reconstruction was ready to report. On the last day of April it proposed a new constitutional amendment dealing with every important aspect of the Southern problem. With some changes at the hands of Congress this eventually became the Fourteenth Amendment. By its first section the principles of the civil-rights act were firmly imbedded in the Constitution, thereby setting at rest all question of its possible unconstitutionality.[1] The second section was an attempt to meet the desires of both the theorists of racial equality and the practical politicians, the states being given the option of enfranchising all adult male citizens or suffering a reduction of representation in Congress. The third section, designed to check the rapid return of rebel leaders into politics, barred from office-holding ex-Confederates who had been federal or state officials before the war, until they should be pardoned by a two-thirds vote of Congress. The next section declared that the war debt of the South should never be paid nor that of the Union repudiated, and further that former masters should never be compensated for their slaves. On June 13, 1866, the amendment was sent to the states. The Radicals were willing to have the Southern governments ratify a constitutional amendment even if they did not deem them "reconstructed" enough to send members to Congress. On July 19 Tennessee ratified, and five days later Congress declared her entitled to representation. The other Southern legislatures rejected the amendment by overwhelming majorities.

Both Congress and the executive had now indicated their conceptions of a proper reconstruction policy, and the fall elections of 1866 gave the people a chance to choose between them. Johnson's friends sought to attract the support of the moderates of both political parties, but their promising efforts were unwittingly defeated by Johnson himself when he undertook a "swing round the circle," making a series of blustering speeches in the large cities of the East and Midwest. His cause was further injured

---

[1] For the wording of this section, see page 277. Though ostensibly evoked by the necessities of the freedmen, its chief effect, as we shall see, has been to enable the federal courts to protect corporations ("persons") by the due-process clause from state and local regulation or interference. This purpose, it appears, was in the minds of certain members of the joint committee, notably J. A. Bingham of Ohio.

by a bloody race riot in New Orleans on July 30, an affray which convinced many that the South did not intend to deal fairly with the freedmen. Both factions exerted themselves to win the soldier vote by assembling special conventions of the veterans, efforts that may be said to mark the formal entry of the old-soldier influence into postwar politics. In the end, the Radicals won an overwhelming triumph, securing more than two thirds of each branch of Congress. Perhaps if the President had stayed in Washington, the outcome would have been different. As it was, the Radicals acclaimed the result as a popular mandate to pursue a repressive policy toward the South.

THE REIGN OF THE RADICALS

When Congress assembled shortly after the election, the Radicals decided to brush aside the governments set up by the President in the ten remaining states, and to exceed their own former demands. Stevens desired to place the South under military government pure and simple, and a bill embodying this idea passed the House. When it reached the Senate, its terms were somewhat softened, though Sumner succeeded in forcing into it the additional requirement of Negro suffrage. Congress accepted Sumner's alteration, notwithstanding the fact that at the very time colored men could vote in but six states of the North — in New York and throughout New England except Connecticut.[1] The new plan was set forth in the basic reconstruction act of March 2, 1867, and in supplementary legislation of March 23 and July 19 and of March 11, 1868. The ten states were to be divided into five military districts under the command of generals, who were charged with preserving order and with continuing or supplanting civil officials as they saw fit. The people of a state might gain representation in Congress when a constitutional convention, chosen by voters of both

[1] Like Lincoln, Johnson would have welcomed a limited Negro suffrage if granted by the Southern states themselves. Even Harriet Beecher Stowe, whom Lincoln called "the little woman who wrote the book that made this great war," disapproved action by Congress to force Negro suffrage on the South. A Negro historian remarks: "Had there been a close coöperation among the best whites in the South and a gradual incorporation of the intelligent freedmen into the electorate, many of the mistakes made would have been obviated; and the recent steps backward towards lynching and peonage would not have been made." See C. G. Woodson, *The Negro in Our History* (Wash., 1922), 256.

races (excluding those disfranchised as former rebels), sho[...]
frame a constitution establishing Negro suffrage; when th[...]
constitution should be ratified by the white and black electorate and accepted by Congress; when the new state legislature
should ratify the Fourteenth Amendment; and, finally, when
this amendment should have become a part of the federal
Constitution.

Meanwhile, the feeling between the President and Congress
had grown constantly more vindictive. Johnson vainly vetoed
all the important reconstruction measures and, in turn, Congress
set about to hamper and defeat his purposes in every conceivable
way. One of their efforts, the tenure-of-office act of March 2,
1867, made the President guilty of a "high misdemeanor" if he
removed an officeholder without the Senate's consent. The
statute specifically included cabinet officers who, unless the
Senate consented to their dismissal, were to hold office "during
the term of the President by whom they may have been appointed and for one month thereafter." Johnson in his unavailing veto declared the act unconstitutional. Not content with
halfway measures, the Radicals determined to depose the President. In their inflamed state of mind, his stubborn resistance
to the measures they thought necessary amounted to nothing
less than treason. The judiciary committee of the House labored
for months to find evidence to justify impeachment on one of
the grounds named in the Constitution — "treason, bribery, or
other high crimes and misdemeanors" — and in December, by a
vote of five to four, reported in favor of such action. But the
House decided to await more specific evidence of misconduct.

Their opportunity came on February 21, 1868, when Johnson,
without consulting the Senate, removed the Secretary of War,
Edwin M. Stanton, who had long been acting in secret league
with his enemies. Three days later the House amid intense excitement voted to impeach the President for "high crimes and
misdemeanors." The charges, set forth in eleven articles, involved much duplication and confusion of thought, but the
principal accusations were that his dismissal of Stanton consti-
tuted a "high misdemeanor" under the tenure-of-office act, and
that he had attempted to bring Congress into contempt in his
"swing round the circle" in 1866. The trial in the Senate began

on March 13, with Chief Justice Chase presiding. It soon appeared that the charge based upon the tenure-of-office act lacked substance, for Stanton, a Lincoln appointee, had continued in service nearly three years after the term of the President who named him. Nothing daunted, the Radicals turned their chief efforts toward removing the President for reasons of general party expediency.

The excitement throughout the North was intense, with popular sentiment against Johnson. Even the General Conference of the Methodist Church, then in session at Chicago, set aside an hour of prayer that the Senators might be directed to do their "high duty." When the vote was taken on May 16, the Senate stood 35 to 19 for conviction, one vote short of the necessary two thirds. Seven Republicans defied public opinion to join with the Democratic minority in making this result possible. To posterity it is clear that Johnson had done nothing to merit removal. As Senator Lyman Trumbull said before casting his ballot for acquittal, "Once set the example of impeaching a President for what, when the excitement of the hour shall have subsided, will be regarded as insufficient causes, and no future President will be safe who happens to differ with a majority of the House and two thirds of the Senate on any measure deemed by them important."

While these stormy scenes were being enacted at Washington, Congress's scheme of military reconstruction had gone into effect in the South. Johnson, despite his deep-seated objections, designated the district commanders as required by law, and these officials proceeded to establish the paramount authority of the federal government in the ten states. Wherever possible, they coöperated with the civil authorities on the spot, but when this proved difficult they did not hesitate to remove governors (as in Louisiana, Texas, Georgia and Mississippi), or to substitute military for the ordinary civil courts. In due course, they provided for registering the voters as a preliminary to holding constitutional conventions. In Georgia the registrants were about equally divided between the two races; in South Carolina, Florida, Alabama, Mississippi and Louisiana the black voters actually outnumbered the white. The elections that ensued produced the most extraordinary constituent assemblies

in American history. All the conventions contained Negroe.
eager to quaff the heady wine of political privilege; in South
Carolina they formed a majority. In the actual transaction of
business, however, they were elbowed aside by the so-called
Carpetbaggers, ambitious Northerners who, packing all their
worldly goods presumably in a carpetbag, had gone South for
purposes of revenue only. Allied with them were a small number
of Southern whites — the detested Scalawags — who had for-
saken their neighbors to espouse the Radical cause. The bulk

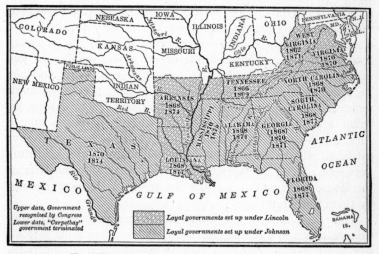

THE PROCESS OF RECONSTRUCTION, 1866–1877

of the colored members were of little consequence save as pawns
in the hands of white or black leaders.

During the late winter and spring of 1868 the conventions
completed their handiwork in all the states but Texas. Surprisingly enough, the constitutions framed under these unpromising
conditions embraced many excellent features, notably the mandatory provisions for setting up free public-school systems. All the
constitutions also guaranteed the civil and political equality of
the two races, and some of them carried the principle of disfranchising ex-Confederates beyond any previous limits. To the
old master class the new frames of government seemed a reversal
of the natural order of society. Acclaiming themselves defenders

of "Caucasian civilization" against the inroads of "African barbarism," they left little undone to stir up popular feeling against ratification. But the hand of the national military authority proved too strong for them. Only in Mississippi, where the white-disfranchisement clause was unusually severe, was acceptance defeated by a majority of the votes cast. Elsewhere — in Arkansas, the Carolinas, Georgia, Alabama, Florida and Louisiana — the constitutions were approved, and the newly installed legislatures promptly ratified the Fourteenth Amendment. All the conditions having been met, Congress in June, 1868, authorized the admission of members from the seven states on the fundamental condition that Negro suffrage forever remain a part of their organic laws. As Virginia and Texas had not yet completed the process of adopting their constitutions, these two states, along with Mississippi, continued under martial rule. An important reason for hurried action in the case of the other seven had been the Radical desire to secure their electoral support in the impending presidential election.

GRANT AND THE RADICALS

On May 20, while the impeachment trial was yet in progress, the Radicals, calling themselves the National Union Republican party, met in convention at Chicago. General Grant and Schuyler Colfax, the latter speaker of the House and an ardent Radical, were nominated on a platform applauding congressional reconstruction and pledging payment of the national debt in gold. Recommended by his war fame, Grant's nomination took place on the theory which came in with Jackson, that any American, particularly a military chieftain, is capable of holding any office, and that special training or aptitude is unnecessary. As a matter of fact, Grant's political affiliations, so far as he had had any, had been Democratic, but shortly before the impeachment trial he had turned to the Radicals, thanks to a bitter quarrel with Johnson.

The Democrats were in a difficult position. Discredited by Southern secession and Northern Copperheadism, the party faced the problem of recovering its former strength. For this purpose they must develop new leaders and new issues, a task hardly to be accomplished in one or even two presidential campaigns.

There was an uncomfortable amount of truth in the remark of Kate Chase, politician-daughter of the Chief Justice, that "when the South seceded, the brains of the party went with it." Meeting in New York on July 4, the Democrats set about to clear their skirts of past offenses and strike out along fresh lines — a course which in time became known in party circles as the "New Departure." As it happened, aside from reconstruction, a brand-new issue lay ready at hand. Certain war-time bonds about to fall due had been issued under a statute requiring the interest to be paid in coin, the principal in "dollars." Hard times in the Midwest, especially in 1867, had caused the farmers to insist that the "bloated bondholders" be paid off in depreciated greenback dollars such as they themselves used. "The same currency for the bondholder and the ploughholder" was their cry, and in the Democrat, George H. Pendleton of Ohio, they found an able champion. The "Ohio Idea," as it was called, had further charm for those Democrats who looked upon the war debt as having been incurred in an unrighteous cause.

Accordingly, the platform, after declaring "the questions of slavery and secession . . . settled for all time to come," berated Radical reconstruction as "unconstitutional" and "revolutionary," and demanded adoption of the "Ohio Idea" in paying the bonds. Andrew Johnson had some support for the nomination, Pendleton considerably more; but August Belmont and other Eastern Democrats, bent on undoing the mischief of the financial plank, succeeded on the twenty-second ballot in naming a sound-money man, ex-Governor Seymour of New York, who reluctantly accepted. F. P. Blair, Jr., of Missouri, was given the second place. The outcome was never in doubt. Republican orators easily diverted attention from the debt issue by "waving the bloody shirt," that is, denouncing the war record of the Democrats. Though both platforms promised pensions to the ex-soldiers, naturally the Republican pledge was looked upon as more certain of results. Grant received 214 electoral votes to 80 for Seymour, though he polled but fifty-three per cent of the popular vote.

The new President was purely a product of the war. A graduate of West Point, he had left the army in 1854 rather than stand trial on a charge of drunkenness. He turned next to farming, then to real estate, but without success. The outbreak of war found him working in his father's leather store at Galena, Illinois, for $800 a year. This short, slouchy, taciturn man was acquainted with neither the theory nor the practice of politics. He had scarcely visited a state capital unless to capture it; and, as President, he turned for advice to men who had selfish and often corrupt interests to serve. "The responsibilities of the position I feel," he said in his brief inaugural address, "but accept them without fear." Honorable himself, loyal to a fault to his friends, he retained unshaken his hold on the public which continued to revere him as the "Hero of Appomattox." The new administration proceeded at once to dispose of the two questions raised by the campaign: the debt issue and reconstruction. On March 18, 1869, Congress formally pledged payment of the public debt in coin. As regards the Southern problem, Grant, inclined at first to follow his own independent judgment, soon fell under the influence of the extremists, notably Benjamin F. Butler of Massachusetts, an unscrupulous demagogue who had mysteriously amassed a fortune while in the army.

These men insisted that, since the Fourteenth Amendment was now a part of the Constitution, the three unreconstructed states be required to ratify the pending Fifteenth Amendment. This amendment, a purely Radical creation, provided that "The right of citizens of the United States to vote shall not be denied or abridged by the United States or by any State on account of race, color, or previous condition of servitude." Its adoption was urged as the only sure way of establishing Negro suffrage, left optional in the previous amendment, and thereby of safeguarding Southern support for the Republicans once the states were again full-fledged members of the Union.[1] The Radicals carried their point, and in the first three months of 1870 Virginia, Mississippi and Texas, complying with the new demands, were declared entitled to representation. But the process of reconstruction was not yet completed, for the newly installed Georgia legislature, under Democratic control, had aroused the ire of the Radicals by expelling all the Negro members. Egged on by Butler,

[1] Furthermore, the action of Ohio, Michigan, Kansas and Minnesota in 1867 of refusing to place Negro suffrage in their state constitutions made the Radicals fearful lest the Fifteenth Amendment fail of ratification.

Congress in December, 1869, placed that state once more under military rule and, after requiring it to ratify the Fifteenth Amendment, allowed its members to return the following July. Congress, in admitting the last four states, affixed a final "fundamental" condition, that Negroes should never be disqualified from holding office. The Fifteenth Amendment went into effect on March 30, 1870.

THE SOUTHERN STRUGGLE FOR WHITE DOMINION

Though all the ex-Confederate states were now back in Congress, the Radical leaders had no thought of allowing them to manage their internal affairs without further interference. The effect of Reconstruction had been to stand the social pyramid on its apex; left alone, it would be sure to try to right itself. The remaking of Southern life and politics by major force had, indeed, been a process monstrous and intolerable to the former dominant class. Even as a penalty for rebellion it seemed irrational, since martial rule and Negro suffrage were imposed two or more years after the peace. Nor was their resentment lessened by the behavior of the ex-slaves. If the rank and file went quietly about their tasks, delusions of power dazzled others who, abetted by mulatto and white leaders from the North, did their utmost to stir the race to self-assertiveness. One outcome was the widespread formation of "Union Leagues," secret oath-bound societies composed mostly of Negroes, and pledged to maintaining the new political order. Their organization was often attended by violence toward the old master class, by the waylaying of men and the burning of houses and barns. The better elements among the whites were at first driven to anger, then to real alarm.

Most exasperating of all was the conduct of the new state governments installed when armed rule was withdrawn. These governments were dominated by Carpetbaggers in the higher offices, by Scalawags and Negroes in the lower. In the seven states reconstructed in 1868, four of the governors and ten of the United States Senators had never seen their respective commonwealths before the war. Every legislature contained a substantial colored contingent, South Carolina's having a majority. In a well-known account James S. Pike, a Northern newspaper man, describes the lawmakers of Calhoun's state: "The Speaker is black, the Clerk is black, the door-keepers are black, the little pages are black, the chairman of the Ways and Means is black, and the chaplain is coal-black. . . . Every one esteems himself as good as his neighbor, and puts in his oar, apparently as often for love of riot and confusion as for anything else." But, he added, "underneath all this shocking burlesque upon legislative proceedings . . . there is something very real to this uncouth and untutored multitude. . . . Seven years ago these men were raising corn and cotton under the whip of the overseer. Today they are raising points of order and questions of privilege. . . . It is their day of jubilee."

The new ruling class had, for the most part, no large property interests. In Alabama the taxes paid by the legislators were said to total less than a hundred dollars. Since the taxes would fall upon the hated aristocracy, the lawmakers saw no reason for staying their hand. Besides, there was real need of unusual expenditures for repairing roads, bridges and government build-ings and for the costly business of setting up a school system. The mounting costs, however, were due chiefly to other reasons — the irresponsible character of those in power, their ignorance of the rudiments of finance and, most of all, downright corruption and fraud. A conservative estimate in 1872 put the increased indebtedness of the eleven states at about $132,000,000, much of it loans and guarantees to wildcat railroad enterprises. The orgy rose highest in Louisiana and South Carolina. In the latter state, a free restaurant and bar was maintained for the legisla-tors, and included in the item, "Supplies," were such articles as hams, perfumes, suspenders, bonnets, champagne and a coffin. The public printing bills during the eight years of Carpetbag rule exceeded by $717,589 the total amount expended for that purpose by South Carolina from 1789.

Southern whites, trained in a different social philosophy, stood aghast at the social and political chaos that threatened to engulf everything in life most dear to them. How could the fine fruits of their civilization be saved from "Africanization"? From Congress no relief could be expected, and the Supreme Court, when appealed to, had turned a deaf ear to their pleas.[1] They

[1] In the cases of Mississippi v. Johnson, Georgia v. Stanton and Ex parte McCardle.

therefore resorted to that mode of secret, terroristic resistance which oppressed peoples are apt to employ against tyrannical rulers. Best known of such organizations, the Ku Klux Klan had started innocently in 1866 at Pulaski, Tennessee, as a means of providing diversion for local youths bored after the excitements of army life. When it was seen that their weird nocturnal ceremonies roused the superstitious dread of the Negroes, the members quickly took advantage of the fact. Appareled in ghostly manner and riding white-sheeted horses with muffled hoofs, they would visit the homes of unruly blacks and obnoxious whites at dead of night, and warn them to behave or flee. The Pulaski idea spread like wildfire, causing similar groups or "dens" to spring up elsewhere in Tennessee and the near-by states. At a secret meeting at Nashville in May, 1867, the dens were brought together into a unified system under the name of the Invisible Empire of the South with officers bearing awe-inspiring titles.

The use of violence became more frequent as time passed, the midnight visitations sometimes ending in floggings, maimings and even death. Criminal bands, too, found it useful to don the disguise for purposes of loot or private vengeance. The situation was already out of hand when in March, 1869, the men at the head of the order decreed its disbandment. But this only made matters worse, for many of the dens refused to obey, and the withdrawal of conservative members gave the turbulent elements full sway. Through a misapprehension of the true state of affairs, Northerners applied the term *Ku Klux* to all secret movements of terrorism in the South. In reality, the largest and probably most powerful of such bodies was the Knights of the White Camelia, which operated in the states from Texas to the Carolinas under nominal control of a supreme council at New Orleans.

The multiplying excesses and disorders led inevitably to a revival of repressive measures by the government at Washington. In a series of statutes, beginning with the force act of May 31, 1870, and followed by the federal elections law and the Ku Klux act on February 28 and April 20, 1871, Congress exerted its power to break up the undercover societies and assure the Negro the civil and political equality guaranteed by the Fourteenth and Fifteenth amendments. The President might, for these purposes, appoint commissioners to supervise congressional elections, employ armed force, or even suspend the writ of *habeas corpus*. In the months that followed, hundreds of men were haled before the federal courts on charges of conspiracy, troops reappeared in many parts of the South and, for a time in the fall of 1871, the privilege of *habeas corpus* was denied in nine South Carolina counties. By the close of 1872 "Ku Kluxing" had virtually disappeared. It is a sufficient commentary on the zeal of the Radicals surrounding Grant that the essential provisions of the force and Ku Klux acts were later declared unconstitutional by the Supreme Court.[1]

In spite of various handicaps the Southern whites were steadily advancing toward their former supremacy. As early as 1869 the obnoxious "Parson" Brownlow government in Tennessee was overturned. After the federal legislation of 1870–1871 they learned to substitute craft for force. A mere threat of violence had the desired effect of frightening Negroes from the polls and usually left no trace on which to base hostile court action. In 1870 and 1871 the Carpetbag governments toppled in North Carolina, Virginia and Georgia. In May of the next year Congress, in the general amnesty act, restored the right of office-holding to most of those disqualified under the Fourteenth Amendment, thereby allowing nearly 150,000 of the South's ablest citizens to resume active political life.[2] Meanwhile the Scalawags, growing weary of their alliance with ex-slaves and Northern adventurers, were beginning to make common cause with their white neighbors. As a result, Alabama, Arkansas, Texas and Mississippi were "redeemed" in 1874 and 1875.

Only the presence of federal bayonets enabled the Carpetbaggers to retain their hold on the three remaining states. The contending elements came to a death grapple there in the presidential campaign of 1876, with the result that the electoral returns were in doubt and the whole nation was thrown into turmoil (see page 167). [The election of Tilden, the Democratic

---

[1] See U. S. *v.* Cruikshank (1875), U. S. *v.* Reese (1875) and U. S. *v.* Harris (1882). An act of 1875 granting equal privileges to both races in hotels, churches, railways, etc., was also held unconstitutional in the civil-rights cases (1883).

[2] About 750 remained unpardoned. Not until June, 1898, when North and South joined in war against Spain, were the last disabilities removed.

candidate, would have meant the withdrawal of the troops, but, as it happened, the seating of Hayes accomplished the same end, for Hayes represented that wing of the Republican party which had grown desperately tired of federal interference in Southern politics. Early in 1877 the troops were removed, and South Carolina, Florida and Louisiana lapsed quietly into the control of the native whites.

Even more than the war itself, Reconstruction left scars that rankled deep in Southern breasts. Besides impeding the process of spiritual reconciliation with the North, so necessary for the restoration of a common love of country, it arrayed the mass of whites against the Republican party in the South as a "nigger party," and helped make the ex-Confederate states thick-and-thin supporters of the Democrats, an example which the old border slave states usually followed. Out of a total of 369 electoral votes in 1880, the "Solid South" cast 95, the border states 35 more — a substantial nucleus about which the Democrats of the North might hope to rebuild their shattered strength. Many years were yet to pass before people came to realize that, however galling Reconstruction had been, it might yet have been worse. The Radicals had avoided the crowning blunders, confiscating virtually no enemy land and putting no one to death for a political offense. After being held for two years as a state prisoner, even Jefferson Davis, though never pardoned, had been left to his own devices; and many other prominent leaders returned to civilian life without any kind of molestation. In James Bryce's opinion, "there was never a civil war or rebellion . . . followed by so few severities."

THE ECONOMIC RECONSTRUCTION OF THE SOUTH

Not only the political but the economic fabric of the South had to be remade as a result of the war. A transition had to be effected from a semifeudal order of society based on slavery to a modern system based on wage labor. Difficult as the process would have been under normal conditions, it was rendered infinitely more so by the ravages of the struggle. Besides the direct damages inflicted on towns, railways and the like, whole fortunes had been wiped out by the collapse of Confederate bonds and currency and the confiscation of slave property, plantations had fallen into ruin, and land depreciated to half its prewar value. Nevertheless, the great planters hopefully set about to reëstablish agriculture on its former large-scale basis. That they should fail was inevitable, for they had to operate on borrowed capital, and were hampered by the excessive taxation of the Carpetbag governments as well as by the irresponsible character of their Negro labor. Salvation seemed possible only through a break-up of the great estates.

Accordingly, the plan was generally adopted of leasing or selling tracts of from forty to eighty acres to Negroes and poor whites. From 1860 to 1880 the number of farms in Dixie more than doubled, reaching a total of 1,500,000, with 300,000 more added in the next decade. As farms increased in number, the average holding shrank in size — from 335 acres at the beginning of the war to 214 in 1870, 153 in 1880 and 139 ten years later. Southern agriculture began rapidly to approach the Northern small-farm system. Yet there were significant differences. Most of the farmers were tenants in process of paying for their land, and in many cases the landlord, through his control over them, managed a whole group of farms as a unit, thus preserving many of the economic benefits of large-scale operation. As the tenants often found it hard to meet the terms of payment, they were constantly tempted to borrow from local money lenders at heavy rates of interest in anticipation of their harvest. This "lazy descent into hell," as Ben Tillman called it, plunged many into a mire of debt-peonage from which extrication was heartbreakingly difficult.

Yet, in the long run, the subdivision of the large estates made possible an independent economic footing for both Negroes and poor whites, the two classes which, as Helper pointed out in *The Impending Crisis*, had borne the yoke of the slavery system. More immediately, it benefited the small yeoman farmers: they were able to outbid their poorer rivals and so acquire the choicest lands. It was these small farmers who, as the old gentry retired from the countryside to the towns, were to seize the reins of political power and, in the 1880's, give Southern public life a distinctly plebeian cast (see page 258). The agricultural reconstruction of the South involved the emancipation of the white masses in as real a sense as the Thirteenth Amendment did that of the Negroes.

Nor, in the long run, were the economic results disadvantageous. The new system caused a more careful husbanding of the soil through crop rotation and the use of fertilizers. Already by 1870 the average cotton yield per acre exceeded that of 1860, though not until 1876 did the total crop reach that at the start of the war. Though cotton remained the principal reliance, increased attention was paid to other products — tobacco, fruits, vegetables, wheat, hay — so that, in time, the total value of the minor crops came to outstrip that of cotton. Moreover, the quickened spirit of enterprise made Southerners vision the possibility of developing manufactures. "If we have lost the victory on the field of fight," declared a South Carolina newspaper in 1881, "we can win it back in the work shop, in the factory, in an improved agriculture and horticulture, in our mines and in our schoolhouses." The industrializing trend of the eighties and nineties, however, really belongs to a broader movement that was sweeping the entire nation, the Economic Revolution, and may best be considered in that connection.

THE POSTWAR SETTLEMENT WITH GREAT BRITAIN

The close of the war left the North a score to settle with Great Britain as well as with the South. Thanks to the legacy of bad feeling, public opinion viewed with complacency the activities of Irish Americans to help free Ireland from British rule. In 1865 leaders of the Fenian movement, as it was called, meeting within the safe confines of Philadelphia, elected a president of the wished-for Irish republic. Large sums were raised by popular appeals, and in June, 1866, a small Fenian band launched a quixotic attack against Canada in the hope of bringing Britain to terms. Acting a bit tardily, the United States authorities nevertheless moved energetically to suppress the lawless effort. The lesson was not lost upon Great Britain. Mistress of many subject peoples, she had a striking demonstration of the importance of strict neutral conduct by other powers when her own sovereign authority was challenged by rebellion and secession.

In January, 1869, she agreed to the Johnson-Clarendon convention for a settlement of the *Alabama* and other claims by means of a joint commission, in cases of disagreement the decision to be left to an umpire chosen by lot. But the Senate rejected the pact by a vote of 44 to 1, holding that the national interest was not adequately safeguarded. In particular, Sumner contended that America was entitled not only to $15,000,000 for direct injuries to our commerce, but also to an additional $2,000,-000,000 for indirect damages, due to the decline of our merchant marine, assistance given Confederate raiders in British colonial ports, and the effect of the premature recognition of Confederate belligerency in prolonging the conflict. To satisfy this debt, he desired Great Britain to cede Canada.

Sumner's extravagant demands temporarily dampened British ardor for a settlement, but early in 1871 the two governments appointed a joint commission to provide for an adjustment of all outstanding differences. The result was the comprehensive treaty of Washington, signed on May 8. This, besides effecting a new twelve-year agreement in regard to the fisheries and granting free navigation of the St. Lawrence and other waters of mutual concern to Canada and the United States, arranged to submit various other questions to special arbitration tribunals. A dispute over the international boundary along the channel separating Vancouver Island from the state of Washington was referred to the German Emperor, who later decided in favor of the United States. The claims of British subjects for damages suffered from military operations during the Civil War were submitted to a tribunal, which eventually made an award of nearly $2,000,000. The most important settlement of all, of course, concerned the question of the British government's conduct during the war. The treaty contained a frank expression of British "regret" for what had happened, and laid down certain principles which were to guide the arbitrators and also to govern the observance of neutrality in the future. In addition to one representative from each country, the court of arbitration comprised three members chosen respectively by Switzerland, Italy and Brazil. Meeting at Geneva, the arbitrators excluded Sumner's indirect claims from consideration, and in September, 1872, awarded direct damages of $15,500,000 for the *Alabama* and other depredations. The outcome was a signal triumph for the cause of international peace and good will. Two great nations had found a better method than the sword for settling their differences.

SELECT BIBLIOGRAPHY

The Postwar South. Besides the wealth of material in Rhodes, *History of the United States*, IV–VII, and Schouler, *History of the United States*, VII, a detailed treatment of Southern Reconstruction appears in the first three volumes of Oberholtzer, *A History of the United States since the Civil War.* In *Essays on the Civil War and Reconstruction* and *Reconstruction, Political and Economic*, Dunning clarifies the constitutional aspects, while Nevins in *The Emergence of Modern America* stresses the social and economic phases. For an understanding of the Southern point of view, Fleming, *The Sequel of Appomattox*, and Hamilton, *The Reconstruction Period*, are useful. Bowers, *The Tragic Era*, is a popular account flavored with melodrama and a Democratic bias.

War-time Efforts at Reconstruction. The most careful discussion of relief work among Negroes is Peirce, *The Freedmen's Bureau*. A different phase of war-time policy is examined in McCarthy, *Lincoln's Plan of Reconstruction*.

Johnson, Congress and the Southern Problem. This theme is developed with a wealth of incident and illustration in Dewitt, *The Impeachment and Trial of Andrew Johnson*. In *The Critical Year* Beale offers the ingenious thesis that the South was kept from representation in order that Northern industrial interests might more easily accomplish their fell designs. The chief contending leaders are treated in Winston, *Andrew Johnson*, and Woodburn, *The Life of Thaddeus Stevens*. Milton, *The Age of Hate*, is a thoroughly documented study, concerned primarily with Johnson's rôle in Reconstruction. The origins of the Fourteenth Amendment are studied in Kendrick, *The Journal of the Joint Committee of Fifteen on Reconstruction*, and Flack, *The Adoption of the Fourteenth Amendment*.

Reign of the Radicals. The actual operation of Reconstruction, chiefly in its political phases, may be studied in a series of monographs on the different Southern states, of which the following are representative: Ramsdell, *Reconstruction in Texas;* Hamilton, *Reconstruction in North Carolina* and Thompson, *Reconstruction in Georgia*. Of a broader scope is Simkins and Woody, *South Carolina during Reconstruction*, which includes industrial as well as political changes. Such treatments should be read in light of two studies by A. A. Taylor, a colored historian: *The Negro in South Carolina during Reconstruction*, and *The Negro in the Reconstruction of Virginia*. A neglected phase receives detailed study in Knight, *The Influence of Reconstruction on Education in the South*.

The Struggle for White Dominion. Coolidge, *Ulysses S. Grant*, and Woodward, *Meet General Grant*, shed light on Grant's participation in politics. Carpetbag rule is thoroughly considered in the series of state studies, while organized Southern opposition receives special treatment in Fleming and Wilson, *Ku Klux Klan; Its Origin, Growth, and Disbandment*.

The Reconstruction of the South. The general lines of development are traced in Chandler and others, *The South in the Building of the*

Nation, especially VI; Thompson, *The New South;* and Bruce, *The Rise of the New South.* Special phases are considered in Hammond, *The Cotton Industry;* Wesley, *Negro Labor in the United States, 1850–1925;* and Brooks, *The Agrarian Revolution in Georgia, 1865–1912.*

The Postwar Settlement with Great Britain. The most extensive treatment appears in Moore, *History and Digest of the International Relations to Which the United States Has Been a Party.*

PART TWO

THE COMING OF MODERN AMERICA

CHAPTER VII

THE ECONOMIC REVOLUTION, 1860–1890

THE OLD ORDER CHANGETH

WHILE the smoke still lingered over the battle-fields of the Civil War and the Carpetbaggers ran their piratical course, mute irresistible forces beneath the surface of events were hurrying the nation on to a new destiny: modern America was in the making. In its lasting effects the Economic Revolution, as it may be called, was more significant than the war itself, for it wrought changes in American life so sudden, so profound, so far-reaching, that even today we have scarcely learned to adjust ourselves to them. The roots of this amazing transformation reached back to the earlier years of the century when steam and machinery first began to invade American industry. Already before the war scattered mill districts had sprung up in the East, and certain kinds of manufacturing had secured a footing in the Midwest and even in parts of the South. Wherever situated, however, such establishments were nearly always of limited size, representing small outlays of capital. Every town, for example, possessed at least one slaughterhouse. New York had more than two hundred; what is now Fifth Avenue was often jammed with cattle wending their way toward great inclosures where today stand hotels, apartment houses and fine retail stores. Several hundred companies in different parts of the land made mowers and reapers; and after the discovery of petroleum, in Pennsylvania in 1859, that business promptly fell into the hands of countless small independent producers. Most manufactured wares bought by the public across the counter came from abroad. Even large supplies of coal and copper were imported, so little had been done to develop America's own splendid resources. Nor, despite the great activity in the fifties, had railway development passed much beyond the period of its infancy. The little wheezy engines, the unheated, dimly lighted coaches, the brittle iron rails and wooden bridges, fairly indicate the progress that was yet to be made. The typical fortunes of prewar days not only were inconsiderable as compared with later times, but derived from shipping, real estate and merchandising rather than from manufactures, railroads and mines.

On these tender industrial growths the Civil War had the effect of a hothouse. For reasons already clear (see page 83), nearly every branch of industry grew lustily, the production of woolen and leather goods and of ready-to-wear clothing scoring particularly notable gains. Pittsburgh, lying in an area rich in coal, petroleum and natural gas, forged rapidly ahead as an iron-manufacturing center, and Chicago now took the lead in pork packing. The heat of war seemed also to quicken inventive talent: from 1860 to 1866 the number of patents annually granted doubled. Meanwhile, the discovery of precious metals, starting with the famous Comstock Lode of gold and silver in 1859 in Nevada, prefigured the enormous mineral development of the Far West in later years. A potent factor in this forward economic thrust was the absence of Southerners from Congress for nearly a decade after 1861. It is not necessary to believe that the Northern industrial and agrarian classes deliberately blocked the South's return in order more easily to impose their will upon the nation; but there can be no doubt that they seized the opportunity to enact far-reaching legislation which Southern opposition had earlier prevented. From these years date the revival of high protection and its conversion into a peace-time policy, the inauguration of free homesteads for settlers, and the adoption of lavish federal aid for the building of transcontinental railways.

Yet the Civil War phase was but the prologue to the drama. In the quarter-century following Appomattox, the Economic Revolution reached its full momentum, energizing man to further and equally amazing triumphs over nature in the years to follow. Everywhere an intensely materialistic spirit reigned — the urge to exploit new sources of wealth, to make fortunes, to grasp power. While the heavy demands levied by the rapidly peopling West and the necessities of the postwar South acted as a stimulus, the transformation was based, more broadly, upon brilliant industrial leadership, American inventive genius, abundant capital (mostly from abroad), mass production, an unmatched natural wealth, and the availability of cheap and plentiful labor. To these should be added, in the words of the census officials of 1900, America's favored position as "the largest area in the civilized world . . . unrestricted by customs, excises, or national prejudice," containing a people who, because of their relatively high standard of living, had "a larger consuming capacity than that of any other nation."

As a result, the United States changed from a country employing mainly primitive methods of tillage and importing the bulk of her manufactures from abroad into an industrialized nation with an export trade in farm and factory products that reached the outer fringes of the globe. "In short," asserted David A. Wells in *Recent Economic Changes* (1889), "to one whose present memory and life-experiences do not extend over a period of time more extensive than . . . a generation, the recital of the economic experiences and industrial conditions of the generation next preceding is very much akin to a recurrence to ancient history." Another economist, Edward Atkinson, writing two years later, added: "There has never been in the history of civilization a period, or a place, or a section of the earth in which science and invention have worked such progress or have created such opportunity for material welfare as in these United States in the period which has elapsed since the end of the civil war."

So swift and momentous a transition could not take place without shaking the foundations of the Old Order and necessitating profound economic and social readjustments. Never before had American society suffered from such a severe attack of "growing pains." The machine rose to its dominant place in industry, the rift between capital and labor dangerously widened, the modern city with all it connotes moved to the forefront of American life, while inventions and conveniences galore came to relieve the drudgery of everyday living. Indeed, the social, political and intellectual consequences of the Economic Revolution form the central themes of American history since the Civil War. Industrial monopoly, the money question, tariff protection, political corruption, immigration, labor discontent, agrarian unrest, imperialism, the unequal distribution of wealth — such questions, new in kind or new in degree, illustrate the variety and gravity

A STATISTICAL VIEW OF CERTAIN ASPECTS OF THE ECONOMIC REVOLUTION

	1860	1880	1890
Population and Wealth			
No. of people	31,443,321	50,155,783	62,622,250
Population per sq. mile	10.4	16.6	20.7
Per cent of population in towns of 8000 or over	16.1	22.6	29.2
National wealth	$16,159,616,000	$43,642,000,000	$65,037,091,000
Wealth per capita	$513.9	$850.2	$1,038.6
Agriculture			
No. of farms	2,044,077	4,008,907	4,564,641
Improved farm land in acres	163,110,720	284,771,042	357,616,755
Value of all farm property	$7,980,493,063	$12,180,501,538	$16,082,267,689
Value of farm implements	$246,118,141	$406,520,055	$494,247,467
Value of farm products	?	$2,212,540,927	$2,460,107,454
Wool production in pounds	60,264,913	232,500,000	276,000,000
Wheat production in bushels	173,104,924	498,549,868	399,262,000
Corn production in bushels	838,792,740	1,717,434,543	1,489,970,000
Cotton production in bales	4,861,292	5,761,252	7,311,322
Cane sugar production in tons	119,040	92,802	136,503
Manufacturing			
No. of plants	140,433	253,852	355,415
Value of domestic manufactures	$1,885,861,676	$5,369,579,191	$9,372,437,283
Capital invested in manufactures	$1,009,855,715	$2,790,272,606	$6,525,156,486
No. of wage-earners	1,311,246	2,732,595	4,251,613
Importation of foreign manufactures	$261,264,310	$423,699,010	$230,685,581
Exportation of Am. manufactures	$48,453,008	$121,818,298	$178,982,042
No. of patents issued in year named	4,778	13,947	26,292
Transportation			
Vessels built for foreign trade (tons)	2,546,237	1,352,810	946,695
Vessels built for domestic purposes (tons)	2,807,631	2,715,224	3,477,802
Railway mileage in operation	30,626	93,267	163,597
Mining			
Production of gold	$46,000,000	$36,000,000	$32,845,000
Silver production (commercial value)	$156,800	$34,717,000	$57,242,100
Tons of coal mined	13,044,680	63,822,830	140,866,931
Gallons of petroleum mined	21,000,000	1,104,017,166	1,924,552,224
Production of pig iron (tons)	821,223	3,835,191	9,202,703
Production of steel (tons)	—	1,247,335	4,277,071
Production of copper (tons)	7,200	27,000	115,966
Communication			
No. of post offices	28,498	42,989	62,401
Mileage of post routes	227,908	343,888	427,990
Postal receipts	$8,518,067	$33,315,479	$60,882,098
No. of telegrams sent	?	29,215,509	63,258,762
Banks and Savings			
No. of national banks	—	2,045	3,214
National bank capital	—	$454,606,073	$607,428,365
Deposits in national banks	—	$833,701,034	$1,521,745,665
No. of savings banks	278	629	921
Deposits in savings banks	$149,277,504	$819,106,973	$1,524,844,506
No. of depositors in savings banks	693,870	2,335,582	4,258,893

of the problems that beset society. In the long run, the nation had to decide whether political agencies and instrumentalities, devised in the eighteenth century by a few million people living under rural conditions with easy means of livelihood, could be adapted to the pressing needs of a teeming population fast growing urbanized and industrialized. The far-reaching character of this revolution can best be understood by examining its influence in the great fields of economic activity where the major changes occurred: agriculture, manufacturing, transportation, mining and communication.

THE DEVELOPMENT OF THE GREAT WEST

The revolution in agriculture and, to a lesser degree, that in transportation and mining stemmed from the occupation of the vast open spaces of the Great West. In 1865 the frontier line, running north through central Texas, followed in a general way the western limits of the states bordering the Mississippi, bulging outward to include the eastern sections of Kansas and Nebraska. Behind this thin edge of pioneer farms was still much unoccupied land, and beyond stretched the unfenced prairies till they merged in the gray, sagebrush plains that extended to the foothills of the Rockies. Then, for nearly a thousand miles, the mountains lifted their enormous bulk, emboweling huge treasures of silver, gold and other metals. On the Pacific side lay other plains and deserts, reaching to the wooded coast ranges and the ocean. Settled districts adjoined San Francisco and San Diego, with others in the Willamette and Columbia valleys. Apart from scattered outposts of whites and notably the Mormon commonwealth in Utah, the vast inland region was inhabited by wild buffaloes and yet wilder Indians. It took twenty-five days to make the overland trip from St. Joseph on the Missouri by the stagecoach line, inaugurated in 1858, and more than ten days to carry mail to San Francisco by the swift pony express, established two years later. The Americans of 1865 looked upon this imperial expanse as a well-nigh inexhaustible reserve which would afford room for growth and provide farms and natural resources for generations to come. Yet, a quarter of a century later, virtually all the country was carved into states and territories, and what was regarded as the last of the arable lands had passed from the government into private possession. Never before had so far-flung a frontier been so quickly overrun by civilization.

Three factors speeded white colonization. One of these, the homestead act adopted in May, 1862, granted free farms of 160 acres to any person who would occupy and improve the land over a five-year period.[1] Already by 1880 nearly 56,000,000 acres had, through this channel, found their way into private hands. The other two influences were the opening of the country by the railways and the subjugation of the redskins. Long agitated, a transcontinental line at last became practicable when Congress on July 1, 1862, voted a charter to the Union Pacific Railroad. While this company pushed its track westward from the Missouri River at Omaha, a California corporation known as the Central Pacific was to build eastward from Sacramento toward an undetermined junction point. Each company, besides obtaining a free right of way through the public domain, should receive vast subsidies in land grants and government loans for every mile of track it laid.[2]

When the active work of construction began in 1866, building operations at the eastern end were directed by the Crédit Mobilier, a company organized by leading stockholders of the Union Pacific, while a similar construction company, headed by Leland Stanford, president of the Central Pacific, had charge in the West. The Orient made its contribution toward success, for Stanford drew his laborers from Chinese coolies who, picturesquely garbed in basket hats and flapping pantaloons, performed even heavier toil in the mountain country than did the Irish "paddies" and ex-soldiers on the plains of Nebraska and Wyoming. Because of Indian hostility, every mile of grading was done under the protection of scouts, and the laborers at a moment's notice had to be ready to drop their picks and shovels for rifles and revolvers. The engineering difficulties were often appalling. In traversing the Sierra Nevadas frequent tunnels and deep rock-cuttings were necessary, or long, high trestles must be swung across ravines and gorges. The construction gangs worked without steam shovels, steam derricks and other modern appliances; it was virtually a "handmade" road.

[1] Alienation of the public lands was further encouraged by the timber-culture act of 1873, the desert-land act of 1877 and the timber and stone act of 1878, which, together with his homestead privilege, enabled a person to acquire a total of 1280 acres. A certain amount of fraud developed in the actual administration of these laws.

[2] The law, as revised in 1864, provided for a gift of ten alternate sections on each side of the track, and for a loan of United States bonds at the rate of $16,000, $32,000 or $48,000 per mile, according as the roadbed traversed plain, plateau or mountain.

The imagination of the whole country was stirred as the two lines steadily closed the gap between them. Greedy for the federal subsidies, each group tried to outstrip the other in the amount of trackage laid. The result was often hasty and wasteful construction, a failure to follow the shortest route, and other practices sufficiently scandalous to provoke a later congressional investigation. Finally, on May 10, 1869, the two tracks met at Promontory Point, northwest of Ogden, Utah, a "wedding of the rails" celebrated with an impressive ceremony. Special arrangements made it possible for the blows of the silver sledge, which drove gold spikes into the connecting rails, to be heard in telegraph stations throughout the land. The great adventure was at an end. Of the completed line, the Union Pacific had built 1086 miles, the Central Pacific 689. The two oceans, hitherto sundered by a month of laborious travel, were now within a week's reach of each other.

The zeal for transcontinental communication did not spend itself with the Union Pacific. Even before it was completed, Congress had granted charters to the Northern Pacific (1864) for linking Lake Superior with Puget Sound; the Southern Pacific (1866), originally called the Atlantic and Pacific, which extended eventually from New Orleans to San Francisco; and the Atchison, Topeka and Santa Fé (1866), which when completed started west from Kansas, reaching San Francisco by way of the desert regions south of the Rockies. These roads, though given no direct financial aid by Congress, received even more princely land subsidies than the Union Pacific. In all, 242,000 square miles, an amount exceeding the area of France or Germany, fell to the transcontinental companies, including the Union Pacific, though some of it had later to be forfeited because of noncompliance with the terms of grant. By 1884 four great lines joined the central valley of the continent with the Pacific tidewater, while a fifth one paralleled them in Canada. The rival companies left no stone unturned to attract settlers. They scattered boom literature throughout the Eastern states and Europe; they advertised special rates and sometimes even offered free transportation. Settled communities not only meant increased traffic but also enhanced the value of railway lands. "Without the railroad," declared a prominent resident of Dakota territory in 1884, not without exaggeration, "it would have required a century to accomplish what has been done in five years under its powerful influence."

Meanwhile, marked progress had been made in allaying the Indian peril. The story is not one to excite pride in the vaunted American spirit of fair play, but it amply illustrates the inexorable character of the conflict between two civilizations, the one dynamic and acquisitive, the other static and unenterprising. In 1860 there were perhaps 300,000 Indians scattered through the Western country. In return for annual gifts of food, munitions and clothing from the government, the bulk of them had agreed to keep the peace, stay within their preserves and allow migration along their trails. But, as settlers penetrated into the region, these solemn treaty stipulations proved mere scraps of paper. The land-hungry or gold-crazy whites viewed the redskin as a bar to the advance of a higher culture and, whenever it suited their purpose, they seized his lands without further ado. In the end, the "Great White Father" at Washington acquiesced, removing the native bands to less desirable tracts. "Many, if not most, of our Indian wars," President Hayes told Congress in 1877, "have had their origin in broken promises and acts of injustice on our part."

Almost incessant conflict prevailed between the two races from 1862 to 1886 — a tangled skein of petty wars which there is no need to unravel. Stung to reprisals by white encroachments or the exactions of greedy government agents, the tribesmen would suddenly take to the warpath, burning, scalping and slaying. Savagery, unhappily, was not always on the one side. On November 28, 1864, a force under Colonel J. M. Chivington fell upon an unsuspecting Cheyenne village on Sand Creek in Colorado, killing and mutilating men, women and children. Most frontier fighters heartily echoed General "Phil" Sheridan's sentiment: "There are no good Indians but dead Indians." Toward the close of the sixties the government sought a more constructive solution of the difficulties. A commission, at work in 1867–1868, not only succeeded in clearing away all legal obstacles to the building of railways through Indian country, but also induced most of the Apache, Comanche and Kiowa bands to remove to Indian Territory and other tribes to diminish their

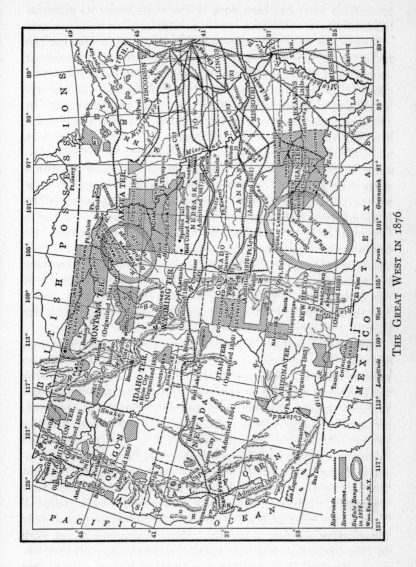

THE GREAT WEST IN 1876

reservations or accept new ones off the beaten tracks. On the initiative of President Grant, a warm advocate of peace on the plains, Congress in 1869 created a board of Indian commissioners to supervise government expenditures for the tribesmen. Though waste and graft were not eliminated, distinct improvement resulted.

Presently, however, hostilities broke out with renewed ferocity, partly because of the decimation of the buffalo herds, the Indian's chief means of livelihood. From the buffalo or bison he obtained food, clothing, bowstrings and harness; the sale of hides provided his principal source of ready cash. Fifteen million of these great, ungainly beasts, it is estimated, were roving the plains at the close of the Civil War. The laborers on the railroads subsisted in large part on buffalo meat, William F. Cody winning his nickname of "Buffalo Bill" for killing 4280 in eighteen months while a scout in the employ of the Kansas Pacific. The worst slaughter, however, occurred at the hands of hunters who, for amusement, killed them by the tens of thousands, leaving their carcasses for coyotes and buzzards. By the end of the hunting season of 1875 the vast Southern herd had been virtually wiped out, and with the building of the Northern Pacific a few years later a similar fate befell the smaller Northern herd. When the Plains Sioux under Sitting Bull donned their war paint in 1876, however, their immediate purpose was to repel the onrush of gold prospectors into the Black Hills which lay within their reservation. Though they annihilated General G. A. Custer's command of 265 men in a battle on the Little Big Horn on June 25, they were soon quelled by superior force and dispossessed of the Black Hill country. Other notable uprisings occurred among the Nez Percé Indians in the Snake River Valley in 1877 and among the Apache in Arizona and New Mexico from 1882 to 1886.

Never before had the United States carried on such extensive Indian warfare. A list of the engagements between 1868 and 1882 alone fills over a hundred pages. The nature of the fighting required eternal watchfulness, instant preparedness and dauntless personal daring. One never knew when, out of the vast treeless expanse, murderous bands would swoop down on the border settlements. No names perhaps stand higher in the annals of plains fighting than those of General Sheridan, General W. T. Sherman and General N. A. Miles. The savages had their great warriors in Sitting Bull, Black Kettle of the Cheyenne, and Red Cloud, a Sioux chieftain, all true patriots from the red man's point of view. Every mile of Western railroad increased the military effectiveness of the dominant race, while the widespread destruction of game also helped reconcile the Indian to a peaceable reservation existence. By the mid-eighties the Indian question was no longer troublesome as a problem of military police, but little or no progress had been made in solving the question in its broader aspects, that is, the assimilation of the tribesman to the white man's way of life. Yet a quarter-century of conflict had made the Great West safe for the more advanced people and placed the best lands at their disposal.

The first great rush of population was into the interior mountainous region, impelled by the discovery of valuable metals, notably gold and silver. The Comstock Lode in Nevada was but the earliest of such fabulous strikes. In the same year (1859) prospectors found the yellow metal in Colorado, causing a headlong stampede from all parts of the nation for "Pike's Peak or Bust." Subsequent years saw the development of rich mineral deposits in Montana, Idaho, Wyoming and Arizona. In the wake of these finds boom towns sprang up like mushrooms in a lush soil. Of Virginia City, Montana, an inhabitant later wrote: "This human hive, numbering at least ten thousand people, was the product of ninety days. Into it were crowded all the elements of a rough and active civilization. . . . Gold was abundant, and every possible device was employed by the gamblers, the traders, the vile men and women that had come in with the miners into the locality, to obtain it. Nearly every third cabin was a saloon. . . . Not a day or night passed which did not yield its full fruition of vice, quarrels, wounds, or murders." These lawless conditions were, of course, only a passing phase, difficult to control because of remoteness from the seats of law and authority. In many cases, the more substantial elements of the community took the law into their own hands, forming bands of "vigilantes" to overthrow the reign of the badman and the desperado. Most of the adventurers failed in their quest of sudden wealth, but many of them remained in the new country, turning farmer or stock raiser to feed their luckier brethren.

Meanwhile almost as powerful a magnet was drawing population into the Great Plains lying to the east. Cattle raising had long been an important industry in Texas; and in 1866 it was discovered, largely by accident, that if Texas longhorns were driven north across the unfenced public domain, feeding as they went, they would arrive at the railway shipping points in Kansas larger and fatter than when they started. Soon the "Long Drive" was a regular event, and for hundreds of miles the trails were dotted with herds of from one to ten thousand cattle moving ceaselessly northward. Dodge City, Kansas, on the newly built Atchison, Topeka and Santa Fé, became the greatest of the "cow towns," the focus of a reckless, turbulent life that won it a dubious repute as the "Bibulous Babylon of the Frontier." At the same time the cattle industry spread rapidly into the trans-Missouri region, thanks to the demand of railway laborers and mining camps for fresh beef and to the improved marketing facilities afforded by the completion of the railroads. Immense ranches appeared overnight, as it were, in Colorado, Wyoming, Kansas, Nebraska and Dakota, while Western cities flourished as centers for the slaughter and dressing of meat.

Ranching introduced a stirring and colorful mode of existence, with the picturesque cowboy as its central figure. "We led a free and hardy life, with horse and with rifle," Theodore Roosevelt wrote in fond reminiscence of his own experiences in Dakota. "We worked under the scorching midsummer sun, when the wide plains shimmered and wavered in the heat; and we knew the freezing misery of riding night guard round the cattle in the late fall round-up. . . . But we felt the beat of hardy life in our veins and ours was the glory of work and the joy of living." The immense profits of the "cattle kings" fruited from the benevolent neglect of the government. After branding their animals the cowboys allowed them to range at will over the public domain, and then, at the spring or summer round-up, sought them out for the drive to market. Cattle, costing only a few dollars, raised in vast numbers, fed on free pasturage and requiring but few men to tend them, were sold several years later for four or five times the original investment. Peace did not always dwell on the ranges. The ranchers often waged petty civil wars with each other over cattle stealing, the changing of brands, and other such matters. Sometimes, to vary the routine, they made common cause against the sheep herders, who soon appeared to appropriate their share of free land and free grass.

By the mid-eighties the halcyon days of the cattlemen were over. Not far behind the rancher creaked the prairie schooner of the farmer or "nester," bringing his womenfolk and children, his draft horses, cows and pigs. Under the homestead act he staked off his claim, fenced it with barbed wire and, backed by the government, ousted the ranchman from the lands of which the latter held illegal possession. The prickly barriers began to render difficult the Long Drive and to destroy the unity of the open range. Moreover, abounding prosperity had caused the cattle industry to expand far beyond market demands, and a succession of severe winters ruined many owners. Hence the romantic "cow country" began to give way to settled communities and prosaic fields of wheat, corn and oats. "It was right and necessary that this life should pass," added Roosevelt to the comment just quoted, "for the safety of our country lies in its being made the country of the small home-maker." In order to survive, the stock raiser had to reorganize his business on a new basis — own his grazing grounds, provide winter feed, and breed fewer and better cattle.

Under these circumstances the agricultural revolution gathered momentum. Including the older settled regions, the farms of America from 1870 to 1880 increased by an area as large as the British Isles and Sweden combined, and in the next two decades they grew by an amount equal to the British Isles and the three Scandinavian countries, with Holland, Belgium and Switzerland thrown in for good measure. Wheat growing was the main reliance in Dakota and Minnesota. South of the wheat belt, in Iowa, Nebraska and Kansas, corn predominated, going to market either as grain or in the converted form of hogs. Many of the farmers were immigrants from Germany and the Scandinavian states, who settled in the new lands in colonies. The production of corn and wheat doubled between 1860 and 1880, doubling once more in the next twenty-year period. Already by 1880 the United States had become the greatest wheat-exporting nation in the world. One of the major causes of agrarian unrest grew out of the difficulties connected with the existence of a crop surplus.

The enormous expansion resulted in part from a greater application of mechanical power to farming. With every husbandman a landowner, machinery was necessary to make up for the dearth of hired labor. Improvement followed improvement, invention followed invention, and many a homestead was mortgaged to secure the new labor-saving tools. Of these implements, the twine binder, patented in 1878 and 1879 by J. F. Appleby of Wisconsin, is particularly noteworthy, for, by increasing eightfold the speed of harvesting, it correspondingly enlarged the quantity of wheat that could profitably be grown. Meanwhile, through the establishment of the federal Department of Agriculture (1862) and the passage of the Morrill act the same year, the government did what it could to change husbandry from a traditional folk exercise to a science. The Morrill act offered each state a generous land grant as endowment for a college devoted chiefly to teaching agriculture and the mechanic arts. The states applied the gift either to enlarging old institutions or to founding new ones. In the Hatch act of 1887 Congress went even further by subsidizing state experiment stations for carrying on original investigative work. Soon important discoveries began to be made in regard to soil fertility, animal breeding, and the methods of combating insect pests and plant and animal diseases. America led the world in developing the scientific principles of farming.

The various influences that had quickened the westward flow of settlement from the early sixties led to the organization of the frontier country into self-governing communities. Between 1861 and 1868 territorial governments were erected in Nevada, Colorado, Dakota, Arizona, Idaho, Montana and Wyoming, leaving only Indian Territory without the usual provision. Nevada was admitted prematurely into the Union in 1864 because of Lincoln's need of support for his policies in Congress; and the state of Nebraska was carved out of the older frontier three years later. The phenomenal increase of population gave rise to the saying that it was impossible to tell the truth about the West without lying. From 1870 to 1890 Idaho grew sixfold, Montana sevenfold, Colorado and Wyoming each tenfold,

Washington fifteenfold. Colorado achieved statehood in 1876, and in 1889–1890 six more states followed: North and South Dakota, Montana, Washington, Idaho and Wyoming. Utah was denied the privilege until 1896 when the Mormon Church finally satisfied Congress that the national laws against polygamy were being enforced. Aside from Oklahoma, formed largely out of lands acquired from the tribes in Indian Territory, New Mexico and Arizona alone continued in a territorial status.

The spectacular rush into the Oklahoma district, when the President threw it open to home seekers on April 22, 1889, heralded the end of the era of good farms for the asking. Twenty thousand "boomers," as they were called, awaited the signal to cross the line. At exactly high noon a bugle shrilled, the troops stood aside, and the impatient throng — on foot, on horseback, in buggies and buckboards — began the mad race for claims. By nightfall Guthrie had sprung into being, a tented city of 10,000 inhabitants, while over the countryside flickering camp fires told of farm homes in the making. The district held 60,-000 people before the year closed. In consequence, Congress in 1890 created the territory of Oklahoma, embracing an irregular area in the western part of Indian Territory, together with "No Man's Land," a narrow rectangular strip bordering the northernmost section of Texas.

Though public lands still remained for occupancy, the unbroken frontier was gone by 1890 and the best available sites were in private hands. From earliest times this reservoir of the people's wealth had served as a recurrent source of economic renewal and as a cradle of robust Americanism. By draining off the restless spirits from the older settled districts it had also acted as a safety valve of discontent. The rugged individualism and incurable optimism which the frontier engendered became a part of the national habit of mind. What had been a great historic force, shaping American life and ideals from the first days of colonization, was thus slowing to a halt. Yet there occurred no sudden shock to the economic and social structure. The years ahead would reveal unsuspected vistas for husbandry as Americans learned the secret of dry farming and the government reclaimed countless acres through irrigation and drainage.[1] Moreover, cheap lands remained everywhere in abundance, while across the international border lay a vast pioneer zone open to those willing to cast in their lot with Canada. But most important of all was the rush of employment and opportunity afforded by the growth of urban centers and the launching of colossal new industries. Even in the 1870's and 1880's the city was beginning to cast its spell over men of spirit and ambition, an enchantment which presently came to exceed that exerted by the great open spaces. If the townward drift meant turning American thought and energy in a new direction, at least it provided equally challenging opportunities for individual initiative, enterprise and achievement.

THE ONWARD PUSH OF INDUSTRIALISM

From the standpoint of posterity the revolution in industry, mining and transportation was even more important than that in agriculture. The progress in manufacturing since the Civil War, according to the United States industrial commission in 1902, was "probably the most rapid change in the methods of industry observable at any time in history." Through the substitution of machinery for men, the widespread introduction of steam for water power, and the application of a minute subdivision of labor to the processes of manufacturing, along with other favoring conditions, factory production advanced at an unparalleled pace. The records of the patent office shed some light upon the rôle played by invention. With less than 62,000 patents granted in all the years before 1865, the number during the remainder of the century reached nearly 638,000. Until the 1880's farming continued to be the chief fount of national wealth, but the census of 1890 gave first place to manufacturing, and ten years later the value of manufactured products was over twice that of agricultural. From less than two billion dollars in 1860, the output of American mills and shops grew more than double in a decade and from 1860 to 1880 trebled. The share of labor-saving machinery in this advance appears in the fact that, though from 1860 to 1890 the number of factory hands increased threefold, the total product increased fivefold. The rate of growth in particular industries was even more astounding. By 1894

[1] As a matter of fact, the homestead entries for the two decades following 1898 were half again as great as those for the three decades preceding.

the United States had leaped from fourth place, her rank as a manufacturing nation in 1860, to first in all the world. At that time her output exceeded the total for both Great Britain and Germany.

The chief development took place in the East, where southern New England, eastern and southern New York and large sections of Pennsylvania and New Jersey became thoroughly industrialized. New England excelled in textiles, the finer grades of paper, and boots and shoes; Pennsylvania in tanning and iron and steel products; New Jersey in silks; New York in the bewildering variety and total value of her wares. At the same time factories spread into the Midwest in such numbers as to cause the center of manufactures in the nation to shift from western Pennsylvania in 1860 to northeastern Ohio (near Canton) in 1890. Broadly speaking, industrial enterprise in Middle America turned to the fabrication of farm implements, railway supplies, building materials, furniture, prepared foods and drinks. Chicago, the center of a great network of transportation facilities, possessed nearly eight hundred woodworking establishments, machine shops and metal works by 1880, besides more than a hundred breweries and distilleries.

During these years, too, the factory system commenced its extensive invasion of Dixie, attracted by abundant raw materials, cheap labor and cheap power. "Bring the mills to the cotton!" was the cry that rang through the seaboard South in the 1880's. Soon the fall line of the rivers began to be dotted with factories, built out of the meager savings of the people near by and manned by poor whites — men, women and children — drawn from the foothill and mountain country. Between 1880 and 1890 the number of spindles and looms almost trebled, and another decade found nearly half the cotton mills of the land clustered there. The manufacture of iron, equally favored by natural conditions, made as notable progress. Great beds of ore were discovered near deposits of coal and limestone, as if nature had purposely associated the necessary ingredients for reducing the crude metal. During the eighties fifty new blast furnaces were erected in Alabama, Tennessee and Virginia.[1] Cottonseed

[1] Here and elsewhere new methods of smelting speeded the manufacture of iron and steel products. Most important was the Bessemer process (named after the

mills, tobacco factories, furniture establishments, vehicle factories and canneries represent other important undertakings. The prime movers in Southern industrialization were usually of the old yeoman strain rather than of the class which had ruled in prewar days, and Northern capital played a negligible part until toward the end of the century when the certainty of profits had been clearly demonstrated. An observer in 1889 scarcely needed to point out that "the nonsense that it is beneath the dignity of any man or woman to work for a living is pretty much eliminated from the Southern mind."

The revolution in manufacturing everywhere rested on the exploitation of vast fields of coal and iron, the two minerals that have most vitally affected modern industrial civilization. Large coal beds were uncovered not only along the Appalachian system but also in Ohio, Indiana and Illinois. With improved transportation facilities and an increased use of steam-driven machinery, production leaped tenfold from 1860 to 1890. Meantime, to meet the voracious demands of industry, the yield of iron ore in western Pennsylvania advanced by leaps and bounds, and in the 1880's great ranges in the Lake Superior region began to be developed. Besides being extremely rich and pure, these new deposits lay near the surface, which made it possible to mine them with labor-saving machines. From 1860 to 1890 pig-iron production multiplied elevenfold. The newest source of subsurface wealth, petroleum, underwent an even more amazing development, increasing in the three decades more than ninetyfold. From the Far West came still other stores of minerals. In the eighties copper mines were opened in Arizona and Montana, rivaling the product hitherto furnished by Michigan. Large-scale silver mining was another undertaking, thanks to the discoveries in Nevada, Colorado and elsewhere. From a value of $157,000 in 1860, the output rose to $36,000,000 in 1873, with an even larger yield in the years to follow — a fact that was to have important political reverberations. Gold production, on the other hand, having reached its peak in 1854, steadily declined from 1872 to 1893.

Englishman Henry Bessemer), introduced into the United States in 1864, by which a cold blast is forced through the molten metal, thereby eliminating carbon impurities. In the next century it was to be supplanted by the open-hearth or Martin process, which is superior for less pure ores.

Meantime, all over the land, a spider web of metal rails was being spun to draw the remotest outposts into the common whole and everywhere give fresh impetus to commercial enterprise. From 30,000 miles of railroad in 1860, the number trebled by 1880, reaching a total of 164,000 ten years later. Not only were the great transcontinental roads built, but rail lines multiplied in the older parts of the North and pushed southward to spur the industrial development of Dixie. The 193,000 miles at the turn of the century greatly exceeded in length the railways of all Europe. Moreover, expansion in mileage was attended by important improvements in service. Iron rails were replaced with steel to insure both heavier carrying capacity and greater safety. The inventor George Pullman in 1864 added to the comfort of travel through his ingenious "palace cars," described by one enthusiast as "gorgeous traveling hotels." In 1872 George Westinghouse took out his first patent on the automatic air brake, a device which permitted the engineer, by means of a steam-driven air pump, to set the brakes simultaneously throughout the whole train. About the same time automatic car coupling came into use. As more and more short roads were linked into through lines and a standard gauge of track was adopted, another improvement resulted. A traveler from the Atlantic Seaboard to the Mississippi before 1870 might have been obliged to change trains a half-dozen times. Now this inconvenience came to be the exception rather than the rule.

No less profound were the changes in communication, a revolution based less on steam than on electricity, whose possibilities were just beginning to be glimpsed. In harnessing electricity to the service of mankind Americans led the way, notably Thomas A. Edison who from 1868 to 1900 took out nearly 800 patents, mostly in this field. His invention of quadruplex telegraphy in 1874 allowed two messages to be sent simultaneously from opposite ends of the same line, thus multiplying the carrying capacity of the wires. Already in 1866 the principle of the telegraph had been applied, after several unsuccessful trials, to cable communication with Europe, a great engineering feat for which Cyrus W. Field was responsible. Ten years later came a new marvel, the telephone, invented by Professor Alexander Graham Bell of Boston University as a by-product of his interest in teaching the

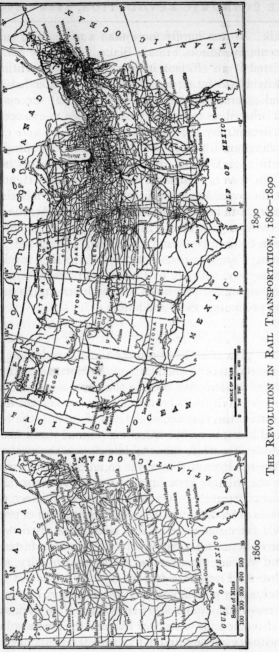

THE REVOLUTION IN RAIL TRANSPORTATION, 1860–1890

In these thirty years the railway attained an importance greater than in any other country of the world. The history of the time might almost be written in terms of railways.

deaf to talk. At first hardly more than a mechanical curiosity, improvements by Edison, Francis Blake, J. J. Carty and others soon rendered it an efficient instrument. The invention of a central switchboard by C. E. Scribner vastly extended its usefulness and assured the telephone's commercial success. The number of subscribers rose from 50,000 in 1880 to 250,000 at the end of the decade. By 1892 Boston and New York were chatting with Washington, Chicago and Milwaukee. As presidential candidate in 1896 William McKinley talked from his home at Canton, Ohio, with his campaign managers in thirty-eight states. Meantime the postal service was placed on a modern basis. Free delivery was introduced in the larger cities in 1863, the system of money orders a year later. In 1883 the rate for single letters was cut from three to two cents a half ounce and, in 1885, to two cents an ounce. These various instrumentalities shed incalculable benefits on society, not only by facilitating business intercourse, but also by helping to break down rural isolation and in countless other ways promoting social solidarity.

THE ADVENT OF GREAT CITIES

Just as the plantation had been the typical product of prewar Southern society and the small farm of the Northern agricultural system, so the modern city became the nerve center of the new industrial order. Within its borders were focused all the dynamic economic forces: the vast accumulations of capital, the business and financial institutions, the spreading railroad yards, the gaunt smoky factories, the white-collar middle classes, the motley army of wage-earners. Recruited from the countryside and from lands across the sea, villages grew into towns and towns sprang into cities almost overnight. In 1830 one out of every fifteen persons lived in places of 8000 or over; in 1860 nearly one out of every six; and in 1890 three out of ten. The older rural districts of the North, caught between the counterattractions of free farms on the frontier and alluring opportunities in the near-by city, suffered shocking losses. From 1880 to 1890 755 townships out of 1316 in Ohio declined in population; 800 out of 1424 in Illinois. Two fifths of Pennsylvania and nearly five sixths of New York state experienced a similar eclipse. In New England the townward exodus left mute witnesses in deserted hill villages and abandoned farms.

No single city had as many as a million inhabitants in 1860, but thirty years later New York had a million and a half and Chicago and Philadelphia each over a million. By that time Brooklyn (which was to be merged with New York in 1898) possessed 800,000, and St. Louis, Boston and Baltimore had attained the half-million class. In the three decades Philadelphia and Baltimore doubled in population, Kansas City and Detroit grew fourfold, San Francisco sixfold, Cleveland ninefold, Chicago tenfold, while certain places like Minneapolis and Omaha, which had been mere hamlets when the Civil War began, grew fifty times or more. Though most towns were of lesser size, everywhere they sought to copy the enterprise and ways of the bigger ones. In Josiah Strong's phrase, the city was "the mighty heart of the body politic, sending its streams of life pulsating to the very finger-tips of the whole land." As the centers of wealth and economic power, moreover, the great cities molded business institutions and transportation facilities to suit their own particular needs and advantage, thus increasing the difficulties from which the farm dwellers suffered during these years.

Earlier American cities had been hardly more than overgrown villages; now, as urban populations thickened, they began to change into modern municipalities. Volunteer fire companies were abandoned by New York in 1865 and by Philadelphia in 1871 in order to make way for full-time, paid fire departments. The urgent need for swifter conveyance, no longer adequately met by horse cars, led New York in 1868 to introduce steam-drawn trains on elevated rails high above the streets. Five years later San Francisco demonstrated the utility of the cable car, contrived by A. S. Hallidie and operated by means of a grappling device reaching downward to an endless steel cable moving in a slotted trench between the tracks. Somewhat later came the even more successful electric trolley car, first installed for public use in 1888 at Richmond, Virginia, and adopted within three years by fifty-one towns. Meanwhile city streets, ill paved when paved at all, showed great improvement with the introduction, particularly in the 1880's, of asphalt and brick surfacing. Serious attention was also given, for the first time, to problems of sewage and garbage disposal, and from 1860 to 1890 the number of public waterworks increased nearly thirteenfold.

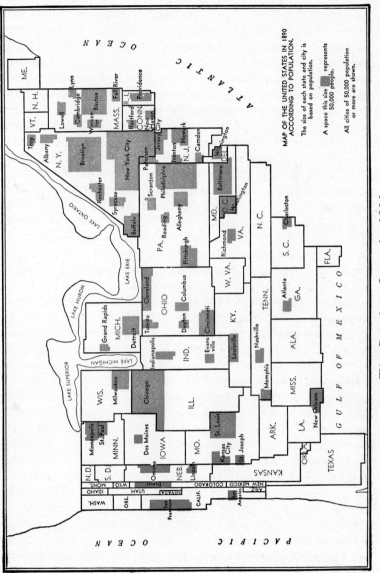

MAP OF THE UNITED STATES IN 1890
ACCORDING TO POPULATION.

The size of each state and city is
based on population.

A space this size represents
50,000 people.

All cities of 50,000 population
or more are shown.

The Populous States in 1890

At the same time, better illumination came to the aid of city dwellers, helping to dispel much of the darkness of night life as well as some of its dangers. Improving upon the experiments of others, C. F. Brush of Cleveland in 1878 devised an arc light, the flame being produced by an electric current passing vertically between two sticks of carbon. It was widely adopted for lighting streets and public squares, but the problem of indoor illumination remained unsolved until Edison two years later patented the first practicable incandescent electric light. Advances were also made in gas illumination, especially after T. S. C. Lowe's discovery in 1875 of the process of making water gas. Though municipalities differed in the quickness with which they adopted the new improvements, yet urban life everywhere assumed a different aspect, causing towns on the advancing frontier to flaunt conveniences and comforts of living which the greatest centers had lacked a generation before.

In the large cities, too, appeared startling contrasts of poverty and riches, squalor matching splendor, urban vice contending with civic virtue. New York reminded one English visitor of "a lady in ball costume, with diamonds in her ears, and her toes out at her boots." In the slums huddled the newly arrived immigrant families, living under conditions which made for diseased minds as well as diseased bodies. Organized crime, long characteristic of frontier communities, now shifted to the great population centers, thanks to the concentration of wealth there and the inadequacy of police protection. It may not be without significance that the bloody repulse of the James Boys' attempt to loot the bank at Northfield, Minnesota, in 1876 was followed two years later by the first great urban criminal exploit, the successful robbery of the Manhattan Savings Institution in New York of nearly $3,000,000 by "Western George" Leslie and his gang. The increase of lawlessness was due, in part, to the collusion of municipal officials with the wrongdoers.

During these years the boss and the machine, abetted by the most vicious elements in city life, rose to a position of dominance. As in national politics, predatory men found opportunities for illicit gain in lax law enforcement, and particularly in obtaining control, by whatever means, of the expanding public utilities. Contracts for municipal works and franchises for the supply of water, lighting and rapid transit were too often granted corruptly to private individuals and companies, with few or no safeguards for the public. One of the sensations of Grant's first term was the exposure of the Tweed Ring in New York City, whose members in two and a half years swelled the city's debt by $70,000,000, most of which lodged in their own pockets.[1] Though Boss Tweed himself was finally brought to justice in 1871, most of his confederates escaped, and later years found New York again wallowing in the mire of Tammany misrule. Other places fared hardly better — Philadelphia with its Gas Ring, Washington with its Real-Estate Ring, St. Louis under the corrupt rule of Boss "Ed" Butler, Minneapolis under "Doc" Ames, San Francisco under "Blind Boss" Buckley. James Bryce, writing in 1888, called the government of cities "the one conspicuous failure of the United States." The truth is that, while long experience had taught Americans how to rule populations scattered over large areas, they had yet to learn how to govern densely packed urban centers. This failure was all the more striking because of the mighty influence which, as we shall see, cities were exerting on American cultural life.

SELECT BIBLIOGRAPHY

The Coming of Modern America. Except for the intricacies of Southern Reconstruction, the standard comprehensive works are less helpful for the period 1865–1900 than for earlier times. Schouler devotes his seventh and last volume to the years 1865–1877. Rhodes, after canvassing certain aspects of the era to 1877 in his seven-volume set, continues his narrative to 1909 in two sketchy volumes. Oberholtzer alone has essayed a large-scale treatment of the entire postwar period to 1900 in *A History of the United States since the Civil War*. The journalist Mark Sullivan, though concerned primarily with the twentieth century, occasionally dips back into earlier years in *Our Times*. The various coöperative works cited at the close of Chapter I all span the period 1865–1900.

The Development of the Great West. Light is shed on the occupation of the last continental frontier in a varied literature. Good general treatments include Paxson, *History of the American Frontier, 1763–1893*, and Riegel, *America Moves West*. For the adoption of the homestead act Stephenson, *The Political History of the Public Lands from 1840 to 1862*, and Du Bois and Mathews, *Galusha A. Grow, the Father of the Homestead Law*, are valuable; for its operation, see Hibbard, *History of Public Land Policies*. Riegel,

---

[1] Thus, by ingenious bookkeeping, the taxpayers were charged $11,000,000 for an uncompleted courthouse which had actually cost $3,000,000. One entry credited a plasterer with earning $138,187 in two days.

Story of the Western Railroads, is a useful summary, which may be supplemented by Haney, *A Congressional History of Railways in the United States, 1850–1887;* Smalley, *History of the Northern Pacific Railroad;* Hedges, *Henry Villard and the Railways of the Northwest;* and Sabin, *Building the Pacific Railway.* Pyle, *The Life of James J. Hill*, tells the story of one of the great railroad builders. Sakolski, *The Great American Land Bubble*, gives many interesting sidelights on land speculation. Border warfare is dealt with in Macleod, *The American Indian Frontier;* Seymour, *The Story of the Red Man;* and Paxson, *The Last American Frontier.* Branch, *Hunting the Buffalo*, considers one aspect of the plight of the Indians. Mining development is treated in Trimble, *The Mining Advance into the Inland Empire*, and Rickard, *A History of American Mining.* Vivid glimpses of life in the mining regions are given in De Voto, *Mark Twain's America.* From a group of studies, most of them recent, emerges a convincing picture of the cattleman and his social and economic significance. Notable among these works are Rollins, *The Cowboy;* Wright, *Dodge City, the Cowboy Capital;* Branch, *The Cowboy and His Interpreters;* Osgood, *The Day of the Cattleman;* Dale, *The Range Cattle Industry;* and Webb, *The Great Plains.* Salient aspects of the agricultural revolution are canvassed in Schmidt and Ross, *Readings in the Economic History of American Agriculture*, and notably in the U. S. Department of Agriculture, *Yearbook for 1899*, a symposium by specialists. The opening of Oklahoma is the theme of Gittinger, *The Formation of the State of Oklahoma.*

The Onward Push of Industrialism. While brief accounts may be found in any of the standard economic histories, the most thorough treatment is Clark, *History of Manufactures in the United States*, which devotes one volume to the years 1860–1914. Particular aspects are dealt with in Woodworth, *American Tool Making and Interchangeable Manufacturing;* Copeland, *The Cotton Manufacturing Industry in the United States;* Cole, *The American Wool Manufacture;* and Smith, *The Story of Iron and Steel.* The industrializing trend in the South is studied in Mitchell, *The Rise of Cotton Mills in the South;* Armes, *The Story of Coal and Iron in Alabama;* and Bruce, *Rise of the New South.* Besides general surveys of technological progress, such as Kaempffert, ed., *A Popular History of American Invention*, and Byrn, *The Progress of Invention in the Nineteenth Century*, there are many special studies, including Casson, *The History of the Telephone;* Husband, *The Story of the Pullman Car;* Martin and Coles, *The Story of Electricity;* Dyer and Martin, *Edison;* and Mackenzie, *Alexander Graham Bell.*

The Advent of Great Cities. Weber, *The Growth of Cities in the Nineteenth Century*, considers the subject in its world-wide aspects. Fairlie, *Municipal Administration*, and Zueblin, *American Municipal Progress*, trace the expansion of municipal functions. Slum conditions in New York are examined in De Forest and Veiller, *The Tenement House Problem*, and criminality in that city is described in Asbury, *The Gangs of New York.* Of special value for the Tweed Ring exposé are Paine, *Th. Nast*, and Bigelow, *The Life of Samuel J. Tilden.* All phases of urban life in the 1880's and 1890's are the special concern of Schlesinger, *The Rise of the City.*

CHAPTER VIII

POLITICAL TRANSITION, 1869–1877

GRANT'S eight years in the White House marked a significant transition in national political life. With sectional animosities as yet unabated, American politics yielded increasingly to the tugs and pressures exerted by leaders of the new capitalistic order bent on extorting special privileges and immunities from the government. Unfortunately, these forces pushed forward at a time when the country was suffering a moral relapse from the lofty idealism of war days, and when the upswing of prosperity, set going during the war, made people careless as regards official rectitude. In the cities extravagance and luxurious living reached a new pitch, while everywhere throughout the North men launched fresh business enterprises and engaged in reckless speculation. Meantime, Tweedism fastened its hold on the great population centers, and the Carpetbaggers busily looted the prostrate South.

Referring to the materialistic trend of politics, Senator Henry Wilson of Massachusetts, ancient foe of the "Slave Power," declared in the *Independent* of June 10, 1869: "The power of wealth, individual and associated, concentrated and diffused, constitutes the new danger that is threatening us with its portentous and increasing dimensions." Another early Republican, George W. Julian of Indiana, cited particularly the "railway power," possessing a "consolidated capital of $5,000,000,000," and "sapping and mining its way through the consciences" of those vested with political control. "Men buy their way into the Senate," wrote James Russell Lowell, "and, of course, expect a profit on their investment." As if to corroborate such views, a congressional investigating committee reported in 1873: "The country is fast becoming filled with gigantic corporations wielding and controlling immense aggregations of money and thereby commanding great influence and power. It is notorious in many state legislatures that these influences are often controlling."

President Grant possessed neither the experience nor the will to stem the rising tide of materialism in political life. Himself a man who had vainly striven against poverty, he readily accepted the dollar sign as the hall mark of success, thus falling in with the sordid ideals of the time. Though his personal integrity was undoubted, he and members of his family received loans from the banks of Jay Cooke at a time when the Northern Pacific and other concerns in which Cooke was interested wanted public favors. He openly consorted with "Jim" Fisk, an unscrupulous stock manipulator, and accepted costly gifts from persons whose motives were dubious, if not corrupt. Nor, aside from two or three members, did his cabinet contribute much to the statesmanlike quality of his administration. His first appointee as Secretary of State, an old personal friend, resigned shortly, making possible the selection of Hamilton Fish of New York, a man of real ability, who gained merited fame for his part in negotiating the treaty of Washington (see page 124). Grant, unaware of an old statute forbidding such a choice, named a wealthy business man as head of the Treasury, then rectified his mistake by appointing G. S. Boutwell, a Massachusetts politician with no special fitness for the office. Of the remaining members only J. D. Cox of Ohio, Secretary of the Interior, and E. R. Hoar of Massachusetts, Attorney-General, had the qualifications usually expected.[1]

Grant's entry into office coincided with the rise of a new generation of political leaders. The giants of the Civil War era were fast passing away: Stevens died in 1868, Stanton in 1869, Seward in 1872, Chase in 1873, Sumner (from whom Grant became estranged as early as 1870) in 1874 and Johnson in 1875. Their places were taken by men of lesser stature and of dissimilar ideals and interests. In Henry Adams's opinion, "No period so thoroughly ordinary had been known in American politics since Christopher Columbus first disturbed the balance of American

---

[1] The original cabinet consisted of Elihu Washburne of Illinois, Secretary of State; A. T. Stewart of New York, Secretary of the Treasury; J. A. Rawlins of Illinois, Secretary of War; A. E. Borie of Pennsylvania, Secretary of the Navy; J. A. Cresswell of Maryland, Postmaster-General; and the other two members named above.

society." It is not unlikely that the men of creative vision and organizing genius — the natural leaders of the time — felt the challenge of the transforming economic life of the country, and renounced politics to become architects of the new industrial order. At any rate, the men who now seized the reins in Congress — Roscoe Conkling of New York, James A. Garfield of Ohio, James G. Blaine of Maine, Samuel J. Randall and W. D. ("Pig-Iron") Kelley of Pennsylvania, and their like — speeded the exploitation of the nation's resources through lavish subsidies, charter grants and tariffs, and were often themselves personally interested as stockholders or lawyers in corporate enterprises which might be affected by their votes as legislators.

At the same time the civil service was in a thoroughly demoralized state. In vogue since Jackson's time, the spoils system had never before borne such evil fruit as during and after the Civil War when the rapid expansion of the public service brought an unusual number of worthless persons into appointive office. Grant was accused by the editor of the *Nation* (New York) of making not only "bad appointments but probably some of the worst ever made by a civilized Christian government." In June, 1870, the President at the instigation of his politician cronies dismissed Attorney-General Hoar, and in October he allowed Cox to resign from the Interior Department where the latter had displayed unwelcome zeal in resisting the demands of grafters and job seekers. Nevertheless, two months later, Grant asked Congress to enact a law for basing federal appointments upon personal fitness as determined by competitive examinations. Such a system, already in operation in England and France, had been urged since 1865 by Thomas A. Jenckes, a member of the House from Rhode Island, and more recently by Carl Schurz, who early in 1870 had entered the Senate from Missouri. Congress granted the desired authority; the President declared the new rules operative in the federal offices at Washington and New York from January 1, 1872. His tardy action undoubtedly smacked of eleventh-hour virtue for the coming presidential election. Indeed, he soon chafed under the restrictions, and in 1873 Congress declined to renew the appropriation for the supervisory commission upon which the success of the plan depended.

Meanwhile, the government dealt with the problem of re-

organizing the national finances on a peace basis. Begun under
President Johnson, a series of enactments converted the war debt
into bonds at lower interest rates, reduced internal-revenue
duties and, after lessening the income tax, in 1872 abolished it.
But a proposal to lower the tariff roused the ire of the industrial
interests, suckled by the war, which were determined to increase
rather than diminish protection. From this time forward, swarms
of lobbyists descended upon Washington whenever tariff measures were under consideration, none shrewder or more effective
than John L. Hayes, agent of the National Association of Wool
Manufacturers. Though no Republican national platform had
ever advocated protection, apart from a passing mention in
1860, Congress raised the rates on wool and woolens in 1867, on
copper in 1869, and on steel rails, nickel and marble in 1870.
As a hostile critic said, the country had advanced from the
five- and ten-per-cent protection of Alexander Hamilton to the
twenty- and thirty-per-cent level of Clay and Webster, and now,
with the duties ranging from thirty to five hundred per cent,
still higher rates were being demanded.

Yet the Republican leaders had reckoned without their farming
constituencies, which felt pinched by the rise of prices. So strong
was the Western protest that in 1870 Congress was obliged to
make a gesture toward tariff reform. The reductions, however,
affected chiefly tea, coffee, wines, spices and certain other articles
in which no domestic manufacturing interest was involved, and
failed to allay the discontent. Desiring to smooth matters over
for the impending presidential campaign, the party chieftains
brought about a new system of rates in acts of May and June,
1872. Besides a sweeping reduction of nonprotective duties, this
legislation provided a horizontal cut of ten per cent on imports
competing with the products of the chief protected industries.
A deficit in revenue caused by the Panic of 1873 led, however, to
a restoration of the protective duties in 1875. At this point they
were permitted to remain until the general tariff revision of 1883.

Though the most shocking misdeeds of the administration
remained as yet undisclosed, certain elements among Grant's
following were already beginning to distinguish between the
"Hero of Appomattox" and the peace-time incumbent of the
White House. As early as 1870 a Republican faction in Missouri,

led by Schurz and aided by the Democrats, carried the state elections. The Liberal Republicans, as they called themselves, favored a more generous treatment of their fellow citizens who had taken the Southern side during the war and, in addition, demanded civil-service reform and tariff revision. The Missouri incident was like a spark to a powder train. As similar bolts from the party occurred in other states, the movement assumed nation-wide proportions. With high hopes the Liberal Republicans convened at Cincinnati on May 1, 1872, to nominate national candidates. The body contained diverse elements: tariff reductionists, civil-service reformers, opponents of federal intervention in the South (see page 121) and disgruntled politicians nursing personal grudges. The proceedings quickly became snarled in a tangle of personalities and politics, which caused the Republicans to call the gathering the "Convention of Cranks." After a savage arraignment of the administration, the platform declared for civil-service reform and home rule in the South, but, in consequence of frankly confessed "irreconcilable differences," it was noncommittal on the tariff. For President the convention made the preposterous mistake of naming Horace Greeley, lifelong foe of the Democrats and a rabid protectionist. Governor B. Gratz Brown of Missouri was made his running mate. Though it was a bitter pill for them to swallow, the Democrats when they convened saw nothing better to do than to indorse the ticket.

The Republicans, meeting on June 5, unanimously renominated Grant, associating with him Henry Wilson of Massachusetts. Their platform, after justifying the administration's Southern policy, pledged tariff protection and paid sanctimonious respects to civil-service reform. The outcome was never in doubt. Many Democrats stayed at home rather than vote for Greeley. Yet, even with a stronger candidate, the Liberal Republican movement could hardly have triumphed, for the average Republican continued to see Grant with his war-time halo, and the Carpetbag governments assured him Southern support. He received an electoral vote of 286 to 62 and a popular majority of almost 56 per cent to 44. Greeley died a broken-hearted man a few weeks later. In the history of the Republican party the campaign was notable as marking the formal adoption of tariff protection as an article of party faith. The campaign also signalized the entry of labor into politics in the guise of the short-lived Labor Reform party. No presidential contest since has been without one or more minor parties devoted to the welfare of the urban or rural workingman.

ECONOMIC COLLAPSE AND POLITICAL SHAME

Six months after Grant's second inauguration the feverish prosperity that had infected the country chilled suddenly to depression, unemployment and distress. Men in their mad strife for gain had forgotten the distinction between possible and impossible. An inflated currency and illimitable credit had caused millions of capital to pour into factories and mills until their productive capacity far outstripped existing needs. In the decade after the incorporation of the Union Pacific over a billion was sunk in rail construction alone. Only the future growth of the country could make many such enterprises profitable, and meantime indebtedness piled up beyond their ability to pay. Moreover, much speculation was sheer dishonesty, foisted on the gullible by rascals. These were the years that Mark Twain and his collaborator, Charles Dudley Warner, called "The Gilded Age." "Beautiful credit!" they jibed, citing a "speculator in lands and mines," who boasted, "I wasn't worth a cent two years ago, and now I owe two million dollars." Even the farmers felt the contagion, heavily mortgaging their lands for tools and improvements.

Much of the business expansion had been financed from abroad; and a panic in Vienna in May, 1873, spreading to other European money centers, caused a withdrawal of a great part of this support. American bankers, already overburdened, were unprepared to carry the additional load. In September came the crash, precipitated by the failure of Jay Cooke and Company, which had invested too heavily in the projected Northern Pacific Railroad. A frenzy of excitement and fear gripped the financial world. The Grant administration was helpless before the storm, and the foundations of credit began to crumble. Banking and business houses toppled, eighty-nine railroads defaulted on their bonds, and the industrial regions were stricken as by a paralysis. In all, more than 5000 concerns failed during the Panic year with an aggregate loss of about $228,500,000. Meantime, more than three million wage-earners were thrown out of work; and the Western farmers, their grain a drug on the market, found themselves without means to meet their mortgage payments.

Five years were to follow the Panic of 1873 before normal conditions returned, years all the more trying because of revelations of the graft and dishonor that honeycombed the federal government. In the opinion of George F. Hoar, Republican Senator from Massachusetts, corruption "never got so dangerous a hold upon the forces of the Government, or upon a great political party, as in the Administration of General Grant." Early in 1873 investigating committees of the House and Senate disclosed that the outgoing Vice-President and a number of Congressmen, including James A. Garfield and "Pig-Iron" Kelley, held stock, for which they had never paid, in the Crédit Mobilier, construction company for the Union Pacific. These shares had been distributed by Oakes Ames, a Congressman and officer of the company, with the assurance given his business associates that he would place them where they would "protect us" and "do the most good" in averting inquiry into the company's affairs. The House, accepting the committee's opinion that most of those involved had acted without "any corrupt motive or purpose," contented itself with censuring Ames and another member. Other exposures followed with almost clocklike regularity, only a few of which need be noted. Thus the Secretary of the Treasury, W. A. Richardson, was found to have grossly abused his authority in order to divert some of the department's funds, through unearned commissions, into the pockets of a political henchman of the notorious Ben Butler. In May, 1874, Richardson hurriedly resigned to avoid a vote of censure by the House.

The public, racked by the hard times, but as yet unaware how far the moral poison had spread, turned on its rulers in the fall elections, giving the Democrats their first victory since before the war. While the Senate continued Republican, the House changed from two-thirds Republican to three-fifths Democratic, a fact which would give administration politicians sleepless nights when the time came to count the returns of the next presidential election. In addition, the Democrats swept twenty-three states out of thirty-five, including New York where Samuel J. Tilden, an active participant in the assault against the Tweed Ring, was chosen governor on a platform of political reform. But this stinging popular rebuke came too late to undo the damage. In 1875 B. H. Bristow, Richardson's successor as head of the Treasury, exposed the rascality of a "whisky ring," made up of wealthy distillers and revenue officers, which since 1870 had been defrauding the government of millions of dollars in taxes. Grant's private secretary, O. E. Babcock, also implicated in the conspiracy, was saved from punishment only through the President's unwise intervention on his behalf. On the heels of these disclosures, in March, 1876, came the precipitate resignation of Secretary W. W. Belknap of the War Department in order to escape impeachment on the charge of receiving an annual bribe since 1870 from an officeholder anxious to avoid removal.

A few weeks more brought another scandal, one which was forever to tarnish the reputation of James G. Blaine, who had been Speaker of the House from 1869 to 1875. The investigation showed that, while holding his powerful office, he had acted as bond salesman for a land-grant railway, and that later he had permitted the Union Pacific and certain other land-grant corporations to relieve him of a large block of the securities at a sum far in excess of their market value. By a trick Blaine got possession of the incriminating evidence, the so-called Mulligan letters, and though he refused to allow the documents to be examined, he made a brilliant speech in the House, which, if it left the critical unsatisfied, at least convinced orthodox Republicans of his innocence. But Blaine's penalty was to be a heavy one, for his connection with this affair was to prevent him in later years from attaining the goal of his ambition, the presidency.

THE GRANGER MOVEMENT AND THE MONEY QUESTION

Meanwhile, economic depression continued unabated, characterized by falling prices, constant bankruptcies and widespread unemployment. In the industrial centers hordes of the jobless crowded the bread lines or, turning hobo, wandered aimlessly about the country, pathetic caricatures of the restless hardy pioneers who had helped conquer the wilderness. Criminality increased, and the violence attending the railroad strikes of 1877 (see page 207) further attested the spread of radicalism and despair. These grim years gave impetus to many a scheme of social and economic redemption — labor amalgamation, "free

silver," socialism, the "single tax" and the like — while rendering clamorous the demands for railway regulation and greenback
inflation.

As early as 1869 Massachusetts had established a commission
with advisory power to deal with the unfair practices of railroads within the state. The chief victims of such abuses, however,
were the Midwestern farmers with produce to market. Already
beset with low prices for their overabundant crops, and obliged
to pay middlemen excessive charges for tools and other supplies,
they considered the rates demanded for hauling their products
beyond all reason. The railroads, on their part, did not hesitate
to impose extortionate charges, or even to discriminate against
certain communities and shippers in favor of others. In 1867 a
secret ritualistic order, named the Patrons of Husbandry but
usually known as the Grange, had appeared among the farmers,
originally for the purpose of fostering a pleasanter social life
among rural dwellers of both sexes. The movement to curb the
railroads is always associated with the rise of this organization,
though the Grange was avowedly nonpolitical and it grew but
slowly until the bad times after 1873 suddenly swelled its membership to two and a half million.

Inspired by "Farmers' Declarations of Independence" and
pledged to emancipate "white slaves from the Slave-Power of
Monopoly," local agrarian parties sprang up in the Midwest and
bent the legislatures to their will. Acts were passed for regulating railroad rates either by direct legislative decree or through
official commissions set up for the purpose. Illinois and Minnesota
led the way in 1870 and 1871, Ohio and Michigan following in
the Panic year, and Iowa, Wisconsin and Missouri in the two
years thereafter. These laws were based upon the then novel
principle that railways should be treated as public-service enterprises, not as mere private businesses for the enrichment of
their stockholders. Some of the legislation was ill wrought or
else tinged with a spirit of vengeance; but the fury of the railway
magnates was directed less against such matters than against
the constitutionality of any mandatory control by the state.
The so-called Granger cases, decided in 1876, set all such doubts
at rest, however. In Munn v. Illinois, the Supreme Court found
in the state's police power (that is, its inherent right to protect

the health, welfare and safety of its citizens) ample authority to regulate businesses "clothed with a public interest." "Property," asserted the court, "does become clothed with a public interest when used in a manner to make it of public consequence and affect the community at large."[1]   In Peik v. the Chicago & Northwestern Railway, the court dismissed a further objection by declaring that, until Congress acted under the interstate-commerce clause, states might even fix rates on shipments passing beyond their limits.

The Grangers, without recourse to politics, also undertook to cure the price evil in respect to both the products they sold and those they bought. They set up central agencies to aid the sale of farm produce; in several states coöperative creameries and grain elevators, operated at cost, saved Grange members thousands of dollars. By pooling their funds farmers also effected great economies through ordering in wholesale lots directly from manufacturers. In Iowa the State Grange established its own factories for making plows and harvesters, sold to members at cost. But by 1876 most of these undertakings were abandoned, having failed for lack of adequate support or skilled business direction or because of the unfair practices of competitors. Yet the widespread interest in coöperation was not without result. Besides making middlemen less ready to ask exorbitant prices, it caused the development of great mail-order houses in Chicago, which, established with Grange sanction, did business directly with rural dwellers over the heads of local dealers. As the seventies drew toward a close, this first great farmers' movement in American history entered on a decline.

Meanwhile, an increasing number of agrarian leaders had turned to currency inflation as a remedy for their ills. Since the early days of the war, it will be recalled, business transactions had been carried on largely in debased greenbacks which the government declined to redeem at face value in gold. When peace came, the substantial business classes in the East demanded the withdrawal of this "cheap money," or at least of enough of it to establish conditions under which all forms of currency

---

[1] Though this law really involved an Illinois law of 1871 for regulating grain warehouses, the principle, of course, applied equally to railway regulation. Further reference to the Granger cases appears on page 277.

would have full gold value. In 1866 Congress authorized its reduction by gradual stages, but this process had to be discontinued two years later, when the amount stood at $356,000,000, because of the outcry from the Midwestern agricultural regions. Many farmers saw in contraction the chief cause of the low price of crops. Moreover, since a large number of farms were heavily mortgaged, they felt intolerably handicapped if, before their debts fell due, the volume of currency diminished. With less money in circulation greenbacks became harder to get, or, to put it differently, their value increased. If paper dollars, borrowed when they were worth sixty-five cents in gold, were repaid in paper dollars worth ninety-five or one hundred cents in gold, the debtor was repaying in principal considerably more than he had received. Many members of the "debtor class" began to insist that the greenbacks be retained as a permanent part of the monetary system.

During the Panic of 1873 the Secretary of the Treasury, as a temporary measure of relief, reissued some of the greenbacks that had been retired, to the extent of $26,000,000. The demand became more insistent and in 1874 Congress passed an inflation bill, designed to increase the total volume to $400,000,000. Though an act of his own party, President Grant courageously vetoed it. When the fall elections of 1874 assured the Democrats control of the next House, the Republicans made use of their remaining months to enact a plan for the renewal, or resumption, of specie payments. The resumption act of January 14, 1875, has been called, not inaptly, the "deathbed repentance of the Republican party." Far from radical, its provisions sought to appease both the greenback notions of the West and the gold-standard sentiment of the East. John Sherman was its chief author. It provided that from January 1, 1879, the government should accept greenback dollars as the equivalent of gold dollars, and that meanwhile, in preparation for the event, the government should retire part of the greenbacks and, at the same time, accumulate a gold reserve through the sale of bonds. The purpose of this reserve was to assure the full specie value of the greenbacks remaining in circulation. The amount of gold was subsequently fixed at $100,000,000, and Congress decided in 1878 that $346,681,016 of greenbacks should form a permanent part of our money supply. The plan proved entirely feasible, for, as it happened, the time of its execution coincided with the return of prosperity. After the date of resumption the full value of the greenback in terms of gold was firmly established.

Grant's veto of the inflation bill incensed the small group of extreme greenbackers in the country, and the passage of the resumption act added to their anger. These persons subscribed to the doctrine of "absolute money"; that is, they contended that money derived its value solely from the stamp (or fiat) of the government, not from its intrinsic value or the fact that it was exchangeable for gold or some other precious metal. Hopeless of winning support from either of the old parties, they organized the National Greenback party in May, 1875, which presented candidates in the next three presidential elections. Their platform demanded repeal of the resumption act, and the establishment of a national legal-tender currency redeemable only in low-interest United States bonds. Though attaining some popularity in the Midwest and in Eastern labor centers, and polling 1,000,000 votes in the congressional elections of 1878, the party never cast an electoral vote. It gradually succumbed to the rising tide of sentiment in favor of unlimited silver coinage.

THE DISPUTED ELECTION OF 1876

Quite content with the resumption act, the mass of voters were thinking of other things as the campaign of 1876 drew near. Already in December, 1875, two thirds of the Republican members of the House had voted with the Democratic majority in condemning the principle of a third presidential term. While this rebuke checked Conkling's scheme to continue Grant in the White House, it also helped fix public attention anew upon the malodorous record of the party in power. What could the Republicans do to avert disaster in the election? Blaine, himself the chief contender for the nomination, pointed the way in January, 1876, when he delivered in the House a violent bloody-shirt speech which goaded Southern members into passionate and ill-considered replies. The Republicans took prompt advantage of the opportunity to frighten voters with the spectacle of an unrepentant South about to ride into power on the back of the Democratic party.

When the Republicans assembled in Cincinnati on June 14, Blaine was the favorite in the balloting, but he failed of success, thanks to opposition both from the reform elements and from Conkling who cherished an invincible personal dislike for him. Instead, the prize went on the seventh ballot to Rutherford B. Hayes, a Civil War veteran of irreproachable character, then serving a third term as governor of Ohio. W. A. Wheeler of New York was named for Vice-President. The platform bristled with bloody-shirt allusions and, as four years before, declared for tariff protection and civil-service reform. The Democrats, meeting two weeks later in St. Louis, chose as their candidate Governor Samuel J. Tilden, who, by reason of his success in destroying the corrupt "Canal Ring" in New York politics, had won nation-wide renown as a reformer. The second place fell to Thomas A. Hendricks of Indiana. The paramount issue, declared the Democratic platform, was reform — financial, tariff, civil-service and administrative — a duty which could not safely be intrusted to a party "honey-combed with incapacity, waste, and fraud."

In the ensuing campaign the Democrats strove valiantly to rivet attention upon the need for change while, to quote James Russell Lowell, a Hayes supporter, "the worst element of the Republican party has got hold of the canvass, and everything possible is done to stir up the old passions of the war." Republican orators even asserted that the Democrats, if elected, would pay the Confederate war debt and compensate the former slaveholders. On the other hand, the hard times following 1873 aided Democratic efforts. On the morning after the election Tilden's victory was almost universally conceded by the newspapers, but the Republican national headquarters stoutly claimed Hayes's success. Within a few days it became clear that, with 185 electoral votes necessary for election, Tilden had unquestioned right to 184, including the usually decisive states of New York, New Jersey, Connecticut and Indiana, while Hayes in like manner had won 165. Twenty votes — one from Oregon, seven from South Carolina, four from Florida and eight from Louisiana — were in doubt.

The difficulty in Oregon was of a technical character. One of the successful Republican electors was, after the election, found to be ineligible. The state law provided, in such case, that the remaining electors should fill the vacancy, but the Democratic governor insisted that the highest Democratic candidate for elector was entitled to the place. In the three Southern states the question was more complicated. There the native whites, engaged in a final desperate effort to dislodge the Carpetbaggers, had, in countless instances, resorted to intimidation and violence to keep Negroes from the polls. But the state election machinery, capped by the famous or infamous "returning boards," was controlled by the Carpetbaggers who from their seats of power could manipulate the election returns as they pleased. The worst conditions prevailed in Louisiana, where the four members of the returning board refused to add a Democratic member as required by law, offered at one stage to sell out to Tilden for $1,000,000, and ended up by rejecting Democratic votes in wholesale lots in order to create the desired majority for Hayes. They actually threw out 13,213 Tilden votes, leaving the Hayes electors a safe margin of 3437 or more.[1]

From each of the four states double sets of returns went to Congress. Unfortunately, the Constitution makes no adequate provision for such a contingency and, since the two branches were controlled by opposite parties, compromise proved necessary. Accordingly, a law was passed on January 29, 1877, to create a special electoral commission of five Senators, five Representatives and five Justices of the Supreme Court, the fifth Justice to be chosen by the four named in the statute. The commission's decisions on disputed returns should be binding upon Congress unless rejected by the two Houses voting separately. It was understood that seven members of the commission would be Republicans and seven Democrats, and it was expected that the unselected Justice would be David Davis, a political free lance. But Davis's unexpected election as United States Senator

---

[1] To give an appearance of fairness, they also rejected 2415 Republican votes. President Grant believed that Tilden was entitled to Louisiana and hence to election. James Ford Rhodes concludes his discussion of the situation by saying, "If Hayes had envisaged the facts as I now do he would have refused to accept the presidency from the Louisiana Returning-Board." *History of the United States*, VII, 236. But another historian, while conceding "grossly partisan and illegal acts," expresses the belief that "in an absolutely fair and free election the state would have gone Republican by five to ten thousand." P. L. Haworth, *The Hayes-Tilden Disputed Election of 1876*, 116, 121.

from Illinois caused the appointment of a third Republican Justice, Joseph P. Bradley, the most acceptable to the Democrats of the remaining members of the bench.

The electoral commission sat throughout the month of February. The time was drawing perilously near to inauguration day, tense excitement pervaded the country, and Grant strengthened the military forces about Washington. Bent on averting the possibility of another terrible civil war, forty-two ex-Confederates in the House took a solemn pledge to oppose all attempts to frustrate the electoral count. Meantime, the commission took cognizance, in turn, of the cases of Florida, Louisiana, Oregon and South Carolina. On all crucial points the decision favored the Hayes electors by a vote of eight to seven and, on March 2, Hayes was formally pronounced victorious with a majority of 185 to 184. The disappointment of the Democrats is indescribable, but, with angry mutterings, they yielded grudging acquiescence. It is hardly too much to say that, in the peaceful acceptance of Hayes's election, the supremacy of the law won the greatest victory in the history of popular government.

SELECT BIBLIOGRAPHY

Public Morals and National Politics, 1869-1872. For all subjects treated in this chapter, valuable material can be found in the general works by Rhodes and Oberholtzer; in Nevins, *The Emergence of Modern America;* and in Dunning, *Reconstruction, Political and Economic.* Postwar financial reorganization is treated compactly in Dewey, *Financial History of the United States.* Tarbell, *The Tariff in Our Times,* emphasizes the political and social forces in tariff making; Stanwood, *American Tariff Controversies in the Nineteenth Century,* is especially good for the legislative history of tariff measures; and Taussig, *The Tariff History of the United States,* gives a scholarly account from the standpoint of an economist. Barclay, *The Liberal Republican Movement in Missouri,* and Ross, *The Liberal Republican Movement,* offer special studies of the revolt against Grantism.

Economic Collapse and Political Shame. Excellent accounts of the Panic of 1873 appear in Burton, *Financial Crises and Periods of Industrial and Commercial Depression,* and Oberholtzer, *Jay Cooke, Financier of the Civil War,* II. The general works cited earlier deal fully with political corruption. For a friendly view of Blaine's involvements, see *James Gillespie Blaine* by Edward Stanwood, a relative of Mrs. Blaine.

The Granger Movement and the Money Question. The standard treatment of the Midwestern agrarian crusade is Buck, *The Granger Movement.* The political aspects of the Greenback movement are sketched in Buck, *The Agrarian Crusade,* and Haynes, *Third Party Movements since the Civil*

War; the more technical aspects in Hepburn, *A History of Currency in the United States;* Barrett, *The Greenbacks and Resumption of Specie Payments;* and Mitchell, *A History of the Greenbacks.*

The Disputed Election of 1876. The most thorough study is Haworth, *The Hayes-Tilden Disputed Presidential Election of 1876.* See also Bigelow, *The Life of Samuel J. Tilden,* and Williams, *The Life of Rutherford Birchard Hayes.*

CHAPTER IX

OLD ISSUES AND NEW ATTITUDES, 1877–1897

REPUBLICANS AND REFORM, 1877–1881

THE narrowness of the Republican victory in 1876 frightened the practical politicians, hitherto overconfident of their hold on public opinion, and gave a strategic advantage to those members who wished to purify the party. Each age has its own abuses that call for cure and, as might be expected, the reformers of the 1870's and 1880's were interested, above all else, in the honest, efficient and economical conduct of government. Alarmed by the ominous creaking of the governmental machinery as operated by unskilled or unscrupulous hands, they feared lest the theory of democracy be defeated by its practices. Their constructive program embraced civil-service reform, prompt punishment of delinquent officials and the abolition of campaign assessments on officeholders. Some of them labored also for tariff reform. Chief among their leaders were Carl Schurz, George W. Curtis, editor of *Harper's Weekly*, Edwin L. Godkin, editor of the *Nation*, and Dorman B. Eaton, a New York lawyer and publicist. If to a later generation they seem to have occupied themselves with symptoms rather than with the disease itself, they at least attacked evils that challenged all civic decency. While most of the reformers were Republicans by preference, they placed their purposes above party, assuming an attitude of independence whenever occasion demanded. Their potential freedom from party restraints, their insistence that parties were merely instruments for the public good, not ends in themselves, enraged the professional politicians. But their example helped gradually to fashion a tradition of independent voting at a period when the fetish of party regularity was stronger than at any other time in American history.

Though he gained office under dubious circumstances, President Hayes earnestly sought to live up to the maxim, announced in his inaugural address, that "he serves his party best who serves his country best." A simple, dignified man, conscientious and hard working, but devoid of qualities of leadership, he gathered about him an unusually able group of advisers, including William M. Evarts of New York as Secretary of State and John Sherman of Ohio as head of the Treasury. To the horror of Conkling and the practical politicians who had surrounded Grant, Carl Schurz, civil-service reformer and an anti-Grant campaigner four years before, was made Secretary of the Interior, and a Tennessee Democrat and ex-Confederate veteran, David M. Key, became Postmaster-General.[1] They found equally unpalatable other of the President's early acts, such as his refusal to lend further military support to the Carpetbag governments, and particularly his zeal for civil-service reform. Soon they began to refer to him as only a "halfbreed" Republican in contrast to their own "stalwart" Republicanism. The names, Halfbreed and Stalwart, clung to the two wings of the party throughout this administration and the next.

President Hayes made a resolute effort to secure administrative efficiency and to weed out dishonesty. Though his repeated appeals to Congress to renew the civil-service appropriation, which had lapsed under Grant, came to naught, he did make progress upon his own authority in reducing the ravages of the spoils system. Schurz placed the Department of the Interior on a merit basis and, in the teeth of bitter opposition from the Stalwarts, Hayes applied the reform to the federal offices in New York City. Besides reappointing to the postmastership there T. L. James, an ardent civil-service champion, he dealt strongly with the situation in the New York customhouse, where an investigating committee had reported incompetency and graft. Other measures failing, he ousted Chester A. Arthur and A. B. Cornell, respectively collector and naval officer. The Senate, incensed, declined for two months to confirm their successors. Hayes's devotion to the cause undoubtedly won popular favor for civil-service reform and helped hasten its final accomplishment.

Though the President's worst enemies were in the house of his friends, the Democrats in Congress left no stone unturned

---

[1] The other members of the cabinet were: George W. McCrary of Iowa, Secretary of War; Richard W. Thompson of Indiana, Secretary of the Navy; and Charles Devens of Massachusetts, Attorney-General.

to discredit him as "Old Eight-to-Seven" and the "*de facto* President." Their purpose was, by keeping the issue alive, to sweep the country in 1880 in a dramatic campaign of vindication. In May, 1878, the Democratic House directed the so-called Potter committee to investigate Hayes's title to his office. After examining over two hundred witnesses concerning conditions in Florida and Louisiana in 1876, the committee by a strict party vote decided that Tilden had been rightfully elected. The edge of the findings was dulled, however, by the enterprise of a Republican Senate committee in unearthing a batch of cipher telegrams that had been sent, or received, by Democratic leaders during the heat of the campaign. These, when decoded, revealed efforts to bribe the Florida and South Carolina returning boards. Thanks to someone's foresight, Republican telegrams sent at the same time could nowhere be found. Most of the Democrats implicated by the "cipher despatches" did not deny the essential charges, justifying their course on the plea that they were merely trying to "ransom stolen property from thieves." Tilden himself was shown to be innocent of any complicity. It was clear that the garments of both parties were soiled, and the "political crime" as a Democratic campaign issue was robbed in advance of much of its effectiveness.

The Democrats also bestirred themselves to bring about a repeal of the force acts, passed in 1870–1871 during the Ku Klux troubles and already enfeebled by Supreme Court decisions (see page 120). By holding up the army-appropriation bill the House in June, 1878, forced the Senate and President to accept a bill barring the use of troops at the polls. Despite the success of the Democrats in winning both Houses in the fall elections of 1878, they could get no further. Hayes vetoed eight different attempts at rescinding other features of the acts. Though rendered harmless by disuse, these last vestiges of the old Reconstruction machinery survived until repealed by a Democratic Congress and President in 1894.

The aggressive tactics of the opposition helped the Republicans, despite internal differences, to present a united front as the presidential election drew near. Tired of too much virtue, Conkling and his group reverted again to the notion of another four years for Grant, who had just returned from a spectacular tour round the globe. The anti-Grant forces, thoroughly alarmed, organized No-Third-Term leagues, and even held a national Anti-Third-Term convention. Nevertheless, when the Republicans convened in Chicago on June 2, 1880, 306 of the 757 delegates voted doggedly for Grant throughout the balloting. They did succeed in preventing the choice of Blaine, who stood second, but the convention on the thirty-sixth ballot stampeded to a "dark horse," James A. Garfield of Ohio. An ex-soldier and moderate Halfbreed, Garfield had seen continuous service in Congress since 1863. As a peace offering to the "Grant Phalanx," the second place was given to Arthur of New York, the recently dismissed customs collector. The platform blended self-laudation with disparagement of the Democrats, praised the protective system and, with evident reluctance, indorsed Hayes's civil-service policy.

The Democrats were in a dilemma. Tilden was not available as a candidate because of ill health and the powerful opposition of Tammany Hall in his own state. Meeting at Cincinnati on June 22, the convention on the third ballot chose General Winfield S. Hancock, with W. H. English of Indiana as his running mate. Hancock's nomination was an attempt to refute the customary Republican charge of disloyalty and, at the same time, to capitalize the popularity of a faithful war veteran. The platform, while demanding civil-service reform and a tariff for revenue only, urged the "great fraud of 1876–77" as the issue that "precedes and dwarfs every other." In the campaign, however, the "great fraud" excited little attention despite the fact that Garfield had served on the commission that seated Hayes. Nor did the efforts to discredit Garfield because of his connection with the Crédit Mobilier and other scandals yield any greater success. The Republicans, on their part, made the most of their nominee's rise from a barefoot canal boy in Ohio, while scoffing at Hancock as "a good man weighing two hundred and forty pounds."[1] Hancock's chief campaign utterance was a repudiation of the Democratic tariff plank on the score that the tariff was necessarily a "local issue." The return of prosperity for the

_____

[1] Appropriately enough, Horatio Alger, past master of the art of portraying the "success" theme in thrilling boys' books, presently produced *From Canal Boy to President, or the Boyhood and Manhood of James A. Garfield.*

first time since 1872 undoubtedly helped the Republicans. Garfield won by an electoral majority of 214 to 155, though polling only 48.3 per cent of the popular vote to 48.23 for his opponent.

SEALING THE DOOM OF THE SPOILS SYSTEM

The announcement of Garfield's cabinet reopened the Republican breach which had closed during the campaign. The choice of Blaine as Secretary of State was regarded by Conkling as a personal affront, while the other cabinet selections were scarcely more to his liking.[1] Even in the case of appointments in Conkling's own state, Garfield went his own way, ignoring the practice of "senatorial courtesy" which customarily bound Presidents to rubberstamp the recommendations of Senators of their own party. Conkling determined to make an issue of W. H. Robertson's nomination as New York customs collector. Not only was the office the most lucrative in the whole government service, but Robertson was a Halfbreed and a Blaine man. When it became clear that his efforts to prevent confirmation by the Senate would be of no avail, Conkling and his fellow Senator, T. C. Platt, resigned their seats, appealing to the New York legislature for reëlection as vindication. To their mortification and the country's amusement both were defeated after fifty-six ballots. Conkling retired permanently to private life, "Me Too" Platt to temporary oblivion. Meanwhile James, the new Postmaster-General, uncovered a nest of corruption in the postal service, involving, among others, T. W. Brady, who since Grant's time had been an Assistant Postmaster-General, and ex-Senator S. W. Dorsey of Arkansas. Brady attempted to block the investigation by threatening the President with unpleasant consequences. Garfield remaining unmoved, he made public a letter — known to fame as the "My dear Hubbell" letter — in which Garfield as a presidential candidate had approved the practice of levying campaign assessments on office-holders. The trials of the conspirators in the "Star Route" frauds, as they were called, dragged on until 1884, when, on technical grounds, the chief culprits managed to escape prison.

---

[1] William Windom of Minnesota, Secretary of the Treasury; Robert T. Lincoln of Illinois, Secretary of War; W. H. Hunt of Louisiana, Secretary of the Navy; Wayne McVeagh of Pennsylvania, Attorney-General; T. L. James of New York, Postmaster-General; and S. J. Kirkwood of Iowa, Secretary of the Interior.

Some good resulted, however, for the ring was broken up, and public attention called anew to the need of better officials.

While still struggling with questions of patronage, Garfield was shot by a disappointed officeseeker on July 2, 1881, four months after his inauguration. At the time the Vice-President was with Conkling and Platt at the New York capital, working for their reëlection; and when Garfield after a gallant fight died on September 19, many people shared the dismay of the man who exclaimed, "Chet Arthur President of the United States! Good God!" Handsome, affable, debonair, the new President was best known to his countrymen as a machine politician. Yet the responsibilities of office revealed him in a new light. As chief executive he displayed unexpected firmness and sagacity and, to the surprise of his erstwhile associates, devoted himself earnestly to the task of reform. Arthur presently reconstituted the cabinet, appointing F. T. Frelinghuysen of New Jersey as Blaine's successor in the State Department. Only Secretary of War Lincoln, son of the martyred President, was permanently retained.[1] Otherwise, most of Garfield's appointees remained undisturbed, including Robertson whose selection as customs collector had prompted Conkling's resignation. Nor did Arthur's devotion to the cause of good government stop here. In 1882, when the Republican Congress voted $19,000,000 for river and harbor improvements in five hundred different localities, he rejected the bill as unwise and extravagant. This first of our modern "pork-barrel" measures had many friends in both parties, however, and his veto was quickly overridden. As we shall see, he also worked for tariff revision.

Most surprising of all was his interest in civil-service reform. In messages of 1881 and 1882 he urged upon Congress suitable legislation. Fifteen years of discussion had created a robust public opinion on the subject, and the President's efforts were reënforced by the agitation of state and national civil-service-reform associations and by countless articles in the *Nation*, *Harper's Weekly* and elsewhere. Revelations of a Senate investi-

[1] The other new appointments were C. J. Folger of New York, Secretary of the Treasury; W. E. Chandler of New Hampshire, Secretary of the Navy; B. H. Brewster of Pennsylvania, Attorney-General; T. O. Howe of Wisconsin, Postmaster-General; and H. M. Teller of Colorado, Secretary of the Interior.

gating committee, showing that the Republicans had collected nearly $100,000 from federal employees in the congressional elections of 1878, touched the public on the raw, as did likewise the knowledge, derived from the "My dear Hubbell" letter and other sources, that this practice had been repeated in 1880. Garfield's death at the hands of a thwarted spoilsman seemed an irrefutable answer to all objections to immediate action; yet the politicians in Congress continued to delay.

In the fall elections of 1882 the Democrats carried the new House, as well as thirteen of the sixteen states in which governors were chosen. Though Republican factionalism helped bring about this result, the failure of the party to reform the public service was a prime contributing factor. In the important state of New York Grover Cleveland, a Democrat and ardent civil-service reformer, was elected governor by the unprecedented plurality of 192,000. The expiring Republican Congress resolved to enact the desired legislation, both in order to propitiate popular sentiment and to protect Republican officeholders from the effects of the severer act which the incoming Democrats were almost certain to favor. The result was the Pendleton act of January 16, 1883, drafted by Dorman B. Eaton of the National Civil Service Reform League and introduced, as it happened, by Senator G. F. Pendleton, an Ohio Democrat. It provided for a bipartisan commission which should set up and administer a system of competitive examinations as a test of fitness for appointment to federal office. It further forbade government officials to solicit campaign contributions from other officeholders and protected the latter from removal for failure to pay. The new plan applied at once only to the executive departments in Washington, the customhouses and the larger post offices (those employing fifty or more); and the President was given discretion to extend the "classified list," as it was called, to other groups of employees.

The statute left much to be desired. The rules affected only future appointments and, at first, less than 14,000 positions, leaving nearly nine tenths of the total still subject to partisan politics. Nevertheless, the Pendleton act has rightly been termed "the Magna Charta of civil-service reform," for, through the provision for enlarging the classified list, Arthur's successors extended the merit system until, at the present time, about three out of every four federal employees enjoy its protection. While idealism contributed to this progress, gross partisanship also played a part, for an outgoing administration oftentimes increased the classified list in order to protect its followers from dismissal by the victors. This practice gave coinage to the saying, "To the vanquished belong the spoils." On the whole, few backward steps have been taken, the most rapid advances being made under Presidents Theodore Roosevelt, Taft and Wilson. Incidentally, the passage of the Pendleton act strengthened the hands of civil-service reformers in local politics, leading Massachusetts and New York within a year to introduce the system for state offices and encouraging many municipalities to try similar measures.

THE EMERGENCE OF GROVER CLEVELAND

The victory for good government, signalized by the Pendleton act, was followed in the campaign of 1884 by further evidence of popular revolt against low political standards. Arthur desired the Republican nomination, but his chances proved slight: he had lost his former Stalwart support without wholly convincing the Halfbreeds of the genuineness of his conversion. The convention, meeting in Chicago on June 3, chose the perennial aspirant, Blaine, on the fourth ballot, though against the bitter opposition of George W. Curtis and of younger delegates like Theodore Roosevelt and Henry Cabot Lodge. As his candidacy lacked the customary recommendation of war service, amends were made by completing the ticket with General John A. Logan of Illinois. To the reform wing of the party Blaine's nomination meant a negation of all the governmental progress that had been achieved since Grant left office. A conference of Independent Republicans denounced the convention's action and called upon the Democrats to offer men whom they could support. Convening in Chicago on July 8, the Democrats rose to the occasion, nominating Grover Cleveland on the second ballot. Hendricks of Indiana, Tilden's running mate in 1876, was given the second place in a feeble effort to resurrect the old "fraud" issue.

Cleveland's nomination admirably met the requirements of the situation. With none of the qualities of the dashing political cavalier or the wiles of the professional intriguer, he had strongly impressed himself upon the people, not only of his state but of the nation at large. As mayor of Buffalo in 1881, he had shown what an incorruptible official could do to stem the tide of municipal misrule, and later, in the governor's chair, he had displayed a similar aggressive devotion to the public weal. In appearance Cleveland was rather unimpressive, his cheeks clean-shaven when most statesmen affected beards. What he lacked in height he made up in bulk, weighing over two hundred and fifty pounds. "We love him most for the enemies he has made," said General E. S. Bragg in seconding his nomination. The Independents at a later meeting indorsed him as an exemplar "of political courage and honesty and of administrative reform," while stigmatizing Blaine as "a representative of men, methods, and conduct which the public conscience condemns."

The platforms of the two parties presented no real points of difference. Both pledged tariff revision without injury to domestic industries, both applauded civil-service reform, and both dangled pension promises before the old soldiers. Accordingly, the contest turned upon the pervasive influence of party loyalty and the personal fitness of the candidates. The Democrats made the most of Cleveland's precept, "Public office is a public trust," while the Republican bolters, contemptuously dubbed "Mugwumps" by the regulars, and captained by men like Schurz, Curtis and Godkin, stumped the East and Midwest, urging public rectitude as the issue paramount to all others. To their assistance came additional Mulligan letters, giving fresh cogency to charges of Blaine's illicit financial relations with privilege-seeking corporations. The force of the attack seemed likely to be nullified, however, when Cleveland, accused of being the father of a seven-year-old illegitimate son, frankly admitted the truth. At once clergymen throughout the North carried the "moral issue" into the pulpit. A middle-class people, deeply imbued with rigid notions of chastity, faced the bitter choice between a candidate of loose private morals and one of loose public morals.

Meantime, the Republican candidate employed his magnificent oratorical powers for waving the bloody shirt, while his campaign managers made heroic efforts to wean Irish Catholic voters from their traditional Democratic allegiance, Blaine's mother being of that faith. Though they gained the fiery support of the *Irish World*, American organ of the Irish Land League, the Democrats had the better of the argument when the Reverend S. D. Burchard, presiding at a New York ministers' gathering a few days before the election, introduced the Republican nominee as leader of the party opposed to "rum, Romanism and rebellion"— a remark which Democratic newspapers promptly attributed to Blaine himself. The contest proved so close that three days passed before the outcome was definitely known. Cleveland received 219 electoral votes to 182 for Blaine, and 48.9 per cent of the popular vote to 48.3. The Democrats carried the usually doubtful states of New Jersey, Connecticut and Indiana by a few thousand each, and the pivotal state of New York by but 1149 out of a total popular vote of over a million. Had Cleveland lost New York with its 36 electoral votes, or had he lost New Jersey and either of the other two states, Blaine would have won a majority in the electoral college and hence the presidency. Many factors helped tip the scale for Cleveland: the lukewarmness of the Stalwarts toward Blaine, the deflection of Republican votes into the Prohibition party, Burchard's injudicious remark, a temporary business depression, and the participation of many new voters grown to manhood since the war. But, in last analysis, the major credit belonged to the Mugwumps who wielded their greatest influence in those states where the Republicans could least afford losses.

Cleveland's election, the first Democratic triumph since Buchanan, evidenced less the strength of his party than a popular rebuke to reactionary Republicanism. Indeed, countless voters who had confidence in the victorious candidate disliked and distrusted his heterogeneous following. For many years the Democrats, itching for power, had relied upon opportunism rather than principles. To Cleveland fell the choice — as once it had to Jackson — of letting the party continue undirected and adrift, or of seizing the helm and steering a bold course. The new President was happily situated to pursue the latter alternative. A newcomer in national affairs, he was not only unhampered by political entanglements, but his temperament rendered him impervious either to flattery or to threats. Possessing little advance knowledge of national problems, he gave them unremitting study, and his conclusions, once formed, became his inflexible chart of conduct. The key to his political thinking appeared in the statement in his inaugural address: "The people demand reform in the administration of the government and the application of business principles to public affairs." As this indicates, he, like the progressive members of the Republican party, was interested mainly in questions of administrative efficiency, being largely indifferent to those profound influences which were already breeding labor unrest and class friction. The opportunity of the Democrats, either for good or ill, was seriously limited, however, for the Senate remained Republican throughout Cleveland's term. The new policies, therefore, did not take the form of statutes, but were embodied in presidential recommendations, executive orders and veto messages.

Cleveland's cabinet, headed by Thomas F. Bayard of Delaware, compared favorably in ability with those of his Republican predecessors. The Solid South was recognized by the appointment of Senators A. H. Garland of Arkansas and L. Q. C. Lamar of Mississippi respectively as Attorney-General and Secretary of the Interior.[1] In dealing with minor appointments the President's sincerity as a civil-service reformer was sorely tried. Old-time party spokesmen, like A. P. Gorman in the Senate and Samuel J. Randall in the House, openly flouted the "Goody Two-Shoes" reform, and even introduced bills to repeal or modify the Pendleton act. Almost alone in its advocacy in his party, Cleveland had to move cautiously to avert factional dissension which might defeat other policies he hoped to accomplish. In general, he stilled the "everlasting clatter for offices" with places from the unclassified service, while quietly applying the merit system to 12,000 more positions and extending the competitive principle to include promotions as well as first appointments. If he failed to realize the lofty ideals of the reformers, he alone knew, as he wrote Eaton in 1885, "the conditions which bound and qualify every struggle for a radical improvement in the affairs of government."

---

[1] The other members were Daniel Manning of New York, Secretary of the Treasury; W. C. Whitney of New York, Secretary of the Navy; W. C. Endicott of Massachusetts, Secretary of War; and W. F. Vilas of Wisconsin, Postmaster-General.

In his desire to apply efficient business standards to governmental operation, he made a determined effort to weed out laxness and fraud in the granting of pensions.   One of the worst abuses was Congress's habit of passing special acts to satisfy individuals whose applications had been, or were likely to be, rejected by the pension bureau.   After painstaking examination the President vetoed 233 such bills.   One applicant, who alleged "long and faithful service," was shown to have spent most of his time in prison for desertion.   Another claimant, a veteran's widow, sought recompense for her husband's death at the hands of a neighbor who was trying to shoot an owl.   In 1887 Congress sought to rebuke Cleveland by passing a general measure, based upon the novel principle of granting pensions to any ex-soldiers of ninety days' service who found themselves unable to make a living.   This he promptly rejected on the ground that its loose phraseology would make the pension list a refuge for impostors instead of a "roll of honor."   Followed shortly by an executive order (later revoked) for returning the captured Confederate battle flags, the veto was hailed by the old-soldier element as proof of the unpatriotic character of the party in power.[1] Yet Cleveland signed many more private pension bills than he vetoed, and in his four years the annual appropriation for pensions grew from $56,000,-000 to $81,000,000.   His determination to keep expenditures within reasonable bounds was further evinced by his refusal to sign an extravagant river-and-harbors bill in 1887, and by his rejection of a measure, passed the next year, for refunding to the states the direct tax of 1861.   In all his vetoes he was rebuking a House, controlled by his own party, as well as a Republican Senate.

THE SURPLUS REVENUE AND THE TARIFF QUESTION

Cleveland's interest in "the application of business principles to public affairs" caused him to devote increasing attention to the tariff, a subject about which he knew little before entering

---

[1] "May God palsy the hand that wrote the order!" shouted the head of the chief veterans' organization, the Grand Army of the Republic. In a public address in 1887, Senator John Sherman termed the Democratic party "the left wing of the new Confederate army." It is worth noting that, when Congress ordered the return of the battle flags in 1905, the act was looked upon as "graceful" instead of "disgraceful."

office. Since 1881 a surplus had been piling up in the treasury at the rate of more than $100,000,000 a year. This excess of revenue over normal expenditures meant that the people were paying needless taxes, and also that money desirable for business development was being kept out of circulation. At the same time, the brimming treasury tempted Congress to intemperate expenditures — "surplus financiering," as it was called. Some of the money went toward diminishing the national debt, but more characteristic were pork-barrel measures, such as Arthur and Cleveland vetoed, and the lavish outlays for pensions. By keeping the surplus expended, the Republicans hoped to avoid reducing the tariff rates of 1875, the mainspring of the difficulty; but a growing popular demand obliged President Arthur to urge action to relieve "industry and enterprise from the pressure of unnecessary taxation."   In May, 1882, Congress, somewhat reluctantly, provided for a special commission which, after studying industrial needs, should propose a revision of the tariff "just to all interests." The nine members appointed were protectionists by conviction, four of them, including the chairman, John L. Hayes of the National Association of Wool Manufacturers, being directly connected with great protected industries. Nevertheless, the tariff commission ended its investigations by recommending reductions averaging from twenty to twenty-five per cent. At once lobbyists flooded the capital, among them Hayes himself who now, as spokesman for the wool manufacturers, set about to defeat the recommendations which he as the commission's chairman had accepted. J. S. Morrill and Nelson W. Aldrich in the Senate, joining with such men as William McKinley of Ohio and "Pig-Iron" Kelley in the House, worked with equal zeal; and, as finally enacted, the tariff of 1883 left the protective system virtually unchanged. While substantial cuts were made in internal-revenue duties, the reductions in import duties averaged less than five per cent, and these concerned manufactures little affected by foreign competition.

The attitude of the Democrats toward the tariff had been wavering and ill defined since the Civil War. Indeed, prominent leaders of the party, like Randall of Pennsylvania who voted for the tariff of 1883, were ardent protectionists. Nor had the Democratic majority in the House from 1875 to 1881 passed any bill to lower duties. Nevertheless, a rising sentiment among party members from the agricultural West and South favored tariff reform, and in the new House, meeting in December, 1883, helped defeat Randall's candidacy for the speakership. Yet a bill, fathered by W. R. Morrison of Illinois early the next year, proposing a twenty-per-cent horizontal cut of most duties, failed of passage, thanks to a coalition of forty-one Randall Democrats with the Republican minority. Even the platform on which Cleveland entered office reflected the protectionist influence, with the result that the party was pledged to tariff revision that would not "injure any domestic industries."

Cleveland was little given to abstract theories and at no time did he espouse that extreme form of doctrine known as "free trade." Confronted, however, by a large annual surplus revenue, he studied the problem assiduously and resolved to attack the evil at its source, a resolution stiffened by the continued success of the Randall Democrats in obstructing action. From a rather vague indorsement of tariff reduction in his message of 1885, he grew more definite in 1886 and finally in December, 1887, defied all precedent and startled the country by devoting his entire annual message to the matter. Branding the tariff of 1883 as "the vicious, inequitable and illogical source of unnecessary taxation," he declared that the surplus revenue would inevitably produce business stagnation. He charged the system of high protection with enhancing the cost of living for the masses in order to give "immense profits" to an exclusive manufacturing class. As a remedy, he proposed "a readjustment" to eliminate the "hardships and dangers" of the present tariff without, however, "imperiling the existence of our manufacturing interests." He excluded theoretical considerations as irrelevant, for, he added in a phrase quick to catch the public ear, "It is a *condition* which confronts us, not a theory." Cleveland's thunderclap cleared the air. The Mills bill, incorporating his ideas, passed the House in July, 1888, with only four Democrats opposing. Since the Senate was Republican, further action awaited the outcome of the presidential election.

Cleveland had already been renominated by the Democrats at their St. Louis convention the month before, with A. G. Thurman of Ohio as his running mate. The platform devoted most space to commending his tariff program. The Republicans lacked an outstanding man, for Blaine declined to allow his name to be considered. Meeting in Chicago on June 19, they finally gave the nomination on the eighth ballot to ex-Senator Benjamin Harrison of Indiana, a war veteran, strong protectionist and grandson of William Henry Harrison. Levi P. Morton of New York was associated with him. The platform resounded with praise of the "American system of protection," besides promising additional pensions from "an overflowing treasury," and declaring that the surplus should be wiped out by repealing internal-revenue taxes. The campaign was the first in American history to turn mainly on the tariff. Though the Democrats advocated merely lower duties, not a tariff for revenue only, Republican spellbinders shouted from every stump that their opponents were "free traders," while the Philadelphia merchant, John Wanamaker, who had had wide experience in raising money for the Y. M. C. A., appealed to the protected manufacturers for financial aid. "If you were confronted with from one to three years of general depression by a change in our revenue and protective methods," he asked them, "what would you pay to be insured for a better year?" Funds rolled in with unprecedented liberality.

Neither party, however, forgot the influence of the Irish vote in the election of 1884, and both platforms feelingly, though prematurely, congratulated the Irish Americans upon the approach of "home rule" in the Emerald Isle. This time the advantage lay with the Republicans, for Democratic tariff reform might be represented as a surrender to British manufacturing interests. A campaign poster displayed the names of the Democratic candidates under the British flag and the Republican ticket under the Stars and Stripes, with the statement, falsely ascribed to the *London Times:* "The only time England can use an Irishman is when he emigrates to America and votes for free trade."[1] Next to the tariff, Cleveland's pension vetoes came in for unrestrained attack. Moreover, he received but half-

[1] In pursuance of the same purpose, the British Minister at Washington was tricked into writing a letter to a supposed former fellow countryman, in which he declared that Cleveland would be the better President for England. This correspondence was given wide publicity by the Republicans.

hearted backing from the professional politicians in his own party, and in New York there is reason to believe that Tammany Hall threw its support to his opponent. In the election Harrison, carrying the large states by small pluralities, secured an electoral majority of 233 to 168, though in the popular vote Cleveland was the favorite, polling nearly 48.7 per cent to 47.8 for his rival. The buying of votes by Republicans in Indiana, Connecticut, West Virginia and certain other close states had been so bold and widespread as to make the campaign of 1888 probably the most corrupt in American history. An important incidental result was the great impetus given the adoption of the so-called Australian ballot system, which required secret voting and the use of uniform, official ballots. Beginning early in the year with Kentucky and Massachusetts, all but four states of the Union adopted the reform, completely or partially, within a decade.

Harrison's chief claim to distinction before taking office had consisted in long and faithful service to his party. As President he shrank from leadership and, though gentle by nature, his cold manner tended to repel even his political friends, and gave point to the saying, "Harrison sweats ice-water." From the outset he leaned heavily upon men high up in the Republican organization: Blaine, who had helped bring about his nomination; Speaker Thomas B. Reed of Maine, whose iron rule of the new House won him the nickname of "Czar"; and, for a time, large-state bosses like Senators Platt of New York and "Matt" Quay of Pennsylvania. Harrison made Blaine head of his cabinet, and rewarded Wanamaker with the office of Postmaster-General.[1] In dispensing patronage he permitted the spoilsmen to have almost unobstructed sway in the unclassified service. J. S. Clarkson of Iowa, Assistant Postmaster-General, fairly won the title of "headsman" by changing thirty thousand officials in a single year before he was himself beheaded. Like Grant, Harrison gave many jobs to relatives by blood or marriage. On the other hand, after waiting two years, he extended

[1] The other members were William Windom of Minnesota, Secretary of the Treasury; Redfield Proctor of Vermont, Secretary of War; W. H. H. Miller of Indiana, Attorney-General; B. F. Tracy of New York, Secretary of the Navy; J. W. Noble of Missouri, Secretary of the Interior; and J. M. Rusk of Wisconsin, Secretary of Agriculture (a cabinet office created in 1889).

the merit system to new classes of offices. His greatest service to the cause, however, was his appointment to the civil-service commission of Theodore Roosevelt, whose aggressive championship of the reform made his name a source of real terror to politicians in both parties during his six-year tenure.

Congress, now Republican in both branches, quickly set about to cope with the problem of excessive revenue. The platform allusion to the "overflowing treasury" was not forgotten, and James ("Corporal") Tanner of New York, upon becoming head of the pension bureau, is reputed to have cried, "God help the surplus revenue!" At any rate, in the six months he was allowed to remain, he recruited new claimants, reopened cases formerly rejected, and increased allowances already granted. In June, 1890, the general pension bill, which Cleveland had vetoed, was repassed by Congress. During Harrison's term the annual outlay for pensions rose from $81,000,000 to $135,000,000. Congress in 1891 did away with $15,000,000 more of the surplus by repassing the bill to refund the direct tax to the states, which Cleveland had also rejected. Increased appropriations for the navy account for other expenditures.

The Republican leaders knew full well that such methods dealt with effects rather than causes, but they were resolved not to reduce the tariff unless they could do so without reducing protection. Under the guidance of William McKinley, head of the House ways-and-means committee, a solution was found. A son and grandson of iron manufacturers, McKinley had long made high protection an object of almost religious veneration. As he read the lesson of the country's growth, "We lead all nations in agriculture, we lead all nations in mining, and we lead all nations in manufacturing. These are the trophies which we bring after twenty-nine years of a protective tariff. Can any other system furnish such evidences of prosperity?" He also believed the customs wall to be the chief bulwark of steady employment and high wages. Though the new tariff of 1890 lifted the general level of duties from thirty-eight per cent to nearly fifty, yet, through ingenious arrangements, a smaller financial yield resulted. Thus, removal of the duty on raw sugar lopped off $50,000,000 from the surplus revenue, while a compensatory bounty of two cents a pound to domestic sugar growers accounted for $10,000,000 more. In other cases, such as cotton and woolen textiles and metal products, the rates were fixed so high as virtually to exclude foreign importations. A further cut in the surplus came from taking the internal taxes off tobacco and alcohol.

In other respects as well the McKinley tariff was unique. Duties on farm products were substantially advanced in the hope of spreading the benefits of protection to the agriculturist in addition to the manufacturer. A second novel feature, that of reciprocity, was introduced at the urgency of Blaine, who charged that the bill as originally drafted disregarded the interests of our growing export trade, and particularly the possibilities of commerce with Latin America. As a result, certain articles commonly imported from Latin-American countries, such as molasses, tea, coffee and hides, were placed on the free list, with the proviso that the President might impose duties on them in the case of any nation which levied "unjust or unreasonable" duties on American products. The generally high rates prescribed by the new tariff were quickly reflected in retail prices, causing widespread dissatisfaction. The fall elections of 1890, coming about a month after the act went into effect, inflicted a stinging defeat on the Republicans, McKinley himself failing to regain his seat. In the new House the Democrats lacked but a few votes of a three-fourths majority. Though this popular rebuke came as a surprise, the law met the expectations of its framers in drying up the source of superabundant revenue. The provisions for revenue reduction, together with Congress's lavish expenditures, rapidly wiped out the surplus, and in Harrison's last months a deficit appeared.

THE TRIUMPH OF PROTECTIONISM

The new Democratic House, standing alone, could not hope to alter the tariff situation, but it passed a succession of "popgun" bills, designed to fasten public attention on the worst spots in the McKinley act as the election of 1892 approached. Under the circumstances Cleveland, who had been quietly practicing law in New York City since his retirement, inevitably became the Democratic candidate, though he was stubbornly opposed by the professional politicians, especially those connected with Tammany in his own state. After naming him on the first ballot, the convention, meeting in Chicago on June 21, added A. E. Stevenson of Illinois to the ticket. The platform, as presented to the convention, reiterated the pledge of 1888 for tariff reduction without injury to "any domestic industries"; but the radical wing induced the delegates to substitute a declaration that any tariff, except for revenue only, was unconstitutional. Though Harrison's renomination was regarded without enthusiasm by the Republicans, the party, hardly daring to repudiate a President of their own choosing, selected him on the first vote at Minneapolis on June 7, along with the New York editor, Whitelaw Reid. On the foremost question of the day the platform contained a ringing reaffirmation of the "American doctrine of protection."

As four years before, the storm center of campaign oratory was the tariff. Cleveland quietly disposed of the extreme utterance in the Democratic platform by declaring in his speech of acceptance, "We need not base our attack upon questions of constitutional permission." Once more the Republicans collected the sinews of war from the great industrialists, but a violent labor outbreak at the Carnegie steel works in Homestead, Pennsylvania (see page 208), helped turn public opinion against the party. The trouble stemmed from wage reductions and, since steel manufacturing enjoyed an unusual measure of protection, the vaunted connection between high pay and a high tariff seemed disproved. Cleveland won a decisive victory, polling 277 votes in the electoral college to 145 for Harrison, and forty-six per cent of the popular vote as compared with less than forty-three. The remaining 22 electoral votes went to a third candidate, James B. Weaver of Iowa, nominee of the People's party. The spectacular rise of this party denoted the emergence of factors and forces with which the old parties had failed to reckon. The story of the Populists, however, can be better understood in connection with the later discussion of the rising demand for silver inflation (see pages 261–265).

Cleveland returned to the White House, heartened by the people's indorsement of tariff reform and their confidence in his own unflinching integrity. At last the way seemed clear for the party to enact its policies into law since, for the first time in nearly a third of a century, the Democrats controlled all branches of the government. Appearances, however, proved deceptive. Cleveland's second term in office was cut across by currents and countercurrents in American political and social life — business stagnation, labor conflict, agrarian unrest (see pages 263–265). These events roused all the President's fighting qualities; but what had formerly been termed sturdiness of character now sometimes appeared to be mere stubbornness, while to many his independence of public opinion seemed indifference to the public welfare. Time, however, has softened such judgments, and has revealed him, in spite of his limitations, as an honest, fearless and patriotic executive.

In express recognition of the low-tariff elements in the Republican and Democratic parties, Cleveland made W. Q. Gresham of Illinois Secretary of State and John G. Carlisle of Kentucky head of the Treasury.[1] As in his first administration, he appeased the hunger for spoils with offices not yet in the classified list, but during the four years he more than doubled the number of positions under the merit system, bringing their total to about 82,000 out of 200,000-odd in the public service. Work on a new tariff bill began at a special session of Congress in August, 1893, under the leadership of W. L. Wilson of West Virginia, chairman of the ways-and-means committee. In striking contrast to the object of the McKinley act, the committee's purpose was to increase the revenue and decrease protection. The Wilson bill, adopted by the House in December, embodied certain principles which, broadly speaking, have guided later Democratic efforts at tariff revision. Basic raw materials used in manufacturing and construction — wool, sugar, lumber, iron ore and the like — were placed on the free list. As this enabled industrialists to lessen costs of production, protective duties on manufactures were generally reduced. In order to offset losses in revenue, new internal duties were placed on domestic liquors, tobacco and other luxuries and, for the first time since Civil War days, an income tax was adopted. This last provision — a two-per-cent levy on incomes above $4000 — was the price the Democrats paid for

[1] The other members were D. S. Lamont of New York, Secretary of War; Richard Olney of Massachusetts, Attorney-General; W. S. Bissell of New York, Postmaster-General; H. A. Herbert of Alabama, Secretary of the Navy; Hoke Smith of Georgia, Secretary of the Interior; and J. S. Morton of Nebraska, Secretary of Agriculture. On Gresham's death in June, 1895, Olney became Secretary of State.

Populist support of the bill, and was championed as a means of shifting the tax burden to those best able to pay.

Once more lobbyists swooped down upon Washington, determined to undo in the Senate the mischief wrought by the House. Their path was eased by the willingness of Democratic members from the industrial sections to join the Republicans in seeking rates beneficial to their own states.   The truth of Hancock's apothegm that the tariff is a "local issue" again found illustration.   Outright corruption may also have played a part.   Senator Quay, among others, admitted to an investigating committee that he had speculated in sugar stock for a rise when the sugar schedule was under consideration.   "I do not feel that there is anything in my connection with the Senate," he asserted, "to interfere with my buying or selling the stock when I please; and I propose to do so."   Under Senator Gorman's guidance 634 amendments were attached to the House bill, altering it not only in detail but also in principle.   The most important articles, including sugar, were taken from the free list, and protective duties generally advanced.   Only the income tax and the internal-revenue duties remained without material change.   After stubborn opposition by the House, the Gorman version was finally accepted; and in August, 1894, the President, bitterly assailing the Senate's action as "party perfidy and party dishonor," allowed the measure to become a law without his signature. The Wilson-Gorman act lowered the general scale of duties to about forty per cent.   Another blow was yet to fall.   In 1895 the Supreme Court by a vote of five to four held the income-tax provision unconstitutional, thereby reversing an earlier decision in 1880.   The majority decided a tax on incomes was a "direct" tax and thus subject to the constitutional limitation of being apportioned among the states according to population.[1]

This series of mishaps, along with the hard times lasting from the Panic of 1893, helped discredit the Wilson-Gorman act with the public.   While the tariff was only a minor issue in the next election, President McKinley when he entered office in

[1] In Pollock v. Farmers' Loan and Trust Company.   All later income taxation by the federal government had to await the adoption of the Sixteenth Amendment in 1913 because, of course, distribution of population is no index of the relative concentration of wealth.

March, 1897, summoned Congress in special session to revise the tariff according to the Republican pattern. The outcome was the Dingley act of 1897, a thoroughgoing protective measure which raised the customs wall to the highest point it had yet reached, an average of fifty-seven per cent. The principle of reciprocity, abandoned by the Democrats, was restored, though in so complicated a form as to be virtually unworkable. After a decade of almost ceaseless controversy victory thus rested with the ultraprotectionists. The remarkable prosperity which shortly burst upon the country was hailed by the Republicans as vindicating their most extravagant claims for the protective system. For ten years the tariff disappeared as a public question.

SELECT BIBLIOGRAPHY

Old Issues and New Attitudes, 1877–1897. Useful surveys, emphasizing party strife and political development, may be found in Dewey, *National Problems;* Peck, *Twenty Years of the Republic, 1885–1905;* Rhodes, *History of the United States*, VIII; and Oberholtzer, *History of the United States since the Civil War*, IV.

Republicans and Reform, 1877–1881. Some of the main actors are portrayed in Williams, *The Life of Rutherford Birchard Hayes;* Smith, *The Life and Letters of James Abram Garfield;* Fuess, *Carl Schurz;* Ogden, *Life and Letters of Edwin Lawrence Godkin;* and Cary, *George William Curtis.* Ostrogorski, *Democracy and the Party System*, gives a connected account of the Independent movement.

Sealing the Doom of the Spoils System. On this subject the best works are Fish, *The Civil Service and the Patronage*, and Stewart, *The National Civil Service Reform League.*

The Emergence of Grover Cleveland. McElroy, *Grover Cleveland*, should be supplemented by Nevins, *Grover Cleveland*, and Thomas, *The Return of the Democratic Party to Power in 1884.* The pension system is clarified by Glasson, *Federal Military Pensions in the United States*, and Oliver, *History of Civil War Pensions.*

The Surplus Revenue and the Tariff Question. For the evolution of tariff legislation and the triumph of protection, see the works by Taussig, Stanwood and Tarbell referred to at the end of Chapter VIII; Barnes, *John G. Carlisle;* and Olcott, *The Life of William McKinley.* On Reed's ascendancy in the House, consult Follett, *The Speaker of the House of Representatives*, and Robinson, *Thomas B. Reed: Parliamentarian.*

CHAPTER X

EMBATTLED INDUSTRY, 1865–1900

THE TREND TOWARD BIG BUSINESS

AS the tariff wall rose higher and higher, manufacturers benefited increasingly from the cutting off of foreign competition, and fresh capital poured into mills and mines. Meantime the expanding network of rails, together with high-pressure advertising, facilitated conquest of the consuming public. To meet the waxing domestic demand as well as the growing export trade, business leaders turned more and more to quantity methods of production. Industry conducted with limited capital on a small scale in a restricted area began to give way to operation with unstinted capital on a large scale for far-flung markets. Whether in manufacturing or transportation, the drift set strongly toward the merging of smaller into larger units with a consequent reduction of competition and a corresponding concentration of control. By the 1880's organization on a nation-wide basis became a distinguishing feature of the economic world. Large-scale operation rendered possible improved processes and great savings: better machinery, more efficient management, quantity purchases of supplies, decreased costs of competitive salesmanship, more effective resistance to the demands of employees. Such a plant could also make profitable use of wastes and by-products that smaller concerns had to discard. As "Mr. Dooley" (F. P. Dunne) with humorous license said of one of the mammoth Chicago packing houses, "A cow goes lowin' softly in to Armours an' comes out glue, gelatine, fertylizer, celooloid, joolry, sofy cushions, hair restorer, washin' sody, soap, lithrachoor an' bed springs so quick that while aft she's still cow, for'ard she may be anything fr'm buttons to pannyma hats." [1]

---

[1] Actually, the by-products include glue, gelatine, fertilizer, soap, leather, felt, knife handles, combs, buttons, brushes, pepsin, albumen, oils, oleomargarine, candles, glycerine, isinglass, lard, tennis strings, hair pins, umbrella handles, dice, perfume-bottle caps and artificial teeth.

With such advantages captains of industry could satisfy the clamor of investors for bigger returns and, in the long run, meet the public's demand for cheaper prices.

In order to command the financial support needful for huge undertakings, corporate organization replaced individual owner-ship and the partnership, forms commonly employed before the Economic Revolution revealed the new possibilities. Through the sale of stock a wide reservoir of capital could be tapped. Besides the expectation of unusual profits, the investor was attracted by the fact that he was liable only to the extent of his stock in case of business failure, a salient consideration in spec-ulative enterprises; in a partnership each member could be held for the firm's full indebtedness. The corporation enjoyed the further advantage of being able to plan its activities without reference to the lifetime of particular individuals. Moreover, if it wished to hide excessive profits from the public, it could "wa-ter" its stock, that is, present additional shares to its stockholders and so disguise the rate of dividend. Thus, a corporation earning twelve per cent might, by doubling the stock held by each in-dividual, cut the nominal rate of return to six per cent without denying each stockholder his full profits. In such case the board of directors could, with a specious show of sincerity, combat the demands both of consumers for lower prices and of wage-earners for better pay. Watering was also a regular practice of unprin-cipled financiers who seized the opportunity to sell stock to gullible investors without warning them of its diminished value. One expert estimated in 1883 that more than a quarter of the railroad capitalization represented water.

The actual process of absorption and consolidation was di-rected by business geniuses who, because of their daring, creative energy and relentless driving power, embodied many of the mythical elements of folk heroes. By common consent they were termed "steel kings," "coal barons," "railway magnates," "Napoleons of finance." Foremost among them were Cornelius and W. H. Vanderbilt, J. Edgar Thomson, Jay Gould, James J. Hill and E. H. Harriman in railroad organization; John D. Rocke-feller, H. H. Rogers and H. M. Flagler in the oil industry; Andrew Carnegie, H. C. Frick and Charles M. Schwab in steel; P. D. Armour, Nelson Morris and G. F. Swift in meat packing;

and Jay Cooke and J. P. Morgan in the financial field. Sprung from obscure origins, unhindered by moral scruples, they were fired by a passionate will to power. Some were builders with far-reaching plans; others were wreckers with no plans at all. The story of their activities is a singular blend of the heroic and splendid with the sordid and sinister.

For the most part, they were free to carry out their schemes without let or hindrance from the government, for the American people traditionally held to the gospel of individualism or *laissez faire*, that is, the right of citizens to be let alone in their economic pursuits. Yet the captains of the new order proclaimed the doctrine with tongue in cheek: while they opposed governmental intervention to their detriment, they constantly advocated interference with the free play of economic forces through tariffs, subsidies and the gift of natural resources. The popular belief in individualism was an inheritance from pioneer days when the doors of opportunity swung wide for all; only gradually did the public come to realize that, under modern conditions, unbridled freedom for the few threatened economic servitude for the many. The philosophy of the new leadership was a primitive one. It may be summed up in the phrase, "everyone for himself," or, in the terse expression attributed to W. H. Vanderbilt, "The public be damned!" "Law!" roared Cornelius the father, founder of the family fortune. "What do I care about the law? Hain't I got the power?" Yet, with all their cynicism, the best of these men were spurred by the conviction that they were laying the foundations of a new America, that the accumulation of colossal wealth by a select class would indirectly benefit all ranks of society.

RAILROAD CONSOLIDATION

Though occasional mergers of railroads had earlier taken place, the close of the Civil War ushered in the era of rapid and extensive amalgamation. Cornelius Vanderbilt was one of the first to vision the possibilities. Already past middle age, the possessor of riches amassed in steamboat traffic, he sold his vessels in 1865 in order to give his whole attention to developing a uniform rail route from the Atlantic Seaboard to the heart of the Midwest. Starting with a line joining New York City with Albany, he acquired the New York Central in 1867, making possible continuous traffic from New York to Buffalo. In 1873 he extended the road to Chicago by leasing the Lake Shore and Michigan Southern. When he embarked on his railway career, Vanderbilt's wealth amounted to about $10,000,000; when he died twelve years later at eighty-three, he left $104,000,000, the first great modern fortune. Much of it came from unscrupulous manipulation of railway stocks and from methods of competition akin to the ethics of the jungle. Meanwhile the Pennsylvania Railroad, under J. Edgar Thomson's leadership, outgrew its line from Philadelphia to Pittsburgh, gaining entry to Chicago and St. Louis in 1869 and establishing connections with New York City. Its business methods, however, formed a welcome contrast to Vanderbilt's. By 1875 three other trunk lines had been completed between the Atlantic and Lake Michigan: the Erie, the Baltimore and Ohio, and the Grand Trunk. Similar mergers took place in the Mississippi Valley. Three through lines linked Chicago and St. Louis by 1870, and others were later established.

It is doubtful whether enough business existed as yet to support all these railways. At any rate, the rival companies engaged in furious strife for traffic between major shipping points. Certain practices resulted that harmed both the companies and the public. Thus in 1869, and again in the years from 1874 to 1876, the trunk lines between Chicago and the seaboard waged relentless rate wars. A standard freight charge of $1.88 per hundred pounds in 1868 was slashed to twenty-five cents in 1869; sometimes the rates did not pay the expense of operating the trains. Such contests proved too costly to the railroads, however, to continue long at a time. Another scheme was to charge higher rates between some places than between others. Intent on taking business from their rivals, the companies held down freight charges between cities having several rail connections, while exacting excessive rates between points on their roads served by but a single line. As a result, it cost less to ship goods from Chicago to New York than to places a few hundred miles east of Chicago. The "long-and-short-haul" device aroused public indignation, especially among rural inhabitants who were the chief sufferers, but the practice enabled the roads to offset losses elsewhere. Equally objectionable was the discrimination against small shippers in the form of secret rebates to dealers in the same city doing a larger freight business. When, as sometimes happened, railroads themselves conducted other businesses, such as coal mining, they had a special incentive to employ unfair methods against independent producers who might compete with them.

To escape the evils of cutthroat competition, railroad managers from time to time tried various schemes of joint action. Rate agreements were entered into for the establishment of uniform charges, only to break down sooner or later for want of mutual confidence. Pooling, a somewhat similar device, proved more successful. By this plan the rival companies divided the freight business according to some prearranged ratio, or placed the total earnings in a common fund for like distribution. The first notable pool, that formed in 1870 by the roads connecting Chicago and Omaha — the Northwestern, the Rock Island and the Burlington — lasted fourteen years. Each line retained about half its earnings on the through traffic, leaving the balance to be shared equally among them. Meanwhile, railroads elsewhere made similar arrangements, their duration determined usually by the willingness of erstwhile competitors to trust one another.

Popular resentment at railroad practices deepened as the years rolled by. While the movement for state regulation, signalized by the Granger laws (see page 162), had a good effect, the transportation problem was, by its very nature, interstate or national in character, calling for action by Congress. As early as 1874 a Senate committee, headed by William Windom of Minnesota, proposed that the government build and operate a double-track freight line from the seaboard to the Mississippi as a means of keeping down charges of private companies. In 1874 and 1878 the House, under Western pressure, passed bills for the federal regulation of railroads, and in 1885 both Houses acted, though without being able to agree on a common measure. Final action was hastened by a decision of the Supreme Court which, reversing its earlier view, forbade individual states to fix rates on shipments passing beyond their borders.[1] In effect, the Wabash decision, announced in 1886, held that the ever increasing volume of

[1] Wabash, St. Louis and Pacific Railway Company v. Illinois. At this time about three fourths of the country's rail traffic was interstate in character. For the earlier decision referred to, see page 163.

interstate traffic could be regulated only by the federal government.

The upshot was the interstate-commerce act which Cleveland signed on February 4, 1887. It forbade excessive charges, pools, rebates and the long-and-short-haul discrimination, and provided for an interstate-commerce commission of five to guard against violations. This body, however, could not fix traffic rates or enforce its own decisions. If a railroad refused obedience, the commission must bring suit in a federal court. The law, being based upon the interstate-commerce clause, did not apply to traffic wholly within a single state. This first experiment in the national supervision of transportation proved a disappointment in many respects. In cases of appeal the Supreme Court was more apt to uphold the companies than the commission. Moreover, repeated decisions restricted the commission's powers within the narrowest bounds. The railways, for the most part, were able to continue their evil ways, though they were obliged to pay greater regard to external appearances than before. For example, since pooling was banned, the companies attained much the same result through traffic associations, which regulated rates and punished disobedient members. When the Supreme Court in 1897 by a vote of five to four held that traffic associations were illegal, a new consolidating movement began, which fruited in the combination of many hitherto independent lines.[1]

By 1900 great railway systems had come into being, designed to control all roads in a particular section of the country. More than half the nation's trackage belonged to six major financial groups, the Vanderbilt, Morgan, Harriman and Pennsylvania interests owning approximately 20,000 miles each, the Gould group 16,000 and the Hill interests 5000. Yet the act of 1887 was not without benefit. It paved the way for a better understanding of the railway problem, while the right of national regulation, at first disputed, was thoroughly established in principle, and a somewhat better adjustment of transportation charges secured. Moreover, official machinery now existed for railway control, machinery which Congress might strengthen and enlarge whenever public opinion should demand.

[1] In this case, involving the Trans-Missouri Freight Association, the court held that the association contravened the Sherman antitrust act of 1890 (see page 200).

CONCENTRATION IN MANUFACTURING

The movement for the consolidation of manufacturing paralleled that of railroad combination. Following the Civil War, industrial establishments, unhindered by legal barriers, waxed rapidly in size and, like the rail companies, waged desperate war with their competitors in the effort to absorb or destroy them. This stage in turn gave way to widespread attempts by the bigger concerns to stabilize particular industries through price agreements, pools and other devices for restricting output and boosting prices. Finally, with public opinion at full tilt against Big Business, both states and nation intervened with restraining laws. The unifying trend, while stronger in some branches than others, left untouched few industries of basic importance.

As one of the earliest and strongest industrial combinations, the career of the Standard Oil Company illustrates the process of concentration in other fields. In 1865 John D. Rockefeller, then a young man of twenty-six, was the guiding spirit in the Standard Oil Company of Cleveland, a concern capitalized at $100,000. Joining hands with powerful capitalists there and in New York, he enlarged his operations, absorbed rival establishments and, in 1870, organized the million-dollar Standard Oil Company of Ohio, which controlled four per cent of all oil refined in the United States. Now began a career of conquest that was Napoleonic in its boldness, scope and execution. By 1872 the Standard owned twenty of the twenty-five independent plants in Cleveland. In the ensuing three years Rockefeller and his associates acquired the biggest refineries in New York, Philadelphia and Baltimore. The Standard next obtained control of the refining business of western Pennsylvania. Thus, within a decade, ninety per cent of all the refineries in the land had passed into its hands.

Many elements, good and evil, made possible this brilliant campaign. Not least was the remarkable group of men who gathered about Rockefeller — Flagler, Rogers, J. D. Archbold and others, who strained every nerve to plan, plot and fight for the Standard, and exacted an equal devotion from their subordinates. Another factor was the superior efficiency attained through large-scale operation. The Standard not only set up factories to make its own barrels and produce its own acids, but it acquired tank cars and great underground mains, or pipe lines, for the transportation of crude oil. It also created selling agencies and, instead of paying large storage charges, erected storage tanks at strategic points. In addition to its main product, kerosene or coal oil, it utilized and popularized many by-products, such as lubricating oils, gasoline, paraffin and vaseline. Its success was further assured by unfair methods of competition, ranging all the way from secret rebates (which it enjoyed for thirty years or more) to bribery and blackmail of public officials. In 1872 the Standard, joining certain Pittsburgh refining companies in the so-called South Improvement Company, induced the railroads to agree to grant them secret rebates not only on their own oil but also on their competitors' shipments. The conspiracy was discovered before the arrangement went into effect and, in the face of a mighty popular wrath, all parties to the agreement disowned it. Before the public exposure, however, agents of the Standard used its existence as a club to force the sale of rival refineries. The Standard's favorite method of crushing competitors was through ruinous price-cutting campaigns, followed by proportionate increases once the object was attained.

By 1882 the Rockefeller group owned fourteen companies outright, besides a majority interest in twenty-six others. Price agreements and pooling arrangements had helped secure harmony of operation in earlier years, but now, with so extensive a control, the Standard undertook a novel form of organization, the trust. It was an old device fitted to new conditions. Adopted in 1879 and revised in 1882, the plan provided for a federation of the several companies under nine trustees to whom was confided all the stock of the individual companies and who thus exercised centralized direction. The original holders, in return for their stock, received "trust certificates," which entitled them to their proportionate share of the earnings of the whole. So successful did the scheme prove in securing unity of management that it prompted the organization of trusts in other fields, notably the American Cottonseed Oil Trust, the National Linseed Oil Trust, the National Lead Trust, the Distillers' and Cattle Feeders' Trust (popularly termed the whisky trust), the Sugar Refineries Company and the National Cordage Association, all formed between 1884 and 1887.

Meanwhile, the popular outcry against Big Business was reaching a climax. The benefits to the public from the improved quality and generally lower prices of commodities were obscured by the evil practices of strangling competition, corrupting legislatures, extorting excessive profits, watering stock and opposing labor welfare. The idea of monopolies had always been abhorrent to the American mind. Now, under the reign of *laissez faire*, not only the comforts but the very necessities of life — "from meat to tombstones," declared Henry Demarest Lloyd — were drifting into the maw of "soulless corporations." In 1884 an Anti-Monopoly party appeared in the national campaign, though with little success. Four years later the platforms of the major parties, recognizing for the first time the presence of the new industrial problem, joined in condemning trusts and combinations. As it happened, however, the first steps toward curbing them were taken by the states. In 1889 and 1890 fifteen commonwealths, mostly in the West and South, passed measures to ban conspiracies or agreements in restraint of free competition. Before the movement spent its force, all but New Jersey, Delaware and West Virginia acted. Unfortunately, remissness on the part of some states proved fatal because a corporation chartered in one of them might trade unmolested across state lines. In order to shut off this means of escape, Congress on July 2, 1890, adopted a national prohibitory law known as the Sherman antitrust act. It declared illegal every "contract, combination in the form of trust or otherwise, or conspiracy, in restraint of trade or commerce among the several States, or with foreign nations."

Passed in response to an imperious popular demand, the statute was drafted in such haste that the meaning of its apparently simple and direct language was, for many years, the subject of impassioned controversy. Should the words be taken literally, it followed that nearly every large business enterprise was illegal since, by its superior efficiency, it tended to be in restraint of competitive trade. If this were the true meaning, then the law aimed to prevent the benefits of large-scale operation as well as its evils, and all industrial combinations were equally at fault. But it was contended by others that, inasmuch as the terms used in the statute had been employed since ancient times in the common law, they had acquired a technical meaning different from their everyday usage. If this were so, acts in restraint of trade, when reasonable and fair, were not intended to be affected.[1] Other obscurities lurked in the statute. Were railway combinations forbidden as well as other kinds? Were labor organizations prohibited along with capitalistic combinations? These and similar questions had to be decided eventually by the Supreme Court.

The antitrust law, in its commonly accepted meaning, was too dangerous a weapon for the innocent to be used freely against the guilty. Largely for this reason the government made little effort to enforce it in the first ten years or so after its enactment. Furthermore, the Supreme Court, as in the case of the interstate-commerce law, took a conservative stand, usually construing the act as narrowly as possible. In reality, the last decade of the century beheld the formation of more industrial combinations than in the entire preceding period. Between 1860 and 1890 twenty-four had been organized with a total nominal capital of $436,000,000, but in the next ten years 157 came into being with a total nominal capital of $3,150,000,000. The years 1898–1901 were particularly prolific, ushering in an era of superconsolidation signalized by the formation of the United States Steel Corporation (1901), the first billion-dollar combination.

The special type of organization known technically as the trust was, however, a thing of the past, thanks to a decision by a New York court in 1890 against a unit of the Sugar Refineries Company and another by the Ohio supreme court two years later against the Standard Oil Trust.[2] But the word itself continued, in popular parlance, to denote any form of Big Business that in size approached a monopoly. In deference to the law the great capitalistic organizations now assumed a different legal framework. Some changed into single huge corporations. Others took the form of holding companies, organized to secure control of corporations in the same branch of industry through the pur-

---

[1] This view was eventually adopted by the Supreme Court in 1911 in the case of the Standard Oil Company *v.* United States (see page 338). The contrary view was upheld by Mr. Justice Harlan's separate opinion in the same case.

[2] The New York decision held that the combination partook of the nature of a partnership of corporations and hence violated the common law. In the Ohio case, the decision rested explicitly on the contention that the object was to form a monopoly.

chase of a majority of their stock. To many people the holding company seemed but the old trust doing business under a different name and with better legal protection. Indeed, changes in legal structure had no perceptible effect on efficiency of operation or the size of earnings. As a trust from 1882 to 1891 the Standard, for example, never made less than $8,000,000 a year; under a system of interlocking directorates from 1892 to 1896 the individual companies totaled from $19,000,000 to $34,000,000; and as a holding company the annual profits from 1899 to 1905 ranged from $34,000,000 to $57,000,000.

The centripetal trend in manufacturing and transportation was symptomatic of a similar movement in almost every other sphere of economic activity. As the century drew to a close, the telephone, telegraph and express businesses gravitated into the hands of a few corporations. The Amalgamated Copper Company, formed in 1899, controlled sixty per cent of all the copper produced in the land; and a few years later the United States Steel Corporation controlled about seventy per cent of the iron and steel production. In the field of banking and finance the Morgan and Rockefeller groups by 1900 dominated to such an extent that it was virtually impossible to launch any large business undertaking without the aid of one or the other. Thus the country was confronted with the spectacle of combinations and monopolies on nearly every hand. Thoughtful people were beginning to wonder how long democratic institutions could withstand the strain.

THE RISE OF ORGANIZED LABOR

If the public at large awoke only slowly to a realization of peril, the wage-earners had long since taken up the gage of battle with the new economic overlords. As industry changed over to large-scale methods and impersonal corporate control, the rift between those who worked for pay and those who paid for work steadily widened. More and more, workingmen lost the sense of being self-respecting craftsmen or masters of their own tiny shops, and became mere tenders of machines, their conditions of toil dictated by managers representing absentee owners. When stockholders clamored for bigger dividends or employers engaged in price-cutting competition, the laborers' pay was the first to suffer. The workday, which in many branches had been cut to ten hours during the short-lived labor movement of the 1830's, tended to grow longer rather than shorter, the employees toiling in gloomy, ill-ventilated structures amidst dangerous unguarded machinery. The rapacious demand for cheap labor drew increasing numbers of women and children into the mills and factories, while the plight of native workingmen was further aggravated by the hordes of immigrant laborers who contended with them for jobs.

Meanwhile, the number of wage-earners advanced with seven-league boots, marking the first appearance of a genuine proletarian class in American history. In 1860 only about one and a third million were employed in factories, mines and rail transportation; thirty years later the total reached four and a quarter million, a rate of growth far exceeding that of the population in general. An aggrieved class in the United States usually turns to political action for relief from wrongs, but for the wage-earners the prospect was not encouraging in an era when government and people were enchained by the doctrine of *laissez faire*. If some optimistic souls did from time to time try to launch labor parties, the shrewder labor leaders, mindful of the successes attained by capital through organized economic effort, devoted their energies to promoting similar combinations among the toilers. The factory system packed workingmen densely in cities where, mingling with their fellows and exchanging ideas, they responded readily to appeals to unite against the enemy.

War-time prosperity had caused a rebirth of the earlier abortive labor movement, resulting in the formation of local unions in many occupations, the setting up of city trade assemblies for the safeguarding of common interests, and the advent of ten or more national unions. In the flush years that followed until the Panic of 1873 the labor forces continued to grow in power. A promising attempt was even made, under the leadership of W. H. Sylvis of the Iron Molders' Union, to federate the various organized groups, together with certain reform bodies, into a single country-wide association called the National Labor Union. This organization, dating from 1866, advocated the eight-hour day, arbitration as a substitute for strikes, and, with particular emphasis, coöperative shops in which the workers should supply the capital and share the profits. Such coöperative experiments as were tried, however, including the iron foundries conducted by Sylvis's own union, failed either from mismanagement or unfair competition. The National Labor Union held seven annual congresses, the last one for the purpose of launching a labor party. But internal dissension rent the organization, and the crash of 1873 administered the finishing blow.

In the somber years that ensued, the labor movement reached a low ebb, most of the local and national groups dissolving or maintaining a bare existence. One of the survivors, however, furnished the nucleus for a second and more successful effort to combine the varied forces of labor on a nation-wide scale. Founded in 1869 at Philadelphia by Uriah S. Stephens and six other garment cutters, the Noble Order of the Knights of Labor differed from the National Labor Union in its insistence that all workers, skilled and unskilled, organized and unorganized, should band together in one comprehensive partnership without distinctions of trade or vocation. Otherwise its objects were much the same — to champion the eight-hour day, advocate arbitration, promote coöperation, abolish child labor and seek other industrial reforms. For ten years it grew but slowly. To protect members from persecution by employers, complete secrecy cloaked its doings, even the order's name being withheld from the public. With the return of prosperity in 1879 and the open use of the order's name two years later, the membership shot upward until in 1886 it reached 700,000, drawn chiefly from the ranks of unskilled labor. A fund to assist coöperative undertakings, established in 1882, helped launch 135 stores and factories, most of them in the mining, cooperage and shoe industries where wages were exceptionally low. These enterprises failed after a time for the usual reasons and, meanwhile, the sudden expansion of membership drew into the order many socialists, radicals and other jangling elements. In spite of their avowed attachment to arbitration, the Knights became embroiled in an increasing number of strikes, boycotts and other disturbances. The disastrous failure of some important railway strikes in 1886 cast further discredit on the order, precipitating it into a decline as rapid as its rise.

Another reason for its collapse was the advent of a rival labor group based upon a wholly different principle of organization. Initiated in 1881 by disgruntled members of the Knights of Labor, this body adopted its present name, the American Federation of Labor, when it reorganized on a broader basis in 1886. Discarding the idea of "one big union," the American Federation, like the British Trades Union Congress upon which it was modeled, was (and is) a confederation of self-governing labor bodies, supervised by a central board of officials. Not only national unions but also city trade assemblies, state federations of labor and local unions lacking national affiliations were eligible to membership. Thus the new organization made due allowance for the special interests of particular labor groups, and protected skilled workers from inundation by the unskilled. The central officials confined their activities to strengthening and extending the union movement, acting in an advisory capacity during industrial conflicts, and agitating for labor legislation. Apart from coöperative undertakings, the Federation sought many of the same objects as the Knights, including the eight-hour day, legislative prohibition of child labor and the improvement of working conditions in factories and mines.

From the outset the dominant figure in the new body was Samuel Gompers, born of Jewish parentage in a London tenement. As a member of the Cigarmakers' Union in New York, he had breathed into it a militant spirit which enabled it to issue from the depression years stronger than when it entered. President of the American Federation almost continuously until his death in 1924, he stamped it with his vigorous personality, being ever distrustful of intellectuals and theorists and firm against all efforts to commit it either to a socialist program or to the experiment of a labor party. The membership of the affiliated bodies grew from 150,000 in 1886 to 200,000 in 1890 and to 550,000 in 1900. One important element of the labor movement, the four Railway Brotherhoods (engineers, conductors, firemen and brakemen), held aloof, however, feeling that, because of their strategic position in American economic life, they had everything to lose and nothing to gain from casting in their lot with the others. Moreover, the Federation, thanks to its peculiar structure, excluded from membership the great bulk of unorganized and unskilled workers, perhaps ninety per cent of the whole. Its strength and opportunity lay in serving as the spearhead of a compactly welded minority.

INDUSTRIAL CONFLICT AND ADJUSTMENT

With the ranks of both labor and capital mobilized for defense and aggression, the stage was set for a trial of strength between the opposing forces. The antagonism usually turned on questions of wages, the length of the workday or the right of employees to organize, but behind such specific issues lay a fundamental difference in point of view. Labor asserted its inalienable right to have a voice in determining working conditions, to share more amply in the profits of industry, to raise its standard of living through better homes and more leisure. In short, labor's spokesmen insisted that the lot of the toilers keep pace with the increase of the wealth they helped create. Employers, on the other hand, viewed labor as but one of many factors in industry, its rate of pay to be governed by the "iron law" of supply and demand, not by humanitarian considerations or notions of fancied right. Indeed, the rôle of the wage-earner seemed to them of small moment as compared with the indispensable part played by financial resources, machinery, managerial ability and business enterprise.

With two such irreconcilable attitudes, protracted industrial warfare was inevitable, particularly in view of what Cleveland told Congress were the "grasping and heedless exactions of employers." Yet neither side was wholly blameless in these encounters, for, in varying degrees, both were actuated by irresponsibility, greed and criminality.[1] Nor did either party envisage such contests as other than purely private affairs, of no concern to the public. It was many years before the American people came to realize that, whichever combatant won a strike, the community was the loser, thanks to business paralysis, enhanced prices and the added costs of police protection and of charity. The first great struggle stemmed from a series of wage reductions on the Pennsylvania, New York Central and Baltimore & Ohio lines during the lean years after the panic. In the latter

---

[1] The extreme of labor lawlessness is illustrated by the Molly Maguires, a secret organization of Pennsylvania anthracite miners, whose career of terrorism and assassination was finally ended in 1876 by the punishment of the ringleaders.

half of July, 1877, rioting and lawlessness convulsed rail centers all the way from Baltimore to St. Louis and San Francisco. At Pittsburgh the contest resembled a pitched battle. State guardsmen in the neighborhood, called to arms, fraternized with the men. When militia from Philadelphia killed nearly twenty strikers, a raging mob besieged the soldiers for twelve hours in a roundhouse. Order was finally restored by patrols of citizens. Meantime, about 1600 cars, 126 locomotives and most of the railway shops and supplies had been destroyed, a loss estimated at $5,000,000. Yet here as elsewhere the strike failed.

If the return of prosperity in 1879 did not lessen the tension between capital and labor, strikers generally found it easier to win their demands, for in boom times industrialists could offset added costs by raising prices. According to statistics compiled by the federal bureau of labor, nearly 24,000 strikes and lockouts of all kinds took place in the score of years from 1881 to 1900, involving about 128,000 establishments and over 6,600,000 wage-earners, at a total loss to employers and employees of $450,000,000 and an incalculable cost to the public at large. The business recession of 1884–1885 yielded a startling harvest of industrial conflicts — strikes, sympathetic strikes, lockouts, nation-wide boycotts — causing the years 1885–1886 to be called the "Great Upheaval." Twice as many disturbances occurred as in any previous two-year period. Three involved the Gould railway system in the Southwest. The first, in March, 1885, resulted in the restoration of a ten-per-cent wage cut. Six months later a second strike, caused by discrimination against workers belonging to the Knights of Labor, also terminated triumphantly for the men. But the third and greatest of the disorders ended in their utter rout. Started as a protest against the discharge of a foreman affiliated with the Knights, the conflagration raged during March and April, 1886, in all parts of the Gould domain, throwing nearly 9000 employees out of work in five states and territories. The same year signalized a country-wide movement for an eight-hour day, a demand given special point by the need of work for the jobless. Sponsored by the American Federation of Labor, trade unions representing 340,000 men took part in it. Before May 1, the date set for a general strike, 150,000 wage-earners secured a shorter day (eight or nine hours) without a demonstration, whereas of those who actually struck but 42,-000 won their point. In many cases, the gains were presently lost through the aggressive activities of employers' associations formed for the express purpose of fighting labor's claims. Yet the conception of an eight-hour day excited wide popular interest, and the public gradually came to accept it as a just demand.

The next historic strike took place in July, 1892, among employees of the Carnegie Steel Company at Homestead, Pennsylvania, confronted with wage reductions and refusal to recognize the union. The arrival of 300 armed Pinkerton detectives, hired to guard the plant, precipitated a fierce battle, resulting in ten deaths and the injury of over sixty. Reënforced by 8000 militia, the company gradually resumed operations with non-union men. The strike dragged to a close in November, and the unions lost their grip on the steel industry. Meanwhile, far to the west, successive wage cuts due to the falling price of silver ore goaded the miners of the Cœur d'Alene district in Idaho to bloody measures. To combat strike breakers imported by the management, they seized the property and harried the "scabs" out of the district. But, at the governor's request, President Harrison sent in troops, martial law was declared, and the strike failed. This affair, however, proved the forerunner of intermittent disorders that ravaged Cœur d'Alene for years.

The widespread unemployment and distress bred by the Panic of 1893 plunged the labor world into another series of struggles which, because of their destructive character, made thoughtful men fear for the stability of the social order. The number of wage-earners involved in strikes during 1894 reached nearly 750,000, surpassing the mark set in 1886. The gravest disturbance took place in Chicago as the outgrowth of a drastic wage cut by the Pullman Palace Car Company. The employees' cause was promptly championed by the American Railway Union, a new organization formed by Eugene V. Debs in the hope of combining all rail workers in a single body. After demanding vainly that the company submit the dispute to arbitration, the American Railway Union ordered its 150,000 members to cease handling Pullman cars on all roads. In the last week of June the strike spread to twenty-three lines, affecting traffic operations in twenty-seven states and territories. The vortex of the storm, however, was Chicago. There, until the United States government took a hand, the principal antagonists were the General Managers' Association, representing the rail companies, and the American Railway Union. Lawless mobs and gangs of hoboes and criminals, always present on such occasions, terrorized the community, burning, looting and killing. The damages, direct and indirect, inflicted on the property and business of the country were later estimated at $80,000,000.

Despite Governor J. P. Altgeld's refusal to ask for federal troops, President Cleveland boldly intervened. On July 2, the government secured a "blanket" injunction from the federal circuit court, which forbade Debs, his fellow strike leaders and "all other persons whomsoever" to interfere in any manner, direct or indirect, with the operation of the railways. The next day 2000 soldiers were dispatched to Chicago. Cleveland found warrant for his unprecedented course in the constitutional obligation to safeguard the mails, protect interstate commerce and uphold the processes of the federal courts. On July 10 Debs was arrested on the charge of conspiracy in restraint of trade under the Sherman antitrust act. Released on bail, he was rearrested a week later on a new charge, contempt of court, that is, violation of the judicial injunction of July 2. The government's vigorous action broke the back of the strike, causing its complete collapse a few weeks later.

Other than as a great labor insurrection, the strike of 1894 is epochal because of the new legal conceptions and practices which issued from it. The employment of United States troops without consent of the state authorities marked a novel and impressive development of national authority. The application of the Sherman antitrust act to labor combinations — later upheld by the courts — threw unexpected light on that law. Perhaps most significant of all was the part played by the judiciary in using the injunction as a weapon in industrial warfare. Though this was not the first time it had so been used, the sweeping character of the injunction in the Pullman strike caused profound concern among the friends of labor. It was denounced as "judicial tyranny" — unjust because it seemed to range the might of the government on the side of the employers, illegal because those violating the court order were sentenced without trial by jury and subjected to penalties not prescribed by statute. Opposition to "government by injunction" became a cardinal issue of the American Federation of Labor, resulting finally in action by Congress under President Wilson intended to restrict its operation (see page 347).

The tumult and lawlessness attending this thirty years' war should not be allowed to divert attention from the constructive forces which, quietly but surely, were breeding saner relations between labor and capital. As trade unions grew in strength and improved in leadership, they were slower to resort to methods of coercion and violence. Amidst the "confused alarms of struggle and flight" they slowly learned lessons of self-control and responsible action in the economic sphere, not unlike the lessons in political self-government which the early colonists had learned through the town meeting and the provincial assembly. Enlightened employers, on their part, betrayed a greater readiness to meet their demands. Gradually, the practice developed in the better organized industries of settling differences through joint conferences instead of the ordeal by battle, the arrangements being embodied in so-called trade agreements. If such adjustment proved impossible, the alternative still remained of peaceful arbitration by disinterested parties.

At the same time, the gains won through trade-union methods were paralleled by an increasing departure by legislatures from a rigorous *laissez faire* attitude. Such concessions, though falling far short of the thoroughgoing statutes in Great Britain and Germany during these same years, attested the ever greater effectiveness of the lobbying activities of labor groups. Before 1879 various states had adopted legislation for shortening the workday, but for one reason or another these acts failed of their purpose, being unenforced or unenforceable.[1] In that year, however, Massachusetts set an example for other commonwealths by making genuinely effective her earlier ten-hour law in regard to children and women in factories. Other industrial states followed, and the evil of child labor declined a third during the eighties, only to thrive again in the next decade as cotton mills

---

[1] In 1868 Congress took an advanced stand by specifying an eight-hour day for workmen employed by the federal government, but for nearly twenty years the law was ineffectively administered when not wholly ignored.

thickened in Dixie. During the eighties, too, acts began to be passed for guarding dangerous machinery, assuring better sanitary conditions in factories, and providing for government inspection.

The ominous proportions of the Great Upheaval elicited, in 1886, the first presidential message devoted solely to the labor problem. Tacitly recognizing the right of employees to organize, Cleveland proposed a national commission to assist in settling industrial controversies of an interstate character. Congress responded in 1888 with a law for arbitrating differences between interstate railways and their employees on condition that both parties should consent and neither be bound by the outcome. Not until ten years later did the Erdman act specify that, once a dispute was submitted to arbitration, the decision should be final. Meantime, fifteen states had enacted legislation for voluntary arbitration and nonenforceable decisions in cases falling within their jurisdictions. Not only these but many other measures for labor welfare left much to be desired, while even adequate laws were seldom adequately enforced. Least progress of all greeted the efforts to secure a shorter workday for men through legislation. When such acts were adopted, the courts invariably held them unconstitutional, save in especially hazardous employments, on the ground that they interfered with the individual's freedom of contract.

SELECT BIBLIOGRAPHY

The Trend toward Big Business. The methods and ideals of the new overlords of business may be glimpsed in biographical treatments, notably Hendrick, *The Life of Andrew Carnegie;* Allen, *Rockefeller;* Harvey, *Henry Clay Frick;* Pyle, *The Life of James J. Hill;* Tarbell, *The Life of Elbert H. Gary;* Hovey, *The Life Story of J. P. Morgan;* Kennan, *E. H. Harriman;* and Burr, *The Portrait of a Banker: James Stillman.* A less favorable view is presented in Myers, *History of the Great American Fortunes.*

Railroad Consolidation. Informing chapters may be found in Sparks, *National Development,* and Dewey, *National Problems.* Riegel, *Story of the Western Railways,* and Moody, *The Railroad Builders,* sketch the history of leading roads. For the legislative background of the interstate-commerce act, Haney, *A Congressional History of Railways in the United States, 1850–1887,* is important. Technical aspects are emphasized in Jones, *Principles of Railway Transportation;* Ripley, *Railroads: Rates and Regulation;* and Daggett, *Railroad Reorganization.* See also references at the end of Chapter VII.

Concentration in Manufacturing. Hendrick, *The Age of Big Business*, and Moody, *The Masters of Capital*, offer excellent popular accounts. Moody, *The Truth about the Trusts*, is a statistical survey of capitalized industry and finance as it existed at the apex of the consolidation movement. For particular industries, see Tarbell, *The History of the Standard Oil Company;* Berglund, *The United States Steel Corporation;* Jones, *The Anthracite Coal Combination in the United States;* Mussey, *Combination in the Mining Industry;* Kuhlman, *Development of the Flour Milling Industry in the United States;* Copeland, *The Cotton Manufacturing Industry in the United States;* Clemen, *The American Livestock and Meat Industry;* and Thornton, *The History of the Quaker Oats Company.*

The Rise of Organized Labor. The fullest treatment of labor development and industrial conflict is Commons and others, *History of Labour in the United States.* Less detailed and briefer in compass are Perlman, *A History of Trade Unionism in the United States;* Orth, *The Armies of Labor;* Beard, *A Short History of the American Labor Movement;* and Ware, *The Labor Movement in the United States, 1860–1895.* For varied aspects, valuable information can be gleaned from Adamic, *Dynamite: The Story of Class Violence in America;* Cahill, *Shorter Hours: A Study of the Movement since the Civil War;* Browne, *Altgeld of Illinois;* and Berman, *Labor Disputes and the President of the United States.* Among the important special studies of organized groups are Lorwin, *The American Federation of Labor*, and Robbins, *Railway Conductors: A Study in Organized Labor.*

CHAPTER XI

HUMANITARIAN STRIVING, 1865-1900

PANACEAS

THE rank and file of organized labor were wage-conscious, not class-conscious. Like the discontented farmers, they sought a more generous share in the fruits of the capitalistic system, not its overthrow. In fine, far from declaring a class war on capitalism, they demanded a better chance to become capitalists themselves. This psychology pervaded not only all trade-union effort, but also the programs of the political labor parties which sprang up from election to election to enjoy a brief moment of life. However roundly they might berate the existing economic order as the "prolific womb" which spawned "the two great classes, tramps and millionaires," they asked but piecemeal reform, the correction of abuses that had become unbearable, such as the long workday, bad factory conditions, the exactions of monopolies, the dearth of money and the inroads of immigrant competition.[1] Polling but a handful of votes, they nevertheless, through their incessant agitation, did something to educate the public to the need for remedial action.

At the same time, however, a radical fringe preached more drastic measures. Through the labor world stalked German Marxian socialists, Irish Fenians, French communards, Russian nihilists, all rankling from Old World wrongs and scornful of the bourgeois aspirations of American labor. Mingling with their compatriots in the industrial centers, the startling extremes of wealth and want confirmed them in their belief that America was going the way of Europe. Socialist parties first became active in New York, Philadelphia, Chicago, St. Louis and other places shortly after the Civil War, making their chief bid to citizens of

---

[1] Of this type were the Labor Reform party (1872), an outgrowth of the National Labor Union; the Greenback-Labor party (1880 and 1884), which sought to combine the interests of rural and urban labor; the Anti-Monopoly party (1884); and the Union Labor and the United Labor parties (1888).

German stock. In 1877, under goad of the depression, the various local groups combined to form the "Socialist Labor party of North America." The socialist purpose was to apply surgery, not poultices, to the body politic. Seeing the source of all evil in the freedom of the few to amass colossal riches and acquire economic mastery over the many, they proposed to abolish the right of private property in the means of transportation and communication and in other public utilities and large-scale industries. They advocated that these be socialized, that is, that the people collectively own them and, in a sort of partnership with the employees concerned, operate them for the good of all. For a number of years the Socialist Laborites shunned ordinary political activities, seeking rather to worm their way into control of the Knights of Labor or the American Federation. At last presenting a ticket in 1892, they mustered but 22,000 votes and only 34,000 in the next election. The party was too foreign in its make-up, too aloof from American ways, to gain wide support. The result was the formation of a rival organization, called at first the Social Democratic party, then simply the Socialist party, which in 1900 won for its candidate, Eugene V. Debs, nearly 95,000 votes. Debs well represented the new influence in the movement. Born in Indiana and a friend of James Whitcomb Riley, thoroughly American to the core, he had imbibed his belief in socialism from reading tracts while jailed for his activities during the Pullman strike. Four times more he was to be the standard bearer, but neither his party nor the older socialist organization ever succeeded in garnering an electoral vote.

During the eighties another foreign philosophy contended for radical support. Anarchism was even more idealistic than socialism: it proposed to abolish the political state, and replace it with loosely federated voluntary groups, each following its own way of life, owning its means of production and exchanging its products with the others. Strongest among Chicago Germans and never numbering more than five or six thousand adherents, it greatly restricted its appeal because of the terroristic methods which most of the leaders advocated. A national gathering of anarchists at Pittsburgh in 1883 issued a "manifesto" vociferating revolution and confiscation, but the people generally remained ignorant of the movement until three years later. Then, on May 4, 1886, at a mass meeting in Haymarket Square, Chicago, addressed by anarchists in protest against the shooting of strikers by the police, an unknown hand hurled a bomb that killed one policeman and wounded many others. The fighting that ensued caused ten more deaths, six of them of policemen. In a burst of popular rage eight anarchist leaders (seven foreign-born) were promptly haled to trial; and although no trace of the bomb thrower could be discovered, nor the fact established that he had been incited by the accused, the jury found all eight guilty.[1] However unjust the conviction, anarchism received a blow from which it did not recover. Alexander Berkman's attempt during the Homestead strike of 1892 to kill H. C. Frick, head of the Carnegie Steel Company, confirmed the popular attitude, and President McKinley's assassination at the hands of another anarchist fruited in a law of 1903 banning anarchists from further admission to the country.

Meanwhile, the philosophy of discontent had been blossoming in native proposals for a perfected society. Between 1884 and 1900 over two-score American novelists indulged in such utopian fancies, works significant less as good literature than as an expression of the popular yearning to escape the chaos and injustices which the Economic Revolution had bred. One of these, Edward Bellamy's *Looking Backward, 2000-1887*, published in 1888, created a veritable sensation. The author visioned a social order in which the gigantic trust development had culminated in one all-embracing trust, owned and operated by the people in their own interest. Under a system of universal service everyone must work, hence everyone had leisure. Poverty and its attendant evil, crime, were unknown; hospitals served in the place of prisons; and the creative energies of mankind were released for unparalleled cultural achievement and the speeding of mechanical invention. Within ten years 400,000 copies were sold in the United States alone; and the proposed system of "Nationalism" proved so alluring that in 1891 there were 163 Nationalist Clubs active in twenty-seven states, though no political party was formed.

[1] Four were hanged, one took his own life and three were committed to prison. In a public statement at the time the usually mild William Dean Howells vigorously denounced the "principle" of killing men because of "their frantic opinions, for a crime which they were not shown to have committed." In 1893 Governor Altgeld braved the fury of mob hysteria by liberating those in the penitentiary.

Neither Bellamy nor any of his fellow utopian novelists used the terms *socialism* or *communism*, a fact that suggests the purely American inspiration of their thinking. All agreed, too, that the changes must come through education and the ballot, not violence.

Less sweeping in its scope, but quite as unacceptable to the bulk of the people, was another native solution, embodied in a book called *Progress and Poverty*, written in 1879 by Henry George, a self-taught economist. Impressed while living in California with the evils flowing from the practice of great proprietors in holding up land prices, he proposed a tax on land so adjusted as to take away the gain ("unearned increment") resulting from unusual natural fertility, mineral deposits, advantages of location and other values not due to the owner's exertions. This plan, he argued, would make it unprofitable for owners to let real estate lie idle; it would also tend to reduce the size of large individual holdings, thus multiplying the number of landholders. So considerable would be the revenue yield that the government could dispense with all other taxes, to the great advantage of business enterprise. The single tax, as it was called, excited wide interest, winning George a surprising vote in his unsuccessful race for mayor of New York in 1886, and forming the cornerstone of the United Labor party, which offered candidates two years later in the presidential election. Over 2,000,000 copies of *Progress and Poverty* had been sold by 1905. Abroad, however, the idea exerted a deeper influence than in the United States, where its chief importance, in the long run, lay in directing attention to more rational methods of local taxation.

The more extreme schemes for social redemption presumed a condition of human misery and despair in America which, save at times and in certain places, did not actually exist. Though the rich were growing richer and the poor had never before been so much in evidence, the middle class was increasing by leaps and bounds, constantly receiving additions from the lower orders and serving as a balance wheel in the social structure. Hence the new faiths made relatively few converts. On the other hand, the ferment of radical ideas helped leaven the thinking of many who had grown too complacent, or too acquiescent in things as they were. Not a few leaders of the progressive movement in the early twentieth century received their initial impulse from youthful reading of Bellamy, the socialist writers or Henry George.

COPING WITH URBAN SOCIAL PROBLEMS

The typical social reformer in the years after the Civil War believed that his proper business was to correct present abuses rather than to draw up blueprints of a future society. The zeal for improving conditions betokened, in part, a resumption of reform energies which the sectional struggle had, for a time, driven into a single channel. Ex-abolitionists and ex-workers in the Sanitary Commission, spurning the notion that to the victor belongs repose, turned briskly to other tasks of uplift, their ranks swelled by younger men and women who beheld shocking evils in the feverish growth of cities and the factory system. Thus, once the Negroes were freed, Gerrit Smith helped found the Prohibition party, and Wendell Phillips occupied his restless spirit with feminism, the temperance cause, colored education, Indian reform and labor rights. The dynamic leadership, however, fell to the newer recruits.

For many years the state and even some local governments had provided almshouses, orphanages, homes for inebriates, insane asylums and institutions for the deaf, dumb and blind. Most cities possessed, in addition, an infinite number of private benevolent societies. The difficulty was that these institutions, whether public or private, were too often run by incompetents; and, in so far as they dealt with the problem of poverty, they contented themselves with old-fashioned methods of indiscriminate almsgiving instead of studying how they might help the needy make a new start. In 1864 Massachusetts led the way toward better things by setting up a state board of charities to supervise and coördinate tax-supported relief institutions. Before the end of the century over half the Union had taken like action. Meanwhile, in 1877, S. H. Gurteen persuaded the private philanthropic agencies in Buffalo to join in a Charity Organization Society after the manner of a similar body in which he had been active in London. The plan involved not only coördination of activities, but also constructive methods of aiding the poor. Other cities swiftly fell into line until the century's close saw 138 such bodies in existence under various names.

Even more significant perhaps was the migration of resident colonies of social workers into the slum districts. There, amidst conditions of squalor and vice, they offered opportunities of instruction and recreation to all ages — kindergartens, boys' clubs, gymnasiums, classes in arts and crafts, and the like — on the principle that a fence at the top of a precipice is better than an ambulance at the bottom. The movement was deeply indebted to the example of Toynbee Hall in London, which many of the first American settlement workers had visited; and the effort appealed particularly to the idealism of young college men and women. From 1886 to 1900 more than a hundred social settlements were planted in American cities, the most famous being Hull House, founded in Chicago in 1889 by Jane Addams and her coworker Ellen G. Starr. Closely related to the general problem of aiding the poor was the question of decent housing. Jacob A. Riis, a reporter on the *New York Sun*, as well as other humane persons, agitated unceasingly for stricter legal regulations. Between 1865 and 1900 the New York legislature made four different attempts to regulate the building of tenement houses; but, thanks to the greed of landlords, faulty laws and lax enforcement, conditions only grew steadily worse. Nor was the situation much better in other large centers.

Directly or indirectly, all such efforts had a vital bearing upon the welfare of the growing generation. As cities walled in an ever greater proportion of America's future citizenship, society for the first time was obliged to give energetic attention to what Kate Douglas Wiggin called "children's rights." The steps taken at first were halting, but grew firmer as the years went on. When a mother was haled before a New York municipal judge in 1874 for beating and starving her nine-year-old daughter, the prosecution was undertaken by the Society for the Prevention of Cruelty to Animals, for as yet the law protected dumb brutes but not human offspring. In that dingy courtroom was born the Society for the Prevention of Cruelty to Children, which quickly developed branches in other places, and everywhere struck blows for more humane laws and better opportunities for the young. The crop of child-labor legislation in the North during the eighties (see page 210) stemmed partly from their agitation. Meanwhile, an awakened public conscience sought to restore to childhood a part of its heritage of outdoor play. In 1877 a minister at Sherman, Pennsylvania, devised the scheme of "country week" for city waifs during the stifling hot season, a plan eagerly adopted by charitable agencies in leading cities and supported by the "fresh-air funds" of enterprising newspapers. A little later, in 1885, a Boston society tried the experiment of providing sand gardens for poor children. From this small beginning rose the public-playground movement, which spread to twenty-one cities by 1900 and was in after years to form a normal provision of every sizable town.

Efforts were also made to deal more intelligently with juvenile delinquency, a problem whose gravity appears in the fact that in 1880 one out of every five prisoners in the land was twenty years old or less. Under the influence of European example, Z. R. Brockway, E. C. Wines and other reformers declared that the purpose of penal discipline should be to regenerate rather than to punish offenders. In 1877 the New York state reformatory was opened at Elmira, under Brockway's direction, to give the new ideas a trial in the case of young men from fifteen to thirty years of age. The inmates, freed from the usual association with confirmed criminals, were encouraged to shorten their stay through good conduct and earnest application to means of self-improvement; then, conditionally released, they continued under supervision long enough to show evidence of the sincerity of their reformation. These two principles, the indeterminate sentence and the parole system, worked so successfully that other Northern and Western states introduced the Elmira plan and, before the end of the century, even applied some of its features to older prisoners.

Urban congestion obliged public authorities to deal increasingly with the problem of contagious diseases. Since colonial times recurrent epidemics had taken their toll of townsfolk, but never before had these scourges had such dense populations on which to feed. Under spur of the peril Louisiana and Massachusetts set up state boards of health in 1867 and 1869, and thirteen other states did likewise before 1878. Then came the terrible yellow-fever pestilence of 1878–1879, which blazed a trail of death through the South, nearly depopulating Memphis. Twelve more commonwealths wheeled into line before 1882, with the rest presently following. To the aid of these state boards and the corresponding municipal bodies came certain epoch-making medical discoveries. In the 1870's and 1880's Louis Pasteur, Robert Koch and other European scientists laid bare the germ theory of the transmission of disease, and thus provided, for the first time, a rational basis for the science of preventive medicine. Armed with the new knowledge, health officers could make early and definite diagnosis of communicable maladies and devise more effective means of control. Quarantine was extended to other ills than the traditional ones of smallpox and yellow fever; and port cities were barred against the entry of imported plagues like cholera and typhus. Progress was made also in providing special hospitals for the isolation and treatment of contagious cases. At the same time, municipal enterprise in constructing water and drainage systems (see page 150) formed an important ally in the public-health campaign. The results, if not as far-reaching as later when the principles of public hygiene became more fully developed, were nevertheless profound, particularly in populous centers. For the country as a whole, the death rate fell nearly ten per cent from 1890 to 1900, while the average age at death rose from thirty-one to thirty-six and a half years. This improvement was due largely to diminishing mortality from tuberculosis, diphtheria and children's diseases. It was fortunate for America that, when the urban age dawned, medical advance made it possible to protect huddled populations from the dire scourges which for so many centuries had ravaged the cities of the Old World.

THE FIGHT AGAINST THE LIQUOR TRAFFIC

Urban growth also attracted acute attention to the liquor problem. The impressive gains for state-wide prohibition made in the 1850's had been mostly lost during the Civil War. Not only did soldiering foster the drink habit anew, but the government gave the traffic a certain respectability by using it, for the first time, as a productive source of national revenue. When the war closed, only Maine and Massachusetts remained "dry," the latter soon falling by the wayside. The capital investment in liquor manufacturing rose from $29,000,000 in 1860 to $67,-000,000 in 1870 and to $269,000,000 in 1890. With so vast a financial stake, producers and retailers entered politics to advance their interests and resist attempts at heavier taxation or prohibitory enactments. As early as 1867 the National Brewers' Congress resolved to "sustain no candidate, of whatever party, in any election, who is in any way disposed toward the total abstinence cause." We have already seen how, during Grant's sway, the whisky distillers were able to reach corrupt hands into the very precincts of the White House. The major parties avoided taking a national stand on the temperance question, fearing either to risk a new and uncertain issue or to lose campaign funds from the liquor magnates.

In the cities were the principal battlements of the "wet" interests. There the drink traffic employed countless persons at every stage of manufacture and sale; there the teeming immigrants saw no reason to forgo cherished folk customs in a land of freedom; there, too, the saloon with its free lunch and rough sociability served as a sort of poor man's club. Dry sentiment, on the other hand, predominated in the farming regions, as it long had. The churches most deeply rooted in rural villages and towns — the Methodist, Baptist and Presbyterian — crusaded tirelessly against "King Alcohol" and lent driving power to such bodies as the Prohibition party, founded in 1869, and the Women's Christian Temperance Union, which came five years later. The Prohibitionists demanded statutory suppression of the traffic, and woman suffrage as the swiftest means to that end. Though they never won an electoral vote, they outrivaled other minor parties by managing at least to keep alive and, by that feat, they furthered the work of temperance propaganda. More important was the W. C. T. U. which, under Frances E. Willard's leadership, became the most militant force in the movement. It waged merciless war against the foe on every front, inducing legislatures to require "scientific temperance instruction" in the schools, and battling everywhere for restriction or destruction of the liquor business. Even in the cities the dry cause gained adherents, notably among those who, unmoved by the usual emotional appeals, turned against the saloon power as the invariable ally of corruption, criminality and political reaction. Here and there, too, large employers were beginning to see the advantages of a sober laboring force. In 1895 a new and aggressive body, the Anti-Saloon League of America, was formed to coördinate the efforts of the various organized groups.

The actual tide of battle swept back and forth, with the saloonless area expanding or contracting as victory perched on one side or the other. Thus the question of state-wide prohibition was submitted to popular vote in at least sixteen commonwealths during the eighties, but only four rural Midwestern states — Kansas, Iowa and the Dakotas — emerged from the decade in company with the three rural New England states — Maine, New Hampshire and Vermont — that had it in 1880. Meanwhile, on the principle of divide-and-conquer, the drys scored greater triumphs, particularly in the rural sections of the Midwest and South, through local option, that is, self-denying regulations adopted by local popular vote. Elsewhere, in the hope of lessening their number, saloons were obliged to operate under high licenses costing from $500 to $1000 a year. One state, South Carolina, from 1893 to 1907 even tried the experiment of exclusive government agencies for dispensing intoxicants. Notwithstanding the increasing restrictions, the per-capita consumption of alcoholic stimulants for the country at large nearly trebled from 1860 to 1900. The most optimistic drys hardly dreamed that within the span of another generation their cause would find lodgment in the federal Constitution.

THE ADVANCE OF WOMEN

The leadership assumed by women in the temperance cause, the social-settlement movement and certain other reform enterprises evidenced their changing rôle in the world of men. The impact of events had jarred them loose from the traditional seclusion of the home, obliging them whether they would or not to take an increasing part in the larger life outside. Thus the Economic Revolution forced more and more of them to find jobs as factory hands, sweatshop workers, telephone operators, typists, clerks and helpers in offices and shops. Between 1870 and 1900 the total number of female breadwinners over sixteen years old leaped from 1,800,000 to 5,300,000. Meanwhile the portals of higher education swung open for middle-class girls as never before. Starting with Vassar in 1865, Wellesley and Smith following a decade later, women's colleges began to offer instruction equal to that of the best men's institutions. More characteristic of the West was coeducation which, though dating from before the war, now enlisted the powerful support of the state universities.   Between 1865 and 1874 at least fourteen state universities, all but three of them in the Middle or Far West, opened their courses to both sexes.   Their number included Michigan which in 1870 admitted girl students after declining to do so for nearly three decades.   The president of the university, at the end of ten years of the new system, solemnly assured an inquiring Englishwoman that "none of the ladies had found the curriculum too heavy for their physical endurance."   By 1880 the number of mixed colleges had grown from twenty-odd at the close of the war to 154.   In another twenty years over seventy per cent of all institutions of higher learning were coeducational.

As higher education reached an ever widening circle of women, they began to push into the professions.   The displacement of men as school-teachers took place so rapidly that in 1900 two out of every three were women.   In law, medicine and theology their path was thornier because of the reluctance of professional schools to afford them training.   Yet by 1879 they were allowed to plead before the Supreme Court, and the final years of the century saw over a thousand women lawyers in the nation, besides nearly as many dentists, more than 3000 ministers, and almost 7500 doctors and surgeons.   As authors, too, they occupied an increasingly important place, and in Emily Dickinson supplied the most talented writer of poetry.   Meanwhile, urban middle-class housewives, finding time for wider interests as a result of the rapid introduction of new household conveniences, took an active part in the development of women's clubs.   From the first two groups in 1868, the Sorosis in New York and the New England Woman's Club in Boston, the number grew so rapidly and spread so far that in 1889 they joined in a nationwide league called the General Federation of Women's Clubs. Such groups, as the years wore on, gave less attention to art, literature and cultural subjects and more to civic and social problems, some becoming centers of agitation for women's rights and equal suffrage.

As a result of the inexorable march of events, the old common-law discriminations against married women, already beginning to crumble before the Civil War, continued to fall before the onslaught of new legislation. Through most of the Union wives were given the right to own and control their property, retain their earnings, make contracts, sue and be sued. In 1900 only a handful of commonwealths — Georgia, Louisiana, New Mexico, the Dakotas and California — still expressly designated the husband as head of the family and the wife subject to him. So generally was the principle of civil equality recognized that it was clear the remaining disabilities would presently be wiped out. Less heartening was the progress toward political equality. The proposal of universal suffrage encountered the inertia, prejudice and active hostility not only of most men but also of a majority of the women themselves. The opponents protested that woman would lose her charm, that sex equality would cause the loosening of family ties, and that the feminine intellect was unfit to cope with problems of state. On the other side were arrayed such forceful figures as Elizabeth Cady Stanton, Susan B. Anthony, Lucy Stone (who refused to take her husband's name of Blackwell), Anna Howard Shaw and Carrie Chapman Catt. They held that each sex had a distinctive contribution to make to public life, and that failure to accept the logic of woman's altered status in society was an attempt to "put the bird back into the egg."

As in the case of temperance, the earlier interest in equal suffrage had been shoved into the background by the Civil War. When peace came, the feminist leaders, arguing from the vantage point of the unstinted war services their sex had rendered, flooded Congress with petitions to obtain the ballot along with the freedmen. Their hopes dashed, they proceeded in 1869, with some difference of opinion, to organize two woman-suffrage associations, the National, which under Mrs. Stanton's leadership strove for the ballot through state action, and the American, which struck boldly for a federal amendment. Besides the clergyman Henry Ward Beecher, who headed the latter body, other prominent men lent their pens and voices to the cause, among them George W. Curtis, Senator Hoar and John Greenleaf Whittier. The Knights of Labor and the American Federation also rallied to the standard. But if the outstanding suffragists hailed from the East, the chief gains were made in the democratic West. Campaign after campaign was fought in state after state. The initial steps, as in Great Britain and the Scandinavian countries during these same years, took the form of the right to vote on certain questions in local elections. Though Kansas's example in 1861 of bestowing the vote in school elections went without emulation for a number of years, from 1875 to 1895 similar action was taken by sixteen commonwealths, representing all parts of the nation but the old Confederacy. Moreover, several states — Kansas and Montana in 1887, Iowa in 1894 and Louisiana in 1898 — gave women the ballot in local bond issues, taxation questions and the like. But full equality, the cherished goal of the feminists, was not attained in any state until Wyoming, which as a territory had practiced it since 1869, entered the Union in 1890. Colorado followed in 1893, Utah and Idaho in 1896. Meanwhile, determined efforts had been made to secure favorable action from the federal government. The great political parties ignored the question, while the Prohibitionists may have hurt it by linking it with their unpopular cause. Nevertheless, between 1878 and 1896, committees of the Senate reported four times in favor of a suffrage amendment, and House committees twice. But action went no further. For some years to come most Americans were to regard universal suffrage as merely an aberration of the wild and woolly West.

THE CHANGING CHURCH

These years, too, brought momentous changes in the field of religion. The growth of cities, the glut of immigrants there, the emergence of a proletarian class, raised problems which the church was ill prepared to meet. In the score of years after 1868, 200,000 more people packed into the district below Fourteenth Street in New York, while seventeen Protestant churches moved out and only two Catholic edifices and one Jewish were added. When Miss Addams founded Hull House in Chicago, the neighborhood contained nine churches and missions and 255 saloons. In the poorer quarters of these and other cities saloons and dens of vice sometimes outnumbered houses of worship a hundredfold. American Protestantism, the product of a rural, middle-class society, was rapidly losing its hold on urban wage-earners. Though the Y. M. C. A. and the Y. W. C. A., both dating from mid-century, provided countless young men and women with decent lodgings, gymnastic facilities and Christian surroundings, these agencies too were middle-class institutions, out of touch with the toiling masses. Even such spirited revivalists as Dwight L. Moody and Ira D. Sankey performed their chief work among laggard members of existing congregations, doing little to reach the many without church affiliations. The growing rift was due partly also to the failure of organized religion to cry out against the malpractices of Big Business, a silence that caused labor leaders to assail the clergy as indifferent, if not antagonistic, to the plain people.

Yet some countervailing influences were at work. The enormous foreign influx brought untold numbers of Catholics and Jews to American shores, and the success of these two faiths in attracting and holding the newcomers formed an object lesson for Protestant sects. In 1879 the Salvation Army, spreading from England to the United States, commenced its evangelistic labors on the city streets, preaching to "rumdom, slumdom and bumdom" the exciting gospel of repentance and reform. Ten years later it branched out into social work, maintaining cheap lodgings, employment agencies and rescue homes. Meanwhile, Protestant churches in the larger centers began to develop "institutional" features, that is, conduct organized philanthropic and educational work among the lowly. Anticipating the first social settlements by a few years, an increasing number of congregations in the eighties provided reading rooms, day nurseries, recreational facilities and manual-training courses for the poor along with religious instruction. Leaps in membership quickly justified their course and by 1894 institutional churches had become numerous enough to form a nation-wide league.

In harmony with these new tendencies, ministers here and there began to insist that Christianity in every way be made a part of, rather than be apart from, life. Notable among these pioneers of the social gospel were Lyman Abbott, Beecher's successor both as editor of the *Christian Century* and as pastor in Brooklyn; Josiah Strong, general secretary of the Evangelical Alliance; and Washington Gladden, Congregational minister in Springfield, Massachusetts, and Columbus, Ohio. Gladden, for example, not only expounded his views in widely read books like *Applied Christianity* (1886) and *Tools and the Man: Property and*

Industry under the Christian Law (1893), but took an active part in the hurly-burly of industrial strife, ever maintaining the "right and necessity of labor organizations." His hoped-for solution was an "industrial partnership" in which the workers would receive "a fixed share in the profits of production." He scourged religious bodies for accepting gifts from possessors of bloated wealth, branding such contributions as "tainted money," defiling the recipient as well as the giver. At the same time Cardinal Gibbons exerted a similar influence within the Roman Catholic fold. In 1886, through intercession at Rome, he saved the Knights of Labor from papal condemnation. Against opposition from within his own ranks he also upheld the right of Catholics to espouse Henry George's panacea of the single tax. His bold course received high sanction in 1891 when an encyclical of Leo XIII, though denouncing socialism, approved of trade unions and called for the application of Christian ethics to the relations of capital and labor. In the case of all faiths such churchmen were the exception rather than the rule. Yet their advent marked a definite turning toward an increased social emphasis in religion. Later years would yield a fuller fruition of their teachings.

As if the problem of social adjustment were not enough, organized religion also faced an intellectual crisis. To defenders of the old-time theology the validity of the Bible itself seemed challenged by new findings of science and scholarship. Religion, in other words, was confronted by one of those recurrent conflicts between orthodoxy and heterodoxy, between fundamentalism and modernism, which historically have formed a law of its growth. Those who led in the effort to socialize religious practice were usually also at the forefront of the effort to liberalize religious thought. One source of dissension was the theory of biological evolution, which gradually had won friends in America after its elucidation by Charles Darwin in *The Origin of Species* (1859). In apparent contradiction to the Biblical account of creation, the Darwinian hypothesis was generally condemned by the clergy as materialistic and atheistic. A growing number of American scientists, however, accepted it; and, following in their train, liberal ecclesiastics like Beecher, Abbott and Gladden insisted that the theory, at the most, imperiled theology, not genuine religion. Indeed, they saw in evolution a new and grander revelation of the mysterious way God moves his wonders to perform. The process of acceptance, however, was slow, particularly in those denominations which stressed emotional above intellectual factors.

Another shock to orthodoxy resulted from the "higher criticism," an attitude fostered by German scholars who had freshly studied the books of the Bible as historical and literary documents. At the same time, an increasing knowledge of Buddhism and other Asiatic religious systems, popularized by James Freeman Clarke's *Ten Great Religions* (1871), seemed to take away from the exclusive character of the Christian faith. As a result of these various influences, sharp divisions occurred among both clergy and laity, fruiting oftentimes in heresy trials and the expulsion of those liberally disposed. Yet, as the years went by, a spirit of tolerance began to make itself felt. If clerics could not always agree on points of theology, they slowly learned that, in the interests of common spiritual service, they could at least agree quietly to disagree. Equally indicative of a new attitude was the gradual admission into theological seminaries of courses on the higher criticism, comparative religion and the relations of science and religion.

Many devout Protestants were also deeply disturbed by the growing secularization of the Sabbath. In the cities six days of grinding toil turned the masses to thoughts of pleasure on the seventh. There, too, the immigrant influence was strong — the Germans accustomed to their Continental Sabbath, the Irish and other aliens with their Catholic Sunday, the Jews with their religious observance of Saturday. In vain did the American Sabbath Union and other similar bodies try to stay the tide, though they were somewhat more successful when they joined with trade unions in resisting employers' demands for Sunday labor.

Yet, despite the many difficulties which beset religion, church membership grew both numerically and relatively. The Catholic gain was particularly notable because of immigrant accessions. A new religious sect also appeared on the scene, Christian Science, based upon *Science and Health*, a book first published by Mrs. Mary Baker G. Eddy in 1875. The latest of a long succession of New England-inspired cults, it rejected medicine as the science of health and substituted therefor a belief in the supremacy of mind over matter. "Disease is caused by mind alone," it taught, and may be banished by working in harmony with Christ's teachings as interpreted by Mrs. Eddy. The new system appealed particularly to nerve-racked urban folk and spread rapidly from Boston to New York and the cities of the Midwest. Outside strictly denominational activities, the religious spirit also pervaded most of the philanthropic efforts of the time. A great majority of the social workers and other humanitarians were church members, and from religion they received an enduring bent toward the service of mankind.

WHITE, BLACK AND RED

While most of the social maladjustments of the time were rooted in urban conditions, two major problems, both affecting race relations, were primarily rural in character. One, the Negro question, concerned the South; the other, the problem of assimilating the Indian, related to the Great West. President Hayes's withdrawal of the last federal garrisons in 1877, after a decade of ceaseless governmental activity on behalf of the ex-slave, was a tacit admission of the South's right to solve the Negro question in its own way, as well as evidence of the North's growing absorption in the complexities of its new industrial order. Moreover, for twelve years the Republicans lacked simultaneous control of both Congress and the presidency and hence could not have interfered if they had wished. The bulk of the Negroes continued to dwell in Dixie, content to work out their destiny in the land where slavery had planted them. Increasing from four million in 1860 to six in 1880, their number advanced to eight million in 1900, a relative growth considerably less than that of the whites about them. Though the colored birth rate was higher than that of the dominant race, this fact was offset by greater infant mortality and by the inroads of diseases which the paternalistic life of the prewar plantation had served to check.

Deserted by their erstwhile Northern allies, the Afro-Americans faced a long, sordid, unremitting struggle with ignorance and poverty. The statesman of this new emancipation was Booker T. Washington, himself a former slave, who in 1881 founded his Normal and Industrial Institute at Tuskegee, Alabama, in the heart of the Lower South. Believing that his people should perfect the mechanical skills for which they had shown an aptitude in slavery, he and his coworkers, assisted by funds from the state legislature and Northern sources, provided training in all the trades and occupations necessary for gaining a foothold in Southern economic life. Deploring the incessant agitation by Negro demagogues for immediate equality, he constantly urged the race to "make itself so valuable to the community in which it lives that it will not merely be tolerated, like a poor relative, but rather welcomed and sought after." "The opportunity to earn a dollar in a factory," he declared, "just now is worth infinitely more than the opportunity to spend a dollar in an opera-house." Washington's leadership influenced the course of colored education everywhere. The rapid extension of teaching facilities was hampered by the postwar poverty of the South, and particularly by the policy of maintaining separate schools for the two races, a costly plan which commonly resulted in inferior instruction for the blacks. Northern philanthropy did something to relieve the situation, notably through the Peabody Fund, established in 1867, the John F. Slater Fund in 1882 and Daniel Hand's generous gift to the American Missionary Association six years later. Despite deterrent conditions Negro illiteracy declined from seventy per cent in 1880 to forty-four in 1900.

The mass of the people continued to live on the land. Handicapped on the one hand by the shiftless habits learned in slavery and, on the other, by the vicious crop-lien system (see page 122), they nevertheless advanced steadily toward the goal of independent farm ownership. By 1890 they owned nearly a fifth of their homes. Ten years later the total value of the farms they operated reached almost half a billion dollars. At that time about 200,000 owned their farms, while about 500,000 more were employed as tenants. This progress was a substantial testimonial to a people who were virtually landless in 1860. Others worked in domestic and personal service, mostly in the towns, where also a growing minority entered the skilled trades. Generally speaking, the Afro-American might walk in the same direction as his white neighbor provided he walked apart. The color line was drawn most rigidly at points where racial association implied social or political equality. To the usual provision for separate schooling and the universal ban against intermarriage, Tennessee in 1881 added a new restriction by passing a so-called Jim Crow law, requiring different coaches or compartments on trains. Other states followed, and presently colored persons throughout the South found themselves compelled, by law or custom, to accept separate and usually poorer accommodations in public conveyances, hotels, restaurants and amusement places, when admitted at all. Violent racial antipathy sometimes broke out in the mob murder of individual Negroes. Between 1882 and 1900 there were over 1800 lynchings, mostly of blacks. Such blots on Anglo-American justice, however, served to emphasize the generally peaceable relations between the races.

Meanwhile, the ruling class proceeded to steal away the political gains which the Reconstruction constitutions had guaranteed the freedmen. Without ceasing to stuff the ballot box and to use intimidation as means of neutralizing the colored vote, they invented discriminatory legal devices such as gerrymandering arrangements to reduce Negro representation and the poll-tax requirement for voting. For the same purpose they devised ingenious electoral regulations like that of South Carolina which, after 1882, rendered difficult the task of the illiterate black by requiring the voter to place each of his many ballots correctly in the eight or more boxes before him. In the next decade the dominant race went even further. The growth of agrarian unrest in the late eighties had divided the white electorate into two factions, with the result that the potential balance of power often lay with the Negroes. To allay this threat to white supremacy, steps were taken to alter the suffrage provisions in the state constitutions, though care had to be exercised not to infringe the letter of the Fifteenth Amendment (see page 116). The three commonwealths in which colored inhabitants predominated were the first to act. Mississippi set the pace in 1890 by limiting the ballot to paid-up taxpayers who were able to read a passage from the state constitution, or understand it when read to them, or give "a reasonable interpretation thereof." The flexible clause was avowedly designed to enable election officials to disfranchise illiterate blacks without disfranchising illiterate whites. Five years later South Carolina followed with a somewhat similar provision, and then, in 1898, Louisiana found a means of exempting whites from the property and educational tests through the so-called grandfather clause. Over a period of several months she admitted permanently to the voting list all male applicants whose fathers or grandfathers had possessed the vote before 1867. Other states presently devised ingenious variants of these restrictions. Under the new arrangements the proportion of colored voters continued to fall. Torn from his giddy heights of Reconstruction times, the Negro became a negligible factor in Southern politics.[1]

The Indian problem was of a different character, though hardly less perplexing. Reduced to a subject people by the 1880's, the vast majority of the red men lived the traditional tribal life within the narrow bounds of government reservations, their health impaired by the white man's diseases and their self-reliance sapped by annuities and rations supplied by the Great White Father in Washington. Many of the government agents to whose care they were confided proved corrupt or incompetent, while the licensed white traders with whom they dealt habitually overcharged and otherwise cheated them. To this record of mistreatment should be added the wholesale disregard of the natives' rights by both the frontiersmen and the government, resulting oftentimes in the grossest inhumanity. On the other hand, Congress, after aiding missionary schools among the tribesmen for over half a century, in 1873 embarked on the policy of providing educational facilities under direct federal auspices. The annual appropriation for this purpose rose in fifteen years from $20,000 to more than a million. As in the case of Negro education, the emphasis was on instruction in agriculture, home economics and other practical pursuits in order to fit the young people for a place in modern economic life. By 1880 over 7000 were attending such schools. Yet education in itself was not enough so long as the Indians continued in the old reservation life with its tribal ownership of land, dependence on government gifts, and other enervating conditions. Congress for many years, however, resisted repeated recommendations by Presidents, Sec-

[1] In Williams *v.* Mississippi (1898) the Supreme Court declined to hold the Mississippi suffrage provision contrary to the Fifteenth Amendment on the ground that the complainants had failed to prove actual discrimination against Negroes in its operation. In 1914, however, the court held grandfather clauses in Oklahoma and Maryland in conflict with the amendment. See Guinn *v.* United States and Myers *v.* Anderson.

retaries of the Interior and Indian commissioners to end the communal system and introduce individual ownership.

That a more enlightened policy was eventually adopted was due to two influences. One was a strong protest on the part of Eastern humanitarians outraged by multiplying instances of Indian wrongs. First finding passionate expression in Helen Hunt Jackson's book *A Century of Dishonor* (1881), this sentiment in the two years following caused the formation of the Indian Rights Association and the annual Lake Mohonk Conference of Friends of the Indians. The other influence was the growing Western demand, as free homesteads grew scarcer, that the reservations be broken up in order to provide additional tracts for whites. The Easterners sought rights for the Indians, the Westerners lands for themselves. President Cleveland, whose sympathies had been deeply stirred by Mrs. Jackson's pathetic recountal, actively interested himself in the problem, and the upshot was the passage in 1887 of a general allotment law, sponsored by Senator Henry L. Dawes of Massachusetts. By the Dawes severalty act the President was authorized to end the tribal government in any reservation whenever time and circumstances seemed appropriate, and parcel out the land among individual owners according to certain fixed amounts.[1] To protect such owners from white avarice, they were denied the liberty to sell or mortgage their holdings for twenty-five years. In all other respects they should enjoy the same rights as white citizens, including the privilege of voting. The land remaining after allotments were made might be bought by the government for sale to actual settlers, the money to be held as a trust fund for educating and civilizing the Indians concerned.

The fruits of the new law justified its popular nickname of the "Emancipation Act of the Indians." Over 21,000,000 acres passed into the hands of 150,000 red men between 1887 and 1906, while the government acquired some 53,000,000 acres for sale to settlers or for use as forest reserves. If members of the older

[1] The first plan was 160 acres for each head of family with lesser allotments for others, the amounts to be doubled in the case of grazing lands. Because this arrangement discriminated against the younger and more educable tribesmen, a supplementary law of 1891 fixed a uniform size of 80 acres. The principles of the Dawes act were not applied to the Five Civilized Tribes in Indian Territory until 1898.

generation clung to tribal customs and traditions, the younger people increasingly broke away from the chief's influence and adopted civilized ways. But experience revealed certain defects in the law. Allotments were sometimes made prematurely. In other instances, capable and self-reliant individuals chafed at the inflexible twenty-five-year restriction. As voters, moreover, the Indians were often preyed upon by corrupt white politicians, and citizenship meant for many a free rein to drink to excess. To check the increase of drunkenness and crime, a supplementary statute in 1897 banned the liquor traffic during the probationary period. When the Supreme Court annulled this law in 1905 as a denial of the equal rights of citizens, Congress proceeded to a revision of the Dawes act. The Burke law, passed in 1906, instructed the executive branch thereafter to bestow full property title upon deserving individuals whenever satisfied of their fitness. At the same time, by postponing citizenship until full ownership was attained, it rendered illegal the drink traffic and helped safeguard the sanctity of the ballot.

In the years that followed, the process of assimilation went on with quickened pace. Increasing numbers of children received instruction in special Indian schools and, as the reservations were gradually broken up, they attended the regular public schools side by side with white youngsters. The vast majority continued to dwell in the West, the typical red man becoming a settled landholder and home builder. Individuals, of course, found the difficulties of adjustment insuperable and acquired the white man's vices without his virtues. In 1924, when over half the Indians had qualified as citizens, Congress signalized the event by extending the boon to all of them. As time passed, the pure strain became more and more diluted through intermarriage with the whites, prefiguring a day when the American aborigine, like many another conquered race, would disappear in the blood of his conqueror.

SELECT BIBLIOGRAPHY

Panaceas. The general account of labor parties and social programs contained in Commons and others, *History of Labour in the United States*, should be supplemented by Fine, *Labor and Farmer Parties in the United States;* Haynes, *Social Politics in the United States;* and Hillquit, *History of Socialism in the United States.* As the title indicates, Schuster, *Native American Anarch-*

ism, stresses American contributions to the antigovernmental philosophy. For socialist interpretations of American history, see Simons, *Social Forces in American History;* Lewis, *The Rise of the American Proletarian;* and Oneal, *The Workers in American History*. The "Prophet of San Francisco" and his doctrine are treated in George, *The Life of Henry George*, and Young, *The Single Tax Movement in the United States*.

Coping with Urban Social Problems. Nevins, *The Emergence of Modern America*, and Schlesinger, *The Rise of the City*, treat urban problems as well as all the other subjects dealt with later in this chapter. For special works on the growth of scientific methods in charity, see Watson, *The Charity Organization Movement in the United States;* Warner, *American Charities;* and Woods and Kennedy, *The Settlement Horizon*. Child welfare is more particularly the concern of McCrae, *The Humane Movement*, and Rainwater, *The Play Movement in the United States*, the latter dealing with playgrounds. Henderson, ed., *Correction and Prevention*, contains authoritative articles, historical and descriptive, on prison reform, preventive agencies and allied topics. For the development of preventive medicine, Ravenel, ed., *A Half Century of Public Health*, is helpful.

The Fight against the Liquor Traffic. The chief phases may be followed conveniently in Cherrington, *The Evolution of Prohibition in the United States of America*, and Colvin, *Prohibition in the United States*, both written with a temperance bias. Simkins, *The Tillman Movement in South Carolina*, contains a brief account of the dispensary system in that state.

The Advance of Women. Bruce, *Woman in the Making of America*, and Irwin, *Angels and Amazons*, are interesting popular sketches. On the entry of women into industry and business, Abbott, *Women in Industry*, and Calhoun, *A Social History of the American Family*, III, are helpful. Woody, *A History of Women's Education in the United States*, treats all levels of education. The rise of woman's clubs is traced in Croly, *The History of the Woman's Club Movement in America*. The contest for legal and political equality may be followed in Wilson, *The Legal and Political Status of Women in the United States*, or, biographically, in Harper, *The Life and Work of Susan B. Anthony*, and Blackwell, *Lucy Stone*.

The Changing Church. Sweet, *The Story of Religions in America*, contains a quick, factual survey of the period, and Rowe, *The History of Religion in the United States*, is a penetrating interpretation of tendencies. Garrison, *The March of Faith*, confines itself to American religious development after 1865. Emotional aspects are set forth in Beardsley, *A History of American Revivals*, and Loud, *Evangelized America*. White, *A History of the Warfare of Science with Theology in Christendom*, includes material on America. Among biographies of outstanding figures are Will, *Life of Cardinal Gibbons;* Hibben, *Henry Ward Beecher;* Bates and Dittemore, *Mary Baker Eddy;* and Powell, *Mary Baker Eddy*.

White, Black and Red. The changing status of the Negro is treated by members of the race in Brawley, *A Social History of the American Negro;* Woodson, *The Negro in Our History;* Nowlin, *The Negro in American National Politics since 1868;* and Wesley, *Negro Labor in the United States, 1850–1925*.

Other useful general treatments include Evans, *Black and White in the Southern States*, and Thompson, *The New South*. Lewinson, *Race, Class, & Party*, deals with Negro disfranchisement, and Cutler, *Lynch-Law*, with mob murder. The standard life of the foremost colored leader is Scott and Stowe, *Booker T. Washington*, written by his secretary in collaboration with the grandson of Harriet Beecher Stowe. Besides the general works on the Indian cited at the close of Chapter VII, the student should consult Moorehead, *The American Indian in the United States;* Schmeckebier, *The Office of Indian Affairs;* and Meriam and others, *The Problem of Indian Administration.*

CHAPTER XII

THE CULTURAL RENEWAL, 1865–1900

THE DIFFUSION OF KNOWLEDGE

IF urban growth begot grave problems of social maladjustment and human misery, it should be remembered that the city also served as the generating center of a dynamic intellectual life. Concentration of wealth and population made possible heavier taxation and greater patronage than rural communities could afford for schools, libraries and the like, while benefactions of the rich added further to the city's cultural opportunities. In the urban communities were to be found the best schools, the best churches, the best newspapers and virtually all the book-stores, circulating libraries, art galleries, museums, theaters, concert halls and opera houses. From 1871 to the close of the century no less than a third of a billion dollars was given by private philanthropists to agencies for cultivating the higher life, half the amount going to colleges and universities. By critics of the economic order this generosity was cynically attributed to love of ostentation, to eagerness for public approbation or, as Dr. Gladden would have said, to the desire to quiet an uneasy conscience. That there was also developing a sense of *richesse oblige* Andrew Carnegie made clear in an article in the *North American Review* in 1889, in which he asserted that a successful capitalist's career should consist of two periods, first, that of acquiring wealth and, second, that of distributing it for the public good. Whatever motives stirred the princely givers, the urban dwellers who reaped most of the benefit profited richly in their cultural life. The city also provided favorable conditions for creative work in letters and the arts. Among its varied inhabitants gifted individuals could find others of similar interests and thus, in an atmosphere of mutual encouragement and stimulating criticism, ripen their powers to the fullest. At the same time, the nearness of publishers, art dealers and wealthy patrons afforded an opportunity to sell the products of their talent.

It is not surprising that the great cultural advances came out of the city or that its influence penetrated to the farthest countryside.

The postwar years witnessed an educational renaissance akin to that of the 1830's and 1840's. In the North, where a system of tax-supported elementary schools was already well established, expansion and development occurred in every part of the system. Among the innovations was the kindergarten: though it had been introduced at Watertown, Wisconsin, as early as 1855 by Mrs. Carl Schurz, a pupil of Froebel, it did not become attached to the regular public schools until St. Louis set the example in 1873. By 1900 there were in the nation nearly three thousand public kindergartens, where play activities enticed youngsters to take the first steps in learning. Methods of instruction improved at every level, partly through the introduction of better textbooks, and even more because an increasing number of commonwealths accepted the responsibility of teacher training by establishing tax-supported normal schools. At the same time the North made school attendance compulsory, thus registering its conviction that education was not merely an opportunity for the individual child but a civic obligation. Meanwhile, free public high schools multiplied, growing from about five hundred in 1870 to six thousand in 1900. As home economics, manual training and other new subjects suited to the times crept into the course of study, the typical secondary school lengthened its term for graduation from three to four years. In this way a twelve-year course of schooling came to be established as the standard period of preparation for college.

In this amazing advance urban America blazed the way, the country districts trailing the towns and cities, the South lagging behind the North. Rural schools even in the East generally remained ungraded, the terms short, and the teachers ill trained and wretchedly paid. As a section primarily rural, Dixie was further handicapped by postwar poverty and by the unusual expense of maintaining separate schools for the two races, a burden borne chiefly by the whites. Moreover, having been little affected by the educational awakening of Horace Mann's time, the people had to build their system from the ground up. Despite such obstacles, before the century closed most of the

Southern states had made adequate provision for elementary instruction. The South at last formed a part of the national educational order. The principle of obligatory attendance was not applied, however, and the real development of high schools had to await the early twentieth century.

In the nation as a whole the ever widening reach of the schools is evidenced by the growth of enrollment from about seven million in 1870 to fifteen and a half in 1900. Yet, because of the newness of the system in many parts of the land and the increasing horde of immigrant newcomers, vast numbers of adults continued to be handicapped by insufficient formal instruction. In 1870 the total amount of schooling received by the average person in his whole lifetime was about three and a third years; in 1900 it amounted to a little more than five. Fortunately educational agencies of a less systematic character were at hand that helped somewhat to offset the deficiencies of youthful opportunity. Of these none more strikingly evinced the popular zeal for knowledge than the rise of the Chautauqua movement. Starting in 1874, great annual summer assemblies on the wooded shores of Lake Chautauqua, New York, listened to authorities lecture on literary, scientific and political subjects, and large numbers who attended were inspired to undertake a four-year plan of home study and reading. Soon many parts of the country began to blossom with "Chautauquas," modest copies of the original, meeting usually under a tent for a week or two during the hot season and acting as a stimulus to small-town intellectual life.

In a different fashion the spread of public libraries served the same purpose. Though circulating libraries for the use of subscribers had been in existence since Benjamin Franklin's time, the legislatures of New Hampshire, Massachusetts and Maine in the mid-nineteenth century were the first to empower local units to set up free tax-supported libraries. In the last year of the Civil War other commonwealths began to follow until the entire Union had fallen into line. Soon libraries free to the public became a normal provision of municipalities. The number of such institutions possessing a thousand or more volumes increased from 2000 in 1875 to nearly 5400 in 1900. Of private philanthropists who aided the cause, the most noteworthy was the ironmaster Carnegie, who in 1881 began the practice of presenting library buildings to towns that provided sites and pledged adequate maintenance through taxation. He gave away ten million dollars by the end of 1900 and a total of sixty million before his death in 1919. Professional leadership in the movement fell to the American Library Association, formed in 1876, which promoted the adoption of progressive methods of service to the public and helped make American libraries the most efficient in the world.

The majority of people, however, kept abreast the changing world by reading newspapers and magazines. American journalism entered a new era. The war had accustomed newspaper owners to lavish outlays of money and had aroused in the public an appetite for exciting news. In the years that followed, the fast tempo and high tension of city life reënforced the popular demand for a lively, colorful treatment of the day's happenings. As a result, editors began to fill their columns with items selected not because of their intrinsic importance but because of their human interest or sensational qualities. Charles A. Dana, becoming editor of the *New York Sun* in 1868, set the new pattern, but his enterprise was presently surpassed by Joseph Pulitzer, a journalist of Hungarian birth, who took charge of the *St. Louis Post-Dispatch* in 1878 and five years later acquired the *New York World*. Pulitzer frankly directed his appeal to the increasing number of wage-earners — the least literate section of the population — shrewdly suiting the form and content of his paper to their mental capacity and tastes. Most of the elements of present-day journalism developed under his hand: flaring headlines, political cartoons, human-interest "stories" of scandal and crime, separate departments for sports, amusements and the interests of women, and, last but not least, the special Sunday edition, divided into many sections for the convenience of the family group and replete with pictures, feature articles and colored "comics."

Within a few years the *World* became the most profitable and widely imitated paper in the land. Pulitzer's example, indeed, was responsible for bringing into the arena a young Californian, William Randolph Hearst, who acquired the *New York Morning Journal* in 1895 and quickly bested Pulitzer at his own game. The battle between these two masters of the craft — involving in part the publication rights of "The Yellow Kid," a daily colored cartoon — gave rise to the term yellow journalism, by which their brand of newspaper enterprise has ever since been known. Yet the influence of the yellow press was not wholly bad. Such newspapers often attacked flagrant political and social abuses in their communities and waged battles for their removal. James Bryce in 1888 testified that in the war against political corruption "the newspapers of New York, Boston, Philadelphia, and Chicago have been among the most effective battalions." It should also be remembered that journals of the new type reached untold millions who in earlier times had read nothing at all.

A different trend was indicated by the transformation of many of the great metropolitan dailies into vast business undertakings. Only rarely was a newspaper the external embodiment of a dominant personality as in Greeley's time. The heavy cost of operation under modern conditions caused them to pass into the hands of newspaper corporations and to be conducted with a main eye to profit. With the enormous growth of retail stores and nation-wide merchandising, revenue from such sources exceeded the receipts from sales, and newspapers tended increasingly to become advertising sheets with a secondary attention to news. Gradually the control of policy shifted from the editorial sanctum to the office of the business manager, with a corresponding loss to the independence of the press. In William Dean Howells's *A Modern Instance* (1881) a newspaper owner loudly asserts that "the press is a great moral engine," but hastily adds, "it ought to be run in the interest of the engineer."

The growing dependence of the average American upon his daily paper is shown by the increase of such journals from less than six hundred in 1870 to nearly twenty-five hundred in 1900 and by the leap in their total daily sales from two and a half million to more than fifteen. To meet the huge jumps in circulation, new mechanical devices and more efficient processes were introduced, such as larger and ever faster presses and cheaper methods of making print paper. In 1885 the setting of type was transformed into a machine process through Ottmar Mergenthaler's invention of the linotype, a mechanical marvel which, under the fingers of a skilled operator, cast from molten lead solid lines of type ready for printing. To the aid of the reporter came the typewriter, devised in 1868 chiefly by C. L. Sholes of Milwaukee and later improved, and also the first practicable fountain pen, placed on the market in 1884 by L. E. Waterman. At the same time newspapers, in the interest of economy and efficiency, began to coöperate in gathering and distributing news. While the original Associated Press dated from before 1860, in the years after the war numerous competing news associations sprang up and contested the field with one another. In the last decade the Western Associated Press, headed by Melville E. Stone of Chicago, gained the position of dominance, and in 1900 reorganized as the present-day Associated Press.

Though less widely read than newspapers, magazines also came to occupy a steadily larger place in American life. From 1860 to 1900 the number of monthlies grew from 280 to over 1800. Never before had they reached so high a plane of general excellence or represented so well the diversified interests of the public. Magazines like the *Atlantic*, dating from 1857, the *Century*, reorganized under that name in 1881, and *Scribner's Magazine*, launched in 1887, welcomed to their pages the new generation of authors and provided them with their chief means of income. Journals appealing to special audiences appeared in abundance, such as *St. Nicholas* (1873) for children, *Outing* (1882) for sport lovers, the *Ladies' Home Journal* (1883) for women, and the *Dial* (1880) in the field of literary criticism. It was particularly fortunate that, in a period of the waning independence of the press, certain weekly magazines were at hand to jar complacency and perform the function of fearless public criticism. Of the free-lance editors the most significant was the Irish American, E. L. Godkin, who directed the *Nation* from 1865 to 1899 and deeply influenced the thinking of the educated minority. In the columns of *Harper's Weekly* Thomas Nast, whose cartoons had helped to expose the Tweed Ring and other frauds, laid the foundations of modern American political caricature, contributing to the political zoo the familiar figures of the Republican elephant, the Democratic donkey and the Tammany tiger. The humorous possibilities of the American scene were even more fully exploited by the comic illustrated weeklies, *Puck, Judge* and *Life*, founded between 1877 and 1883. The nineties brought the culminating development, the advent of a group of monthlies — *McClure's*, *Munsey's* and others — which, without sacrificing good standards, sold for ten or fifteen cents a copy instead of the traditional twenty-five or thirty-five. Cheaper manufacturing processes, large-scale production and a greater reliance on advertising revenues made this development possible, and the result was seen in a vast expansion in the number of magazine readers.

THE PROGRESS OF KNOWLEDGE

In the field of higher learning the number of students, the improvement of instruction and equipment and the founding of additional universities attested both the ardor for knowledge and the wider-felt need of education beyond the high school to prepare for the exacting tasks of a complex civilization. Many of the new institutions, such as Vanderbilt (1873), Johns Hopkins (1876), Leland Stanford (1885), Clark (1889), the University of Chicago (1892) and the Armour Institute of Technology (1893), were the creation of private philanthropists. Under spur of the Morrill act of 1862 (see page 142) twenty more state universities opened between 1865 and 1900, mostly in the Middle and Far West, while the older foundations increasingly freed themselves from denominational influences on the one hand and political entanglements on the other. Everywhere the cause of higher education was quickened. To give depth and direction to the new forces a remarkable group of university presidents came to the fore, including Andrew D. White of Cornell, James McCosh of Princeton, Charles W. Eliot of Harvard, James B. Angell of Michigan, Noah Porter of Yale, Daniel Coit Gilman of Johns Hopkins and William Rainey Harper of the University of Chicago.

Under the leadership of men of this caliber the traditional college curriculum, besides being enriched with new subjects of instruction, was extended upward to include training for research and the granting of graduate degrees. Since the 1860's increasing numbers of American college graduates had been frequenting German university centers where they drank deep of the learning of some of the greatest scholars and scientists the world afforded.

In the eighties the exodus reached flood tide, embracing over two thousand. Imbibing the Teutonic ideal of patient specialization, of knowing all about a few things instead of a little about many, these eager young pilgrims returned to America resolved through their efforts to enlarge the world's store of knowledge as well as to disseminate it. Johns Hopkins University, devoting itself primarily to graduate work, numbered among its faculty scarcely a professor who had not had German training. Under its tonic influence other institutions rapidly expanded their advanced instruction, the total number of American-enrolled students increasing from about 400 in 1875 to nearly 5700 in 1900. By the century's close a dozen universities offered as rich opportunities for graduate training as could be found anywhere in the world. It is worth noting that, in a supposedly materialistic age, a larger proportion of American youth than ever before consecrated themselves to careers in which the financial rewards at best were small.

The zeal for extending the bounds of knowledge reminded James Bryce of "the scholars of the Renaissance flinging themselves into the study of rediscovered philology." For the first time, American research workers began to hold their own with the scientists and scholars of the Old World. To keep abreast the latest discoveries specialists in the different fields banded together in great nation-wide associations like the American Chemical Society (1876), the Modern Language Association (1883) and the American Economic Association (1885). The general government, too, turned to the active promotion of research, not only by means of the agricultural experiment stations (see page 142), but also through such agencies as the federal geological survey and the bureau of ethnology, both established in 1879. In nearly every branch of investigation the evolutionary hypothesis helped dispel the darkness surrounding ancient problems and light the way to new results. G. Stanley Hall, himself a contributor to the new study of experimental psychology, called it "the greatest intellectual stimulus of the modern age." While some of the older scientists like Louis Agassiz at Harvard sided with leading theologians against the theory, far more typical was the course of two of his colleagues: Asa Gray who eagerly lent it the great weight of his reputation as a botanist, and John Fiske who, reaching a wider intellectual audience through his popular lectures and writings, taught that the evolutionary process explained man's social as well as his biological development.[1]

Though the growth of knowledge stemmed primarily from the minute investigations of myriad workers, certain names stand out as of special note. Among such men in the natural sciences were A. A. Michelson who in 1879 began his epoch-making experiments in measuring the velocity of light; Simon Newcomb, famed for his recomputation of the elements of the solar system; and O. C. Marsh and E. D. Cope whose excavations of vast fossil beds of prehistoric beasts in the American West enriched the world's knowledge of paleontology. Greater than any of these, however, was J. Willard Gibbs who laid the foundations for a new branch of research, physical chemistry, and who is generally termed the foremost scientist America has yet produced. Towering figures also appeared in the social sciences; for example, Francis A. Walker and Richard T. Ely in economics, Lester F. Ward in sociology, Lewis H. Morgan in anthropology, John W. Burgess and Woodrow Wilson in political science, J. B. Mc-Master, James Ford Rhodes, Henry Adams and Henry C. Lea in history. Frederick J. Turner, a member of this last group, in 1893 gave a fresh direction to historical study for years to come by pointing to the profound influence that the frontier, then rapidly vanishing, had exerted upon American development from the earliest days of settlement. In psychology William James was a dominant factor, as he also was in philosophy where he developed the theory of method known as pragmatism. These men and their kind were as truly discoverers, explorers, pioneers, in the intellectual realm as were their forbears who had hewn a path through the physical wilderness of forest and mountain. On their tireless labors and penetrating insights rests the vast superstructure of American scientific achievement in the twentieth century.

LETTERS AND THE ARTS

No less fruitful were the forces at work in letters and the fine arts. In 1871 Walt Whitman published his most noteworthy

[1] Though deeply indebted to the contemporary English philosopher Herbert Spencer, Fiske differed from his master in insisting that evolution implied the working out of a divine plan for the betterment of mankind.

prose work *Democratic Vistas*. Boldly he called for a literary culture springing from the common life, one begot of the people, by the people and for the people. His challenge to the new era was what Ralph Waldo Emerson's *The American Scholar* had been to the generation of the thirties and forties. But where the Concord sage had pleaded for an aristocracy of literature — for the lone man thinking his own thoughts — Whitman pleaded for a democracy of literature, one "fit to cope with our occasions, lands, permeating the whole mass of American mentality, taste, belief, breathing into it a new breath of life." Know you not, he asked, "that the people of our land may all know how to read and write, and may all possess the right to vote, and yet the main things may be entirely lacking?" He himself, scorning rhyme, meter and other conventional poetic embellishments, sounded the new note in verse, free, ardent and spacious, its *leitmotif* the praise of common people and common things.

As if evoked by his trumpeting, there trooped forth from every corner of the land young writers eager to record their impressions of a many-sided rural civilization fast disappearing before the standardizing influences of urbanism and industrialism. Impatient with the bookishness and fastidious diction of their predecessors, they told their stories simply, often with unconscious idealization, and always with a careful attention to dialect and local color. Never before had American fiction so faithfully mirrored the amazing diversity that typified the human geography of the nation. Edward Eggleston in *The Hoosier School-Master* (1871) and later novels depicted mid-century conditions in rural Indiana. "Mark Twain" (Samuel L. Clemens), drawing on his own earlier experiences, gave a broadly humorous account of life along the Mississippi, producing his masterpiece in *The Adventures of Huckleberry Finn* (1884). With Bret Harte and the poet Joaquin Miller he also helped make memorable the picturesque life of the Far West, while Helen Hunt Jackson in *Ramona* (1884) recalled the romance and drama of the passing of the old Spanish order in California.

Nor were other sections of the nation less ably represented. There was a literary New South as well as a political and industrial one. In finely wrought sketches George W. Cable, Grace King and Kate Chopin introduced a wondering America to the exotic, orange-scented atmosphere of Creole life in Louisiana; the chivalry of the old Virginia gentry lived again in the pages of Thomas Nelson Page and F. Hopkinson Smith. By contrast, *In the Tennessee Mountains* (1884) and other stories by "Charles Egbert Craddock" (Mary N. Murfree) told of the humble folk dwelling amidst the grandeur of the interior highlands, and Joel Chandler Harris revealed a new aspect of the Negro in his charming versions of animal myths as narrated by Uncle Remus. In authors like Sarah Orne Jewett and Mary E. Wilkins New England had its regional spokesmen, but they were concerned not with a colorful past but with the dun hues of the present, giving sympathetic portrayals of narrow, introspective lives in the era of New England's rural decline.

Still other writers found their themes in the main stream rather than in the backwaters of American life. In a series of novels distinguished by such works as *The Rise of Silas Lapham* (1884) and *A Hazard of New Fortunes* (1889) William Dean Howells dealt with the trials and foibles of middle-class urban people, with ever sharpening emphasis upon the "economic chance-world" which governed human destinies under modern conditions. Henry James, residing abroad and employing a style marked by painstaking precision, discovered rich literary opportunities in the clash of Old World culture upon Americans in Europe. Both men strove to achieve realism, but, unlike the contemporary realists in France and Russia, they concerned themselves with life's normalities instead of its abnormalities. A harsher temper pervaded the pages of Hamlin Garland, who in *Main-Travelled Roads* (1891) stressed the repellent aspects of Midwestern rural life, and of Stephen Crane whose *Maggie, a Girl of the Streets* (1892) exposed one of the tragic failures of the vaunted urban civilization. Even Mark Twain indirectly leveled deadly shafts at the inhumanity and injustices of modern industrialism in his burlesque on the Middle Ages, *A Connecticut Yankee in King Arthur's Court* (1889). The 1880's marked the full bloom of the new literary growths, with a greater number of good novels published than in any other American decade. Yet the epoch was even more distinctive for its profusion of short stories, "literature in small parcels," a form which this generation molded into a finished work of art. It was peculiarly adapted to the taste of the hurrying, scurrying people who filled the cities. Through the short story America has made perhaps her greatest contribution to world literature.

Equally significant was the renaissance in the arts of line, color and form. Just as young American scholars were flocking to Germany, so fledgling painters, sculptors and architects were besieging the studios of Paris, the world's art center. During the seventies, as they returned in ever increasing numbers, their advent was like a fresh wind on a sultry day, clearing the atmosphere of muggy traditions and introducing breadth, freedom and vigor. In the field of painting the clash of schools was so sharp as to cause the "Younger Men" in 1877 to form the Society of American Artists in opposition to the long-established National Academy of Design. Into their ranks they quickly drew some of the more progressive older men like George Inness and John La Farge. The years that followed brought an epoch of creative achievement in painting such as the nation had never before known. A few names will illustrate both the quality and variety of the work performed. In Inness America discovered perhaps her greatest landscape painter, an artist with a poet's insight into nature's vagrant moods. By contrast Winslow Homer painted bold, realistic canvases of the sea. James A. McNeill Whistler's genius appeared best in his nocturnes, which conveyed inimitably the hue and mystery and quiet of night. His well-known painting, "The Artist's Portrait of His Mother," a study in grays, was bought in 1891 by the French government. A. P. Ryder devoted his brush to legendary and often nocturnal subjects, which he interpreted with great imaginative power. La Farge transformed American mural painting into a fine art and, through his invention of opalescent glass, helped revive the ancient glories of medieval stained-glass work. In response to the new interest in painting, art schools increased from less than forty in 1880 to nearly one hundred and twenty at the century's close. The establishment of public art museums by Washington, New York and Boston in the postwar decade led other large cities presently to make similar provision. In a less obvious way the waxing popularity of the camera, especially after the simplifications introduced in the eighties by George Eastman of Rochester, helped to awaken in many a latent artistic sense.

In sculpture gifted men like Daniel Chester French, Frederick W. MacMonnies and G. G. Barnard pushed to the front and exerted a profound influence for higher standards. The foremost practitioner, however, was Augustus Saint-Gaudens, whose statue of Admiral Farragut (1881) in Madison Square Garden, New York, first revealed his genius to the public. His symbolic figure, "The Peace of God," erected at the tomb of Mrs. Henry Adams in Washington in 1891, is generally accounted the greatest sculpture America has yet produced. In no other branch of art had the national traditions been so poor. These men and their like raised it to a plane comparable with the best work of contemporary Europe.

The new influences made slower headway in architecture, partly because of the enormous new construction required to accommodate the needs of the swift-growing cities, partly also because people did not discriminate between ostentation and good taste. Even men of wealth and note oftentimes lived in houses disfigured with towers, turrets, Moorish arches and fantastic jigsaw work in wood and iron. It was Henry Hobson Richardson who ushered in a better day. Employing the heavy Romanesque style of southern France, he taught the superiority of sturdiness, unity and restraint as elements of design. His crowning achievement was Trinity Church, Boston, in 1877, for which John La Farge provided the murals and much of the stained-glass work. Before Richardson died in 1886, many fellow craftsmen had risen up to foster the superior standards, and from plans published in magazines like the *Ladies' Home Journal* the ordinary person might learn how to build an inexpensive house in approved taste. The younger men wrought characteristically in the classic mode or some of its Renaissance derivatives. The Chicago World's Fair of 1893 — largely the architectural creation of D. H. Burnham, C. B. Atwood, R. M. Hunt and the firm of McKim, Mead and White — marked the supreme attainment of the classic style, the effect being a poignant dream of loveliness. Louis Sullivan, one of the World's Fair group, possessed a more individual genius. His work prefigured the functional architecture of a later time, so strikingly exemplified by the Chicago exposition of 1933.

A special problem was presented by the need to economize

ground space in the congested business quarters of big cities. The obvious solution was lofty perpendicular structures, whose use the recent introduction of the fast elevators rendered practicable. Masonry construction, however, required supporting piers so huge as to devour much of the desirable space in the lower floors. The upshot was the invention of the skyscraper, a building riveted securely in a metal frame and employing brick or stone merely to screen off the weather. Less trammeled by tradition than the Eastern centers, Chicago first ventured upon the new departure, the original "skyscraper" being the Home Insurance Building (1885) which rose to what then seemed the dizzy height of ten stories. Soon Chicago and New York engaged in pushing their office buildings higher and higher until in 1898 the Ivins Syndicate Building in the latter city achieved twenty-nine floors, a mere hint of what awaited in the next century. These "proud structures, defiant in their altitude," fittingly symbolized the titanic energy, the willingness to experiment, the superb engineering competence, that characterized the age. Since historical research has denied to Americans the credit of devising the log cabin, the skyscraper stands as the nation's unique architectural gift to the world.

If progress in musical composition was less brilliant, still the nation began in a modest way to repay its debt for the rich stores of melody it had long derived from Europe. The principal composers had all received their training in Germany. John Knowles Paine, George W. Chadwick and Horatio Parker won a transatlantic reputation for their orchestral and choral scores, while Edward A. MacDowell composed piano selections distinguished by originality and haunting beauty. More significant perhaps was the heartening growth of popular musical appreciation. Conservatories of music sprang up in the more important cities; artists' recitals enjoyed a profitable patronage; choral societies flourished, particularly in German centers; the founding of the New York Symphony Orchestra in 1878 and of the Boston Symphony Orchestra three years later signalized a new era in orchestral music. Grand opera, too, secured a firmer footing with the opening in 1883 of the Metropolitan Opera House in New York. Such evidences of public support and improving taste augured well for future musical attainments.

RECREATION AND SPORT

All classes in the cities faced the problem of making use of the increasing leisure at their disposal, even the wage-earners whom the gradual reduction of the workday gave unwonted freedom. Life under pioneer conditions had taught the people how to work but not how to relax. They therefore turned to pleasure with the same fierce energy that they devoted to money making. In Bryce's contemporary phrase, they "make amusement into a business." Society life in the greater cities became characterized by frantic display, especially on the part of the newly rich determined to climb into the ranks of the exclusive. If Patrick O'Riley, formerly a familiar of the shirt-sleeved saloon gang, would win social recognition as Patrique Oreillé, his womenfolk must somehow or other perform the miracle. Ways and means lay at hand. Palatial mansions and lavish entertaining helped obscure the rise from humble origins; liberal patronage of fashionable charities smoothed the path; proper "ancestors" were always procurable from the right genealogists. But the supreme goal was a brilliant international marriage. So successful were ambitious mothers in this quest that toward the end of the century it was estimated that over $200,000,000 had been exported to replenish the coffers of impoverished European nobility.

For the ordinary man no use of leisure better suited his taste than to join one or more of the secret fraternal orders that sprang up as if by spontaneous generation. Attaining their greatest numerical strength in the urban centers, these lodges not only provided a substitute for the neighborliness of rural communities, but, through their elaborate ceremonialism, enabled members to recover a sense of self-importance lost in the solitude of crowds. A further attraction appeared in the sickness and death benefits usually provided. Between 1880 and 1901 no less than 490 different fraternal organizations were founded. By the latter date America had fairly won its title of a "nation of joiners," with over six million names on the rosters of its secret societies.

At the same time, the multiplication of city dwellers rendered possible new developments in the theater. The serious drama probably has never been better presented than by such native players as Edwin Booth, Clara Morris and Lawrence Barrett and by such foreign visitors as Sarah Bernhardt and Helena Modjeska. More characteristic of the times, however, was the enthusiastic patronage accorded to the minstrel show and the circus, and similarly to the endless series of blood-curdling melodramas that pleased a public taste whetted by the dime novel and the sensational press. Yet no form of stage entertainment so well embodied the restless urban spirit as vaudeville, which Tony Pastor, B. F. Keith and others made into a great success. Vaudeville, observed a contemporary, "belongs to the era of the department store and the short story." By the 1890's it accounted for the attendance of perhaps half the theatergoers. Comic opera also made its appearance, floated into general favor on the wave of popularity that greeted "Pinafore" and other delightful concoctions of the Britishers, Gilbert and Sullivan. The tunes from such musical performances swiftly became known from one end of the country to the other, thanks to the invention of the talking machine or phonograph. Devised by Edison in 1877–1878, the original crude instrument, consisting of a tinfoil cylinder record turned by hand, was presently improved by Edison and others through the adoption of flat waxlike disks and the use of spring or electric motors. Soon it was furnishing amusement and recreation in countless homes.

These years also saw the rise of organized sport. As rural life receded into the background, as more and more people slaved long hours in office and factory, some form of outdoor diversion became indispensable. Unhappily, softened muscles did not encourage active personal participation. Most people therefore were content to take their more violent exercise vicariously, a tendency zealously abetted by sport promoters who coveted the gate receipts that professional contests made possible. The "audience habit," nurtured by the theater, thus came to infect sport lovers as well. Many of the new games were imported from Great Britain where an athletic revival had been proceeding since the mid-century; in the United States, however, they were deemed not a special perquisite of the upper classes but a boon to be enjoyed by everyone. In the case of basketball, invented in 1891, Americans contributed a game all their own.

Of the older sports thoroughbred racing enjoyed an era of

unparalleled prosperity. Prize fighting, though viewed askance by the respectable elements, brought to the fore a succession of world's heavyweight champions in John L. Sullivan (1882), James J. Corbett (1892), "Bob" Fitzsimmons (1897) and James J. Jeffries (1899). Baseball, long a favorite amateur pastime, began to assume its aspect as "America's national game" when the Cincinnati Red Stockings in 1869 turned themselves into a professional team. Soon professional baseball overspread the land, leading to the formation of intercity leagues and, in 1884, to the first "World Series" between the pennant-winning teams of the two major leagues. Football, an American version of the English game Rugby, developed somewhat more slowly, being closely associated with the growth of college athletics. The first intercollegiate contest occurred between Princeton and Rutgers in 1869. Seven years later the American Intercollegiate Football Association was formed by Columbia, Harvard, Princeton and Yale; and in the next score of years the game, under constantly changing rules, spread to nearly all the colleges and most of the high schools of the country. At Connecticut Wesleyan Professor Woodrow Wilson in his odd hours helped coach a team that in 1889 defeated Pennsylvania, Amherst, Williams, Rutgers and Trinity.

Lawn tennis, golf and polo were among the new sports introduced in the seventies. In these and other games, differences as to rules caused the formation of national associations to establish uniform regulations and often also to conduct annual tournaments. All classes took part in this new play life of the nation. The well-to-do signified their approval by the establishment of athletic clubs, country clubs and yacht clubs. In between his political activities Theodore Roosevelt found time to box, wrestle, fish, hunt and play polo, exemplifying in these early years his later championship of the "strenuous life." President Hayes found relaxation in shooting at a mark in Rock Creek Park, and his successors, Arthur and Cleveland, were among the country's most expert fishermen.

In the eighties the modern bicycle began its amazing career of popularity. Bicycling had been confined earlier to riders whose courage was undaunted by an occasional fall from the lofty perch over the high front wheel. But the introduction in

1884 of the "safety" bicycle — possessing two medium-sized wheels of equal height — and the later substitution of pneumatic tires for solid rubber ones produced a cycling craze that ramified to every part of the nation. By 1893 a million bicycles were in use. Spurred by the League of American Wheelmen, over half the states enacted laws for improving their highways, a movement later to be accelerated by the advent of the automobile. For untold thousands cycling renewed the forgotten pleasures of open road and countryside. It also helped bring about more rational fashions for women. The generation little dreamed that the rattling, snorting "horseless carriage," with which inventors in the nineties were hopefully beginning to tinker, would presently spell the doom of the universally popular "bike."

SELECT BIBLIOGRAPHY

The Diffusion and Progress of Knowledge. The varied phases of civilization treated in this chapter are dealt with in Nevins, *The Emergence of Modern America*, and Schlesinger, *The Rise of the City*. Such works as Cubberley, *Public Education in the United States*, Dexter, *A History of Education in the United States*, and Knight, *Public Education in the South*, sketch the expansion of the public school system. The latest and best survey of newspaper development is Bleyer, *Main Currents in the History of American Journalism*. Among the ablest of the individual newspaper histories are Davis, *History of the New York Times*, and Nevins, *The Evening Post*. The fathers of the yellow press are treated in Seitz, *Joseph Pulitzer*, and Winkler, *W. R. Hearst*, and another phase of journalism forms the theme of Rosewater, *History of Coöperative News-Gathering in the United States*. Ogden, *Life and Letters of Edwin Lawrence Godkin*, is concerned with the New York *Nation* and its editor. On major trends in higher education the writings of Thwing are enlightening, notably *A History of Education in the United States since the Civil War* and *The American and the German University*. Outstanding contributors to the advancement of knowledge are considered biographically in Jordan, ed., *Leading American Men of Science*, and Odum, *American Masters of Social Science*.

Letters and the Arts. Of the many surveys of American literature, Pattee, *A History of American Literature since 1870*, and Parrington, *The Beginnings of Critical Realism in America*, devote detailed attention to postwar developments. Hartmann, *A History of American Art*, which briefly reviews both painting and sculpture, should be supplemented by fuller treatments like Isham, *The History of American Painting*, and Taft, *The History of American Sculpture*. Weitenkampf, *American Graphic Art*, considers the various forms of illustrative art. Tallmadge, *The Story of American Architecture*, is an engaging presentation of the subject. The student will want to consult the excellent pictorial reproductions in Mather and others, *The American Spirit* *in Art*, and Hamlin, *The American Spirit in Architecture.* Howard, *Our American Music: Three Hundred Years of It*, is informing and accurate.

Recreation and Sport. Theatrical development is canvassed in Hornblow, *A History of the Theatre in America;* Crawford, *The Romance of the American Theatre;* and Mayorga, *A Short History of the American Drama.* A particular phase is treated in Wittke, *Tambo and Bones: A History of the American Minstrel Stage.* Krout, *Annals of American Sport*, offers the best general historical discussion. For two major sports Weyand, *American Football*, and Spalding, *America's National Game* (baseball), are of special value.

CHAPTER XIII

THE FARMERS TAKE THEIR STAND, 1880–1900

THE REVIVAL OF RURAL UNREST

AS the eighties wore on, rural life lagged ever farther behind the van of urban progress. The gains of the Economic Revolution accrued primarily to city dwellers. Few of the new mechanical inventions ameliorated life on the countryside. From their city ramparts captains of industry, as we have seen, directed the course of economic conquest heedless of how rural welfare might be affected. In the increase of national wealth the husbandman secured a rapidly dwindling share. Whereas the value of farms in 1880 just equaled that of urban real estate, ten years later city real estate had advanced to double the value of farm land. The contrast was even sharper if other forms of property were included. A contemporary economist estimated that in 1890 the average wealth of rural families did not exceed $3250, while that of urban families surpassed $9000. This disparity in worldly goods and economic progress was emphasized by the many human advantages that city life afforded — opportunities for choosing from among a variety of occupations, for working shorter hours, for social commingling, for educational and cultural development, for amusement and recreation. Under the provision of the homestead law for four different farms to each square mile, isolation and loneliness were the almost inescapable conditions of existence in the newer West, a fact that worked a special hardship on womenfolk and members of the growing generation. Though many country dwellers continued to value farming above every other type of life, the phenomenal migration from country to town suggests how greatly such contrasts affected rural psychology. "The farm youth sees only the dazzling, gaudy side of city life," lamented one student of conditions. "He sees not that for every success there are scores, nay hundreds, who sink into darkness and misery."

This growing sense of rural inferiority, this deepening conviction that the tillers of the soil were losing their ancient heritage of economic independence and equal opportunity, needed only specific bread-and-butter grievances to precipitate organized movements for farm relief. Such grievances the eighties provided in abundance. The return of prosperity in 1879 (see page 173), after five years of depression, chiefly benefited the urban and industrial sections. Because of the enormous expansion of Western agriculture and of stiffer competition in the world's markets with the wheat-growing regions of Russia, Australia and the Argentine, farm prices fell disastrously during the decade. Corn, which commanded 63 cents a bushel in 1881, sold for 28 in 1890. Wheat averaged but 73 cents a bushel from 1883 to 1889, oats 28. The farmer himself blamed the increasing woes of agriculture not on "overproduction," but on the profits which middlemen garnered from his labors, the high transportation charges imposed by the railroads, and the heavy interest rates that his creditors (mostly Easterners) exacted. "There are three great crops raised in Nebraska," wrote one embittered agricultural editor. "One is a crop of corn, one a crop of freight rates, and one a crop of interest. One is produced by farmers who by sweat and toil farm the land. The other two are produced by men who sit in their offices and behind their bank counters and farm the farmers." As if the situation were not bad enough, an almost uninterrupted decade of drought, beginning in 1887 and attended by infestations of chinch bugs, destroyed the plantings of countless settlers who had taken up homesteads in the semiarid zone embracing the western halves of Kansas, Nebraska and the Dakotas. It seemed as though the hand of both man and nature was raised against the husbandman. By 1890 mortgages averaged one for every two persons in Kansas and North Dakota, one for every three in Nebraska, South Dakota and Minnesota. In some counties ninety per cent or more of the land was under mortgage.

Meantime, the Southern agriculturist complained of similar difficulties: low farm prices, excessive transportation costs, heavy taxes, grinding debts. The market price of cotton, the principal staple, averaged less than nine cents a pound during the decade. The crop-lien system, by which the farmer mortgaged his growing crop at high interest charges, enmeshed perhaps eighty or ninety per cent of the cotton growers, reducing them to a condition of "debt-peonage." Throughout the South agricultural land tended to gravitate into the hands of money lenders, loan companies and a few of the financially stronger farmers. In the nation as a whole the mortgage indebtedness of farm lands grew from $343,000,000 in 1880 to $586,000,000 in 1890.

Meanwhile evidences of agrarian unrest multiplied. Under a bewildering variety of names farmers' clubs, associations, unions, alliances, sprang up in the South and West to consider common grievances and propose means of relief. In this manner two great organizations grew up in the cotton belt — the National Farmers' Alliance, started in 1879, and the Agricultural Wheel three years later — which in 1889 joined to form a body with over a million members, known popularly as the Southern Farmers' Alliance. Meanwhile a Northern Farmers' Alliance, founded in 1880, rose to a dominant position among the agricultural bodies of the trans-Mississippi West. At first the organized farmers pinned their faith to nonpolitical measures. Taking a leaf from the experience of the Grangers, they tried to cultivate a pleasanter rural life through picnics, lodge meetings and other neighborhood gatherings of one sort or another. Like the Grangers, too, local groups adventured in the field of economic coöperation, setting up their own stores, cotton yards, grain elevators, creameries, insurance companies and the like. But when these coöperative undertakings collapsed, as most of them did because of poor business direction or cutthroat competition, the farmers began to seek legislative remedies for their ills. In a number of Southern states new leaders "fresh from the soil," like "Ben" Tillman in South Carolina and "Jim" Hogg in Texas, leaped into prominence and, by rousing the rural masses against the leadership of the upper classes and the towns, captured the Democratic party in their states. In the strongly Republican commonwealths of the West the agrarian elements usually formed independent parties, sometimes through fusion with the Democrats. Such successes, however, promised only limited relief; the ultimate goal was the control of Congress. From the national government the agrarians hoped to secure their chief means of salvation: currency inflation, a graduated income tax on the rich and public ownership of railroads.

While the greenback notion still lingered fondly in the minds of many, the circumstances of the time directed chief attention to another form of money inflation, "free silver." Until 1873 the country had been on a bimetallic standard, that is, the government stood ready to coin into dollars all the gold and silver that might be brought to the mint. Congress in that year reorganized the monetary system and, among other things, omitted the standard silver dollar from the list of authorized domestic coins. The act excited little attention at the time because, thanks to the scarcity of silver metal, the amount of bullion required for a silver dollar exceeded its legal value, and hence none had actually been in circulation for forty years. Almost at once events occurred that put a different face on affairs. The law which had been passed by default gained an ugly repute as the "Crime of 1873," and in the political discussions of the next quarter-century the demonetization of silver was ascribed to a sinister and corrupt plot of Big Business and Wall Street. This sudden change of attitude was due partly to an enormous and unexpected leap in the world's supply of silver ore as a result of the fabulous finds in the mountain states of the West. At about the same time several European countries, deciding to adopt the gold standard, melted their larger silver coins and thus further increased the supply available.[1]

With the nation wallowing in a slough of hard times, agrarian spokesmen in the West and South, abetted by labor groups in the Eastern industrial centers, demanded a return to free silver; in other words, a resumption of the unlimited coinage of the historic silver dollar as in the years before 1873. Confident that their troubles stemmed from a shortage of circulating medium, they cited not only the "Crime of 1873," but also the fact that the world's annual production of gold was virtually stationary. By enlarging the volume of money in use, they believed the government would indirectly help them to get higher prices for farm crops and better wages in industry, and make it easier for them to pay their debts. They reckoned without the waxing strength of the Eastern business classes, which shrank from any measure that might diminish the pur-

[1] Germany demonetized silver in 1871, Denmark, Sweden and Norway in 1873. In the latter year the Latin Union, composed of France, Italy, Belgium, Switzerland and Greece, limited silver coinage.

chasing power of their incomes and enable debtors to discharge their obligations in "cheap money." To the aid of the inflationists, however, came the small but energetic group of silver-mine owners in the Far West, who saw the market price of the bullion content of the old dollar drop from $1.02 in 1872 to 96 cents in 1875, and to 82 in 1885, with the downward trend unchecked. If the government could again be induced to purchase all the bullion brought to the mint for coinage, they reasoned that the market price of the metal and the profits of silver production would rise in response to the unlimited demand. The money question did not become an issue between the parties for many years. Within each party, however, it produced jangling discord, the members from the West and South generally opposing those from the moneyed East and the manufacturing sections of the Midwest.

The first trial of strength between the forces came in November, 1877, when a free-silver bill passed the House of Representatives with Western and Southern support. Its father was "Silver Dick" (Richard P.) Bland, whose advocacy bespoke his experiences in the Western mining country as well as his sympathy with his debt-ridden farmer constituents. Unwilling to go so far, the Senate at the instance of W. B. Allison of Iowa amended the bill by directing the Treasury Department to buy only from two to four million dollars of silver bullion each month for coinage. President Hayes rejected the measure on the ground that, in the case of money borrowed after 1873, it involved a virtual scaling down of debts and hence a breach of contract. But the bill was easily carried over his veto in February, 1878. As a compromise settlement, the Bland-Allison act had the effect of allaying further agitation for several years, though both Arthur and Cleveland recommended repeal of the law. The least amount of bullion permitted by the statute was purchased and coined each month, adding about $31,000,000 annually to the circulating medium.

Toward the end of the eighties the movement sprang to life again. The reasons were various. For one thing, the government, bent on reducing the surplus revenue, was actively engaged in retiring the war bonds; and since the volume of national bank notes varied with the amount of federal bonds the banks owned, this course of action caused these notes to shrink from a total of $359,000,000 in 1882 to $186,000,000 in 1890. At the same time that this money was being taken out of circulation, the admission of six new plains and mountain states in 1889 and 1890 (see page 143) strengthened the hand of the silver forces, particularly in the Senate. Besides, the Farmers' Alliances now loomed big on the national political horizon. Party politicians were scarcely surprised when the fall elections of 1890 placed fifty-three "Alliance men" in Congress. When the question of a new monetary law was taken up early in that year, it appeared that, contrary to their earlier attitudes, the Senate now favored free silver while the House wanted no change. The silverites in the House, however, finally forced the majority to make concessions by threatening to vote against the McKinley tariff bill, then in course of passage. In July, 1890, the so-called Sherman silver-purchase act went into effect. Though not providing for free silver, it required the Treasury Department to buy 4,500,000 ounces of bullion each month (nearly twice as much as had been coined before), and to issue in payment therefor treasury notes of full legal-tender character, redeemable in either gold or silver at the government's option. William McKinley, who had supported the Bland free-silver bill in 1877 as a member of the House, advocated the new law as the next best thing to unlimited coinage.

POPULISM AND THE PANIC OF 1893

Unlike the Bland-Allison act, no respite of agitation followed the new silver law. Almost at once began another downward plunge in the prices of cotton, grain and livestock. An investigation, made by the Department of Agriculture in 1893, showed that under existing conditions the cost of raising wheat and corn exceeded the prices received. In the single year 1891 no less than 18,000 covered wagons crossed from the Nebraska to the Iowa bank of the Missouri River in full flight before the scorpion-whips of disaster. Between 1889 and 1893 more than 11,000 mortgages were foreclosed in Kansas alone. Meanwhile, despite the greater absorption of silver by the mint, the bullion value of the dollar fell from 81 cents in 1890 to 60 three years later. A wave of despair swept over the West and South. Hamlin Garland, who studied the phenomenon at first-hand, wrote many years later, "As ten-cent corn and ten per cent interest were troubling Kansas, so six-cent cotton was inflaming Georgia — and both were frankly sympathetic with Montana and Colorado whose miners were suffering from a drop in the price of silver." The new spirit was exemplified by Mrs. Mary E. Lease of Kansas, who, exhorting the farmers to "raise less corn and more hell," shouted to great audiences, "The West and South are bound and prostrate before the manufacturing East." The effect on conservative Easterners was reflected in the caustic comment of the *New York Evening Post*, "We don't want any more states until we can civilize Kansas."

Flushed by their successes in the November elections of 1890, the Farmers' Alliances laid plans to bring the urban wage-earners into the movement, and thereby enable the manual workers of the nation to present a united front to the old parties. In May, 1891, over fourteen hundred representatives of various agrarian, labor and reform groups, meeting in Cincinnati, resolved to enter the national political arena as the People's party, and a mammoth convention in Omaha on July 2, 1892, made preparations for the impending presidential election. The platform charged the Republicans and Democrats with sacrificing "our homes, lives, and children on the altar of Mammon," and promised that the Populists would restore the government "to the hands of the plain people with whose class it originated." To this end it pledged such measures as free silver, greenbacks, a graduated income tax, government ownership of railways and telegraphs, a shorter workday for urban laborers, direct election of United States Senators, and the initiative and referendum. The adoption of the platform, according to an observer, evoked "cheers and yells which rose like a tornado . . . and raged without cessation for thirty-four minutes, during which women shrieked and wept, men embraced and kissed . . . , marched back and forth, and leaped upon tables and chairs in the ecstasy of their delirium." James B. Weaver of Iowa, veteran inflationist, who had headed the Greenback ticket in 1880, was named for President, with J. G. Field of Virginia as his running mate. In the ensuing election the new party amazed old-party leaders by polling twenty-two electoral votes and more than a million popular votes. For the first time since the birth of the Republican party, a minor party won representation in the electoral college.

Nevertheless, as we have seen, Cleveland was elected by an enormous majority on the tariff issue and, should economic conditions improve, it seemed likely that the political stream would subside once more into its customary banks. But such did not prove to be the case. No sooner did the new President enter office than a panic crashed upon the country, which in its destructive effects rivaled that of 1873. The disaster of 1893 was bred of a complication of causes. Overinvestment in railways and industrial combinations, including too many of a highly speculative character, was a prime factor. Widespread depression in Europe since 1889, involving leading nations like Great Britain, Germany and France, had its influence by causing a withdrawal of part of the gold which foreign capitalists had invested in American enterprises. But most serious of all was the growing fear of the business classes that the flood of silver inflation under the Sherman act would sweep the government off a gold basis and force a suspension of gold payments.

Though the Sherman law permitted the government to redeem the new treasury notes in either gold or silver, gold was a popular symbol of the nation's financial integrity, and refusal to pay in the more precious metal would have destroyed public confidence. Yet no provision had been made in the act for enlarging the gold reserve. Hence, this fund of $100,000,000, established in 1875 to protect the greenbacks left outstanding (see page 164), must now serve, in addition, to back up the new treasury notes that were being issued at a rate of $50,000,000 a year.[1] Indeed, since the gold reserve was not held separate from other public funds, there was the further danger that, under pressure of need, the government might use some of it for current operating expenses. Such an emergency confronted Cleveland when he took office. Thanks to lavish appropriations by Harrison's outgoing Congress and the meager revenue produced by the McKinley tariff, the gold reserve within six weeks fell below the $100,000,000 mark, greatly to the alarm of the business and

---

[1] Greenbacks to the amount of nearly $347,000,000 were outstanding. The 378,000,000 silver dollars issued under the Bland-Allison act were not, by law, redeemable in gold.

financial classes. People everywhere rushed to get their treasury notes redeemed in gold, and foreign investors redoubled their efforts to secure prompt settlement of their American accounts in the only metal used in international trade.

Even a sounder commercial structure might not have withstood this shock to public confidence. As it was, a paralysis of terror gripped the business world. More than 8000 commercial concerns failed between April 1 and October 1, with liabilities of nearly $285,000,000. Many banks also toppled, particularly in the West and South, and 156 railways went into receivership, including the Erie, the Union Pacific and the Northern Pacific. In the urban centers the problem of unemployment became acute, challenging all the resources of the new generation of social workers in the bestowal of relief. The farmers were now plunged even deeper into the abyss of adversity, wheat selling for but 49 cents a bushel in 1894.

Cleveland, a hard-money man, was determined at all hazards to maintain the gold standard. This he planned to accomplish by two courses of action. In order to stop additional silver purchases and thus ease the strain upon the already overburdened gold reserve, he induced the House on August 28, 1893, to adopt a bill repealing the Sherman act. The upper chamber was in a more recalcitrant mood. Utilizing their opportunity of unlimited debate, the silver Senators for a time succeeded in delaying passage through filibustering. On one occasion, W. V. Allen, the Nebraska Populist, held the floor for fourteen hours. Another persistent opponent was H. M. Teller, a Colorado Republican. But the majority eventually prevailed, and on November 1 the repeal bill became law.

As a second measure, Cleveland proposed to borrow gold faster than it was drained from the treasury for redemption. In this way he hoped to protect the reserve of yellow metal without suspending gold payments. Unhappily, paper currency presented for redemption had to be paid out again to defray the government's running expenses, and this money the recipients promptly exchanged for gold. Under the operation of what the President called "an endless chain," the gold fund dwindled from $95,000,-000 at the end of June, 1893, to $65,000,000 a year later. Congress, inspired in part by silver arguments, refused to authorize bond issues to maintain the reserve, whereupon Cleveland, discovering authority in an earlier statute, sold $50,000,000 worth of bonds to the public for gold in January, 1894, and another $50,000,000 worth in November. Yet only temporary relief resulted, for the bonds were bought, in large part, with gold that had been drawn out of the treasury by the presentation of paper currency for redemption. In the quest for more substantial relief, the administration in February, 1895, arranged with J. P. Morgan and a financial syndicate for a loan of $65,000,000 worth of gold in return for government bonds. The unusual conditions were affixed that at least half the metal be procured from abroad, and that the bankers exert their influence to protect the gold reserve against further depletion. As a result, the strain on the government relaxed for the next four or five months, though the Populists and radical Democrats, embittered against capitalistic greed, charged Cleveland with allowing the financial group to take the bonds on too easy terms and thus make an excessive profit on the transaction. The peak of the financial crisis now was passed. Normal conditions, however, did not return until the next year, when they were assisted by a fourth bond sale — this time directly to the public — of $100,000,000 in January, 1896, and by a widespread improvement of business.

THE BATTLE OF 1896 AND ITS AFTERMATH

When the bill repealing the Sherman law passed the House, "Silver Dick" Bland proclaimed that the struggle had but begun, and that it would end only in the establishment of free coinage. The events of the next few years made this prediction seem anything but an idle boast. The air was full of revolt against things as they were. The wage reductions and bread lines of 1893 produced a harvest of labor outbreaks in the spring of 1894, of which the Pullman strike was but the most portentous (see pages 208-210). Among the two million unemployed the social contagion spread rapidly. Presently organized bands of the jobless began a march on Washington to make a personal presentation of their grievances. These "petitions in boots" moved slowly across the country, afoot and on horseback, sometimes stealing trains for faster transit, frightening some of the communities through which they passed and cheered on by others. They came from many points of the compass — from Los Angeles, San Francisco, Seattle, St. Louis, Chicago, as well as from towns along the way and in New England. The "army" led by "General" J. S. Coxey of Massillon, Ohio, though by no means the largest, excited the most attention. With depleted numbers, about twelve hundred men straggled into Washington from May to July, 1894. There they were able to accomplish nothing. Coxey himself was arrested on the technical charge of trespassing on the Capitol grounds, and his footsore comrades, facing starvation and harassed by the police, presently scattered for parts unknown. The failure of the movement, however, did not heal the conditions that had given it rise.

Popular suspicion of the overweaning power of Big Business was deepened by the Senate's betrayal of Cleveland's tariff policy in the Wilson-Gorman act in 1894 (see pages 189–190), and the Supreme Court's disallowance of the income tax in 1895 provoked the greatest outburst of wrath against that tribunal since the Dred Scott decision. As Mr. Justice Harlan recalled many years later in the course of a judicial opinion, "a deep feeling of unrest" stirred the people. "The Nation had been rid of human slavery," he said, ". . . but the conviction was universal that the country was in real danger from another kind of slavery, . . . namely, the slavery that would result from aggregations of capital in the hands of a few . . . controlling, for their own . . . advantage exclusively, the entire business of the country."

Under the circumstances the battle over free silver took on the semblance of a holy war, arraying the West and South against the East, the countryside against the city, the debtor class against the creditor class. As a writer in the *Arena* magazine put it, the real meaning of the contest "lies far deeper than any question of one metal or two for a monetary base. It is a question of entrusting Federal power to men in hearty sympathy with the great common people or to men in sympathy with Wall Street." The growing enthusiasm for unlimited coinage displayed many of the elements of a mighty religious revival, and in 1894 appeared the Bible of the new faith in the form of a yellow-colored, paper-bound book entitled *Coin's Financial School*, written by W. H. Harvey. This little volume, enlivened with caricatures and addressed to the simplest understanding, set forth cogently the main silver arguments, and skillfully played upon the prejudices of the poor against the rich. Attaining a sale in 1895 of more than 100,000 copies a month, it undoubtedly made numberless converts. In ten thousand schoolhouses throughout the West and the South the people assembled to debate the absorbing question — not only the politician and the farmer, but the small merchant and the workingman, the preacher and the school-teacher. Organized labor rallied to the cause, the American Federation of Labor warmly indorsing free silver.

The old parties were badly frightened, but knew not what to do. In their state conventions before the autumn elections of 1894, the platforms of both Republicans and Democrats varied from ambiguous generalities to forthright declarations for unlimited coinage. A significant demonstration among Western Democrats took place in June at Omaha where, under the leadership of William Jennings Bryan of Nebraska, a monster convention demanded the immediate adoption of free silver. Handicapped by Cleveland's unpopularity, the Democrats suffered severe losses at the polls. The Republicans were the chief gainers, but the Populists elected six Senators, and increased their popular vote over that of 1892 by nearly fifty per cent.

On the heels of the election the silver Democrats began to make plans to cast off Eastern control and commit the party unequivocally to free coinage in the forthcoming presidential campaign. During 1895 numerous conferences were held, organizations formed, speeches made, pamphlets circulated. When the national convention assembled at Chicago on July 7, 1896, triumph was assured. A platform was adopted which acclaimed free silver as the question "paramount to all others," assailed the income-tax decision, and denounced federal interference in labor disturbances. While the platform was before the convention for discussion, there occurred one of the most exciting debates ever held on such an occasion. Senator David B. Hill of New York ably championed the cause of gold and the East, ending his address with an appeal not "to drive old Democrats out of the party who have grown gray in the service, to make room for a lot of Republicans and Populists, and political nondescripts." After other speakers had entered the lists, the debate reached a dramatic climax in the concluding address of the youthful Bryan of Nebraska. Speaking with a full-toned, richly modulated eloquence unmatched in his generation, he presented the free-coinage question as "a cause as holy as the cause of humanity." Turning to those who opposed the silver plank, he declared: "You tell us that the great cities are in favor of the gold standard; we reply that the great cities rest upon our broad and fertile prairies. Burn down your cities and leave our farms, and your cities will spring up again as if by magic; but destroy our farms and the grass will grow in the streets of every city in the country." His closing defiance to the gold adherents brought the vast audience in a frenzy to its feet: "You shall not press down upon the brow of labor this crown of thorns; you shall not crucify mankind upon a cross of gold." The "Boy Orator of the Platte" had made himself the man of the hour. Without strength before the convention met, he won the nomination on the fifth ballot, the second place going to Arthur Sewall of Maine. Most of the Eastern delegates abstained from voting.

When the Republicans convened at St. Louis on June 16, their ranks were divided among advocates of the gold standard, those who preferred the customary policy of noncommittalism, and a resolute minority from the Far West bent upon a free-silver plank. The leading aspirant for the nomination was ex-Governor McKinley of Ohio, known to the public chiefly as an ardent protectionist. For his prominence before the convention he was indebted to the tireless exertions of his friend Marcus A. Hanna. The latter, an Ohio capitalist, had found in "practical politics" an indispensable tool for amassing a fortune in mines, banking and street railways, but later became enamored of the political game for its own sake. Hanna's efforts and money had facilitated McKinley's election as governor in 1891 and, when two years later McKinley became involved in heavy financial obligations, Hanna, Carnegie, Frick and others supplied the $100,000 that saved him from bankruptcy. In preparing the way for McKinley's nomination Hanna spent not less than $100,000 in a campaign of publicity and personal canvass among the delegates.

The monetary issue presented serious difficulties for McKinley. After having long championed free silver, in his campaign for

governor in 1891 he had upheld the limited coinage provided by
the Sherman act as preferable to unlimited coinage. By temperament, as well as by previous conviction, he wished the party
to straddle the question and focus all attention on the tariff.
Furthermore, he feared that a less conciliatory course would lose
him votes needed for the nomination.   Hanna, sinking the
business man in the politician, assented to the plan, but not so
the powerful leaders from the industrial regions, who made a gold
declaration the price of their support. The outcome of many
secret conferences between the factions was a skillfully con-
structed plank, which read in part: "We are . . . opposed to the
free coinage of silver except by international agreement . . . ,
which we pledge ourselves to promote, and until such agreement
can be obtained the existing gold standard must be preserved."
Taken literally, the platform declared for international free silver,
but since international conferences in 1878, 1881 and 1892 had
demonstrated the unwillingness of European countries to depart
from the gold standard, the plank was rightly construed by the
silverites as a repudiation of free coinage. Thirty-four delegates
with Senator Teller of Colorado at their head withdrew from the
convention in protest. In the completed platform the money
plank occupied an inconspicuous place in the middle, the first
nine paragraphs being devoted to disparaging the Democrats and
praising the protective system. McKinley was named on the
first ballot, with G. A. Hobart of New Jersey as his running mate.

   The decision of the major parties led to a disruption of party
loyalties comparable only to the effect of the slavery issue on the
voters of 1860. A convention of old-school Democrats, acting
with Cleveland's approval, reaffirmed the gold standard, and put
up J. M. Palmer of Illinois and S. B. Buckner of Kentucky as
their candidates. Had the Republican platform been less em-
phatic on the tariff question, McKinley might have received their
support. The Republican irreconcilables, calling themselves the
National Silver party, gave their formal indorsement to Bryan
and Sewall. As was to be expected, the People's party also backed
Bryan, though for Vice-President they nominated one of their
own followers in preference to the Maine banker. Even the
Prohibitionists were affected by the all-absorbing issue, and
broke into two parties with different platforms and candidates.

The contest was unique and sensational to the end. Fearful of further defections from their ranks, Republican orators at first avoided the monetary question, placing all stress upon "Bill McKinley and the McKinley Bill." But it was Bryan who set the pace for the campaign when he undertook a remarkable stumping tour of eighteen thousand miles, addressing nearly five million people in twenty-nine states in fourteen weeks, and everywhere preaching free silver and the doctrine of discontent. Gompers and other leaders of organized labor exerted themselves on his behalf. Of no little influence were Homer Davenport's cartoons in Hearst's *New York Journal*, which portrayed Hanna as an ogrelike figure checkered with dollar signs and leading the child McKinley by a string. For campaign funds the Democrats leaned heavily upon the silver-mine owners, somewhat over a half-million dollars being subscribed in all. To checkmate the efforts of the opposition, Hanna as head of the Republican national committee collected from the great banking and business interests an election fund of unknown amount, probably between three and four million dollars, and launched a mammoth campaign of popular education. A small army was organized to address rallies, send out literature in ten different languages, and distribute campaign buttons. Besides, over five hundred different posters were prepared, the most popular being a lithograph of McKinley bearing the inscription, "The Advance Agent of Prosperity." Most, though not all, leading economists and financiers were against Bryan on the money question, and the veteran independent, Carl Schurz, threw his influence to the Republican ticket. The candidate himself remained at home, delivering from his front porch in Canton, Ohio, impressive set addresses to visiting delegations.

As the campaign drew to a close, the excitement of the country became intense. Manufacturers made contracts contingent upon McKinley's election, and wage-earners were told the factories would close in the event of Democratic success. By such newspapers as the *New York Tribune* Bryan was reviled as a "demagogue," an "anarchist" and a "madman." One Republican spellbinder, commending the designation, "Boy Orator of the Platte," asserted that that river was "six inches deep and six miles wide at the mouth." Even so sober an organ as the

New York Evening Post characterized the contest as one between "the great civilizing forces of the republic" and "the still surviving barbarism bred by slavery in the South and the reckless spirit of adventure in the mining camps of the West." A rise in the price of wheat, due to crop failures in Russia, South America and elsewhere, occurred a few weeks before election day and, by easing the farmers' distress, aided the Republican cause. The outcome was decisive. McKinley received fifty-one per cent of the popular vote to less than forty-seven for his opponent, the largest majority since Grant's victory over Greeley. His preponderance in the electoral college was far greater, 271 to 176. In general, the industrial and older grain-growing states supported McKinley as against the cotton, prairie and silver-mining states. It was noteworthy, too, that all the great cities outside the former Confederacy cast Republican majorities.[1] The immediate issue, that of silver coinage, was conclusively settled; the farmers' attempt to beat back the new urban and industrial civilization had turned to rout. Yet the future was to disclose that the campaign marked the entry of novel and dynamic social forces into American political life.

The new President went into office with both branches of Congress safely Republican. A man of quiet dignity, with deep-set eyes under a Websterian brow, he brought to public affairs qualities that sharply set him off from his Democratic predecessor: affability, tact, patience and a desire to keep in step with his party. To further Hanna's ambitions, he promoted Senator John Sherman to the office of Secretary of State, so that Hanna might succeed to the vacant senatorship.[2] Advanced years and mental impairment presently obliged the replacement of Sherman by William R. Day, another Ohioan, and the latter in turn re-

---

[1] "Moreover," added the *Nation*, November 12, 1896, "the cities having the largest population and the largest percentages of foreign-born citizens cast the heaviest majorities in support of sound money and social order." E. L. Godkin, the editor, made no allowance for the effect of economic coercion in producing this result.

[2] Other than Sherman, the members of the original cabinet were L. J. Gage of Illinois, Secretary of the Treasury; R. A. Alger of Michigan, Secretary of War; Joseph McKenna of California, Attorney-General; J. A. Gary of Maryland, Post-master-General; J. D. Long of Massachusetts, Secretary of the Navy; C. N. Bliss of New York, Secretary of the Interior; and James Wilson of Iowa, Secretary of Agriculture.

tired in August, 1898, to make way for John Hay, also of Ohio, one of the ablest men who ever held the post.

In spite of an apparently clear popular verdict against silver, McKinley chose to interpret his victory as primarily a mandate for tariff protection (see page 190). The fact was that Republican ranks remained divided notwithstanding the united front displayed at the election, and it seemed to McKinley and his advisers the part of wisdom to let well enough alone so far as monetary reform was concerned. However, to carry out the platform pledge, an official commission was dispatched to France and Great Britain in 1897 to confer in regard to the establishment of free silver by international action. The anticipated refusal of Great Britain, followed presently by the distracting effects of the Spanish-American War, eased the path for the gold advocates. Other events also were working in their behalf. After 1896 a period of bewildering prosperity burst upon the country. Harvests were generous and prices ample, thereby making agriculture profitable again and gladdening the heart of the farmer. At the same time, the introduction of rural free delivery of mail beginning in 1896, the spread of farmers' mutual telephone companies with the lapse of the basic Bell patents, the advent of interurban electric railways and the extension of the good-roads movement did something to relieve the loneliness of country life and appease the sense of rural inferiority.[1] Most important of all was an enormous increase in available gold as a result of the new cyanide process of extracting the metal from low-content ores and the opening up of mines in Alaska and South Africa. The world's annual production, which had averaged between five and six million ounces from 1860 to 1890, reached nearly eleven and a half million in 1897 and twenty-two in 1910. Paper currency also grew in volume, thanks to the purchase by national banks of government bonds issued to finance the war with Spain and to liberalization of the national banking act. With prosperity widely diffused and all reasonable fear of the scarcity of money removed, the argument for silver inflation collapsed.

On March 14, 1900, the gold-standard act was adopted. This

[1] Rural-free-delivery routes lengthened from 1800 miles in 1897 to nearly 29,000 in 1900 and 950,000 in 1916.

statute definitely established the single standard by declaring other forms of money redeemable in gold on demand. It also enlarged the gold redemption fund to $150,000,000. In order to avoid the difficulties that had vexed the Cleveland administration, the law made the gold reserve a separate and distinct fund, not to be drawn upon to meet current deficiences in the revenue, and it provided further that, when paper notes were offered for redemption, they should not be paid out again except for gold. Thus the war of the standards closed, leaving to the next generation the solution of certain knotty problems arising from other imperfections of the circulating medium, notably its inelastic character.

SELECT BIBLIOGRAPHY

The Farmers Take Their Stand, 1880-1900. Hicks, *The Populist Revolt*, traces with impartial hand the history of the Farmers' Alliances and the People's party. Laughlin, *The History of Bimetallism in the United States*, deals with the technical aspects of the silver question. Lauck, *The Causes of the Panic of 1893*, and Weberg, *The Background of the Panic of 1893*, are special studies of the financial collapse. In *Coxey's Army* McMurry presents a graphic account of the march of the jobless on Washington. Leading figures in the controversy over free silver are portrayed in Nevins, *Grover Cleveland;* Barnes, *John G. Carlisle;* Long, *Bryan;* Croly, *Marcus Alonzo Hanna;* and Olcott, *The Life of William McKinley*. These biographies treat the campaign of 1896 from varying points of view.

CHAPTER XIV

THE STRENGTHENING OF NATIONALITY, 1865–1900

THE DRIFT TOWARD CENTRALIZATION

THE presidential campaign of 1896 bore striking testimony to the firmness of the Union that had come into being since the Civil War. Though the farmers' grievances were no less real than had been those of the slaveholders, there was no talk of nullification or secession, no Calhoun or Davis brandishing the shibboleth of state sovereignty. On the contrary, the agrarian spokesmen demanded an enlargement, not a limitation, of the powers of the general government. This new attitude toward federal supremacy was one of the most significant developments of the postwar era. The overthrow of the Confederacy in 1865 not only had insured the geographic unity of the country, but had also strongly stimulated the sense of national consciousness. The adventure of Western exploitation after the war further exalted the people's faith in the greatness of American destiny. Meanwhile the Economic Revolution, by knitting the nation together with bonds of steel and ties of mutual business interest, caused men to become forgetful of state boundaries and to think in terms of the nation as a whole. As James Bryce remarked in 1888, "The South and the West need capital for their development, and are daily in closer business relations with the East. The produce of the West finds its way to the Atlantic through the ports of the East. Every produce market, every share market, vibrates in response to the Produce Exchange and Stock Exchange of New York."

Other influences — the increasing urbanization and standardization of American life, the extension of the public-school system to all parts of the land, the broad appeal of the new literature, the country-wide absorption in athletic sport — worked to the same end. In a different way, the new spirit found vent in the formation of an endless number of voluntary continent-wide bodies, not only those of capital and labor, but also, it will be recalled, similar organizations of scholars, scientists, artists, social and political reformers, sport lovers and secret-society "joiners." America had never beheld such a banding together of the like-minded regardless of geography.   As the nation reached the centenary of its birth, the heightened pride of nationality exulted in a series of patriotic celebrations, beginning with the anniversary of Concord and Lexington in 1875 and the Centennial Exhibition at Philadelphia in 1876, and continuing year after year until the setting up of the Supreme Court was commemorated in 1890 with due pomp and circumstance. It is little wonder that Edward Freeman, the English historian, visiting the United States in 1883, noted that "where the word 'federal' used to be used up to the time of the civil war or later, the word 'national' is now used all but invariably. It used to be 'federal capital,' 'federal army,' 'federal revenue,' and so forth. Now the word 'national' is almost always used instead."

Nothing more clearly revealed the pervasive strength of the nationalizing process than the changed attitude of the South. Nearly every year yielded fresh evidence that the Southern people accepted their defeat in good faith, while an ever larger number rejoiced that the "Lost Cause" was indeed lost. Even Jefferson Davis, writing in 1881 without apology for the past, expressed the earnest hope that "there may be written on the arch of the Union, *Esto perpetua*." In that year, veterans' organizations of the former blue and gray hosts began occasionally to hold joint reunions in order to compare war-time experiences in a spirit of amity and mutual esteem. The Virginian, John S. Wise, probably voiced the thought of most of his erstwhile comrades-in-arms when he wrote a few years later, "Through our tears, and without disloyalty to the dead, in the possession of freedom and union and liberty, true Confederates, viewing it all in the clearer light of to-day, ought to thank God that slavery died at Appomattox." Behind this growth of national good will lay a number of causes, among them the recovery of white rule in the South; the cessation of Northern intrusion in Southern race relations; the mingling of Northerners and Southerners as a result of free intermigration; the crowding in of new industrial and agricultural problems that increasingly identified Dixie with the national economic order; and, not of least importance, the healing balm of time and the coming of a new generation. Southern contributions to local-color fiction (see page 246) did much to restore sectional self-esteem, while at the same time they gave Northerners a mellow and romantic picture of Southern life and ideals to offset the abolitionist exaggerations of bygone years. All these tendencies reached a climax in the Spanish war of 1898. For the first time, the former foemen were called upon to face a common national enemy. None could doubt the completeness of the response or the attainment of a single, undivided country.[1]

In the sphere of national politics the new centripetal tide swept parties and leaders before it. Republicans welcomed it, Democrats deplored it; but even the latter, when in power, could not successfully resist it. Whether men sought to promote or to curb the mighty forces remaking the economic order, they turned to Washington, not to their state governments, as the effective agency for action. The Republicans, as we have seen, speeded national consolidation through the Thirteenth, Fourteenth and Fifteenth amendments, federal supervision of state elections, extreme tariff protection, lavish grants for railroad, river and harbor development, and the Sherman law for abolishing trusts. A Democratic House initiated and a Democratic President signed the interstate-commerce act, which embodied a startling new assumption of national authority. A few years later when Cleveland defied the state-rights view of the Constitution at the time of the Pullman strike by sending troops to Chicago (see page 209), Governor Altgeld of Illinois felt obliged to remind the President that "the principle of local self-government is just as fundamental in our institutions as is that of Federal supremacy." Yet there was no time when Altgeld and other men of progressive or radical opinions would not gladly have used the federal government to implement policies which they themselves deemed desirable. Bryce acutely pointed out that, though the state had once been a "self-sufficing commonwealth," it "is now merely a part of a far grander whole, which seems to be slowly absorbing its functions and stunting its growth, as the great tree stunts the shrubs over which its spreading boughs have

[1] It was at this time that Congress expunged from the statute books the remaining disabilities imposed upon ex-Confederate leaders by the Fourteenth Amendment.

begun to cast their shade." The twentieth century was to bring an even greater exaltation of national at the expense of state power, notably during the administrations of Woodrow Wilson and Franklin D. Roosevelt.

The Supreme Court yielded more slowly to the nationalizing current. The "convenient vagueness" of the first section of the Fourteenth Amendment admitted of a variety of interpretations, but the court's early decisions looked backward rather than forward. "No State," reads the amendment, "shall make or enforce any law that shall abridge the privileges or immunities of citizens of the United States; nor shall any State deprive any person of life, liberty, or property, without due process of law; nor deny to any person within its jurisdiction the equal protection of the laws." In the Slaughterhouse cases (1873) certain butchers of New Orleans appealed to the Supreme Court to annul the monopoly rights that the corrupt Carpetbag legislature had granted to a local slaughterhouse company. They alleged that the law in question abridged the privileges and immunities of "citizens of the United States" and that, further, it deprived them as "persons" of property without due process of law and denied them the equal protection of the laws. By a majority of five to four, the court held that there was a difference between state citizenship and national citizenship and that, since the privileges and immunities in dispute belonged to state citizenship, the complainants must look for relief to Louisiana, not to the federal government. The court dismissed the other charges by denying that the Louisiana statute involved a taking of property without due process of law, and by asserting that the provision for equal protection was intended to apply to Negroes.[1] Three years later, as we have already seen (page 162), the tribunal took a somewhat similar stand in the Granger cases, declaring Illinois's untrammeled right under her police power to fix rates for businesses "clothed with a public interest," and denying that the complainants had been deprived of property without due process of law. The court displayed an equally conservative attitude in 1882 in the case of San Mateo County v. Southern

---

[1] As the majority opinion pointed out, the "one pervading purpose" of the framers of the Fourteenth Amendment had been to protect the rights of the ex-slave. See earlier, page 109.

Pacific Railroad Co. by deciding that a corporation was not a "person" whose actions fell within the purview of the Fourteenth Amendment. In other words, the whole tendency of the Supreme Court was to restrain the federal authority from interfering with the activities of state and local governments.

After the mid-eighties, however, the judiciary began to assert a boldly national point of view. Revising its opinion of four years before, it declared in the case of Santa Clara County *v.* Southern Pacific Railroad Co. (1886) that a corporation was a "person" and hence entitled to the protection of the amendment. The same year it held in the Wabash case (see page 196), contrary to its judgment in the Granger cases, that states could not regulate rates that affected interstate commerce. In the Minnesota Rate case three years later, it went even further and denied the state's uncontrolled right to fix rates of any kind, declaring in effect that, under the due-process clause, the court was the final authority as to the reasonableness of the rates imposed.[1] In these and other later decisions the tribunal arrogated to itself the power of reviewing all state and local legislation affecting the rights of private property. That its influence generally favored the great business interests is less important in the present connection than the fact that the court, responsive at last to the centralizing trend, assumed the high function of arbiter and censor of the shifting national economic order.

THE NEW ATTITUDE TOWARD IMMIGRATION

The heightened sense of nationality led also to a changed attitude toward unrestricted immigration. Since colonial times migrants from across the sea had flocked to America without let or hindrance. The bulk of the newcomers consisted of farmers and petty shopkeepers from the British Isles, Germany and, more recently, the Scandinavian countries. Of the seven million foreigners living in the United States in 1880, the Germans and Irish numbered about a million each, the Canadians 717,000, the English 664,000 and the Scandinavians 440,000. Most of them, the Irish excepted, took up farming as a livelihood, and in 1880 a higher proportion of immigrants dwelt in the upper Mississippi

---

[1] Chicago, Milwaukee and St. Paul Railway Co. *v.* Minnesota, a six-to-three decision.

Valley than in any other section of the country. Such folk were easily assimilated, for they represented the racial strains from which the Anglo-Saxon stock had originally sprung. So greatly were they desired that the newer commonwealths maintained official bureaus to encourage their coming. With plenty of land

EUROPEAN SOURCES OF AMERICAN IMMIGRATION IN THE LATE NINETEENTH AND EARLY TWENTIETH CENTURIES

for settlement their addition to the population caused no shock to the economic structure.

The year 1882 marks a turning point in the history of immigration. In that year the influx from Western and Northern Europe reached its crest, arrivals began to appear in noticeable numbers from Eastern and Southern Europe, and Congress enacted the first significant restrictive law. The hosts from south Russia, Italy, Austria-Hungary and other Mediterranean countries increased steadily year by year until in 1896 they exceeded in volume those of the older type. Many influences account for the "new immigration," notably overcrowded conditions in Southern and Eastern Europe, anti-Semitic persecution in Russia beginning about 1881, the opening of direct steamship connections between Mediterranean ports and the United States, and the unexampled opportunities for employment in the new mines and factories. Steamship companies stimulated the inflow to the extent of their advertising ability, while agents representing American corporations stood ready to prepay the passage of laborers agreeing in advance to work in their plants.

The new immigrants contrasted sharply with the old in almost every respect. Hiving in the industrial centers, they formed self-contained communities that tended to perpetuate the peculiar institutions, folk customs and foreign-language newspapers of the homeland. Unused to the American standard of living, they vastly complicated the problems of sanitation, health and housing for municipal authorities. For the same reason, they gladly toiled for wages and upon terms that native workingmen scorned; and since one out of every three planned to go back home after laying aside a little money, many remained indifferent, when not actually hostile, to the efforts of organized labor to improve conditions. Moreover, most of them lacked familiarity with democratic institutions and ideals, and over thirty-five per cent were illiterate as against three per cent in the case of the older immigrant class. They were widely charged with responsibility for municipal misrule; but this could hardly be maintained when "American" cities like Philadelphia and Portland, Oregon, disclosed as wretched conditions as New York and Chicago with their far higher proportion of foreign-born citizens. Individuals among the recent comers were equal to the best that the older strain produced; the bulk of these Slavs, Magyars, Poles, Russian Jews, Italians and Greeks provided the heavy labor upon which rested the remarkable development of mill and mine during these years.

The swelling tide of immigration from Mediterranean Europe hastened the adoption of a new national policy toward incoming aliens. There was as yet no desire on the part of the United

States to relinquish its historic rôle as a refuge for the oppressed of all lands, but the conviction was growing that, with the dwindling of the open frontier and the increasing problems raised by the herding of immigrants in cities, national self-protection called for some measure of selective immigration. Organized labor urged the same course as a means of safeguarding native workers against unfair competition. The first important restrictive act, that of 1882, excluded lunatics, convicted criminals and persons likely to become public charges. Three years later the alien-labor-contract law forbade employers to import foreign workingmen under previous contract. Every few years saw the adoption of additional restraints until by 1903 the excluded classes embraced physical, mental and moral defectives of all kinds, professional beggars, assisted immigrants, polygamists and anarchists. As a special discrimination against the more recent comers, a strong sentiment developed for a literacy test, but this was as vigorously opposed by persons who insisted that ability to read was a test of youthful opportunity, not of mental capacity. A bill for this purpose was vetoed by President Cleveland before he left office in 1897. Among other things, he dismissed the charges as to the inferior character of the new immigrants by saying, "The time is quite within recent memory when the same thing was said of immigrants who, with their descendants, are now numbered among our best citizens."

The sheer magnitude of the immigration after 1865 is a source of amazement. In the period to 1900 no less than 13,260,000 foreigners of all kinds entered the United States, nearly enough to populate New England twice over today; and the volume was to become bigger in the opening years of the present century. It is unlikely that this great influx did much to enlarge the total population, for, by increasing competition for employment, it tended to encourage late or childless marriages on the part of natives and thus to retard the growth of the old American stock. The mounting stream caused the racial complexion of certain sections to change in startling ways. As *Donahoe's Magazine* pointed out as early as 1889, "Boston is no longer the Boston of the Endicotts and the Winthrops, but the Boston of the Collinses and the O'Briens." In that year sixty-eight towns and cities of Massachusetts, including many of the largest, were governed by the Irish. Greater New York in 1890 was the world's chief center of immigrants, a veritable amalgam of nations, with half as many Italians as Naples, as many Germans as Hamburg, twice as many Irishmen as Dublin and two and a half times as many Jews as Warsaw. Chicago was hardly less cosmopolitan, having more Bohemians, Poles and Canadians than New York, while the great agricultural empire to its northwest was rapidly turning into a new Scandinavia. Yet everywhere, even in the dense population centers and among the new type of immigrants, the "melting pot" was performing its work. Sometimes unusual business success or the liberalizing effect of membership in a labor union hastened the process. More often it was the democratic school system that brought the influences of the new land into the immigrant home. The American-born children were apt to intermarry with other racial stocks, and accept American ways and ideals so zealously as wholly to forget their alien cultural heritage.

Though the government raised ever higher bars against the undesirable individuals from Europe, it did not go so far as to exclude whole peoples as undesirable. This more drastic course, however, it adopted to cope with the problem of Oriental immigration on the Pacific Coast. The earliest Chinese coolies in California in the fifties and sixties had been in such demand, as cheap labor, that Leland Stanford and other captains of industry imported whole shiploads of them. By 1870 they numbered between fifty and sixty thousand. While this cordial attitude still continued, the United States made the Burlingame treaty of 1868 with China, which explicitly recognized the "inalienable right of man to change his home and allegiance, and also the mutual advantage of the free migration and emigration" between the two countries. Almost at once local sentiment began to change. White immigrant laborers, multiplying in California as the transcontinental lines were completed, found themselves obliged to compete for jobs with a people whose low standard of living enabled them to work for a mere pittance. As Robert Louis Stevenson, who resided for a time in California, wrote, "Hungry Europe and hungry China, each pouring from their gates in search of provender, had here come face to face." Racial differences and a strong belief as to the unassimilability of the

Orientals further sharpened the antagonism. In 1871 a riot in Los Angeles ended in the death of twenty-one Asiatics and, for ten years, the question was of burning importance in state politics. A newly formed political party adopted the slogan, "The Chinese must go," mob attacks took place upon the Chinese quarter of San Francisco, and the legislature passed discriminatory laws, though most of these were set aside by the courts.

In time the violence of the agitation excited national attention. In 1879 the Democratic House of Representatives and the Republican Senate, vying with each other for the electoral vote of California, passed a bill revoking the Burlingame treaty and restricting Chinese immigration. President Hayes, disapproving the method but not the purpose of this action, vetoed the measure and, instead, negotiated a new arrangement with China. The treaty of 1880 permitted the United States to "regulate, limit, or suspend," but "not absolutely prohibit," future coolie immigration. Under its terms Congress two years later adopted the first Chinese exclusion law, to remain in effect for ten years. Subsequent acts renewed the suspension from time to time, and in 1902 Congress made the prohibition indefinite. Though China in 1904 declined to give the practice further treaty sanction, the United States continued the exclusion upon its own authority.

THE CRUMBLING OF NATIONAL ISOLATION

With the enhanced nationalism at home came a new attitude in international relations. Though pledges of "isolation" and fear of "entangling alliances" continued to mark the utterances of statesmen, the deep pull of events steadily loosened the nation from ancient moorings. As the Economic Revolution gained full momentum, industrialists found they needed to look elsewhere to market their growing surplus of goods, while capitalists began to scan the globe for opportunities to supplement their domestic investments.[1] Other motives operated to the same end.

[1] Lyman J. Gage, McKinley's Secretary of the Treasury, pointed out in 1900 that, while the American population had doubled from 1870 to 1899, exports had increased 212 per cent, pig-iron production 607 per cent and the output of steel over 1200 per cent. In the same period American foreign investments rose from a negligible amount to more than $500,000,000, over half of it in Latin-American countries.

Overseas missionary activity, particularly in the Pacific islands and the Orient, had long been a feature of American life, and the possibility of carrying the blessings of Christianity to the "benighted heathen" under protection of the Stars and Stripes touched a responsive chord in many hearts. Equally important was the fact that the national spirit of adventure and acquisition, thwarted by the occupation of the last continental frontier, sought fresh channels for expression. "In our infancy," wrote Captain A. T. Mahan, one of the early protagonists of American imperialism, "we bordered upon the Atlantic only; our youth carried our boundary to the Gulf of Mexico; to-day maturity sees us upon the Pacific. Have we no right or no call to progress farther in any direction?"

Sensitive to the broadening international outlook, heads of the Navy Department throughout the eighties pressed forward plans to enlarge and modernize the fleet. Other powers had gone over to steel warships, but the American navy remained upon a wooden basis. In 1883, during Arthur's administration, Congress made a start with four steel cruisers. Cleveland vigorously lent his support, bringing about the construction of additional steel vessels, improvements in armament, the establishment of a naval ordnance plant and a strengthening of coast defenses. Under Harrison the first first-class battleships were built, and the total number of modern steel vessels in commission grew to twenty-two. The United States by 1893 had advanced from twelfth to fifth place as a naval power, and by 1900 to third.

In a different way, the new spirit was mirrored in the willingness of the United States to join with groups of other nations in a series of treaties dealing with subjects like submarine cables, patents, weights and measures, and suppression of the African slave trade. Without precedent in earlier American diplomacy, the government signed fifteen such agreements between 1865 and 1900. In 1880 it also joined nine European powers in a pact defining and protecting the rights of foreigners in Morocco. Of the various treaties, none aroused such wide interest at home as the adherence of the Arthur administration in 1882 to the Geneva convention for establishing the International Red Cross Society. This agreement, made originally by sixteen nations in 1864, provided that, in every country signing it, there should be set up civilian organizations to coöperate in time of war with the army medical corps in caring for the sick and wounded. Long indifferent to the matter, the American government was finally brought to action through the persistent advocacy of Clara Barton of Massachusetts, who from her services with the Red Cross in the Franco-Prussian War (1870–1871) had learned its superiority to the Sanitary Commission in the Civil War. To her, too, belongs credit for the "American Amendment" to the Geneva convention in 1884, which extended the scope of the Red Cross to peace-time humanitarian work in connection with floods, earthquakes and other public disasters.

Meanwhile, the government at Washington made efforts to promote American commerce and investments in two widely separate parts of the world, the Pacific area and Latin America, both of them rich in natural resources and both of them — to use the language of diplomacy — "backward regions." Such steps were taken hesitantly and without a definite program, but they quickly carried the country to the edge of the powerful current of imperialism that late in the seventies began to envelop Europe. Far more than America, these transatlantic powers felt driven to capture new markets for trade, secure fresh fields for investment, acquire territories in which to colonize their surplus populations, and otherwise enhance their national prestige. Before 1890 Great Britain, France and Germany had carved up most of Africa among them, with tidbits for Italy and Belgium.[1] In the Pacific, as we shall see, the advancing outposts of Europe and America clashed, necessitating an accommodation of interests. In this international rivalry the United States enjoyed the advantage of being the only Occidental power with a front on the great ocean. In Latin America, on the other hand, the American government was able to play virtually a lone hand, thanks to the Monroe Doctrine, which held Europe at arm's length. Not only economic interest, but historic reasons and geographic proximity, impelled the United States to seek active leadership there.

During the Civil War American trade in the Pacific had

[1] From 1870 to 1900 the British Empire grew by about 5,000,000 square miles exclusive of spheres of influence, while France added 3,500,000 and Germany 1,000,000 square miles to their possessions.

suffered a setback, only to be followed by a revival in the years thereafter. As a halfway stop between Asia and California the Hawaiian Islands had long been of special interest to the United States (see page 5). They were well situated to serve as a commercial coaling station, a naval base and a cable landing. Yankee missionaries had reduced the native language to writing and helped modernize the government; many of their children became landholders and sugar planters. In 1875 a reciprocity treaty was concluded, which granted sugar and other Hawaiian products free access to the United States and pledged the insular king not to dispose of any territory to another country. This was followed in 1884 by the lease of Pearl Harbor, near Honolulu, as a naval station. By 1890 American sugar plantations attained a value of $25,000,000. But the McKinley tariff of that year, by putting all imported sugar on the free list, took away Hawaii's favored position in that respect, and heightened sentiment among the local sugar growers for annexation to the United States and a share in the American sugar bounty (see page 186). In January, 1893, the opportunity came. The illiberal queen was deposed by a revolt engineered by American residents and receiving moral support, at least, from the presence of United States marines landed for that purpose. The revolutionary government, headed by an American, promptly negotiated a treaty of annexation, but Harrison's term expired before the Senate could act. President Cleveland withdrew the treaty from the Senate and, when official inquiry disclosed the complicity of the American Minister at Honolulu in the revolt, he denounced the whole transaction. Yet his action only delayed the inevitable. Japan cast hungry eyes upon the little Hawaiian republic; and when the Republicans returned to power and the Philippine operations of the Spanish-American War emphasized the naval advantages of ownership, Congress on July 7, 1898, acquired the islands by joint resolution.[1] "Annexation," declared McKinley, "is not a change; it is a consummation."

Meantime another series of events was preparing a foothold for the United States far to the south. About five thousand miles from San Francisco, on the direct trade route to Sidney,

[1] While the negotiations were in progress, Japan protested vigorously on the ground that American annexation would "disturb the *status quo* in the Pacific."

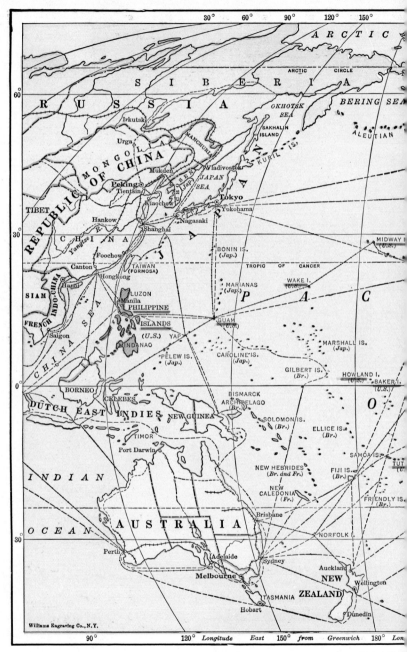

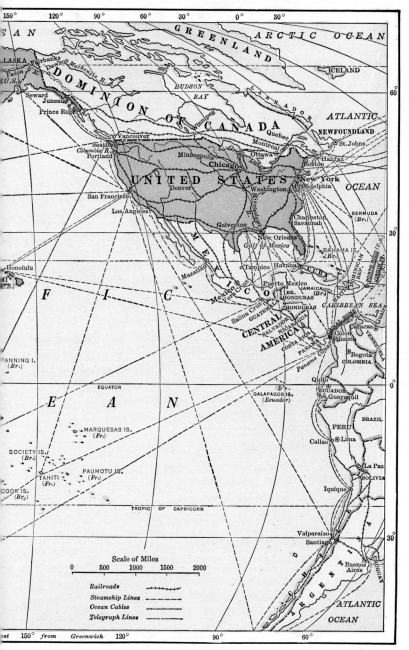

Australia, lay the Samoan Islands, possessing in Pago-Pago, in the island of Tutuila, the finest harbor of the south Pacific. In 1872 a naval officer secured from a native chief permission to establish a coaling station there. Six years later this arrangement was embodied in a treaty and the United States, in return, pledged "its good offices" to adjust difficulties between the Samoan king and other nations. British and German commercial interests also made their appearance, and the islands soon became a tiny storm center of international intrigue and conflict. In 1886, to block German designs, the American consul proclaimed a protectorate, an act promptly disavowed, however, by President Cleveland. Germany continuing aggressive, all three powers hurried warships to the scene in March, 1889. A hurricane, inflicting widespread damage and distress, swept away hostile feeling for the moment, and led to an agreement of the powers to guarantee Samoan independence and neutrality under a tripartite protectorate. This arrangement, indubitably an "entangling alliance," did not work well. Finally, in 1899, the three countries agreed upon a division of the islands, the United States receiving Tutuila, Germany taking the rest, and Great Britain being compensated with other Pacific islands belonging to Germany.

Besides these more notable acquisitions, the United States in the eighties and nineties asserted jurisdiction over more than fifty scattered small islands in the Pacific. Some of these were hardly more than rocks or coral reefs, but they were valuable for guano, for use as relay cable stations or for other purposes. Among the largest of them were Wake, Christmas, Gallego, Starbuck, Penrhyn, Phœnix, Midway, Palmyra, Howland, Baker, Johnston, Gardner, Morell and Marcus.

TOWARD LEADERSHIP IN THE AMERICAS

In Latin America the United States sought leadership rather than dominion. In earlier years the government had stressed the negative implications of the Monroe Doctrine, the obligation to prevent military or political interference by Europe with the free nations to the south. Now it assumed positive political responsibilities and, in addition, endeavored to forge closer commercial bonds. To establish its political primacy among the

New World republics, it repeatedly tendered its good offices as mediator in controversies arising among them and between them and European powers. Thus in 1876 the United States arbitrated a boundary difference between Argentina and Paraguay. In 1881 it kept France from seizing Venezuelan customhouses to compel payment of a debt, protested against the plan of Colombia and Costa Rica to submit a boundary dispute to Spain for arbitration, helped settle boundary difficulties between Mexico and Guatemala, and tried vainly to stop a war waged by Chile against Peru and Bolivia for possession of the nitrate district, Tacna and Arica.

In these efforts James G. Blaine, Secretary of State during Garfield's brief administration in 1881 and again under Harrison from 1889 to 1892, played an energetic part. His chief interest, however, was in promoting commercial relations with the southern republics, a field which Great Britain had actively exploited, with France, Spain and, somewhat later, Germany as her chief rivals. Never large in amount, the export trade of the United States to Latin America had actually decreased between 1860 and 1880. Blaine's plan took the form of a new kind of Pan-Americanism, primarily economic in purpose rather than political, as in the case of the ill-fated Panama Congress of 1826 in which Henry Clay and John Quincy Adams had been interested. In answer to his tireless advocacy, the first Pan-American Congress assembled in Washington in 1889 with Blaine as presiding officer. Among the subjects discussed were the formation of a customs union, a uniform system of trademarks and patents, improved railway and steamship communication among the various states, the creation of a monetary union and, finally, a thoroughgoing scheme for arbitrating inter-American disputes. The sole tangible results were the naming of a committee to report on an intercontinental railway, and the establishment in Washington, at the joint expense of the several countries, of the Bureau of American Republics (subsequently the Pan-American Union) as a clearing house of commercial information. Nevertheless, the discussion of common problems did much to dispel mutual jealousies and suspicions, and caused the congress to be the forerunner of a series of similar conferences in later years.

This propitious beginning of Pan-American accord suffered a

temporary setback, however, as a result of Blaine's handling of certain difficulties arising out of the Chilean civil war of 1890–1891. The United States Minister in Chile, Patrick Egan, long conspicuous in America as an agitator for Irish home rule, assumed an unfriendly attitude toward the victorious rebels, apparently because their success gratified English residents in Chile. Blaine, perhaps with an eye on the Irish-American vote in the next presidential election, upheld him in this. Other incidents followed. Finally, on October 16, 1891, sailors from the United States ship *Baltimore* fell to quarreling with Chilean sailors in a saloon in Valparaiso. In the ensuing riot two Americans were killed and several wounded. Blaine, declining to regard the affair as a mere sailors' brawl, adopted a high-handed policy. The provisional government of Chile, equally defiant, refused to accord any sort of satisfaction. For a time the countries teetered on the brink of war, but the election of a new government in Chile led to a change of attitude. Ample apologies and reparation followed.

The boldest assertion of American primacy in New World affairs came not at the hands of Republicans, but at those of President Cleveland. His pronouncement was the by-product of a long-standing controversy between Venezuela and British Guiana as to their common frontier. Like so many other South American boundaries, this one had never been accurately determined. After long years of sterile argument Venezuela began to insist that the matter be left to arbitration, a proposal which the United States gladly supported but which Great Britain steadily resisted. The conviction gained ground in Washington that Britain by bullying tactics aimed to enlarge her borders at the expense of a weak and relatively defenseless neighbor. With the discovery of gold in the disputed area in 1888, a settlement of the question became imperative. Hostile encounters took place during the next few years between British settlers and the Venezuelan police, and the appeals of Venezuela for protection grew increasingly insistent. Such pleas were reënforced by American consular representatives who saw in intervention a means of promoting trade.

Cleveland, whose acquaintance with the trouble dated from his first administration, decided in 1895 that the time had arrived for decisive action. At his behest, Secretary of State Olney in a dispatch of July 20 warned Great Britain that her failure to submit the dispute to arbitration would lead to grave consequences. The conduct of the British government, he declared, looked like an attempt to encroach upon the territory of a free American nation and, accordingly, came within the purview of the Monroe Doctrine. If, encouraged by America's silence, other powers should follow Britain's example, "it is not inconceivable that the struggle now going on for the acquisition of Africa might be transferred to South America." Britain was further told that "today the United States is practically sovereign on this continent" and, thanks to its "infinite resources combined with its isolated position," is "practically invulnerable against any or all other powers." This dispatch, blunt, aggressive and provocative, elicited a reply from Lord Salisbury, the British Foreign Minister, on November 26 to the effect that the Monroe Doctrine was not applicable to the controversy, and that the United States was wholly unwarranted in interfering.

The President now took the question out of diplomatic channels. Announcing to Congress on December 17 that the Monroe Doctrine was in jeopardy, he asked for authority to appoint a boundary commission whose findings the United States should, if need be, enforce against any counterclaims of Great Britain. "In making these recommendations," he stated, "I am fully alive to the responsibility incurred and keenly realize all the consequences that may follow." Congress, promptly acceding to the President's wishes, unanimously voted funds for the commission's expenses. To the general public in both nations, ignorant of the international crisis, Cleveland's peremptory message came like a bolt from the blue. Evidences soon appeared on every hand that the two English-speaking peoples were resolved to avert the war which the rashness of their rulers had brought near. Leading American newspapers criticized the President's extreme position. Thirteen hundred British authors sent an appeal to their brethren in America to exert every effort to prevent fratricidal conflict. In both countries prominent public figures, including the Prince of Wales and the Bishop of London, threw their influence on the side of conciliation.

Joseph Chamberlain, an influential member of the cabinet,

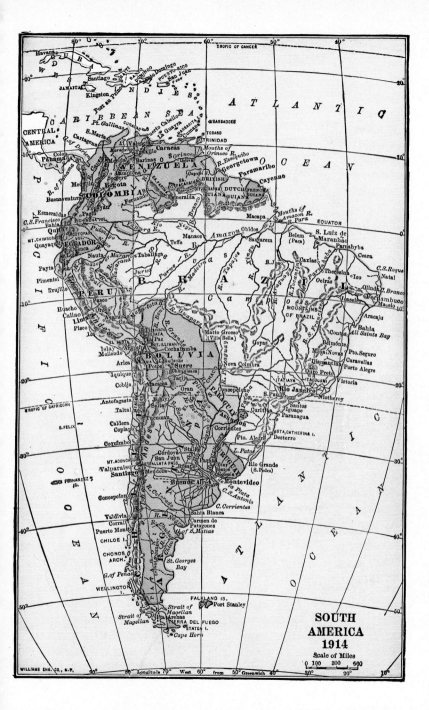

SOUTH
AMERICA
1914

Scale of Miles

0   100   300   500

voiced British official opinion when he declared in a speech at Birmingham in January, 1896, "We do not covet one single inch of American territory. War between the two nations would be an absurdity as well as a crime. . . . The two nations are allied and more closely allied in sentiment and in interest than any other nations on the face of the earth." Indeed, with continental Europe already dividing into hostile alliances, British statesmen realized the folly of unnecessarily making an enemy of the principal non-European power.[1] An impending clash with the Boers in South Africa served further to make it prudent to avoid a rupture with the United States. Accordingly, though the American boundary commission had already begun its work, Great Britain signified her willingness to submit the dispute to international arbitration. When a treaty for this purpose was drafted in February, 1897, the American commission ceased its labors. In 1899 the new tribunal, much to British satisfaction, awarded to British Guiana the larger part of the disputed area. Yet, whatever the outcome, Great Britain's yielding did much to vindicate Olney's boastful claim of the supremacy of the United States in the Western Hemisphere. In the eyes of the world the Monroe Doctrine gained new prestige. The incident is equally significant in marking the adoption of a systematic policy on the part of Great Britain to cultivate closer relations between the two English-speaking powers. The fruits of this policy became amply evident in the international developments of the ensuing years.

SELECT BIBLIOGRAPHY

The Drift toward Centralization. Aspects of this movement are considered in Bryce, *The American Commonwealth;* Merriam, *American Political Ideas, 1865–1917;* Malin, *An Interpretation of Recent American History;* and Schlesinger, *The Rise of the City.* For the expanding power of the Supreme Court Warren, *The Supreme Court in United States History*, is good.

The New Attitude toward Immigration. Such works as Fairchild, *Immigration*, Stephenson, *A History of American Immigration*, and Garis, *Immigration Restriction*, deal with the new inflow from Europe and Asia and its effects upon American governmental policy. Some of the newer immigrant

---

[1] The Triple Alliance, formed in 1882 by Germany, Austria and Italy, was renewed from time to time. Russia and France entered into the so-called Dual Alliance in 1891. Great Britain, possessing interests apart from either coalition, held aloof until 1904 when she formed an Entente Cordiale with France and, three years later, with Russia.

elements from Europe have received special study, as in Foerster, *The Italian Emigration of Our Times;* Burgess, *Greeks in America;* Joseph, *Jewish Immigration to the United States;* and Balch, *Our Slavic Fellow Citizens*. For the Asiatic phases Coolidge, *Chinese Immigration*, is detailed and authoritative.

The Crumbling of National Isolation. Coolidge, *The United States as a World Power*, Faris, *The Rise of Internationalism*, and Moon, *Imperialism and World Politics*, all contribute to a larger understanding of America's changing position in world affairs. The story of the founder of the American Red Cross is told by her son W. E. Barton in *The Life of Clara Barton*. Foster, *American Diplomacy in the Orient*, needs to be supplemented by Kuykendall, *A History of Hawaii*, and Ryden, *The Foreign Policy of the United States in Relation to Samoa*.

Toward Leadership in the Americas. Accounts of a survey character include Latané, *The United States and Latin America;* Robertson, *Hispanic-American Relations with the United States;* and Thomas, *One Hundred Years of the Monroe Doctrine*. Tyler, *The Foreign Policy of James G. Blaine*, illuminates certain aspects. Henderson, *American Diplomatic Questions*, Nevins, *Grover Cleveland*, and James, *Richard Olney and His Public Service*, are important for the Venezuelan boundary dispute.

PART THREE
DEMOCRACY AND EMPIRE

CHAPTER XV

AMERICA BECOMES A WORLD POWER

THE UNITED STATES AND THE CUBAN QUESTION

THE closing years of the nineteenth century brought to fruition the new tendencies in American foreign policy. The United States rose to the position of a world power with insular possessions in two hemispheres and a potential voice in the affairs of Asia and Europe. Brimming nationalism spilled over into imperialism. For this turn of events, unanticipated even by statesmen, American intervention in the revolt of Cuba against Spain was directly responsible. This fertile island, just about the size of Virginia, and occupied by a population two-thirds white and one-third black or mixed, was, except for its smaller neighbor Puerto Rico, the sole remnant of Spain's once magnificent empire in the New World.[1] Cuba had interested Americans even before Democratic politicians in the mid-century had pressed for its acquisition as additional slave territory. Its commanding position at the entrances of the Gulf of Mexico and the Caribbean Sea gave it strategic naval importance from the standpoint of the United States, and its economic penetration by American capital in the period after the Civil War occasioned concern for the maintenance of orderly political and business conditions there.

Spain, learning nothing from the revolt of her other colonies early in the century, continued her despotic rule in Cuba, exploiting the natives both politically and economically. From 1868 to 1878 ceaseless civil strife harassed the island, marked by atrocities and irregular methods of warfare on both sides. Filibustering expeditions, clandestinely fitted out by Cuban agents, slipped away from American ports to lend help. When one such vessel, the *Virginius*, was captured outside Cuban waters in October, 1873, by a Spanish gunboat and eight Americans on board were shot, war was nearly precipitated between the two

---

[1] The name of Porto Rico was changed to Puerto Rico by act of Congress in 1932.

countries. The United States admitted the illegal nature of the expedition, but maintained that, so long as the *Virginius* remained on the high seas, the American government alone might restrain the lawbreakers. After a time Spain offered an apology with suitable indemnity and reparation. In 1875 President Grant sounded European powers on the subject of American intervention in the struggle, but the proposal was not well received. When the Ten Years' War dragged to a close three years later, the insurgents won some paper concessions for a small measure of self-government. As a matter of fact, however, the government continued to be a thinly veiled military autocracy. Meanwhile the burden of taxation borne by the natives grew heavier, for they were saddled with the whole expense of their unsuccessful revolt.

Their kindling wrath burst forth into a new war for independence in February, 1895.[1] The event was hastened by a severe depression of the sugar industry, caused by the repeal in 1894 of the McKinley tariff which had allowed Cuban sugar free entry into the United States (see page 190). Great barbarism and widespread destruction of sugar plantations and other property marked the progress of the hostilities. The plan of the insurgents was to avoid open battle, but to fight incessant skirmishes and devastate the country, with the purpose either of exhausting Spain or of bringing the United States into the conflict. Unable to distinguish friend from foe, the Spaniards adopted the scheme of herding the rural inhabitants into the *reconcentración* camps, which quickly became pestholes filled with starving and diseased unfortunates. In the province of Havana alone over 50,000 perished.

The course of the uprising was watched in the United States with growing concern. Apart from America's traditional interest in Latin-American struggles for independence, United States investments in Cuban plantations, mines and railways now amounted to no less than $50,000,000, and trade with the island annually reached $100,000,000. These pecuniary interests were

[1] In an effort to forestall the insurrection, Spain at the eleventh hour authorized a "council of administration" for the island. But since this body was to have advisory powers only, and would consist one half of Spanish appointees and the remainder of persons chosen under a severely restricted franchise, the only effect was to fortify the rebels in their resolution.

placed in grave jeopardy by the civil strife. Moreover, American humanitarianism was outraged by the cruel methods of warfare, particularly the suffering inflicted on the *reconcentrados*. The yellow press, led by the *New York Journal* and the *New York World*, broke out in a rash of inch-high type, page-wide streamer headlines, and blood-curdling full-page illustrations concerning alleged Spanish atrocities. In 1897 a party organized by the *Journal* actually effected the escape from a Havana prison of Evangelina Cisneros, a Cuban girl sentenced for treason. It was not wholly journalistic brag that explained this sheet's effrontery in daily asking its readers after America's entry, "How do you like the *Journal's* war?" Early in 1898 the American Red Cross responded to the call of humanity by engaging in work among the sick and starving *reconcentrados* near Havana.

Resolved not to be stampeded into war, President Cleveland as long as he remained in office put forth every effort to preserve the attitude of impartial friend. Official vigilance succeeded in stopping most, though not all, of the expeditions that Cuban agents fitted out in American ports. In his last annual message to Congress (December, 1896), however, he declared that, should it presently appear that Spanish authority was "extinct in Cuba for all purposes of its rightful existence," America might feel compelled to intervene because of her "higher obligations" in the affair. The McKinley administration began to pursue the more aggressive policy foreshadowed by Cleveland. Partly in response to American protests, Spain modified somewhat the policy of *reconcentración* in October, 1897, and offered the natives a larger share of self-government, to become effective upon ratification by the *Cortes*. Granted three years earlier, the concession might have assured a peaceful solution. However, after more than two years of relentless warfare, the revolutionists, suspicious of Spanish good faith, were unwilling to accept anything short of complete independence.

Now occurred two incidents which raised war sentiment in the United States to a fever pitch. Thanks to the enterprise of the *New York Journal*, the American public on February 9, 1898, learned that Dupuy de Lôme, the Spanish Minister at Washington, had declared in a private letter that McKinley was a tricky politician and, further, had admitted his own duplicity in certain commercial negotiations then under way with the United States. Spain refused to make a formal disavowal of the utterances and, instead of dismissing De Lôme, permitted him to resign. Of graver import was the destruction of the United States warship *Maine* on February 15 while lying peacefully at anchor in Havana Harbor. The vessel was sunk and 260 men killed. An American court of naval experts ascribed the disaster to an external explosion, but a similar board appointed by Spain found the cause in an explosion of one of the ship's forward magazines. Though the American findings were later confirmed when the vessel was raised in 1911, it remains unknown whether the destruction was due to an overzealous Spanish subordinate, to a Cuban patriot intent on precipitating intervention, or to a mere accident.

The outburst of patriotic feeling was unlike anything since 1861. Abetted by the sensational press, the slogan, "Remember the *Maine!*" was echoed in public gatherings throughout the land. Even the churches, hitherto the mainstay of the organized peace movement, hailed the prospect of a war "for humanity's sake." Congress was seething with bellicose spirit, but the President, who had declared in his inaugural address that "peace is preferable to war in almost every contingency," seemed resolved at this juncture to avert hostilities, if possible, provoking Roosevelt's impatient remark, "McKinley has no more backbone than a chocolate éclair." On March 29 he demanded of Spain the complete abandonment of *reconcentración*, and the establishment of an armistice in Cuba preliminary to peace negotiations to be conducted through himself. The first demand was promptly granted, but national pride and a deep-rooted habit of procrastination caused Spain to temporize in regard to the second. Nevertheless, the American Minister in Madrid cabled McKinley his conviction that the Spanish government and people sincerely desired peace. With a few months' delay, he promised, "I will get peace in Cuba, with justice to Cuba and protection to our great American interests." On April 6 the Washington representatives of Great Britain, Germany, France, Austria-Hungary, Russia and Italy joined in an appeal to the President for a continuance of peaceful negotiations. Four days later Spain informed him that, at the Pope's solicitation, the Queen had acceded to the demand for an armistice.

By this time, however, McKinley had experienced a change of heart. Perhaps he doubted Spain's good faith in complying and felt that, after all, war was the only real solution. But it seems more likely that he was frightened by the clamor of the war faction in Congress and feared a serious rupture in his own party. At any rate, on April 11, he sent a message to Congress, in which, after scant mention of Spain's latest concession, he recommended armed intervention.[1] The grounds, he asserted, were the interests of common humanity, the need to protect the "commerce, trade, and business of our people" in the island, and the ending of a conflict that was "a constant menace to our peace." Eight days later Congress responded by authorizing the President to employ force for the establishment of Cuban independence. At the same time, on motion of Senator Teller, Congress assured an incredulous world that the United States would claim no "sovereignty, jurisdiction, or control over said Island except for the pacification thereof," and, when that was accomplished, would "leave the government and control of the Island to its people."

European powers observed these developments with mixed feelings. In Germany and France public opinion was frankly hostile to the United States, and talk was rife of a joint European intervention on behalf of Spain. British sentiment was mirrored in a widely quoted sentiment of the *London Spectator* on April 9, 1898: "If America were really attacked by a great Continental coalition, England would be at her side in twenty-four hours." President McKinley took occasion early in the war to thank the *London Times* for its hearty advocacy of the American cause. In reality, all the powers observed an official neutrality toward the two belligerents, although at one juncture, shortly to be described, it seemed possible that the contest might develop into a wider international conflict.

[1] "We may rest assured that if Mark Hanna had been President there would have been no war with Spain," says James Ford Rhodes in his *McKinley and Roosevelt Administrations*, 64. "To his dying day Mr. Cleveland never believed that the war with Spain was necessary," states his personal friend George F. Parker in the *Saturday Evening Post*, November 10, 1923. Pulitzer, who in 1898 demanded a "short and sharp" war, admitted in 1907, when deploring President Roosevelt's proposal to send battleships into the Pacific to impress Japan, that "Spain had granted to Cuba all that we had demanded, but passion in Spain and here forced the hands of the government." D. C. Seitz, *Joseph Pulitzer*, 312.

THE WAR WITH SPAIN AND ITS FRUITS

Blithely the United States entered upon a war that brought quick returns in martial glory, some unexpected scandals, and new and heavy responsibilities. Unlike most previous conflicts, the naval arm proved of paramount importance, land operations being subsidiary thereto. The champions of a new navy now won complete vindication. For the immediate state of preparedness, however, credit was due largely to the energetic foresight of Theodore Roosevelt, McKinley's Assistant Secretary of the Navy. In sad contrast was the condition of the army. The regular forces were enlarged from 28,000 to 62,000; and in April and May the President called for 200,000 volunteers, most of whom it was eventually unnecessary to send out of the country. Politics entered into the appointment of officers; and mismanagement, lack of plans and general confusion interfered seriously with the mobilization, feeding and transport of troops. Moreover, the men were sent to fight in a tropical country outfitted in heavy winter uniforms, without due attention to the need of a diet adjusted to a hot climate, and lacking proper hospital equipment. A picturesque feature of the volunteer cavalry was a regiment of "Rough Riders," recruited from among cowboys, ranchers, Indians and college athletes by Roosevelt, who presently became their colonel.

The actual hostilities proved swift and decisive, lasting four months in all. The chief sphere of operations was the West Indies. Cuba was promptly placed under blockade in order to prevent the arrival of reënforcements and supplies from Spain. Nevertheless, on May 19, a fleet under Admiral Pasqual Cervera succeeded in reaching Santiago, which had rail connections with Havana. Santiago was at once placed under close blockade by Rear Admiral W. T. Sampson and, in the ensuing weeks, troops under General W. R. Shafter assembled for a land attack on the city. On July 1 they took El Caney and San Juan Hill, its outer defenses. Santiago now was doomed. In order to avoid capture, Cervera's fleet made a gallant attempt to escape on July 3, but as the warships steamed out of the harbor, one by one they were engaged by the blockading vessels and either captured or destroyed. Sampson being absent at the moment on an official errand, Commodore W. S. Schley had actual command. The fall of Santiago quickly followed. Shortly afterwards, an army under General Nelson A. Miles began the occupation of the near-by island of Puerto Rico.

Meantime, the Americans had successfully attacked the Spaniards in a different quarter of the globe. Immediately upon the outbreak of war Commodore George Dewey, then at Hong Kong, had proceeded with his squadron of six vessels to the

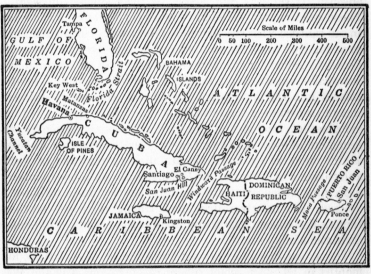

THE THEATER OF WARFARE IN THE WEST INDIES, 1898

Philippine Islands, under orders to incapacitate the Spanish fleet there for operations in American waters. Though his nearest base was 7000 miles away, Dewey, trained in the school of Farragut, executed his instructions with boldness and dispatch. Before dawn on May 1 he ran the batteries of Manila Bay and, by high noon, he had destroyed the entire Spanish fleet without losing an American life. His main purpose accomplished, Dewey proceeded to blockade Manila and its environs preparatory to a combined attack upon the city when land forces should arrive.

As is usual on such occasions, men-of-war of neutral powers gathered on the scene to look after their national interests. The

German force under Otto von Diederichs was actually stronger than Dewey's own fleet, and its commander showed every disposition to embarrass the blockading squadron to the advantage of the Spaniards. Time and again Dewey's patience was sorely tried and an open rupture narrowly averted. On one occasion the German, inquiring of Sir Edward Chichester, the British commander, as to his attitude, was told briefly "that only Admiral Dewey and himself knew what would happen if the situation came to the worst." When the American troops arrived and Dewey prepared to bombard Manila, Chichester moved his vessels into position between the German warships and the American fleet as a precaution against possible interference. The whole conduct of the Germans suggests not merely partiality for Spain, but also a design to secure a foothold in the Philippines at the conclusion of the war. The British government was resolved to prevent such an outcome.

During July and early August the reënforcements from the United States arrived. The city was invested with the aid of the Filipinos who, under the leadership of Emilio Aguinaldo, were fighting for independence. On August 13, after a joint sea and land attack, Manila capitulated. Meanwhile, in June, the cruiser *Charleston* had quietly secured the surrender of Guam and the other Ladrone Islands, tiny Spanish possessions lying 1500 miles east of the Philippines.

The war was tremendously popular with the American people, partly perhaps as an emotional escape from the economic distresses that had so long burdened their spirits. A special bond issue of $200,000,000, offered in amounts as small as twenty dollars, was readily subscribed, and the government raised additional money from a wide variety of internal-revenue duties. The Red Cross amply demonstrated its war-time efficiency, extending its activities to all parts of Cuba, to the mobilization camps in southern United States and, eventually, to the Philippines and Puerto Rico. At home nearly two thousand branches were formed from coast to coast to coöperate in collecting money and supplies. By contrast, the almost criminal negligence of the War Department in safeguarding soldier health and welfare provoked sharp public criticism. Malaria and typhoid fever made their inroads on the unseasoned troops about Santiago in the early weeks, Shafter reporting on August 3 that seventy-five per cent of his command were sick. After his general officers signed a "round-robin" protest insisting that the army be removed to the United States before it was exterminated by that dreadful tropical scourge, yellow fever, the government acquiesced.

Despite such conditions it is only fair to note that, thanks to the progress of medical science in the intervening years, the percentage of deaths from disease was only about three fifths as great as during the first year of the Civil War. Moreover, comparatively few amputations proved necessary. An epochal consequence of this first contact of American science with the tropics was the discovery, made in 1900 by an army medical board headed by Major Walter Reed, that yellow fever was transmitted by the female *Stegomyia* mosquito.[1] By means of this knowledge, the disease was soon banished from the island through the efforts of Major Reed and Major W. C. Gorgas. Potentially at least, tropical life the world over was relieved of one of its terrors.

After hostilities had been under way about three months, Spain asked France to ascertain peace terms from the United States. An armistice, signed on August 12, foreshadowed the settlements of the peace treaty, save in regard to the disposition of the Philippines, which was left undetermined. In the final negotiations at Paris, William R. Day acted as head of the American delegation. Since the United States stood in a position to demand whatever it wanted, the negotiations proved the simplest in which the government had ever engaged. The outcome was the treaty of December 10, 1898. Spain transferred Cuba to the United States for temporary occupation preliminary to insular independence. It ceded Puerto Rico and Guam in lieu of war indemnity, and the Philippines on payment of $20,000,000. The civil and political rights of the native inhabitants of the ceded islands were to be determined by Congress.

The acquisition of Puerto Rico was a natural fruit of the war, and the annexation of Guam might be justified as a desirable coaling and cable station. But the taking of the Philippines

---

[1] In his report as Secretary of War, Elihu Root declared in 1902, "The name of Dr. Jesse W. Lazear, contract surgeon, who voluntarily permitted himself to be inoculated with the yellow fever germ in order to furnish a necessary experimental test . . . and who died of the disease, should be written in the list of the martyrs who have died in the cause of humanity."

marked a new and not wholly welcome innovation in American policy. These islands, aggregating an area as large as Arizona, not only formed a part of the coast line of Asia, but were thickly inhabited by a people alien in race, language and institutions, who were not likely ever to achieve statehood. Moreover, the islands could not be expected to furnish room for the expanding American population, though it was hoped they might supply openings for trade and the export of capital. Before the peace conference McKinley had been undecided as to the wisdom of the step, but strong pressure was brought to bear upon him by chambers of commerce and Protestant missionary bodies. There was, besides, a well-founded conviction that, if America did not annex the islands, Germany, a dangerous trade rival in the Orient, would do so.[1]

When the treaty came before the Senate for consideration, certain members violently attacked this feature of the settlement. G. C. Vest of Missouri denied that constitutional authority existed "to acquire territory to be held and governed permanently as colonies." The staunch Republican Senator Hoar of Massachusetts made much of the fact that, since the Filipinos had declared their independence, annexation would occur without "the consent of the governed," and thus violate a precious American tradition. In the end, the vote of ratification was accompanied by the McEnery resolution which declared, in effect, that the treaty provision should not be deemed a final settlement of the Philippine question. Since the resolution received a mere majority vote, however, it had no validity as an act of the treaty-making power.

In the light of earlier history the war was significant chiefly because it marked the final expulsion of Spain from the Western Hemisphere. From a prospective point of view, however, it signalized a momentous departure in American policy. The United States, for the first time, became a colonial power in the New World and, through acquiring the Spanish holdings in the Pacific, besides Hawaii and Tutuila, it became an Asiatic power as well. The nation took under its wing nearly a million subjects of Spanish and Negro blood in Puerto Rico. It shouldered

---

[1] As a matter of fact, Germany did purchase Spain's remaining possessions in the Pacific.

certain as yet undefined responsibilities in regard to Cuba. It was master and protector of seven and a half million people in the Philippines, ranging from the civilized Tagalogs of Manila to the primitive Moros of the Sulu Peninsula and the head-hunting Igorots of northern Luzon. Like the Great Powers of Europe, the United States had at last chosen the path of empire.

COMBATING THE POWERS IN CHINA

This fateful decision embroiled the United States almost at once in grave international rivalries on the Asiatic mainland. Japan's success in wresting Formosa and other territorial concessions from China in the war of 1894–1895 had served as an open invitation to Europe to join in the spoils. In the next five years the various powers had busied themselves with acquiring naval bases, so-called leased territories and spheres of influence at China's expense. Through these devices they secured not only monopolistic rights of trade, but usually also exclusive concessions for the investment of capital by their subjects in railway construction and mining development in adjoining regions. Thus in 1898, a banner year, Germany obtained control of the Shantung Peninsula in northern China; Russia secured the important harbor of Port Arthur, which dominated the sea approaches to Peiping (then Peking); Great Britain established its rights to Wei-hai-wei, lying between the acquisitions of Germany and Russia; and France took over Kwangchow Bay in southeastern China.[1]

From the standpoint of the United States, newly intrenched in the Philippines, this game of grab threatened to frustrate hopes of a vigorous development of trade with China. In its earlier diplomatic relations with Oriental countries the American government had always insisted upon equality of commercial privileges for all nations. If this principle were now to be preserved, a bold course was necessary. Moreover, the British government was willing to lend support, even going so far in 1898 as to suggest an Anglo-American alliance for the purpose. In spite of British aggression in China that country's commercial interests demanded a policy that would freely admit her

[1] As a result of the Russo-Japanese War in 1904, Port Arthur was transferred to Japan.

manufactures to all ports. As in the case of the Monroe Doctrine in 1823, however, the Washington government preferred to act

FOREIGN CONCESSIONS IN CHINA

independently. In September, 1899, Secretary of State John Hay addressed a circular note to the powers, asking them to subscribe to the doctrine of the "open door" for all nations in China, that is, equality of trading opportunities (including equal tariffs, harbor duties and railway rates) in the areas they controlled. The policy proposed was only a halfway measure, for it ignored the important subject of investments in mines and rail construction. To Hay's note Great Britain, Germany, France, Italy and Japan agreed on condition that the other powers do likewise, while Russia gave a qualified assent. In order to clinch matters, Hay announced that the understanding would be regarded "as final and definitive." The future was to disclose, however, that many difficulties remained.

The year 1900 furnished opportunity for a further development of American policy. The Chinese, increasingly hedged in by encroachments from without, took matters into their own hands and, with secret connivance from the authorities, struck out blindly against the "foreign devils." In June the insurgents, known as Boxers, seized Peiping and besieged the legations there. To deal with the situation, an international relief expedition was organized, including 6000 American troops. Hay, fearing that the presence of foreign armies would result in a naked dismemberment of China, promptly announced to the powers that the United States would oppose any disturbance of Chinese territorial or administrative rights or of the open door. Once the rebellion was quelled, however, it required all his skill to carry through the American program, and to protect China from crushing indemnities. His considerable measure of success was due largely to the distrustful attitude of the several countries toward one another. In October Great Britain and Germany signified their adherence to the open-door policy and the preservation of Chinese independence, and the others presently followed.

Finally, on December 22, the powers announced the basic terms of their withdrawal: punishment of the rebel leaders, indemnities to foreign individuals and states, and the adoption of measures to prevent future outbreaks. The details were embodied in a treaty of September 7, 1901. Despite Hay's efforts, the total indemnity amounted to nearly twice as much as the American government deemed proper. Even the $24,000,000 awarded to the United States exceeded the actual American losses by nearly $11,000,000, and in 1907 the balance was given back. This investment in international good will bore noble returns, for China set aside the money as a fund for sending students to

American colleges. Russia's retention of troops in Manchuria, contrary to the peace treaty, made it clear that China still had perils to face, and caused Great Britain and Japan to form a defensive alliance in 1902 for the protection of their respective interests in China and the Pacific.

"IMPERIALISM" AND THE ELECTION OF 1900

Meanwhile, the presidential election of 1900 gave the electorate a chance to pass judgment on the McKinley administration's policy of foreign adventure and colonial aggrandisement. Meeting at Philadelphia on June 19, the Republicans expressed jubilation over the war with Spain, the insular annexations, the restoration of prosperity, and the effort to "obtain new markets" through "the policy of the open door." McKinley's renomination was a foregone conclusion, the second place going to Governor Theodore Roosevelt of New York, hero of the Rough Riders. Roosevelt had not wanted the honor; but "Boss" Platt was determined to rid his state of an energetic and self-willed executive, and the genuine enthusiasm of the Western delegates made declination almost impossible.

The foes of overseas expansion rallied to the Democratic standard. The fact that since the previous February the Filipinos had been waging a war for independence against American rule affected public opinion at home, and placed the United States in the position of imposing its dominion upon an unwilling people. At the same time, American tobacco and beet-sugar growers viewed with dislike the possibility of Philippine competition in the domestic market. When the Democratic convention assembled at Kansas City on July 4, the platform declared that "the paramount issue" was "imperialism," that is, "the seizing or purchasing of distant islands to be governed outside the Constitution and whose people can never become citizens." After affirming that "no nation can long endure half republic and half empire," the party further condemned the entry of the United States into "so-called world politics, including the diplomacy of Europe and the intrigue and land grabbing in Asia." Bryan was unanimously renominated and, at his behest, the platform also contained a perfunctory plank for free silver. A. E. Stevenson, Cleveland's former Vice-President, was chosen as his running mate.

As in 1896, Bryan's candidacy was indorsed by the Populists and the Silver Republicans, and reverberations of the silver question served somewhat to confuse the main issue. Hanna, once more in charge of McKinley's campaign, ascribed the return of prosperity to Republican supremacy, and everywhere might be found campaign emblems and posters of the "Full Dinner-Pail." In spite of Bryan's eloquent condemnations of imperialism, the policy of overseas dominion struck most voters as a happy fulfillment of American destiny. Though fewer popular ballots were cast than in the preceding election, McKinley received a larger proportion of them, 51.6 per cent to 45.5 for Bryan. The electoral vote stood 292 to 155.

LINKING THE ATLANTIC AND THE PACIFIC

McKinley did not live long to enjoy his victory. On September 6, 1901, while attending an exposition at Buffalo held to symbolize Pan-American unity, he was shot by an anarchist. Eight days later his gentle spirit passed away. His death brought to the presidential chair the most picturesque and dynamic figure since Andrew Jackson. "Teddy's" very appearance suggested divergence from the familiar type of White House incumbent, his body stocky and athletic, his face mobile with expressive teeth, his voice easily slipping into the falsetto. At the age of forty-two, Roosevelt was the youngest man ever to take up the reins of office. Though he devoted his chief energies to domestic problems, it fell to him to cap the new national imperial structure with an interoceanic waterway through Central America.[1]

To accomplish this purpose a series of diplomatic obstacles had to be surmounted. The American government had long contemplated such a canal, either across the Isthmus of Panama, a Colombian possession, or through the Republic of Nicaragua.

---

[1] Roosevelt retained McKinley's cabinet, composed at this time of John Hay, Secretary of State; L. J. Gage of Illinois, Secretary of the Treasury; Elihu Root of New York, Secretary of War; Philander C. Knox of Pennsylvania, Attorney-General; C. E. Smith of Pennsylvania, Postmaster-General; J. D. Long of Massachusetts, Secretary of the Navy; E. A. Hitchcock of Missouri, Secretary of the Interior; and James Wilson of Iowa, Secretary of Agriculture. In 1904 William H. Taft of Ohio was appointed Secretary of War and, upon Hay's death in 1905, Root succeeded to his place. Numerous other changes were made.

As early as 1846 a treaty with Colombia had granted American citizens "open and free" right of passage across the isthmus on condition that the United States "guarantee positively and efficaciously . . . the perfect neutrality" of the isthmus and Colombia's "rights of sovereignty and property" there. Four years later the Clayton-Bulwer treaty (see page 5) evidenced a further development of American policy. The United States and Great Britain agreed that any canal which might be dug should be neutral, unfortified and under international guarantee. In a treaty of 1867 with Nicaragua concerning a route through its territory, the United States again assented to the principle of an international guarantee.

But the upsurge of American nationalism in the years thereafter put a different face on affairs. In a message of March 8, 1880, President Hayes declared, "The policy of this country is a canal under American control. The United States cannot consent to the surrender of this control to any European power or to any combination of European powers." Neither his administration nor the next, however, despite persistent efforts, could induce Britain to recast the Clayton-Bulwer treaty. Meanwhile, American interest in a possible canal increased as a result of the economic development of the Pacific Coast states and complaints of the high freight charges of the transcontinental railroads. The desire for an exclusively American waterway further deepened when it appeared that a French company, headed by Ferdinand de Lesseps, builder of the Suez Canal, might steal a march upon American enterprise. Chartered in 1879, this company obtained the exclusive privilege of constructing a canal across Panama, the rights of the United States under the treaty of 1846 remaining unimpaired. Though the French government was not officially concerned, the project occasioned misgivings in the United States. De Lesseps from 1881 to 1889 spent $260,000,000 on the undertaking; but gross financial irregularities and unexpected engineering difficulties impeded operations, and forced the company into bankruptcy. Several interested Frenchmen then reorganized the company in order to keep alive its franchises and to salvage the canal equipment.

Meantime, stimulated by this competition, an American syndicate set about to dig a rival waterway in Nicaragua. The Maritime Canal Company, chartered by Congress, began excavation at Greytown on the Atlantic side in 1890, only to have its work abruptly ended three years later by the Panic. Appeals to Congress for financial aid proved unavailing, for, though official commissions reported favorably on the Nicaragua route in 1895 and 1897, the government was unwilling to proceed further under the chafing Clayton-Bulwer restrictions. Nevertheless, the acquisition of dependencies in the two hemispheres during 1898–1899 made an interoceanic canal not only important for shortening trade routes, but also vital from the standpoint of naval defense. Both political parties demanded prompt steps to that end in the campaign of 1900, and fortunately the British government, true to her policy of cultivating American good will, was now well disposed. The outcome was the Hay-Pauncefote treaty of November 18, 1901, which expressly revoked the Clayton-Bulwer treaty, and granted the United States "exclusive" control over any canal that might be built. Though the "general principle of neutralization" received nominal recognition, the United States was authorized to maintain "military police" along the canal adequate for its protection.

Further action now awaited the selection of a route. President Roosevelt strongly championed a Panama canal as both cheaper to build and shorter than the Nicaraguan alternative. Advocates of the latter urged the superior advantages to be derived from using Lake Nicaragua and the San Juan River as connecting links. After considerable debate Congress in June, 1902, passed the Spooner act which instructed the President to proceed with the Panama route if "within a reasonable time and upon reasonable terms" he could reach an agreement with the French company and also with Colombia; otherwise he should undertake a canal through Nicaragua. The moribund French company, whose sole remaining interest was to sell out its canal rights before they expired in 1904, promptly reduced its former exorbitant figure of $109,000,000 to the acceptable one of $40,000,000.

Arrangements with Colombia, however, proved more difficult. By the Hay-Herran treaty of January 22, 1903, the United States was granted, on indefinite lease, a six-mile-wide belt of land across the isthmus in return for $10,000,000 and an annual rental of $250,000. But in August the Colombian senate, acting within its undoubted constitutional rights, unanimously rejected the treaty. The members felt that Colombia would surrender too much authority in the canal strip, and that, in any case, the compensation was too little as compared with the sum offered the French company. This action enraged Roosevelt. As he said later, "I did not intend that any set of bandits should hold up Uncle Sam." Others shared his indignation. The people in Panama saw their chance of standing at one of the great cross-roads of the world's commerce blasted, and to the leaders of the French company Colombia's decision involved an almost certain loss of $40,000,000.

Here were the combustibles for a conflagration, and the rapid march of events in November, 1903, bears eloquent testimony to the unity of purpose which actuated the several interested parties. On November 2 the United States cruiser *Nashville* arrived in the harbor of Colon. On the next evening occurred a bloodless revolution in the City of Panama, at the opposite side of the isthmus. On the fourth, marines from the *Nashville* prevented the rail transportation of five hundred Colombian troops from Colon to the seat of the trouble. Two days later Washington recognized the new Republic of Panama, and on November 18 a canal treaty was arranged.[1] The United States was granted perpetual use and control of a zone ten miles wide across the isthmus, in return for the payments which Colombia had spurned and for an American guarantee of independence. Philippe Bunau-Varilla, former chief engineer of the French company, represented the isthmian government in these negotiations.

In a message to Congress Roosevelt later brilliantly defended the part played by the United States. Denying that the American government had fomented the revolution, he claimed justification for the actions in November on three grounds: "First, our treaty rights; second, our national interests and safety; and, third, the interests of collective civilization." By barring the use of the railway to Colombian troops, he asserted that the United States was merely executing its pledge of 1846 to protect the "perfect neutrality" of the right of passage. He disposed of

---

[1] "If they had not revolted," Roosevelt wrote in a private letter, "I should have recommended to Congress to take possession of the Isthmus by force of arms."

the correlative treaty obligation — to protect Colombia's owner-ship of the isthmus — by insisting that this guarantee held only against external aggression. His further contentions — that transcendent interests of national and world import were in-volved in an interoceanic canal — no one could deny, but his critics did not fail to point out that a waterway through Nic-aragua, the alternative authorized by the Spooner act, would have served these grand purposes equally well.

Three years later, in 1906, the work of excavation began. Discarding the earlier idea of having a construction company carry it through, the government intrusted the task to the War Department. As an engineering feat, it was comparable in this new age to the transcontinental railway of four decades earlier. Eight years were required for completion, the cost reaching $194,000,000 in 1914 and $354,000,000 in 1920. "It is," said James Bryce, "the greatest liberty man has ever taken with nature!" Yet the dearth of labor, questions of sanitation and the task of stamping out yellow fever and malaria offered diffi-culties nearly as great as the strictly engineering problems.

Meanwhile, Colombia's resentment over her high-handed treat-ment continued unabated. To allay this feeling, the Democrats when they came into power under Woodrow Wilson negotiated a treaty in 1914, which expressed for the United States "sincere regret that anything should have occurred" to cause ill will, and provided a payment to Colombia of $25,000,000. In return that government agreed to recognize the independence of Pan-ama. A militant Republican minority in the Senate blocked ratification, however. Finally, under President Harding, the expression of apology, though not the payment, was eliminated from the treaty, and in this modified form it went through in 1921. But no stroke of the pen or giving of money could easily allay the fears of the "Colossus of the North," which Roosevelt's course had implanted throughout Latin America.

SELECT BIBLIOGRAPHY

Democracy and Empire. No professional historian has yet done for the first two decades of the twentieth century what Channing, McMaster and Schouler did for earlier periods. Rhodes, *The McKinley and Roosevelt Ad-ministrations*, while useful, falls far short of that historian's earlier work. Volumes of the *American Nation*, *The Chronicles of America Series* and *A*

History of American Life cover all or most of the years from 1900 to 1919. The only large-scale treatment is Sullivan, *Our Times: The United States, 1900–1925*, intended for popular consumption, but containing much of value to the student.

The Cuban Question and the War with Spain. These and the other subjects treated in this chapter are dealt with in Latané, *America as a World Power*. Among the more important works devoted specifically to Cuban conditions and the American intervention are Millis, *The Martial Spirit;* Chadwick, *The Relations of the United States and Spain;* Flack, *Spanish-American Diplomatic Relations Preceding the War of 1898;* and Benton, *International Law and Diplomacy of the Spanish-American War*. The European background is made clear in Reuter, *Anglo-American Relations during the Spanish-American War*, and Keim, *Forty Years of German-American Political Relations*, chap. vi. Wilkerson, *Public Opinion and the Spanish-American War*, studies the part played by American newspapers in generating hostile feeling.

Combating the Powers in China. Dennett, *Americans in Eastern Asia*, is a thorough and authoritative work covering the period to 1901. Additional material appears in Bau, *The Open Door Doctrine in Relation to China*. Thayer, *The Life and Letters of John Hay*, is concerned more with praise than appraisal.

Linking the Atlantic and the Pacific. The question of a Central American canal is discussed from various angles in Arias, *The Panama Canal;* Williams, *Anglo-American Isthmian Diplomacy;* Bennett, *History of the Panama Canal;* and Thomson, *Colombia and the United States*. Roosevelt's rôle is assessed in Pringle, *Theodore Roosevelt*. Rippy, *The Capitalists and Colombia*, sheds light on the later relations with that country.

CHAPTER XVI

THE RISE OF THE PROGRESSIVE MOVEMENT, 1901-1908

THE ADVENT OF THE MUCKRAKERS

IN domestic as well as in international affairs Roosevelt's accession coincided with the dawn of a new age in American political life. The incumbent of the White House, however, was less the maker of an era than the beneficiary of an awakening sentiment that welled up from nearly every village and community of the land. Since the early days of the Economic Revolution the farmers had been fighting a losing battle against the cities and the rising industrial magnates. Now the spirit of unrest and revolt reached the cities, and aroused not only the wage-earners, who had long known how to wage war against their employers, but also members of the middle class, notably the white-collar workers and small business men. As a distinguished conservative (William Howard Taft) later admitted, "For thirty years we had [had] an enormous material expansion in this country, in which we all forgot ourselves in the enthusiasm of expanding our material resources and in making ourselves the richest nation on earth. We did this through the use of the principle of organization and combination, and through the development of our national resources. In the encouragement of the investment of capital we nearly transferred complete political power to those who controlled corporate wealth and we were in danger of a plutocracy."

To many thoughtful people the danger of which he spoke appeared an accomplished fact. It seemed as though America, in ironical perversion of Lincoln's words at Gettysburg, had come to be a government of the corporations, by the corporations and for the corporations. Organized wealth was active in municipal, state and national government, the laws to restrain railways and trusts were openly flouted, and a spirit of unbridled materialism infected every branch of business and society.[1] The tocsin of revolt, sounded in 1896 against Wall Street and Big Business, had been hushed by the thronging of new and bewildering national problems as a result of the Spanish-American War, and in 1900 the "vested interests" were more firmly intrenched than ever.

Indeed, the turn of the century saw Big Business take on Brobdingnagian size. In the single year 1899 ninety-two combinations were formed, including the Standard Oil Company of New Jersey, a holding corporation controlling the far-flung properties of the Standard group, and the Amalgamated Copper Company capitalized at $175,000,000. Two years later followed the billion-dollar United States Steel Corporation; the next year brought the International Harvester Company, which absorbed the five leading manufacturing concerns in its field; and similar huge monopolistic structures grew up in other branches of business. Invariably the guiding hand in such amalgamations was some dominant banking group, which thus imposed outside financial direction in place of management by the operators of the industries and railroads. To such an extent did the Morgan, Rockefeller and similar groups prompt, control and exploit the processes of business consolidation that the Pujo committee of the House of Representatives in 1913, after a painstaking study, attested the existence of a "money trust," that is, a "well-defined identity and community of interest between a few leaders of finance . . . held together through stock holdings, interlocking directorates, and other forms of domination over banks, trust companies, railroads, public-service, and industrial corporations, and which has resulted in a vast and growing concentration of control of money and credit in the hands of a comparatively few men."[2]

Toward this condition of affairs most people in the opening

[1] As late as 1906, Roosevelt credited E. H. Harriman with saying that "he could buy a sufficient number of Senators and Congressmen or State Legislators to protect his interests, and when necessary he could buy the Judiciary."

[2] As the most powerful banking units, the committee named three concerns, J. P. Morgan and Company, the Morgan-controlled First National Bank and the Rockefeller-controlled National City Bank, estimating their combined assets in New York City at over two billion dollars. Four allied financial institutions, it asserted, held 341 directorships in banks, transportation, insurance and public-utility companies, whose aggregate resources were over twenty-two billion.

years of the century had a fatalistic attitude; they were oppressed with the hopelessness of battling against the evil. Only through bold and spectacular methods could the nation be aroused from its lethargy and the old, confident spirit of American democracy be revived. As someone has said, when people are deaf, you have to shout at them. To this mission a group of young journalists dedicated themselves. Newspapers and popular magazines led the van; fledgling novelists took up the hue and cry; and presently the crusade was given a practical turn by aspiring political reformers, including the new master of the White House. The agitation eventually bred individuals who purveyed sensation for sensation's sake, and it was this fact that led Roosevelt to liken such persons to the Man with the Muckrake in *Pilgrim's Progress*, whose absorption in the filth on the floor caused him to refuse a celestial crown. Though the term was unfair to most of the crusaders, they seized upon it as a badge of distinction.

The period of greatest activity of the Muckrakers extended from 1902 to 1908. Of the countless articles, one of the outstanding was Ida M. Tarbell's "History of the Standard Oil Company." Beginning in *McClure's* late in 1902, and based upon three years' study of congressional reports, court testimony and similar evidence, the series month after month relentlessly unfolded the record of the Standard's methods toward independent producers, the public and the government. During 1904-1905 appeared Thomas W. Lawson's trenchant articles on "Frenzied Finance" in *Everybody's*, concerned particularly with the Amalgamated Copper Company. The author, a notorious Boston stock-market operator, purported to reveal, in realistic detail, the inner workings of the gigantic financial "System" which held the nation's economic and political life by the throat. In 1905 Upton Sinclair, using fiction as his medium, published a novel entitled *The Jungle*, which exposed unsanitary conditions in the great Chicago packing houses, and told of the grip of the beef trust on the nation's meat supply. The railways came in for their share of the onslaught because of unfair manipulation of traffic rates, one of the notable series being Ray Stannard Baker's "The Railroads on Trial" in *McClure's* during 1905 and 1906. The fulminations against trust-controlled government reached their climax in David Graham Phillips's articles on "The Treason of the Senate" in the *Cosmopolitan* during 1906–1907. The members of that body were considered one by one, and the sensational conclusion reached that seventy-five of the ninety served the railways, the beef and sugar trusts, the Standard Oil and steel interests.

The activities of the Muckrakers extended to other phases of American life as well. Two series by Lincoln Steffens appeared in *McClure's* under the titles, "The Shame of the Cities" and "Enemies of the Republic," which laid bare fetid conditions in municipal and state government. Samuel Hopkins Adams in *Collier's* gave aggressive attention to the fraudulent claims and injurious ingredients of patent medicines. In like fashion, articles were published to expose the unscrupulous practices of banking and insurance companies, the immoral traffic in women, food adulteration, the evil effects of child labor, the appalling number of unnecessary industrial accidents. The Muckrakers did not fail to make their accusations specific and to name names. Hence light is thrown upon the substantial correctness of their charges by the fact that few of them were ever found guilty of libel. On the other hand, their exposures of corruption and knavery led to court proceedings and legislative action to rectify some of the worst abuses. The most beneficial effect of this "literature of exposure," however, was the moral awakening of the masses. In growing numbers they gave their support to a new group of political leaders who fought to restore government to the people.

THE GROUND SWELL OF REFORM

The first battles for reform were waged in municipal and state politics. Thus the field of local government again proved its utility as a laboratory of political and social experimentation. Conditions in the cities could hardly have been worse (see page 151). Whether one scanned the teeming immigrant centers of the Atlantic Seaboard or the newer municipalities in the West, everywhere corruption, inefficiency and boss rule held sway. Yet, as the sequel showed, the civic conscience was dormant, not dead. Under the spur of mayors like "Golden Rule" (Samuel M.) Jones and Brand Whitlock in Toledo and Tom L. Johnson in Cleveland, the citizens turned on their oppressors, fought for municipal ownership of public utilities, and checked the power of the boss and the ring. Johnson, in Steffens's phrase, became the "best mayor of the best governed city in the United States." In a similar manner Joseph W. Folk between 1900 and 1904, as district attorney and then governor, attacked corruption in St. Louis, and Judge Ben B. Lindsey of the Denver children's court waged war against machine domination of the Colorado capital. In Minneapolis H. C. Clarke, foreman of a grand jury, uncovered the misdeeds of the Ames Ring in 1902 and freed the city from its toils. The election of Emil Seidel as Socialist mayor in 1910 began a new era for Milwaukee. Even New York secured a brief respite of honest government by making Seth Low, president of Columbia, its mayor in 1901.

Other influences worked to a like end. As the result of a tidal wave in 1900 that destroyed about a third of the city, Galveston in its extremity reorganized its municipal government and, departing radically from the conventional pattern, devised the commission plan in place of the more complicated mayor-and-council type. The advantages of this simpler arrangement excited emulation, and presently led other cities to add the feature of a city manager, employed by the commission to conduct the government. This departure implied a tardy recognition that the complex organism of a modern city may be more efficiently run after the fashion of a business corporation than in the usual analogy to the state government, and also that training and expertness are prime requisites for the chief executive official. By 1912 the commission plan in some form had spread to over two hundred communities and was still growing in favor. Its rapid adoption was facilitated by yet another reform, the introduction by various states of the scheme of municipal home rule. By being granted the right to frame their own charters, cities were freed from legislative meddling, often corrupt in character, and at the same time enabled to deal more adequately with their own special local problems. The number of state constitutions with home-rule provisions rose from four in 1900 to eleven in 1915, most of them in the Middle and Far West. The net effect of the civic renaissance was a notable improvement in the standards of municipal government. Much remained to be done, of course, and the voters soon learned that even a superior system required eternal vigilance to beat back the encroachments of self-seeking politicians.

Meanwhile the wave of reform brimmed over into state politics. Riding into power on the stream of protest, young men like Folk of Missouri, Robert M. La Follette of Wisconsin, A. B. Cummins of Iowa, Charles E. Hughes of New York and Hiram Johnson of California boldly took up cudgels against intrenched privilege, the party bosses and all those whom Mark Hanna meant to compliment with the term "standpatters." As in the case of municipal reform, the new spirit coursed most rapidly through the more recently settled parts of the country. It infected both parties, and bred internal differences which in time divided each of them into progressive and conservative, or "standpat," wings. In many a legislative contest the progressives of the two parties fought shoulder to shoulder against the conservatives of the same parties — a fact which lent increasing unreality to the significance of party labels.

One salient point of attack was the state nominating convention, another the legislature, for in these bodies the bosses and the special interests they represented had their strongholds. In place of the convention method of naming candidates, the progressives advocated "direct nominations" through popular vote of the party membership in advance of the regular election. Wisconsin adopted the first state-wide primary law in 1903; seven other commonwealths followed in 1907. From these beginnings the system spread through most of the Union. As a democratic check on the legislature, the reformers championed the initiative and referendum, a dual arrangement long in use in democratic Switzerland.[1] After Oregon set the pace in 1902, the next ten years saw fifteen other states adopt the system of "direct legislation" in some form or other, and presently half the Union was committed to the plan. As a further measure to implement popular control, the progressives demanded that the voters enjoy the right to recall officials who no longer possessed the public's confidence. Oregon gave the plan state-wide application in 1908, ten other commonwealths following before the end of 1914, all but one of them west of the Mississippi. The

---

[1] The referendum is a device to enable the electorate to approve or reject, by popular vote, laws adopted by the legislature. The initiative allows the voters themselves to propose laws, either for action of the legislature or for submission to popular vote.

recall was even more generally adopted in the field of municipal government, where, too, the initiative and referendum flourished. The legislatures also took action to curb the lavish and corrupt expenditure of money in elections. By 1911 thirty-five commonwealths had enacted laws for this purpose.

At the same time, the deep-seated distrust of the federal Senate as a "rich man's club" revived the old Populist demand that its members be chosen directly by the people, not by the legislatures, as the Constitution provided. On several occasions the Senate blocked efforts of the House to secure an amendment to effect the change. But the rising democratic tide could not so easily be stayed. Beginning with Nevada in 1899, various states passed laws which pledged the members of the legislature to elect, as Senator, the candidate who won indorsement in a state-wide primary election. By 1912 three fourths of the states were operating under this system, in one form or another, and it was only a question of time until the Senate should consent to its formal incorporation in the Constitution.

At the inception of the progressive movement, the leaders fought primarily to democratize the machinery of government. But, under the hammering impact of the Muckrakers, they came to concern themselves increasingly with laws to ameliorate the conditions under which the masses lived and worked. As a result, more social legislation was passed in the first fifteen years of the century than in all previous American history. Laws in regard to child labor were strengthened, and new ones adopted, raising the age limits, shortening the hours, restricting night work, closing dangerous trades to minors, and requiring better opportunities for school attendance. By 1912 child-labor laws were to be found in thirty-eight states, the South lagging behind the rest of the Union. In the same period twenty-eight commonwealths enacted legislation limiting the number of hours a woman wage-earner might work; and certain states provided pensions for destitute mothers.

Progress was also made in shortening the workday for men. Most of the larger cities and more than half the states had provided an eight-hour day for labor on public works by 1912. In certain especially hazardous employments, such as mining and rail transportation, the workday was likewise subjected to legislative regulation.   Thus, in the single year 1907, no less than twenty-three states passed acts of this character.   Hardly less important was the crop of employers' liability (or working-men's compensation) laws, which, contrary to the old common-law doctrine, made employers legally responsible for injuries sustained by employees in the course of their work.   Maryland led the way in 1902, and by 1917 all but ten states had set up insurance systems, optional or compulsory, for administering the plan.

Renewed efforts were made by the states to tighten their control over corporations and railways operating within their boundaries.   Beginning in Ohio in 1906, a wave of passenger-rate regulation overran the South and the Midwest, reaching its height in 1907.   Some of these acts were admirable, but most of them overshot the mark.   Oftentimes passenger rates were fixed so low as to hamper the roads in making needed repairs and extensions.   New revenue laws were also enacted, which, by taxing inheritances, incomes and the property or earnings of corporations, sought to place the burden of government on those best able to pay.

The new body of social and economic legislation ran counter to the old *laissez faire* doctrine which had usually guided legislatures and courts in the past.   Accordingly, the judiciary at first invalidated many of the laws as contrary to the Fourteenth Amendment, alleging either that the employers were being deprived of "property without due process of law" or that the wage-earners were being denied the "liberty" to work under any conditions they chose.   Much popular dissatisfaction resulted and criticism of the judicial system became rife.   In time, however, a more liberal view prevailed among the judges.   The bench began to sustain the new acts on the ground that a state, under that vague authority known as the police power, possesses ample power to promote the health, morality and welfare of the people as opposed to special privilege.   Thus, in Lochner *v.* New York, the Supreme Court in 1905 had annulled a New York ten-hour statute for bakers, finding "no reasonable foundation for holding this to be necessary or appropriate as a health law," whereas twelve years later, in Bunting *v.* Oregon, it upheld an Oregon ten-hour act for all factory workers as falling within a justifiable exercise of the police power. This yielding of the *laissez faire* attitude to the doctrine of social responsibility was perhaps the most valuable advance made by the new generation.

Notwithstanding the great avalanche of social legislation, certain types of laws common in Western Europe made little headway in the United States. Such, for example, were the minimum-wage acts, provisions for health and unemployment insurance and old-age pensions. Moreover, during the first decade of the century, the reformers, in spite of constant agitation by the women, were, on the whole, indifferent to the demand for equal suffrage. As it became increasingly clear, however, that the women might prove valuable allies in the political struggle, the cause sprang to life again. In 1910 and 1911 Washington and California gave them the franchise, and by the end of 1914 they enjoyed full voting rights in eleven states, all west of the Mississippi. Not much longer could the major parties afford to ignore their demand for national political enfranchisement.

ROOSEVELT AND REFORM

Against this background of social aspiration and constructive achievement must be placed the stiff, uphill fight to render the general government responsive to the new democratic ideals. Without federal coöperation and support many of the reforms were partial and ineffective. Thus, the curbing of corporations and railroads, in so far as they functioned across state lines, fell to Congress. The same held true of the transportation of adulterated foods and the restriction of expenditures in national elections. Yet Big Business and the great financial interests had a grip upon the federal government and the national Republican organization that seemed unshakable.

To Roosevelt fell the task of breaking this hold and heralding a new and better day. Equipped by long experience in political life, and endowed with a temperament sensitive to shifts in popular opinion, he possessed buoyant self-confidence, a flair for pungent utterances and an unusual gift of dramatizing his actions. His past career had shown him, in turn, an opponent of Blaine's nomination in 1884 but not a Mugwump, an ardent civil-service reformer, an energetic police commissioner in New York City, a bitter foe of Populism, a big-navy man and hot nationalist, a Rough Rider, governor and Vice-President. More than any of his predecessors since the early days of the republic, he was the scholar in politics, having won distinction in such varied fields as natural history, literature and historical writing. Whatever this apostle of the "strenuous life" did, he did with high emotional voltage. With the nation in a mood to swing to the left, Roosevelt readily responded to the new democratic aspirations. Yet he proved an enigma to many. Schooled in the old order of politics, a strict party man, he never flinched from working with the bosses, and he seldom fought through a proposed reform to its full attainment, accepting something less than the whole. Uncompromising fighters like La Follette found in his devotion to the progressive cause a strong element of opportunism and charlatanry. On the other hand, none of his successors during the period faced such stubborn resistance in Congress, and his leadership grew in decision and independence when, in his second term, he was President "in his own right."

In his first message to Congress (December, 1901), Roosevelt stressed the "serious social problems" growing out of the "tremendous and highly complex industrial development which went on with ever accelerated rapidity during the latter half of the nineteenth century." Acclaiming business concentration as a natural and desirable evolution, he opposed the policy of trust prohibition, and demanded legislation to eliminate the evils, while retaining the advantages, of large-scale enterprises. He also recommended broader powers for the interstate-commerce commission in regulating railways, and directed attention to the need of conserving the nation's natural resources. Law-abiding labor unions received his approval, and he declared for protective legislation for women and children in federal employment. The program elicited widespread popular approval, but it roused no answering chord in Congress, where stolid conservatism reigned under Speaker Cannon's leadership in the House and that of Aldrich and Hanna in the Senate. During the summer of 1902 the President carried his message directly to the people, making speeches in New England and the Midwest. Everywhere he urged his policy of federal regulation, and demanded a "square deal" for all — for labor, for capital and for the public.

The outbreak of a great strike in the Pennsylvania anthracite fields in May, 1902, called attention to corporate selfishness in an impressive manner, and lent strength to the President's cause. The miners asked a reduction of the workday from ten to nine hours, a twenty-per-cent wage increase and recognition of the union. Although the United Mine Workers were one of the best managed unions in the country, the mine owners refused to negotiate. The resulting strike involved nearly 150,000 men and a total loss to miners and operators of almost $100,000,000. As winter approached, the East faced a terrible coal famine, and Roosevelt decided to intervene in the affair on behalf of the public whose interests transcended those of either of the contending parties. Though admitting privately that there was "literally nothing" which the federal government had "any power to do," early in October he urged the owners and the miners to submit their dispute to arbitration. When the former, denying his right to interfere, flatly refused, he let it be known that, if necessary, he would operate the mines with troops, and meantime appoint an arbitration board whose findings he expected Congress to support with appropriate legislation. J. P. Morgan and other New York financiers at once exerted strong pressure on the operators, and on October 23 the strike ended with an agreement that the controversy should be arbitrated by a board appointed by the President. The subsequent arbitral award was a substantial victory for the strikers, who received a ten-per-cent increase in pay and the shorter workday. In the settlement, provision was also made for adjusting future difficulties by a board of conciliation, representing equally the operators and the organized workers, with final appeal to the federal judge of the circuit.

Under spur of an aroused public sentiment, Congress now made grudging concessions to Roosevelt's demands for extending government regulation. In mid-February, 1903, it passed the Elkins act in an attempt to cure the evil of railway rebates, which the interstate-commerce law of 1887 had vainly sought to stop. The new statute forbade variations from published rates and, in cases of violation, inflicted fines not only on the railway and its officers but also on shippers who accepted special favors. The general power of rate-fixing, however, was left exclusively in the hands of the railways, as hitherto, notwithstanding the strong popular feeling that charges were unreasonably high. A few days later Congress created the new Department of Commerce and Labor, with membership in the cabinet, and having as one of its divisions a bureau of corporations empowered to investigate the affairs of large business aggregations. Its function was not to prosecute offenders, but to provide data for the use of the Attorney-General and of Congress.

Aided by this legislation, the administration pressed for a stricter enforcement of the antitrust and interstate-commerce acts. Earlier judicial decisions, it will be recalled, had narrowed the scope of these laws and rendered difficult the conviction of offenders. In the case of the Northern Securities Company in 1904, which involved an attempt of the Morgan and Hill interests to unite the management of two transcontinental railways by means of a holding company, the Supreme Court reversed a previous decision in regard to holding companies and, by a vote of five to four, dissolved the merger as a combination in restraint of trade. Encouraged by this friendlier attitude, the Attorney-General pushed other prosecutions. In January, 1905, the court rendered a decision against the beef trust. All together, the Roosevelt administration in its seven and a half years secured twenty-five indictments.

Already in 1904 Teddy, as he was fondly called, had become the idol of the Republican rank and file. Even children in the nursery took to playing with "Teddy bears." His striking personality, his "trust-busting" activities, his use of the "big stick" in taking the Canal Zone, captured the imagination of the man on the street. Nor did the machine politicians, left leaderless by Hanna's death in February, 1904, dare stand out against giving him a second term. The national convention in Chicago on June 21 named him by acclamation, with C. W. Fairbanks of Indiana for Vice-President. The influence of the standpatters, however, appeared in the platform, which was largely a eulogy of the past achievements of the party. On the trust question it declared simply that combinations of capital and labor "are alike entitled to the protection of the laws, . . . and neither can be permitted to break them." For the first time since 1892, Democrats of the Cleveland stamp dominated the national convention of that party at its St. Louis meeting on July 6.

Against Bryan's fierce opposition, the nomination went to Judge Alton B. Parker of New York, an utterly respectable gentleman of conservative convictions, hitherto unknown to the nation. H. G. Davis of West Virginia was named for second place. The platform called for prohibition of capitalistic monopolies and for augmenting the powers of the interstate-commerce commission. Roosevelt was berated for his "executive usurpation of legislative and judicial functions," and his whole course as President written down as "erratic, sensational, spectacular, and arbitrary."

"Rooseveltism," rather than any specific public question, proved the decisive factor in the campaign. Like Andrew Jackson, Teddy possessed an unusual capacity for exciting passionate devotion or fanatical antagonism, and people voted accordingly. Parker represented, on the whole, the conservative elements, but the certainty of Roosevelt's success caused the great corporations to contribute to the Republican campaign chest as before. Progressive Democrats were drawn more to Roosevelt than to their own party candidate, though Bryan himself gave Parker lukewarm support. The abounding prosperity of the country was another influence making for Republican victory. The outcome was an extraordinary testimonial of public confidence in the President. He received 56.4 per cent of the popular ballots to 37.6 for Parker, and 336 electoral votes as compared with 140 for his opponent. Incidentally the result was a vindication of the new-school Democrats, for in both 1896 and 1900 Bryan polled over a million more votes than did the conservative Parker in 1904. When Roosevelt was notified of his victory, he declared in a statement to the press, "The wise custom which limits the President to two terms regards the substance and not the form, and under no circumstances will I be a candidate for or accept another nomination."

THE CONTEST RENEWED

Emboldened by his sweeping triumph, Roosevelt returned to office with fresh determination to advance the cause of reform. In his first annual message he called in particular for more drastic regulation of the railroads. Though his proposal was fought at every turn by the rail interests, who asserted that their charges were the cheapest in the world, the small shippers and the traveling public rallied to the President's standard. The House promptly passed a bill granting the interstate-commerce commission unrestricted power to fix interstate rates, but the standpatters in the Senate would not yield the point. In the end, a compromise was reached in the Hepburn act, adopted in June, 1906. This measure gave the commission provisional authority to substitute fair rates for unreasonable ones in interstate commerce, the commission's orders to be binding unless set aside by a federal court. Despite the disappointment of the progressives, the new law marked an advance over the act of 1887, for the burden of initiating litigation to test the validity of the commission's orders now rested upon the railways, not upon the commission as hitherto. The Hepburn act also extended the commission's authority to express and sleeping-car companies and pipe lines. Free passes, long an insidious source of political corruption, were forbidden except under strict limitations. In addition, the commission was empowered to prescribe the methods of bookkeeping and accounting which the roads must follow, a regulation prompted in part by the practice of certain companies of concealing corrupt expenditures through manipulating book entries.

Other measures of Congress carried the principle of federal control beyond these limits. In response to the Muckrakers' crusade against patent medicines and adulterated foods, the pure-food law of 1906 prohibited the use of any "deleterious drug, chemical or preservative" in prepared medicines or preserved foods sold in interstate commerce. This measure was presently reënforced by an act requiring federal inspection of all meats shipped from one state into another. An employers' liability act for interstate transportation companies was also passed in 1906. When the Supreme Court declared it unconstitutional, a law which met the court's objections was adopted in April, 1908. In 1907 the question of the relationship of Big Business to politics was taken up, and a statute enacted forbidding corporations to make campaign contributions in federal elections. A sister bill providing for publicity of campaign funds and expenditures encountered defeat, however.

Meantime, the administration took active steps to assure enforcement of the regulatory laws. In 1907 it was discovered that the American Sugar Refining Company had defrauded the government out of a large amount of import duties. The resulting legal actions led to the recovery of over $4,000,000 and the conviction of several of the company's officials. In the same year the Standard Oil Company of Indiana, a subsidiary of the Standard of New Jersey, was indicted for receiving secret rebates on shipments over the Chicago and Alton Railroad. The changed spirit of the times was reflected in the fine imposed by Judge K. M. Landis of the federal district court, amounting to $29,240,000 on 1462 separate counts. To thoughtful people it seemed that the decision was actuated by a desire for retaliation rather than a spirit of justice, and the case was subsequently dismissed by a higher court.

Next to corporation control, Roosevelt gave chief attention to the conservation of the nation's natural wealth. While the last of the desirable farm lands had passed into the hands of settlers in the late eighties, powerful private interests had been acquiring, often through fraud, great tracts valuable for minerals or timber or as irrigation sites. The result was the selfish exploitation and waste of raw materials and natural advantages that should have been utilized over a long period of years for the greatest good of the greatest number. At the turn of the century it was estimated that, at the current rate of consumption, the forests would last about thirty years longer, anthracite coal maybe fifty years, bituminous perhaps a century. Furthermore, wide stretches of land regarded as worthless needed only proper attention from the government to become fit for occupation. In the nineties Congress had adopted some preliminary measures looking toward the husbanding of natural resources. A statute of 1891 gave the President discretion to reserve from sale and settlement public lands bearing forests. Three years later the Carey act offered gifts of arid tracts to states agreeing to irrigate them and open them to settlers at reasonable prices.

Upon these beginnings President Roosevelt greatly enlarged. Starting with his first annual message in 1901, he lost no occasion to preach the gospel of conservation until the masses came to understand the relationship between public-land policy and national welfare. His actions suited his words. Where his predecessors had set aside 47,000,000 acres of timberland, Roosevelt increased the area by 148,000,000 acres and, through Gifford Pinchot, chief of the division of forestry, began systematic efforts to prevent forest fires and to retimber denuded tracts. The close of his presidency saw most of the great forests remaining on the public lands in the Pacific and Rocky Mountain states set apart to be used perpetually in the interest of the whole nation.

Important progress was made in reclaiming unproductive agricultural lands and in the protection of mineral resources. Because the Carey act had accomplished little, the Newlands reclamation act in 1902 provided that the proceeds of public-land sales in sixteen semiarid Western states and territories should constitute a revolving fund to assist the construction of irrigation works. Soon one important project after another was undertaken, large dams and reservoirs were built, and great thirsty tracts supplied with water by irrigation. Steps were also taken to reclaim swamp or overflowed lands which were subject to interstate control. In order to safeguard mineral wealth, Roosevelt withheld from sale a total of 64,000,000 acres containing oil, coal and other subsurface riches.

Still another phase of his conservation program concerned the waterways. It was becoming increasingly apparent that, in order to relieve the congestion of the railways, the public must make greater use of water transportation. Furthermore, the destructive effects of the recurrent floods on the Mississippi and elsewhere called for preventive measures by the government. In 1907 Roosevelt appointed an inland-waterways commission to study the problem from all angles; and on the basis of their report appropriations began to be made for a systematic development of the nation's rivers, lakes and canals. Realizing that the success of conservation required whole-hearted coöperation by the states, the President set a precedent by summoning the governors of the states to a conference on the subject in 1908. Within eighteen months after its adjournment forty-one state conservation commissions were appointed and in active operation. Roosevelt's efforts had the effect of making conservation a major national policy. Only at their peril did his successors in office fail to give unstinted devotion to the cause.

As the campaign of 1908 drew near, he was at the peak of his popularity. His great service to the country had consisted, not

CONSERVATION AND RECLAMATION TO 1917

Forest Reserves
National Parks
National Monuments
Irrigation Projects
Reservoirs

in specific additions to the statute book, but in helping give the nation new faith in itself. Furthermore, at a time when labor and capital were ready to leap at each other's throats, his voice declared with ringing emphasis, "The corporation has come to stay just as the trade union has come to stay," and, he unfailingly added, both must bow to the will of the public. Conservatives who thought him too radical and radicals who thought him too conservative failed to perceive that he sought to hold an even balance between the contending elements in modern society. Always deeply indebted to the pioneer efforts of the Muckrakers and to the labors of the reform leaders in city and state, he gave the prestige of his high office to the view that between the two extremes of unbridled individualism and paternalistic socialism lay the middle path of intelligent social control.

SELECT BIBLIOGRAPHY

The Advent of the Muckrakers. Brandeis, *Other People's Money*, summarizes and interprets the findings of the Pujo committee, and Regier, *The Era of the Muckrakers*, offers the fullest account of the "literature of exposure." In *Farewell to Reform* Chamberlain characterizes and adversely criticizes the ideology of the Muckrakers and of the progressive movement in the light of later developments.

The Ground Swell of Reform. The struggle to improve conditions in municipal and state politics may be followed in Faulkner, *The Quest for Social Justice*, DeWitt, *The Progressive Movement*, Haynes, *Third Party Movements since the Civil War*, and his *Social Politics in the United States*, volumes which also treat other topics dealt with later in the present chapter. Particular phases are presented in Munro, *The Initiative, Referendum and Recall*; Carlton, *The History and Problems of Organized Labor*; Commons and Andrews, *Principles of Labor Legislation*; Groat, *Attitude of American Courts in Labor Cases*; and Mangold, *Problems of Child Welfare*.

Roosevelt and Reform; The Contest Renewed. Ogg, *National Progress*, Rhodes, *The McKinley and Roosevelt Administrations*, and Sullivan, *Our Times*, I–III, discuss the main events of Roosevelt's presidency. Additional material may be found in Pringle, *Theodore Roosevelt*, and Bishop, *Theodore Roosevelt and His Time*. The Roosevelt envisaged by the public is shown in Shaw, ed., *A Cartoon History of Roosevelt's Career*. The standpat attitude is studied in Croly, *Marcus Alonzo Hanna*, and Stephenson, *Nelson W. Aldrich*. The best general exposition of conservation problems is Van Hise and Havemeyer, *The Conservation of Our Natural Resources*, which should be supplemented by Teele, *Irrigation in the United States*, and Hibbard, *History of Public Land Policies*.

CHAPTER XVII

PROGRESSIVISM AT FLOOD TIDE, 1908–1917

TAFT INHERITS THE PRESIDENCY

AS the presidential election of 1908 approached, Roosevelt sternly repelled all suggestions of a "second elective term," throwing his support to William Howard Taft of Ohio, who had been Secretary of War since 1904. Taft had consistently supported the President's policies in public and private, and he knew the insular dependencies as no other American. Nevertheless Roosevelt's preference occasioned considerable surprise and, among progressive Republicans, distrust, for Taft in his earlier career as federal judge had displayed marked conservative tendencies. They bowed to the judgment of their chief, however; and the latter, by adept management of the federal patronage and manipulation of the Southern delegates, won his point on the first roll call of the party convention at Chicago in the middle of June. J. S. Sherman of New York was nominated for Vice-President. The platform praised Roosevelt's record in combating "the abuse of wealth and the tyranny of power," and called for ampler regulation of trusts. Recognition was accorded the growing demand for tariff reform by a pledge for "a revision of the tariff," to be based on the difference between "the cost of production at home and abroad, with a reasonable profit to American industries."

The disastrous defeat suffered by the candidate of the conservative Democrats in 1904 brought the progressive wing strongly to the fore. At its convention in Denver on July 7 the party on the first ballot gleefully named Bryan for his third trial at the presidency, giving the second place to J. W. Kern of Indiana. "The overwhelming issue," declared the platform, is "Shall the people rule?" — an issue forced on the nation by Roosevelt's dictation of his successor, Speaker Cannon's "absolute domination" of the House and the grip of the predatory interests on the party in power. Stigmatizing the Republican tariff plank as belated and insincere, the Democrats pledged themselves definitely to tariff "reduction." They also demanded the destruction of capitalistic monopolies.

In the ensuing campaign both Taft and Bryan made long stumping tours. Chief stress was laid on the tariff question, and Taft was forced by Bryan to interpret the Republican plank as meaning revision downward. For the first time, organized labor took official part, the American Federation of Labor indorsing the Democrats because of their plank for restricting the use of injunctions in labor disputes. In harmony with the new political ethics, the Democrats during the campaign made public all individual contributions received above $100, and both parties issued postelection statements. Taft proved the victor, receiving 321 electoral votes to 162 for Bryan, and 51.6 per cent of the popular ballots to 43 per cent for his opponent. Afterwards, in explaining his defeat, Bryan ruefully declared that the Republican party had enjoyed the unfair advantage of running two candidates: Taft the progressive who swept the West, and Taft the conservative who won the East. The Republicans also carried both branches of Congress.

Events quickly revealed that Roosevelt was mistaken in his judgment of Taft. Left to his own devices by Roosevelt's departure on an African hunting trip, the new President speedily reverted to his naturally conservative outlook on public questions. It is likely that, without conscious disloyalty to his former chief's policies, he believed the country needed time for recuperation and reflection after seven years of incessant agitation. If Teddy was essentially a man of action, "Big Bill" was essentially a man of deliberation. At any rate, the kindly nature and imperturbable good humor embodied in his 350 pounds inclined him to conciliate the powerful party leaders whom his predecessor had antagonized; but progressive Republicans were soon convinced that he was a deliberate traitor to the cause they cherished.[1]

---

[1] Taft's cabinet consisted of P. C. Knox of Pennsylvania, Secretary of State; Franklin MacVeagh of Illinois, Secretary of the Treasury; J. M. Dickinson of Tennessee, Secretary of War; G. W. Wickersham of New York, Attorney-General; F. H. Hitchcock of Massachusetts, Postmaster-General; G. von L. Meyer of Massachusetts, Secretary of the Navy; R. A. Ballinger of Washington, Secretary of the Interior; James Wilson of Iowa, Secretary of Agriculture; and Charles Nagel of Missouri, Secretary of Commerce and Labor. Only two, Meyer and Wilson, were holdovers from Roosevelt's cabinet.

The most urgent problem the new administration faced was tariff revision, a question which Roosevelt had refrained from taking up. A growing number of people had come to believe that the Dingley act of 1897 was the nursing mother of trusts, and responsible for the high cost of living, which had been steadily rising since the century opened. The center of this sentiment was the great grain-growing Midwest, which had cradled the progressive movement. Summoned in special session to deal with the problem, the House at the President's behest passed the Payne bill lowering the tariff. But under Aldrich's direction the Senate mangled the measure, adding 847 amendments, most of them increasing duties. The outcome of the differences was the Payne-Aldrich act, signed by Taft in August, 1909, which raised the average rate on dutiable goods about one per cent. In addition, the President was empowered to impose much higher rates on imports from countries that discriminated against American trade. The law also levied a one-per-cent tax on the net earnings of corporations above $5000, and provided for a bipartisan tariff board. At every step the increases had been fought by La Follette, Cummins, A. J. Beveridge of Indiana and other progressive Senators of the party, but to no avail. Schedule K was a particular abomination in their eyes, for it left virtually unchanged the high duties on wool and woolens at a time when woolen manufacturers were declaring dividends up to fifty per cent. Even President Taft did not defend these duties, though in an address at Winona, Minnesota, he pronounced the tariff as a whole "the best the country ever had."

The Payne-Aldrich act was the first step in Taft's downfall. Hard on its heels came two other events that alienated Roosevelt's old followers. One appeared to involve the President's good faith toward the conservation of natural resources. In the summer of 1909 Gifford Pinchot, the chief forester, charged Secretary of the Interior Ballinger with lack of zeal in the protection of water-power sites and coal lands. Taft, siding with Ballinger, dismissed Pinchot for insubordination. In consequence, the administration's situation became so intolerable that presently Ballinger was "permitted" to resign. Reform sentiment was further outraged by the President's failure to aid the Western Republicans in their fight to unhorse Speaker Joseph G.

Cannon. In the course of many years the presiding officer of the House had come not only to appoint all committees, but also, through his domination of the rules committee, to limit debate and control the whole course of lawmaking. A confirmed standpatter, Cannon used his autocratic authority to thwart the desires of the progressives. Consequently, on March 19, 1910, a group of Republican insurgents joined with the Democratic minority in a successful effort to curb the Speaker's powers. Though permitted to retain his office, Cannon was shorn of the right to appoint the rules committee and to act as one of its members. When the Democrats came into control the next year, they went further and made all committees elective.

The revolution in the House foreshadowed a greater one in the fall elections. On the issues of tariff reform and "Cannonism" the Democrats won decisive victories in all sections of the country, and gained a majority of 53 in the new House. Roosevelt, once more in the United States, made a long speaking tour and, though not yet openly hostile to the administration, directed his efforts mainly toward the election of progressive Republican candidates. Even New Jersey, a boss-ridden Republican state hitherto the despair of reformers, placed in the governor's chair a progressive Democrat, Woodrow Wilson, recently president of Princeton University.

The lesson of the election was not lost upon Taft. In January, 1911, the President in an effort to meet part way the low-tariff sentiment proposed to Congress a reciprocity pact with Canada, providing for free entry or reduced rates in the case of certain Canadian food products and raw materials in return for similar concessions on American farm implements and other specified commodities. The measure pleased Eastern Republicans, since it left duties on their manufactures untouched; but it roused a whirlwind of protest from the farming and lumbering interests of the Middle and Far West, which feared the consequences of Canadian competition. Under the astute leadership of Oscar W. Underwood of Alabama, head of the House ways-and-means committee, the Democrats took prompt advantage of this new breach in their opponents' ranks. Viewing Canadian reciprocity as an entering wedge for general tariff reduction, they helped the President carry his scheme through Congress in July, 1911.[1] Then, to offset the displeasure of the progressive Republicans, the Democrats combined with them to pass a number of bills for lowering the tariff on Eastern manufactured articles. A "farmers' free-list bill" was enacted, the notorious Schedule K revised, and bills were carried to scale down the duties on cotton goods, chemicals, iron and steel. All these ran afoul the President's veto, an act that served further to increase his unpopularity both within and without the party.

Yet, despite Taft's inept leadership and the growing revolt against him, the administration had done much in a quiet, untheatrical way to further the cause of reform. In 1910 Congress put new teeth into the interstate-commerce law by passing the Mann-Elkins act, which extended the commission's authority to telegraph and telephone companies, and amended the Hepburn act so as to make the commission's orders for lower rail rates immediately effective, even when a court investigation was being conducted into their reasonableness. In a similar fashion, Congress tackled the question of campaign contributions, adopting legislation in 1910 and 1911 limiting the amount of money a candidate might spend in running for the House or Senate and requiring that all receipts and expenditures be published before and after both primaries and elections.[2] The dust raised by the Ballinger-Pinchot affair obscured the fact that Congress in 1911 enlarged the scope of conservation by providing for the purchase of forest lands near the headwaters of navigable streams in the White Mountains and the southern Appalachians. In addition, in 1910, the public-land laws were improved, stricter provision was made for safety appliances on railways, and a bureau of mines established. Two years later a children's bureau was set up to study problems of child welfare and a parcels-post law was enacted. The following year saw the creation of a Department of Labor with membership in the cabinet.

[1] Taft's victory, as it turned out, was short-lived because Canada later rejected the terms.

[2] In Newberry v. the United States (1921), the Supreme Court held unconstitutional that part of the law of 1910 which sought to regulate the expenditures of senatorial candidates in primary elections. Since the statute was enacted prior to the adoption of the Seventeenth Amendment this decision does not necessarily determine the power of Congress under that amendment.

Nearly twice as many prosecutions were conducted against business combinations as under Roosevelt. In May, 1911, the Supreme Court ordered the dissolution of the Standard Oil Company of New Jersey and also of the American Tobacco Company. The immediate rise in the value of Standard stock indicated that the decision was of slight practical consequence. The court in these two decisions betrayed a conviction as to the undesirability of reckless attempts to break up large-scale enterprises. This appeared in a new construction it placed upon the Sherman act. Where that statute had outlawed "every" contract or combination "in restraint of trade" (see page 200), the Supreme Court now interpreted the prohibition to apply only to *undue* or *unreasonable* restraints of trade.

Perhaps most important of all was the initiation of two new amendments to the Constitution. The controversy dating from the Supreme Court decision of 1895 against the federal income tax (see page 190) was solved, once and for all, by the Sixteenth Amendment, submitted to the states in 1909. By its provisions Congress was empowered to levy an income tax without the necessity of apportioning it among the states according to population. The Seventeenth Amendment, proposed by Congress in 1912, represented the climax of the popular demand for a reconstitution of the Senate. By its terms Senators were made elective by popular vote of the state instead of by the legislature. The income-tax amendment was ratified by the state legislatures in 1913 shortly before Taft left office, and the other amendment soon thereafter. It was significant of the changed outlook of America that the Taft administration should clothe with constitutional sanction two reforms which the Populists had first brought to national notice.

THE PRESIDENTIAL ELECTION OF 1912

Had Taft possessed his predecessor's qualities of showmanship, he might have capitalized these constructive achievements to political advantage. As it was, the progressive Republican leaders began to lay plans as early as January, 1911, to prevent his renomination. With some misgivings they fixed upon Senator La Follette as their choice. "Fighting Bob's" lifelong battle for popular rights had placed him at the van of the progressive cause, but he had never made the same appeal to the popular imagination as the colorful Roosevelt, and the feeling grew that he lacked the vote-getting qualities necessary to unseat Taft in the convention. Such lukewarm supporters cast longing eyes toward the ex-President, who had not yet identified himself un-reservedly with the antiadministration movement. Yielding to their importunities as well as to his own combative instincts, Roosevelt in a speech in February, 1912, declared his adherence to those items of the progressive creed he had earlier ignored or opposed, and a few days later, following an opportune but temporary breakdown in La Follette's health, he announced his candidacy for the nomination. Though La Follette stayed in the race, he was almost forgotten as the country beheld the dis-tressing spectacle of the President and ex-President, recently devoted friends, engaging in a campaign of caustic personal recrimination. Taft denounced Roosevelt's "explosive incon-sistencies" and warned the people against "political emotional-ists" about to plunge the country "into a condition that would find no parallel except in the French Revolution," while Roosevelt charged Taft with reaction and added bitterly, "It is a bad trait to bite the hand that feeds you."

The advantage by no means lay wholly on Roosevelt's side. If he commanded a wider popular following, the President's supporters dominated the party machinery for selecting delegates in most of the states, and absolutely controlled the South where the delegates were usually federal officeholders. But in the twelve states where preferential primaries prevailed, Roosevelt won 278 delegates, Taft 46 and La Follette 36. Elsewhere Taft was gen-erally the favorite, though there was an unusually large number of contested seats. When the convention assembled in Chicago on June 18, the administration-controlled national committee, employing what the progressives called "steamroller tactics," awarded most of the disputed seats to Taft delegates, and con-structed a majority which renominated Taft and Sherman on the first ballot. Three hundred and forty-four Roosevelt support-ers, representing a third of the delegates, refused to vote, though critics unkindly pointed out that Roosevelt himself had jammed through Taft's nomination by similar methods four years before. The platform, while declaring for a "self-controlled representative democracy," carefully skirted questions provocative of factional bitterness. The chief planks called for a federal commission to regulate trusts, a "readjustment" of the tariff with the aid of a board of experts, and a reformation of the monetary system. The Roosevelt followers, unappeased, prepared to carry their case directly to the people.

The Republican schism lent unusual interest to the proceedings of the Democrats in Baltimore on June 25. For the first time in many years the Democrats felt confident of victory, and, emboldened by this circumstance, the conservative forces and professional politicians made a desperate effort to regain mastery of the party. Either Governor Judson Harmon of Ohio or Congressman Underwood would have been acceptable to them as a candidate, and they resolved at all costs to prevent the nomination of Woodrow Wilson, who as governor of New Jersey had shown himself a militant progressive. A fourth candidate, Speaker Champ Clark of Missouri, flirted with both factions, and on the tenth ballot actually polled a majority of the votes. That he failed of the requisite two thirds was due to the energy and skill of William Jennings Bryan of the Nebraska delegation, who distrusted Clark's equivocal attitude. At every turn he fought the "predatory interests," meanwhile keeping the outside public constantly informed of his plans, with the result that thousands of approving telegrams poured in upon the delegates. The long balloting concluded with Wilson's nomination on the forty-sixth trial, Governor T. R. Marshall of Indiana being named to run with him. The platform blamed the high cost of living on the Republican tariff, pledged "immediate downward revision," repeated the injunction plank of 1908, promised to restore the Sherman act to its original vigor, and demanded revision of the banking and currency laws.

Meantime, the disappointed Roosevelt supporters had been organizing their forces and, at a convention in Chicago on August 5, they launched a new party, the Progressive party. Amid scenes of high excitement, Roosevelt and Governor Hiram Johnson of California were named as the standard bearers. The platform was the most unusual ever framed by a party having reasonable hopes of victory. Its keynote was the pledge to "build a new and nobler commonwealth." To that end the platform championed not only such political devices as direct primaries, equal suffrage, the initiative, referendum and the recall, but also a referendum on court decisions that annulled state laws. As economic reforms, it advocated a federal commission to regulate combinations, tariff revision along protective lines through an expert commission, and an overhauling of the banking and currency laws. In addition, it indorsed a wide range of measures for "social and industrial justice," including an eight-hour day, the assurance of a "living wage," prohibition of child labor and safeguards against industrial accidents and occupational diseases.

In view of its dramatic prelude the campaign proved surprisingly quiet. Roosevelt was inevitably the central figure. His followers assumed the nickname of Bull Moosers from a chance expression dropped by their leader. His opponents flayed him for his unbounded ambition and egotism in seeking a third term. The most startling incident was the attempt made on his life by an insane man in Milwaukee. Though the Progressive program was widely condemned as radical and socialistic, the ticket commanded warm support from certain well-known capitalists, who saw in the elaborate provisions for government control of industrial conditions the best hope for an efficient and contented labor force. It is significant that Gompers, as in 1908, called on organized labor to back the Democrats; indeed, the Progressive platform nowhere definitely affirmed the wage-earner's right to organize and strike. Wilson's dignified and well-phrased utterances won growing favor with thoughtful people who came to regard him as standing midway between candidates of extremist tendencies — "a progressive with the brakes on." In any case, the divided opposition insured Democratic success. Many Republicans refrained from voting, but the bulk of them rallied to their old idol, Teddy. Wilson mustered 435 electoral votes, Roosevelt 88, Taft 8. But the distribution of popular ballots mirrored the situation more accurately, Wilson winning 41.8 per cent, Roosevelt 27.4 and Taft 23.2. In fact, the victor received one and a third million less than the total polled by his two rivals, and fewer than Bryan had commanded in any of his three candidacies. Benefiting from the unrest, the Socialists headed by Eugene V. Debs and Emil Seidel doubled their popular vote of 1908, reaching nearly a million. The remarkable showing made by the new party promised to give it a permanent place in American politics if, indeed, its strength represented anything more than attachment to a brilliant chief.

THE TRIPLE ASSAULT ON PRIVILEGE

The new President embodied the finest traditions of the party that elected him. A Virginian by birth, he had spent his mature years in the North, serving rom 1890 on as professor and then president of Princeton. Like Jefferson, he was a student and philosopher of political institutions; his works on political science laid the foundations of the modern study of that subject in America. In common with Jackson, he was a militant believer in democracy, and possessed an intuitive understanding of the unspoken hopes of the plain people. His unvarying self-command and obstinate courage, derived perhaps from his Scotch Presbyterian ancestry, recalled Cleveland, whose neighbor he had been at Princeton. Unlike all these, however, he surveyed the world with singular mental detachment, with the eyes of a student accustomed to probe beneath the immediate flux of events and to seek for guiding principles. His espousal of popular rights, it is not too much to say, sprang from his head rather than from his heart. His high forehead, narrow, ascetic face and aggressive jaw denoted the special qualities that gave character and force to his leadership. His hold on the people rested more on their growing confidence in his disinterested and penetrating intelligence than on a devotion to his personality, though he was deeply loved by his intimates. Not the least of his gifts was a literary style that made his public utterances a fine tapestry woven of noble and luminous phrases. His intellectual aloofness and stubborn independence proved a constant irritation to his political opponents and often to his own party leaders and, in the end, contributed to his defeat in the last great battle of his career, that for ratification of the League of Nations.

The election of 1912 was a victory for progressivism if not for the Progressives. Wilson showed no disposition to evade or straddle any of the urgent questions of the time. He felt a solemn mission to commit the Democrats unalterably to reform and, by appointing Bryan Secretary of State, he served notice at the outset of his open alliance with the liberals of his party.[1] In any case, this course was the part of political wisdom, for through it the President might hope to undermine the strength of the Progressive party and win for his administration the majority support in the country that had been lacking in the election. Though the Democrats controlled both Houses of Congress, the party, long out of power, was wanting in cohesion and responsible leaders. To Wilson this was no deterrent. For many years as a student of government he had maintained that the chief executive should be not a mere presiding officer of the nation, but an active and aggressive director of public policy, bearing a relationship to his party and the people akin to that of the Prime Minister in Great Britain. Accordingly, he frankly assumed the reins of leadership, revived the custom, abandoned by Jefferson, of reading his messages to Congress, and in other ways enhanced the prestige of his office, even to a greater degree than had Roosevelt. In accounting for his legislative achievements, however, it must always be remembered that his administration was the beneficiary of all the agitation for democratic reform that had occurred since the opening of the century.

Summoned in special session, the new Congress proceeded to carry through a legislative program which, in scope and importance, was one of the most notable in American history. Its first task was tariff revision. To safeguard their vested interests, agents of the protected manufacturers followed their usual course of gathering from far and near to press their special claims; but the President promptly put them to rout by exposing to the public the activities of the "insidious and numerous lobby." The Underwood tariff, as signed on October 3, 1913, provided substantial reductions in the rates on important raw materials and foodstuffs, cotton and woolen goods, iron and steel and other com-

---

[1] The other members of the cabinet were W. G. McAdoo of New York, Secretary of the Treasury; L. M. Garrison of New Jersey, Secretary of War; J. C. McReynolds of Tennessee, Attorney-General; A. S. Burleson of Texas, Postmaster-General; Josephus Daniels of North Carolina, Secretary of the Navy; F. K. Lane of California, Secretary of the Interior; D. F. Houston of Missouri, Secretary of Agriculture; W. C. Redfield of New York, Secretary of Commerce; and W. B. Wilson of Pennsylvania, Secretary of Labor. The indebtedness of the Democratic party to the Solid South was evidenced by the appointment of five members, including McAdoo, who were natives of ex-slave states. Robert Lansing of New York succeeded Bryan in June, 1915.

modities, and removed the duties from more than a hundred items.) Although the act retained many protective features, a real attempt had been made to lower the cost of living. In order to make up for the certain loss of revenue, advantage was taken of the recent Sixteenth Amendment to levy a graduated tax on net incomes in excess of $3000, with an additional exemption of $1000 for married persons. The actual fiscal effects of the Underwood act were never fairly tested, for the outbreak of the World War in 1914 caused a sharp decline of imports and of customs revenue. The law did not continue the tariff board established in 1909, but agitation in favor of such a body presently became so strong that in 1916 Congress created a bipartisan commission of six to assist in tariff legislation.

The second item on the Democratic program was a reorganization of the banking and currency system. The act of 1900, while establishing the gold standard, had left unaltered another serious defect of the monetary system: its lack of elasticity. With the currency the product of a variety of fortuitous historical conditions, it was ill adapted to meet the normal ebb and flow of business needs.[1] There was no way to expand or contract its volume as busy times required more or dull times less. This and other faults were dramatically projected on the public consciousness by a sharp financial panic in November, 1907. Speculation had been rife for several years, particularly in trust development, and many industrial securities were selling far above their real value. Yet the blow fell with little warning. Most banks were in excellent condition, industries were flourishing, and labor was fully employed. Suddenly, however, confidence became impaired, runs started on banks, mills shut down, and business generally became paralyzed. Thirteen banks failed in New York City alone. To afford relief, pay-roll checks and other substitutes for money were put into circulation, gold was imported from Europe, and the national treasury poured its surplus into banks of deposit. By the middle of January, 1908, confidence was again restored. Other than overspeculation, the

[1] The amount of greenbacks, treasury notes, and silver certificates was stationary, and the quantity of national bank notes, being based upon ownership of government bonds by the banks, showed little fluctuation. Though the volume of gold varied from time to time, its movements were governed by the demands of international trade and had no relation to domestic needs.

basic cause of the trouble seemed to be the inability of national banks to enlarge the volume of their currency in a time of money stringency. Many business concerns with adequate resources failed through inability to convert their assets into ready money. An important contributory cause was the fact that each bank had to meet the crisis substantially alone. Although few of the stronger institutions were without ample funds in their vaults, they hesitated to part with their cash for fear of being themselves left in the lurch. The difficulties were increased by the unscrupulous activities of certain big financiers in New York, the nation's money center. The crisis left a trail of indictments and suicides in high financial circles.

Shocked into action by the crash, Congress in 1908 passed the Aldrich-Vreeland act which, as a temporary expedient, provided means by which national banks in times of emergency might issue additional bank notes. These should be guaranteed by the government and be taxed on a graduated scale to insure their retirement as soon as the stringency ceased. The act further authorized the creation of a monetary commission to investigate the whole problem of currency and credit and to propose a permanent reformation of the system. In 1912 the commission submitted its report which, among other things, recommended a great central reserve bank, to be owned and controlled by private banking interests. To the Wilson administration, however, this proposal was wholly unacceptable. Nevertheless the Democrats found the commission's investigations of great service in framing their own solution.

This solution appeared in the federal reserve act, adopted on December 23, 1913. The law was designed to cure glaring flaws that experience had revealed in the system of money and credit; notably, lack of coöperation among banks in crises, inelasticity of the currency supply and concentration of power in the hands of a few financial magnates. Upon the existing banks the act superimposed a new system of organization. The country was divided into twelve districts or regions with a federal reserve bank in each. These regional institutions should serve as depositories for the cash reserves of the national banks and of such state banks and trust companies as might join the system. Their primary function, in other words, was to act as a bank for banks. Under strict regulations it was made possible for the funds thus accumulated to be used to assist individual local banks in moments of temporary embarrassment. To accomplish the second object — greater flexibility of the money supply — provision was made for the issuance of federal reserve notes to meet business demands. Local banks might deposit with the federal reserve banks approved commercial paper (for example, promissory notes of reliable business concerns), receiving in exchange federal reserve notes for use during the period of need. Finally, to curb the unlimited control hitherto exerted by large private bankers, the delicate and complicated machinery of the new banking plan was intrusted to the immediate oversight of the governing boards of the regional reserve banks and to the general supervision of a federal reserve board, made up of the Secretary of the Treasury, the comptroller of the currency and five (later six) presidential appointees.[1]

The new scheme was a landmark in American banking history comparable to Hamilton's financial plan and the national banking system established during the Civil War. Though its passage had been bitterly resisted by the private banking interests, and though it went into effect under the abnormal conditions caused by the outbreak of the World War, it quickly demonstrated its utility. By mid-November, 1914, the extensive financial machinery had been set up, and the system put into operation. The regional banks worked harmoniously with each other; currency demands were promptly met; crop-moving difficulties, notably in the South, were overcome; and progress was made toward unifying the basic banking resources of the nation. After America entered the war, the plan gave indispensable aid to the government itself. "Without it," says Professor H. Parker Willis, "the war could not have been financed with anything like the success actually attained." Yet, despite the notable forward step, many evils remained in the American banking system, as the Great Depression of 1929 and later was to reveal.

---

[1] The act discontinued the subtreasury system, a Democratic reform of the forties, by providing that the government should deposit its funds in the federal reserve banks. Provision was also made for the eventual replacement of national bank notes with federal reserve bank notes. The federal reserve banks were located in Boston, New York, Philadelphia, Richmond, Atlanta, Cleveland, Chicago, Minneapolis, St. Louis, Kansas City, Dallas and San Francisco.

The next important task of the Democrats was trust regulation. Experience commended a system of control similar to that of the interstate-commerce commission over the railways, but it required Wilson's most vigorous efforts to secure appropriate legislation. The results were embodied in two laws. One, passed on September 26, 1914, abolished the bureau of corporations, dating from 1903, and transferred its powers of investigating corporate abuses to a new body, the federal trade commission, of five appointive members. In addition, the commission was given authority to issue orders prohibiting "unfair methods of competition" by business concerns in interstate trade. In cases of disobedience it was empowered to seek aid from the courts to enforce its orders. A second law, the Clayton antitrust act of October 15, forbade many corporate practices that had thus far escaped specific condemnation by federal statute, such as interlocking directorates, price discriminations among purchasers and the ownership by one corporation of stock in similar enterprises.

Other provisions of the Clayton act dealt with labor grievances going back at least as far as the Pullman strike of 1894. Thus it exempted from antitrust prosecution all labor and agricultural organizations "lawfully carrying out the legitimate objects thereto." It proclaimed that strikes, peaceful picketing, and boycotting were not violations of any federal law. It also prohibited injunctions in labor disputes growing out of the terms and conditions of employment "unless necessary to prevent irreparable injury to property," and required jury trial for contempt of court, except when the offense was committed in the judge's presence. The public at large greeted the new trust legislation with high satisfaction. In labor circles the elation was unexampled. Decisions of the Supreme Court, however, tended to chip away many of the benefits of the labor clauses, and to rob the unions of immunities which they had believed theirs. In one notable case, that of the Duplex Printing Press Company v. Deering (1921), the court upheld an injunction issued by a lower court to prevent the membership of a national union from boycotting an employer. The decision was based upon the view that the exemptions of the Clayton act applied only to the employees immediately and directly involved in a controversy, not to members of their union throughout the country who, by order of the national officers, joined in the boycott. Again, in the case of the United Mine Workers *v.* the Coronado Coal Company (1922), the court held that unions, although unincorporated, were in every other respect like corporations, and hence liable for damages, including triple damages under the Sherman anti-trust act.

OTHER REFORM MEASURES OF THE DEMOCRATS

The congressional elections of 1914 gave the voters a chance to pass judgment on the President's masterful course. At the same time, they had an opportunity to declare whether, upon sober second thought, they wished to abandon the historic Republican party for the new Progressive party. On both points the outcome was clear. The Progressives revealed startling weaknesses all along the line, polling less than half their strength of 1912. Thanks to Republican gains, the Democratic majority in the House fell from 147 to 29; but the administration had cause for rejoicing, for it had maintained its control of Congress in what was essentially a two-party contest. It was evident that large numbers of Progressives had gone over into the President's following.

If foreign affairs, notably the great conflict in Europe, occupied increasing attention during the second half of Wilson's administration, the Democrats nevertheless proceeded energetically to the task of rounding out their program of economic and social legislation. In 1915 a seamen's act, sponsored by La Follette, provided for improvement of the living and working conditions of employees on ocean-going vessels and on lake and river craft. The federal workingmen's compensation act in 1916 authorized a government allowance to civil-service employees during periods of disability. In the same year a rural-credits law was enacted. Its purpose was to give farmers credit facilities equal to those extended by the federal reserve system to manufacturers and merchants. Under general administration of a federal farm-loan board, named by the President, agriculturists were enabled to borrow from federal land banks on farm-mortgage security over long periods of time at a lower rate of interest than an ordinary commercial bank would charge.

Congress also attacked the thorny problem of child labor. Though most of the states had laws to restrict such employment, others were notoriously laggard. Notwithstanding the silence of the Constitution on the subject, the need to improve the situation through federal action was urgent. Hence Congress in 1916, stretching to the utmost its power to regulate interstate commerce, excluded from interstate transportation the products of factories employing workers under fourteen years. Only about 150,000 children fell directly within the scope of the law, but it was hoped that the example would indirectly benefit the nearly two million beyond reach of the national authority. The Supreme Court, however, by a vote of five to four declared the law unconstitutional. Thereupon Congress, not to be balked, tried another scheme, and in 1919 imposed a ten-per-cent tax on the net profits of factories employing children under the age of fourteen. Again the judicial lightning struck.[1] At once a demand developed for a child-labor amendment to the Constitution. Congress in 1924 finally took the desired action, submitting to the states a proposal to give it the "power to limit, regulate, and prohibit the labor of persons under eighteen years of age." Had the amendment been submitted when the progressive movement was at its peak, it doubtless would have been speedily put into effect. But coming in the period of postwar reaction, it excited little public favor outside of labor and humanitarian circles, whereas Southern employers of child workers, Northern investors in Southern mills and conservatives generally united to arouse opinion against it. Though a few states ratified the proposal, not until the hard times beginning in 1929 brought widespread unemployment did interest in the amendment begin to evidence real vitality.[2] Prohibition of child labor then seemed a means of creating jobs for adults.

[1] The two cases were Hammer v. Dagenhart (1918) and Bailey v. Drexel Furniture Company (1922).

[2] Before the crash of October, 1929, but five states — Arizona, Arkansas, California, Montana and Wisconsin — had ratified the amendment, and twenty-four had rejected it. By the middle of October, 1933, a total of fifteen had taken favorable action. In addition to the five already named they were Colorado, Illinois, Michigan, New Hampshire, New Jersey, North Dakota, Ohio, Oklahoma, Oregon and Washington.

SELECT BIBLIOGRAPHY

Progressivism at Flood Tide, 1908–1917. Besides the works of Faulkner, Ogg and Sullivan cited at the close of Chapter XVI, the student will find useful material in Duffy, *William Howard Taft;* Stephenson, *Nelson W. Aldrich;* Pringle, *Theodore Roosevelt;* Bowers, *Beveridge and the Progressive Era;* Dodd, *Woodrow Wilson and His Work;* and Baker, *Woodrow Wilson.* The following studies shed light on special phases of governmental policy: Knauth, *The Policy of the United States toward Industrial Monopoly;* Jones, *Principles of Railway Transportation;* Willis, *The Federal Reserve System;* Warburg, *The Federal Reserve System;* Henderson, *The Federal Trade Commission;* and Frankfurter and Greene, *The Labor Injunction.*

CHAPTER XVIII

SOCIAL AND INTELLECTUAL FERMENT, 1900–1914

THE MARCH OF LABOR

NOT only in legislative gains but also in other respects the waxing power of organized labor was reflected in American life. The membership of the American Federation of Labor rose from 550,000 in 1900 to 2,000,000 in 1914, exclusive of unaffiliated bodies, like the Railway Brotherhoods, which at the latter date totaled 700,000. The return of good times after 1897 energized the unions to press their claims upon a scale hitherto unknown. In the five-year period 1901–1905 more strikes took place than in the whole preceding decade, with victory usually perching on the side of the workers, as in the anthracite-coal strike of 1902 (see page 324). Despite the opposition of the National Association of Manufacturers and other employers' organizations, wages advanced, and the workday shortened until eight hours became the rule in most occupations. Ten hours continued to prevail in rail transportation, however, and the steel industry remained absolutely closed to unions. Progress also occurred in the spread of trade agreements. The acceptance of a joint partnership of labor and capital in fixing conditions of employment afforded heartening evidence of saner relations between the two contending forces in modern industry.

In 1906 the American Federation made its first tentative plunge into active politics by backing prolabor candidates for Congress, and, as we have seen, two years later it began the practice of indorsing one of the major-party tickets in the presidential race. As earlier, it flinched from launching a separate party of its own, nor did it view with friendly eyes the growing strength of the Socialists. How effective was the policy of "Reward your friends and punish your enemies" is problematical. The Wilson administration, however, bestirred itself to justify the Federation's support. Not only did the President appoint W. B. Wilson, a former official of the United Mine

Workers, to the new post of Secretary of Labor, not only did Congress pass the Clayton act which Gompers acclaimed "labor's Magna Carta," but Congress in the Newlands law of 1913 set up a permanent board of mediation and conciliation to assist in settling railway labor troubles. Though the board lacked compulsory powers, the provision marked a decided advance over that of the Erdman act of 1898 (see page 211), and already by October, 1916, the new body had helped in the adjustment of sixty-one disputes.

Yet in March, 1916, when the four great Railway Brotherhoods made a joint demand for a basic eight-hour day, they declined to submit the matter to the board's adjudication. Instead, they threatened to precipitate a country-wide strike unless the rail companies gave them the shorter day at the same pay as for ten hours, with a time-and-a-half rate for working overtime. Labor in the saddle was no more disposed to resort to arbitration than were employers when they held the whip hand. To obviate the calamity of a general tie-up of transportation, President Wilson, after exhausting other expedients, went before Congress on August 29 and asked the immediate enactment of a law granting ten hours' pay for the first eight hours of work, with a proportionate additional wage for overtime. In defending his unusual action, he declared that "the eight-hour day now undoubtedly has the sanction of the judgment of society in its favor." Within exactly one hundred hours the Adamson law was passed, embodying his proposals. He had also urged that the Newlands act be so amended as to make it illegal to call a strike or lockout while a government investigation was pending; but this recommendation was ignored. Critics of the administration believed the "surrender" of the government to be a precedent fraught with grave consequences for the future.

Though organized labor greatly extended its membership and strength, the American Federation ignored the bulk of ill-paid, unskilled, foreign-speaking toilers in the factories and the migratory workers in the Great West who followed the harvest and cut the lumber. To take care of their interests, a new organization, the Industrial Workers of the World, sprang up in 1905 under the leadership of "Big Bill" (W. D.) Haywood, a fighter trained in the savage industrial warfare of the Cripple Creek

mining district in Colorado. Like the old Knights of Labor, the
I. W. W. proposed to unite all workingmen, skilled and unskilled,
regardless of trade, in "one big union," but to this program it
added two significant features. It announced, in the first place,
that the "struggle must go on until the workers of the world . . .
take possession of the earth and the machinery of production
and abolish the wage system." In addition, it advocated "direct
action" (the general strike, the boycott and sabotage) as the
way to victory.[1] Probably at no time did the "wobblies" exceed
60,000; but for nearly ten years they kept the Pacific Northwest
in a state of unrest, and in 1912 and 1913 they reached eastward
to conduct desperate strikes among the sweated textile workers
in Lawrence, Massachusetts, Paterson, New Jersey, and Little
Falls, New York. Only the Lawrence effort proved victorious.
Their violence frightened a public used to the more orderly
methods of the old-line unions, and sometimes provoked communities to lawless or extralegal reprisals to rid themselves of
the disturbing element. In 1917 the opposition of the I. W. W.
to America's entry into the European war arrayed the government against it and hastened its collapse. Yet its brief and
stormy career called attention to a grave failure of the older
labor movement, and caused the American Federation to extend
its activities increasingly among unskilled and unorganized wage-
earners.

IMMIGRATION POLICY

The radical fringe of the labor movement consisted largely of
workingmen of foreign birth. The American Federation's demand
for ever greater restriction of immigration rested less on this
fact, however, than on the effect of the incoming horde in providing employers with cheap labor and holding down the standard
of living. From 1900 to 1914 a total of thirteen and a third
million migrated to the United States, somewhat more than in
the preceding three and a half decades. In the latter year, just
before the war brought a sharp decline, the number stood at
1,218,500, the highest on record. The arrivals from Italy,
Austria-Hungary and Russia in 1914 were three times as many
as when the century began, and exceeded four fifths of the

---

[1] Sabotage may be peaceable, such as loafing on the job, or it may involve violent
tactics like destroying property.

total. As the inflowing stream swelled in volume, all the earlier fears as to assimilability of the newer type of immigrant deepened, while organized labor became clamorous on the subject. Under these circumstances the device of a literacy test, which Cleveland had blocked in 1897 (see page 281), revived in favor. It was argued that the requirement of a reading knowledge of English or some other language would sort the old from the new immigrants since the bulk of the latter were illiterate. But when Congress passed such a bill in 1913, Taft rejected it, and two years later Wilson did likewise. Illiteracy, they asserted, implied not absence of natural capacity, but lack of youthful opportunity. In 1917, however, shortly before America entered the war, Congress passed the measure over Wilson's objections.

Meanwhile, the question of Oriental immigration had arisen in a fresh form. Though an effective curb had already been put upon Chinese arrivals, growing numbers of Japanese appeared on the Pacific Coast in the early years of the century. Thrifty, hard-working, inured to a bare subsistence, they began to displace white workers, notably in agriculture. Talk soon became rife of a new "yellow peril," organized labor demanded Japanese exclusion, and the people of California gave hearty support. Yet California's fears looked to the future rather than to the present, for the newcomers numbered only two per cent of the population in 1910. It was also true that a federal statute had long barred Japanese and other Asiatics from naturalization, though, of course, their American-born offspring acquired citizenship under the Fourteenth Amendment. In 1906 the antagonism flared up in an order of the San Francisco board of education to restrict Japanese children to a separate building, this despite the fact that there were but 93 in the schools out of a total of 25,000 pupils. The home government promptly protested the action as a violation of its treaty with the United States. Though the question of state rights was involved, President Roosevelt induced the board to withdraw its decree and took steps to bring about an understanding between the two countries in regard to the larger issue. The upshot was the "Gentlemen's Agreement" in 1907 by which Japan contracted on its own motion to prevent the future emigration of laborers to the United States.

Anti-Japanese feeling in California persisted, however, and in 1913 led the legislature, over President Wilson's protest, to pass the Webb act, which forbade aliens ineligible to citizenship to own agricultural land in the state. In operation, its purpose was to some extent defeated by the practice of Japanese in taking out the title in the name of their American-born offspring, and also by their holding stock in land corporations. To plug these holes, the Asiatic land law in 1920 expressly forbade such practices. Japan continued to remonstrate, but the American government, insisting that no actual treaty rights were denied, proposed to leave the question to the Supreme Court. In 1923 the court affirmed the constitutionality of the Webb act and of a similar statute of the state of Washington. In the following year, as we shall see, Congress gave statutory backing to the Gentlemen's Agreement by excluding all immigration from Japan. This needless offense to Japan's dignity became a disturbing factor in the future relations of the two powers.

THE ADVANCE OF SOCIAL REFORM

Meanwhile, in the urban centers, the pioneer work of the humanitarians in the 1880's and 1890's bore fruit in wide-flung efforts to relieve poverty and distress. The conservation of human resources, no less than of natural resources, became a watchword of the age, one ably maintained by the fast-growing profession of welfare workers. Charity-organization societies and social settlements multiplied, spreading to the smaller cities and extending westward and southward until the whole nation was covered. At the same time, the slum evil was attacked with fresh zeal. Prompted by the fact that no city in the world housed its poor as wretchedly as New York, the legislature in 1901 enacted a tenement-house code that was a model of its kind. It not only worked substantial improvement in all the larger centers of the state, but led Pennsylvania, New Jersey, Connecticut and other commonwealths, as well as many cities, to establish similar regulations. The increase of playgrounds further evidenced the renewed interest in children's rights. By 1910 more than 150 cities had made such provision; only five years later the total had risen to 432 and the number of playgrounds to nearly 3300. By providing wholesome outlets for children's energies it was hoped, on the one hand, to promote their health and pleasure and, on the other, to lessen juvenile delinquency. The introduction of the Boy Scouts from England in 1910 and the establishment two years later of the Girl Scouts and the Campfire Girls represented yet other efforts to turn the gang spirit natural to youth into constructive channels.

New gains also came to the temperance movement. The widening reach of the social settlements and the increase of urban recreational facilities steadily undermined the saloon as the "poor man's club"; and the pecuniary importance of sober employees was driven home to business men by the spread of workingmen's compensation laws (see page 322). Though nearly every religious denomination had its temperance committee or teetotal society, the brunt of the attack was borne by the W. C. T. U., the Temperance Society of the Methodist Church and a relatively new and markedly militant body, the Anti-Saloon League. These groups left little undone to mold public opinion to their will, and to press forward every advantage against the liquor interests. As the century opened, only Kansas, North Dakota, Maine, New Hampshire and Vermont possessed state-wide prohibition, and the last two reverted to local option in 1903. In other directions, however, the increase of dry territory was startling. For the first time, the South took state-wide action, spurred by the desire to keep strong drink from the Negroes; between 1907 and 1915 eight Southern commonwealths adopted prohibitory measures. The movement swung into the Great West in 1915 and 1916, scoring victories in Arizona, Oregon, Washington, Colorado and Idaho. Meanwhile Iowa joined the state-wide group, and local option had largely dried up other rural parts of America. Nearly everywhere, however, there were serious difficulties of enforcement; and in 1913 the temperance forces induced Congress to pass the Webb-Kenyon law to protect dry areas from liquor shipments from outside the state. The larger cities stubbornly resisted the efforts of the prohibitionists. Nor, until America's entrance into the war, were the drys able to accomplish their purpose of imposing their reform upon unwilling communities through a national constitutional amendment.

At all points the quest for community betterment received

support from persons affiliated with churches and, to an increasing extent, from the churches themselves. During the first decade and a half of the century most of the leading Protestant denominations set up social-service commissions and issued declarations of social purpose. Institutional churches broadened their scope and grew in number; ministers' conferences sent fraternal delegates to city trade assemblies; congregations established helpful relations with various types of welfare agencies. Not all religious groups advanced with equal pace, but few failed to devote greater attention to the social teachings of Jesus. In 1908 the Federal Council of Churches, which had been formed by thirty-three evangelical sects to bring about closer coöperation especially for applied Christianity, adopted a social creed which, in a sense, anticipated and outdistanced the Progressive platform of 1912. It declared for labor's right to organize, for old-age insurance, for the abolition of child labor and suppression of the sweating system, for a living wage, shorter hours and a six-day week, and for "the application of Christian principles to the acquisition and use of property" and "the most equitable division of the product of industry that can ultimately be devised." The Federal Council's function, however, was not so much to accomplish results itself as to stimulate other religious bodies to greater activity and to correlate their efforts. To that end it diligently fostered the formation of state and local interchurch federations.

Meanwhile the Catholic Church, strong in its organization, alert to its opportunities, employed its energies to conserve the gains that came to it from the mounting immigration from Catholic countries of Europe. The problem of rural communities also commanded increasing attention from religious leaders. Drained of much of their best blood by the exodus to the cities, such places were apt to be overstocked with Protestant churches whose listless spiritual life was galvanized occasionally by temporary revivals. Improvement began to appear, however, as dwellers on the countryside forgot ancient doctrinal differences and joined in federated or union churches. Theological seminaries aided by providing special courses for the training of country ministers. As a result, better men were attracted into the service and rural religion took on new vitality.

INTELLECTUAL LIFE

In deepening the spirit of social unrest the newspaper press played an important part. The ever increasing emphasis on yellow journalism made editors the natural allies of the Muck-rakers, particularly in local campaigns for civic betterment. At the same time, the business of coöperative news gathering grew in comprehensiveness and efficiency as rivals of the Associated Press appeared in the International News Service (1906) and the United Press (1907), the former sired by William Randolph Hearst. The tendency toward standardization of news presentation was further strengthened as a result of the formation of newspaper chains under one control, an application to the journalistic field of a well-tried principle in the business world. The Scripps-McRae (later Scripps-Howard) League, founded in 1895 with four dailies in the Midwest, had gathered in eleven by 1906 and in 1925 embraced twenty-three in many parts of the land. Hearst meantime reached out until in 1925 he owned twenty-five journals in seventeen cities.

As prodders of the public conscience, however, the low-priced magazines, as we have seen, were more active than the newspapers. Never before had they been so widely or so attentively read. While Lawson's "Frenzied Finance" was running in *Everybody's*, the circulation leaped in a year from 150,000 to more than 750,000. Yet the dinosaur among periodicals was of a different ilk, being less concerned with voicing social and economic criticism than with expressing the traditional ideals of the comfortable middle class. This was the *Saturday Evening Post*, for which Cyrus H. K. Curtis had paid a thousand dollars in 1897, and which within a decade mustered nearly a million weekly buyers. Through its stories and articles, and even its advertising columns, the *Post* appealed to such familiar American traits as optimism, nationalistic feeling, the gospel of hustle, and glorification of material success. Some of the best fiction of the time appeared in its pages.

The restless mood of the generation pervaded much of the literature that these years begot. Under spell of the Spanish-American War there was a temporary flurry of interest in historical novels, and books like Paul Leicester Ford's *Janice*

Meredith (1899), Mary Johnston's *To Have and To Hold* (1900), Winston Churchill's *The Crisis* (1901) and Owen Wister's *The Virginian* (1902) enjoyed an enormous vogue. As the rumblings of insurgency became louder, however, makers of fiction deserted the glamorous past for the grim present. Frank Norris in *The Octopus* (1901) pictured the struggle between the farmers and the rail magnates. The socialist Jack London, after writing adventure stories about the Arctic North, heralded an impending social revolution in *The War of the Classes* (1905) and *The Iron Heel* (1910). David Graham Phillips added *The Plum Tree* (1905) and other novels exposing the flaws and injustices of a money-mad society. Churchill contributed *Coniston* (1906), a tale of the railroads in politics, while Upton Sinclair and many other writers brewed a similar mixture of love interest and social propaganda. It was only as a relief from such fare that readers turned to the scintillating short stories of "O. Henry" (W. S. Porter), who deftly and humorously portrayed the changing prism of metropolitan life.

The drama went through a somewhat similar cycle. Content at first with dramatizations of successful historical novels and with the society pieces of Clyde Fitch, Augustus Thomas and others, the public soon gave an enthusiastic patronage to plays that dealt trenchantly with contemporary problems. Among the more popular offerings were Charles Klein's "The Lion and the Mouse" (1906), written after the dramatist had read Miss Tarbell's *History of the Standard Oil Company;* C. R. Kennedy's "The Servant in the House" (1908), which revealed how far the practice of Christianity might fall short of its theory; Eugene Walter's "The Easiest Way" (1909); Charles Kenyon's "Kindling" (1911), a play dealing with slum life; and Edward Sheldon's "The Boss" (1911), which concerned the struggle between capital and labor. Players like Mrs. Minnie Maddern Fiske, John Drew, Richard Mansfield, Otis Skinner, Julia Marlowe and E. H. Sothern did much to sustain the high standards of acting inherited from the previous generation.

Meanwhile, the schools quietly carried on their work of eradicating illiteracy and handing on the torch of knowledge. The task became ever greater as untold numbers of immigrant children stormed the doors; but public and private funds streamed into the educational system in unprecedented volume, and physical equipment and teaching excellence reached a new high-water mark. The total enrollment grew from 15,500,000 in 1900 to more than 19,000,000 in 1914, embracing an ever larger proportion of American childhood; the total expenditures rose two and a half times. While the cities continued to set the pace, notable progress was made toward equalizing educational opportunity in the country districts. Aided by the good-roads movement and the introduction of the motor bus, rural inhabitants began to abandon the scattered "little red schoolhouses" with their ungraded methods, and to pool their resources in a centrally located "consolidated" school where better instruction, modern equipment and separate grades were provided. Especially striking was the advance made in the South. Throughout the section compulsory-attendance laws were at last enacted, public appropriations were greatly enlarged, and high schools were added to round out the system. Yet, despite the impressive gains everywhere manifest in the nation, the total schooling which the average person received in his entire lifetime increased only from a little more than five years in 1900 to a bit more than six in 1914. Much remained for the future to do.

In tune with the times, outstanding educational leaders emphasized the function of the school in preparing young America for an intelligent part in a civilization growing ever more complex and dynamic. Professor John Dewey, the most outspoken critic of the older pedagogy, maintained that social utility and not mere knowledge should be the goal of education. In such works as *The School and Society* (1899) and *Democracy and Education* (1916) he taught that "the primary business of the school is to train children in coöperative and mutually helpful living," and that the school should "reproduce on the child's level the typical doings and occupations of the larger, maturer society into which he is finally to go forth." These and other principles that he set forth served gradually to modify educational aims and procedures not only in the United States, but in many other countries as well.

Though the public schools increasingly stressed preparation for life above preparation for college, university enrollments advanced by leaps and bounds, growing from 114,000 at the start of the century to nearly a quarter of a million in 1914. In the organization of higher education, the chief divergence from earlier practice came in the development of the so-called junior college, usually through either the addition of two years to the public-school system or the elimination by weaker colleges of the upper two years. Such provision not only afforded opportunity for advanced study nearer home, but also supplied a shorter unit of training for those who could not complete the regular college course. The din of the economic conflict echoed in academic halls, heightening the interest of undergraduates in the social sciences, and causing professors to take an increasing part as advisers in the development of social and economic reforms by city, state and nation. The nation did not hesitate to make a former college professor its chief magistrate, nor had it been surprised when his predecessor retired from the White House to a chair of law at Yale. Even scholarly work showed the impress of the times, notably in the penetrating analyses of the physiology and psychology of capitalist society made by Thorstein Veblen, the economist, the brilliant forays into the economic interpretation of history by Charles A. Beard, historian and political scientist, and the all-embracing view of human development — the "new history" — championed by the historian James Harvey Robinson. Such contributions helped to give point and direction to a mass of scholarly production exceeding anything the nation had before known.

In a quite different way, science played an ever larger part in the daily life of society. Chemists manifested their wizardry by creating many new articles and by showing how familiar natural products might be concocted through artificial means. Coal tar, for example, was turned into commodities ranging all the way from coloring matter for cake frosting to high explosives. They also discovered a world of new knowledge in regard to food constituents, thereby causing the public to give greater attention to vitamins as an element of diet, and arming medical scientists for a fresh attack on scurvy, rickets and other ills supposed to be due to improper food. Equally important advances were made in other phases of the healing art. Aside from American enterprise in finding the transmitting source of yellow fever (see page 303), Dr. H. T. Ricketts of the University of Chicago found that

Rocky Mountain fever was a tick disease and, with R. M. Wilder's collaboration, proved that typhus was carried by body lice. American ownership of Puerto Rico prompted a scientific inquiry under Major B. K. Ashford into the cause of anæmia, which held ninety per cent of the islanders in its grip. The discovery that a tiny intestinal parasite called the hookworm was responsible led to Dr. C. W. Stiles's identification of the species as one also prevalent in the rural South, where its ravages helped to explain the backwardness of the poor-white class.

In these and similar instances, new knowledge of the causation of disease equipped medical scientists with ampler means of prevention, control and cure, and greatly strengthened the effectiveness of the public-health agencies that had been growing up since the Civil War. Between 1900 and 1920 the average length of life in the United States increased from thirty-six and a half years to forty-three and a half. Decline in the death rate was particularly notable in such maladies as typhoid, diphtheria, croup, tuberculosis and scarlet fever. The enlarging American contribution to world progress in science thrice won signal recognition during these years when the Nobel Prize was awarded in 1907 to the physicist, Professor A. A. Michelson of the University of Chicago, in 1912 to the surgeon, Dr. Alexis Carrel of the Rockefeller Institute for Medical Research, and in 1914 to the chemist, Professor T. W. Richards of Harvard.[1]

Progress in the fine arts stemmed from the beginnings made in the eighties and nineties. Many of the master figures of the earlier era now reached the full bloom of their powers, while younger men introduced fresh vigor and originality. In painting the bent toward a bolder realism, prefigured by the marine scenes of Winslow Homer, found development in the work of Robert Henri, W. J. Glackens, George W. Bellows and Eugene Speicher. In a special sense, Joseph Pennell's etchings of skyscrapers, the great locks of the Panama Canal and other feats of the new technology tingled with the life of the age. The masses, however, derived their knowledge of art mainly from the popular magazines, in which illustrators like Charles Dana Gibson and How-

[1] Dr. Carrel, a Frenchman by birth and training, had been in the United States since 1905.

ard Chandler Christy portrayed idealized types of American girls and men that excited untold thousands in real life to eager imitation. Meanwhile, the parks and public squares of the cities became studded with statuary fashioned by sculptors whose work ranked with the best offered by contemporary Europe. These compositions usually commemorated warriors and statesmen, but, more and more, themes typifying a broader national achievement crept in, as betokened by Solon Borglum's spirited delineations of frontier scenes, G. G. Barnard's "Hewer" (1902) at Cairo, Illinois, C. H. Niehaus's "The Driller" (1902), erected by the Standard Oil Company at Titusville, Pennsylvania, and Lorado Taft's grand plan of sculptured decoration for Chicago, beginning with "The Spirit of the Lakes" (1913).

Architecture expressed itself most strikingly in the urban apartment houses, which increased in number as they grew higher and handsomer in appearance; in the monumental passenger terminals like the Union Station (1907) in Washington, the Pennsylvania Station (1910) in New York and the Kansas City Union Station (1914); and in the steel-framed office buildings which, dwarfing the skyscrapers of the 1890's, pushed steadily upward into the clouds. The Singer and Woolworth buildings in New York, completed in 1908 and 1913, and soaring respectively forty-one and fifty-one stories, revealed possibilities of the majestic beauty which the future would further unfold. A new note was also struck in domestic architecture, particularly by Louis Sullivan's pupil Frank Lloyd Wright who, scorning mere decorative convention, endeavored to develop the natural qualities of the materials and to set his structure in "the embrace of rock and tree and shrub." For better or for worse, the old regional traditions of building faded rapidly away before the architectural types popularized by the cities. A hotel or schoolhouse or bank in Atlanta might just as well have been in Philadelphia or Minneapolis so far as externals went. Even in domestic architecture the contagious spread of the New England Georgian style and the Midwestern "bungalow" to all parts of America served to make residential and suburban districts everywhere look more and more alike. Yet, whatever its drawbacks, it is well to remember that standardization of architecture usually denoted better architectural standards.

THE CHANGING STANDARD OF LIVING

Despite the uneven race between wages and the advancing cost of living, the mass of the people, particularly in the cities, enjoyed advantages and opportunities such as their predecessors had never known. This was due in part to the general undertakings that taxpayers supported on an ever increasing scale, like schools, parks, sewerage, public-health protection and good roads. Such measures helped to diffuse the benefits of the rapid production of wealth. Even more striking was the voluntary diversion of a part of the huge private fortunes to broad social purposes, usually through the setting up of "foundations," managed by self-perpetuating boards of trustees, and staffed by experts charged with the responsibility of advising how the funds should be spent. Between 1902 and 1911 Carnegie created five such bodies: the Carnegie Institution, designed to encourage "research and discovery, and the application of knowledge to the improvement of mankind"; the Carnegie Hero Fund Commission; the Carnegie Foundation for the Advancement of Teaching; the Carnegie Endowment for International Peace; and the Carnegie Corporation, whose endowment of $125,000,000 should be devoted to causes which succeeding generations of trustees might find most significant. Rockefeller benefactions, amounting to $400,000,000 by 1921, went into four great foundations: the Rockefeller Institute for Medical Research (1901); the General Education Board (1903); the Rockefeller Foundation (1913), established "to promote the well-being of mankind throughout the world"; and the Laura Spelman Rockefeller Memorial Foundation (1918), created also for the large purpose of advancing human welfare. In addition, scores of lesser foundations made their appearance to give lift and drive to humanitarian enterprises, education and scientific research. Critics did not fail to flay an economic system that allowed a few individuals to amass stupendous wealth and then dole it back in the form of charity, but the fact remained that such private accumulations increasingly found their way into the channels of general welfare.

More directly, the comfort of daily life was influenced by countless labor-saving devices that relieved housework of much of its drudgery and added to the pleasure of living. Many of these resulted from the application of electricity to the traditional tasks of the housewife. Mechanical invention also invaded the field of amusement, scoring its greatest triumph during these years in the motion picture, but already preparing the way for the coming of the radio and the "talkie." Crude animated films had been projected on screens in the United States as early as the mid-nineties, but not till 1905, when Edison set up the first studio for indoor production, did they begin to attain a perfection that presently caused the "movie" to become a major form of popular entertainment, reaching multitudes who seldom, if ever, attended the regular theater. The stage, however, showed as yet no signs of suffering from the competition. Particularly successful commercially were musical comedies, not delightfully satirical operas of the Gilbert and Sullivan type, but too often hodgepodges compounded of expensive stage settings, an aimless plot, vaudeville stunts, a few high-paid principals and a large prancing chorus. Through such means a kind of syncopated music called ragtime laid its spell upon the masses, symbolizing as it did the increasing tempo and nervousness of American life. It is only fair to add, however, that at the same time the more serious forms of music commanded an ever growing patronage. This interest came in part from the activities of the National Federation of Musical Clubs, formed in 1898, and led to the organization of symphony orchestras, hitherto restricted to a few leading centers, in cities as far removed as Minneapolis, New Orleans and Seattle.

Meanwhile, outdoor recreation attained Gargantuan proportions. The trend toward professionalization of sports grew continually stronger, attracting tremendous crowds who were content to take their exercise visually instead of muscularly. In a similar fashion college athletics, notably football, became so hedged about with highly paid coaches and so dominated by gate receipts as to render it more of a business than a pleasure even for the participants. Signs of a reaction appeared in the increasing popularity of amateur golf. For many years a fad of the wealthy few, golf promised to become a sport of the many as inexpensive courses began to be laid out and even municipalities provided facilities for their citizens.

The chief transforming influence in the open-air life of the people, however, was a new mechanical marvel, the self-propelling motor vehicle. As far back as 1893 ingenious young mechanics — C. E. Duryea in Chicopee, Massachusetts, Henry Ford in Detroit, R. E. Olds in Lansing — had devised crude gasoline-driven cars, but European inventors had anticipated them and, for over a decade, the French and English produced more and better cars than did Americans. As American manufacturers made progress in standardizing the processes, however, and resorted increasingly to mass production, the price was steadily brought within reach of the average purse, and the automobile swung into a tremendous popularity. The number in use rose from 300 in 1895 to 78,000 in 1905 and to 2,446,000 in 1915. The motor car ceased being a luxury of the rich — of the "automobility," as a wag put it — and rapidly became a part of the normal equipment of American life. The social effects were incalculable. Not only did it restore the forgotten delights of the open country to growing numbers of urban dwellers, not only did it help break down provincial barriers and mitigate rural isolation, but it built up a whole new cluster of industries, provided employment for millions, gave a new push to the good-roads movement, accelerated suburban development and, in countless ways, increased the momentum of American civilization. The widespread introduction of the self-starting device in 1913 and 1914 insured that the future would see women vie with men as drivers of cars.

Even more spectacular was the progress made in navigating the heavens. Long a dream of mankind and vainly attempted by numberless inventors, flying in heavier-than-air machines was made practicable through the ingenuity of Orville and Wilbur Wright, two bicycle mechanics in Dayton, Ohio.[1] Familiar with what other experimenters had done, and undaunted by a series of failures, they succeeded in contriving a gasoline-driven airplane that on December 17, 1903, remained aloft for a distance of 852 feet in a trial flight at Kitty Hawk, North Carolina. The

---

[1] S. P. Langley, secretary of the Smithsonian Institution in Washington, had devised a small steam-propelled model that flew 3000 feet in 1896, but his later experiments with a man-carrying, gasoline-driven craft in 1903 proved unsuccessful because of difficulties in launching it.

secret of the eagle was now within grasp. In the years that followed, they and other inventors, notably in France, introduced
changes and greatly improved the mechanism of flying; but avi-
ation required the furnace heat of war to bring about its most
notable development. Few people failed to appreciate the revolutionary import of the dramatic shortening of distances when
Ezra Meeker, who had taken six months to cover the Oregon
Trail to Washington by ox team in 1852, winged the distance in
1924, at the age of ninety-three, in twenty-four hours.

The multiplied uses of electricity, its increasing application to
the work of home and factory, to lighting, heating, traction and
communication, led to a tremendous development of the sources
of electrical energy. The generating capacity of power plants
grew nearly sixfold from 1902 to 1914; the number of customers
from less than 600,000 to more than 5,000,000. Particularly
noteworthy was the rapid spread of hydroelectric projects until
every state possessed one or more. Water-power sites assumed
an enormous importance, and were acquired by corporations,
usually without adequate safeguards to assure good service and
cheap rates for the public. As in other branches of industry,
the desire for economical operation and the hope of bigger profits
led to a consolidation of ownership and to the weaving of a
network of transmitting cables over great areas. An ampler
public regulation of power companies was one of the problems
which this generation, hardly realizing its importance, bequeathed
to its successors.

Into every department of life, power and the machine extended
their sway. Historically, Americans had always displayed mechanical ingenuity and a flair for tinkering; the twentieth century with its flowering of technology seemed the culmination of a
long-cherished dream. No one could doubt the beneficent effects.
Machinery freed mankind from an incalculable amount of back-
breaking toil; it pointed the way to shorter working hours
without loss of productive capacity; it turned out more and
cheaper goods; it conferred a measure of material comfort such
as people had never before enjoyed; it widened horizons, created
new pleasures for the many, enlarged the range of activity, and
added color and variety to everyday life. Moreover, through
curtailing distances, it linked all parts of the land in closer

comradeship and forged stronger bonds of nationality. As the century advanced, however, thoughtful persons began to ask whether these gains did not come at too high a price, whether man's servant was not usurping the rôle of master. The monotony of machine tending in the mill, the tremendous speeding up of industry, the displacement of faithful workers by the introduction of new machines, the wastage of natural resources through mass processes, the loss of individual craftsmanship in standardized commodities, the growing dependence of people upon mechanical aids instead of upon their inner resources in the use of leisure — all these bulked large on the debit side of the ledger. Yet no bold voice cried out for a return to a machineless age. The fault indeed lay not in machinery, but in man's attitude toward it. Sooner or later, if he would achieve a more wholesome life, he must learn how to conserve the benefits of his extraordinary mastery over nature and to combat its evils.

SELECT BIBLIOGRAPHY

The March of Labor. On this and the other topics in the present chapter, the best general discussion is Faulkner, *The Quest for Social Justice.* Perlman, *A History of Trade Unionism in the United States*, is good but brief. Two contrasting labor bodies of the period are described and interpreted in Lorwin, *The American Federation of Labor*, and Brissenden, *The I. W. W.: A Study of American Syndicalism.*

Immigration Policy. Jenks and Lauck, *The Immigration Problem*, is particularly valuable as a summary of the *Report* of the federal immigration commission. The new Oriental immigration is treated at length in Ichihashi, *Japanese in the United States*, and in Buell, *Japanese Immigration.*

The Advance of Social Reform. Watson, *The Charity Organization Movement in the United States*, Woods and Kennedy, *The Settlement Horizon*, and Rainwater, *The Play Movement in the United States*, sketch leading phases of welfare work. Cherrington's general treatment of the temperance movement in *The Evolution of Prohibition in the United States* should be supplemented by Odegard, *Pressure Politics*, and Steuart, *Wayne Wheeler, Dry Boss.* Main trends in religion are set forth in Rowe, *The History of Religion in the United States;* Garrison, *The March of Faith;* Smith, ed., *Religious Thought in the Last Quarter Century;* and Macfarland, *The Progress of Church Federation.*

Intellectual Life. For the various topics treated under this head, references cited at the close of Chapter XII will be found useful. In addition, attention is directed to Pattee, *The New American Literature;* Van Dorens, *American and British Literature since 1890;* Kandel, ed., *Twenty-Five Years of American Education;* Barnes, *The New History and the Social Studies;* Stieglitz, *Chem-*

istry and Recent Progress in Medicine; and Starrett, *Skyscrapers and the Men Who Build Them.*

The Changing Standard of Living. Kaempffert, ed., *A Popular History of American Invention,* discusses many of the new inventions. Particular ones are treated in Lubschez, *The Story of the Motion Picture;* Epstein, *The Automobile Industry;* Barber, *The Story of the Automobile;* and Lougheed, *Vehicles of the Air.* For music, the theater and athletic recreation, consult the references listed at the end of Chapter XII.

CHAPTER XIX

THE FORMATION OF A COLONIAL EMPIRE

ADAPTING THE CONSTITUTION TO AN IMPERIAL SYSTEM

THE political and social ferment that penetrated every phase of life was responsible for a remodeling of the organic laws of many states. Between 1900 and 1914 five of the older commonwealths framed new constitutions, while other states attained much the same result through the process of amendment.[1] When Oklahoma (including within her borders Indian Territory) entered the Union in 1907, she also ranged herself on the side of the newer tendencies; her constitution embraced virtually all the radical democratic reforms of the day. Five years later the last of the continental domain was organized for statehood. The original territory of New Mexico, created in the stormy days of the Compromise of 1850, had been subdivided into Arizona and New Mexico in 1863 at the time of the discovery of precious minerals. The population of the twin territories grew but slowly, though a new era opened toward the close of the century with the progress of irrigation and of large-scale mining. As in the case of Oklahoma, the constitutions proposed for the two new states reflected the democratic idealism of the times, and the Arizona instrument even included a provision for the popular recall of judges. Congress, upon President Taft's recommendation, declined to complete the act of admission in the latter instance until this innovation should be removed. Arizona acceded, but only to restore it as soon as full statehood was achieved.

The admission of the forty-seventh and forty-eighth members of the Union completed, for the time at least, the process of state building and federal integration that had been going on since the nation was formed. For a number of years, however, the United States — "in a fit of absent-mindedness," as Seeley once said of Great Britain — had been acquiring colonial holdings in distant

[1] In the first two decades of the century 1500 amendments were proposed and about 900 adopted.

parts of the globe. These lands contained peoples of diverse races and religions in every state of cultural and political progress; their historical traditions and governmental ideals were totally unlike those of the American stock. The nation therefore must face the problem whether the usual large powers of self-rule should be granted these dependencies as a preparation for eventual statehood, or whether they should be governed permanently as provinces. To this question publicists and statesmen gave anxious attention. Its solution was inextricably entangled with motives of political expediency as well as with considerations involving historic American ideals, and, in final analysis, it devolved upon the judiciary to say whether any departure from ancient practice was warranted by the Constitution.

In the so-called Insular cases, most of which arose in 1900 and 1901, the Supreme Court made its position clear.[1] In reply to the basic question, "Does the Constitution follow the flag?" it decided "yes," but with important and sweeping qualifications. The Constitution was held to consist of two kinds of provisions, "fundamental" and "formal," only the former of which applied to the dependencies. The court intimated that, from time to time as specific cases arose, it would declare which provisions possessed this "fundamental" character. The cases then under consideration enabled the court, however, to settle at once some of the most important points involved. In the light of this series of decisions, the inhabitants of these scattered possessions were not to be citizens of the United States unless and until Congress should expressly confer citizenship on them. The constitutional guarantees enjoyed by citizens, such as indictment by grand jury and trial by jury, did not belong to them unless and until Congress should so provide. As respects tariff laws, duties might be freely imposed on their commerce with the United States. In other words, Congress might, for all practical purposes, administer the acquisitions as it saw fit. Accordingly, the government was able, without hampering restrictions, to work out a colonial policy in which diversity, rather than uniformity, was the guiding principle. In each case, an effort was made to legislate

[1] Downes v. Bidwell (1900), De Lima v. Bidwell (1900), Dooley v. the United States (1901), Pepke v. the United States (1901), Hawaii v. Mankichi (1901), Dorr v. the United States (1904).

in accordance with the special needs of the dependency, and to suit the regulations to its state of political and economic progress.

THE IMPERIAL SYSTEM IN OPERATION

As the system gradually rounded into shape, it came more and more to resemble the structure of the British Empire. Attached to the continental cluster of self-governing states were the outlying organized territories, inhabited by alien peoples enjoying a large share of home rule. Whether or not these territories might expect eventual membership in the Union remained an unsettled question. On a plane below these were the numerous insular possessions, comparable to Britain's Crown Colonies, which were under direct tutelage of the Washington government with little or no rights of self-management. A few of the subject races, one notably, were held against their desires, and longed for independence; but nearly everywhere the extension of American sovereignty produced striking improvements in the living conditions of the masses. Nor did the resemblance end here. The imperial structure was given the final touch by the establishment of a fringe of political and economic protectorates in the Caribbean.

Where circumstances seemed to warrant, territorial status was accorded after a suitable period of probation. Between 1900 and 1917 this boon was conferred upon three widely separated possessions: Hawaii, Alaska and Puerto Rico. The Filipinos also received large powers of representative government, but, as we shall see, their situation differed in essential respects from that of the others. In the case of Hawaii the organic act of 1900 granted American citizenship to the inhabitants, bestowed the vote on all men who could read, write and speak either the Hawaiian or English language, and authorized an elective legislature with a governor appointed from Washington. Under American rule the new territory, half the size of Maryland, made steady progress as American capital stimulated the development of sugar production and the growing and canning of pineapples. Its yield of sugar cane per acre exceeded that of any other country. The population, amounting in 1930 to 370,000, sprang from divers origins, over a third being Japanese, with strong contingents of

Filipinos, Portuguese, Chinese and Americans. The pure native stock formed a dwindling minority, partly because of intermarriage with other strains. To offset this racial diversity, an excellent school system was established, capped by the tax-supported University of Hawaii. The literacy qualification on the suffrage served to keep the political power largely in the hands of the English-speaking islanders.

Alaska, an American possession since 1867, and embracing an area over twice that of Texas, had for many years lived up to its reputation as "Seward's Ice-Box." Its chief springs of wealth were the fur-seal industry and the fisheries, but it had been left to the initiative of outsiders, rather than to that of the native Eskimos and Indians, to exploit them. By the treaty of purchase all the rights of American citizenship belonged to the inhabitants, the uncivilized tribes excepted, but it was not till 1884 that Alaska was given a resident civil government, and then without any local popular control. In the ensuing years white penetration of the interior gradually laid bare its wealth of natural resources. The finding of gold on Klondike Creek in 1896, on the Canadian side of the border, precipitated a rush from all parts of the world, which soon led to the discovery of valuable deposits in American territory — along the Yukon, around the head of Cook Inlet, and about Nome, near Bering Strait. Before 1921 this treasure-trove yielded $320,000,000 in gold from American sources alone. Few of the adventurers, however, became permanent settlers.

Nevertheless, increasing knowledge of Alaska's resources caused the question of safeguarding this reservoir of potential riches to loom large in Roosevelt's conservation program. The best timberlands were set aside as national preserves, and efforts were made to protect coal and other mineral lands from unlawful encroachment. With the gradual growth of a settled white population, Congress in 1912 granted Alaska territorial status with the usual provision for an elective legislature and an appointive governor. The first legislature extended the suffrage to women. Poor transportation facilities continued to hamper the territory's development; and, in default of other means, Congress in 1914 provided for the governmental construction and operation of a railroad, which eventually stretched some 500 miles from Seward to Fairbanks. Never before had the United States essayed the rôle of railway owner and operator in time of peace. The population continued small, numbering but 59,000 in 1930, of whom the whites formed less than a majority. With many difficulties yet to overcome, there could be no doubt that under favorable conditions Alaska would turn out to be one of America's most profitable acquisitions.

Five years after Alaska, Puerto Rico became a territory. This sunny island, half again as big as Delaware, had been relieved of military rule in April, 1900, by the Foraker act which, though failing to declare the inhabitants American citizens, allowed them to elect the lower house of the legislature, the upper house and the governor to be appointed by the President. American dominion brought vast improvements in social and economic life. In the score of years after 1899, the highways lengthened from 430 miles to more than 1900, while the number of public school buildings increased from none at all to well over 500. Meanwhile illiteracy declined from eighty per cent to fifty-five. Public-health agencies, including sewerage, quarantine regulations and hospitals, were introduced, and such scourges as yellow fever, smallpox and anæmia were almost completely banished. Economic progress was quite as marked, sugar-cane culture outstripping coffee growing as the chief occupation, with tobacco ranking third. The population was largely white, and in 1930 numbered a million and a half, over half again as many as when the United States took possession.

While the Puerto Ricans assisted whole-heartedly in the advances made, they were discontented because they had not gained American citizenship or a larger measure of local control. In 1914 President Wilson reconstructed the upper house so as to give the natives a majority of the appointments, and three years later their demands were more fully met by the boon of territorial standing and the bestowal of American citizenship. Nevertheless, restiveness continued among the islanders, partly because of the growing centralization of land ownership in a relatively few hands and the corresponding increase of tenancy. A rising sentiment favored statehood, or some equivalent status that would give the people unrestricted right to deal with their local problems in their own way.

Other parts of the overseas empire had to remain content

with simpler and less democratic forms of government. In Guam and in American Samoa all political authority was vested in a resident official of the Navy Department, and the Panama Canal Zone was similarly put under a governor appointed by the War Department. In 1917 the insular area was enlarged by the purchase of the Danish West Indies or Virgin Islands. This group, situated sixty miles east of Puerto Rico, consists of St. Thomas, St. Croix and St. John, and of about fifty smaller islands, mostly uninhabited. Attracted by the splendid harbor of St. Thomas, Secretary of State Seward had attempted to buy the islands in 1867, only to have the treaty fail in the Senate. The strategic value of American ownership became increasingly apparent with the progress of the isthmian-canal plans. A treaty of annexation was approved by the Senate in 1902, but was rejected by the Danish upper chamber. A third attempt in 1916, however, resulted in the transfer of the islands to the United States the next year for $25,000,000. The acquisition was placed under a governor appointed directly by the President. The people, mostly Negroes, were allowed limited rights of local self-government, and in 1927 were declared citizens of the United States. Unlike other possessions, the dependency made only halting progress. The population actually fell fifteen per cent from 1917 to 1930, thanks largely to attractions of employment in the United States. After a visit in 1931, President Hoover called the colony "an effective poorhouse," adding, "Viewed from every point except remote naval contingencies, it was unfortunate that we ever acquired these islands." As for the host of petty Pacific islands — Midway, Wake, Howland, Baker and the others — they contained few or no inhabitants and were given no resident form of government.

AMERICA IN THE PHILIPPINES

The special position of the Philippines in the imperial system was due to the expectation, voiced in the McEnery resolution at the time of annexation in 1899 (see page 304), that the islands would eventually be set free. When America took them over, the Filipinos resumed against the United States the war for independence they had been waging against Spain. The odds, however, were badly against the insurgents, who lacked not only military skill but also sufficient weapons and ammunition. Repeatedly overcome in pitched engagements, they resorted to guerrilla tactics, laying waste fields, and surprising and massacring small troop detachments. The Americans, angered by the barbarous treatment of captive comrades, often inflicted reprisals in kind. Finally, in March, 1901, a small party under Brigadier General Frederick Funston captured Emilio Aguinaldo, the rebel chieftain, through a daring exploit, and the latter presently issued a proclamation to his followers to give up the fight. But it was not until July 4 of the next year that President Roosevelt officially declared the islands pacified. Even afterward, sporadic outbreaks occurred, notably among the Moros and other wild tribes. The cost of subduing the Philippines amounted to $170,000,000, more than eight times the purchase price.

Under American tutelage the islands advanced steadily toward the goal of political autonomy. In July, 1901, the military government gave way to an American civil commission of five, headed as governor-general by William Howard Taft, the future President, and enlarged a few months later to include three appointed native members. The commission promptly set about to reorganize the local governments; and, for this purpose, the suffrage was bestowed upon all men of twenty-three and over who were taxpayers or property owners or former municipal officeholders, or who could speak, read and write English or Spanish. After one year of this system Congress made more permanent provision for the islands in the organic act of July 1, 1902. It declared the inhabitants "citizens of the Philippine Islands, and as such entitled to the protection of the United States." Most of the constitutional guarantees for the protection of life, liberty and property were extended to them, except trial by jury which could not easily be grafted onto the old Spanish legal system. Though the civil governor and commission were continued in sole control for the time, the act provided for the eventual creation of a legislature. In 1907 this pledge was fulfilled, the commission becoming the upper house and the lower being chosen by the voters.

Meanwhile, the islands awakened from their long tropical sleep to a new interest in the bustling life of the modern world.

One long-standing native grievance had been the economic and political power wielded by three Roman Catholic orders, which owned great tracts of fertile land. The Filipinos hated the friars so bitterly that, during the revolt, they had expelled them from the islands with great cruelty. When the establishment of American authority led the friars to reassert their legal rights, the natives generally continued to ignore them. As a way out, Governor Taft took up the matter with the papal authorities in Rome in person, and in 1903 the United States purchased the 410,000 acres for $7,239,000. In addition, a currency system was established, and a comprehensive program of public works carried on, including highways, bridges, port improvements, lighthouses and irrigation works. With the aid of American capital agriculture made rapid strides, notably in the cultivation of sugar, cocoanuts and hemp. The mineral resources of the islands, however, were hardly scratched.

Public order was assured through an able native constabulary, and prison administration was reorganized. There remained, however, insufficient provision for public health, sanitation and hospitals. Public education, on the other hand, made notable progress, culminating in the tax-supported University of the Philippines. To get the system under way, hundreds of young American men and women went to the islands and taught Filipino children, and the normal school at Manila was greatly enlarged to speed the training of native teachers. With 200,000 pupils in the schools in 1902, the number more than doubled by 1907, and reached the surprising total of a million and a quarter in 1930. Illiteracy fell from fifty-six per cent in 1903 to thirty-seven in 1921. English gradually supplanted the numerous native dialects and languages, much to the relief of the Filipinos themselves who, divided by speech barriers, saw in a common tongue a necessary basis for the achievement of national solidarity. The population, which numbered less than seven million under Spain, exceeded twelve and a half in 1930.

In all the reforms that were undertaken the islanders warmly coöperated. Keenly aware of their own political inexperience, they sought to learn what they could from this intimate contact with a progressive Western people. In return, the American officials placed natives in positions of trust and responsibility as rapidly as circumstances seemed to justify.[1] They never forgot their aspirations for national freedom, however. After the first few years every Philippine political party unfurled the banner of immediate independence. In America their cause was championed by the Democrats. President Wilson upon entering office insured full native control of the insular legislature by appointing Filipinos to a majority of the seats in the upper house. Three years later, in 1916, Congress adopted the Jones act, which granted the islands what was, in many respects, a territorial status. Both houses were made elective and the governor-general was continued in executive charge. The extension of the suffrage to all men of twenty-one and over, who could read and write a native dialect, trebled the number of voters in the first election. American citizenship was not conferred, however, since the Philippines were not considered a permanent possession.

The preamble of the Jones act further stated the purpose of the United States to recognize the independence of the islands "as soon as a stable government can be established therein." Almost at once the Filipinos were confronted with a severe test of their capacity for self-rule, thanks to the financial and economic disturbances attendant upon the World War. Hostile critics saw evidences of governmental incompetence on every hand. Nevertheless, President Wilson in his message of December 2, 1920, declared that the people, having "succeeded in maintaining a stable government," were ready for independence. The accession of the Republicans a few months later held up action for a number of years. A special commission appointed by President Harding, after surveying conditions on the spot, recommended "that the present general status . . . continue until the people have had time to absorb and thoroughly master the powers already in their hands." Each year the insular legislature adopted a unanimous resolution for immediate freedom, and in 1927 President Coolidge vetoed an act of that body, which called for a popular referendum on the question. In a communication to a Philippine leader he declared that the best case for independence "is not the argument that it would benefit the Filipinos" — which he denied — "but that it would be of ad-

[1] By 1930 Filipinos held 20,332 offices out of a total of 20,811 in the insular civil service.

vantage to the United States." The beneficent policy of the government had indeed failed to pay in dollars and cents, but, added to the altruistic motive implied in the expression, "the white man's burden," was the fear that, if the United States let go, Japan would seize the islands.

Nevertheless, sentiment in Congress steadily veered back toward the pledge given in the Jones act. Economic considerations lent it force, for the domestic sugar and tobacco growers had long objected to Philippine competition, and until 1913 had succeeded in maintaining restrictions on the importation of these products. American dairying interests, too, found that cocoanut oil came into competition with their commodities. There was, besides, a growing opposition on the Pacific Coast to the free admission of Philippine immigrants, of whom 45,000 dwelt in the United States in 1930. Finally, in January, 1933, a Republican Senate and Democratic House passed over President Hoover's veto the Hawes-Cutting bill, which set forth specific conditions of separation. Within two years, if the local legislature approved, the islanders should frame a constitution which must be acceptable both to the President and to a popular vote of the Filipinos. A ten-year transitional period should then follow before independence, during which time restrictions would be placed upon the amounts of sugar, cocoanut oil and hemp products imported free of duty into the United States, the Philippine government must levy an increasing tariff on goods shipped to America, and emigration to the United States would be limited to an annual quota of fifty. American commodities, however, should have free entry into the islands. Upon the attainment of independence the new republic should be outside American tariff walls, and the United States be permitted to retain certain military and naval stations. One of President Hoover's several objections to the act concerned its failure to define the future responsibilities of the United States as regards insular independence in case of foreign attack. Thanks chiefly to the onerous economic restrictions, the law was regarded by the Filipinos themselves with mixed feelings. Yet the special Philippine delegation, which had lobbied for its passage, did not hesitate to declare in a public statement that the action of Congress was "unprecedented in the history of dependent peoples," and that

"No nation heretofore has been able to win its independence in the manner it will come to the Philippines under this law, through the orderly processes of self-government and peace."

THE CARIBBEAN SPHERE OF INFLUENCE

Meanwhile, events had caused the United States to extend its power to certain Caribbean lands whose ownership it did not seek to acquire. The first impulse toward the establishment of protectorates came as a result of the responsibilities which the government assumed toward Cuba under the Spanish-American peace treaty. When the American military administration took charge on January 1, 1899, the island was disorganized politically and economically. Furthermore, two thirds of the inhabitants could neither read nor write. To Major General J. R. Brooke and his successor, Major General Leonard Wood, fell the task of introducing order into the chaos. Emergency relief was afforded the destitute, far-reaching sanitary reforms were introduced, order was established, the legal system reorganized, and an extensive program of highway construction begun. Likewise, church and state were separated, and the educational system was renovated and extended. On Wood's initiative, a constitutional convention assembled at Havana on November 5, 1900, and framed a basic law for the new republic modeled on that of the United States. Despite his urgent representations, the proposed instrument was silent as to the future relations of Cuba with the United States. Congress met the situation through the Platt Amendment to the army-appropriation act of March 2, 1901, which instructed the President to prolong the military occupation until certain specified provisions should be inserted in the insular constitution. These included Cuba's pledge never to allow a foreign power to impair her independence or territorial integrity, her agreement never to contract indebtedness beyond the capacity of her ordinary revenues to pay, and her express recognition of America's right to intervene to preserve the island's independence or orderly government. In addition, Cuba must permit the United States to acquire naval bases within her borders.[1] Reluctantly the convention made the re-

[1] Such stations were presently leased at Bahia Honda and Guantanamo, but the former was abandoned in 1913.

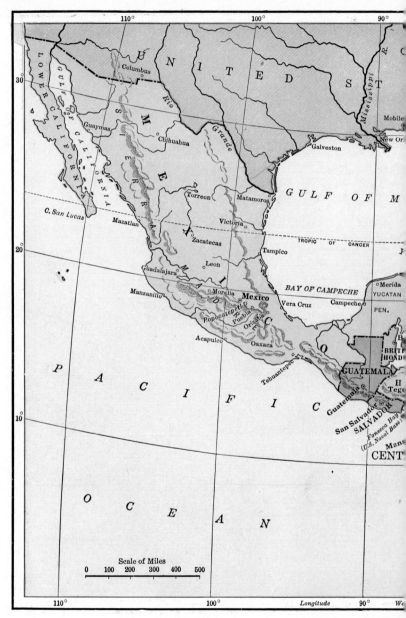

Scale of Miles

| 0 | 100 | 200 | 300 | 400 | 500 |

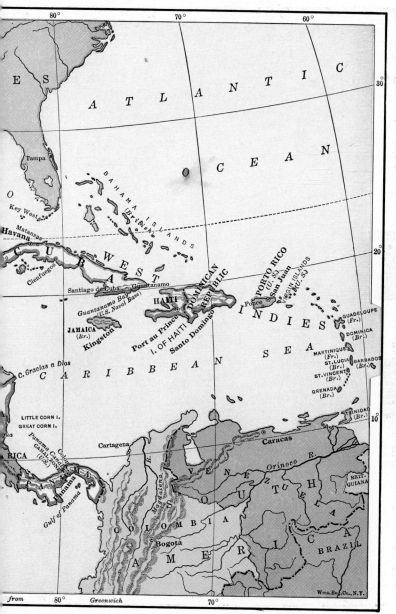

quired concessions and, two years later, the stipulations were embodied in a "permanent" treaty.

On May 20, 1902, the government of independent Cuba was formally installed. Handicapped by a bad heritage, the people were slow to value the ballot over the bullet as a means of settling public issues. Civil disorders fruiting from the presidential election of 1906 led to a military occupation of the island under the Platt Amendment, which lasted from September of that year to January, 1909. In his message to Congress on December 3, 1906, Roosevelt made it clear that, though the United States had no desire to annex Cuba, it was "absolutely out of the question" for the island to continue independent should the "insurrectionary habit" become "confirmed." The warning, however, was soon forgotten. In 1912 marines were landed for several weeks near Santiago to protect American-owned mines and sugar plantations during a Negro uprising. Five years later a revolt, provoked by a disputed election of 1916, caused forces to be landed at Santiago, Camaguey and elsewhere for the preservation of order, the detachment at Camaguey remaining until 1922. To prevent a recurrence of such disturbances, a new electoral code, drafted with the help of the American general, E. H. Crowder, was adopted by the insular legislature in 1919. The conduct of the election of 1920 showed little improvement, however, and Crowder had to return in order to effect a peaceable seating of the successful candidate. At his instance, also, the Cuban congress two years later undertook an extensive program of governmental reform, designed to do away with financial corruption and extravagance, and to improve the administration of justice. Yet, under President Gerardo Machado, who took office in 1925, conditions reverted to a worse state of turbulence than at any time since Spanish days. After inducing the congress to emasculate the Crowder code, he seized dictatorial powers and perpetuated his sway through terrorism, assassination and martial law. Violent opposition to his rule developed in 1931, and again in 1933. In August of the latter year the American Ambassador presented the demand of the several antiadministration groups that Machado abdicate and, when the armed forces two days later joined the movement, he decamped in haste. Carlos Manuel de Cespedes succeeded to the presidency, but a revolutionary group of students and soldiers soon replaced him with Grau San Martin. The shift of power was an earnest of the troubles which would attend the task of restoring orderly government.

From an economic point of view, Cuba as the century advanced became more and more an appanage of American capitalists. American investments grew from $80,000,000 in 1901 to $220,-000,000 at the outbreak of the World War and to $1,500,000,000 in 1928, the largest amount of United States money invested in any Latin-American country. Aided by preferential tariffs in the United States as well as by American capital, Cuba became the "sugar bowl of the world," sending the great bulk of its supply to the United States. Real estate, railways, government bonds, public utilities, manufacturing and tobacco represented other significant ramifications of the economic penetration. Similarly, American financial houses extended their dominion, the National City Bank of New York establishing over twenty branches in the island. To some Cubans it seemed that they had won independence from Spain only to turn over the country to American business interests; but there could be no doubt that this economic relationship, plus the political balance wheel of the Platt Amendment, gave the island a measure of prosperity, and also of governmental stability, that it could not otherwise have attained.

Shortly after Cuba accepted the Platt Amendment, a second protectorate came into being under circumstances quite as natural. The Panama revolution in 1903 (see page 312) put the infant republic in need of a defender against Colombia; and the United States sought a controlling hand in the territory bordering on the Canal Zone. As a result, the American government agreed in the treaty of November 18 to guarantee Panama's independence in return for the constitutional privilege of intervening with armed force whenever necessary "for the reëstablishment of constitutional peace and order." Under this arrangement the United States landed forces in Panama five times between 1908 and 1921. American investments rose to $5,000,000 in 1913 and to $46,500,-000 in 1930.

Even before this new protectorate was set up, a dramatic incident foreshadowed further and unexpected applications of the Platt Amendment principle. In December, 1902, Great

Britain, Germany and Italy undertook a blockade of Venezuela, on the south shore of the Caribbean, in order to compel payment of long-standing debts to their subjects. Although the United States had been notified in advance, the presence of a hostile European fleet boded ill for a weak Latin-American country, and the American government bestirred itself successfully to have the claims referred to arbitration and to lift the blockade. The moral of the episode was clear. As President Roosevelt informed Congress in December, 1904, "Chronic wrongdoing . . . may in America, as elsewhere, ultimately require intervention by some civilized nation, and in the Western Hemisphere, the adherence of the United States to the Monroe Doctrine may force the United States, however reluctantly, . . . to the exercise of an international police power." In other words, according to the so-called Roosevelt corollary of the Monroe Doctrine, the American government in the future must ward off European intervention by itself assuming responsibility for the financial good faith of defaulting republics. A doctrine of noninterference by Europe in the affairs of the New World thus came to involve a doctrine of unmistakable interference by the United States.

In line with this new policy and with the desire to establish additional outposts for the protection of the isthmian canal, the circle of protectorates widened in the ensuing years and the Caribbean Sea acquired its character of the "American Mediterranean." The inflow of United States capital into the region speeded the process. Not only in Cuba and Panama, but also in other Caribbean lands, American investments and trade rapidly mounted. American capital was particularly active in the exploitation of sugar, fruit, coffee, public utilities, asphalt and oil.[1] Commerce with the United States grew from $195,000,000 in 1900 to $545,000,000 in 1927, Mexico excluded.

The Dominican Republic in the eastern part of the island of Santo Domingo was the first country to which the Roosevelt corollary was applied. In order to avert possible foreign inter-

---

[1] According to Max Winkler, the leading authority, American capital investments in the Dominican Republic rose from $4,000,000 in 1912 to $24,000,000 in 1929; in Haiti from $4,000,000 in 1914 to $31,000,000 in 1929; and in Nicaragua they reached $24,000,000 in 1929.

vention for the collection of debts long overdue, President Roosevelt in 1905, with the consent of the insular government, placed an American financial expert in charge of its revenues, with power to arrange for the progressive payment of the foreign bondholders. Two years later, the stipulations were embodied in a treaty, the United States receiving authority to accord "such protection" to the general receiver and his staff as might "be requisite for the performance of their duties." Under this vague grant American representatives supervised the Dominican elections of 1913, and three years later marines landed for the purpose of quelling a revolt. The intervention quickly grew into a complete military occupation. The American administration restored peace to the country, enforced sanitary measures, reorganized and extended the school system, and undertook an elaborate program of good roads and public works. Wrathy at outside interference in their domestic affairs, the natives insisted again and again upon a termination of the occupation. In June, 1921, President Harding announced that withdrawal would occur only when the insular government agreed to a treaty ratifying all the acts of the military régime and enlarging the powers of the general receiver of the customs. These terms, though deeply resented, were eventually accepted. American evacuation occurred in the summer of 1924, though the customs receivership continued.

Meanwhile, the neighboring Negro republic of Haiti was subjected to a similar supervision. Following a revolutionary outbreak early in 1915, marines took possession of the chief towns. The outcome was a treaty in September, which established American management of Haitian finances, provided for a constabulary officered by Americans, and empowered the United States to intervene when necessary for the preservation of Haitian independence or an orderly government. The American administration, with characteristic efficiency, carried through extensive sanitary, fiscal and governmental reforms, and stabilized political and economic conditions. Bitter native antagonism, however, resulted from the revival in 1917–1918 of the *corvée* system of forced labor on the roads, and from alleged abuses of authority by the marine corps. A Senate committee, after investigating conditions at first-hand, recommended unanimously in 1922 that the military occupation continue for an indefinite period. In 1930, however, President Hoover after another investigation began a policy of gradually withdrawing the American régime, with the purpose of ending it completely in 1936 when the treaty arrangements lapsed. His successor, President Franklin D. Roosevelt, went further, agreeing to recall the last marines by November 1, 1934.

In 1911 the Taft administration, following in Roosevelt's footsteps, had negotiated treaties for fiscal receiverships in Honduras and Nicaragua, only to have them rejected by the Senate. Nevertheless, Nicaragua the same year, with the approval of the State Department, put her customs in charge of an American financial expert as the price of securing a loan from certain New York banking houses. In August, 1912, marines were landed to allay civil disorder, and remained until 1925 as a legation guard at the capital. In the interval order was preserved at elections with the aid of American bayonets. A treaty of 1914 granted the United States exclusive and perpetual right to build a canal through Nicaragua, turned over to America certain naval bases, and stipulated a payment of $3,000,000 for these privileges. In December, 1926, the marines returned in order to protect American lives and property, and this time stayed on until January, 1933, fighting rebels and bandits, supervising elections and helping to train a native constabulary. Thus, without express treaty stipulations, Nicaragua found herself, in fact if not in law, an American protectorate.

In 1922 Salvador, tiniest of the Central American nations, followed Nicaragua's example of obtaining a loan from American bankers at the cost of turning over the management of her customs to an American official chosen with the approval of the State Department. This whole line of policy was variously regarded in the United States as an altruistic assumption of the "white man's burden," as an ungrateful task imposed by considerations of national safety and as an ugly manifestation of economic and financial imperialism. Doubtless all these elements figured in the unfolding of the program. Nothing more clearly evinced the limited objectives of the progressive movement than the failure of these crusaders for democracy at home to insist upon applying the democratic principle of self-determination to the Caribbean. Only in the case of Mexico, which we shall next consider, did an American President attempt a policy that presumably harmonized with the new governmental ideals.

THE UNITED STATES AND MEXICO

Though the United States made no move to establish protectorates south of Central America and the Caribbean, the outward thrust of Yankee dominion produced great uneasiness throughout the Latin-American world. If, as Roosevelt asserted, the southward advance found its justification in the Monroe Doctrine, then it looked as though a policy originally forged as defensive armor had turned into a weapon of imperialistic aggrandisement.[1] ❨Resentment against "Monroeism" burned especially fiercely among the peoples of Argentina, Brazil and Chile, the so-called A. B. C. Powers, who felt that their political stability and cultural progress entitled them to freedom from alien tutelage.❩ As a result, a powerful sentiment developed for a Pan-American Doctrine, which would replace the United States as sole interpreter and guarantor of the Monroe Doctrine with a league of New World republics. A Pan-American Doctrine, of course, would act as a curb on the "Colossus of the North" as well as on European powers.

To allay Latin-American apprehensions aroused by his cavalier treatment of Colombia during the Panama revolt, President Roosevelt solemnly avowed in his message of December 5, 1905, that "under no circumstances will the United States use the Monroe Doctrine as a cloak for territorial aggression." Subsequent administrations reiterated the assurance. But the acid test of American good faith came when a prolonged reign of anarchy began in Mexico in 1911 at America's very doors. United States citizens at the time held Mexican investments, mostly in oil properties, mines, railways and ranches, amounting to a billion dollars. Fifty or sixty thousand of them carried on business there, and the bulk of Mexico's commerce lay with her northern neighbor. Nevertheless, President Wilson made

---

[1] It is noteworthy that a memorandum made public by the State Department in 1930 denied that the Roosevelt corollary was "justified by the terms of the Monroe Doctrine, however much it may be justified by the application of the doctrine of self-preservation." But to many Latin Americans this seemed a distinction without a difference.

it clear from the outset that the administration's policy would not be controlled by selfish economic considerations. "We have seen material interests threaten constitutional freedom in the United States," he declared in a speech at Mobile in 1913. "Therefore we will now know how to sympathize with those in the rest of America who have to contend with such powers, not only within their borders but from outside their borders also." As his program took form, he established a further precedent by calling on Latin-American nations, at critical junctures, to co-operate in the settlement of Mexican difficulties. Only the future can disclose whether these were the first steps toward the development of a Pan-American Doctrine.

Since 1877 Mexico had been almost continuously under the iron rule of Porfirio Diaz, nominally president but actually dictator. Representative government existed in form only, and the agrarian masses, mostly of Indian blood, were tied to the soil by a system of peonage. But peace and order prevailed, foreign capital was welcomed, and the country experienced a wonderful material transformation. Native dissatisfaction increased to a dangerous pitch, and the eighth "election" of Diaz in 1910 proved the signal for a popular uprising headed by Francisco Madero, a sincere democrat. In 1911, when the aged Diaz fled to Europe, Madero became his successor. The tide of lawlessness, however, still ran strong. In February, 1913, General Victoriano Huerta, supported by the old Diaz faction, overturned the new government and, there is good reason to believe, instigated Madero's assassination. Once more Mexico plunged into anarchy with Venustiano Carranza leading the insurgent bands as Madero's political heir.

Though European powers promptly recognized Huerta, Wilson declined to follow suit, justifying his course on the novel ground that the régime rested on force and murder. Convinced that Huerta's authority would soon collapse without American recognition and financial aid, he notified Congress that his policy would be one of "watchful waiting." Meantime the destruction of life and property continued, and American interests bent on armed intervention savagely denounced the President as an impractical idealist. In fact, even Wilson found the game of waiting a trying one. When Huerta failed to make suitable apology for arresting some American marines at Tampico, the President ordered the seizure of Vera Cruz in April, 1914. He then accepted an offer of the A. B. C. governments to mediate the difficulties. This action, however, proved of little practical consequence, for Huerta, overwhelmed by his enemies, fled Mexico almost at once. Carranza, the chief insurgent leader, succeeded to his place, and in November the American forces evacuated Vera Cruz.

With the popular party once more in control, the situation assumed a new aspect, for the victors fell to quarreling among themselves. Francisco Villa, a former bandit chieftain, proved the chief disturbing element, and so fierce was the ensuing strife that Mexico City changed hands thrice in a single month. His patience sorely taxed, Wilson once more turned to Latin America for counsel. An inter-American conference of Bolivia, Uruguay, Guatemala, the A. B. C. Powers and the United States decided in October, 1915, to recognize Carranza as the true head of Mexico. This action immeasurably strengthened Carranza's hold, but Villa succeeded in continuing his stormy career for over a year. In a spirit of pique against the United States, he raided across the border in March, 1916, killing seventeen persons in Columbus, New Mexico. A punitive expedition under General J. J. Pershing went in pursuit; and although Villa managed to elude capture, many lawless bands were dispersed, and Villa himself was forced to cease his activities. Meanwhile, Wilson called out 150,000 state militiamen to guard the international frontier. In January, 1917, the forces were withdrawn.

Later differences between the two nations centered in the interpretation of a new Mexican constitution, adopted in 1917. This instrument was designed to accomplish a radical economic and social reconstruction of the country. Besides devoting much attention to the welfare of industrial workers, it provided for breaking up the great landed estates, and asserted national ownership of all oil and other mineral resources. The provision (Article 27) in regard to property rights vitally affected the security of American investments, and provoked sharp protests from Washington. Finally, Mexico in 1923 gave assurance that Article 27 would not be so applied as to work the confiscation of American mineral rights acquired under the previous constitution, and agreed further to compensate American citizens whose estates had been seized and partitioned. A month later certain other difficulties were cleared away by the signing of two conventions setting up mixed claims commissions to determine the amount of American damages suffered during the revolutionary disturbances and for the adjustment of Mexican losses growing out of the Vera Cruz and Pershing expeditions. After yet further diplomatic exchanges, the Mexican congress in 1927 liberalized its petroleum and land laws in such a way as to render greater justice to foreign holdings acquired before 1917. Though it was likely that the revolutionary fever was checked rather than cured, relations between the two countries were at last on a satisfactory basis, and augured well for the future.

THE NEW PEACE MOVEMENT

The rising tide of democracy throughout the world, the new value placed upon the welfare of the common man, the incessant internationalist agitation of the socialists, the tightening network of financial and commercial ties among the powers, the staggering cost of national armaments — influences such as these smoothed the way for the growth of a powerful world peace movement in the first decade of the twentieth century. In this enterprise the United States took an energetic part. Indeed, no other country had done more in the past to encourage the pacific settlement of international difficulties. But it was at the suggestion of the Czar of Russia that twenty-six leading powers conferred at The Hague in 1899 on the possibility of limiting armaments and promoting universal amity. This body drafted certain principles to govern the conduct of warfare on land and sea, and established a Permanent Court of Arbitration to sit at The Hague. In 1907 a second Hague conference of forty-four states, held this time at the instance of President Roosevelt, adopted additional rules to mitigate the horrors of war, reorganized the court, and indorsed the principle that the debts of one country to another should not be collected by force.

In the ordinary sense, the Permanent Court of Arbitration was not a court, being a list of judges selected by the several countries, from which special courts might be composed with the consent of the governments directly concerned, whenever specific cases arose. Though the submission of cases was left optional and the machinery of adjustment proved somewhat cumbersome, its establishment was an important move in the right direction. The tribunal settled seventeen disputes between 1902 and the end of 1914, and to four of these the United States was a party. The most notable case involved the long-standing question of the rights of Americans in the fisheries off Newfoundland and Labrador; the decision, rendered in 1910, was favorable to the United States.

Private endeavors were being made along similar lines. Although the hopeful efforts of the American Peace Society in the mid-nineteenth century had been blasted by the Civil War, the movement had slowly got under way again, notably with the help of various church groups. But it was not until the new century came and practical men of affairs lent their support that the agitation assumed large consequence. Thanks to the benefactions of Andrew Carnegie, Edwin Ginn and others, foundations were set up to investigate and promote the cause. Peace agencies multiplied, their literature received wide distribution, and the greater universities aided by creating international exchange professorships. Such exertions did not go unchecked. Thus the Navy League, formed in 1903 largely by retired navy officers and armor-plate manufacturers, and closely interlocked with New York banking firms, kept up an incessant propaganda for bigger armaments. Besides, the increase of investments abroad did not always promote a pacific disposition. Not only did it lead to unacknowledged wars in the Caribbean, but American bankers found it profitable to supply the financial sinews for other nations' conflicts. In 1901 they lent $50,000,000 to help defray the expenses of the British government in conquering the Boers. A few years later their loans assisted Japan at Russia's cost to extend her sway into southern Manchuria. By 1909 American investments in various parts of the globe had climbed to two billion dollars, and four years later to over two and a half billion, of which a seventh was placed in Europe itself.

Nevertheless, Roosevelt struck a responsive chord in 1904 when he assumed leadership in an effort to enlarge the authority of the Hague court beyond the limits set. He submitted to the Senate a group of treaties, which, departing from the existing arrangement, *obligated* the United States and the contracting powers to submit all their disputes to the tribunal, save those involving vital interests, independence or national honor. An unhappy quarrel between the President and the Senate prevented ratification in a form acceptable to him, and the matter hung fire until 1908–1909 when the United States entered into twenty-two agreements of this kind. As a promoter of peace, however, Roosevelt did not subscribe to many of the tenets of the professional pacifist. Even his arbitration treaties, through their reservation of certain large subjects, left the gate wide open for a resort to force. Ever an ardent nationalist, he held that heavy armaments were, after all, the best guarantee of peace. Nor did he hesitate to plunge into the hurly-burly of world politics in pursuit of his objective. In January, 1906, when the peace of Europe was menaced by a controversy between Germany and France over the latter's claims to Morocco, the United States joined with ten other governments in a conference at Algeciras in Morocco to compose the differences. The Senate in ratifying the act of settlement cautiously disclaimed any "purpose to depart from the traditional American foreign policy which forbids participation . . . in the settlement of political questions which are entirely European in their scope."

Meanwhile, without consulting the Senate and in the greatest secrecy, Roosevelt had launched upon an even bolder course. Fearing lest the Russo-Japanese War of 1904–1905 develop into a general international conflict, he warned Germany and France that, if either of them intervened on the side of Russia, he would bring in America on the side of Japan. Knowledge of this unprecedented, if not unconstitutional, action did not become public until many years later. As Japan drew near the end of her resources, he persuaded the warring powers to join in a peace conference at Portsmouth, New Hampshire, from which Japan as the victorious combatant issued with the former Chinese holdings of Russia.

Yet, in the ensuing years, the gravest threat to American peace, Mexico excepted, proved to be the increasing tension with Japan. Roosevelt's pressure on Japan's delegates at Portsmouth not to insist upon a war indemnity, discriminations against her subjects on the Pacific Coast, and the enlarging influence of

America in the Far East, all fed the flames of Japanese resentment. The United States on its part suspected the island kingdom of designs upon China subversive of her independence and the preservation of the open door. The question of Japanese immigration was presently set at rest, at least for the time (see page 354), and in 1908 an endeavor was made to dispose of the larger and more fundamental problem. In the Root-Takahira agreement, the two powers, "uninfluenced by any aggressive tendencies," pledged themselves to respect each other's territorial possessions in the Pacific and to support "by all pacific means" Chinese independence and the open door. The understanding partook of the nature of a gentlemen's agreement, and hence was not acted upon by the Senate. In 1917, in the Lansing-Ishii agreement, the two powers reaffirmed these assurances, with the imprudent admission by America that "territorial propinquity" gave Japan "special interests" in China. Innocently intended by Secretary Lansing, the phrase was construed by Japan to sanction new aggressions.

In the meantime President Taft had bent his efforts to create larger opportunities for the export of capital to China. Hay's open door, it will be remembered, applied to trade, not to investments. Nevertheless, from 1900 to 1914, American investments there increased from seventeen and a half million to forty-two. To accelerate the process, Taft's State Department encouraged American financial groups to unite with bankers of other countries in joint loans to the Chinese government for railway construction and other internal purposes. A six-power consortium for a loan of $125,000,000 to the new-fledged Chinese republic was thus being formed when President Wilson appeared on the scene in 1913. Disapproving certain of the terms and particularly the "implications" of governmental responsibility, he withdrew administration support and the American syndicate dropped out. Several years later, however, he saw the problem from a different angle — as a means of checking Japan's financial advance into China. Hence American bankers, with the government's full blessing, took the lead in forming the four-power consortium of 1920.

The advent of the Democrats led to a notable extension of the arbitration principle beyond the limits of the Roosevelt treaties. Long before becoming Secretary of State, Bryan had advocated referring every sort of dispute, even those involving national honor or vital interest, to arbitration. With Wilson's approval, in April, 1913, he invited the governments of the world to sign treaties with the United States committing the parties to submit their controversies "of whatever kind" to an investigating commission, and to refrain from hostilities until after the commission's report had been made. By allowing time for bellicose passions to subside he believed most wars could be prevented. The plan was so well received that thirty-one governments agreed to enter "cooling-off" treaties, and twenty-one ratifications were eventually exchanged. The dawn of a new era of world brotherhood seemed to be at hand when suddenly, almost without warning, the glittering dream was shattered by the outbreak of the great European war in 1914.

SELECT BIBLIOGRAPHY

Adapting the Constitution to an Imperial System. State activity in constitutional revision is sketched in Dealey, *Growth of American State Constitutions*. For an understanding of the Insular cases, two books by Willoughby are helpful: *Territories and Dependencies of the United States*, and *The Constitutional Law of the United States*.

The Imperial System in Operation. Reinsch, *Colonial Administration*, is a useful early work of general scope. For further light on particular dependencies, see Kuykendall, *A History of Hawaii;* Nichols, *Alaska;* Clark, *History of Alaska;* Mixer, *Porto Rico: History and Conditions;* Clark and others, *Porto Rico and Its Problems;* Westergaard, *The Danish West Indies;* and Tansill, *The Purchase of the Danish West Indies*.

America in the Philippines. Most of the works on this subject are controversial, having been written by Americans for or against insular independence, or by Philippine patriots. Much enlightening information may be gleaned from Forbes, *The Philippine Islands;* Worcester, *The Philippines, Past and Present;* LeRoy, *The Americans in the Philippines;* and Reyes, *Legislative History of America's Economic Policy toward the Philippines*.

The Caribbean Sphere of Influence. Latané, *The United States and Latin America*, and Robertson, *Hispanic-American Relations with the United States*, include discussions of the American advance into the Caribbean. Winkler, *Investments of United States Capital in Latin America*, deals with an essential aspect. For the Venezuelan incident, see Hill, *Roosevelt and the Caribbean*, which punctures a widely accepted earlier version. Particular protectorates receive detailed treatment in Chapman, *A History of the Cuban Republic;* Jenks, *Our Cuban Colony;* Knight, *The Americans in Santo Domingo*, which concerns the Dominican Republic; Millspaugh, *Haiti under American Control, 1915–1930;* and Cox, *Nicaragua and the United States, 1909–1927.*

The United States and Mexico. Haring, *South America Looks at the United States,* presents the Latin-American attitude toward the new rôle of the United States. Priestley, *The Mexican Nation,* Gruening, *Mexico and Its Heritage,* and Callcott, *Liberalism in Mexico, 1857–1929,* make clear Mexico's internal situation. For American relations Hackett, *The Mexican Revolution and the United States, 1910–1926,* Rippy, *The United States and Mexico,* Callahan, *American Foreign Policy in Mexican Relations,* and Dunn, *The Diplomatic Protection of Americans in Mexico,* are important.

The New Peace Movement. Significant phases of the revived interest in world peace are discussed in Beales, *The History of Peace;* Allen, *The Fight for Peace;* anon., *Arbitration and the United States;* Scott, *The Hague Peace Conferences of 1899 and 1907;* and Curti, *Bryan and World Peace.* On Japanese-American relations, consult Dennett, *Theodore Roosevelt and the Russo-Japanese War;* Hornbeck, *Contemporary Politics in the Far East;* Treat, *Japan and the United States, 1853–1921;* Norton, *China and the Powers;* and Remer, *Foreign Investments in China.*

CHAPTER XX

AMERICA AND THE WORLD WAR

THUNDER ACROSS THE SEA

THE seeds of the European war were sown as early as 1870 when the Germans imposed a drastic peace on their vanquished foe at the close of the Franco-Prussian War. The ground was fertilized by the intense nationalism which, in the same decade, started the Great Powers on strenuous imperialistic careers, involving a world-wide scramble for territory, spheres of influence, raw materials, markets and trade routes. As part of the drift of events there occurred an ominous division of Europe into two armed camps, each with its own ambitions, fears, secret treaties and unrecorded commitments — Russia, France and Great Britain heading one coalition, Germany and Austria-Hungary the other. An exhausting competition in armaments took place, leading to the creation of ever bigger armies and navies, undertaken quite as much from the rival powers' dread of each other as from motives of aggression.

By 1914 Europe had become a powder magazine which needed only a careless match to set it off. This spark fell on June 28 when the Austro-Hungarian heir-apparent was assassinated by a youth belonging to one of the many subject peoples composing the empire. Without proof, Austria-Hungary charged Serbia with being a party to the crime and, after making certain of the German Kaiser's support, declared war on Serbia a month later. Such was the tenseness of feeling and the obligation of alliances that all the Great Powers quickly plunged into the conflict, with the Central Empires — Germany and Austria-Hungary — captaining one set of belligerents, and the Entente Allies — Russia, France and Great Britain — the other.[1]

---

[1] Between July 28 and November 5 Austria-Hungary, Germany and Turkey entered the war on the one side, Serbia, Russia, France, Great Britain, Belgium, Montenegro and Japan on the other. Italy joined the Allies in May, 1915. Smaller states followed.

The people of America were stunned. Notwithstanding the rapid advance of the United States as a world power since 1898, the progressive movement had chained public attention to domestic problems, leaving the people blind to the forces that were driving Europe to disaster. On August 4, when five nations had taken up arms, President Wilson issued a proclamation of neutrality, which he repeated as successive countries joined the conflict. Later in August he made a special appeal to his countrymen to be "impartial in thought as well as action." The former measure accorded with a century and a quarter of consistent practice; the latter, however desirable, was impossible of fulfillment.

Of the hundred million people in the United States when the war began, a third were foreign-born or American-born of alien parentage. Of the total number of immigrants the Central Empires contributed a third, Great Britain and Canada a sixth. Next in order stood the Russians, the Irish (who generally sided with Germany because of hatred of England) and the Italians, each of whom numbered well above a million. These peoples, hitherto dwelling peaceably together in the land of their common adoption, were soon deeply stirred by emotions born of racial attachments, family relationships and rekindled patriotisms. The older American stock had its prejudices as well. The "ancient grudge" against Great Britain, nourished by school histories, was by no means offset by the multiplying evidences of Anglo-American accord. From the start, however, the business and banking interests, notably in the Atlantic states, sympathized with Britain, thanks to close financial ties and to their disapproval and fear of German commercial methods. Despite such differences the people generally eagerly supported the President's position of official neutrality, viewing the European conflict as something horrible and unclean. The stronghold of pacifist feeling was the Midwest, hitherto the breeding ground of progressivism.

THE USES AND ABUSES OF NEUTRALITY

The European struggle placed America in somewhat the same position she had occupied during the Napoleonic wars. With German shipping swept from the seas and a large part of Brit-

ain's merchant marine devoted to military uses, the United
States became the chief carrier of the world's commerce. The
derangement of European industry and agriculture and the in-
satiable demand for munitions, metal products, foodstuffs and
raw materials poured a flood of gold into America, especially
from the Allied countries whose markets were easily reached.
The value of explosives exported rose from $6,300,000 in 1914
to $803,000,000 in 1917; of chemicals, dyes, drugs and the like
from $22,000,000 to $181,000,000; of iron and steel from $252,-
000,000 to $1,134,000,000; and of wheat from $88,000,000 to
$298,000,000. The country's shipping proved unequal to the
demands. In an effort to remedy the situation, Congress in
August, 1914, enacted a law to facilitate the purchase of merchant vessels built in neutral nations by admitting such ships
to immediate registry without the former five-year restriction.
A few weeks later it instructed the government to set up a bureau
of war-risk insurance in order to keep marine insurance charges
within reasonable limits.

These measures, though helpful, failed to meet the real need:
the construction of more ships. Accordingly, the administration
proposed that the government itself engage in the business.
Congress, slow to act through fear of foreign complications and
dislike of government ownership, waited until September, 1916,
to set up a shipping board, with authority to build, buy or lease
merchant vessels and to operate them for a period not longer
than five years after the war. In addition, the board was granted
permanent powers to regulate private vessels engaged in interstate or foreign commerce. It thus attained a footing similar
to the interstate-commerce commission and the federal trade
commission. Unfortunately the law came too late to be of
much use before America's entry into the war; but thereafter
the board was given virtual control of the entire shipbuilding
resources of the nation and, in that capacity, performed indispensable service.

The war also stimulated an extraordinary export of capital
to embattled Europe. From August 1, 1914, to January 1, 1917,
several months before the nation's entry, Americans had purchased foreign securities to the amount of $2,325,000,000, of
which $1,900,000,000 consisted of loans to the Allies. The

workingmen shared in the good times. Since the abnormal expansion of industry occurred at a time of sharply declining immigration, organized labor was in a position to demand higher wages and other concessions, which employers found it easy to pass on to the public in the form of higher prices.

As in Napoleon's time, along with the tide of material prosperity came grave perils to the maintenance of national security. Neither Great Britain nor Germany was disposed to allow the interests of countries at peace to endanger its chances of victory. Accordingly, as the principal power not engaged in war, America was obliged once more to assume her historic rôle as champion of neutral rights. Britain's infringements consisted chiefly in arbitrary interruptions of commerce between the United States and neutral countries bordering on the Teutonic states. Perceiving that war materials were thus finding a backdoor entry into enemy territory, she freely seized cargoes of contraband. Though the United States, asserting the right of neutrals to absolute freedom in trading with other neutrals, denounced the interferences as illegal, the seizures continued. Already before the end of 1914 the British had taken over thirty-one cargoes of copper to a value of $5,500,000. Partly to obviate American objections, Britain in March, 1915, adopted a policy that amounted to a blockade of the German coast and near-by neutral ports. This move was likewise protested by the President as "illegal and indefensible" on the score that, under international law, countries at peace were not subject to blockade. Again Britain, pleading the law of national self-preservation, declined to abandon her course. The British government also extended the list of contraband articles greatly beyond those tentatively agreed to at a conference of ten maritime powers at London in 1909. Early in 1915 it even forbade the shipment of foodstuffs to the civil population of Germany, alleging that a recent German order nationalizing the food supply made it impossible to distinguish provisions intended for noncombatants from those destined for the army.

Vexatious and unlawful as such practices were, they inflicted property losses merely; but the troubles that developed with the Central Empires involved, in addition, plots against American domestic tranquillity and the destruction of lives on the high seas. Since German success required that the Allied shortage in munitions should not be replenished from other sources, Teutonic agents in the United States undertook a vigorous propaganda to induce Congress to place an embargo on war supplies. The government, however, was not to be persuaded, for the munitions trade was fully sanctioned by international law, and it was not America's fault that Germany was unable to buy in the American market. Thwarted at this point, the Central Empires undertook to accomplish their purpose through a campaign of terrorism. "It is my impression," boasted the Austrian Ambassador, Dr. Constantin Dumba, to his government in August, 1915, "that we can disorganize and hold up for months, if not entirely prevent, the manufacture of munitions in Bethlehem and the Middle West." At the instigation of Teutonic agents and pro-German sympathizers, explosions and incendiary fires damaged or destroyed munition plants, bombs were concealed aboard vessels carrying cargoes to the Allies, and strikes were set afoot among seamen and munition workers. The federal authorities apprehended most of the individual culprits, and soon managed to establish a connection with the Teutonic embassies in Washington. In September, 1915, the President forced the recall of Dumba and, three months later, that of two German naval and military attachés.

Along the sea lanes the Central Empires engaged in an even more desperate attempt to prevent shipments to the Allies. Outmatched by the British on the ocean's surface, Germany had developed undersea craft ("U-boats") to a point of perfection hitherto undreamed of. The use of submarines, though sanctioned by international law, was subject to severe restrictions. A merchant or passenger vessel must not be attacked unless, after being warned, it refused to allow visit and search, and under no circumstances should it be destroyed without safeguarding the lives of those on board. From Germany's unwillingness to abide by these restrictions stemmed all the difficulties that arose over submarine warfare. In justification, she pleaded the inability of undersea craft to carry additional passengers, and contended that, by rising to the surface to give warning, the frailty of the vessel exposed it to quick destruction from hostile gunfire. The United States, on its part, maintained that, if the new instrument could

not be used according to the well-established rules, then the submarine should be abandoned, not the rules.

Germany began her U-boat operations with a proclamation
that from February 18, 1915, she would destroy every enemy mer-
chantman found in the waters about the British Isles without
regard to the safety of passengers or crew, and that even neutral
vessels might, through accident, meet with like treatment. At
once Wilson replied that, if this course caused the loss of American
vessels or lives, he would hold Germany to "strict accountabil-
ity." Nevertheless, in March an American was drowned by the
torpedoing of the British steamer *Falaba*, and on May 1 the
Gulflight, an American ship, was sunk. Six days later occurred
the most shocking incident of all when the British transatlantic
liner *Lusitania*, carrying military supplies and nearly 2000 people,
was sent to the bottom unwarned, with a loss of more than a
thousand, including 114 United States citizens.

America blazed with resentment, and war might at once have
followed had a less resolute friend of peace been in the White
House. In a series of diplomatic dispatches, Wilson demanded
that the German government disavow her lawless practices, take
prompt steps to prevent their recurrence, and make all possible
reparation for losses already inflicted. But the only immediate
result was Bryan's resignation as Secretary of State. With a
large body of American sentiment, especially strong in the Midwest, he felt that citizens should travel at their own risk on
munition-carrying ships, and he wished the difficulties with
Germany to be settled according to the principle of the "cooling-
off" treaties (see page 393). Meanwhile the depredations continued, culminating on August 18 in the sinking of the British
liner *Arabic* and the loss of two more American lives. Fearful
of the consequences, Germany nine days later gave the definite
pledge that "Liners will not be sunk by our submarines without
warning and without safety of the lives of noncombatants." In
October she offered apologies and indemnity for the *Arabic*
disaster.

Wilson had won a diplomatic victory, but its edge was somewhat dulled by lack of confidence in Germany's good faith.
Thus, in February, 1916, when Germany made indemnity for the
lives lost in the *Lusitania*, she refused to admit the illegality of

the destruction. This was followed on March 24 by a further loss of American lives through the sinking of the French passenger ship *Sussex*. As an outright violation of the *Arabic* pledge, the President declined to accept the German excuse that the submarine commander had made an unfortunate mistake. In a note of April 18 he delivered an ultimatum to the effect that, unless unrestricted submarine attacks ceased, the United States would sever diplomatic relations. Convinced at last of the aroused state of American opinion, Germany grudgingly made the concession demanded. The crisis was over, at least for the moment. For the next nine months relations between the two nations showed less tension than at any time since hostilities had begun.

FROM SPECTATOR TO PARTICIPANT

When the war opened in 1914, it had seemed remote from the ordinary concerns of American life. But successive incidents, such as British interferences with American trade, German plots against American industry and the ruthless submarine operations, had gradually caused the people to think of the conflict as a concrete reality affecting intimately their own comfort and happiness. Moving westward from the Atlantic Seaboard, a strong pro-Ally sentiment began to envelop the people. Its spread was assisted not only by the greater enormity of Teutonic infractions of American neutrality, but also by disapproval of the invasion of neutral Belgium at the start of the war, and notably by skillful British manipulation of American opinion.[1] The British had complete control of the transatlantic cables, and hence censored all messages that passed over them. Besides, as one of their number later divulged, they supplied newspapers with a weekly pro-Ally review of the war, established connections with "eminent people of every profession in the United States, beginning with university and college presidents, professors and scientific men and running through all the ranges of the population," and also streamed their "documents and literature" into public libraries, clubs, Y. M. C. A. branches, colleges and news-

---

[1] American interest in the plight of Belgium was greatly stimulated by the leadership of Herbert Hoover, an American mining engineer, in organizing food relief for the people. As head of the Commission for the Relief of Belgium, he secured widespread financial support in the United States, obtained much-needed food and, in spite of many hindrances, provided for its effective distribution.

paper offices. Through such channels were disseminated appalling tales of Teutonic war atrocities and barbarities, and a growing number of people came to fear a triumphant Germany as a definite menace to the United States itself.

As the Teutonic cause lost favor in America, its supporters, led by the widespread German-language press, grew more and more strident in their efforts to stem the tide. The nation, as it were, turned into a vast and vociferous debating society, with the President a somewhat lonely figure bent on avoiding intervention save as a last resort. Increasingly he became a target for acrid criticism from "hyphenated" Americans, both pro-Germans who accused him of dealing too gently with Great Britain, and pro-Allies who charged him with weakness toward Germany. Inspired by Roosevelt, Leonard Wood and the recently organized National Security League (subsidized mostly by munitions and armor-plate interests and international bankers), an active agitation began early in the war for a stronger army and navy. Wilson was at first averse, for, like many of his countrymen, he attributed the demand to hysteria. Convinced at last by the thickening dangers, he advocated "preparedness" in his annual message of December, 1915, and even toured the Midwest to educate public sentiment on the question.

Under spur of the President's insistence, Congress in June, 1916, adopted the Hay act to strengthen the military department. It provided for augmenting the regular army by five annual accessions, for enlarging the state militia and placing it under federal control, and for establishing civilian training camps and introducing military instruction into schools and colleges. In protest against the bill Secretary of War Garrison, who thought it too mild, resigned, being replaced by Newton D. Baker of Ohio. In August Congress turned its attention to the navy, adopting a three-year program embracing the construction of ten dreadnaughts, six cruisers and 140 minor war craft, and making provision for a government-owned armor-plate plant. At the same time, Congress authorized a council of national defense of six cabinet members, to be set up in case of war as a board of strategy for industrial mobilization.

With Wilson preparedness for war represented a sober second thought. From the beginning of hostilities he had devoted his

chief energies to meeting the international crisis through the
healing methods of diplomacy. Nor had he been content to confine his efforts to safeguarding the rights of neutrals. On the
contrary, he endeavored to attack the evil at its source by repeatedly offering his good offices to the belligerents to end the
conflict. In these transactions his confidential agent was Colonel
E. M. House of Texas, a man of wide acquaintance abroad
and of unusual ability as a diplomat. Wilson made an even
bolder gesture in February, 1916, while the opposing armies
lay deadlocked on the western front. Through House he assured the British government that he stood ready to call a
peace conference at which he would act as mediator, and that,
if Germany declined, the United States "would probably enter
the war against Germany." [1] This offer the English leaders
rejected, possibly because they hoped through continuing the
struggle to secure better terms, possibly because Walter Hines
Page, the pro-Ally American Ambassador at London, openly
scoffed at the administration's sincerity, and perhaps also because the word, "probably," did actually leave the way open
for Wilson to recede from his position. At any rate, America's
delay in entering the conflict, so bitterly criticized by Allied
statesmen, may in considerable part be laid at their own door.

But already the President was arriving at a new conception
of peace terms. Thanks to the activities of an organization
called the League to Enforce Peace, founded at Philadelphia in
1915, he adopted as his own the notion of a world federation
for the prevention of war. The idea also made a ready convert
of ex-President Taft and of other public figures irrespective of
party. Believing that the European conflict might be made
into a war to end war, Wilson on December 18, 1916, requested
the belligerents to state "their respective views as to the terms
upon which the war might be concluded, and the arrangements
which would be deemed satisfactory as a guarantee against its
renewal." On January 22, 1917, he reported the results to the
Senate in an address intended for the whole world to hear. The

---

[1] According to a memorandum of Sir Edward Grey, approved by Wilson, the
President had in mind as peace terms "the restoration of Belgium, the transfer of
Alsace and Lorraine to France, and the acquisition by Russia of an outlet to the
sea," with compensation to Germany for her territorial losses in "concessions to her
in other places outside Europe."

Central Empires, he said, had refused to define peace terms; the reply of the Allies had been more satisfactory, and had outlined "indispensable conditions." As a neutral whose rights the struggle had put "in constant jeopardy," he asserted America's vital interest in a righteous and enduring peace — not "a victor's terms imposed upon the vanquished," provocative of future bloodshed, but "a peace without victory." The settlement must embrace such principles as the right of self-determination, freedom of the seas, limitation of armaments and a league to safeguard peace. Through the President's efforts, the United States was rapidly attaining the moral leadership of the world. At home, however, the address exposed him to fresh volleys of execration because of the expression, "peace without victory," which was interpreted by his critics as a confession of weakness and indecision. In reality, the conception underlying the phrase remained the essence of America's purpose even as a belligerent, though, in view of the altered circumstances and his certainty of direct participation in the peace negotiations, Wilson later changed the expression to a "peace of justice."

Before the President sent his formal request to the warring powers, the campaign of 1916 had taken place. At the outset the Republicans and the Progressives met in Chicago on the same day (June 7), in the hope that the two conventions might unite upon a single ticket. But the passions of four years before had not yet sufficiently cooled. The older party proposed the nomination of Charles E. Hughes who, as a member of the Supreme Court since 1910, had kept free from partisan embroilments; but the Progressives, despite Hughes's earlier reform record in New York, would have none other than Roosevelt. In the end, each side named its own candidate, the Republican ticket being completed by the addition of C. W. Fairbanks of Indiana. The Republican platform stigmatized Wilson's foreign policy as one of "phrase-making" and "shifty expedients," indorsed thoroughgoing preparedness, and promised a "strict and honest neutrality between the belligerents." Roosevelt, who had no liking for lost causes, waited until the Progressive convention had adjourned and then declined to run, urging his supporters to follow him back into the Republican party. His running mate, J. M. Parker of Louisiana, however, declared for Wilson. The

Democrats, convening at St. Louis on June 14, renominated their ticket of 1912. For the first time in many years they could point to a record of actual achievement. After rehearsing the party's epoch-making economic and humanitarian measures, the platform condemned "hyphenism," pledged adequate preparedness, and vaunted the President's diplomatic victories in dealing with the European belligerents.

The ensuing canvass proved close and exciting. As the "Outs," the Republicans brought all their batteries to bear upon the shortcomings of the "Ins." The pro-Germans, urged on by an organization called the German-American Alliance, helped by bitterly denouncing Wilson, and until the last week of the campaign Hughes avoided saying anything that might alienate their support. In the words, "He kept us out of war," Democratic orators found an effective vote-getting slogan, especially in the case of the women who now possessed the franchise in eleven states. Wilson's own speeches, however, contained nothing to justify an expectation that peace would necessarily continue. The American Federation of Labor advocated his reëlection and, as the campaign wore on, the independent voters began to turn to him, largely because of Hughes's lukewarmness toward social and economic reforms. The outcome was in doubt for several days after the election. The President received 277 electoral votes to 254 for his opponent, and 49.2 per cent of the popular ballots to 46. The Democratic ticket swept the South and the Far West, including nearly all the woman-suffrage states. For the first time in almost fifty years, if the Hayes-Tilden contest be excepted, a candidate won without the electoral vote of New York.

The significance of the result was misunderstood in the Central Empires. "The Germans," later declared J. W. Gerard, the American Ambassador at Berlin, "believed that President Wilson had been elected with a mandate to keep out of war at any cost, and that America could be insulted, flouted, and humiliated with impunity." Hence they redoubled the secret exertions already begun for the most extensive and destructive submarine campaign within their resources. On January 31, 1917, Germany abruptly informed the United States that thereafter, in disregard of the *Sussex* pledge, she would sink on sight all vessels, neutral as well as belligerent, found in certain specified waters about the British Isles and in the Mediterranean. At once, in conformity with his ultimatum on the former occasion, Wilson broke off diplomatic relations, and appealed, vainly, to all neutral countries to follow America's example so that the weight of world opinion might be thrown against Germany. Meanwhile, seeing a possibility of halting that power in her reckless course by drawing Austria into a separate peace, he exerted pressure upon the Allies to make known to Austria their willingness to accept milder terms than they had hitherto contemplated. Though Britain met his wishes part way, Austria proved obdurate. As a result, Wilson on February 26 asked Congress to authorize a policy of armed neutrality. The House promptly responded, but in the Senate eleven Western and Southern members, led by La Follette, managed to block action before the session ended a few days later. Nevertheless, the President, by authority of an almost forgotten statute, directed the arming of merchant ships.[1] Meantime, Teutonic ruthlessness was taking its toll. From February 3 to April 1, eight American vessels were sent to the bottom with a loss of forty-eight lives. Armed neutrality was fast proving its futility when Wilson called a special session of Congress for April 2.

Before that date two new events helped further to clarify the popular mind in regard to the issues at stake. One was the so-called Zimmermann note, whose contents were made public on March 1 through the enterprise of the British intelligence service. This document, signed by the German Foreign Minister on January 19, instructed the German Minister in Mexico to urge that government to attack the United States in case the latter declared war on Germany, and to offer as inducements "general financial support" and the opportunity to recover "the lost territory of New Mexico, Texas and Arizona." The American people, deeply shocked by the disclosure, were alarmed anew by the menace of German militarism to their own safety and peace. The other event was the news of the Russian revolution and the setting up of a republican government. By the overthrow of the Czar the principal Allies all became exponents of popular govern-

[1] On the Attorney-General's advice, Wilson resorted to a law of 1819 which, however, had specific reference to piratical vessels.

ment, leaving to the Teutonic states and Turkey the dubious distinction of being the last strongholds of military autocracy. There can be no doubt, further, that American financial interests deeply involved in Allied bonds, along with the merchants and manufacturers who had fattened on the war-swollen export trade, were badly frightened lest a German triumph imperil their chances of repayment. Economic interests thus lent fervor to political and idealistic considerations.

When the special session assembled, President Wilson in words that profoundly stirred the nation asked Congress to recognize the existence of a state of war with Germany. He recited the submarine depredations and the conspiracies against American national security culminating in the Zimmermann note, picturing these as the inevitable accompaniments of "autocratic governments backed by organized force which is controlled wholly by their will, not by the will of their people." The United States, he said, would battle for the rights of mankind, "for the ultimate peace of the world and for the liberation of its peoples, the German peoples included." And he added, in a phrase that rang round the globe, "The world must be made safe for democracy."

The period of indecision was at an end. After three years of unexampled forbearance, Wilson led the nation into the conflict when the people were fully convinced that no alternative remained. Moreover, he made the fateful choice turn not on motives of revenge or of selfish national gain, but on the opportunity to extend traditional American ideals to oppressed peoples. On April 6 Congress by overwhelming majorities voted to back up the President. A declaration of war against Austria-Hungary was withheld until December 7, in the hope that meantime she might still be weaned from her alliance with Germany. America's entry was a signal for similar action by many other neutral countries. The response of the republics of the New World was particularly significant for the light it shed upon Pan-American solidarity. In the ensuing months Brazil, Cuba, Panama, Guatemala, Costa Rica, Honduras, Haiti and Nicaragua declared war, while most of the other countries, not wishing to go so far, severed diplomatic relations.

A NATION IN ARMS

The World War was not the first but the eighth general international conflict in which the American people had taken part — the fourth since national independence.[1] Every major European war involving operations in the Atlantic had, sooner or later, drawn America into it. When she entered the lists against Germany, the war had been raging two years and eight months. At the outset the Germans had tried for a speedy decision, but, after getting within sight of Paris, they had been turned back at the battle of the Marne. Since then, in spite of titanic Allied exertions, they had retained possession of most of Belgium and an important section of northern France. Besides fighting on the western front, the contending forces struggled on the Russo-Austrian frontier and, after the spring of 1915, on the Austro-Italian frontier as well. On land the advantage lay everywhere with the Central Empires. But their commerce had been swept from the seas, and nearly all the German colonies had been captured.

The war had developed along unprecedented lines. With millions of soldiers engaged on the two sides, open-field fighting proved out of the question, and trench warfare on a vast scale took its place. Moreover, mechanisms and discoveries that had been developed in peace time to promote human happiness were now converted to purposes of human destruction. Chief among these were the motor car, which not only quickened the movement of men and materials but, in the form of armored tanks, became itself an engine of warfare; and the airplane which, developed by the combatants to new perfection, rendered indispensable service in scouting, bombing and combat. Among other inventions, wireless telegraphy (devised in 1895 by Guglielmo Marconi, an Italian) proved valuable for keeping the many units of the gigantic armies in constant communication, while the beneficent peace-time discoveries of the world's chemists were utilized in the manufacture of explosive bombs and clouds of poison gas. The new machinery of warfare

[1] Though it is often forgotten, the following conflicts were merely American phases of greater international struggles: the four intercolonial wars with the French; the Revolutionary War following the French alliance of 1778; the naval defense of neutral rights against France from 1798 to 1800; and the War of 1812–1815.

gave unexpected importance to petroleum or gasoline, which
supplied motive power for conveyances on land, in the air and
under the water, and was even displacing the use of coal on warships. It "is as necessary as blood in the battles of tomorrow,"
wrote Georges Clemenceau, the French Premier, to President
Wilson shortly after America's entry.

The intervention of the United States placed at the disposal
of the Allies not only an unplumbed reservoir of man power,
but also unlimited quantities of money, foodstuffs, minerals,
manufactures, shipyards and material resources of every kind.
Perhaps even more significant was the fresh enthusiasm and
ardent idealism that America brought to the struggle, for a
spirit of exhaustion and defeatism lay heavily on the Allied
peoples. Official missions, hastening to Washington, made clear
the extent of the Allied need, and urged the greatest possible
speed in the sending of troops. While American preparations
were getting under way, the United States before the close of
1917 lent the Allied governments $885,000,000, a mere earnest
of the huge sums that were to follow. These loans were not
advanced in gold, but in credits in American banks with which
to purchase war supplies in the United States. Resolved to
coöperate in every practicable way, the American government
did not forget that it had joined the war for American, not European, reasons, and it refrained therefore from entering a formal
alliance, preferring to regard the Allies officially as "Associates"
in a common effort.

However remiss the government may have been in forearming
against war, it sought now to make up for lost time by organizing the nation on a war basis with a thoroughness and on a
scale unparalleled in American annals. Under Wilson's compelling
leadership, and against fierce opposition from leaders of his own
party, Congress on May 18, 1917, adopted the selective-service
act. The President was empowered to conscript a million men
from between the ages of 21 and 30 inclusive, with exemption
or deferred classification for public officials, clergymen, members
of religious sects opposed to war, persons engaged in employments essential to military success, men upon whom others were
dependent, and physical and mental defectives.[1] No one was

---

[1] The draft age was lowered to 18 and raised to 45 inclusive on August 31, 1918.

permitted to purchase exemption or hire a substitute, as in Civil War times. The President justified the measure on the democratic principle "that there is a universal obligation to serve and that a public authority should choose those upon whom the obligation of military service shall rest, and also in a sense choose those who shall do the rest of the nation's work." Without loss of time the men of draft age were registered, and this, with the subsequent enrollment of youths later coming of age, soon made available more than ten million. From this body the names of the first half million to be called to the colors were drawn on July 20. The operation of the draft occasioned local protests, but, unlike Civil War times, no serious disturbances. The act of May 18 also increased the regular army to 287,000, and incorporated the entire national guard in the federal service. With these additions, the total military strength at the end of 1917 attained one and a quarter million men and more than 100,000 officers.

The problem of assembling the elements of an army was less difficult than that of fitting them for the grim business ahead. Sixteen great tent-camps in the South served as training quarters for the augmented national guard, while a similar number of cantonments in various parts of the country was provided for the national or draft army. Swiftly constructed to meet the need, these cantonments resembled full-fledged towns more than camps. Each comprised a thousand or more frame barracks and other buildings to care for about 48,000 men, and was amply equipped with sewers, running water, artificial light, camp newspapers, libraries, theaters, laundries and hospitals. Here, thanks to able direction and conscientious devotion to duty, the men prepared for active service in an average period of six months. Officers were supplied through special training camps, the best known being that at Plattsburg, New York. The curse of political appointments, which had marred the conduct of earlier wars, was avoided by the adoption of a scientific rating system, designed to recognize ability and experience. Even the colleges were formed into training schools, and ultimately about 170,000 youths in five hundred institutions joined the so-called students' army training corps.

Simultaneously with the creation of an army, thoroughgoing

measures were taken to mobilize the country's material resources. "Under modern conditions" — to quote Secretary of War Baker — "wars are not made by soldiers only, but by nations. . . . The army is merely the point of the sword." The council of national defense, authorized before America's entrance, assumed general charge, though much of the actual work was carried on through an advisory commission composed of seven men thoroughly familiar with the nation's industrial, professional and labor potentialities. Thus Daniel Willard, president of the Baltimore and Ohio Railroad, acted as expert in transportation; Julius Rosenwald, head of a Chicago mail-order concern, in clothing and similar supplies; and Samuel Gompers in labor matters. From this group as a generating center there developed from time to time, as occasion demanded, numerous subcommittees and special technical boards. The elaborate national organization was, in many of its features, paralleled by the states. Every state had its special council of defense, and some of them a network of local councils as well. Everywhere the people showed that capacity for practical coöperation in face of an emergency which had distinguished them time and again in their earlier history.

Of the committees of the council of national defense, that on munitions attained such importance that in July, 1917, it was reorganized as the war-industries board. Under the chairmanship of Bernard M. Baruch it exercised dictatorial powers over the processes of manufacture. It bought supplies for the Allies as well as for the American government, fixed prices and determined priorities of production and delivery. At the war's close its efforts were estimated to have increased the nation's industrial capacity at least twenty per cent. For heavy artillery, machine guns and airplanes, however, the United States was forced to rely largely upon the French and British.

America had hoped to make her distinctive contribution in aëronautics, for in the large-scale manufacture of aircraft the mechanical and organizing genius of the nation would have full play. Moreover, the prospect of fighting above the clouds appealed to the imagination of a people accustomed to frontier warfare and displays of personal daring. In July, 1917, the government formulated a plan for building 11,500 combat planes before the following summer, besides a large number of training craft. Unfortunately no American factories were equipped to turn out combat planes, and this fact, along with other delays and difficulties, some of them avoidable, prevented the execution of the program, greatly to the public's exasperation. Not until well into the second year did the plans begin to yield substantial results, though when the armistice was signed only about 12,000 planes had been completed, a third of them service planes.

Another committee of the council of national defense, that on food supply, derived its importance from a dangerous shortage of foodstuffs in the Allied countries and the need to collect huge supplies to feed the American forces. This committee, headed by Herbert Hoover, famed as the organizer of Belgian relief, at first lacked adequate authority, but on August 10, 1917, the food and fuel-control act gave Hoover as food administrator practically unlimited power to stimulate agriculture and conserve food. To assist him, subordinate food administrators were appointed in the states and local subdivisions. The problem centered mainly in wheat, meat, sugar and fats. In order to increase production, every effort was exerted to expand the existing cultivated acreage. Farmers were encouraged to make extensive plantings by the government's agreement to buy all wheat raised in 1918 at two dollars a bushel. Even city dwellers converted their yards and near-by vacant lots into "war gardens" and, by consuming their own produce, lessened the demand on the grocer. In order to curtail domestic consumption, the food administration resorted both to official regulations of wholesalers and retailers and to the encouragement of voluntary coöperation by the public. The slogan, "Food Will Win the War," was spread over the billboards of the country, and a new verb, "to hooverize," entered the vocabulary. Housewives hung cards in their windows to proclaim their fidelity to the regulations, and showed patriotic zeal in the use of substitutes and the observance of "meatless meals" and "wheatless days." It was a movement of general renunciation such as no country had ever undertaken except at the urge of biting necessity.

The results amply justified the self-denial. In the four summer months of 1918 the American people through savings from their regular consumption sent abroad half a million tons of sugar. The autumn saw an increase of nearly a million tons of pork products over that available the preceding year. In general, during the crop year of 1918, America doubled the average amount of food exported to Europe immediately before the war. By such means the United States was able not only to feed the Allied armies, but also to save their peoples (and later much of Central and Southeastern Europe) from almost certain starvation.

The food administration hardly began its work before it was paralleled by the establishment of a fuel administration, authorized in the same law. As in the case of food, the coal problem involved both increased production and frugal use. Miners and operators zealously coöperated, while householders observed unwonted domestic economy. Difficulties of distribution were heightened by congested rail conditions and by the cruelly cold winter of 1917–1918 which held up transportation and imprisoned coal barges in icebound harbors. At one juncture H. A. Garfield, the fuel administrator, ordered a temporary shutdown of industry in the trans-Mississippi region in order that the coal might be diverted to more essential purposes. Attention was also given to oil production, which in 1918 increased fourteen per cent over the yield of 1914. The motoring public reduced pleasure riding to a minimum, and willingly heeded the request for "gasless Sundays."

As the fuel situation made evident, success in industrial mobilization required the most efficient utilization of rail facilities. The problem of troop movements was similarly involved. Because the railways, obliged to carry an unprecedented volume of traffic and hampered by long-established habits of rivalry, could not rise to the emergency, the President on December 26, 1917, put them in charge of Secretary of the Treasury McAdoo as director-general, an act later validated by Congress. Calling to his aid experienced rail executives, McAdoo operated the chief lines as a single system. Arbitrary control of the routing and distribution of traffic relieved the congestion on certain roads, and obtained ampler service from others. Terminals, equipment, repair shops and other facilities were used wherever needed irrespective of ownership. The sole object was the hurrying of wanted supplies to their destination, and in this respect McAdoo's success was remarkable. But he found it necessary to raise wages by an aggregate sum of more than $600,000,000, and to effect substantial advances in freight and passenger rates. Despite the higher transportation charges, the greatly enhanced costs caused the railways to be operated at a deficit throughout the period of federal control. In July, 1918, the Postmaster-General, by direction of the President, took over the telephone and telegraph lines, and later extended his authority to cables. In a similar fashion the express business was placed under federal management in November. At the behest of Mars the government, for the time being, moved far in the direction of state socialism.

SELECT BIBLIOGRAPHY

America and the World War. Among general accounts are Frothingham, *The American Reinforcement in the World War;* Bassett, *Our War with Germany;* McMaster, *The United States in the World War;* and Seymour, *Woodrow Wilson and the World War.* America's situation as a neutral is discussed from various angles in Ogg, *National Progress;* Scott, *A Survey of International Relations between the United States and Germany, August 1, 1914–April 6, 1917;* Jones and Hollister, *The German Secret Service in America;* and Grattan, *Why We Fought,* an unorthodox treatment. The "nation in arms" is portrayed in Crowell and Wilson, *How America Went to War,* a comprehensive account devoted chiefly to economic mobilization; Willoughby, *Government Organization in War Time and After;* Van Hise, *Conservation and Regulation in the United States during the World War;* Dixon, *Railroads and Government;* Hines, *The War History of American Railroads;* Surface, *The Grain Trade during the World War;* Powell, *The Army behind the Army;* Clarkson, *Industrial America in the World War;* and Kolbe, *The Colleges in War Time and After.* Biographies of leading figures include Dodd, *Woodrow Wilson;* Palmer, *Newton D. Baker;* Seymour, *The Intimate Papers of Colonel House;* Synon, *McAdoo;* and Hendrick, *The Life and Letters of Walter H. Page.*

CHAPTER XXI

THE STRUGGLE FOR PEACE

ARMED OPERATIONS OVERSEAS

THE naval forces were the first to begin operations. Within eighteen days after America's entry, six destroyers started for Europe where, under Admiral W. S. Sims's command, they at once set about to aid the British navy in chasing and sinking submarines. Battleships and cruisers followed until, at the close of the war, 5000 naval officers and 70,000 enlisted men were serving abroad. The three-year construction plan, adopted in 1916 as part of the preparedness program, was accelerated and expanded. The government also commandeered private vessels and took over German ships that had been interned in American ports. In the first nine months of 1918, no less than eighty-three new destroyers were launched. During the war period the total number of vessels in commission increased from less than 200 to more than 2000. Among other exploits, the navy, with British assistance, laid a great mine barrage, extending 245 miles from the Norwegian coast to the Orkney Islands, in the effort to prevent German U-boats from reaching the high seas. Also with British coöperation, it performed indispensable service in protecting troop ships while crossing the Atlantic from submarine raids. The results amply attested Anglo-American naval efficiency, for of the whole number of transports only six were torpedoed, and of these two managed to make port.

Shortly after the declaration of war General John J. Pershing, fresh from his punitive operations across the Mexican border, went to France to act as chief of the American Expeditionary Force (A. E. F.). At the urgent request of the French, a division of regulars followed in June and July, as a visible symbol of the hosts which were to come later. These hosts, however, were still in course of training and, by the end of 1917, only 195,000 troops had reached France. But then their numbers increased rapidly. During the four months from

May to August, 1918, more than a million made the overseas trip.

To look after the multifarious needs of these arrivals, colossal preparations were made by the Services of Supply, an organization formed by Pershing in February, 1918. From its headquarters at Tours, the S. O. S. was responsible for securing, organizing and distributing all the food, equipment and other materials required for the A. E. F. Besides building gigantic docks at the ports of arrival, it constructed 1000 miles of railroad and more than 100,000 miles of telegraph and telephone, and erected great hospitals and warehouses. Supplies of all kinds had to be brought in from the United States — everything from bags of cement to monster locomotives ready to run from the hatch of a vessel under their own steam. Before the armistice, over five million tons of materials had thus been transported, including more than 17,000 freight cars and 34,500 motor trucks. The fighting forces as they arrived usually underwent a month or so of further training before going to the front and then, brigaded with French or British troops, spent another month in a quiet part of the line. But in January, 1918, Pershing began to gather the scattered fragments of his command, though it was not until August that he established a distinct American army.

While America was organizing her strength, Germany, fearful of the might of the western giant when fully aroused, had endeavored to end the war with a series of crushing blows. A terrific defeat at Caporetto in October, 1917, at the hands of the Austrians demoralized Italy. In March, 1918, war-weary Russia, now dominated by socialist extremists or Bolshevists, concluded an inglorious peace with the Central Empires at Brest-Litovsk. Rumania, left in the lurch by Russia's defection, had little choice but to follow her example, which she did the same month. Free at last to concentrate their armies in the western theater of warfare, the Central Empires under Erich von Ludendorff made gigantic preparations for a smashing drive. In March, 1918, as the offense got under way, the Allies for the first time buried their national jealousies and gave supreme command of the several armies to a single person, the French general, Ferdinand Foch.

Though the Americans had hitherto done little besides joining in nocturnal raids and occasional attacks, now, inured to the novel conditions of warfare and eager to get into the fray on their own account, they played their full part, along with the seasoned Allied veterans, in resisting the terrific German onslaughts. Of the American participation certain phases stand out. On May 28 the first division took Cantigny. Three days later the third division helped the French check the Teutonic advance at Château-Thierry on the Marne River, only forty miles from Paris. Near by, enemy forces occupied a densely forested tract known as Belleau Wood. After six days of furious hostilities, marked by hand-to-hand fighting, the marines of the second division ejected them on June 11. A new assault by the Germans on July 14 brought the third division into action again, and on the next day a Franco-American charge drove the enemy back a mile and captured the villages of Chezy and Montlevon.

The Teutonic offensive, as the sequel proved, was a gambler's last throw. The enemy not only failed to win a decisive victory, but suffered irreplaceable losses in men, equipment and morale. Unexpectedly, in mid-July, Foch launched a mighty counteroffensive. Once more the Americans contributed to victory. On the eighteenth, in coöperation with picked French troops, they made a successful drive on Soissons. The following weeks found them almost continually in action until, on August 30, they assumed sole responsibility for a section of the front about 85 miles in length. From this position of vantage on September 12–15 they succeeded, against feeble resistance, in capturing the St. Mihiel salient, a triangle of enemy ground jutting into Allied territory. About 550,000 Americans engaged in this battle — five and a half times as many as the Union army at Gettysburg. But the most important action in which they participated was the Meuse-Argonne offensive. The goal of the attack was a four-track railroad running parallel to the front and forming a main supply line of the enemy. In point of sheer size this battle was the greatest ever fought by American troops. From September 26 it proceeded with little abatement and increasing success for forty-seven days. A total of 1,200,000 Americans, besides 840 airplanes and 324 tanks, took part. At last, in the first week of November, a section of the coveted railway passed into the hands of the French and Americans. In Pershing's words,

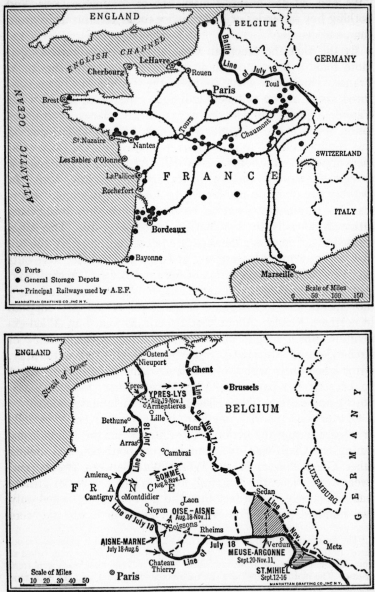

(*Courtesy of the U. S. War Department*)

THE A. E. F. IN FRANCE, 1918

"We had cut the enemy's main line of communications, and nothing but surrender or an armistice could save his army from complete disaster."

By this time the American army at home and abroad totaled more than 3,500,000, of whom 1,390,000 saw active service in France. During the whole course of the war the Americans captured about 44,000 prisoners and 1400 guns of all kinds, while Yankee aviators brought down 755 enemy planes, themselves losing nearly half that number. Though American participation was confined chiefly to operations in France, United States soldiers appeared on other fronts as well. At Italy's urgent request a regiment went to the Austro-Italian front in July, 1918. In October two divisions reënforced the French in Belgium. America also became involved in hostilities with the Bolshevists, although officially the two nations were at peace. The Allies refused to acknowledge the separate peace concluded by the Soviet government with Germany at Brest-Litovsk, and were outraged by Russia's cancellation of her foreign debt. Accordingly, they sent armed forces to assist anti-Bolshevist insurrectionary movements and to safeguard large stores of military supplies in northern Russia. About 5000 Americans joined an Allied expedition which fought minor engagements in the vicinity of Archangel and Murmansk from September, 1918, until May, 1919, when their withdrawal began. Another force of about 10,000 served as part of an Allied expeditionary force to Vladivostok and eastern Siberia, being recalled in January, 1920.

Of every one hundred Americans in the war two died of wounds or disease during the period of hostilities.[1] In the Union army during the Civil War, the number was about ten, and among other Great Powers in the World War between twenty and twenty-five. That the American losses in battle were not greater was due largely to the fact that the heavy fighting lasted only two hundred days. For every man killed in battle, six were

---

[1] The American deaths from all causes totaled 125,000, of which about 10,000 occurred in the navy. In the A. E. F. more than twice as many died from battle as from disease, but, for the army as a whole, almost half the total losses were from disease. The mortality rate from disease amounted to 110 a year for each 1000 men in the Mexican War; 65 in the Civil War; 26 in the Spanish-American War; and 19 in the A. E. F. The total battle deaths for all countries in the World War exceeded all deaths in all wars in the preceding century.

wounded and, of these, five eventually returned to duty. Romance has always portrayed the soldier as shot through the heart, but in every earlier war of the United States more had died from disease than from battle. The health record would have been even more creditable but for a dreadful epidemic of influenza-pneumonia which swept through the country during the fall and winter of 1918, taking its heaviest toll in the crowded camps and cantonments. The remarkable record in combating disease attested the great advances which had been made in medical science in recent years as well as the completeness of hospital facilities. Into the medical corps of 2000 were drawn over 31,000 physicians and surgeons from civilian life, among them the foremost leaders of the profession. They not only facilitated the adoption of the most recent methods for the prevention and cure of disease, but themselves made new discoveries of vast human benefit. The main preventive measures involved thorough camp sanitation and control of drinking water, and compulsory vaccination against typhoid fever. Intestinal disorders, such as dysentery, typhus, cholera and typhoid, which had ravaged armies in the past, were virtually eliminated as causes of death.

While war still raged on the several battle fronts, President Wilson renewed his efforts, begun as a neutral, to turn the greatest war in history into an instrument for lasting peace. To him military victory was an opportunity not for vengeance, but for securing a settlement that would preclude the possibility of future bloodshed. By common consent he became the spokesman of the powers fighting Germany. If they did not subscribe to all his lofty idealism, they at least believed his utterances might have the useful effect of weakening the hold of the military clique on the war-weary Teutonic peoples and thus shorten the struggle. In an address to Congress on January 8, 1918, he set forth Fourteen Points that embodied the most complete statement he had yet made of an acceptable peace. The first five struck at three of the deeper causes of the conflict: secret diplomacy, militarism and imperialism. He demanded the abandonment of secret international understandings, a guarantee of freedom of the seas, the removal of economic barriers between nations, reduction of national armaments, and an adjustment of colonial claims with due regard to the interests of the inhabitants affected. Next followed eight points, more specific in character but all concerned with assuring European nationalities rights of self-rule and unhampered economic development. The German-conquered sections of Belgium, France, Russia, Rumania, Serbia and Montenegro, he said, should be evacuated and restored; the oppressed nationalities of Austria-Hungary and Turkey must gain political autonomy;[1] an independent Poland should be created out of German, Austrian and Russian territory; and the Franco-German and Austro-Italian frontiers be readjusted along lines of nationality. For his fourteenth point Wilson reserved the keystone of his arch of peace: the formation of an association of nations to afford "mutual guarantees of political independence and territorial integrity to great and small states alike." In closing his address he intimated that America and the Allies would be unwilling to make peace with a government which spoke for the military party rather than for the people of Germany.

But it required the great Allied offensive of the summer of 1918 to convince Germany that she faced unavoidable disaster. Her allies, hemmed in on every side, their morale shattered, were preparing to give up the fight with or without her consent. The German people were seething with revolution, and the Kaiser was about to abdicate and flee. On October 4 the government at Berlin asked Wilson to take steps toward peace on the basis of the Fourteen Points. After assuring himself that the request came from representatives of the people rather than of the military clique, the President conferred with the Allies, who acceded to the German proposal subject to reservations as to freedom of the seas and to an explicit admission of German obligation for all damages to civilian life and property. On this basis an armistice was concluded on November 11.

THE WAR AND THE AMERICAN PUBLIC

In no previous conflict had the American people given such whole-hearted support to the government. Earlier differences of opinion as to the relative merits of the European belligerents

[1] Later, however, he altered his formula in the case of Austria-Hungary to one of political independence for the subject peoples.

were drowned in a swelling tide of patriotism. Customary party lines vanished, though the Republicans reserved the right to insist on a vigorous conduct of the war and grew increasingly restive under what they termed Wilson's "dictatorial" methods. Organized labor rallied strongly to the support of the government. Even citizens of Teutonic origin, almost without exception, made America's cause their own. In Congress the President found them among his most zealous supporters. Hundreds of thousands of their number fought valiantly on the field of battle.

As a force for unifying and invigorating popular opinion, the committee on public information played an important part. Created by executive order on April 14, 1917, with the liberal journalist George Creel as chairman, it gave out news concerning war activities, withholding such as might aid the enemy. It also carried on a mammoth campaign of popular education regarding America's objects in the war and the dangers of German imperialism. For these purposes, it published a daily newspaper, issued millions of pamphlets, produced patriotic films, directed countless speakers, and established press agencies in Allied and neutral countries.

Notwithstanding the unexampled unity of opinion, unanimity, of course, did not exist. The farmers of the upper Mississippi Valley retained some of their earlier pacifism, and occasional individuals came into conflict with the law. But the chief dissent rose from the Socialists who, meeting at St. Louis on April 7, branded America's entry as a crime of the capitalist class against the people, and pledged a "continuous, active and public opposition to the war through demonstrations . . . and all other means within our power." Though their position was anticapitalistic and antimilitaristic rather than pro-German, the public generally refused to recognize a distinction. Many prominent Socialists, including Allan Benson, the presidential candidate in 1916, bolted the party in protest.

In order to cope with this and kindred situations, Congress in June adopted the espionage act. This statute provided severe penalties for willful attempts to obstruct recruiting or to "cause insubordination, disloyalty . . . or refusal of duty" among the armed forces. It also gave the Postmaster-General authority to exclude from the mails any matter deemed seditious or treasonable. A year later, in May, 1918, the law was strengthened by the sedition act, which amplified the list of crimes, including among them abusive utterances in regard to the government, the Constitution or the flag.[1] A third statute followed in October, empowering the Secretary of Labor to deport, without jury trial, aliens who "believe in or advocate" the forcible overthrow of government, or who advocated the unlawful destruction of property, or who belonged to organizations holding such views.

All three measures, while in course of passage, were assailed as infringements of the constitutional rights of free speech and free press, and they were vigorously denounced as exceeding the alien and sedition acts of 1798 in severity. As in the case of the Civil War, however, the real or fancied rights of the individual were not suffered to hamper the will of the majority. The federal authorities systematically prevented supposedly objectionable Socialist activities, censoring and suppressing their newspapers, raiding their meetings and prosecuting their speakers. Debs, four times Socialist candidate for President, was among those sentenced to prison. In all, over 1900 judicial proceedings were brought against Socialists and other offenders up to July 1, 1919. About half the cases resulted in convictions. There can be little doubt that the zeal of the authorities often outran their judgment. Thus one Socialist speaker, Rose Pastor Stokes, received a ten-year sentence for saying, "I am for the people, and the government is for the profiteers." Men were even imprisoned for excited remarks made in the heat of private altercation. Higher courts set aside a number of such judgments, as they also did that involving Mrs. Stokes.

One of the fantastic offshoots of excessive patriotism was the war on the German language. Many states banned the teaching of German in the schools, or attained the same result through local administrative action, while in the colleges students shunned the subject. Fifteen years after the armistice German had not recovered its former position in the curriculum. Some wanted to go further and suppress all public use of the enemy tongue, even in religious worship. In the two war years the number of periodicals published in German fell from about 500 to less than

[1] Many states enacted similar and even more drastic laws of their own.

350. Bands and orchestras played German music at their peril, and many families and even towns bearing Teutonic names hastened to anglicize them to avoid trouble or to attest their loyalty.

Without an ardent public support of the war it would have been difficult to raise the huge sums necessary for its prosecution. From the first of April, 1917, through April, 1919, the United States spent considerably more than $1,000,000 an hour on the war, or a total of $21,850,000,000. In addition, loans to the Allies occurred at the rate of nearly half a million an hour, amounting in the same period to $8,850,000,000. The expenditures arising from these two sources were almost three times as great as the total outlay of the government for all purposes during the first century of its existence. The proportion of war revenue secured from taxation — about one third of the whole — exceeded that in any earlier war and, indeed, that of any other power in the World War. Income taxes were greatly increased, with the heaviest burdens falling upon the largest amounts (rising to sixty-seven per cent in the case of incomes of $2,000,000 and over). In like fashion corporation profits in excess of normal prewar earnings were taxed on a progressive scale. Aside from these chief founts of revenue, taxes were laid upon inheritances, the postage rates were raised, and internal-revenue duties were expanded until they touched virtually all the luxuries and many of the necessities of life. The tariff, long the mainspring of government receipts, contributed less than five per cent.

In order to borrow the money needed to defray two thirds of the war expenditures, the government authorized five great bond issues, the first four known as Liberty loans and the last, floated after the armistice, as the Victory loan. Campaigns of publicity such as had never been seen in America popularized the bond issues, which sold in denominations as small as $50. In the fourth loan 21,000,000 subscribers responded, nearly one for every family in the population. Though the design of the government was to tap every available source of revenue, almost equally important was the desire to give a maximum number of people a financial stake in the war. These purposes were further served by the sale of war-savings certificates in denominations of $5, and of so-called thrift stamps as low as twenty-five cents. Local sales committees sometimes overshot the mark and coerced unwilling buyers, particularly if they possessed Teutonic names. In such cases, reluctant purchasers might be haled before self-constituted "courts," or their front doors be smeared with yellow paint. In the end, hardly a man, woman or child in the entire population had failed to contribute a "silver bullet" toward victory.

At the same time, the government set a new standard in humane legislation for the soldiers and their dependents. An act of October, 1917, provided that the sum of $15, or half the pay of a private, should be sent home each month as an "allotment," the government increasing the sum by an "allowance," which normally amounted to $15 or more according to nearness of kin and the number of the dependents. The maimed soldier was promised vocational training at national expense in case he should be unable to resume his former employment. In addition, the war-risk insurance plan provided means whereby the soldiers, at low cost, could take out government insurance against death or disability. It was hoped that these provisions might prevent a repetition of the pension abuses that had followed the Civil War.

Meanwhile, voluntary organizations appeared on every hand to befriend the soldiers and sustain the national morale. Chief among these was the American Red Cross, which scaled new heights of service to distressed mankind. Besides safeguarding the interests of needy soldiers' families at home, it took charge of sanitary conditions in civil districts adjoining the camps, distributed comfort articles among the fighting forces and aided civilian refugees outside the war zone. It also recruited ambulance companies, trained and directed vast numbers of nurses and organized great base hospitals. On March 1, 1919, Henry P. Davison, chairman of the Red Cross War Council, reported that in the preceding twenty-one months the American people had given $400,000,000 toward the cause in cash and supplies — "by far the largest voluntary gifts of money, of hand and heart, ever contributed purely for the relief of human suffering." Scarcely less important was the work of other civilian agencies, notably the Young Men's Christian Association, Young Women's

Christian Association, National Catholic War Council of the Knights of Columbus, Jewish Welfare Board, Salvation Army, American Library Association and War Camp Community Service. These bodies carried on their work without class, racial or sectarian bias and, as in the case of the Red Cross, the public sustained their efforts with an unexampled financial support.

Such support could not have been forthcoming save for the widespread and dazzling prosperity, which formed a fitting climax to the industrial revival of the period of neutrality. To the insistent call of the Allies for foodstuffs, manufactures and munitions was added the imperative need of the American government for such supplies. Heroic efforts were made to meet the demands. In order to stimulate production, the banks freely lent money, and the government added the inducement of exceptionally high prices. Meantime, thanks to the abnormal trade relations with Europe, sales abroad vastly exceeded purchases, the position of the United States changed from a debtor to a creditor nation, and each year saw an increasing inflow of gold available for investment. As a result, every nerve of industry was quickened. The farmer shared in the general well-being, receiving prices beyond his wildest dreams of a few years before. The chief benefits of the war-puffed prosperity, however, fell to business men whose rapidly mounting profits permitted them to keep safely ahead of the advancing costs of operation. It is significant that from 1917 to 1920 the ranks of American millionaires increased from 16,000 to 20,000.

As prices swung upward, the cost of living sharply advanced, rising seventy-seven per cent above that of 1913. To meet the increased living expenses, wage-earners demanded higher pay. The government at Washington, unlike previous administrations, exerted constant pressure on employers to improve wages and working conditions. To this end the American Federation of Labor was given representation on the council of national defense, the war-industries board and other important official bodies. In April, 1918, President Wilson appointed a war-labor board which formulated a set of principles essential to a sound national labor program, including recognition of the right to organize, maintenance of factory codes, equal pay for women, a basic eight-hour day and a living wage. The years 1916 and 1917 had been unusually stormy ones in the labor world, the latter witnessing 4450 strikes and lockouts involving 2,350,000 toilers. But in 1918, because of the new machinery for mediation and the mounting pay of rail, shipyard and munition workers, the number of strikes fell to 3350 and the number of strikers to 1,930,000. Before the war closed, real wages had reached a higher level than ever before in American history. Meanwhile, a half-million new members streamed into the American Federation, raising the total at the end of 1918 to 2,726,000. One unexpected result of the abnormal demand for labor was the exodus of hordes of Negroes from the South to better paid jobs in Northern mills. It is estimated that 400,000 migrated in the years 1916–1919, and an equal number from 1921 to 1923. To industrial centers like Chicago, East St. Louis, Cleveland and Detroit they resorted in dense colonies. Soon Northern communities began to have their first direct experience with the problem of race relations.

WILSON AND THE PEACE SETTLEMENT

While the American President in the days before the armistice acted as spokesman for the world, he was already beginning to lose the right to speak for his own countrymen. The accumulating resentment of Wilson's political opponents against his imperious leadership found unrestricted vent for the first time in the election of a new Congress in November, 1918. His appeal to the voters to name a Democratic majority fell on unheeding ears, and the Republicans won both Houses of Congress. Undeterred by this event, the President turned his attention to the approaching peace negotiations at Paris. As author of the Fourteen Points, he decided, in defiance of unbroken precedent, to attend the peace conference in person, taking as fellow commissioners Secretary of State Lansing, Henry White, a retired diplomat, Colonel House and General T. H. Bliss. The group as a whole was not a strong one. White, the only Republican, figured little in the party counsels, and many felt that the Senate should have had representation. To this delegation was added a host of legal, economic, historical, geographic and military experts, who had spent many months compiling an enormous mass of pertinent information under House's direction.

From the moment he reached France in mid-December till the peace conference began on January 18, 1919, Wilson enjoyed a triumphal progress through Western Europe such as no man in history had ever known. Everywhere the populace acclaimed him as the savior of humanity, and showered him with gifts and honors. But when the veteran Allied statesmen sat down to deliberate peace terms, the atmosphere chilled. While thirty-two nations nominally participated in the proceedings, all the major decisions fell to Great Britain, France, the United States and Italy and, to a less extent, to Japan. The vanquished foemen were denied representation until summoned to learn what fate had been allotted them. From the outset Wilson strove tirelessly to secure an idealistic basis for the settlement — that "peace of justice" which he believed essential to world stability. But his purpose, however exalted, quickly partook of the quixotic. The very air of Paris reeked with fear and hatred of Germany. Moreover, the broad principles enunciated in the Fourteen Points often lent themselves to differing, or even conflicting, interpretations when applied to concrete situations, a fact which the President's antagonists promptly exploited to their own advantage.[1] Finally, despite Wilson's example and their own lofty professions, the victors were resolved, true to time-honored custom, on a division of the enemy spoils. Some, notably England, France, Italy, Japan and Rumania, had driven advance bargains through secret treaties, and every nation had its own special necessities, jealousies and aspirations.

Wilson's chief adversary in the negotiations was the French Premier, Georges Clemenceau, grim, grizzled and determined — an uncompromising representative of the old diplomacy. David Lloyd George, the British Prime Minister, who reminded Americans in many ways of their own Roosevelt, usually sided with the President, but he was not to be relied upon. Vittorio Orlando of Italy played a lesser rôle, though at one juncture the Italian claim to the Adriatic port of Fiume, at Yugoslavia's expense, led to an open clash with Wilson. The Italian delegation actually

[1] Thus the Poles demanded the application of Point 13 promising them "a free and secure access to the sea," but, in order to accord this to them, it was necessary to include a million or more Germans within Polish borders, an arrangement which violated the spirit of the principle of self-determination that animated Points 6–13.

left the conference temporarily, but subsequently negotiated a compromise. The Japanese, watchful and assertive where their own interests were involved, took little part in the strictly European settlements. As for the smaller nations, each lifted a piping voice, and accepted such crumbs as fell to its lot. While the discussions proceeded behind closed doors, starvation spread over half the continent, Bolshevism was gaining new adherents in Central Europe, and nearly a score of little fires of war, left over from the great one, still burned fiercely. As Lloyd George declared later to the House of Commons in a vivid figurative passage, "We had to . . . work crowded hours, long and late, because, while we were trying to build, we saw in many lands the foundations of society crumbling into dust. . . . I am doubtful whether any body of men with a difficult task have worked under greater difficulties, with stones crackling on the roof and crashing through the window, and sometimes wild men screaming through the keyholes."

As the weeks went by and the President felt obliged to make one concession after the other, many of the Fourteen Points went by the board.[1] Yet, notwithstanding the inconsistencies and injustices that found lodgment in the treaty, its terms would have been far more punitive and imperialistic but for Wilson's presence at the peace table. On one critical occasion, when the tide of reaction ran unusually strong, he summoned the *George Washington* to take home the American delegation. This threat of withdrawal had the desired effect of causing an immediate toning down of demands. Against all attempts to tamper with Point 14 the President stood firm as a rock. In an "association of nations" he saw an opportunity to repair the mistakes and inequities of the treaty as well as to insure future world peace. "This is the central object of our meeting," he told the conference. "Settlements may be temporary, but the actions of the nations in the interests of peace and justice must be permanent. We can set up permanent processes. We may not be able to set up permanent decisions." On February 14 the conference took the vital

---

[1] For example, Point 4 (pledging an effective reduction of national armaments) was abandoned. Likewise, the fate of enemy territory and colonies was determined with little or no regard to the principle of self-determination or the interests of the native inhabitants.

step of establishing a League of Nations by adopting a provisional Covenant, or constitution, largely the handiwork of Lord Robert Cecil of England and General Jan Smuts of the South African Union. Wilson sailed on the next day for America in order to take counsel with leading Senators and with distinguished publicists like Hughes, ex-President Taft and Elihu Root. Armed with their comments, he returned to Paris and succeeded in incorporating in the document an explicit recognition of the Monroe Doctrine as well as certain other changes they had suggested. By these alterations he believed he had assured American adherence.

In the form finally adopted and embodied in the treaty, the Covenant provided for international machinery at Geneva consisting of an Assembly in which each country in the League should have an equal voice, a Council composed of representatives of the four chief Allied powers and America together with four (later increased to nine) other members chosen by the Assembly, and a permanent Secretariat or business office. The purpose of the League should be "to achieve international peace and security by the acceptance of obligations not to resort to war." To this end secret treaties were outlawed, and authority was vested in the Council to propose plans for reducing national armaments. Provision was also made for the creation of a Permanent Court of International Justice (see page 455). It was further declared the "friendly right" of any country in the League to call attention to "any circumstance whatever" inimical to international peace. If war should threaten anywhere in the world, the League was empowered to "take any action that may be deemed wise and effectual to safeguard the peace of nations." More specifically, the members agreed, in conformity with the Bryan "cooling-off" plan, that when diplomatic means failed they would submit their differences to arbitration, and in no case declare war until three months after the decision was rendered. Violation of this provision subjected the offending nation to drastic international boycott. If armed coercion proved necessary, the Council would "recommend" what armed forces each country should furnish. Article X, framed by President Wilson as an additional guarantee of peace, pledged the League members "to respect and preserve as against external aggression the territorial integrity and existing political independence of all members of the League. In case of any . . . danger of such aggression, the Council shall advise upon the means by which this obligation shall be fulfilled." Another section asserted that "regional understandings like the Monroe Doctrine" were in no wise affected by the Covenant.[1] The League was granted general supervision of the administration of the former enemy colonies, though these were placed directly in charge of various powers in the capacity of trustees or "mandatories." It was also authorized to seek improvement in labor conditions throughout the world, and to assist in certain other humanitarian reforms of international concern. No important decisions could be made without unanimous vote of the Assembly and Council, and no amendment to the Covenant without the consent of all the nations represented in the Council.

On June 28 representatives of the new German Republic in great bitterness signed the treaty, which they denounced as contrary to the Fourteen Points and intolerably severe.[2] On July 10 President Wilson submitted it to the Senate for ratification. At once a tempest of protest and denunciation, which had been gathering strength for several months, broke loose in the Senate and, only to a less degree, in the country at large. This hostility stemmed from a variety of sources, personal, partisan and racial. Part of it was due to Wilson's characteristic aloofness and self-assurance, which had become intensified under the stress of war-time exigencies. Besides, Republican leaders perceived a strong party advantage in advertising the treaty's defects and their own efforts to "Americanize" it by means of amendments. The Irish-American section of the population was antagonistic for fear that Article X would block Irish independ-

---

[1] It is noteworthy that Mexico entered the League in 1931 on the express understanding that she did not subscribe to this declaration in regard to the Monroe Doctrine. Argentina, reëntering the next year, made a similar declaration.

[2] Known as the treaty of Versailles, the document contained 80,000 words, and was about two fifths the size of the present volume. It served as a pattern for similar pacts with the other enemy powers. Among other things the several treaties broke up the conglomerate empire of Austria-Hungary, and created three independent governments: Austria, Hungary and Czechoslovakia, the remainder of the territory being distributed among various adjoining countries. Poland was also erected as an independent nation. Representatives of the United States signed the treaties with Austria and Hungary on September 10, 1919, and June 4, 1920.

ence, and their hostility was reënforced by German-American indignation because of the treaty's harshness and the initial exclusion of the German Republic from the League.[1] Beneath these springs of opposition, however, lay a deep-seated and sincere hesitation of many Americans to depart from what they believed to be the traditional national policy of abstention from European entanglements.

Out of the storm and fury of controversy there gradually emerged certain definite groupings among the Senators: those who, like Wilson himself, demanded ratification without material change; those who were willing to accept mild reservations; those who insisted on amendments or strong reservations; and, lastly, the irreconcilables who opposed ratification in any form. The first two groups were predominantly Democratic in complexion, the latter two Republican. The two midway groups were led respectively by G. M. Hitchcock, a Democrat from Nebraska, and Henry Cabot Lodge, the Republican chairman of the foreign-relations committee. Though few in number, the irreconcilables were singularly fortunate in having as spokesmen such men as Johnson of California, La Follette of Wisconsin and W. E. Borah of Idaho, long known to the public as persistent champions of popular rights.

On September 10, 1919, Senator Lodge, acting for the foreign-relations committee, recommended ratification with forty-two amendments and reservations (subsequently reduced to fourteen). The principal changes concerned certain features of the League Covenant, notably Article X which, in its existing form, was alleged to guarantee the *status quo* and to obligate the United States, at the League's behest, to send troops to defend even unjust territorial settlements. The Lodge amendments expressly repudiated any such obligation except in cases where Congress should specifically authorize. In anticipation of this action, the President had left Washington a week before on a stumping tour to arouse popular backing for unqualified ratification. But the effort proved too great for a physique worn by months of fearful strain and terrific responsibility. On September 26, while in Colorado, he suffered a paralytic stroke which ended the tour and confined him to the sick room for most of the remainder of his presidency.

[1] Germany was finally admitted in 1926.

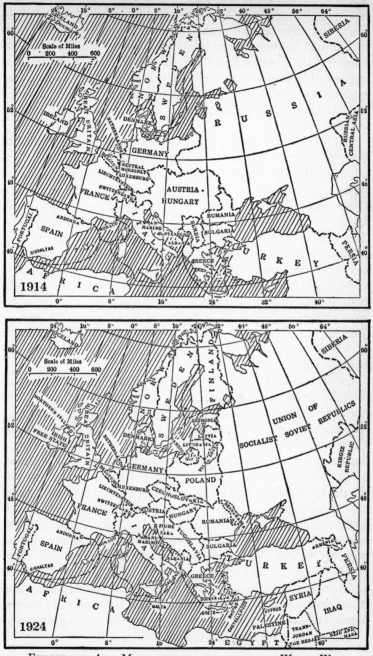

Europe and Asia Minor before and after the World War

433

By this catastrophe the pro-League forces lost their commanding general, and the way was cleared for the ultimate triumph of the opposition.

The Senate discussions continued with increasing rancor through the succeeding weeks. When the treaty came up for vote on November 19, it failed to command a majority vote either with or without reservations. Had the spirit of acrimony been less intense or President Wilson more amenable, it is possible that the requisite two-thirds majority might even then have been secured through compromise. Senator Hitchcock, on behalf of the Democrats, did indeed offer a series of reservations which differed from the Lodge set chiefly in details of phraseology; but on the eve of a presidential election neither party was willing to yield to the other the credit of saving the peace. On March 19, 1920, the treaty came up a second time, modified in this instance by fifteen Lodge reservations. Once more ratification failed though the vote stood 49 to 35 in favor. The minority consisted of a combination of the irreconcilables with those Democrats who stood squarely by the President. Pleading the impossibility of action through the treaty-making process, the Republicans set about to conclude a separate peace by means of a majority vote of the two Houses. The Knox resolution, repealing the declarations of war, was passed on May 27, only to be vetoed promptly by the President. The question of peace was at a deadlock so far as the American government was concerned. Further action awaited an expression of the popular will in the approaching election, which Wilson asked should take "the form of a great and solemn referendum."

SELECT BIBLIOGRAPHY

Armed Operations Overseas. Besides the general accounts of America's relation to the war listed in Chapter XX, the student will wish to consult such works as Sims and Hendrick, *The Victory at Sea;* Harbord, *America in the World War;* Beamish and March, *America's Part in the World War;* Ayres, *The War with Germany*, a statistical summary; Chambrun and Marenches, *The American Army in the European Conflict*, a French view; Thomas, *The History of the A. E. F.;* Marcosson, *S. O. S.;* Johnson, *Without Censor;* Graves, *America's Siberian Adventure, 1918–1920;* and Palmer, *Newton D. Baker*.

The War and the American Public. Slosson, *The Great Crusade and After*, gives a vivid picture of war-time life in the United States. Particular phases receive treatment in Creel, *How We Advertised America*, describing the work of the committee on public information; Chafee, *Freedom of Speech;* Thomas, *The Conscientious Objector in America;* Bogart, *War Costs and Their Financing;* Clark, *The Costs of the World War to the American People;* Davison, *The American Red Cross in the Great War;* Mayo, *"That Damn Y,"* dealing with the Y. M. C. A.; Bing, *War-Time Strikes and Their Adjustment;* Lorwin, *The American Federation of Labor;* and Wesley, *Negro Labor in the United States, 1850–1925.*

Wilson and the Peace Settlement. American participation in the peace conference is treated in Baker, *Woodrow Wilson and World Settlement;* House and Seymour, eds., *What Really Happened at Paris;* Baruch, *The Making of the Reparation and Economic Sections of the Treaty;* and Nevins, *Henry White.* On the conflict over the treaty in America, the best work is Fleming, *The United States and the League of Nations, 1918–1920.*

PART FOUR

SINCE THE WORLD WAR

CHAPTER XXII

THE REPUBLICANS AND THE NEW WORLD ORDER

POSTWAR READJUSTMENTS, SOCIAL AND ECONOMIC

THE bitterness displayed in the fight over the treaty reflected the spirit of intolerance and political bigotry that raged throughout the land. National sentiment had been effectively mobilized for war purposes; it now proved a difficult task to demobilize it and prevent its turning into blind and cruel fanaticism. In particular, many persons feared the effects of Russian Bolshevist propaganda on radical elements in the United States, and seemed to see their suspicions confirmed in the adoption of communistic views by the left-wing faction of the Socialist party in 1919. Consequently, Attorney-General A. M. Palmer and his assistants frankly devoted their attention to the suppression of unorthodox political and social opinions, whether concerned with the war or not.

In many states the authorities, abetted by local feeling, were equally active. One incident bred of the hysteria eventually attracted international notice. In the spring of 1920 two Italian immigrants, Nicola Sacco and Bartolomeo Vanzetti, were charged with murdering a paymaster and his guard near Boston. Though the evidence against them was flimsy and contradictory, the trial disclosed that they were draft dodgers, atheists and philosophical anarchists and, as in the case of the Chicago Haymarket trial in 1886 (see page 215), loosed the passions of those who thought "reds" ought to be strung up on general principles. Convicted of the murder charge, and unable to get their case retried in a higher Massachusetts court despite new evidence that rendered their guilt even more doubtful, the two men were finally executed in 1927. During the long seven-year wait people throughout the country and in many parts of the world came to take an intense interest in the case — not only radicals of various brands, but also many conservatives who, though unsympathetic with the men's opinions, defended their right to a fair and impartial trial. Their death occurred to the accompaniment of demonstrations all over the United States and in lands across the sea.[1]

While the red scare was still at its height, the New York legislature in April, 1920, went so far as to expel five duly accredited members because they were Socialists. The incident challenged nation-wide attention. In a ringing protest, former Justice Hughes of the Supreme Court asserted, "This is not, in my judgment, American government. . . . I count it a most serious mistake to proceed, not against individuals charged with violation of law, but against masses of our citizens combined for political action, by denying them the only resource of peaceful government; that is, action by the ballot box and through duly elected representatives in legislative bodies." Though the ejected members were not restored to their seats, no other legislature emulated New York's example. Meanwhile, champions of intolerance banded together in an organized movement, choosing the name of the Ku Klux Klan for the purpose. While like the old Reconstruction organization in habiliments and methods, in its aims the new K. K. K. more nearly resembled mid-century Know Nothingism, its slogan being "100 percent Americanism," that is, native, white, Protestant supremacy. Founded five years before in Georgia, it did not command a nation-wide membership until 1920. To carry out its objects, the masked, white-robed members did not hesitate to resort to threats, floggings, tar-and-feathering and even murder. Its following became so great, particularly in the South and Midwest, that in 1922 it entered politics, backing friendly candidates of the old parties, carrying local and state elections and, as we shall see, figuring in the Democratic national convention of 1924.

---

[1] Another case almost as widely discussed grew out of the arrest of Thomas Mooney, a radical laborite, in 1916 on the charge of killing several people in a bomb explosion during a "preparedness" parade in San Francisco. Condemned to death, the sentence later being commuted to life imprisonment, Mooney made persistent but vain attempts to secure a retrial. Responsible persons, including the trial judge and the state attorney-general, later asserted that perjured testimony had produced the conviction. Finally, in 1933, Mooney managed to get a first trial on a related murder indictment that had stood against him since his conviction, and he was promptly acquitted. But the earlier judgment caused his return to prison.

Part of its strength was doubtless due to the inability of many Americans to resist the temptation of joining another secret society. As time passed, the Klan became the foe not only of immigrants, Negroes, Catholics and Jews, but also of prohibition repeal, birth control, the League of Nations, pacifism and other expressions of minority opinion. Before entering on a decline, the order in 1925 attained a membership of between four and five million.

The cessation of hostilities also threw the labor world into turmoil. Industry, freed from war-time restraints, tried to recover lost ground, while the wage-earners, harried by the ever ascending cost of living, fought back on every front. During 1919 more than four million took part in labor upheavals at an aggregate cost to employees of over $800,000,000 and to employers of $1,300,000,000 or more.[1] An ominous feature of the situation was the great number of "outlaw" strikes — strikes undertaken against the wishes of the national unions — which involved a fourth of the total number of strikers. Among the gravest disturbances were the walkout of 125,000 wage-earners in the building trades in New York City in February, the railway shop workers' strike in August involving 250,000, the strike of 367,000 iron and steel employees in September, and the walkout of 435,000 bituminous-coal miners in November. The coal strike marked a reversal of the earlier sympathetic attitude of the government. Attorney-General Palmer, taking advantage of the fact that the country was still technically at war with Germany, secured two court injunctions to prevent the United Mine Workers and "all persons whomsoever" from supporting the strike. Though bitterly protesting against this action, the union officials on November 11 felt obliged to acquiesce. In two or three states the governors temporarily took over the mines and called for volunteers to work them. Through federal mediation the men eventually secured a wage advance of twenty-seven per cent, but no change in hours or conditions of labor. During the year the membership of the American Federation of Labor greatly increased, reaching in 1920 its high-water mark, 4,000,000, twice the number in 1914.

[1] The total duration of these strikes and lockouts was 57,885 days as compared with 28,779 days in 1918.

The soaring prices indicated a continuance of the war-time business boom. With her industries still badly deranged, Europe continued to stand in need of American exports, while in the United States the people, made gay by unwontedly fat purses and the sudden relaxing of the war strain, engaged in an orgy of extravagant buying and fast living. Overexpansion, speculation and swollen prices were carried to new extremes both in industry and agriculture. But during 1920 the foreign demand began to fall off, the products of mill, mine and farm soon glutted the domestic market, prices dropped, and a depression set in that lasted somewhat over two years in the industrial regions and many years longer among the farmers. About 20,000 business firms failed in 1921, the number of workingmen actively employed fell off a third, and wages generally declined. Thanks to the efficient working of the federal reserve system, however, bank failures were kept at a minimum, and the deflation, though severe, failed to attain the proportions of a panic.

As steps toward restoring normal conditions, Congress in 1920 passed two important laws. One, the Esch-Cummins act in February, fixed the terms upon which the railways should be handed back to private ownership and management. Passed after much controversy, it embodied certain new principles that had been discovered as a result of government operation. The idea that competition must be enforced among railways was abandoned. Pooling, hitherto forbidden, was legalized under supervision of the interstate-commerce commission, and plans were authorized for ultimately consolidating the lines into a limited number of systems. To the commission was granted the power of fixing minimum as well as maximum rates, so that the roads would be assured a fair profit at the same time that they would be prevented from obtaining an excessive one. Other provisions authorized special tribunals to deal with railway labor difficulties. In the merchant-marine act, passed in June, Congress declared its policy in regard to the fleet of 1500 merchantmen which the shipping board (see page 397) had acquired during the war. The law ended further shipbuilding by the board, but continued temporarily the experiment of government ownership and operation. The board, at its discretion, was empowered to dispose of the vessels from time to time to American purchasers, and to accumulate out of its profits a fund from which loans might be made to private builders. By such means it was hoped — vainly, as the sequel was to show — that America might recover her earlier importance in the carrying trade.[1]

Meanwhile the upheaval of war had brought two changes in the nation's fundamental law. The first had to do with the long-agitated question of prohibition. By the time the United States entered the conflict thirty-two commonwealths had outlawed

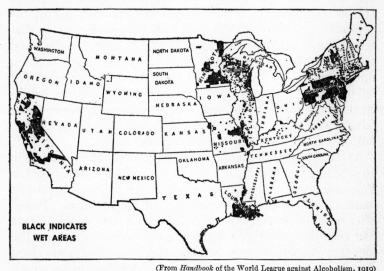

(From *Handbook* of the World League against Alcoholism, 1919)

Dry Territory on the Eve of National Prohibition

the liquor traffic, while much of the remaining territory was dry under local option. More than three fourths of the national area was saloonless. In most parts of the country only the large cities and mill towns remained wet, Chicago possessing more saloons than the whole group of Southern states. Aside from other factors, the increasing menace of drunken automobile drivers on the highways lent strength to the prohibition cause. War conditions provided a favorable opportunity for enlisting federal ac-

[1] Disappointment with the results of the law of 1920 led to the passage of the merchant-marine act in 1928, which enlarged the loan fund and also, through generous mail contracts, provided a substantial subsidy to private owners. In 1933 the shipping board was abolished, and its thirty-eight remaining vessels transferred to the Department of Commerce.

tion. To stimulate grain and coal conservation, Congress in August, 1917, forbade food products to be used in the making of distilled beverages, and gave the President power, which he later exercised, to restrict the manufacture of beer. In November, 1918, Congress provided that from the following July 1 no intoxicants should be sold so long as a state of war continued. Meantime, the ownership of so many breweries and distilleries by persons of German origin had helped to sharpen public resentment against the drink traffic and to prepare the way for the adoption of the Eighteenth Amendment by Congress in December, 1917. This amendment, the first to seek to regulate a citizen's strictly personal habits, provided for the prohibition of the manufacture, transportation and sale of intoxicating beverages one year after its ratification. On January 16, 1919, it became a part of the Constitution and, before the wave of popular interest subsided, all but two states — Rhode Island and Connecticut — passed resolutions of ratification. The apparent finality of the decision is further indicated by the fact that 78.5 per cent of the total vote cast by the lower houses of the state legislatures was in favor, and about 85 per cent of the vote of the upper houses.

The Nineteenth Amendment granted the long-sought boon of country-wide equal suffrage. Its adoption was prompted largely by a heartfelt appreciation of the indispensable war services rendered by the women. They had played their full part, not only in food production and conservation and in Red Cross workrooms, but also as patriotic speakers and as workers in munition plants and other essential industries. Thousands of them had accompanied the A. E. F., serving in a wide variety of capacities from ambulance drivers and nurses to office clerks and Y. M. C. A. entertainers. Earlier content with the extension of the suffrage through state action, Wilson began to champion a federal amendment after the outbreak of the war. He viewed it not merely as an act of justice, but also as a measure required to convince the world of the thoroughgoing character of American democracy.[1] After considerable delay Congress submitted the Nine-

[1] Though a pioneer in the movement, the United States had been outdistanced during the war period by many foreign countries. In 1917 woman suffrage was granted in Russia and Mexico; in 1918 in Austria, Germany, Hungary, Poland, Czechoslovakia, England, Scotland, Wales, Ireland and Canada; and in 1919 in Belgium, Luxemburg, Sweden, Iceland, British East Africa and Rhodesia.

teenth Amendment to the states in June, 1919, and it was proclaimed a part of the Constitution on August 18, 1920, in time for the women to take part in the national election.

THE RETURN OF THE REPUBLICANS

As the presidential campaign of 1920 approached, the temper of the people strongly favored a change of rulers. All over the world the war governments had been swept out of power on a tide of accumulating resentment because of the hardships which the conflict entailed. In America the cause of the Democrats was further prejudiced by the unpopularity of Wilson's stubborn stand on the ratification of the peace treaty and by the blight that had fallen on the nation's economic life. When the Republicans met in Chicago on June 8, the convention's proceedings were dominated by the senatorial clique which had conducted the fight against the treaty. They blandly ignored a widespread outside sentiment for Herbert Hoover, the only American connected with the war who had captured the popular imagination; and when neither of the leading aspirants, General Leonard Wood and Governor F. O. Lowden of Illinois, could obtain a majority, they steered the nomination on the tenth ballot to Senator Warren G. Harding of Ohio, a Lodge reservationist and safe organization man. The second place went to Governor Calvin Coolidge of Massachusetts, whose part in suppressing a policemen's strike in Boston had attracted national notice. The platform, after assailing "executive autocracy," promised governmental econ· omy, farm relief, the return of prosperity and, in language designed to satisfy all shades of opinion on the League question, declared "for agreement among the nations to preserve the peace of the world."[1] In San Francisco on June 28, the Democrats nominated Governor James M. Cox of Ohio on the forty-fourth ballot after a hot three-cornered contest in which Attorney-General Palmer and Wilson's son-in-law, W. G. McAdoo, were his chief rivals. Franklin D. Roosevelt of New York, a fifth cousin of the Republican "Teddy," was named for Vice-President.

[1] This section of the platform was very long and involved a constant restatement of the Republican position on the League, the last one being: "We pledge . . . such agreements with the other nations . . . as shall meet the full duty of America to civilization and humanity . . . without surrendering the right of the American people to exercise its judgment and its power in favor of justice and peace."

The platform lauded Wilson's domestic and foreign policies, promised farm betterment, and declared for immediate ratification of the peace treaty without material reservations.

As usual, minor parties entered the lists. The Socialists, for the fifth time, nominated Eugene V. Debs, although he was still behind the bars in the Atlanta prison. A new group, the Farmer-Labor party, offered candidates in the hope of crystallizing the growing discontent of the rural and industrial classes. Neither major candidate was an outstanding figure, and one organ of liberal opinion suggested the choice lay "between Debs and dubs." But the result of the campaign was clear from the start. The action of the American Federation of Labor in indorsing the Democratic ticket did little to help it. The public was in a captious mood and eager to lay all its troubles at the door of the party in power. In regard to the League question the Republicans succeeded in befuddling the issue. Leading irreconcilables like Hiram Johnson maintained that Harding's election would mean repudiation of the treaty. On the other hand, thirty-one Republican notables, including Hughes, Root and Hoover, assured the public in a joint statement that "the true course to bring America into an effective league" was through Republican success. Harding's own speeches, if somewhat ambiguous, indicated his preference for "an association of nations," based possibly on a modification of the Covenant. The election was a Republican landslide. The huge plurality of nearly 7,000,000 was due in part to the new women voters. In the electoral college the vote stood 404 to 127, while Harding received 60.3 per cent of the popular ballots to 34.2 for Cox. Even the Solid South was shaken, Tennessee deserting to the enemy for the first time since Carpetbag days. The Republicans also elected substantial majorities in both Houses of Congress.

The new President had had a long but undistinguished career in Ohio politics where he had always lent himself to conservative views and purposes. A handsome man with heavy features and a large frame, he possessed the modesty and amiability of a Taft without the latter's brains or singleness of devotion to the public weal. He was better known for his gifts of good fellowship than for any inklings of statesmanlike ability. As if to offset his own ordinary qualities of mind and character, he placed in his cabinet three men of conspicuous ability: Charles E. Hughes as head of the State Department, A. W. Mellon, a Pittsburgh millionaire, as Secretary of the Treasury, and Herbert Hoover as Secretary of Commerce. Some of his other choices, however, were less happy, being dictated by an undiscriminating personal friendship. Thus ex-Senator A. B. Fall of New Mexico, a pronounced anticonservationist, became Secretary of the Interior, and H. M. Daugherty, an Ohio machine politician, Attorney-General.[1] Several months after entering office, Harding paid a graceful compliment to the only living Republican ex-President, Taft, by appointing him Chief Justice of the Supreme Court.

In dealing with the major issue raised by the campaign, the President yielded to the most vociferous element in his party and abandoned his own earlier attitude. Summoned in special session, Congress revived the Knox resolution which Wilson had vetoed (see page 434), and on July 2, 1921, repassed it in somewhat modified form. This act, after declaring the war at an end, reserved to the United States all the rights and advantages which it would have received as a signatory of the treaty of Versailles, and provided that all enemy property seized by the government during the war should be retained until Germany, Austria and Hungary agreed by treaty to a satisfaction of America's war claims.[2] The resolution, of course, involved repudiation of the League of Nations. In August treaties with the enemy powers expressed assent to these terms. One year later Germany and the United States set up a mixed commission to determine the amount of American losses from submarine depredations and other causes.

Harding's election introduced an era of Republican supremacy that was to last for twelve years. The tapering off of the depression in 1922 ushered in a boom period which increased year after

[1] The remaining members of the cabinet were J. W. Weeks of Massachusetts, Secretary of War; W. H. Hays of Indiana, Postmaster-General; Edwin Denby of Michigan, Secretary of the Navy; H. C. Wallace of Iowa, Secretary of Agriculture; and J. J. Davis of Pennsylvania, Secretary of Labor.

[2] Exclusive of forty German vessels, the property sequestrated during the war amounted to $400,000,000. The United States was eventually awarded $120,000,000.

year and on which the party claimed a private patent.[1] Neither
Harding nor his successor in office, Coolidge, possessed reform
inclinations or the itch for strong executive leadership. The
economic policies fostered by Congress accorded with the desires of Big Business, and Mellon, one of the country's richest
men, continued at the helm of the Treasury Department until
1932. Though at times sorely tried, the ordinary voter preferred
to let well enough alone while he, too, nibbled at the fat ears of
prosperity. The Democrats, on their part, seemed singularly
lacking in leadership and cohesion, sacrificing through factional
differences whatever chance they might have had for success
in 1924 and 1928. As for the newly enfranchised women, the
evidence indicates that those who bestirred themselves most
actively came from communities and states with strong Republican traditions and, during these years, their votes increased
the preponderance of the majority party.

But for these favoring conditions the Republican sway might
not have outlasted the term for which Harding was elected.
Able and disinterested as were certain members of his cabinet,
in domestic affairs he gave greater heed to the advice of a coterie
of intimates, the so-called Ohio Gang, who had hastened to
Washington to be near him when he entered the White House.
The extent of the corruption in which they involved his administration was not revealed until after the President's unexpected
demise in San Francisco on August 2, 1923, while returning from
a trip to Alaska. Though ugly rumors long persisted as to the
cause of his death, probably the true reason was a stroke of
apoplexy induced by worry over his criminal failure to safeguard
the public interest and the certainty of its becoming known.[2]

[1] Thus, in accepting the presidential nomination in 1928, Herbert Hoover declared, "But it is not through the recitation of wise policies alone that we demon-
strate our progress under Republican guidance. . . . During this less than eight
years . . . our national income has increased by over thirty billions of dollars
per year. . . . The barriers of time and distance have been swept away and life
made freer and larger by the installation of six million more telephones, seven
million radio sets, and the service of an additional 14 million automobiles. Our
cities are growing magnificent with beautiful buildings, parks, and playgrounds.
Our countryside has been knit together with splendid roads."

[2] Hoover, who accompanied him on the Alaska trip, declared in 1931 in a speech
dedicating the Harding Memorial at Marion, Ohio, "We saw him gradually weaken
not only from physical exhaustion but from mental anxiety. Warren Harding had
a dim realization that he had been betrayed by a few of the men whom he had

The disclosures of wrongdoing came as a result of Senate investigations, the unsavory record surpassing anything like it since Grant's time. The first notable scandal fruited from C. R. Forbes's activities as director of the veterans' bureau, an agency which had taken over the functions of the bureau of war-risk insurance. In his two years in office, the Senate committee found him guilty of "almost unparalleled waste, recklessness and misconduct" in the handling of construction contracts and the purchase of supplies and equipment. The losses sustained by the government were estimated at more than $200,000,000. In 1924 Forbes was indicted by a federal grand jury for conspiracy and fraud, and subsequently convicted.

Close on the heels of this exposure came startling revelations involving members of the cabinet. The evidence showed that in 1921 Secretary Denby of the Navy Department had, with Harding's approval, transferred to Secretary of the Interior Fall the administration of certain oil reserves which had been set apart by Taft and Wilson for exclusive use of the navy. In 1922 Fall, without seeking competitive bids, secretly leased Reserve No. 3 (Teapot Dome) near Casper, Wyoming, to H. F. Sinclair, and another and larger reserve at Elk Hills, California, to E. L. Doheny. Though in each case the government reserved a royalty on the oil extracted, the fluid itself was by these leases diverted from its intended purpose, to the enormous gain of private commercial interests. However unwise, the transactions bore no sinister aspect until a Senate committee, headed by T. J. Walsh of Montana, discovered that late in 1921 Doheny had loaned Fall $100,000 without interest or security, and that, after Fall's retirement from the cabinet in March, 1923, Sinclair had similarly loaned him $25,000. Government suits ultimately secured the return of the reserves in 1927 and, two years later, the conviction of Fall for bribe taking. While the oil scandal was still under investigation, another Senate committee brought to light shocking facts concerning Daugherty's record as Attorney-General. The testimony, which was of a highly sen-

trusted. . . . It was later proved in the courts of the land that these men had betrayed not alone the friendship and trust of their staunch and loyal friend but they had betrayed their country. That was the tragedy of the life of Warren Harding."

sational character, tended to support the charges that he had surrounded himself with bribe takers and other disreputable characters, and that the department's activities had been subject to corrupt influences.

It was on the eve of these disclosures that Calvin Coolidge became President. Thin-faced, tight-lipped, with a nasal twang that smacked of his Vermont forbears, he was a conscientious, matter-of-fact man who, in Dryden's celebrated phrase, had mastered the art of "saying much in little and often in silence." Though not well-known to the public in general, Coolidge had shown himself a shrewd and competent executive while governor of Massachusetts. He was the first native New Englander to reach the presidency since Arthur's succession under similar circumstances. Faced with the exposures of graft in high places, he displayed an unruffled calm; but, yielding at last to the popular clamor, in February, 1924, he accepted the resignation of Denby, whose chief fault had been negligence, and a month later he dismissed Daugherty. In the long run, his simplicity, Yankee caution and patent sincerity won him the firm confidence of a public unwilling in the midst of prosperity to dwell long on the unpleasant aspects of governmental affairs. His sentiment, "The business of America is business," was attuned to the times.

Hoping to capitalize the Harding scandals to their own advantage, the Democrats in high glee made preparations for the election of 1924. Their convention in New York City on June 24, however, turned into a pitched battle between two closely matched cohorts, the one led by Governor Alfred E. Smith of New York, a wet and a Roman Catholic, the other by W. G. McAdoo, now of California, a dry, a Protestant and the recipient of Ku Klux Klan support. When neither contestant could secure the prize, the tired, sweltering delegates stampeded on the hundred and third ballot to John W. Davis, an able New York corporation lawyer and former Ambassador. Governor C. W. Bryan of Nebraska, brother of William Jennings Bryan, was added to temper the conservatism of the ticket. The platform denounced Republican corruption and incapacity, promised legislation to restore rural prosperity, and favored a popular referendum on the League of Nations. Meanwhile, Coolidge had been nominated without opposition by the Republicans in Cleveland on June 10, the second place going to Charles G. Dawes of Illinois. The platform pointed with pride to Republican retrenchment and tax reduction, the nation's recovery from the depression, and the administration's success in promoting international peace without the entanglements of the League.

Discontented with the thorough conservatism of both major candidates, some of the more radical trade unions and farmers' organizations met with various middle-class reform groups in Cleveland on July 4 to form a new Progressive party. Senator La Follette, veteran leader of the earlier progressive movement, was named for President on a platform assailing official corruption and private monopoly, and pledging farm relief, public ownership of water power and railroads, and a constitutional amendment to enable Congress to override Supreme Court decisions. To widen the party's appeal, B. K. Wheeler, Democratic Senator from Montana, was nominated for Vice-President. The ticket was promptly indorsed by the Socialist party, the Farmer-Labor party, the American Federation of Labor and many national unions and state federations. The campaign that followed proved singularly apathetic. A novel feature was the extensive use which the candidates made of the radio, a means of lightning communication developed during the war, and already beginning to be an indispensable appurtenance to the average American home. On every occasion Republican spellbinders besought the voters to "Keep Cool with Coolidge," and, by focusing attention on the Progressives, they maintained — in the President's words — that the vital issue was "whether America will allow itself to be degraded into a Communistic and Socialistic state, or whether it will remain American." The wounds inflicted on Democratic unity by the convention rancors impaired the effectiveness of the efforts for Davis. Coolidge scored a decisive victory, winning 382 electoral votes to 136 for Davis and 13 for La Follette — his own state of Wisconsin. He had behind him 54 per cent (15,725,000) of the popular ballots as compared with 28.7 (8,386,000) and 16.5 (4,823,000) for his two rivals, and his party retained control of both Houses of Congress by large majorities.

President Coolidge's good fortune attended him during his

second administration.[1] He favored the policies which business leaders favored and opposed those which they opposed; peace and plenty prevailed; and general contentment reigned. Had he been willing once more to bear aloft the Republican standard in an election, his party would have rejoiced. But this he would not do; and when the convention met in Kansas City on June 12, 1928, the nomination went on the first ballot to Secretary of Commerce Hoover, the ticket being completed with the name of Senator Charles Curtis of Kansas. The Democrats meeting in Houston, Texas, on June 26 faced as easy a choice. Since 1924 "Al" Smith had gained steadily in popularity in the country at large as well as in New York, where he had been elected governor for the fourth time in 1926 by a plurality of nearly 250,000. He too was named on the first ballot, Senator J. T. Robinson of Arkansas being chosen as his running mate. The two platforms offered few points of contrast, both promising agrarian relief, prohibition enforcement, reduction of armaments, protection to labor and care for the war veterans. The Republicans assured the country that "A continuation of this great public peace of mind now existing, which makes for our material well-being, is only possible by holding fast to the plans and principles which have marked Republican control," while the Democrats abandoned their traditional hostility to protection, pledging a tariff based on the "actual difference between the cost of production at home and abroad, with adequate safeguard for the wage of the American laborer." Though the Progressive party had not survived its first baptism of fire, other minor parties offered candidates, the Socialists naming Norman Thomas of New York and the Workers (Communists) W. Z. Foster of Illinois.

While the canvass at first promised to be as dull as that of 1924, Governor Smith proved a colorful campaigner, whipping a laggard electorate into a new interest in governmental affairs, and flaying the administration for what he regarded as its veiled partnership with Big Business, particularly the public-utility interests. Departing from the Houston platform, he called for

[1] In 1925 he made four changes in the cabinet, appointing F. B. Kellogg of Minnesota, Secretary of State; D. F. Davis of Missouri, Secretary of War; J. G. Sargent of Vermont, Attorney-General; and W. M. Jardine of Kansas, Secretary of Agriculture.

a liberalization of the prohibition (Volstead) law, and pledged his efforts to secure a repeal of the amendment with safeguards against the return of the saloon. But the "Happy Warrior" faced insuperable odds. Hoover, dismissing his opponent's utterances on farm relief, hydroelectric power and prohibition as "state socialism," dwelt fondly on the country's phenomenal prosperity under Republican rule, and heralded the speedy day "when poverty will be banished from this nation." The Democrat, moreover, suffered from severe personal handicaps, especially in the rural South and West — his religious affiliations, his Tammany connections, his occasionally ungrammatical speech and his hostility to prohibition. The "three P's" — prosperity, prohibition and prejudice — prevailed, giving Hoover a smashing victory. Forty of the forty-eight states cast their electoral votes for him, a total of 444, leaving but 87 for Smith. The latter lost not only his own state, but every border state and five states of the former Confederacy. The popular ballots, however, were somewhat more evenly distributed, Hoover receiving 58 per cent (over 21,000,000) and Smith 40.7 (15,000,000). The Democrats derived what satisfaction they could from polling the largest popular support a candidate of their party had ever obtained. Large majorities also assured a continuance of Republican control of the legislative branch.

The new President, going into office under such auspicious circumstances, had a past career which seemed amply to justify the unstinted popular confidence. A mining engineer of international reputation and experience, Hoover had demonstrated during the war his unusual constructive abilities, first as head of Belgian relief and then as federal food administrator. Under his direction, too, the Department of Commerce had rapidly expanded its functions, showing industries how to cut costs through simplifying products and processes, and itself becoming — in the language of the *Republican Campaign Text-Book* — "the world's most formidable engine of foreign trade conquest." The purpose of government, Hoover held, should be to guide and foster, not to coerce and restrain, business and finance, thus insuring free play for what he termed "rugged individualism." His chubby face suggested geniality, but most of those who came in contact with him found his manner cold and indifferent.

By promoting him to the White House the voters believed they had ended the Harding-Coolidge era of drift. Unhappily, however, Hoover despite his long public record had never held an elective office; he had dealt with subordinates, not with equals. It remained to be seen whether he was master of the difficult art of party leadership and political accommodation.[1] And not far ahead loomed the clouds of the Great Depression.

THE REPUBLICAN QUEST FOR WORLD STABILITY

Meanwhile, their uninterrupted lease of power had enabled the Republicans to develop a program for international peace in place of that sponsored by Woodrow Wilson and the Democrats. In his inaugural address in 1921 President Harding had enunciated its guiding principles: "We seek no part in directing the destinies of the world. . . . We are ready to associate ourselves with the nations of the world, great and small, for conference and counsel, for the suggestion of plans of mediation, conciliation, and arbitration; but every commitment must be made in the exercise of our national sovereignty." The new formula thus became "coöperation without entangling alliances." Toward the League itself the United States had quickly to determine its attitude. Thriving without the sun of official American approval, the League had speedily gathered into its fold fifty-four nations, including seventeen in the New World. Many of its activities and decisions involved matters in which the government at Washington had a vital interest.

After six months during which Secretary of State Hughes did not so much as answer communications from Geneva, the administration began hesitantly to send "observers" to conferences where questions of concern to America were at stake. They were authorized to present the government's viewpoint,

[1] His original cabinet consisted of H. L. Stimson of New York, Secretary of State; A. W. Mellon of Pennsylvania, Secretary of the Treasury; J. W. Good of Iowa, Secretary of War; W. D. Mitchell of Minnesota, Attorney-General; W. F. Brown of Ohio, Postmaster-General; C. F. Adams of Massachusetts, Secretary of the Navy; R. L. Wilbur of California, Secretary of the Interior; A. M. Hyde of Missouri, Secretary of Agriculture; J. J. Davis of Pennsylvania, Secretary of Labor; and R. P. Lamont of Illinois, Secretary of Commerce.

but not to vote in determining the outcome.[1] Meantime, non-governmental coöperation went much further, for American experts in law, medicine and finance in their private capacities freely accepted important League appointments. Thus, Henry Morgenthau headed the committee to provide an international loan to Greece, and Norman H. Davis of New York presided over the commission which settled a boundary dispute between Poland and Lithuania. In 1924 the government itself took a further step by sending official delegates to participate fully in League conferences when the national interest seemed to warrant. By March, 1930, America had dispatched observers to over twenty such meetings and official delegates to twenty-two more. Before the end of another year she had adhered to a total of thirteen international agreements sired by the League, had five permanent officials stationed at Geneva and, under circumstances shortly to be related, even appointed a representative to sit with the League Council itself during the Manchurian crisis. Many people saw in this steady drift of events ultimate membership in the League. But if party spokesmen and presidential campaigns indicated future policy, this eventual outcome seemed far from certain.

Toward the Permanent Court of International Justice Harding and his successors took a bolder attitude, though ever fearful lest American concurrence bear the appearance of a backdoor entrance into the League. This tribunal, authorized by Article XIV of the Covenant, had been set up at The Hague in January, 1922, in conformity with a plan which Elihu Root had helped draft; and one of the members of the original bench was an American, Professor John Bassett Moore of Columbia. Unlike the earlier Hague tribunal (see page 389), it was an actual court with a fixed personnel and always open to litigants. The judges were selected by the League Council and Assembly from nominations made by the older Hague body. The World Court, as it was popularly called, had jurisdiction over "any dispute of an international character which the parties thereto submit to it"; in addition, it might issue advisory opinions when called

---

[1] In this manner, for example, the United States attached observers to League committees on health, the opium trade, the traffic in arms, communications and transit, and the traffic in women and children.

upon to do so by the Council or Assembly. In February, 1923, Harding recommended American adherence on conditions which Coolidge later somewhat amplified. The irreconcilables blocked favorable action, however, until January, 1926, when the Senate voted to join with reservations along the lines that had been suggested. These included the right of the United States to participate in the choice of judges, an American veto over any amendment of the statute of the court, an American veto over requests for advisory opinions touching any question "in which the United States has or claims an interest," and, finally, a disclaimer that adherence to the World Court involved any obligations under the League Covenant or the treaty of Versailles.

In September the fifty-odd nations in the World Court, meeting at Geneva, agreed to all the reservations save the one on advisory opinions. The deadlock thus created was finally broken in 1929 when Elihu Root, on invitation of the League Council, devised a formula that proved acceptable to the State Department and to the other governments concerned. In essence, it provided that the court should not, without American consent, render an advisory opinion in any dispute to which the United States was a party; should cases arise in which the United States claimed merely "an interest," the American government might, if it thought necessary, withdraw from the court "without any imputation of unfriendliness." There the matter rested. The Senate failed to take action, though both parties in the next presidential election declared for American participation. The United States and Soviet Russia continued to be the only large nations outside the court.

The American government meantime had launched a series of efforts to scale down national armaments. Under spur of a resolution fathered by Senator Borah, Harding called a conference of nine nations — China, Belgium, Holland and Portugal in addition to the five Great Powers — which met in Washington on November 12, 1921. The deliberations were dominated by the conviction that the greatest threat to world peace lay in the disturbed conditions and international rivalries of the Pacific and the Orient. On the opening day Secretary Hughes dramatically proposed a drastic reduction in navies, following which the United States, Great Britain, Japan, France and Italy presently signed a treaty that established virtual parity in battleships between the British Empire and the United States, with smaller contingents for the other three countries. The quotas were fixed in accordance with the ratio 5 : 5 : 3 : 1.75 : 1.75. The treaty should remain in effect until the end of 1936, and beyond that time unless one of the signatories should desire to withdraw. By this agreement a new balance of sea power was established, with the two English-speaking powers assured a combined strength greater than that of the other three. The five nations also agreed to limit their relative strength in aircraft carriers, and they joined in a declaration condemning unrestricted submarine warfare and the use of poisonous gas.

In the effort to remove Far Eastern incitements to war, Great Britain, Japan, France and the United States pledged themselves to respect each other's possessions in the Pacific Ocean and, if danger threatened from some outside power, to confer "as to the most efficient measures to be taken, jointly or separately." While reassuring to all the signatories, from the standpoint of the United States the four-power treaty quieted popular fears that Japan cherished aggressive designs against the Philippines. The open-door policy, which had been weakened during the war by the aggressive nature of the "Twenty-one Demands" which Japan had imposed on China, attained full international sanction through the nine-power treaty to respect Chinese independence and maintain "the principle of equal opportunity for the commerce and industry of all nations" there. No power, furthermore, should seek "special rights or privileges which would abridge" those of the subjects of other countries.[1]

Important as were the gains for international peace, the American government had failed in its effort to apply the principle of restriction to minor naval craft such as cruisers, destroyers and submarines. Competition in these vessels, particularly in 10,000-ton cruisers, promptly began among the powers. To

[1] Other Far Eastern sources of irritation were dealt with. Japan agreed to restore to China the German-leased territory of Shantung, which she had acquired under the peace treaty. A nine-power treaty established the principle of China's control over her own tariff. In 1923, a year after the conference, Secretary Hughes induced Japan to cancel the troublesome Lansing-Ishii agreement of 1917 (see page 392).

stop this new arms race, President Coolidge called a conference at Geneva in 1927; but only Great Britain and Japan accepted, and agreement proved impossible even among these three. In 1930 President Hoover made a fresh effort. The London naval conference, attended by the five Great Powers, resulted in a treaty limiting all auxiliary naval vessels of the United States, Great Britain and Japan, the two former on a basis of parity and Japan on a more favorable ratio than that fixed for battleships at the Washington conference. Franco-Italian jealousies prevented those governments from joining in the arrangement. In the case of both the Washington and London conferences America was allowed a larger navy than Congress was willing to build. Encouraged by the substantial progress in curtailing naval strength, the League called a world disarmament conference at Geneva in February, 1932, to consider plans for limiting the other two major branches of national offense and defense, those of land and air. Thirty-one nations took part, many far-reaching proposals were offered, and the sessions continued with adjournments into 1933. While the outcome seemed uncertain, there could be no doubt that the process of clarifying ideas would, in any case, be helpful in arriving at an eventual solution of the problem.[1]

Meantime the Coolidge administration had helped organize a peace offensive of a different kind. When Aristide Briand, the French Premier, in 1927 proposed to Washington a treaty to outlaw war between the two powers, Secretary of State Kellogg countered with a proposal to widen the declaration to include all nations. The upshot was the pact of Paris in August, 1928, signed in first instance by fifteen countries, and pledging them to renounce war "as an instrument of national policy" and never to seek to settle their "conflicts of whatever nature . . . except by pacific means." By August, 1932, sixty-two of the sixty-

---

[1] In May, 1933, Norman H. Davis, speaking for the new Democratic administration, assured the delegates that, should an international conference "determine that a State has been guilty of a breach of the peace in violation of its international obligations and take measures against the violator, then if we concur in the judgment rendered as to the responsible and guilty party, we will refrain from any action tending to defeat such collective effort which these States may make to restore peace." This policy, if supported by Congress, involved a significant further move into the orbit of the League.

four nations of the world had signed. To many the Briand-Kellogg pact seemed a pious gesture or, as Senator James Reed of Missouri put it, "an international kiss." It provided no explicit means of enforcement, and the State Department had informed the signatories that the "right of self-defense" — a pretext often used to cloak aggression — was not affected. But others felt that this voluntary pledge by the united governments of the globe was of profound import, that it haled the nations "not into a court of law, but into the forum of conscience." President Hoover went further in a joint statement with Ramsay MacDonald, the British Prime Minister, during the latter's visit to America in October, 1929: "Both our Governments resolve to accept the Peace Pact not only as a declaration of good intentions, but as a positive obligation to direct national policy in accordance with its pledge."

Events in northern China presently put the matter to a test. The invasion of Manchuria by Japanese armed forces led the United States in October, 1931, to send a representative to sit with the League Council to consider a basis for common action under the pact of Paris. Japan, sternly reminded of her obligations to renounce war, nevertheless continued her career of conquest. In November, Stimson, Hoover's Secretary of State, further protested Japan's course as a violation of the nine-power treaty guaranteeing Chinese territorial integrity. Meanwhile the League bestirred itself in the attempt to restore peace, but shrank from applying coercive measures. When in spite of these varied efforts Japan occupied all Manchuria, Secretary Stimson on January 7, 1932, formally notified that country and China that America would not "recognize any situation, treaty, or agreement which may be brought about by means contrary to the covenants and obligations of the Pact of Paris." Two months later the League Assembly (Japan and China not voting) unanimously indorsed this action. But Japan denied any culpability, advancing the plea of self-defense, and setting up the "independent" state of Manchukuo in February to prove that the Chinese in Manchuria remained free to exercise the right of self-determination. Whether the "Stimson Doctrine" would prove effective in the long run, only the future could disclose.

From the outset it had been apparent that the postwar structure of peace was conditioned by the dual question of debts and reparations, the former involving repayment to the United States of the war-time borrowings of the Allied governments, and the latter Germany's payment to the Allies of her crushing war indemnity. Of the $10,000,000,000 due the United States, more than 90 per cent was owing from Great Britain, France and Italy. America early assured the debtor countries of her willingness to take into account capacity to pay in the terms of settlement. Between June, 1923, and May, 1930, seventeen nations entered arrangements, Russia, Nicaragua and Armenia alone holding aloof. Great Britain, for example, agreed to repay over a period of sixty-two years on the basis of an interest rate estimated at 3.3 per cent; Belgium similarly at 1.8 per cent; France at 1.6; and Italy at 0.4 per cent.

For the wherewithal to discharge these obligations the leading powers relied upon the reparation payments from Germany. This latter sum had not been fixed in the peace treaty, but in 1921 a special commission had set the figure at $33,000,000,000. The burden, however, proved too heavy for Germany; and the Dawes plan in 1924 and the Young plan in 1929 — named respectively after Charles G. Dawes and Owen D. Young, two Americans who helped draw them up — provided progressively smaller amounts and easier terms. The Young plan frankly coupled reparations and intergovernmental debts by arranging for a still further reduction of German payments to the extent that America might in the future relax her demands on the Allies. This provision flew in the face of the American contention that the two transactions had no relationship to each other. But when presently depression settled on the world and an overstrained Germany seemed on the point of financial collapse, President Hoover in June, 1931, announced a one-year moratorium, or postponement, of both debt and reparation payments. His action was widely interpreted as a tardy official admission that the two financial operations were interlocked.

In the summer of 1932, as the moratorium drew to a close, a conference of European powers at Lausanne decided that, if a "satisfactory" debt settlement could be reached with America, they would let Germany end further reparation payments with a lump sum of $714,000,000. The resolution, obviously squinting at cancellation by the United States, caused the latter promptly to affirm that its policy remained unchanged. Both at home and abroad the agitation, long under way, for canceling or drastically revising the debts reached new proportions. Some argued that the act would be amends for America's delay in entering the war, while American economists maintained that repayment could occur only at the cost of deluging the home market with commodities that would injure domestic industries. European bitterness was represented by newspapers that spoke of Uncle Sam as Uncle Shylock. The official attitude of the United States was compounded of the feeling that generous terms had been accorded the debtor countries, and that they would find it possible to foot the bill if they would only spend less on national armaments. In December, 1932, France, Poland, Belgium, Estonia and Hungary defaulted their semiannual payments, as they did again, along with other governments, in June, 1933.

Despite the growing irritation caused by the debt situation, the years from 1921 had beheld an impressive collective effort by the nations toward the goal of a warless world. The American government's contribution to this advance had been abetted by an eager public opinion. Once the war ended, the various peace bodies had resumed their activities with redoubled zeal, and new organizations joined their ranks. A noteworthy indication of revived interest in the cause was afforded by a nation-wide poll of Protestant clergymen in 1931. Of the total number of over 19,000 responding, 12,000 (sixty-two per cent) declared that the churches should go on record as refusing to sanction or support any future war, while more than 10,000 (fifty-four per cent) stated that they personally would not sanction any future war or participate in it as armed combatants. Though such sentiments were opposed by other elements in the population, notably by veterans' groups and the hereditary patriotic societies, yet the most significant plan to strike at the war evil through purely domestic action originated with the American Legion, the chief ex-soldiers' organization. At its prompting, Congress created a war-policies commission including five cabinet officials. This body in 1932, after consulting with industrial and labor leaders, army officers and spokesmen for civilian groups, recommended a plan to eliminate the profiteering motive as an incentive to war.[1] It proposed a constitutional amendment giving the government unrestricted war-time power to fix prices and, further, the enactment of legislation which, when war should break out, would automatically subject individuals and corporations to a tax of ninety-five per cent on all income above the previous three-year average. Congress, its hands tied with pressing domestic problems, took no action.

SELECT BIBLIOGRAPHY

Since the World War. Two general surveys by historians touch on these years: Slosson, *The Great Crusade and After*, which stresses social aspects, and Malin, *The United States after the World War*, concerned primarily with political events. Allen, *Only Yesterday*, justifies its subtitle of "an informal history of the nineteen-twenties." Two coöperative works of the utmost value are Committee on Recent Economic Changes, *Recent Economic Changes in the United States*, and President's Research Committee on Social Trends, *Recent Social Trends in the United States*. As aids in linking current events with recent history, the following annual compilations will be found useful: Lippmann, *The United States in World Affairs; The American Year Book; The New International Year Book; The Americana Annual; The American Labor Year Book;* and *The World Almanac*. Of the quarterly periodicals, *Foreign Affairs*, the *Political Science Quarterly, American Political Science Review, American Journal of International Law, American Economic Review* and *Quarterly Journal of Economics* are valuable in their respective fields, as is also the bimonthly *Social Forces*. Among monthly magazines *Current History* and the *Monthly Labor Review* are particularly helpful. The *Literary Digest* and *Time* are two of the best weeklies that chronicle history in the making; the *Nation*, the *New Republic* and the *New Survey* offer critical and interpretative comments.

Postwar Readjustments, Social and Economic. On postwar hysteria and its manifestations, consult Chafee, *Freedom of Speech;* Irwin, *How Red Is America?;* Hays, *Let Freedom Ring;* Frankfurter, *The Case of Sacco and Vanzetti;* Mechlin, *The Ku Klux Klan;* and Williams, *The Shadow of the Pope*. Lorwin, *The American Federation of Labor*, discusses the impact of peace on the labor movement. McVeagh, *The Transportation Act, 1920*, is valuable for the Esch-Cummins law; Zimmermann, *Zimmermann on Ocean Shipping*, for the merchant-marine act.

The Return of the Republicans. Apart from the general surveys listed in the first paragraph, parties and elections during the 1920's have as yet re-

---

[1] The American Legion said in its official statement to the commission: "That wars in the past have been immensely profitable to many of those who have been unable to serve is a fact known to everyone. It is probably true that, subconsciously, the public opinion which has so much to do with war or peace is affected by the knowledge that if war does come, it will be a time of great prosperity for those who are unable to serve."

ceived little study from historians. Ravage, *The Story of Teapot Dome*, describes one of the amazing pieces of official rascality. Peel and Donnelly, *The 1928 Campaign, an Analysis*, studies a particular election on which further light may be gained from Williams, *The Shadow of the Pope*.

The Republican Quest for World Stability. The various phases are treated in Geneva Research Information Committee, *American Coöperation with the League, 1919–1931;* Jessup, *The United States and the World Court;* Buell, *The Washington Conference;* Ichihashi, *The Washington Conference and After;* Williams, *The United States and Disarmament;* Myers, *Origin and Conclusion of the Paris Pact;* Moulton and Pasvolsky, *War Debts and World Prosperity;* and Lippmann, *The United States in World Affairs,* the volumes for 1931 and 1932.

CHAPTER XXIII

DOMESTIC PROBLEMS OF THE TWENTIES

REPUBLICAN ECONOMICS

NOT only on foreign but also on domestic policies the twelve-year Republican tenure made a deep impress. Economy in government, the promotion of business enterprise, and tax reduction were the slogans that issued from the White House; and, in considerable part, the program found fulfillment. At the very outset President Harding, succeeding where his predecessor Taft had failed, induced Congress in June, 1921, to create a budget bureau in the Treasury Department, headed by a director buttressed with authority, under the President, to prepare estimates of revenue and to recommend expenditures. It was further provided that all requests for appropriations must go to the bureau, not directly to Congress. The new system marked a sharp break with the time-honored practice by which requests for funds, arising from the several executive departments and commissions and from sundry committees of Congress, were voted by Congress without sufficient scrutiny or adequate attempt to coördinate outgo with income. Under Charles G. Dawes as first director the plan quickly demonstrated its utility.

Congress in the same session turned to the customary Republican task of increasing protection. In an effort to obviate the competition of low-priced Canadian grain, it enacted an emergency tariff, which imposed high duties on wheat and corn, along with meat, wool, sugar and certain other farm products. This piece of legislation was supplemented in 1922 by a general tariff revision in which the industrial interests shared. The Fordney-McCumber act was the highest protective measure so far passed. The effect of the excessive rates was, however, somewhat tempered by the provision that, upon advice of the tariff commission, the President might raise or lower duties as much as fifty per cent in order to equalize costs of production in the United States and competing foreign countries. As a matter of fact, Harding and his successors made extensive use of the flexible provision, but usually to enhance rates. A majority of the Democrats in Congress condemned the law: it was a tax extorted by the manufacturers from the people, and it was certain to discourage foreign trade at the very time when the huge debts due from Europe would have to be paid chiefly in commodities. But the country's abounding prosperity served to discount all such outcries.

Yet, as the decade drew toward a close, the evil plight of the Western farmers caused the beneficence of the Fordney-McCumber act increasingly to be questioned. To the rising chorus of criticism the Republican answer was the need of more protection, not less. When Congress reopened the subject in the spring of 1929, representatives of the manufacturing interests — lawyers, publicity experts, professional agents — packed the lobbies. Joseph R. Grundy, president of the Pennsylvania Manufacturers' Association, frankly declared before a committee that industrialists had contributed funds to elect President Hoover and that Congress should take full cognizance of the fact. In November Grundy was appointed to a vacancy in the Senate in time to aid powerfully in putting his ideas into effect. After months of what the staunchly Republican *Boston Transcript* called "the unrestrained play of selfishness and of petty politics," the Hawley-Smoot bill finally emerged in June, 1930. Contrary to President Hoover's desire to limit action to a few mainly agricultural schedules, the measure was a general revision pushing protection to still higher levels, an average of perhaps twenty per cent above the rates of 1922. In the case of certain articles, notably automobiles, duties were retained when a majority of the manufacturers had no wish for them. A protest signed by over a thousand economists from 179 colleges and universities urged the President to veto the bill. They stressed the harmful effects of high rates on living costs, foreign trade and investments and the debt situation. But Hoover signed the measure, believing he could remedy its worst features through the flexible clause that the bill retained. The most startling result of the law appeared in reprisals by foreign governments. By the spring of 1932 more than twenty had raised their tariffs, some explicitly avowing their purpose to retaliate against America.

That the foreign trade of the United States steadily increased through most of these years (from 1922 to 1929 inclusive), despite the lofty customs wall, was due partly to the enormous sums that Americans loaned abroad, much of which was used to pay for American exports. Foreign investments by United States citizens rose from $8,500,000,000 in 1922 to over $12,000,000,000 in 1927, while investments by foreigners in America advanced from $2,800,000,000 to but $3,700,000,000. The transactions assumed such great size that in 1921 the State Department began the practice of having banking houses get its approval before floating foreign loans in the United States.[1] The American government's announcement of the moratorium in 1931 (see page 460) was inspired in part by the fact that Germany's bad financial situation imperiled American investments there estimated at around $2,000,000,000. In order to make the Department of Commerce "the world's most formidable engine of foreign trade conquest," Secretary Hoover among other things induced Congress in 1927 to supplement the regular consular officers with a world-wide network of high-powered special agents working under his supervision to search out openings for American commerce and the export of capital. One unanticipated consequence of the international tariff situation, as Professor James Harvey Rogers pointed out in 1929, was that "substantial portions of our most highly developed and most profitable industries" found it expedient to migrate to alien lands, "carrying with them not only American organization and methods but also American talent, with all the resultant loss of purchasing of American domestic products and of the stimulus to American business in general." Thus American automobile plants sprang up in Canada, cork factories in Spain, glove works in France, burlap mills in India. This condition helped to account for the growing opposition of mercantile exporters to excessive protection.

Obedient to the Republican purpose of stimulating industrial enterprise, both the Attorney-General's office and the federal

[1] In explanation of this practice an official of the State Department declared in 1924, "The Department of State could not be expected to view with favor the utilization of American capital abroad in such a manner as to prevent or make difficult the carrying out of essential American policies, nor to promote the carrying out abroad of policies inimical to the proper interests of the United States."

trade commission displayed a much friendlier attitude toward the methods of Big Business than in the days of militant progressivism. A new consolidating movement began, usually taking the form of holding companies. Because of the bewildering complexity of their internal structure, such supermergers lent themselves readily to stock watering, speculation and dishonest accounting methods.[1] These vast growths proved particularly striking in the electric-power industry where the courts had ruled that the holding companies were not public utilities and hence were free from regulation by state public-utility commissions. That industry quickly fell under the control of four major capitalistic groups, the General Electric, Insull, North American, and Stone and Webster. Since American homes, factories and transportation lines used as much electricity as all the rest of the world combined, the conservation question raised its head in a new and acute form. More than a tenth of the total electric power moved across state lines and therefore gave opportunity for federal regulation in the interest of the public. Yet only in the case of water power did Congress take action. In 1920 Wilson had signed a law creating a federal power commission, consisting of three cabinet officers, with authority to license hydroelectric projects on navigable waters and on the public lands, and also to supervise security issues and, in certain instances, the rates charged. In the next ten years it issued licenses for 449 projects, chiefly in the West, but the licensed plants in 1930 represented only a sixteenth of the total power generated in the nation.

Agitation for more drastic federal control meantime grew, its chief source being the rural sections of the Midwest, and its chief spokesman the veteran Republican progressive, Senator George W. Norris of Nebraska. The principal bone of contention was the question of the disposition of the government properties on the Tennessee River at the foot of Muscle Shoals near Florence in northern Alabama. Authorized by Congress as a war-time measure, President Wilson in 1918 had directed the construc-

[1] The full extent of the financial jugglery and dishonesty possible became public in 1932 with the collapse of the Insull group of public utilities, which furnished power, light and heat to nearly 5000 communities in 30 states. The crash inflicted a staggering loss on the investing public of nearly $700,000,000.

tion there of plants for the production of nitrates for explosives and fertilizers and of dams to generate electric power for their operation. The national expenditure at Muscle Shoals totaled $145,000,000. The progressive elements in both parties demanded government ownership and operation of the nitrate plants and the hydroelectric station; the industrial East insisted on turning them over to private companies. After prolonged controversy, two bills framed to accomplish the purpose of the progressives, one in 1928, the other in 1931, were killed by presidential vetoes. President Hoover, faithful to his creed, denounced the nation's entrance into commercial competition with its own citizens, and maintained that regulation of power utilities belonged properly to the states.

Out of the welter of discussion and conflict emerged two concessions to the progressives. One was Congress's authorization in 1928 of the Boulder Canyon project for erecting a dam across the Colorado River at the Arizona-Nevada boundary line. The purpose was to insure flood control, provide water for irrigation and furnish electric power to the seven states of the Southwest, preference being given to state and municipal agencies over private companies. The act provided for creating an artificial lake more than a hundred miles long, at a total cost of $165,000,000, to be repaid to the government over a period of fifty years by the users of water and power. Actual construction began two years later. Less important was the law of 1930, which reconstituted the federal power commission with five members appointed by the President, but left the scope of its authority unaltered. Settlement of the Muscle Shoals question awaited the advent of the Democrats.

Meanwhile the Republicans had bent their energies toward scaling down the public debt and lowering the high war-time taxes. So successful was Secretary of the Treasury Mellon in the former regard that the national indebtedness shrank from $24,000,000,000 in 1920 to about $16,000,000,000 in 1930, a decline of approximately one third. In tax reduction, too, Mellon made substantial progress, Congress usually accepting his recommendation to slash most heavily the rates on the biggest incomes (those in the "upper brackets"), with slighter decreases for smaller ones. The chief stumblingblock to the smooth working

out of this double-headed program was the ceaseless clamor of
the ex-soldiers for further compensation. Through the veterans'
bureau in Washington the government already provided medical and hospital care for totally disabled soldiers, offered vocational training to partially disabled ones, granted allowances to
their dependents, and administered a vast insurance business on
behalf of the ex-service men. In addition, at the close of the
World War, a discharge bonus totaling $256,000,000 had been
paid the soldiers.

Yet the veterans, led by the American Legion, insisted that
the government owed them a further bonus to help offset the
fabulous war-time wages they might have earned in civilian
employments. A bonus bill passed in 1922 was stopped by Harding's veto, but another one, in 1924, was carried over Coolidge's
veto. It provided for the issuance of adjusted-service certificates
in the form of paid-up insurance policies, with the stipulation
that the principal should be paid in twenty years. Other acts
from time to time liberalized the compensation provisions of the
earlier laws, and one in 1930 authorized payments for disabilities
even though they had been contracted after the war closed.
When the country began to feel the pinch of unemployment in
1930, the ex-soldiers started an agitation for immediate redemption of the adjusted-service certificates. Over President Hoover's
ringing veto Congress in February, 1931, granted a part of the
demand by increasing the loan value of the certificates from
twenty-two to fifty per cent of their face value. Expenditures
for World War veterans, which had cost the American people
$402,000,000 in 1921, reached an annual total of over $860,000,000
in 1932.[1]

LABOR, IMMIGRATION AND THE FARM PROBLEM

While capital reaped the lush fruits of prosperity, labor issued from the dark years of the early 1920's into the sunlight
of ampler wages and a better standard of living. As long as the
depression lasted, however, wage cuts, strikes and unemployment marked the scene. The year 1920 saw nearly 3300 strikes
and lockouts, the next year about 2400. In July of the following

[1] This was at the rate of about $2668 for every American soldier killed or wounded
in action; the comparable figure for Germany, France, Great Britain, Italy and
Canada combined was about $54.

year began a nation-wide strike of 400,000 railway shopmen as a result of wage reductions ordered by the federal railway-labor board. After President Harding made several fruitless attempts to end the trouble through mediation, Attorney-General Daugherty on September 1, alleging the need of protecting the mails and interstate commerce, obtained a blanket injunction against the strikers. It was the most sweeping decree of the kind ever issued. Under its terms they could not even use peaceful argument or moral suasion to induce fellow employees to cease work. It was bitterly denounced as an infringement of labor's rights and of the Clayton antitrust act. Though not the decisive factor, the government's move hastened the conclusive defeat of the strikers.

Yet 1922 and the return of good times ushered in an era unusually free from industrial upheavals. The number dropped from approximately 1000 in that year to as few as 629 in 1927. Many factors helped account for this unwonted peace: on the one hand, the increasing use of injunctions to break strikes, and the resolute drive of employers for the open or nonunion shop and for introducing local company unions in place of labor organizations affiliated with national bodies; on the other hand, the ascending scale of pay, profit-sharing plans, and employer's welfare programs involving such features as recreational facilities, sickness and death benefits and retirement pensions. As the profits of industry climbed ever upward, employers not only exerted themselves to insure a contented labor force, but many of them accepted the doctrine that high wages (and hence enhanced purchasing power) formed an essential element in the reigning prosperity. The membership of the American Federation of Labor fell away, numbering but 2,900,000 in 1929 as against 4,000,000 in 1920.

Though a declining force in the industrial world, the American Federation left its mark on legislation. Many states were induced to strengthen the enforcement of their workmen's compensation acts, raise the scale of payments, and make better provision for medical and hospital care. A new type of social legislation appeared in old-age pensions, for which seventeen states had made provision by 1930. But the Federation's principal efforts were directed toward limiting the use of injunctions, and toward securing protection of workingmen from so-called yellow-dog contracts, a means by which employers bound their employees not to join outside labor organizations during their term of service. The Federation's zeal increased as new Supreme Court decisions, notably the Bedford Cut Stone case in 1927, further weakened the anti-injunction provisions of the Clayton act (see pages 347–348). Finally, after extended controversy, Congress in February, 1932, passed a law, sponsored by Senator Norris, which declared yellow-dog contracts unenforceable before the federal courts, and also explicitly set forth certain forms of activity in labor conflicts that should be immune from injunctions. In general, it provided that "no persons participating in, or affected by, such disputes shall be enjoined from striking, or from striving for the success of the strike by customary labor union effort, short of fraud or violence." The immunity extended to all persons "in the same industry, trade, or occupation," thus considerably enlarging the benefits of the Clayton act which the court had construed as applying only to employers and their own employees.

The American Federation found it an easier matter to marshal popular support for tightening the clamps on immigration. The intense nationalism bred by the war, the dread of a deluge of low-grade newcomers from devasted Europe, the waxing power of the Ku Klux Klan — such influences impelled Congress to give ready ear to labor's fears of competition with hordes of underpaid foreign workingmen. Prompt measures seemed called for by the appearance of over 800,000 immigrants in the twelve months before July 1, 1921. In May of that year Congress took action, limiting the quota any European or African country could send in a single year to three per cent of the number of its people in the United States in 1910. The law accomplished a dual purpose. It not only insured a reduction in the total number of arrivals, but also discriminated in favor of those from Northern and Western Europe. The restriction, however, did not go far enough to satisfy public opinion; and in 1924 the Johnson act fixed the quota of each nation at two per cent, based upon the number of its immigrants in the United States in 1890.[1] The

[1] Each nation, however, was allowed an irreducible annual minimum of one hundred immigrants and, under certain circumstances, near relatives of recent comers might be admitted in excess of the quota.

naming of the earlier census year involved even greater partiality for the older immigration. The law further provided that from July 1, 1927 (later postponed to 1929), the total annual number of newcomers should be held to 150,000, and that they should be apportioned among the several countries according to the relative strength of the various foreign stocks represented in the American population in 1920. These restrictions, however, did not apply to native-born citizens of Canada and Latin America. Finally, in a clause aimed at Japan, the Johnson act totally excluded immigrants ineligible to citizenship. President Coolidge had tried in vain to keep this last provision out of the bill, for it involved abrogating the Gentlemen's Agreement of 1907, which Japan had observed in good faith. Its inclusion drew a sharp protest from that power.

IMMIGRATION RESTRICTION UNDER THE QUOTA LAWS

	2% Quota Act of 1924	3% Quota Act of 1921	Immigrants Admitted 1913
Italy	3,845	42,057	265,542
Russia	2,248	34,284	291,040
Germany	51,227	68,059	34,329
United Kingdom	62,574	77,342	88,204
All countries	164,667	356,995	1,092,442

This legislation attested that the melting pot no longer worked to the nation's satisfaction, while the national-origins clause registered the government's purpose to stabilize the racial composition of the population as it stood in 1920. Because of this latter fact, it is a matter of considerable importance to note that the statisticians reported the blood of white America as being forty-one per cent British and north Irish in origin, over sixteen per cent German, over eleven from central and southern Ireland, with the remaining thirty-one drawn chiefly from Canada, Poland, Italy, Sweden, the Netherlands, France, Czechoslovakia, Russia, Norway, Mexico and Switzerland in the order named. No longer was the United States to offer free refuge and opportunity to the peoples of the world. An untoward effect of the increasing restraints on European immigration was the flocking in of unskilled laborers from Mexico, particularly to the mines, construction camps, fruit groves, beet and cotton fields of trans-Mississippi America. In 1925 more than 89,000 crossed the international border. By 1929, however, the Department of Labor began actively to check this inflow, mainly through exercising its authority to turn back immigrants who were likely to become public charges.

Meanwhile, with prosperity heavily blanketing the country in general, the agricultural sections had failed to recover from the postwar depression. During the World War the farmers had not only rapidly mechanized agricultural work and expanded their acreage to the tune of ever higher prices, but they had, in many instances, reorganized their methods of marketing.[1] The radical Farmers' Nonpartisan League, centering in North Dakota, induced that commonwealth in 1919 to embark on a program of state-owned and operated flour mills, grain elevators and a bank. More typical was the widespread interest in coöperative undertakings. From 1914 to 1919 the number of such associations increased from about 2975 to nearly 5780, most of them dealing in grain, dairy products, fruits, vegetables and livestock. In the latter year over half a million husbandmen in this manner sold products valued at $722,000,000, while more than 300,000 made purchases of $84,000,000 through a similar pooling of resources. Unlike earlier experiments, these new coöperatives were conducted with businesslike efficiency, and bade fair to remain a permanent instrument of the farmers' economic operations. The war period also witnessed a revival of the more familiar type of agrarian organizations, groups like the Farmers' National Council, the United Farmers of America and notably the American Farm Bureau Federation, which acted as watchdogs over the farmers' interests and well-being.

From the dizzy heights of boom times the postwar slump plunged the agriculturists into a slough of starvation prices, grinding debts, mortgage foreclosures and bankruptcies. A prime source of their difficulties sprang from the fact that, with the falling off of the European demand, agricultural production greatly surpassed domestic needs; and prompt readjustment to the new conditions was difficult, if not impossible. Their plight was aggravated by the greatly increased taxes, the high freight rates continuing from the war, and the difficulty of borrowing

[1] The number of farm tractors sold annually in the United States increased from less than 28,000 in 1916 to more than 136,000 in 1919.

money to tide over the bad times. Moreover, when conditions in the urban business world returned to normal, the situation of the farmer remained as before, except that he was obliged to pay higher prices for the goods he needed. Data collected by the Department of Agriculture in 1922 showed that the cost of producing a bushel of wheat or oats exceeded the average selling price.

The Harding administration, partial to urban industrialists, displayed little interest in the situation; but, at the prompting of the Farm Bureau Federation with its million members, a bipartisan group in Congress, mostly Westerners, formed a so-called farm bloc in the spring of 1921 to secure remedial legislation. Holding the balance of power between the two major parties, they steered through Congress (1921–1923) a series of laws that was designed, on the one hand, to improve rural credit facilities and, on the other, to curb the power of the middlemen. To accomplish the first purpose, Congress in 1921 temporarily revived the war-finance corporation, authorizing it to assist in financing the exportation of farm products. In the twelve months from December 1, 1921, $433,500,000 was advanced in this manner in thirty-seven states. Congress also increased the capacity of the federal land banks (see page 348) to lend on farm mortgages, and the intermediate-credits act in 1923 enabled farmers to borrow on livestock and crops on their way to the market. A second group of measures aimed to reduce the great disparity between the small price paid the farmer and the high price charged the public. An act in August, 1921, gave the Secretary of Agriculture supervision of the packing houses, stockyards and commission merchants, with authority to correct price manipulations and other unfair practices. The grain-futures law several days later empowered the same official to prevent improper speculation upon the exchanges in regard to grain sold for future delivery.[1] In the Capper-Volstead act in 1922 Congress expressly exempted coöperative associations in interstate commerce from prosecution under the antitrust laws, and charged the Secretary of Agriculture to see that they did not become monopolies ex-

---

[1] Held unconstitutional, it was replaced in 1922 by a new act, which was based on the interstate-commerce clause instead of the taxation clause as in the former case.

torting unfair prices. Besides these laws, the tariff acts of 1921 and 1922 threw sops to the agrarians.

All such legislation, however, virtually ignored the heart of the farmers' difficulties: overproduction. So long as they raised more products than could command a profitable market, prices could not return to a paying level. Yet in America land utilization was unrelated to broad policies of general welfare, nor had it ever been subjected to comprehensive public control. Moreover the farmers, widely scattered and traditionally individualistic, were not themselves in the position of an industrial combination to regulate production in the interests of better prices. As a way out, agrarian leaders proposed that the federal government should create a huge loan fund with which to buy up the agricultural surplus and send it abroad for sale. From 1924 on, this scheme was the subject of bitter controversy in Congress, the farm spokesmen insisting on their right to the same benevolent governmental care that tariff protection had long accorded the industrialists. As embodied in the McNary-Haugen bill, the plan provided that through a federal farm board the government should purchase each year's surplus in certain agricultural branches, collecting from the growers of each staple an "equalization fee" to defray any losses resulting from the difference between the domestic and foreign selling prices. The bill passed Congress in 1927 and, in slightly modified form, again in 1928, each time to run afoul Coolidge's veto. With unwonted heat he denounced the scheme as price-fixing, a grant of special favors, an abuse of the taxing power and an incentive to overproduction. The question of farm relief figured in the election of 1928, as it had in the two preceding ones, and Hoover as President moved at once to put into execution the counter-proposal he had offered during the campaign. The agricultural-marketing act in June, 1929, established a federal farm board which should stimulate the formation of coöperatives, propagate the doctrine of crop limitation, and use its fund of $500,000,000 to stabilize agricultural prices. In this last effort it bought up, through subsidiary agencies, 330,000,000 bushels of wheat and 1,320,000 bales of cotton, but these operations failed to stay the downward trend of prices. The situation evidently called for a more fundamental solution.

PROHIBITION IN PRACTICE

While the country was occupied with such varied and far-reaching problems, it had embarked upon one of the boldest social experiments of all time. Backed at the outset by an apparently overwhelming popular sentiment, the effort through constitutional edict to change deep-rooted personal habits over a continent-wide area seemed almost certain of success. In the Volstead act, effective on January 17, 1920, Congress defined as intoxicating, and hence illegal, all beverages containing more than half of one per cent of alcohol. But the federal government was without either the experience or the prior organization to administer a law of this character; and as time went on and public opinion evidenced increasing doubt concerning the wisdom of the war-time decision, difficulties of enforcement multiplied. A brisk smuggling trade along the Atlantic Coast and an overland traffic southward from Canada brought in much foreign liquor, while within the national borders illicit distilling and the diversion of industrial alcohol formed an even greater source of supply. Though Congress from time to time strengthened the machinery and increased the appropriations for enforcement, the task was staggering, thanks to the vast territory to be covered, the frequent failure of states and localities to coöperate, and oftentimes the venality of the prohibition agents themselves. From 1920 to 1932 a grand total of nearly 600,000 cases was brought into the federal district courts, and the number of persons killed in the course of enforcement was 254, including 79 government agents.

The results proved most successful in the rural sections and small towns. In the big cities bribery of officials, "racketeering," "hijacking" and other forms of organized criminality thrived on the profits of making supplies available to "bootleggers," "speakeasies" and "roadhouses," which in turn dispensed the liquor, good or bad in quality, to consumers. Defiance of the Volstead act by otherwise law-abiding citizens became in many circles almost a matter of pride. Particularly alarming was the seeming demoralization of the young people, who found in carrying a hip flask the spice of adventure and sophistication. Imperfect statistics suggest that the total consumption of alcoholic beverages fell off under the Eighteenth Amendment, but both wets and drys testified to a change from the preprohibition preference for beer and light wines to hard drinks like whisky, gin and brandy. Prohibitionists, however, claimed credit for the reduction of poverty, the increased savings deposits, the greatly enlarged consumption of candy, milk and soft drinks, and the generally improved condition of the poor.

With characteristic timidity the major parties avoided making an issue of the question until "Al" Smith, true to his city upbringing and contrary to the spirit of the Democratic platform, boldly injected the demand for repeal into the campaign of 1928 (see page 452). The results of the election seemed hardly to warrant a repetition of such hardihood. Yet, as the future was to disclose, the "experiment, noble in purpose" — to use President Hoover's phrase — could hardly have been launched at a time less likely to attain success. Urban sentiment had always been the mainstay of the wet cause, and the decade from 1920 to 1930 saw the proportion of people living in cities of 10,000 and upward increase from a little more than forty-two per cent to nearly forty-eight.[1] Moreover, the trial was made when the recoil from war-time self-sacrifice brought a relaxation of morals in personal behavior as well as in public life, a tendency prolonged by the hectic living and easy-going standards of an era of extraordinary prosperity. It was the fate of national prohibition to be blamed for all the excesses and crime of flush times, and then, as we shall see, to be doomed by the depression as a cause of high taxes and denial of employment.

THE GREAT DEPRESSION BEGINS

As a matter of fact, prosperity failed to include not only agriculture, but also coal mining and cotton and woolen textile manufacturing. But elsewhere the nation basked in the sunshine of unexampled opulence. The expansion of the radio, motion-picture, automobile, rayon, chemical, electrical and construction industries surpassed the fondest hopes of their sponsors, while other forms of business showed a comparable develop-

[1] Perhaps even more significant was the fact that the percentage dwelling in centers of 25,000 or more rose from 35.8 to 40.2 and that, through the newspapers, magazines, talkies and the radio, cosmopolitan notions and prejudices penetrated to the remotest corners of the land.

ment. Real-estate booms overspread the country; a fever of installment buying infected untold millions, causing them to spend beyond their means; shopgirls and washerwomen wore fur coats and drove to work in their own cars. At the same time expenditures by governmental agencies, municipal, state and federal, vastly increased. Responsible public men and business leaders spoke of a "New Economic Era," a dream of good wages, high prices, inflated credits and fat profits from which there would be no awakening. In 1928 and 1929 values in the stock market soared to heights out of all rational relationship to earnings present or prospective. A craze for speculation akin to that of the South Sea Bubble in eighteenth-century England seized upon rich and poor alike. Early in 1928 President Coolidge bestowed his blessing by stating publicly that he did not consider brokers' loans too far extended. Bankers who should have given their clients conservative advice became high-pressure salesmen for investments, domestic and foreign, of which they knew little beyond what the roseate prospectuses imparted. People withdrew their lifelong savings and even mortgaged their homes in the hope of doubling and trebling their money through the financial legerdemain. In 1929 the daily volume of trading in the New York stock exchange averaged nearly 4,000,000 shares. In vain did the federal reserve system, by restricting bank credits, seek to stem the flood of speculation. In late October the crash came. Good securities and bad tumbled down like a house of cards. The Great Depression had begun.

Flashes and mutterings of the impending storm might have forewarned a people less befogged with the mirage of sudden wealth. Not only had certain branches of business failed to share in the prevailing prosperity, but technological unemployment, due to the introduction of labor-saving machines, had rendered at least 700,000 jobless during the years 1920–1927, while industry, abetted by the government, geared itself to a volume of output that exceeded any existing demand. The building boom ended late in 1928; automobile and steel production began to slacken in the summer of 1929. Moreover, the federal government's postwar program of nursing business enterprise had largely ignored the economic interdependence of the modern world. Economic nationalism as expressed most strikingly in the mounting tariff wall prompted other countries to similar measures, the intergovernmental debt situation operated to the detriment of American trade, and political and economic unrest in many lands endangered the unexampled amount of private American investments abroad. Added to these factors were certain others domestic in character: the reckless or fraudulent nature of many of the new business enterprises; the mountainous taxes levied by state and municipal governments; and the wasteful habits of living of all classes. The United States had experienced protracted depressions before — in 1837, in 1873, in 1893 — but it had then had free land to absorb its unemployed and an expanding domestic and foreign market to aid recovery. The hard times presaged by the stock-market panic in 1929 not only lacked these saving circumstances, but, to an unprecedented extent, spread ruin deep and wide through every part of the country and every section of the population. "Experience as measured in statistics of prices, production, foreign and domestic trade, and unemployment," wrote Professor Edwin F. Gay in July, 1932, "shows nothing comparable in intensity." In other lands, too, the creeping paralysis of stagnation was at work, and in the summer of 1931 the débâcle definitely became world-wide.

The full extent of the catastrophe in America became apparent as the year 1930 advanced. Prices shrank; business fell off; factories and mines shut down; agriculture lay prostrate. Commercial and bank failures during the year totaled over 26,000 with liabilities of more than $668,000,000. Among their number was the largest bank failure in American history, that of the Bank of United States in New York City, which before the run on it began held deposits of $200,000,000 in the vaults of its sixty-two branches. Winter found men tramping the streets, bread lines forming in the industrial centers, charitable agencies straining to keep even with the widening circle of want and woe. In all, 5,000,000 men were thrown out of work during this first year. Summer brought further suffering, for a prolonged drought, the worst recorded in the nation's history, blighted the corn, hay and other crops in thirty states from Virginia to Montana and from Pennsylvania to Texas. In fifteen of them the average rainfall was about half the normal.

In the months following the stock-market crash Secretary Mellon and business leaders generally viewed the situation with unquenched optimism.   President Hoover read the portents quite as badly, asserting in January, 1930, that the "trend of business" was "upward," and assuring the people as late as December that "there are many factors which give encouragement" and that the nation had already weathered the worst of the storm.   This faith in the recuperative powers of "rugged individualism" and the "New Economic Era" made the administration slow to propose decisive measures to cope with the crisis.   In November, 1929, the President called a conference of industrial and labor leaders, which declared against a policy of wage cuts, but already by March wage reductions had begun.   Hoover also speeded up the government's construction program in order to provide new jobs, and appointed a federal committee to stimulate and coördinate the relief activities of the states and local communities.   At his recommendation, Congress cut the income-tax rates as a boon to business enterprise — a curtailment of federal revenues soon to be repented. As late as March, 1931, he vetoed a bill, sponsored by Senator R. F. Wagner of New York, for creating a national employment system which should help to finance and coöperate with state employment agencies in the effort to improve conditions.

Meanwhile, certain new factors entered the situation and nerved the administration to bolder action.   In Congress the progressives of both parties demanded with increasing vehemence direct federal subsidies for the relief of distress as well as other strong measures that enlisted a growing outside support. In November, 1930, popular discontent with the President's mild course fruited in a Democratic majority in the House and in a Senate almost exactly balanced between the parties — the first Republican setback since Wilson's time.   As 1930 drew to a close and the new year began, the depression instead of lifting grew steadily deeper.   In May the Austrian *Kredit Anstalt* crashed; in June the German financial system collapsed; and England's abandonment of the gold standard in September served as a signal for thirteen other countries to follow before the year ended.   In America during 1931 business and bank failures mounted to over 28,000 with liabilities of nearly $700,-

000,000; foreign trade reached its lowest point since 1914; the jobless totaled 7,000,000 or more; and the end of the fiscal year in June showed a deficit in the federal revenues of $900,000,000 and an even larger one in prospect.

When Congress met in December, Hoover announced that "the time is ripe for forward action to expedite our recovery," and to that end he submitted a sheaf of far-reaching proposals. Unhappily, his relations with Congress, which had never been harmonious, grew constantly more rancorous as the weeks passed and his program ran the gauntlet of searching criticism from his old progressive foes and the newly victorious Democrats. From January to July, 1932, the measures were all enacted into law, though some were much modified at Congress's hands. The most important one provided for creating a reconstruction finance corporation, modeled on a closely similar war-time body, and empowered to use funds of $2,000,000,000 for making emergency loans to banks, life-insurance companies, savings institutions, farm-mortgage associations, livestock associations, railroads and the like. Three other acts strengthened the federal land banks, enlarged the credit facilities of the federal reserve system, and set up a special home-loan banking system to assist building-and-loan associations and other concerns that disbursed money for residential construction.

Apart from these moves to bolster up business and credit, the President had no wish to involve the government in unemployment relief, maintaining that this responsibility rested on the states and localities. Yet he who had roundly declared in December that "I am opposed to any direct or indirect Government dole," and who later vetoed one measure of the kind he disliked, felt obliged on July 21 to accept another bill that authorized a total appropriation of $2,122,000,000, of which $1,800,000,000 was to be loaned to states and municipalities for the relief of distress and for self-liquidating public works, and the remainder to be spent on federal construction projects. A controversy almost as bitter took place over the question of new taxes to offset the deficit in revenues or, in the current phrase, to "balance the budget." The act finally passed increased the income tax all along the line, with rates on incomes above $1,000,000 reaching fifty-five per cent, and at the same time imposed a bewildering variety of excises. Since the levies fell short of Hoover's object, he next proposed economy measures to reduce the cost of government. Once more occurred a pitched battle, and the act as accepted, though effecting substantial savings, did not wipe out the deficit. Meanwhile the system of government help went into effect as quickly as circumstances permitted. By October 1 the reconstruction finance corporation had advanced funds to nearly 6000 banks, other financial institutions and railroads, and had similarly made loans to thirty-seven states for public works and relief of the jobless.

SELECT BIBLIOGRAPHY

Republican Economics. For most of the topics treated in this section and in the rest of the chapter, the two composite works, *Recent Economic Changes* and *Recent Social Trends*, are useful, and Malin, *The United States after the World War*, is a dependable guide to federal administrative and legislative action. Special phases are discussed in Dunn, *American Foreign Investments;* Williams, *Economic Foreign Policy of the United States;* Laidler, *Concentration of Control in American Industry;* and Berle and Means, *The Modern Corporation and Private Property.*

Labor, Immigration and the Farm Problem. The first two topics are treated in Lorwin, *The American Federation of Labor;* Frankfurter and Greene, *The Labor Injunction;* Garis, *Immigration Restriction;* and Gamio, *Mexican Immigration to the United States.* Various aspects of the farmers' situation are canvassed in Fossum, *The Agrarian Movement in North Dakota;* Wiest, *Agricultural Organization in the United States;* Williams, *Power on the Farm;* Forrester, *Report on Large Scale Coöperative Marketing in the United States;* Capper, *The Agricultural Bloc;* Nourse, *American Agriculture and the European Market;* and Black, *Agricultural Reform in the United States.*

Prohibition in Practice. The interesting chapters on prohibition in Slosson, *The Great Crusade and After*, and Allen, *Only Yesterday*, should be supplemented by fuller treatments like Feldman, *Prohibition, Its Economic and Industrial Aspects;* Bruère, *Does Prohibition Work?;* and Merz, *The Dry Decade.*

The Great Depression Begins. A cogent analysis of the causes of the economic débâcle is Gay, "The Great Depression," *Foreign Affairs*, X (1931–1932), 529–540. An account of the early stages of the depression may be found in Seldes, *Years of the Locust.*

CHAPTER XXIV

THE DEMOCRATS AND THE "NEW DEAL"

WHILE the federal machinery for fighting the depression got under way, the condition of the country continued to grow worse. More banks and business houses toppled; the federal deficit at the end of June, 1932, reached the stupendous figure of $2,880,000,000; the decline of state and local revenues necessitated shorter school terms and the slashing of teachers' salaries. Colleges and universities suffering from diminished resources joined commercial employers in cutting salaries and other expenses. With ten million or more wage-earners idle, many a city dump saw "depression villages" spring up overnight bearing such resentful names as Hooverville and Hoover Heights. In rural America wheat plumbed 42 cents, said to be the lowest level in over three hundred years; and farmers presently began to rally in armed bands to protect their homes from foreclosure sales. During midsummer more than ten thousand unemployed ex-soldiers gathered in Washington to make personal presentation of their demand for immediate cash payment of their adjusted service certificates. There the Bonus Expeditionary Force, as it was promptly dubbed, lingered to the annoyance of the police and the administration until the authorities at last drove it out, unresisting, with army tanks and gas bombs.

Despite occasional stirrings of unrest the scene as a whole was singularly free from the labor conflicts and social upheavals that had marked earlier prolonged depressions. Labor groups agitated for a six-hour day and a five-day week, while many employers accepted the new basis in order to keep more men on the pay roll and relieve privation. Proposals for unemployment insurance attracted wide notice after a Wisconsin law of this character was signed by Governor Philip F. La Follette, a son of the late Senator and brother of Robert M., Jr., who had succeeded to his father's seat in 1925. More significant perhaps was the increasing attention which intellectuals and enlightened business leaders, fired by the example of Soviet Russia, gave to the subject of long-range economic planning. Through such means, either sponsored by the government or industrial groups or both, they saw the only cure for the progressive chaos of modern economic society and perhaps the only certain bulwark against the deep-lying forces threatening the whole capitalistic order.

As the party chieftains turned to preparations for the impending presidential election one thing was undeniably true: the people were in a sullen mood, and disposed to ascribe all their troubles to the man in the White House who, they believed, had failed them in foresight and leadership. In Chicago on June 14 the Republicans in a convention containing an unusually high proportion of federal officeholders renominated Hoover on the first ballot, with Vice-President Curtis as his running mate. The platform resounded with praises of the President's policies, and endeavored to compromise internal differences over prohibition by pledging the party to submit a repeal amendment while leaving individuals free to support or oppose ratification as they liked. Meeting in the same hall on June 27, the Democrats on the fourth ballot named Franklin D. Roosevelt, the popular governor of New York — much to the chagrin of his erstwhile friend "Al" Smith, who went to the convention with few votes but with high hopes of a stampede in his own direction. John N. Garner of Texas, Speaker of the House of Representatives, was given the second place. The platform, the shortest ever framed, pictured the hard times as the evil and inevitable fruit of Republican postwar measures, and promised thoroughgoing steps to lift the depression, a twenty-five-per-cent cut in federal expenditures, and a "competitive tariff for revenue." As regards the Eighteenth Amendment, the party demanded immediate repeal and, until that could be accomplished, a higher alcoholic content of beverages than the Volstead act allowed.

Informed of his nomination, Governor Roosevelt violated all political precedents by flying to Chicago to deliver his speech of acceptance to the assembled delegates. In September he launched forth on an aggressive campaign of speech making that eventually carried him into thirty-seven of the forty-eight states. Everywhere he charged the Republicans with favoring Big Business to the detriment of the "forgotten man," denounced their helplessness in face of the economic crisis, and promised that the Democrats would inaugurate a "new deal." His opponents derided his proposals for betterment as the glittering generalities of a charming but superficial gentleman, but many people found in the fundamentals of public policy that he set forth a tonic assurance of old-time Wilsonian liberalism. Even the demand for prohibition repeal, which four years before had encumbered his predecessor, commended itself to countless voters who had come to associate the Eighteenth Amendment with gangsterism, unnecessary taxes and the problem of urban unemployment. Some believed, further, that repeal would aid agricultural recovery by increasing the demand for barley, hops, corn, sugar and other ingredients used in the manufacture of intoxicants.

Saddled with the blame for the depression, the Republicans faced a task rendered more hopeless by a bad split in their ranks, for most of the leading progressive Senators of the party — Bronson Cutting of New Mexico, Hiram Johnson of California, "Young Bob" La Follette of Wisconsin, Norris of Nebraska and others — openly declared for Roosevelt. Republican spellbinders harped on the theme, "It might have been worse," while Hoover himself cited sixteen different remedies he had applied to heal the nation's wounds, and warned that under a Democratic tariff "The grass will grow in the streets of a hundred cities, a thousand towns." To his aid came many large employers of labor, men like Henry Ford who posted bulletins in his wide-strewn plants announcing, "To prevent times from getting worse and to help them to get better President Hoover must be elected." On election day Roosevelt carried the country in a landslide comparable to that on which Hoover had ridden into office. He won 472 electoral votes — every state in the Union but six — to 59 for his opponent, and received 57.4 per cent (22,800,000) of the popular ballots to 39.7 per cent (15,760,000) for Hoover. The Democrats also swept both Houses of Congress. Particularly surprising, in view of the widespread discontent, was the small popular support accorded the Socialists and Communists: Norman Thomas for the former polled but 880,000 votes and W. Z. Foster for the latter slightly more than 100,000.

Before the victors took over the reins, the Twentieth Amendment became imbedded in the fundamental law of the land. Championed by Senator Norris since 1923, and seven times approved by the Senate before the House accepted it early in 1932, the amendment provided for doing away with the so-called lame-duck session of Congress — that session which an outgoing Congress held from December to March 4 after a new membership had been chosen. The advocates of the change contended that the old system was undemocratic and that, furthermore, the lame ducks, being no longer subject to popular control, often yielded to the temptation of passing legislation harmful to the public interest. The amendment was ratified in record time, being officially proclaimed on February 6, 1933. It specified that, instead of on March 4, Representatives and Senators should take office on January 3 following the election, and the President and Vice-President on January 20. Since the plan was to go into effect on October 15 following ratification, the transition to the new arrangement involved somewhat foreshortened terms for Roosevelt, Garner and the newly elected members of Congress. Other sections of the amendment provided for certain contingencies overlooked by the Constitution, thus that Congress should have full power to deal with the situation should both the President-elect and Vice-President-elect die or be otherwise unable to qualify for the office. These latter provisions assumed a sudden importance in the public mind when President-elect Roosevelt narrowly escaped death at the hands of a mentally unbalanced person on February 15 while in Miami, Florida. One of the assailant's shots ended the life of a member of his party, Mayor A. J. Cermak of Chicago.

THE DEMOCRATS ATTACK THE DEPRESSION

In both political experience and personality the new chief executive contrasted strikingly with his predecessor. After serving a few years in the New York state senate as an anti-Tammany Democrat, Roosevelt had become Assistant Secretary of the Navy under Woodrow Wilson, a post he resigned in 1920 to conduct his spirited campaign for Vice-President. Stricken the following year with infantile paralysis, he gallantly and patiently fought the dread disease until, with lamed legs, he returned to active political life in time to present Alfred E. Smith's name to the Democratic convention of 1924. Four years later he was chosen governor of his state by a majority that in 1930, when he ran a second time, swelled to the unprecedented total of 725,000. His policies as governor embraced such liberal measures as farm betterment, unemployment relief, a program of reforestation and the public development and operation of water-power facilities. Square-shouldered, athletically inclined, his face radiating cheer and good will, he possessed a prodigious capacity for work and unusual skill in dealing with both friend and foe.

The presidency gave him an opportunity to employ on a nation-wide scale many of the devices of leadership that had served him well in the lesser post. In recognition of the bipartisan make-up of his vast majority in the election, he placed in his cabinet three former Republicans — W. H. Woodin of New York, Secretary of the Treasury, H. L. Ickes of Illinois, Secretary of the Interior, and H. A. Wallace of Iowa, Secretary of Agriculture — and he set a precedent by including a woman, Secretary of Labor Frances Perkins, who had served him in a similar capacity in New York state.[1] For advice as to legislation, however, he usually relied upon a small group of college professors, the so-called Brain Trust, of whom Assistant Secretary of State Raymond Moley, recruited from the Columbia faculty, bulked largest in the public eye. With their help he worked out the details of the "new deal," communicating his proposals to the special session of Congress in short crisp messages that the man on the street might read, and accompanying the messages with bills ready for passage. None of his predecessors had so nearly approached the ideal of responsible parliamentary leadership. To keep his huge party following in Congress whipped into line, he withheld the bulk of the patronage until his major purposes were accomplished. At the same time, through the newspapers, radio and the talkies, he kept the electorate constantly informed of his plans, difficulties, hopes and accomplish-

[1] The other cabinet officers were Cordell Hull of Tennessee, Secretary of State; G. H. Dern of Utah, Secretary of War; H. S. Cummings of Connecticut, Attorney-General; C. A. Swanson of Virginia, Secretary of the Navy; J. A. Farley of New York, Postmaster-General; and D. C. Roper of South Carolina, Secretary of Commerce.

ments. The people rallied zealously to his support. Having failed to solve their difficulties under Hoover, they insisted that the new incumbent be given every chance.

On March 4, 1933, the day Roosevelt took office, the country was in the throes of a bank depositors' panic that shut the doors of nearly every bank and stock exchange in the land. Within thirty-six hours he issued two proclamations, one to declare a bank holiday for the nation and stop the withdrawal and export of gold, the other to summon Congress at once to Washington. Meeting on March 9 for a session that lasted to June 16, Congress under the President's spur enacted a series of momentous laws with breath-taking rapidity. The first task was to preserve and strengthen the foundations of banking and credit. To this end the banks of the country were virtually put under a licensing system and permitted to reopen only after satisfying the Treasury Department as to their soundness. Pursuant to this plan the great bulk of them quickly resumed operations and popular distrust was allayed. The Glass-Steagall act, passed toward the end of the session, forbade commercial banks to carry on an investment business, provided for insurance of deposits up to certain amounts, added savings banks to the federal reserve system, and regulated bank loans, investments and interest rates. Congress also authorized the creation of a home owners' loan corporation with large financial resources for the relief of mortgage-burdened small home owners. Another law required of corporations truthful information and full publicity in regard to security issues.

In order to balance the federal budget, Congress, on the one hand, imposed additional taxes without advancing the normal rates on incomes and, on the other, instructed the President to effect drastic governmental economies. Under this warrant Roosevelt cut $125,000,000 from the federal pay roll and, to the amazement of the old-time politicians, reduced payments to the ex-soldiers by more than $300,000,000. The government had never hitherto decreased pensions once granted. As a further measure to enlarge revenues as well as to stimulate employment, the platform pledge regarding prohibition was put into effect. The outgoing Congress on February 20 had already proposed a constitutional amendment repealing the Eighteenth Amendment and prohibiting alcoholic shipments into any state contrary to its laws. In conformity with the promises of both party platforms, the requirement was attached that the amendment be approved by special state conventions instead of by the legislatures, as had been the invariable previous practice. The special session rounded out the program by legalizing and taxing beverages containing 3.2 per cent of alcohol. In state after state all over the country the voters instructed their convention delegates to ratify the repeal proposal, and it seemed clear that by December, 1933, the Twenty-first Amendment would be incorporated in the Constitution.

In order to enhance the public's purchasing power and promote business activity, the government resorted to sundry expedients. On April 19 the nation abandoned the gold standard, not from an immediate dearth of gold, the usual reason, but as a means of competing on more favorable terms with other nongold-standard countries in world commerce and, at the same time, of boosting wages and prices and quickening trade at home. In addition, Congress provided for expanding the credit of the federal reserve system by $3,000,000,000, and gave the President discretionary power to issue a similar amount of treasury notes in small denominations in payment for government bonds. Besides, if he deemed it desirable, he might lower the gold content of the dollar, and even establish unlimited coinage of silver — the dreaded free silver of 1896. This act represented a compromise in which Roosevelt checkmated the extreme inflationists by obtaining authority to employ any of the several methods which, in his judgment, he might deem best.

Even more unprecedented were the steps taken to revive industry, transportation and agriculture. The national industrial-recovery act, adopted on June 16 and limited by its terms to two years, provided for federal control of industry by compelling industry to regulate itself in regard to quantity of output and in accordance with certain enlightened standards as to hours, wages, the right of employees to bargain through their own representatives, and protection of the interests of consumers. For these purposes every branch of industry was required to draw up a code which should become effective upon the government's approval. Uniform action throughout an industry, declared

Roosevelt, was the only means of protecting well-disposed employers from "cutthroat underselling by selfish competitors." To safeguard the process of national recovery from competition with cheaply made foreign goods, the President was empowered, should he deem it necessary, to curtail or bar all imports from abroad. The same act authorized a bond issue of $3,300,000,000, to be used by the federal government and to be loaned to states and municipalities for building highways, developing hydroelectric power, clearing slums and for other projects of a public character. The railroad legislation aimed to reduce the huge wastes of competition by providing for mergers and coöperation among the roads under a federal coördinator of transportation, so that they might jointly use the same terminals, coördinate train service and effect many other economies for the benefit of investors and shippers. In a fresh assault on the farm problem, the agricultural-adjustment act vested the federal authorities for two years with a wide variety of powers to restrict acreage and prevent overproduction, including subsidies to staple growers who agreed to limitation and government leasing and withdrawal of inferior lands from tillage. In addition, provision was made for easing the debt burden resting on forty per cent of the nation's farms by refinancing agricultural mortgages on better terms with federal help.

To afford immediate relief to those suffering from unemployment, Congress set aside $500,000,000 for grants to state and local governments, many of which were in a condition of bankruptcy. It also adopted the Wagner bill, which Hoover had vetoed, establishing a coördinated system of federal and state employment exchanges. Another measure created a civilian conservation corps, which quickly recruited 300,000 jobless men for the work in the national forests.[1] As if this budget of legislation were not sufficiently great, Congress settled the long-standing controversy over Muscle Shoals by providing for the government's development of the Tennessee Valley on a scale surpassing the hopes of even Senator Norris, its battle-scarred

[1] In view of President Hoover's earlier experience, it is worth noting that in May a new bonus army, three thousand strong, appeared in Washington. The administration, after providing them with shelter and food, offered to enlist them in the civilian conservation corps or pay their fares back home. The demonstration promptly collapsed.

champion. The act set up a federal board to build dams, power stations and transmission lines, provide for flood control, manufacture electricity, fertilizers and explosives, and develop the agricultural and industrial possibilities of the region.

The middle of June saw this epochal special session come to an end. Never before in time of peace had the government embarked on so gigantic and audacious a program of social and economic control. In his radio talk to the people after the adjournment, Roosevelt emphasized that the legislation was not "just a collection of haphazard schemes, but rather the orderly component

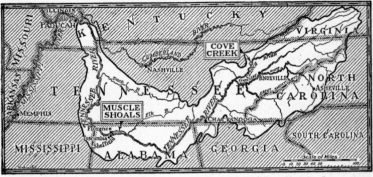

MUSCLE SHOALS AND THE TENNESSEE RIVER VALLEY

parts of a connected and logical whole." The new measures, directly or indirectly, touched the welfare and daily round of every man, woman and child in the land. For the time, the country moved onto a basis of national planning, with the President as supreme manager and coördinator. *Laissez faire*, even in its attenuated twentieth-century form, was discredited; rugged individualism, said a newspaper humorist, had produced ragged individualism. As during the stress of the World War, the people eagerly turned to decisive collective action against the common foe. Roosevelt was dictator of the national destinies, but his was a dictatorship in the American tradition, one backed by law and public opinion, limited in certain essential respects as to duration and, in any case, accountable to the voters on election day. The success of the mighty experiment depended, in considerable part, on the ability of the myriad officials who were to guide and direct the new administrative machinery. As the tired members of Congress left Washington, signs were already appearing of a revival of industry: factories opening, wages increasing, men returning to work. Whether these betokened a genuine turning of the tide only the future could reveal.

SELECT BIBLIOGRAPHY

The Democrats and the "New Deal." For the election of 1932 and the eventful hundred days of the special session, the student should consult the periodical publications listed at the end of Chapter XXII.

APPENDIX

CONSTITUTION OF THE UNITED STATES

We The People of the United States, in Order to form a more perfect Union, establish Justice, insure domestic Tranquillity, provide for the common defence, promote the general Welfare, and secure the Blessings of Liberty to ourselves and our Posterity, do ordain and establish this Constitution for the United States of America.

ARTICLE I

Section 1. All legislative Powers herein granted shall be vested in a Congress of the United States, which shall consist of a Senate and a House of Representatives.

Section 2. The House of Representatives shall be composed of Members chosen every second Year by the People of the several States, and the Electors in each State shall have the Qualifications requisite for Electors of the most numerous Branch of the State Legislature.

No Person shall be a Representative who shall not have attained to the Age of twenty-five Years, and been seven Years a Citizen of the United States, and who shall not, when elected, be an Inhabitant of that State in which he shall be chosen.

Representatives and direct Taxes shall be apportioned among the several States which may be included within this Union, according to their respective Numbers, which shall be determined by adding to the whole Number of free Persons, including those bound to Service for a Term of Years, and excluding Indians not taxed, three fifths of all other Persons. The actual Enumeration shall be made within three Years after the first Meeting of the Congress of the United States, and within every subsequent Term of ten Years, in such Manner as they shall by Law direct. The Number of Representatives shall not exceed one for every thirty Thousand, but each State shall have at Least one Representative; and until such enumeration shall be made, the State of New Hampshire shall be entitled to chuse three, Massachusetts eight, Rhode-Island and Providence Plantations one, Connecticut five, New-York six, New Jersey four, Pennsylvania eight, Delaware one, Maryland six, Virginia ten, North Carolina five, South Carolina five, and Georgia three.

When vacancies happen in the Representation from any State, the Executive Authority thereof shall issue Writs of Election to fill such Vacancies.

The House of Representatives shall chuse their Speaker and other Officers; and shall have the sole Power of Impeachment.

Section 3. The Senate of the United States shall be composed of two Senators from each State, chosen by the Legislature thereof, for six Years; and each Senator shall have one Vote.

Immediately after they shall be assembled in Consequence of the first Election, they shall be divided as equally as may be into three Classes. The Seats of the Senators of the first Class shall be vacated at the Expiration of the second Year, of the second Class at the Expiration of the fourth Year, and of the third Class at the Expiration of the sixth Year, so that one-third may be chosen every second Year; and if Vacancies happen by Resignation, or otherwise, during the Recess of the Legislature of any State, the Executive thereof may make temporary Appointments until the next Meeting of the Legislature, which shall then fill such Vacancies.

No Person shall be a Senator who shall not have attained to the Age of thirty Years, and been nine Years a Citizen of the United States, and who shall not, when elected, be an Inhabitant of that State for which he shall be chosen.

The Vice President of the United States shall be President of the Senate, but shall have no Vote, unless they be equally divided.

The Senate shall chuse their other Officers, and also a President pro tempore, in the Absence of the Vice President, or when he shall exercise the Office of President of the United States.

The Senate shall have the sole Power to try all Impeachments. When sitting for that Purpose, they shall be on Oath or Affirmation. When the President of the United States is tried, the Chief Justice shall preside: And no Person shall be convicted without the Concurrence of two thirds of the Members present.

Judgment in Cases of Impeachment shall not extend further than to removal from Office, and disqualification to hold and enjoy any Office of honor, Trust or Profit under the United States: but the Party convicted shall nevertheless be liable and subject to Indictment, Trial, Judgment and Punishment, according to Law.

Section 4. The Times, Places and Manner of holding Elections for Senators and Representatives, shall be prescribed in each State by the Legislature thereof; but the Congress may at any time by Law make or alter such Regulations, except as to the Places of chusing Senators.

The Congress shall assemble at least once in every Year, and such Meeting shall be on the first Monday in December, unless they shall by Law appoint a different Day.

Section 5. Each House shall be the Judge of the Elections, Returns and Qualifications of its own Members, and a Majority of each shall constitute a Quorum to do Business; but a smaller Number may adjourn from day to day, and may be authorized to compel the Attendance of absent Members, in such Manner, and under such Penalties as each House may provide.

Each House may determine the Rules of its Proceedings, punish its Members for disorderly Behavior, and, with the Concurrence of two thirds, expel a Member.

Each House shall keep a Journal of its Proceedings, and from time to time publish the same, excepting such Parts as may in their Judgment require Secrecy; and the Yeas and Nays of the Members of either House on any question shall, at the Desire of one fifth of those present, be entered on the Journal.

Neither House, during the Session of Congress, shall, without the Consent of the other, adjourn for more than three days, nor to any other Place than that in which the two Houses shall be sitting.

Section 6. The Senators and Representatives shall receive a Compensation for their Services, to be ascertained by Law, and paid out of the Treasury of the United States. They shall in all Cases, except Treason, Felony and Breach of the Peace, be privileged from Arrest during their Attendance at the Session of their respective Houses, and in going to and returning from the same; and for any Speech or Debate in either House, they shall not be questioned in any other Place.

No Senator or Representative shall, during the Time for which he was elected, be appointed to any civil Office under the Authority of the United States, which shall have been created, or the Emoluments whereof shall have been encreased during such time; and no Person holding any Office under the United States, shall be a Member of either House during his Continuance in Office.

Section 7. All Bills for raising Revenue shall originate in the House of Representatives; but the Senate may propose or concur with Amendments as on other Bills.

Every Bill which shall have passed the House of Representatives and the Senate, shall, before it become a Law, be presented to the President of the United States; If he approve he shall sign it, but if not he shall return it, with his Objections to that House in which it shall have originated, who shall enter the Objections at large on their Journal, and proceed to reconsider it. If after such Reconsideration two thirds of that House shall agree to pass the Bill, it shall be sent, together with the Objections, to the other House, by which it shall likewise be reconsidered, and if approved by two thirds of that House, it shall become a Law. But in all such Cases the Votes of both Houses shall be determined by Yeas and Nays, and the Names of the Persons voting for and against the Bill shall be entered on the Journal of each House respectively. If any Bill shall not be returned by the President within ten Days (Sundays excepted) after it shall have been presented to him, the Same shall be a Law, in like Manner as if he had signed it, unless the Congress by their Adjournment prevent its Return, in which Case it shall not be a Law.

Every Order, Resolution, or Vote to which the Concurrence of the Senate and House of Representatives may be necessary (except on a question of Adjournment) shall be presented to the President of the United States; and before the Same shall take Effect, shall be approved by him, or being disapproved by him, shall be repassed by two thirds of the Senate and House of Representatives, according to the Rules and Limitations prescribed in the Case of a Bill.

Section 8. The Congress shall have Power To lay and collect Taxes, Duties, Imposts and Excises, to pay the Debts and provide for the common Defence and general Welfare of the United States; but all Duties, Imposts and Excises shall be uniform throughout the United States;

To borrow Money on the credit of the United States:

To regulate Commerce with foreign Nations, and among the several States, and with the Indian Tribes;

To establish an uniform Rule of Naturalization, and uniform Laws on the subject of Bankruptcies throughout the United States;

To coin Money, regulate the Value thereof, and of foreign Coin, and fix the Standard of Weights and Measures;

To provide for the Punishment of counterfeiting the Securities and current Coin of the United States;

To establish Post Offices and post Roads;

To promote the Progress of Science and useful Arts, by securing for limited Times to Authors and Inventors the exclusive Right to their respective Writings and Discoveries;

To constitute Tribunals inferior to the supreme Court;

To define and punish Piracies and Felonies committed on the high Seas, and Offences against the Law of Nations;

To declare War, grant Letters of Marque and Reprisal, and make Rules concerning Captures on Land and Water;

To raise and support Armies, but no Appropriation of Money to that Use shall be for a longer Term than two Years;

To provide and maintain a Navy;

To make Rules for the Government and Regulation of the land and naval Forces;

To provide for calling forth the Militia to execute the Laws of the Union, suppress Insurrections and repel Invasions;

To provide for organizing, arming, and disciplining the Militia, and for governing such Part of them as may be employed in the Service of the United States, reserving to the States respectively, the Appointment of the Officers, and the Authority of training the Militia according to the discipline prescribed by Congress;

To exercise exclusive Legislation in all Cases whatsoever, over such District (not exceeding ten Miles square) as may, by Cession of particular States, and the Acceptance of Congress, become the Seat of the Government of the United States, and to exercise like Authority over all Places purchased by the Consent of the Legislature of the State in which the Same shall be, for the Erection of Forts, Magazines, Arsenals, dock-Yards, and other needful Buildings; — And

To make all Laws which shall be necessary and proper for carrying into Execution the foregoing Powers, and all other Powers vested by this Constitution in the Government of the United States, or in any Department or Officer thereof.

Section 9. The Migration or Importation of such Persons as any of the States now existing shall think proper to admit, shall not be prohibited by the Congress prior to the Year one thousand eight hundred and eight, but a Tax or duty may be imposed on such Importation, not exceeding ten dollars for each Person.

The Privilege of the Writ of Habeas Corpus shall not be suspended, unless when in Cases of Rebellion or Invasion the public Safety may require it.

No Bill of Attainder or ex post facto Law shall be passed.

No Capitation, or other direct, tax shall be laid, unless in Proportion to the Census or Enumeration herein before directed to be taken.

No Tax or Duty shall be laid on Articles exported from any State.

No Preference shall be given by any Regulation of Commerce or Revenue to the Ports of one State over those of another: nor shall Vessels bound to, or from, one State, be obliged to enter, clear, or pay Duties in another.

No Money shall be drawn from the Treasury, but in Consequence of Appropriations made by Law; and a regular Statement and Account of the Receipts and Expenditures of all public Money shall be published from time to time.

No Title of Nobility shall be granted by the United States: And no Person holding any Office of Profit or Trust under them, shall, without the Consent of the Congress, accept of any present, Emolument, Office, or Title, of any kind whatever, from any King, Prince, or foreign State.

Section 10. No State shall enter into any Treaty, Alliance, or Confederation; grant Letters of Marque and Reprisal; coin Money; emit Bills of Credit; make any Thing but gold and silver Coin a Tender in Payment of Debts; pass any Bill of Attainder, ex post facto Law, or Law impairing the Obligation of Contracts, or grant any Title of Nobility.

No State shall, without the Consent of the Congress, lay any Imposts or Duties on Imports or Exports, except what may be absolutely necessary for executing it's inspection Laws: and the net Produce of all Duties and Imposts, laid by any State on Imports or Exports, shall be for the Use of the Treasury of the United States; and all such Laws shall be subject to the Revision and Controul of the Congress.

No State shall, without the Consent of Congress, lay any Duty of Tonnage, keep Troops, or Ships of War in time of Peace, enter into any Agreement or Compact with another State, or with a foreign Power, or engage in War, unless actually invaded, or in such imminent Danger as will not admit of delay.

ARTICLE II

Section 1. The executive Power shall be vested in a President of the United States of America. He shall hold his Office during the Term of four Years, and, together with the Vice President, chosen for the same Term, be elected, as follows

Each State shall appoint, in such Manner as the Legislature thereof may direct, a Number of Electors, equal to the whole Number of Senators and Representatives to which the State may be entitled in the Congress: but no Senator or Representative, or Person holding an Office of Trust or Profit under the United States, shall be appointed an Elector.

The electors shall meet in their respective States, and vote by ballot for two Persons, of whom one at least shall not be an Inhabitant of the same State with themselves. And they shall make a List of all the Persons voted for, and of the Number of Votes for each; which List they shall sign and certify, and transmit sealed to the Seat of the Government of the United States, directed to the President of the Senate. The President of the Senate shall, in the Presence of the Senate and House of Representatives, open all the Certificates, and the Votes shall then be counted. The Person having the greatest Number of Votes shall be the President, if such Number be a Majority of the whole Number of Electors appointed; and if there be more than one who have such Majority, and have an equal Number of Votes, then the House of Representatives shall immediately chuse by Ballot one of them for President; and if no Person have a Majority, then from the five highest on the List the said House shall in like Manner chuse the President. But in chusing the President, the Votes shall be taken by States, the Representation from each State having one Vote; A quorum for this Purpose shall consist of a Member or Members from two-thirds of the States, and a Majority of all the States shall be necessary to a Choice. In every Case, after the Choice of the President, the Person having the greatest Number of Votes of the Electors shall be the Vice President. But if there should remain two or more who have equal Votes, the Senate shall chuse from them by Ballot the Vice-President.

The Congress may determine the Time of chusing the Electors, and the Day on which they shall give their Votes; which Day shall be the same throughout the United States.

No Person except a natural born Citizen, or a Citizen of the United States, at the time of the Adoption of this Constitution, shall be eligible to the Office of President; neither shall any Person be eligible to that Office who shall not have attained to the Age of thirty five Years, and been fourteen Years a Resident within the United States.

In Case of the Removal of the President from Office, or of his Death, Resignation or Inability to discharge the Powers and Duties of the said Office, the same shall devolve on the Vice President, and the Congress may by Law provide for the Case of Removal, Death, Resignation or Inability, both of the President and Vice President, declaring what Officer shall then act as President, and such Officer shall act accordingly, until the Disability be removed, or a President shall be elected.

The President shall, at stated Times, receive for his Services, a Compensation, which shall neither be encreased nor diminished during the Period for which he shall have been elected, and he shall not receive within that Period any other Emolument from the United States, or any of them.

Before he enter on the Execution of his Office, he shall take the following Oath or Affirmation: — "I do solemnly swear (or affirm) that I will faithfully execute the Office of President of the United States, and will to the best of my Ability, preserve, protect and defend the Constitution of the United States."

Section 2. The President shall be Commander in Chief of the Army and Navy of the United States, and of the Militia of the several States, when called into the actual Service of the United States; he may require the Opinion, in writing, of the principal Officer in each of the executive Departments, upon any Subject relating to the Duties of their respective Offices, and he shall have Power to grant Reprieves and Pardons for Offences against the United States, except in Cases of Impeachment.

He shall have Power, by and with the Advice and Consent of the Senate, to make Treaties, provided two thirds of the Senators present concur; and he shall nominate, and by and with the Advice and Consent of the Senate, shall appoint Ambassadors, other public Ministers and Consuls, Judges of the supreme Court, and all other Officers of the United States, whose Appointments are not herein otherwise provided for, and which shall be established by Law: but the Congress may by Law vest the Appointment of such inferior Officers, as they think proper, in the President alone, in the Courts of Law, or in the Heads of Departments.

The President shall have Power to fill up all Vacancies that may happen during the Recess of the Senate, by granting Commissions which shall expire at the End of their next Session.

Section 3. He shall from time to time give to the Congress Information of the State of the Union, and recommend to their Consideration such Measures as he shall judge necessary and expedient; he may, on extraordinary Occasions, convene both Houses, or either of them, and, in Case of Disagreement between them, with Respect to the Time of Adjournment, he may adjourn them to such Time as he shall think proper; he shall receive Ambassadors and other public Ministers; he shall take Care that the Laws be faithfully executed, and shall Commission all the Officers of the United States.

Section 4. The President, Vice President and all civil Officers of the United States, shall be removed from Office on Impeachment for, and Conviction of, Treason, Bribery, or other high Crimes and Misdemeanors.

ARTICLE III

Section 1. The judicial Power of the United States, shall be vested in one supreme Court, and in such inferior Courts as the Congress may from time to time ordain and establish. The Judges, both of the supreme and inferior Courts, shall hold their Offices during good Behaviour, and shall, at stated Times, receive for their Services, a Compensation, which shall not be diminished during their Continuance in Office.

Section 2. The judicial Power shall extend to all Cases, in Law and Equity, arising under this Constitution, the Laws of the United States, and Treaties made, or which shall be made, under their Authority; — to all Cases affecting Ambassadors, other public Ministers and Consuls; — to all Cases of admiralty and maritime Jurisdiction; — to Controversies to which the United States shall be a Party; — to Controversies between two or more States; — between a State and Citizens of another State; — between Citizens of different States, — between Citizens of the same State claiming Lands under Grants of different States, and between a State, or the Citizens thereof, and foreign States, Citizens or Subjects.

In all Cases affecting Ambassadors, other public Ministers and Consuls, and those in which a State shall be Party, the supreme Court shall have original Jurisdiction. In all the other Cases before mentioned, the supreme Court shall have appellate Jurisdiction, both as to Law and Fact, with such Exceptions, and under such Regulations as the Congress shall make.

The Trial of all Crimes, except in Cases of Impeachment, shall be by Jury; and such Trial shall be held in the State where the said Crimes shall have been committed; but when not committed within any State, the Trial shall be at such Place or Places as the Congress may by Law have directed.

Section 3. Treason against the United States, shall consist only in levying War against them, or in adhering to their Enemies, giving them Aid and Comfort. No Person shall be convicted of Treason unless on the Testimony of two Witnesses to the same overt Act, or on Confession in open Court.

The Congress shall have Power to declare the Punishment of Treason, but no Attainder of Treason shall work Corruption of Blood, or Forfeiture except during the Life of the Person attainted.

ARTICLE IV

Section 1. Full Faith and Credit shall be given in each State to the public Acts, Records, and judicial Proceedings of every other State. And the Congress may by general Laws prescribe the Manner in which such Acts, Records and Proceedings shall be proved, and the Effect thereof.

Section 2. The Citizens of each State shall be entitled to all Privileges and Immunities of Citizens in the several States.

A person charged in any State with Treason, Felony, or other Crime, who shall flee from Justice, and be found in another State, shall on Demand of the executive Authority of the State from which he fled, be delivered up to be removed to the State having Jurisdiction of the Crime.

No Person held to Service or Labour in one State, under the Laws thereof, escaping into another, shall, in Consequence of any Law or Regulation therein, be discharged from such Service or Labour, but shall be delivered up on Claim of the Party to whom such Service or Labour may be due.

Section 3. New States may be admitted by the Congress into this Union; but no new State shall be formed or erected within the Jurisdiction of any other State; nor any State be formed by the Junction of two or more States, or Parts of States, without the Consent of the Legislatures of the States concerned as well as of the Congress.

The Congress shall have Power to dispose of and make all needful Rules and Regulations respecting the Territory or other Property belonging to the United States; and nothing in this Constitution shall be so construed as to Prejudice any Claims of the United States, or of any particular State.

Section 4. The United States shall guarantee to every State in this Union a Republican Form of Government, and shall protect each of them against Invasion; and on Application of the Legislature, or of the Executive (when the Legislature cannot be convened) against domestic Violence.

ARTICLE V

The Congress, whenever two thirds of both Houses shall deem it necessary, shall propose Amendments to this Constitution, or, on the Application of the Legislatures of two thirds of the several States, shall call a Convention for proposing Amendments, which, in either Case, shall be valid to all Intents and Purposes, as Part of this Constitution, when ratified by the Legislatures of three fourths of the several States, or by Conventions in three fourths thereof, as the one or the other Mode of Ratification may be proposed by the Congress; Provided that no Amendment which may be made prior to the Year One thousand eight hundred and eight shall in any Manner affect the first and fourth Clauses in the Ninth Section of the first Article; and that no State, without its Consent, shall be deprived of its equal Suffrage in the Senate.

ARTICLE VI

All Debts contracted and Engagements entered into, before the Adoption of this Constitution, shall be as valid against the United States under this Constitution, as under the Confederation.

This Constitution, and the Laws of the United States which shall be made in Pursuance thereof; and all Treaties made, or which shall be made, under the Authority of the United States, shall be the supreme Law of the Land; and the Judges in every State shall be bound thereby, any Thing in the Constitution or Laws of any State to the Contrary notwithstanding.

The Senators and Representatives before mentioned, and the Members of the several State Legislatures, and all executive and judicial Officers, both of the United States and of the several States, shall be bound by Oath or Affirmation, to support this Constitution; but no religious Test shall ever be required as a Qualification to any Office or public Trust under the United States.

ARTICLE VII

The Ratification of the Conventions of nine States, shall be sufficient for the Establishment of this Constitution between the States so ratifying the Same.

DONE in Convention by the Unanimous Consent of the States present the Seventeenth Day of September in the Year of our Lord one thousand seven hundred and Eighty seven, and of the Independence of the United States of America the Twelfth.

ARTICLES IN ADDITION TO, AND AMENDMENT OF, THE CONSTITUTION OF
THE UNITED STATES OF AMERICA, PROPOSED BY CONGRESS, AND RATIFIED
BY THE LEGISLATURES OF THE SEVERAL STATES PURSUANT TO THE FIFTH
ARTICLE OF THE ORIGINAL CONSTITUTION.

ARTICLE I

(The first ten Articles declared in force December 15, 1791)

Congress shall make no law respecting an establishment of religion, or
prohibiting the free exercise thereof; or abridging the freedom of speech,
or of the press; or the right of the people peaceably to assemble, and to
petition the Government for a redress of grievances.

ARTICLE II

A well regulated Militia, being necessary to the security of a free State,
the right of the people to keep and bear Arms, shall not be infringed.

ARTICLE III

No Soldier shall, in time of peace, be quartered in any house, without
the consent of the Owner, nor in time of war, but in a manner to be prescribed by law.

ARTICLE IV

The right of the people to be secure in their persons, houses, papers,
and effects, against unreasonable searches and seizures, shall not be violated, and no Warrants shall issue, but upon probable cause, supported by
Oath or affirmation, and particularly describing the place to be searched,
and the persons or things to be seized.

ARTICLE V

No person shall be held to answer for a capital, or otherwise infamous
crime, unless on a presentment or indictment of a Grand Jury, except in
cases arising in the land or naval forces, or in the Militia, when in actual
service in time of War or public danger; nor shall any person be subject for
the same offence to be twice put in jeopardy of life or limb; nor shall be
compelled in any Criminal Case to be a witness against himself, nor be
deprived of life, liberty, or property, without due process of law; nor shall
private property be taken for public use, without just compensation.

ARTICLE VI

In all criminal prosecutions, the accused shall enjoy the right to a speedy
and public trial, by an impartial jury of the State and district wherein the
crime shall have been committed, which district shall have been previously
ascertained by law, and to be informed of the nature and cause of the ac-

cusation; to be confronted with the witnesses against him; to have compulsory process for obtaining Witnesses in his favor, and to have the Assistance of Counsel for his defence.

ARTICLE VII

In suits at common law, where the value in controversy shall exceed twenty dollars, the right of trial by jury shall be preserved, and no fact tried by a jury shall be otherwise re-examined in any Court of the United States, than according to the rules of the common law.

ARTICLE VIII

Excessive bail shall not be required, nor excessive fines imposed, nor cruel and unusual punishments inflicted.

ARTICLE IX

The enumeration in the Constitution, of certain rights, shall not be construed to deny or disparage others retained by the people.

ARTICLE X

The powers not delegated to the United States by the Constitution, nor prohibited by it to the States, are reserved to the States respectively, or to the people.

ARTICLE XI

(January 8, 1798)

The Judicial power of the United States shall not be construed to extend to any suit in law or equity, commenced or prosecuted against one of the United States by Citizens of another State, or by Citizens or Subjects of any Foreign State.

ARTICLE XII

(September 25, 1804)

The Electors shall meet in their respective states, and vote by ballot for President and Vice-President, one of whom, at least, shall not be an inhabitant of the same state with themselves; they shall name in their ballots the person voted for as President, and in distinct ballots the person voted for as Vice-President, and they shall make distinct lists of all persons voted for as President, and of all persons voted for as Vice-President, and of the number of votes for each, which lists they shall sign and certify, and transmit sealed to the seat of the Government of the United States, directed to the President of the Senate; — The President of the Senate shall, in the presence of the Senate and House of Representatives, open all the certificates and the votes shall then be counted; — The person having the greatest number of votes for President, shall be the President, if such number be a majority of the whole number of Electors appointed; and if no person have such majority, then from the persons having the highest numbers not exceeding three on the list of those voted for as President, the House of Representatives shall choose immediately, by ballot, the President. But in choosing the President, the votes shall be taken by states, the representation from each state having one vote; a quorum for this purpose shall consist of a member or members from two-thirds of the states, and a majority of all the states shall be necessary to a choice. And if the House of Representatives shall not choose a President whenever the right of choice shall devolve upon them, before the fourth day of March next following, then the Vice-President shall act as President, as in the case of the death or other constitutional disability of the President. The person having the greatest number of votes as Vice-President, shall be the Vice-President, if such number be a majority of the whole number of Electors appointed, and if no person have a majority, then from the two highest numbers on the list, the Senate shall choose the Vice-President; a quorum for the purpose shall consist of two-thirds of the whole number of Senators, and a majority of whole number shall be necessary to a choice. But no person constitutionally ineligible to the office of President shall be eligible to that of Vice-President of the United States.

ARTICLE XIII

(December 18, 1865)

Section 1. Neither slavery nor involuntary servitude, except as a punishment for crime whereof the party shall have been duly convicted, shall exist within the United States, or any place subject to their jurisdiction.

Section 2. Congress shall have power to enforce this article by appropriate legislation.

ARTICLE XIV

(July 23, 1868)

Section 1. All persons born or naturalized in the United States, and subject to the jurisdiction thereof, are citizens of the United States and of the State wherein they reside. No State shall make or enforce any law which shall abridge the privileges or immunities of citizens of the United States; nor shall any State deprive any person of life, liberty, or property, without due process of law; nor deny to any person within its jurisdiction the equal protection of the laws.

Section 2. Representatives shall be apportioned among the several States according to their respective numbers, counting the whole number of persons in each State, excluding Indians not taxed. But when the right to vote at any election for the choice of electors for President and Vice President of the United States, Representatives in Congress, the Executive and Judicial officers of a State, or the members of the Legislature thereof, is denied to any of the male inhabitants of such State, being twenty-one years of age, and citizens of the United States, or in any way abridged, except for participation in rebellion, or other crime, the basis of representation therein shall be reduced in the proportion which the number of such male citizens shall bear to the whole number of male citizens twenty-one years of age in such State.

Section 3. No person shall be a Senator or Representative in Congress, or elector of President and Vice President, or hold any office, civil, or military, under the United States, or under any State, who, having previously taken an oath, as a member of Congress, or as an officer of the United States, or as a member of any State legislature, or as an executive or judicial officer of any State, to support the Constitution of the United States, shall have engaged in insurrection or rebellion against the same, or given aid or comfort to the enemies thereof. But Congress may by a vote of two-thirds of each House, remove such disability.

Section 4. The validity of the public debt of the United States, authorized by law, including debts incurred for payment of pensions and bounties for services in suppressing insurrection or rebellion, shall not be questioned. But neither the United States nor any State shall assume or pay any debt or obligation incurred in aid of insurrection or rebellion against the United States, or any claim for the loss or emancipation of any slave; but all such debts, obligations and claims shall be held illegal and void.

Section 5. The Congress shall have power to enforce, by appropriate legislation, the provisions of this article.

ARTICLE XV

(March 30, 1870)

Section 1. The right of citizens of the United States to vote shall not be denied or abridged by the United States or by any State on account of race, color, or previous condition of servitude.

Section 2. The Congress shall have power to enforce this article by appropriate legislation.

ARTICLE XVI

(February 25, 1913)

The Congress shall have power to lay and collect taxes on incomes, from whatever source derived, without apportionment among the several States, and without regard to any census or enumeration.

ARTICLE XVII

(May 31, 1913)

The Senate of the United States shall be composed of two senators from each State, elected by the people thereof, for six years; and each Senator shall have one vote. The electors in each State shall have the qualifications requisite for electors of the most numerous branch of the State legislature.

When vacancies happen in the representation of any State in the Senate, the executive authority of such State shall issue writs of election to fill such vacancies: *Provided*, That the legislature of any State may empower the executive thereof to make temporary appointments until the people fill the vacancies by election as the legislature may direct.

This amendment shall not be so construed as to affect the election or term of any senator chosen before it becomes valid as part of the Constitution.

ARTICLE XVIII

(*January 16, 1920*)

After one year from the ratification of this article, the manufacture, sale, or transportation of intoxicating liquors within, the importation thereof into, or the exportation thereof from the United States and all territory subject to the jurisdiction thereof for beverage purposes is hereby prohibited.

The Congress and the several States shall have concurrent power to enforce this article by appropriate legislation.

This article shall be inoperative unless it shall have been ratified as an amendment to the Constitution by the legislatures of the several States, as provided in the Constitution, within seven years from the date of the submission hereof to the States by Congress.

ARTICLE XIX

(*August 26, 1920*)

The right of citizens of the United States to vote shall not be denied or abridged by the United States or by any States on account of sex.

The Congress shall have power by appropriate legislation to enforce the provisions of this article.

ARTICLE XX

(*February 6, 1933*)

Section 1. The terms of the President and Vice-President shall end at noon on the twentieth day of January, and the terms of Senators and Representatives at noon on the third day of January, of the years in which such terms would have ended if this article had not been ratified; and the terms of their successors shall then begin.

Section 2. The Congress shall assemble at least once in every year, and such meeting shall begin at noon on the third day of January, unless they shall by law appoint a different day.

Section 3. If, at the time fixed for the beginning of the term of the President, the President-elect shall have died, the Vice-President-elect shall become President. If a President shall not have been chosen before the time fixed for the beginning of his term, or if the President-elect shall have failed to qualify, then the Vice-President-elect shall act as President until a President shall have qualified; and the Congress may by law provide for the case wherein neither a President-elect nor a Vice-President-elect shall have qualified, declaring who shall then act as President, or the manner in which one who is to act shall be selected, and such person shall act accordingly until a President or Vice-President shall have qualified.

Section 4. The Congress may by law provide for the case of the death of any of the persons from whom the House of Representatives may choose a President whenever the right of choice shall have devolved upon them, and for the case of the death of any of the persons from whom the Senate may choose a Vice-President whenever the right of choice shall have devolved upon them.

Section 5. Sections 1 and 2 shall take effect on the 15th day of October following the ratification of this article.

Section 6. This article shall be inoperative unless it shall have been ratified as an amendment to the Constitution by the legislatures of three-fourths of the several States within seven years from the date of its submission.

ARTICLE XXI

(*Pending*)

Section 1. The eighteenth article of amendment to the Constitution of the United States is hereby repealed.

Section 2. The transportation or importation into any State, Territory or possession of the United States for delivery or use therein of intoxicating liquors, in violation of the laws thereof, is hereby prohibited.

Section 3. This article shall be inoperative unless it shall have been ratified as an amendment to the Constitution by convention in the several States, as provided in the Constitution, within seven years from the date of the submission hereof to the States by the Congress.

ARTICLE XXII

(*Pending*)

Section 1. The Congress shall have power to limit, regulate, and prohibit the labor of persons under eighteen years of age.

Section 2. The power of the several States is unimpaired by this article except that the operation of State laws shall be suspended to the extent necessary to give effect to legislation enacted by the Congress.

LIST OF BOOKS CITED

Abbott, Edith, *Women in Industry*. New York, 1910.
Adamic, Louis, *Dynamite: The Story of Class Violence in America*. New York, 1931.
Adams, C. F., Jr., *Charles Francis Adams (American Statesmen, XXIX)*.
Adams, E. D., *Great Britain and the American Civil War*. 2 v. New York, 1925.
Adams, W. F., *Ireland and Irish Emigration to the New World (Yale Historical Publications. Miscellany, XXIII)*. New Haven, 1932.
Allen, Devere, *The Fight for Peace*. New York, 1930.
Allen, F. L., *Only Yesterday*. New York, 1931.
Allen, W. H., *Rockefeller*. New York, 1930.
American Crisis Biographies. See Oberholtzer, E. P., ed.
American Nation, The. See Hart, A. B., ed.
American Political Leaders. See Nevins, Allan, ed.
American Statesmen. See Morse, J. T., Jr., ed.
——, 2d ser. 7 v. Boston, 1905–1916.
Anon., *Arbitration and the United States* (World Peace Foundation, *Pamphlets*, IX, nos. 6–7). Boston, 1926.
Arias, Harmodio, *The Panama Canal*. London, 1911.
Armes, Ethel M., *The Story of Coal and Iron in Alabama*. Birmingham, 1910.
Asbury, Herbert, *The Gangs of New York*. New York, 1928.
Auchampaugh, P. G., *James Buchanan and His Cabinet on the Eve of Secession*. Lancaster, Penn., 1926.
Ayres, L. P., *The War with Germany*. Washington, 1919.
Baker, R. S., *Woodrow Wilson*. 4 v. Garden City, 1927–1931.
——, *Woodrow Wilson and World Settlement*. 3 v. Garden City, 1922.
Balch, Emily G., *Our Slavic Fellow Citizens*. New York, 1910.
Bancroft, Frederic, *The Life of William H. Seward*. 2 v. New York, 1900.
——, *Slave-Trading in the Old South*. Baltimore, 1931.
Barber, H. L., *The Story of the Automobile*. Chicago, 1927.
Barclay, T. S., *The Liberal Republican Movement in Missouri, 1865–1871*. Columbia, Mo., 1926.
Barnes, H. E., *The New History and the Social Studies*. New York, 1925.
Barnes, J. A., *John G. Carlisle (American Political Leaders)*.
Barrett, D. C., *The Greenbacks and Resumption of Specie Payments, 1862–1879 (Harvard Economic Studies, XXXVI)*. Cambridge, 1931.
Bartlett, R. J., *John C. Frémont and the Republican Party* (Ohio State University, *Contributions in History and Political Science*, no. 13). Columbus, 1930.

Barton, W. E., *The Life of Abraham Lincoln.* 2 v. Indianapolis, 1925.
——, *The Life of Clara Barton.* 2 v. Boston, 1922.
Baruch, B. M., *The Making of the Reparation and Economic Sections of the Treaty.* New York, 1920.
Bassett, J. S., *Our War with Germany.* New York, 1919.
Bates, E. S., and Dittemore, J. V., *Mary Baker Eddy.* New York, 1932.
Bau, M. J., *The Open Door Doctrine in Relation to China.* New York, 1923.
Baxter, J. P., 3d, *The Introduction of the Ironclad Warship.* Cambridge, Mass., 1933.
Beacon Biographies, The. See Howe, M. A. DeW., ed.
Beale, H. K., *The Critical Year.* New York, 1930.
Beales, A. C. F., *The History of Peace.* New York, 1931.
Beamish, R. J., and March, F. A., *America's Part in the World War.* Philadelphia, 1919.
Beard, Mary R., *A Short History of the American Labor Movement.* New York, 1920.
Beardsley, F. G., *A History of American Revivals.* New York, 1912.
Bemis, S. F., ed., *The American Secretaries of State and Their Diplomacy.* 10 v. New York, 1927–1929.
Bennett, I. E., *History of the Panama Canal.* Washington, 1915.
Benton, E. J., *International Law and Diplomacy of the Spanish-American War.* Baltimore, 1908.
——, *The Movement for Peace without Victory during the Civil War* (Western Reserve Historical Society, *Collections,* no. 99). Cleveland, 1918.
Berglund, Abraham, *The United States Steel Corporation* (Columbia University, *Studies,* XXVII, no. 2). New York, 1907.
Berle, A. A., Jr., and Means, G. C., *The Modern Corporation and Private Property.* New York, 1933.
Berman, Edward, *Labor Disputes and the President of the United States* (Columbia University, *Studies,* CXI, no. 2). New York, 1924.
Beveridge, A. J., *Abraham Lincoln.* 2 v. Boston, 1928.
Bidwell, P. W., and Falconer, J. I., *History of Agriculture in the Northern United States, 1620–1860* (Carnegie Institution, *Contributions to American Economic History*). Washington, 1925.
Bigelow, John, *The Life of Samuel J. Tilden.* 2 v. New York, 1895.
Bing, Alexander, *War-Time Strikes and Their Adjustment.* New York, 1921.
Bishop, J. B., *Theodore Roosevelt and His Time.* 2 v. New York, 1920.
Black, J. D., *Agricultural Reform in the United States.* New York, 1929.
Blackwell, Alice Stone, *Lucy Stone.* Boston, 1930.
Blegen, T. C., *Norwegian Migration to America, 1825–1860.* Northfield, Minn., 1931.
Bleyer, W. G., *Main Currents in the History of American Journalism.* Boston, 1927.
Bogart, E. L., *An Economic History of the American People.* New York, 1930.
——, *War Costs and Their Financing.* New York, 1921.
Bonham, M. L., Jr., *The British Consuls in the Confederacy* (Columbia University, *Studies,* XLIII, no. 3). New York, 1911.

Bowers, C. G., *Beveridge and the Progressive Era.* Boston, 1932.
——, *The Tragic Era.* Boston, 1929.
Bradlee, F. B. C., *Blockade Running during the Civil War and the Effect of Land and Water Transportation on the Confederacy.* Salem, Mass., 1925.
Branch, E. D., *The Cowboy and His Interpreters.* New York, 1926.
——, *The Hunting of the Buffalo.* New York, 1929.
Brandeis, L. D., *Other People's Money.* New York, 1914.
Brawley, B. G., *A Social History of the American Negro.* New York, 1921.
Brissenden, P. F., *The I. W. W.: A Study of American Syndicalism* (Columbia University, *Studies*, LXXXIII). New York, 1919.
Brockett, L. P., and Vaughan, Mary C., *Woman's Work in the Civil War.* Philadelphia, 1867.
Brooks, R. P., *The Agrarian Revolution in Georgia, 1865–1912* (University of Wisconsin, *Bulletin*, no. 639). Madison, 1914.
Browne, W. R., *Altgeld of Illinois.* New York, 1924.
Bruce, H. A., *Woman in the Making of America.* Rev. edn., Boston, 1928.
Bruce, P. A., *The Rise of the New South* (*The History of North America*, XVII).
Bruère, Martha B., *Does Prohibition Work?* New York, 1927.
Bryce, James, *The American Commonwealth.* 3 v. London, 1888.
Buck, S. J., *The Agrarian Crusade* (*The Chronicles of America Series*, XLV).
——, *The Granger Movement* (*Harvard Historical Studies*, XIX). Cambridge, 1913.
Buell, R. L., *Japanese Immigration* (World Peace Foundation, *Pamphlets*, VII, nos. 5–6). Boston, 1924.
——, *The Washington Conference.* New York, 1922.
Burgess, Thomas, *Greeks in America.* Boston, 1913.
Burr, Anna R., *The Portrait of a Banker: James Stillman.* New York, 1927.
Burton, T. E., *Financial Crises and Periods of Industrial and Commercial Depression.* New York, 1902.
——, *John Sherman.* Boston, 1906.
Byrn, E. W., *The Progress of Invention in the Nineteenth Century.* New York, 1900.
Cahill, M. C., *Shorter Hours: A Study of the Movement since the Civil War.* New York, 1932.
Calhoun, A. W., *A Social History of the American Family.* 3 v. Cleveland, 1917–1919.
Callahan, J. M., *American Foreign Policy in Mexican Relations.* New York, 1932.
——, *Cuba and International Relations* (Johns Hopkins University, *Studies*, extra vol. XXI). Baltimore, 1899.
——, *The Diplomatic History of the Southern Confederacy.* Baltimore, 1901.
Callcott, W. H., *Liberalism in Mexico, 1857–1929.* Stanford University, 1931.
Capper, Arthur, *The Agricultural Bloc.* New York, 1922.
Carlton, F. T., *The History and Problems of Organized Labor.* Boston, 1920.

Carpenter, J. T., *The South as a Conscious Minority, 1789–1861.* New York, 1930.

Cary, Edward, *George William Curtis* (C. D. Warner, ed., *American Men of Letters*). Boston, 1894.

Casson, H. N., *The History of the Telephone.* Chicago, 1910.

Chadwick, F. E., *The Relations of the United States and Spain.* 3 v. New York, 1909–1911.

Chafee, Zechariah, Jr., *Freedom of Speech.* New York, 1920.

Chamberlain, John, *Farewell to Reform.* New York, 1932.

Chambrun, Colonel de, and Marenches, Captain de, *The American Army in the European Conflict.* New York, 1919.

Chandler, J. A. C., and others, *The South in the Building of the Nation.* 12 v. Richmond, 1909–1910.

Channing, Edward, *A History of the United States.* 6 v. New York, 1905–1925.

Chapman, C. E., *A History of the Cuban Republic.* New York, 1927.

Charnwood, Lord, *Abraham Lincoln* (Basil Williams, ed., *Makers of the Nineteenth Century*). London, 1917.

Cherrington, E. H., *The Evolution of Prohibition in the United States of America.* Westerville, Ohio, 1920.

Chronicles of America Series, The. See Johnson, Allen, ed.

Clark, A. H., *The Clipper Ship Era, 1843–1869.* New York, 1910.

Clark, H. W., *History of Alaska.* New York, 1930.

Clark, J. M., *The Costs of the World War to the American People* (J. T. Shotwell, ed., *Economic and Social History of the World War*). New Haven, 1931.

Clark, V. S., *History of Manufactures in the United States* (Carnegie Institution, *Contributions to American Economic History*). 3 v. Rev. edn., New York, 1929.

——, and others, *Porto Rico and Its Problems.* Washington, 1930.

Clarkson, G. B., *Industrial America in the World War.* Boston, 1923.

Clemen, R. A., *The American Livestock and Meat Industry.* New York, 1923.

Cole, A. C., *The Irrepressible Conflict, 1850–1865* (*A History of American Life,* VII).

——, *The Whig Party in the South.* Washington, 1913.

Cole, A. H., *The American Wool Manufacture.* 2 v. Cambridge, Mass., 1926.

Colvin, D. L., *Prohibition in the United States.* New York, 1926.

Committee on Recent Economic Changes, *Recent Economic Changes in the United States.* 2 v. New York, 1929.

Commons, J. R., and Andrews, J. B., *Principles of Labor Legislation.* New York, 1920.

——, and others, *History of Labour in the United States.* 2 v. New York, 1918.

Coolidge, A. C., *The United States as a World Power.* New York, 1908.

Coolidge, L. A., *Ulysses S. Grant.* Boston, 1917.

Coolidge, Mary R., *Chinese Immigration.* New York, 1909.

Copeland, M. T., *The Cotton Manufacturing Industry of the United States* (*Harvard Economic Studies*, VIII). Cambridge, 1912.

Coulter, E. M., *The Civil War and Readjustment in Kentucky*. Chapel Hill, 1926.

Cox, I. J., *Nicaragua and the United States, 1909–1927* (World Peace Foundation, *Pamphlets*, X, no. 7). Boston, 1927.

Crandall, A. W., *The Early History of the Republican Party, 1854–1856*. Boston, 1930.

Craven, A. O., *Edmund Ruffin, Southerner*. New York, 1932.

Crawford, Mary C., *The Romance of the American Theatre*. Rev. edn., Boston, 1925.

Creel, George, *How We Advertised America*. New York, 1920.

Croly, Herbert, *Marcus Alonzo Hanna*. New York, 1912.

Croly, Jane C., *The History of the Woman's Club Movement in America*. New York, 1898.

Crowell, Benedict, and Willson, R. F., *How America Went to War*. 6 v. New Haven, 1921.

Cubberley, E. P., *Public Education in the United States*. Boston, 1919.

Curti, M. E., *Bryan and World Peace* (Smith College, *Studies*, XVI, nos. 3–4). Northampton, 1931.

Curtis, E. N., *The French Assembly of 1848 and American Constitutional Doctrines* (Columbia University, *Studies*, LXXIX, no. 2). New York, 1918.

Curtis, G. T., *Life of James Buchanan*. 2 v. New York, 1883.

Cutler, J. E., *Lynch-Law*. New York, 1905.

Daggett, Stuart, *Railroad Reorganization* (*Harvard Economic Studies*, IV). Cambridge, 1908.

Dale, E. E., *The Range Cattle Industry*. Norman, Okla., 1930.

Davis, Elmer, *History of the New York Times*. New York, 1921.

Davison, H. P., *The American Red Cross in the Great War*. New York, 1919.

Dealey, J. Q., *Growth of American State Constitutions*. Boston, 1915.

De Forest, R. W., and Veiller, Lawrence, *The Tenement House Problem*. 2 v. New York, 1903.

Dennett, Tyler, *Americans in Eastern Asia*. New York, 1922.

——, *Theodore Roosevelt and the Russo-Japanese War*. Garden City, 1925.

De Voto, Bernard, *Mark Twain's America*. Boston, 1932.

Dewey, D. R., *Financial History of the United States* (A. B. Hart, ed., *American Citizen Series*). Rev. edn., New York, 1931.

——, *National Problems* (*The American Nation*, XXIV).

DeWitt, B. P., *The Progressive Movement*. New York, 1915.

Dewitt, D. M., *The Impeachment and Trial of Andrew Johnson*. New York, 1903.

Dexter, E. G., *A History of Education in the United States*. New York, 1904.

Dixon, F. H., *Railroads and Government*. New York, 1922.

Dodd, E. W., *Jefferson Davis* (*American Crisis Biographies*).

——, *Woodrow Wilson and His Work*. Rev. edn., Garden City, 1932.

Dodge, T. A., *A Bird's-Eye View of Our Civil War*. Rev. edn., Boston, 1897.

Du Bois, J. T., and Mathews, Gertrude S., *Galusha A. Grow, the Father of the Homestead Law*. Boston, 1917.

Duffy, H. S., *William Howard Taft*. New York, 1930.

Dumond, D. L., *The Secession Movement, 1860–1861*. New York, 1931.

Dunbar, C. F., *Economic Essays* (O. M. W. Sprague, ed.). New York, 1904.

Dunn, F. S., *The Diplomatic Protection of Americans in Mexico*. New York, 1933.

Dunn, R. W., *American Foreign Investments*. New York, 1926.

Dunning, W. A., *Essays on the Civil War and Reconstruction*. Rev. edn., New York, 1904.

——, *Reconstruction, Political and Economic* (*The American Nation*, XXII).

Dyer, F. L., and Martin, T. C., *Edison*. 2 v. Rev. edn., New York, 1929.

Eggleston, G. C., *The History of the Confederate War*. 2 v. New York, 1910.

Epstein, R. C., *The Automobile Industry*. Chicago, 1928.

Ettinger, A. S., *The Mission to Spain of Pierre Soulé, 1853–1855* (*Yale Historical Publications. Miscellany*, XXII). New Haven, 1932.

Evans, M. S., *Black and White in the Southern States*. New York, 1915.

Fairchild, H. P., *Immigration*. Rev. edn., New York, 1928.

Fairlie, J. A., *Municipal Administration*. New York, 1901.

Faris, J. C., *The Rise of Internationalism*. New York, 1915.

Faulkner, H. U., *American Economic History* (G. S. Ford, ed., *Harper's Historical Series*). Rev. edn., New York, 1931.

——, *The Quest for Social Justice* (*A History of American Life*, XI).

Faust, A. B., *The German Element in the United States*. 2 v. Boston, 1909.

Feldman, Herman, *Prohibition, Its Economic and Industrial Aspects*. New York, 1927.

Fine, Nathan, *Labor and Farmer Parties in the United States, 1828–1928*. New York, 1928.

Fish, C. R., *American Diplomacy* (C. H. Haskins, ed., *American Historical Series*). Rev. edn., New York, 1919.

——, *The Civil Service and the Patronage* (*Harvard Historical Studies*, XI). Cambridge, 1905.

Fite, E. D., *The Presidential Campaign of 1860*. New York, 1911.

——, *Social and Industrial Conditions in the North during the Civil War*. New York, 1910.

Flack, H. E., *The Adoption of the Fourteenth Amendment*. Baltimore, 1908.

——, *Spanish-American Diplomatic Relations Preceding the War of 1898* (Johns Hopkins University, *Studies*, XXIV, nos. 1–2). Baltimore, 1906.

Fleming, D. F., *The United States and the League of Nations*. New York, 1932.

Fleming, W. L., *The Sequel of Appomattox* (*The Chronicles of America Series*, XXXII).

Flippin, P. S., *Herschel V. Johnson of Georgia*. Richmond, 1931.

Foerster, R. F., *The Italian Emigration of Our Times* (*Harvard Economic Studies*, XX). Cambridge, 1919.

Follett, Mary P., *The Speaker of the House of Representatives*. New York, 1896.

Forbes, W. C., *The Philippine Islands*. 2 v. Boston, 1928.

Forrester, R. B., *Report on Large Scale Coöperative Marketing in the United States*. London, 1925.

Fossum, P. R., *The Agrarian Movement in North Dakota* (Johns Hopkins University, *Studies*, XLIII, no. 1). Baltimore, 1925.

Foster, J. W., *American Diplomacy in the Orient*. Boston, 1903.

Fox, D. R. See Schlesinger, A. M., and Fox, D. R., eds.

Frankfurter, Felix, *The Case of Sacco and Vanzetti*. Boston, 1927.

——, and Greene, Nathan, *The Labor Injunction*. New York, 1930.

Frederick, J. H., *The Development of American Commerce*. New York, 1932.

Frothingham, T. G., *The American Reinforcement in the World War*. Garden City, 1927.

Fuess, C. M., *Carl Schurz* (*American Political Leaders*).

Gabriel, R. H., ed., *The Pageant of America*. 15 v. New Haven, 1925–1929.

Gamio, Manuel, *Mexican Immigration to the United States*. Chicago, 1930.

Garber, P. N., *The Gadsden Treaty*. Philadelphia, 1923.

Garis, R. L., *Immigration Restriction*. New York, 1927.

Garrison, W. E., *The March of Faith*. New York, 1933.

Gay, E. F., "The Great Depression," *Foreign Affairs*, X (1931–1932), 529–540.

Gazley, J. G., *American Opinion of German Unification, 1848–1871* (Columbia University, *Studies*, CXXI). New York, 1926.

Geneva Research Information Committee, *American Coöperation with the League of Nations, 1919–1931* (*Geneva Special Studies*, II, no. 7). Geneva, 1931.

George, Henry, Jr., *The Life of Henry George*. New York, 1900.

Gittinger, Roy, *The Formation of the State of Oklahoma* (University of California, *Publications*, VI). Berkeley, 1917.

Glasson, W. H., *Federal Military Pensions in the United States* (David Kinley, ed.). New York, 1918.

Grattan, C. H., *Why We Fought*. New York, 1929.

Graves, W. S., *America's Siberian Adventure, 1918–1920*. New York, 1931.

Gray, L. C., *History of Agriculture in the Southern United States to 1860* (Carnegie Institution, *Contributions to American Economic History*). Washington, 1933.

Groat, G. G., *Attitude of American Courts in Labor Cases* (Columbia University, *Studies*, XLII). New York, 1911.

Gruening, E. H., *Mexico and Its Heritage*. New York, 1928.

Hackett, C. W., *The Mexican Revolution and the United States* (World Peace Foundation, *Pamphlets*, IX, no. 5). Boston, 1926.

Hamilton, J. G. de R., *Reconstruction in North Carolina* (Columbia University, *Studies*, LVIII). New York, 1914.

Hamilton, P. J., *The Reconstruction Period* (*The History of North America*, XVI).

Hamlin, T. F., *The American Spirit in Architecture* (*The Pageant of America*, XIII).

Hammond, M. B., *The Cotton Industry* (American Economic Association, *Publications*, n.s., no. 1). New York, 1897.

Haney, L. H., *A Congressional History of Railways in the United States, 1850–1887* (University of Wisconsin, *Bulletin*, no. 342). Madison, 1910.

Harbord, J. G., *America in the World War*. Boston, 1933.

Haring, C. H., *South America Looks at the United States*. New York, 1928.

Harper, Ida H., *The Life and Work of Susan B. Anthony*. 3 v. Indianapolis, 1898–1908.

Harris, T. L., *The Trent Affair*. Indianapolis, 1896.

Hart, A. B., ed., *The American Nation: A History*. 28 v. New York, 1904–1918.

——, *Salmon Portland Chase* (*American Statesmen*).

Hartmann, Sadakichi, *A History of American Art*. 2 v. Rev. edn., Boston, 1932.

Harvey, George, *Henry Clay Frick*. New York, 1928.

Haworth, P. L., *The Hayes-Tilden Disputed Presidential Election of 1876*. Cleveland, 1906.

Haynes, F. E., *Social Politics in the United States*. Boston, 1924.

——, *Third Party Movements since the Civil War*. Iowa City, 1916.

Haynes, G. H., *Charles Sumner* (*American Crisis Biographies*).

Hays, A. G., *Let Freedom Ring*. New York, 1928.

Heathcote, C. W., *The Lutheran Church and the Civil War*. New York, 1919.

Hedges, J. B., *Henry Villard and the Railways of the Northwest*. New York, 1930.

Henderson, C. R., ed., *Correction and Prevention*. 4 v. New York, 1910.

Henderson, G. C., *The Federal Trade Commission*. New Haven, 1924.

Henderson, G. F. R., *Stonewall Jackson and the American Civil War*. 2 v. New York, 1898.

Henderson, J. B., *American Diplomatic Questions*. New York, 1901.

Hendrick, B. J., *The Age of Big Business* (*The Chronicles of America Series*, XXXIX).

——, *The Life and Letters of Walter H. Page*. 3 v. Garden City, 1922–1925.

——, *The Life of Andrew Carnegie*. 2 v. Garden City, 1932.

Hepburn, A. B., *A History of Currency in the United States*. New York, 1915.

Hibbard, B. H., *A History of the Public Land Policies* (R. T. Ely, ed., *Land Economics Series*). New York, 1924.

Hibben, Paxton, *Henry Ward Beecher*. New York, 1927.

Hicks, J. D., *The Populist Revolt*. Minneapolis, 1931.

Hill, H. C., *Roosevelt and the Caribbean*. Chicago, 1927.

Hillquit, Morris, *History of Socialism in the United States*. Rev. edn., New York, 1910.

Hines, W. D., *War History of American Railroads* (J. T. Shotwell, ed., *Economic and Social History of the World War*). New Haven, 1928.

History of American Life, A. See Schlesinger, A. M., and Fox, D. R., eds.

History of North America, The. See Lee, G. C., and Thorpe, F. N., eds.

Hodder, F. H., "Genesis of the Kansas-Nebraska Act," Wisconsin Historical Society, *Proceedings for 1912*, 69–86.

Holst, Hermann von, *The Constitutional and Political History of the United States* (J. L. Lalor, A. B. Mason and Paul Shorey, trs.). 8 v. Chicago, 1876–1892.

Hornbeck, S. K., *Contemporary Politics in the Far East*. New York, 1916.

Hornblow, Arthur, *A History of the Theatre in America*. 2 v. Philadelphia, 1919.

Hosmer, J. K., *The Appeal to Arms* (*The American Nation*, XX).

——, *Outcome of the Civil War* (*The American Nation*, XXI).

House, E. M., and Seymour, Charles, eds., *What Really Happened at Paris*. New York, 1921.

Hovey, Carl, *The Life Story of J. Pierpont Morgan*. New York, 1911.

Howard, J. T., *Our American Music: Three Hundred Years of It*. New York, 1931.

Howe, M. A. DeW., ed., *The Beacon Biographies*. 31 v. Boston, 1899–1910.

Huidekoper, F. L., *The Military Unpreparedness of the United States*. New York, 1915.

Husband, Joseph, *The Story of the Pullman Car*. Chicago, 1917.

Hutchinson, W. T., *Cyrus Hall McCormick, Seed-Time, 1809–1856*. New York, 1930.

Ichihashi, Yamato, *Japanese in the United States*. Stanford University, 1932.

——, *The Washington Conference and After*. Stanford University, 1928.

Ingle, Edward, *Southern Sidelights* (R. T. Ely, ed., *Library of Economics and Politics*). New York, 1896.

Irwin, Inez H., *Angels and Amazons*. New York, 1933.

Irwin, Will, *How Red Is America?* New York, 1927.

Isham, Samuel, *The History of American Painting* (J. C. Van Dyke, ed., *The History of American Art*, III). Rev. edn., New York, 1927.

James, Henry, *Richard Olney and His Public Service*. Boston, 1923.

Jenks, J. W., and Lauck, W. J., *The Immigration Problem*. 6th edn., New York, 1926.

Jenks, L. H., *Our Cuban Colony*. New York, 1928.

Jessup, P. C., *The United States and the World Court* (World Peace Foundation, *Pamphlets*, XII, no. 4). Boston, 1929.

Johnson, Allen, ed., *The Chronicles of America Series*. 50 v. New Haven, 1918–1921.

——, *Stephen A. Douglas*. New York, 1908.

——, and Malone, Dumas, eds., *Dictionary of American Biography*. 20 v. New York, 1928, in progress.

Johnson, E. R., and others, *History of the Domestic and Foreign Commerce of the United States* (Carnegie Institution, *Contributions to American Economic History*). 2 v. Washington, 1915.

Johnson, T. M., *Without Censor*. Indianapolis, 1928.

Jones, Eliot, *The Anthracite Coal Combination in the United States* (*Harvard Economic Studies*, XI). Cambridge, 1914.

——, *Principles of Railway Transportation*. New York, 1924.

Jones, J. P., and Hollister, P. M., *The German Secret Service in America*. Boston, 1918.

Jordan, Donaldson, and Pratt, E. J., *Europe and the American Civil War*. Boston, 1931.

Jordan, D. S., ed., *Leading American Men of Science* (W. P. Trent, ed., *Biographies of Leading Americans*). New York, 1910.

Joseph, Samuel, *Jewish Immigration to the United States* (Columbia University, *Studies*, LIX, no. 4). New York, 1914.

Kaempffert, Waldemar, ed., *A Popular History of American Invention*. 2 v. New York, 1924.

Kandel, I. L., ed., *Twenty-Five Years of American Education*. New York, 1924.

Keim, Jeannette, *Forty Years of German-American Political Relations*. Philadelphia, 1919.

Kendrick, B. B., *The Journal of the Joint Committee of Fifteen on Reconstruction* (Columbia University, *Studies*, LXII). New York, 1914.

Kennan, George, *E. H. Harriman*. 2 v. Boston, 1922.

Kirkland, E. C., *A History of American Economic Life*. New York, 1932.

——, *The Peacemakers of 1864*. New York, 1927.

Knauth, O. W., *The Policy of the United States toward Industrial Monopoly* (Columbia University, *Studies*, LVI, no. 2). New York, 1914.

Knight, E. W., *The Influence of Reconstruction on Education in the South* (Teachers College, *Contributions to Education*, no. 60). New York, 1913.

——, *Public Education in the South*. Boston, 1922.

Knight, M. M., *The Americans in Santo Domingo*. New York, 1928.

Kolbe, P. R., *The Colleges in War Time and After*. New York, 1919.

Krout, J. A., *Annals of American Sport* (*The Pageant of America*, XIV).

Kuhlmann, C. B., *The Development of the Flour-Milling Industry in the United States*. Boston, 1929.

Kuykendall, R. S., *A History of Hawaii*. New York, 1926.

Laidler, H. W., *Concentration of Control in American Industry*. New York, 1931.

Latané, J. H., *America as a World Power* (*The American Nation*, XXV).

——, *A History of American Foreign Policy*. Garden City, 1927.

——, *The United States and Latin America*. Garden City, 1920.

Lauck, W. J., *The Causes of the Panic of 1893*. Boston, 1907.

Laughlin, J. L., *The History of Bimetallism in the United States*. New York, 1910.

Lee, G. C., and Thorpe, F. N., eds., *The History of North America*. 20 v. Philadelphia, 1903–1907.

LeRoy, J. A., *The Americans in the Philippines*. 2 v. Boston, 1914.

Lester, J. C., and Wilson, D. L., *Ku Klux Klan: Its Origin, Growth and Disbandment* (W. L. Fleming, ed.). New York, 1905.

Lewinson, Paul, *Race, Class, & Party*. London, 1932.

Lewis, Austin, *The Rise of the American Proletarian*. Chicago, 1907.

Linn, W. A., *Horace Greeley* (*Appletons' Historic Lives Series*). New York, 1903.

Lippmann, Walter, *The United States in World Affairs*. New York, 1931, in progress.

Long, J. C., *Bryan, the Great Commoner*. New York, 1928.

Lonn, Ella, *Desertion during the Civil War*. New York, 1928.

Lorwin, L. L., *The American Federation of Labor; History, Policies and Prospects*. Washington, 1933.

Loud, G. C., *Evangelized America*. New York, 1928.

Lougheed, Victor, *Vehicles of the Air*. Chicago, 1919.

Lubschez, B. J., *The Story of the Motion Picture*. New York, 1920.

McCarthy, C. H., *Lincoln's Plan of Reconstruction*. New York, 1901.

McCrae, R. C., *The Humane Movement*. New York, 1910.

McElroy, John, *The Struggle for Missouri*. Washington, 1909.

McElroy, Robert, *Grover Cleveland*. 2 v. New York, 1923.

Macfarland, C. S., *The Progress of Church Federation*. New York, 1917.

MacGill, Caroline E., and others, *History of Transportation in the United States before 1860* (Carnegie Institution, *Contributions to American Economic History*). Washington, 1917.

McGregor, J. C., *The Disruption of Virginia*. New York, 1922.

Mackenzie, Catherine, *Alexander Graham Bell*. Boston, 1928.

Macleod, W. C., *The American Indian Frontier* (C. K. Ogden, ed., *The History of Civilization*). New York, 1928.

McMaster, J. B., *A History of the People of the United States*. 8 v. New York, 1883–1913.

——, *A History of the People of the United States during Lincoln's Administration*. New York, 1927.

——, *The United States in the World War*. 2 v. New York, 1918–1920.

McMurry, D. L., *Coxey's Army*. Boston, 1929.

McVeagh, Rogers, *The Transportation Act, 1920* (R. C. McCrea, ed., *American Business Series*). New York, 1923.

Mahan, A. T., *Admiral Farragut* (J. G. Wilson, ed., *Great Commanders*). New York, 1892.

Malin, J. C., *An Interpretation of Recent American History*. New York, 1926.

——, *The United States after the World War*. Boston, 1930.

Mangold, B. B., *Problems of Child Welfare*. New York, 1914.

Marcosson, I. F., *S. O. S.* New York, 1919.

Marraro, H. R., *American Opinion on the Unification of Italy, 1846–1861*. New York, 1932.

Martin, P. F., *Maximilian in Mexico*. New York, 1914.

Martin, T. C., and Coles, S. L., eds., *The Story of Electricity*. 2 v. New York, 1919–1922.

Mather, F. M., and others, *The American Spirit in Art* (*The Pageant of America*, XII).

Maurice, Frederick, *Robert E. Lee, the Soldier*. Boston, 1925.

Mayo, Katherine, *"That Damn Y."* Boston, 1920.

Mayorga, Margaret G., *A Short History of the American Drama*. New York, 1932.

Mechlin, J. M., *The Ku Klux Klan*. New York, 1924.

Meneely, A. H., *The War Department: 1861* (Columbia University, *Studies*, no. 300). New York, 1928.

Meriam, Lewis, and others, *The Problem of Indian Administration* (Institute for Government Research, *Studies in Administration*). Baltimore, 1928.

Merriam, C. E., *American Political Ideas, 1865–1917*. New York, 1920.

Merritt, Elizabeth, *James Henry Hammond* (Johns Hopkins University, *Studies*, XLI, no. 4). Baltimore, 1923.

Merz, Charles, *The Dry Decade*. New York, 1931.

Millis, Walter, *The Martial Spirit*. Boston, 1931.

Millspaugh, A. C., *Haiti under American Control, 1915–1930*. Boston, 1931.

Milton, G. F., *The Age of Hate*. New York, 1930.

Mitchell, Broadus, *The Rise of Cotton Mills in the South* (Johns Hopkins University, *Studies*, XXXIX, no. 2). Baltimore, 1921.

Mitchell, W. C., *A History of the Greenbacks* (Chicago University, *Decennial Publications*, 2d ser., IX). Chicago, 1903.

Mixer, Knowlton, *Porto Rico: History and Conditions*. New York, 1926.

Moody, John, *The Masters of Capital* (*The Chronicles of America Series*, XLI).

——, *The Railroad Builders* (*The Chronicles of America Series*, XXXVIII).

——, *The Truth about the Trusts*. New York, 1904.

Moon, P. T., *Imperialism and World Politics*. New York, 1926.

Moore, A. B., *Conscription and Conflict in the Confederacy*. New York, 1924.

Moore, J. B., *History and Digest of the International Relations to Which the United States Has Been a Party*. 6 v. Washington, 1898.

Moorehead, W. K., *The American Indian in the United States*. Andover, Mass., 1914.

Morison, S. E., *The Maritime History of Massachusetts, 1783–1860*. Boston, 1921.

Morse, J. T., Jr., ed., *American Statesmen*. 32 v. Boston, 1898–1900.

Moulton, H. G., and Pasvolsky, Leo, *War Debts and World Prosperity*. New York, 1932.

Mueller, H. R., *The Whig Party in Pennsylvania* (Columbia University, *Studies*, CI, no. 2). New York, 1922.

Munro, W. B., *The Initiative, Referendum and Recall*. New York, 1912.

Mussey, H. R., *Combination in the Mining Industry* (Columbia University, *Studies*, XXIII, no. 3). New York, 1905.

Myers, D. P., *Origin and Conclusion of the Paris Pact* (World Peace Foundation, *Pamphlets*, XII, no. 2). Boston, 1929.

Myers, Gustavus, *History of the Great American Fortunes*. 3 v. Chicago, 1909–1910.

Nevins, Allan, ed., *American Political Leaders*. New York, 1930, in progress.

——, *The Emergence of Modern America* (*A History of American Life*, VIII).

——, *The Evening Post*. New York, 1922.

——, *Frémont, the West's Greatest Adventurer*. 2 v. New York, 1928.

——, *Grover Cleveland* (*American Political Leaders*).

——, *Henry White: Thirty Years of American Diplomacy*. New York, 1930.

Nichols, Jeannette P., *Alaska*. Cleveland, 1924.

Nichols, R. F., *Franklin Pierce*. Philadelphia, 1931.

Norton, H. K., *China and the Powers*. New York, 1927.

Nourse, E. G., *American Agriculture and the European Market*. New York, 1924.

Nowlin, W. F., *The Negro in American National Politics since 1868*. Boston, 1931.

Oberholtzer, E. P., ed., *American Crisis Biographies*. 14 v. Philadelphia, 1905–1915.

——, *A History of the United States since the Civil War*. 5 v. New York, 1917, in progress.

——, *Jay Cooke, Financier of the Civil War*. 2 v. Philadelphia, 1907.

Odegard, P. H., *Pressure Politics*. New York, 1928.

Odum, H. W., ed., *American Masters of Social Science* (same ed., *American Social Science Series*). New York, 1927.

Ogden, Rollo, *Life and Letters of Edwin Lawrence Godkin*. 2 v. New York, 1907.

Ogg, F. A., *National Progress* (*The American Nation*, XXVII).

Olcott, C. S., *The Life of William McKinley*. 2 v. (*American Statesmen*, 2d ser., VII).

Oliver, J. W., *History of the Civil War Military Pensions, 1861–1885* (University of Wisconsin, *Bulletin*, no. 844). Madison, 1917.

Oneal, James, *The Workers in American History*. New York, 1921.

Orth, S. P., *The Armies of Labor* (*The Chronicles of America Series*, XL).

Osgood, E. S., *The Day of the Cattleman*. Minneapolis, 1929.

Ostrogorski, M., *Democracy and the Party System in the United States*. New York, 1910.

Owsley, F. L., *King Cotton Diplomacy*. Chicago, 1931.

——, *State Rights in the Confederacy*. Chicago, 1925.

Packard, F. R., *The History of Medicine in the United States . . . to the Year 1800*. Philadelphia, 1901.

Pageant of America, The. See Gabriel, R. H., ed.

Paine, A. B., *Th. Nast, His Period and His Pictures*. New York, 1904.

Palmer, Frederick, *Newton D. Baker*. 2 v. New York, 1931.

Parrington, V. L., *The Beginnings of Critical Realism in America* (*Main Currents in American Thought*, III). New York, 1930.

Pattee, F. L., *A History of American Literature since 1870*. New York, 1915.

——, *The New American Literature*. New York, 1930.

Paullin, C. O., *Atlas of the Historical Geography of the United States* (J. K. Wright, ed., Carnegie Institution, *Publications*, no. 401). Washington, 1932.

Paxson, F. L., *The Civil War* (*The Home University Library*). New York, 1911.

——, *History of the American Frontier, 1763–1893*. Boston, 1924.

——, *The Last American Frontier*. New York, 1910.

Peck, H. T., *Twenty Years of the Republic, 1885–1905*. New York, 1906.

Peel, R. V., and Donnelly, T. C., *The 1928 Campaign, an Analysis.* New York, 1931.

Peirce, P. S., *The Freedmen's Bureau* (University of Iowa, *Studies*, III, no. 1). Iowa City, 1904.

Pendleton, Louis, *Alexander H. Stephens* (*American Crisis Biographies*).

Perkins, Dexter, *The Monroe Doctrine, 1826–1867.* Baltimore, 1933.

Perlman, Selig, *A History of Trade Unionism in the United States* (R. T. Ely, ed., *Social Science Text-Books*). New York, 1922.

Phillips, U. B., *Life and Labor in the Old South.* Boston, 1929.

——, *The Life of Robert Toombs.* New York, 1913.

Porter, D. D., *The Naval History of the Civil War.* New York, 1886.

Powell, E. A., *The Army behind the Army.* New York, 1919.

Powell, L. P., *Mary Baker Eddy.* New York, 1930.

President's Research Committee on Social Trends, *Recent Social Trends in the United States.* 2 v. New York, 1933.

Priestley, H. I., *The Mexican Nation.* New York, 1923.

Pringle, H. F., *Theodore Roosevelt.* New York, 1931.

Pyle, J. G., *The Life of James J. Hill.* 2 v. Garden City, 1917.

Rainwater, C. E., *The Play Movement in the United States.* Chicago, 1921.

Ramsdell, C. W., *Reconstruction in Texas* (Columbia University, *Studies*, XXXVI, no. 1). New York, 1901.

Randall, J. G., *Constitutional Problems under Lincoln.* New York, 1926.

Ravage, M. E., *The Story of Teapot Dome.* New York, 1924.

Ravenel, M. P., ed., *A Half Century of Public Health.* New York, 1921.

Ray, P. O., *The Repeal of the Missouri Compromise.* Cleveland, 1909.

Regier, C. C., *The Era of the Muckrakers.* Chapel Hill, 1932.

Reinsch, P. S., *Colonial Administration.* New York, 1905.

Remer, C. F., *Foreign Investments in China.* New York, 1933.

Reuter, Bertha A., *Anglo-American Relations during the Spanish-American War.* New York, 1924.

Reyes, J. S., *Legislative History of America's Economic Policy toward the Philippines* (Columbia University, *Studies*, CVI, no. 2). New York, 1923.

Rhodes, J. F., *History of the Civil War.* New York, 1917.

——, *History of the United States from the Compromise of 1850 to the McKinley-Bryan Campaign of 1896.* 8 v. New York, 1892–1919.

——, *The McKinley and Roosevelt Administrations.* New York, 1922.

Rickard, T. A., *A History of American Mining.* New York, 1932.

Riegel, R. E., *America Moves West.* New York, 1930.

——, *The Story of the Western Railroads.* New York, 1926.

Ripley, W. Z., *Railroads: Rates and Regulation.* New York, 1912.

Rippy, J. F., *The Capitalists and Colombia.* New York, 1931.

——, *The United States and Mexico.* Rev. edn., New York, 1931.

Robbins, E. C., *Railway Conductors: A Study in Organized Labor* (Columbia University, *Studies*, LXI, no. 1). New York, 1914.

Robertson, W. S., *Hispanic-American Relations with the United States* (*Carnegie Endowment Publications*). New York, 1923.

Robinson, W. A., *Thomas B. Reed: Parliamentarian.* New York, 1930.

Rollins, P. A., *The Cowboy.* New York, 1922.

Rosewater, Victor, *History of Coöperative News-Gathering in the United States.* New York, 1930.

Ross, E. D., *The Liberal Republican Movement.* New York, 1919.

Rowe, H. K., *The History of Religion in the United States.* New York, 1924.

Russel, R. R., *Economic Aspects of Southern Sectionalism, 1840–1861* (University of Illinois, *Studies*, XI, no. 1). Urbana, 1922.

Ryden, G. H., *The Foreign Policy of the United States in Relation to Samoa.* New Haven, 1933.

Sabin, E. L., *Building the Pacific Railway.* Philadelphia, 1919.

Sakolski, A. M., *The Great American Land Bubble.* New York, 1932.

Sanborn, J. B., *Congressional Grants of Land in Aid of Railways* (University of Wisconsin, *Bulletin*, no. 30). Madison, 1899.

Scharf, J. T., *History of the Confederate States Navy.* Albany, 1886.

Schlesinger, A. M., *The Rise of the City* (*A History of American Life*, X).

——, and Fox, D. R., eds., *A History of American Life.* 12 v. New York, 1927, in progress.

Schmeckebier, L. F., *The Office of Indian Affairs* (Institute for Government Research, *Service Monographs*, no. 48). Washington, 1927.

Schmidt, L. B., and Ross, E. D., eds., *Readings in the Economic History of American Agriculture.* New York, 1925.

Schouler, James, *History of the United States of America, under the Constitution.* 7 v. Rev. edn., New York, 1895–1913.

Schuster, Eunice M., *Native American Anarchism* (Smith College, *Studies*, XVII). Northampton, 1931–1932.

Schwab, J. C., *The Confederate States of America, 1861–1865: A Financial and Industrial History.* New York, 1901.

Scisco, L. D., *Political Nativism in New York State* (Columbia University, *Studies*, XIII, no. 2). New York, 1901.

Scott, E. J., and Stowe, L. B., *Booker T. Washington.* Garden City, 1916.

Scott, J. B., *The Hague Peace Conference of 1899 and 1907.* 2 v. Baltimore, 1909.

——, *A Survey of International Relations between the United States and Germany, August 1, 1914–April 6, 1917.* New York, 1917.

Scrugham, Mary, *The Peaceable Americans, 1860–1861* (Columbia University, *Studies*, XCVI, no. 3). New York, 1921.

Seitz, D. C., *Joseph Pulitzer.* New York, 1924.

Seldes, Gilbert, *The Years of the Locust.* Boston, 1933.

Seymour, Charles, *The Intimate Papers of Colonel House.* 4 v. Boston, 1926–1928.

——, *Woodrow Wilson and the World War* (*The Chronicles of America Series*, XLVIII).

Seymour, Flora W., *The Story of the Red Man.* New York, 1929.

Shannon, F. A., *The Organization and Administration of the Union Army.* 2 v. Cleveland, 1928.

Shaw, Albert, ed., *A Cartoon History of Roosevelt's Career.* New York, 1910.

Siebert, W. H., *The Underground Railroad from Slavery to Freedom*. New York, 1898.

Simkins, F. B., *The Tillman Movement in South Carolina* (Duke University, *Publications*). Durham, 1926.

——, and Woody, R. H., *South Carolina during Reconstruction*. Chapel Hill, 1932.

Simons, A. M., *Social Forces in American History*. New York, 1911.

Sims, W. S., and Hendrick, B. J., *The Victory at Sea*. Garden City, 1920.

Slosson, P. W., *The Great Crusade and After* (*A History of American Life*, XII).

Smalley, E. V., *History of the Northern Pacific Railroad*. New York, 1883.

Smith, E. C., *The Borderland in the Civil War*. New York, 1927.

Smith, G. B., ed., *Religious Thought in the Last Quarter Century*. Chicago, 1927.

Smith, J. R., *The Story of Iron and Steel* (*The Library of Useful Stories*). New York, 1908.

Smith, T. C., *The Life and Letters of James Abram Garfield*. 2 v. New Haven, 1925.

——, *Parties and Slavery* (*The American Nation*, XVIII).

Spalding, A. G., *America's National Game*. New York, 1911.

Sparks, E. E., *National Development* (*The American Nation*, XXIII).

Spears, J. R., *The Story of the American Merchant Marine*. Rev. edn., New York, 1918.

Spring, L. W., *Kansas; the Prelude to the War for the Union*. Boston, 1907.

Stanwood, Edward, *American Tariff Controversies in the Nineteenth Century*. 2 v. Boston, 1903.

——, *A History of the Presidency*. 2 v. Boston, 1916.

——, *James Gillespie Blaine* (*American Statesmen*, 2d ser.).

Starrett, W. A., *Skyscrapers and the Men Who Build Them*. New York, 1928.

Stephenson, G. M., *A History of American Immigration*. Boston, 1926.

——, *The Political History of the Public Lands from 1840 to 1862*. Boston, 1917.

Stephenson, N. W., *The Day of the Confederacy* (*The Chronicles of America Series*, XXX).

——, *Lincoln*. Indianapolis, 1922.

——, *Nelson W. Aldrich*. New York, 1930.

Steuart, Justin, *Wayne Wheeler, Dry Boss*. New York, 1928.

Stewart, F. M., *The National Civil Service Reform League*. Austin, 1929.

Stieglitz, Julius, *Chemistry and Recent Progress in Medicine*. Baltimore, 1924.

Stillé, C. J., *History of the United States Sanitary Commission*. Philadelphia, 1866.

Sullivan, Mark, *Our Times: The United States, 1900–1925*. 5 v. New York, 1926, in progress.

Surface, F. M., *The Grain Trade during the World War*. New York, 1928.

Sweet, W. W., *The Methodist Episcopal Church and the Civil War*. Cincinnati, 1912.

——, *The Story of Religions in America*. New York, 1930.

Synon, Mary, *McAdoo: The Man and His Times*. Indianapolis, 1924.

Taft, Lorado, *The History of American Sculpture* (J. C. Van Dyke, ed., *The History of American Art*, I). Rev. edn., New York, 1924.

Tallmadge, T. E., *The Story of American Architecture*. New York, 1927.

Tansill, C. C., *The Purchase of the Danish West Indies*. Baltimore, 1932.

Tarbell, Ida M., *The History of the Standard Oil Company*. 2 v. New York, 1904.

——, *The Life of Elbert H. Gary*. New York, 1925.

——, *The Tariff in Our Times*. New York, 1911.

Taussig, F. W., *The Tariff History of the United States*. Rev. edn., New York, 1931.

Taylor, A. A., *The Negro in South Carolina during Reconstruction*. Washington, 1924.

——, *The Negro in the Reconstruction of Virginia*. Washington, 1926.

Teele, R. P., *Irrigation in the United States*. New York, 1915.

Thayer, W. R., *The Life and Letters of John Hay*. 2 v. Boston, 1915.

Thomas, B. P., *Russo-American Relations, 1815–1867* (Johns Hopkins University, *Studies*, XLVIII, no. 2). New York, 1930.

Thomas, D. Y., *One Hundred Years of the Monroe Doctrine*. New York, 1923.

Thomas, H. C., *The Return of the Democratic Party to Power in 1884* (Columbia University, *Studies*, LXXXIX, no. 2). New York, 1919.

Thomas, N. M., *The Conscientious Objector in America*. New York, 1923.

Thomas, Shipley, *The History of the A. E. F.* New York, 1920.

Thompson, C. Mildred, *Reconstruction in Georgia* (Columbia University, *Studies*, LXIV, no. 1). New York, 1915.

Thompson, Holland, *The New South* (*The Chronicles of America Series*, XLII).

Thomson, Norman, *Colombia and the United States*. London, 1914.

Thornton, H. J., *The History of the Quaker Oats Company*. Chicago, 1933.

Thwing, C. F., *The American and the German University*. New York, 1928.

——, *A History of Education in the United States since the Civil War*. New York, 1906.

Treat, P. J., *Diplomatic Relations between the United States and Japan, 1853–1895*. 2 v. Stanford University, 1932.

——, *Japan and the United States, 1853–1921*. Boston, 1921.

Trimble, W. J., *The Mining Advance into the Inland Empire* (University of Wisconsin, *Bulletin*, no. 638). Madison, 1914.

Tyler, Alice F., *The Foreign Policy of James G. Blaine*. Minneapolis, 1927.

Underwood, J. L., *The Women of the Confederacy*. New York, 1906.

Vander Velde, L. G., *The Presbyterian Churches and the Federal Union, 1861–1869* (*Harvard Historical Studies*, XXXIII). Cambridge, 1932.

Van Doren, Carl and Mark, *American and British Literature since 1890*. New York, 1925.

Van Hise, C. R., *Conservation and Regulation in the United States during the World War*. Washington, 1917.

——, and Havemeyer, Loomis, *The Conservation of Our Natural Resources*. New York, 1930.

Villard, O. G., *John Brown, 1800–1859*. Boston, 1910.

Warburg, P. M., *The Federal Reserve System*. 2 v. New York, 1930.

Ware, N. J., *The Labor Movement in the United States, 1860–1895*. New York, 1929.

Warner, A. G., *American Charities*. Rev. edn., New York, 1922.

Warren, Charles, *The Supreme Court in United States History*. 2 v. Rev. edn., Boston, 1932.

Watson, F. D., *The Charity Organization Movement in the United States*. New York, 1922.

Webb, W. P., *The Great Plains*. Boston, 1931.

Weber, A. F., *The Growth of Cities in the Nineteenth Century* (Columbia University, *Studies*, XI). New York, 1899.

Weberg, F. P., *The Background of the Panic of 1893*. Washington, 1929.

Weitenkampf, Frank, *American Graphic Art*. Rev. edn., New York, 1924.

Wendell, Herbert, *Southern Commercial Conventions* (Johns Hopkins University, *Studies*, XLVIII, no. 4). Baltimore, 1930.

Wesley, C. H., *The Collapse of the Confederacy* (Howard University, *Studies*, no. 2). Washington, 1922.

——, *Negro Labor in the United States, 1850–1925*. New York, 1927.

West, W. R., *Contemporary French Opinion on the American Civil War* (Johns Hopkins University, *Studies*, XLII, no. 1). Baltimore, 1924.

Westergaard, W. C., *The Danish West Indies*. New York, 1917.

Weyand, A. M., *American Football*. New York, 1926.

White, A. D., *A History of the Warfare of Science with Theology in Christendom*. 2 v. New York, 1896.

White, Laura A., *Robert Barnwell Rhett*. New York, 1931.

Wiest, Edward, *Agricultural Organization in the United States* (University of Kentucky, *Studies in Economics and Sociology*, II). Lexington, 1923.

Wilkerson, M. M., *Public Opinion and the Spanish-American War* (Louisiana State University, *Studies*, no. 8). Baton Rouge, 1932.

Will, A. S., *Life of Cardinal Gibbons*. 2 v. New York, 1922.

Williams, Arthur, *Power on the Farm*. New York, 1927.

Williams, B. H., *Economic Foreign Policy of the United States*. New York, 1929.

——, *The United States and Disarmament*. New York, 1931.

Williams, C. R., *The Life of Rutherford Birchard Hayes*. 2 v. Boston, 1914.

Williams, Mary W., *Anglo-American Isthmian Diplomacy, 1815–1915*. Washington, 1916.

Williams, Michael, *The Shadow of the Pope*. New York, 1932.

Willis, H. P., *The Federal Reserve System*. New York, 1923.

Willoughby, W. F., *The Constitutional Law of the United States*. 2 v. New York, 1910.

——, *Government Organization in War Time and After*. New York, 1919.

——, *Territories and Dependencies of the United States*. New York, 1905.

Wilson, Jennie L., *The Legal and Political Status of Women in the United States*. Cedar Rapids, Iowa, 1912.

Winkler, J. K., *W. R. Hearst*. New York, 1928.

Winkler, Max, *Investments of United States Capital in Latin America* (World Peace Foundation, *Pamphlets*, XI, no. 6). Boston, 1928.

Winston, R. W., *Andrew Johnson*. New York, 1928.

Wittke, Carl, *Tambo and Bones: A History of the American Minstrel Stage*. Durham, 1930.

Wood, William, *Captains of the Civil War* (*The Chronicles of America Series*, XXXI).

Wood, W. B., and Edmonds, J. E., *A History of the Civil War in the United States*. London, 1905.

Woodburn, J. A., *The Life of Thaddeus Stevens*. Indianapolis, 1913.

Woods, R. A., and Kennedy, A. J., *The Settlement Horizon*. New York, 1922.

Woodson, C. G., *The Negro in Our History*. Washington, 1922.

Woodward, W. E., *Meet General Grant*. New York, 1928.

Woodworth, J. V., *American Tool Making and Interchangeable Manufacturing*. New York, 1911.

Woody, Thomas, *A History of Women's Education in the United States* (J. M. Cattell, ed., *Science and Education*, IV). 2 v. New York, 1929.

Worcester, D. C., *The Philippines, Past and Present*. 2 v. New York, 1914.

Wright, R. M., *Dodge City, the Cowboy Capital*. Wichita, Kan., 1913.

Young, A. N., *The Single Tax Movement in the United States*. Princeton, 1916.

Zimmermann, E. W., *Zimmermann on Ocean Shipping*. New York, 1921.

Zueblin, Charles, *American Municipal Progress* (R. T. Ely, ed., *The Citizen's Library of Economics, Politics, and Sociology*). New York, 1902.

INDEX

A. B. C. Powers, and Monroe Doctrine, 386; and Mexican imbroglio, 388.

Abbott, Lyman, and social religion, 226; and evolution, 227–228.

Abolition, Lincoln's attitude toward, 53, 88–89, 91; during Civil War, 88–93; and freedmen's bureau, 104. *See also* Emancipation.

Adams, C. F., as Minister to Great Britain, 97, 98.

Adams, Henry, on politics, 155–156; as historian, 245.

Adams, S. H., attacks patent-medicine fraud, 318.

Adamson law, passed, 352.

Addams, Jane, founds Hull House, 218, 225.

Africa, struggle for acquisition of, 285; Boer War in, 291, 390.

Agassiz, Louis, against evolution, 244.

Agrarianism, increases in 1880's, 256–261; and silver crusade, 259–265; during World War, 473. *See also* Granger movement, People's party.

Agricultural-adjustment act, provisions of, 490.

Agricultural-marketing act, provisions of, 475.

Agriculture, mid-century, 3, 6–7; Panic of 1857 affects, 37; during Civil War, 83; in South after Civil War, 121–123, 257–258; compared in 1860, 1880 and 1890, 132; in West after Civil War, 133–134, 141–142, 256–257; Economic Revolution in, 141–142; growth of scientific, 142, 143–144, 244; Department of, 142, 261, 474; in Philippines, 377; during World War, 412–413, 473; postwar, 473–475; and Capper-Volstead act, 474–475; and McNary-Haugen bill, 475; and agricultural-marketing act, 475; and agricultural-adjustment act, 490; and Great Depression, 479, 483. *See also* Agrarianism, Farmers.

Aguinaldo, Emilio, and Spanish-American War, 302; captured, 376.

Airplane, development of, 366–367; in World War, 408, 411–412, 417, 419.

Alabama, as Confederate cruiser, 83, 98; claims, 123–124.

Alabama, secedes, 48; postwar taxes in, 118; "redeemed," 120; manufacturing in, 145.

Alaska, purchased, 99; as American possession, 373–374.

Aldrich, N. W., and tariff, 182, 335; conservatism of, 324.

Aldrich-Vreeland act, passed, 345.

Alexander II, frees serfs, 99; supports Union, 99.

Alger, Horatio, writes biography of Garfield, 173n.

Alien-labor-contract law, passed, 281.

Allison, W. B., and free silver, 260.

Altgeld, J. P., and Pullman strike, 209, 276; and Haymarket riot, 215n.

Amalgamated Copper Company, formed, 202, 316; controls copper, 202; exposed, 317.

American Chemical Society, founded, 244.

American Economic Association, formed, 244.

American Expeditionary Force, in France, 415–420.

American Federation of Labor, formed, 205; objects of, 205; growth of, 205–206; and eight-hour-day strike, 207–208; opposes injunctions, 210, 470; and Socialist Laborites, 214; for woman suffrage, 224; for free silver, 267; enters politics, 351; indorses Democrats, 334, 405, 446; indorses Progressives, 451; against immigration, 353, 471; during World War, 426; increased membership of, 427, 441; decreased membership of, 470; influence of, 470–471.